LAFAYETTE IN
THE FRENCH REVOLUTION

From the October Days through the Federation

LAFAYETTE IN THE FRENCH REVOLUTION

From the October Days through the Federation

By

LOUIS GOTTSCHALK

and

MARGARET MADDOX

THE UNIVERSITY OF CHICAGO PRESS

CHICAGO & LONDON

The University of Chicago Press, Chicago 60637
The University of Chicago Press, Ltd., London

International Standard Book Number: 0–226–30547–3
Library of Congress Catalog Card Number: 72–94731

To the memory of

ANDREW CUNNINGHAM McLAUGHLIN

TABLE OF CONTENTS

THIS IS the second in a series of four studies on the career of Lafayette during the French Revolution (to 1792). The first dealt (to quote its Preface) "with approximately the first nine months of Lafayette's career in 1789—up to the climax of October 5 and 6," ending "with his becoming the principal guardian of the king's person, the real power behind the toppling Bourbon throne." This one begins with the dawn of October 7, 1789, and ends with the night of July 14, 1790—another nine-month period. Its major theme is the struggle for leadership and power in a time of rapid reform, popular violence, and unstable government. The symbol of governmental authority during that time still was the monarch, but real power lay with the police, and Lafayette controlled the police in the form of the National Guard, which he organized and commanded in Paris and which his prestige largely dominated elsewhere in the monarchy. Hence, if he had wanted to do so, he might have become (as some of his contemporaries nevertheless called him) a dictator.

If during this period Lafayette was not "the man on horseback," he was "the one to beat," and several tried to beat him or, failing that, to join him. Hence he generally was in the position of "the man in the middle." What he wanted for France was a strong but constitutional monarchy, brought about by tempered reform through the willing cooperation of a benevolent king with a moderate constituent assembly, the military preserving public order under the control of civil authorities; from France, he intended, these liberal ideas should spread abroad. Other influential figures, however, while they might have accepted such a policy in general terms, did not agree with him on specifics or semantics. So a large part of the time that he could spare from his obligations as commandant general of the Paris National Guard went into trying to hold the moderate reformers together and keep either the opponents of reforms he considered reasonable or the advocates of reforms he considered extreme from gaining predominance. The greater danger to his purposes as yet lay with the opponents of reform— that is, with Queen Marie Antoinette and the so-called "Austrian Cabal," supported by some of the aristocracy, whether courtiers at home or émigrés abroad, and one of Lafayette's principal aims at this stage was to dissuade King Louis XVI from casting his lot with them. With the triumphant Federation of July 14, 1790, the gala event with which this volume terminates, he seemed to have gloriously succeeded. He had done so despite cross fire from two sides. He had successfully encountered, on the one hand, the maneuvers of Orléans, Mirabeau, Bouillé, and others who perhaps did not wholly disagree with his political philosophy but had ambitions of their own, resented his power, or doubted his capacity, and, on the other, the apprehension of the "Triumvirate," the Paris districts, and some of the popular press that, even if he were not personally ambitious, he was creating a potentially tyrannical executive dependent upon a praetorian guard. The gloom that gradually overshadowed the blaze of the Federation will be the theme of our subsequent volumes.

The late Margaret Maddox prepared a first draft from which this volume was developed. In the several decades that have passed since the initiation of these Lafayette studies many institutions and persons have contributed in some way, great or small, to the production of this volume, and in the prefaces and the footnotes of this and earlier studies we have generally tried to acknowledge our indebtedness wherever our records indicate the creditors. Sometimes our records are faulty in that regard, and we owe some debts to persons and institutions that regretfully will have to remain nameless here. In the recent past Liliane O. Ziegel, Charles R. Bailey, Robert Carden, Alexander De Grande, Edgar Newman, Lee Grugel, Mary-Susan Abelow, and David Foldi have been particularly helpful, and we extend our special thanks to them. Professors Fruma Gottschalk and Shirley A. Bill have helped both in the preparation of the manuscript and in the reading of proof. My friend Charles A. Bill prepared the index. And since we have regularly received support from the Social Science Research Committee of the University of Chicago, the staff of the University of Chicago

Libraries, and that of the University of Chicago Press we remain continually in their debt, while warning them that, as a wise man has somewhere said, gratitude is a lively sense of favors yet to come.

LOUIS GOTTSCHALK

CHICAGO, 1971

CHAPTER I

Outmaneuvering Orléans and Mirabeau

WHEN, on October 6, 1789, King Louis XVI of France and his family yielded to the demands of a sullen troop of Parisians and, escorted by a triumphant party of his subjects, reluctantly left Versailles to take up residence at the Tuileries Palace in Paris, the French Revolution, having already run a turbulent course for five crisis-packed months, entered a new phase. Until the preceding May, Louis had been an absolute monarch who, seemingly out of his own free will and royal grace, had called the representatives of his people together in an Estates General to consult with him on some knotty problems of general import. The next July an insurrection in Paris had made it politic for him to concede that that Estates General, which up to that time he had considered his creature, was a self-propelling National Assembly with authority to draw up a new constitution for France. And now another insurrection, soon to be known as the October Days, had made him little better than a captive, obliged by violence and bloodshed to change his royal abode, to accept unwelcome constitutional provisions which until October 5 he had sidetracked, and to contemplate the likelihood that a new constitution of which he might not approve would ultimately come to him for a sanction which he would hardly dare to refuse. Were he to offer resistance, in his new, undignified position he ran not merely the risk of personal danger, which he might have been willing to incur, but also the risk of widespread national disruption, which in several previous crises he had made genuine if constrained concessions to avert and in which now the odds were patently against him.

If the unhappy king had had sufficient force at his disposal, he might conceivably have dug in his heels, refusing to make further concessions. But he had no force strong enough to rely upon. His army, largely infected by the new revolutionary spirit, was disorganized, and his courtiers were divided in views and loyalties. His personal popularity was still great, but the younger of his two brothers had emigrated, the older was suspect, some of his advisers were distrusted, and even among his loyal subjects his wife was disliked. That an appeal to his people would be successful was highly dubious, while few could doubt that such an appeal would lead to serious conflict, even civil war. Discretion dictated that Louis temporarily follow the line of least resistance, counting upon moderate leaders to head the Revolution down the narrow path between radical extremists and counterrevolutionaries.

One man stood out as a potential guarantor of order, reason, and political moderation. That man was the Marquis de Lafayette, commandant general of the Paris National Guard, hero of the populace, and idol of his troops—or at least most of them. It was he who had restored order during the terrifying morning hours of October 6 when resentful Parisians had attacked the Château of Versailles, who had rescued the King's Bodyguard from wholesale slaughter as overzealous royalists, and who had brought the royal family safely to the Tuileries. As the principal military officer of the Paris Commune he was legally obliged, and he was personally ready, to supervise the policing of Paris, which must now become at least temporarily the royal residence.

Lafayette's political views were well known in the royal family. Though a court noble he was one of that faction of self-styled Patriots in the National Assembly who envisaged a governmental structure which the king and his retinue might consider less odious than that which some other Patriots wanted. Lafayette intended that the National Assembly should draw up a moderate constitution in an orderly atmosphere, free from interference from either the court party or its opponents, but whatever the constitution was to be, he hoped that it would be accepted by all parties gracefully, subject to peaceful amendment. He no longer expected the new constitution to be exactly the one that he would himself have made if he had had a free hand. Under the leadership of less moderate Patriots the National Assembly had recently decided that the new French legislative body was to have only one elective house, having scarcely considered his preference for an upper house representing the provinces and having definitely rejected an upper house of peers such as others had proposed. Furthermore, it had compromised between those who wanted to vest the king with an absolute veto of legislation and those who wanted him to have no veto power whatsoever, granting him instead a suspensive veto. But Lafayette, having all along contended that the veto was not an irreconcilable issue, now felt bound by that compromise. Most important for him, the Assembly had drawn up a Declaration of Rights based in large part upon principles that he had been the first deputy to propose publicly, sometimes couched in phrases that he had composed. He was persuaded that a constitution with these provisions left the monarch a chief executive with ample dignity and power to assure the future welfare of France.

Yet only upon the display of popular force had Louis XVI now unconditionally accepted the suspensive veto and the Declaration of Rights, and events were soon to show that he still had misgivings. How much more of the social and political structure, particularly the absolute power, which he had inherited from his ancestors would he have to surrender? If the king had paused a moment amid the excitement of his compulsory migration from Versailles to Paris to canvass his plight, he perhaps speculated, for he was not a stupid man, that Lafayette seemed to have as good a chance as any, and better than most, to head off further disaster. As "the hero of two worlds" he appeared to have enough personal popularity to dissuade the people from following a more dangerous leader, and he had an armed force at his back probably strong enough to prevent those who might undertake to do so.

Before quitting the royal residence on October 6, Lafayette placed himself at Louis' disposal.[1] In view of the horror through which they had just passed, both men could hardly have failed to realize that this was much more than a traditional military gesture.

---

[1] Comte de Seneffe to M. de Doué, Oct. 7, 1789, Pierre de Vaissière, *Lettres d' "Aristocrates," la Révolution racontée par des correspondances privées, 1789–1794* (Paris, 1907), p. 150. (Hereafter, unless otherwise indicated, the year—1789 or 1790—will be omitted from the dates given in these footnotes.)

The commandant general of the Paris National Guard, now directly and personally responsible for the safety of the royal family, recognized that he must make his command more efficient than ever before and, what their recent defiance had shown might be even more difficult, more obedient to his orders. He must, besides, try to win the king away from his counterrevolutionary advisers, so that the royal influence might become an ally and not a potential enemy of a moderate program and so that the king might avoid the political errors which previously had roused popular hostility. Convinced that unknown leaders had instigated the recent attack upon Versailles, he must seek them out, not merely to punish them as fomenters of past disorders but also to dampen any purpose to obtain the king's future cooperation by duress. Moreover, he must persuade the National Assembly, still meeting in Versailles, that he could keep it free from undue public pressure so that even the most indignant or fearful deputies might come to condone the violence of October 5 and 6 and feel that if they followed the king to Paris, they could proceed in a peaceful atmosphere and an orderly fashion with their sworn task of drawing up a constitution.

Lafayette did not, as the victor, exult over the discomfiture of the King's Bodyguard on October 5 and 6. He attributed their humiliation as defenders of the Château of Versailles not to any lack of military gallantry on their part but to the negligence of their officers.[2] One of the wounded bodyguards had been taken to Lafayette's house on the Rue de Bourbon and had been nursed by Adrienne, his wife; and before leaving home on the morning of October 7, Lafayette arranged an escort to take the wounded man to the hospital.[3] Then, accompanied by "a numerous suite," he started out toward the Tuileries to attend the king's levee. A short ride to the river's left bank took him to the bridge which crossed to the Place de

[2] Louis Gottschalk and Margaret Maddox, *Lafayette in the French Revolution: Through the October Days* (Chicago, 1969), pp. 366, 369, and *Mémoires, correspondance, et manuscrits du Général Lafayette* (Paris, 1837) (hereafter called *Mémoires*), II, 351; III, 237; and IV, 203.

[3] *Mémoires*, II, 351, and *Procédure criminelle instruite au Châtelet de Paris,* etc. (Paris, 1790) (hereafter called *Procédure au Châtelet*), I, 197–98 (testimony of F.-N. Gueroult du Berville). Dorothée Talleyrand-Périgord, *Chronique de 1831 à 1862* (Paris, 1909), I, 100, says Bishop Talleyrand told her that Lafayette calmly had his picture painted on the morning of Oct. 7, but we have found no evidence to corroborate this story.

Louis XV (now Place de la Concorde), by which he could reach the main entrance to the extensive Tuileries Gardens paralleling the Seine. On the way he and his suite encountered the Duc de Villeroi, one of the captains of the King's Bodyguard. Villeroi apparently felt called upon to account for himself to Lafayette. He had taken no part, he explained, in the errors of his subordinates the day before—to which Lafayette responded: "So much the worse for you, sir, for they conducted themselves very well indeed."[4]

Good-humored crowds had gathered outside the Tuileries, some drawn by curiosity, some to show their loyalty to the monarchy, and all acclaiming the royal pair who had come to live among them. That the National Guard had taken the King's Bodyguard under its protection was also plain as men from both corps walked arm-in-arm in the public squares. When Lafayette entered the palace, he was well received, and the queen personally expressed to him her gratitude for having stood by her on October 6 in her hour of danger.[5]

Amid the disorders of the October Days, Louis XVI had promised a deputation of distressed women who had gone to Versailles to seek reassurance about the bread shortage in Paris that he would do all he could to maintain an adequate supply. The mayor of Paris, Jean-Sylvain Bailly, also attended the royal levee on October 7, and the king asked him for information regarding measures to provision the capital. Later that day the king promised to give whatever orders the Commune might request "through Monsieur the Mayor or through Monsieur de La Fayette."[6] Thus all Paris learned that His Majesty seemed to place the commandant general on an equal footing with their mayor.

Sometime before the day was over, the king expressed his confidence in Lafayette in a still more concrete fashion. He ordered him "to take general command of all the military forces located in Paris

---

[4] At least so Lafayette remembered the episode forty years later: see *Mémoires*, II, 345.

[5] Seneffe to Doué, Oct. 7, Vaissière, p. 150; Lord Robert Fitzgerald to the Duke of Leeds, Oct. 8, J. M. Thompson (ed.), *English Witnesses of the French Revolution* (Oxford, 1938), p. 72. Cf. Adrien Duquesnoy, *Journal . . . sur l'Assemblée constituante* (Paris, 1894), I, 466.

[6] Sigismond Lacroix, *Actes de la Commune de Paris pendant la Révolution*, II (Paris, 1895), 201–3.

and within a radius of fifteen leagues [*ca.* 45 miles] . . . for the purpose of provisioning the capital."[7] In addition, the minister of the royal household requested Lafayette to deny to deserters from other branches of the king's service the right to enroll in the National Guard.[8] In short, the commandant general of the Paris National Guard, a semi-civilian organization, was now by royal order the commander also of the king's regular forces in the vicinity and charged with part at least of the responsibility for keeping the rest of the king's army from disintegrating.

From the very outset of Louis XVI's residence in Paris Lafayette tried to surround the royal family with a courteous, loyal, and adequate guard. Anticipating that he himself might be able to give little attention to supervising the patrol of the Tuileries, he deputed his able chief of staff, Jean-Baptiste Gouvion, to take charge there, and Gouvion soon moved from Lafayette's house, where he had previously lived, to quarters in the Tuileries. In due course a system was devised that seemed to work satisfactorily. Lafayette placed the chiefs of the city's six divisions on palace duty under Gouvion, each serving twenty-four hours in rotation as head of the palace guard, during which time the Swiss Guards, the Cent Suisses, and a battalion of the National Guard relieved each other in prescribed turns.[9] Lafayette intended that the King's Bodyguard should also take part in this service, but the court, supported by the Bodyguard's aristocratic officers, seemed to object. He afterward suspected that they wanted it to appear that the king was not a free agent, but at the time the ill will of the Paris populace toward the Bodyguard in fact made it wise to give them temporary leave.[10]

For a few days after the insurrection of October 5–6 quiet

---

[7] Fogg Museum of Art, *Exhibition, Washington, Lafayette, Franklin* (Cambridge, Mass., 1944), p. 49, item 108. Cf. the report of Comte de Salmour, envoy of Saxony, to his government, Oct. 9, in Jules Flammermont (ed.), *Les Correspondances des agents diplomatiques étrangers en France avant la Révolution* (Paris, 1896), p. 273; *Journal de Paris*, Oct. 10, p. 1299; and Alexandre Tuetey, *Répertoire général des sources manuscrites de l'histoire de Paris pendant la Révolution française* (Paris, 1890–1914), I, 105, Nos. 990, 991.

[8] Tuetey, II, 435, No. 4130.

[9] Comte de Vergennes to M. de Bellejeant, Oct. 12, Vaissière, pp. 97–98, and Duchess de Tourzel, *Memoirs* (London, 1886), pp. 48–49.

[10] *Mémoires*, II, 342, and Vergennes to Bellejeant, Oct. 12, Vaissière, p. 97.

seemed to the casual observer to prevail in Paris. William Short, the American chargé d'affaires, reported: "A calm reigned through the streets . . . and . . . to the astonishment of every body bread became as abundant as ever."[11] But if Short had known all that was going on, he might have been less sanguine. Restlessness developed throughout the city as the horror of the October insurrection receded. As early as October 7 rumors of new plots to curtail the sale of food dictated sending extra guards to the flour market, to suspend the issuance of passports until further notice,[12] and to consider new regulations to tighten discipline in the National Guard.[13]

On the following morning restlessness continued, and people poured into the environs of the Tuileries Palace. Word came to the Hôtel de Ville that a big crowd had also collected outside the Mont-de-Piété (the city pawnshop) and was demanding the return of the property deposited there. The Representatives, convinced that some public enemies were conspiring to start a new insurrection, ordered Lafayette "to deploy the military force confided to him" to prevent "dire consequences"[14] and solicited the king's cooperation in the preservation of order. Louis issued a proclamation authorizing "the commandant of the national militia" to preserve peace and inviting "all good and loyal citizens to give him aid and succor."[15]

The crowd at the Tuileries was well disposed, but rumors persisted that the Faubourg Saint-Antoine planned to march upon Versailles and burn the recently abandoned royal palace there. This time Lafayette was not caught unawares, as he had been by the insurrection on October 5. He warned the Versailles authorities of the danger and offered aid if a crowd should break through,[16]

---

[11] William Short to Thomas Jefferson, Oct. 9, Julian Boyd (ed.), *The Papers of Thomas Jefferson*, XVI (Princeton, 1961), p. 5 n.

[12] Lacroix, II, 198–99.

[13] *Ibid.*, p. 200.

[14] *Ibid.*, p. 208.

[15] *Ibid.*, pp. 207–8.

[16] Duquesnoy, I, 421, and Thompson, p. 72. J.-J. Mounier, "Exposé de ma conduite dans l'Assemblée nationale" in M.-J. Mavidal and M. E. Laurent (eds.), *Archives parlementaires de 1787 à 1860* (Paris, 1862—) (hereafter cited as *AP*), IX, 579, mentions a letter from Lafayette on Oct. 8 apologizing for stopping deputies at the city gates.

and in Versailles every approach from Paris was put under heavy guard.

After a midday dinner at home[17] Lafayette returned to the Hôtel de Ville for the five o'clock session of the Assembly of Representatives, arriving late. This was his first appearance at the Assembly since he had left for Versailles with his army on October 5. The Representatives received him with an ovation that expressed their satisfaction with the "noble, firm, and conciliatory line of conduct which he had followed during the past few days." "In a simple and touching manner"[18] he thanked them for their confidence and took the occasion to turn the Assembly's attention again to the vital problem of preserving order. Since the king had consented to receive a deputation from the Assembly of Representatives the next morning,[19] he recommended that the Assembly take that opportunity to ask that His Majesty announce his intention to stay in Paris permanently and to thank him for having already prompted the National Assembly to join him there. Lafayette proposed further that the Representatives issue an address to the provinces reaffirming the capital's continued respect for the National Assembly, loyalty to the monarchy, and fraternal sentiments for the provinces. His purpose was obvious; he meant to show all doubters that the events of October 5 and 6 had not split king from subjects, National Assembly from king, or capital from province. The Representatives unanimously approved of his suggestions.[20]

The Parlement of Paris, France's most celebrated law court, had earlier informed Lafayette that it too wished to send a deputation to wait upon the king and meant to proceed to the Tuileries with its traditional police escort, the Robe-courte, and he now presented that request to the Assembly of Representatives. That the Parlement of Paris, which at times had defied the kings of France, should thus seek his permission to march in the streets of Paris but that he should prefer to submit their request to the civil authorities was perhaps unintended, but no less revealing, evidence of the new

[17] See below, p. 10.
[18] Lacroix, II, 212–13.
[19] *Ibid.*, pp. 211–12, 220–22.
[20] *Ibid.*, pp. 212–13.

hierarchy of prestige in Paris. After due deliberation the Representatives authorized the procession.[21]

The Assembly's consideration of further police details was interrupted by a deputation of market women who announced that they repudiated the "unbecoming behavior" of the women who on October 5 had reviled the mayor and the commandant general and had invaded the Château of Versailles. "Far from speaking evil of M. Bailly and M. de la Fayette," they declared, "they had spoken only good of them and would defend them to the last drop of their blood." The Representatives applauded their patriotic words, awarded them tricolor ribbons and cockades, and ordered their address printed and given wide publicity.[22]

Before they adjourned for the night, the Representatives turned their attention to the "scandalous and incendiary" press. Despite earlier measures to prevent the sale of inflammatory literature, attacks upon prominent citizens were becoming alarmingly frequent. They sounded at times as if they came from royalists but at other times as if from those who feared that some of the leaders of the Revolution were royalist. Prominent among the anti-royalists was the journalist Jean-Paul Marat, the proprietor and editor of the *Ami du peuple*. Although he claimed to be still hopeful that Lafayette would act as a patriot, he looked with suspicion upon the transformation of the National Guard into "automatons under the order of a chief."[23] The Representatives decided to reconfirm a previous ordinance which forbade the public hawking of publications dangerous to the capital's tranquility and ordered the commandant general to enforce it strictly.[24]

On the morning of October 9 the mayor and a deputation of Representatives proceeded in state to an audience with the king. Just as Bailly was ready to lead the deputation into the king's presence, the commandant general and some of his staff joined them. The royal master of ceremonies conducted them into the

[21] *Ibid.*, p. 213.

[22] *Ibid.*, pp. 214–15, 222–24.

[23] *Ami du peuple,* Sept. 29, p. 164. See also *ibid.,* Sept. 25 and Oct. 5–8, pp. 132, 217–18, 226, 233–34, 239–40.

[24] Lacroix, II, 215–16.

royal presence through the antechamber, between lines of Paris National Guards presenting arms. Wearing a hat and seated in an armchair, Louis XVI, surrounded by his advisers, awaited them, but as the deputation advanced, the king honored them by removing his hat for a moment. Bailly then formally delivered a florid address, based upon Lafayette's unadorned motion of the preceding evening, requesting that His Majesty make Paris his principal residence and that the National Assembly join him. Louis repeated his readiness to cooperate in the provisioning and policing of the city and not only promised to fix his residence in Paris but also had his keeper of the seals hand the mayor a copy of a letter he intended to send to the National Assembly asking it to hold its meetings there. Even before the deputation retired, the king's letter was on its way to the National Assembly by one of Lafayette's aides.[25]

The deputation then went to pay its respects to Queen Marie Antoinette. Accompanied by her children and surrounded by her retinue of ladies, the queen awaited the Paris officials. She rose to greet them and then reseated herself to listen to Bailly's brief, respectful address. In reply, she said she would gladly follow the king wherever he chose to go "and especially here." Their mission accomplished, the deputation returned to the Hôtel de Ville.[26] Official Paris had once more shown its solidarity with its king and queen, and it had good reason to believe that it reflected the reactions of Parisians in general against the excesses of the October Days. But more than ceremonies was needed to make good will endure.

Arriving home for dinner, Lafayette found among his guests, as was becoming increasingly common, one who had a political axe to grind.[27] Their conversation was interrupted by the entrance of Lafayette's trusted friend the Duc de La Rochefoucauld, fresh from Versailles, where he was a deputy in the National Assembly.[28]

[25] *Ibid.*, 231, and *AP,* IX, 290. *Journal de Paris,* Oct. 11, p. 1304, puts this episode on Oct. 8, but Oct. 9 is correct.

[26] Lacroix, II, 233–34.

[27] See below, pp. 28–29.

[28] B. C. Davenport (ed.), *A Diary of the French Revolution by Gouverneur Morris* (Boston, 1939), I, 250 (Oct. 9).

He had come directly from the morning session, which had opened with a heated debate whether to leave Versailles because of the danger of violence in that now inadequately policed region. The debate took a decisive turn when Lafayette's aide arrived with the king's letter asking that the Assembly move to the capital, and the Assembly finally decided to do so as soon as a meeting place became available.[29]

Upon learning this decision, Lafayette went off to the evening session of the Assembly of Representatives, again arriving late. As soon as he entered, he delivered the good news that the National Assembly had decided to come to Paris. The Representatives' pleasure over this development was quickly dampened, however, by a warning that an insurrection to force down the price of bread impended. The Representatives forthwith enjoined any demand upon bakers to sell bread at less than the fixed price of twelve sous for four pounds and instructed the commandant general to give force to that injunction.[30]

That night Lafayette confessed to having some cause for satisfaction and yet some cause for anxiety also. His own staff was apparently reliable and efficient, his aides active and loyal. The National Guard appeared obedient and seemingly tireless. The Representatives were alert and determined to do their part to control the city. Louis XVI seemed to be sympathetic and cooperative, even if some of his ministers were found wanting. The majority of the National Assembly were ready to accept the October revolution and to join the king in his "permanent" residence in Paris. Nevertheless, reports of inflammatory addresses, complaints of poverty and hunger, and the threats of riot kept pouring in from first one section of the city and then another, and the entire National Guard would now have to remain under arms on special duty. "It is pretty hard," Lafayette apologized to his confidante Comtesse Adelaïde de Simiane, "to exchange a supper with you for a revolt," but the danger of a popular outbreak, he explained, obliged him to stay on guard at the Hôtel de Ville. "Someone is trying to reduce us to starvation, and we are in a rather dark

[29] *Ibid*. Cf. *AP*, IX, 388–90.
[30] Lacroix, II, 234–35.

cloud."[31] Once again, it appeared to him, the populace was led "by an invisible hand."[32]

In spite of their all-night vigil, when Saturday morning (October 10) came, the National Guard reported that terrorists had again been at work. During the night the doors of many houses had been marked with chalk colored red, white, or black, and it was whispered that red marked a house to be burned, white one to be pillaged, and black one whose inmates were to be assassinated.[33] The homes of the Representatives of the Commune and the principal officers of the Paris National Guard had received the terrorists' special attention, although when the episode was discussed that evening, the Representatives were apparently not overly concerned.[34]

It seemed more urgent, in conformity with Lafayette's suggestion of the evening before, to reinforce the confidence of any whom the events of the October Days had shocked. A committee appointed to elaborate his views submitted that morning a statement for the Representatives' approval. "Enemies of the public welfare," it declared, had attempted to thwart the new order, but "thanks to the activity of the Paris national troops and to the wisdom of their commander, the odious plot had been turned against the very ones who had hatched it"; in permitting his palace to be guarded by the Paris National Guard His Majesty had acquired a fresh title to the loyalty of all Parisians, and to promote unity among "the free and equal citizens of a single empire" the Representatives of the Commune now bound themselves to "an inviolable pledge of profound respect for the National Assembly, of inalterable fidelity to the person of the king, and of sincere and confident fraternity with all the communes of the realm."[35] They made a direct appeal also to the National Assembly, hoping to calm the uneasiness of those deputies at Versailles who still opposed the transfer to Paris.

[31] [Oct. 9], *Mémoires*, II, 414.

[32] Lafayette to [Mme de Simiane], July 24, *ibid.*, p. 320.

[33] *Courier national*, Oct. 11, pp. 7–8.

[34] Lacroix, II, 250.

[35] *Ibid.*, pp. 245–47.

Before the colleagues who were delegated to present those addresses to the National Assembly[36] could depart, the Assembly of Representatives learned that the National Assembly would soon approve a revised code of criminal procedure.[37] This was a measure upon which Lafayette had long insisted. He had hesitated to press charges against prisoners accused of political offenses until some code had been adopted granting them counsel, access to the evidence, confrontation with witnesses, and public trial.[38] A little later in the day the Hôtel de Ville learned that a new code had actually been passed the night before, and Lafayette dispatched an aide to the National Assemby to get a copy of it, obviously meaning to hasten the royal sanction of the revised proceedings so that the trial of prisoners accused of fomenting insurrection might soon begin.[39]

In the Assembly of Representatives that evening (October 10) someone announced that Louis XVI had just signed an order releasing some of the King's Bodyguard.[40] In the face of the Commune's efforts to make *peace* and *fraternity* the watchwords of a new regime this alleged act smacked of Louis' concern for his guards' safety from the people's hostility and of their officers' innuendo that he had become a ward of the Paris National Guard.[41] After considering several suggestions, the Representatives postponed discussion until the commandant general could get more precise information. Lafayette discovered that the King's Bodyguard in fact had been stationed outside of Paris, and he became convinced that its officers intended to make Louis look like the National Guard's prisoner.[42] Some of Paris' sixty district assem-

---

[36] *Ibid.*, pp. 247–48, 254–55, 259–61, 264, and *AP*, IX, 405–6.

[37] *Lacroix*, II, 249.

[38] Morris diary, Davenport (ed.), I, xxiv; *Mémoires*, III, 246; P.-V. de Besenval, *Mémoires* (Paris, 1821), II, 374–75; Comte de Mirabeau, *Mémoires biographiques, littéraires et politiques* [ed. Gabriel Lucas de Montigny], (Paris, 1841), VI, 164 n.; and Gottschalk and Maddox, pp. 247–48.

[39] *Courrier de Versailles à Paris et de Paris à Versailles*, Oct. 12, p. 156.

[40] Lacroix, II, 251.

[41] Cf. Lafayette to J.-J. Mounier, Oct. 23, *Mémoires*, II, 417–18 and n. See also above, p. 6 and n. 10.

[42] Lacroix, II, 251, 257, 262, and Lafayette to Mounier, Oct. 23, *Mémoires*, II, 417–18 n.

blies also excitedly debated the issue, and it bade fair to kindle a public flare-up,[43] but Lafayette doubled and trebled the patrols, giving them strict orders to keep the streets cleared, and so Saturday and Sunday (October 10 and 11) passed without serious disturbances.[44] On the twelfth, having found that the appeal to the provinces had not yet gone out, he urged the Assembly of Representatives to hasten its dispatch so that the whole realm might discover the king's "truly paternal intentions," and he was promised speedy action.[45]

The continual threats of disorder, Lafayette was inclined to infer, were attributable to some conspirator's manipulations. He had long suspected a prince of the blood, the Duc d'Orléans, like more than one of his ancestors, of plotting to make himself the ruler (*de facto* if not *de nomine*) of France in its time of troubles, and he even believed that behind Orléans lurked the British government as well as the eloquent deputy Comte de Mirabeau, and other cronies.[46] He had no evidence, however, that would convince a court of the prince's guilt although he was earnestly looking for it.[47] In fact, his zeal in tracking down plots and subversive activity led to an expansion of the police powers of search. He had found that police agents were sometimes foiled because certain places such as the Château at Versailles were traditionally privileged against police investigation, and so he and the police authorities appealed to the National Assembly for removal of the privilege. One of his aides put the matter before the National Assembly's Comité des Recherches (Investigations Committee), and the National Assembly shortly (October 13) passed a resolution opening every area in the realm to investigation in case of *lèse-nation* (a recent substitute for *lèse-majesté*).[48] It was probably at this time

---

[43] Lacroix, II, 256.

[44] *Patriote français*, Oct. 13, pp. 2–3, and *Courrier de Versailles*, Oct. 13, p. 163.

[45] Lacroix, II, 268–69.

[46] See Gottschalk and Maddox, pp. 307–8.

[47] *Mémoires*, II, 358; Lafayette to Mounier, Oct. 23, *ibid.*, p. 416; Comtesse de Genlis, *Mémoires inédits* (Paris, 1825), III, 270–71; and *Révélations privées . . . ou mémoires (inédits) de Sénart . . .* , ed. Alexis Dumesnil (Paris, 1824), p. 9.

[48] *Courrier de Versailles*, Oct. 16, p. 228; *AP*, IX, 440; and Duquesnoy, I, 438–39.

that Lafayette began to receive from the Comité des Recherches moneys that eventually were to add up to 173,600 livres, derived from the royal treasury, to pay for the surveillance of plotters, agitators, hoarders, forgers, unfriendly foreigners (including certain ambassadors), deserters, émigrés, and other suspects.[49]

Shortly after the October Days Lafayette decided that his duty as Paris' chief police officer required him to circumvent Orléans, if he was indeed a conspirator, or to remove him as a rallying point, if he was merely a symbol for other malcontents. Even if (though Lafayette was far from certain) Orléans had had no hand in fomenting the recent outbursts of violence, who could tell when he or his supporters would indeed make trouble? Obviously the thing to do was to have a clear understanding with the prince. On October 9 Lafayette sent him a polite message stating that he had "some words to say that might interest him" and suggesting that they meet the next afternoon at the home of a mutual friend, Marquise de Coigny.[50] Orléans received the message in Versailles, shortly after he arrived to attend the meeting of the National Assembly, of which he was a member. He accepted the invitation.[51]

Accordingly on the afternoon of October 10 Lafayette went to the home of Mme de Coigny. Enough had happened to assure him, if he needed assurance, that the Commune of Paris agreed with him that the violence of recent days was the result of none too subtle instigation by unnamed plotters. Moreover, a prevalent sentiment in the National Assembly implied that he need no longer scruple—in fact, should make every effort—to bring such plotters to trial if he could build a case against them. For the sake

---

[49] Papiers du Comité des Recherches, Archives Nationales (hereafter called AN), Dxxix^bis 34, dossier 357. See Appendix I below.

[50] Lafayette to Orléans, "ce vendredi" [Oct. 9], Étienne Charavay, *Le général La Fayette, 1757–1834* (Paris, 1898), pp. 191–92. Charavay thinks this letter is the request for the second of the three interviews of the two men on this matter, but he has been misled by Lafayette's own predating of the first interview. In *Mémoires*, II, 357 (written apparently long after the event) Lafayette placed his first invitation on Oct. 7, and *ibid.*, III, 201 (written in 1799) he placed the actual meeting on Oct. 8, and *ibid.*, II, 416 (Lafayette to Mounier, Oct. 23, 1789) he placed it on Oct. 9. The contemporary testimony referred to below (n. 53), however, places the first interview on Oct. 10. The letter published by Charavay is obviously a request for that first interview.

[51] "Exposé d'Orléans, rédigé par lui-même," *AP*, XVI, 733.

of public order at least (and he could hardly have failed to identify the cause of public order with his own political prestige) he must get rid of Orléans' presumed (and rival) influence. A public accusation, however, would never do, since Orléans had influential supporters, and Lafayette had little evidence that would stand up in court. The solution of the dilemma seemed obvious—the prince must be sent out of the country on a mission he could not tactfully refuse to undertake, and Lafayette could count on the minister of foreign affairs, his friend Comte de Montmorin, to fall in with that stratagem.

Having arrived at Mme de Coigny's, Lafayette engaged the prince in a conversation which, as Lafayette himself afterward admitted (echoing Mirabeau's description of it), was "very imperious on one side and very resigned on the other."[52] Whether or not Lafayette brought up all the current charges against him, Orléans could not have been ignorant of them. Some charged that Orléans was responsible for the shortage of bread, others that he had sought to drive the king to flight in order to place himself in power, others that he had distributed money among the Parisian crowd and the National Guard to foment the disorders of October 5–6, and still others that the Orleanists were plotting to infiltrate the Guard with malcontents and to assassinate Bailly and Lafayette.[53] Lafayette pointed out frankly that the prince's presence in France was in any case a source of political unrest, because ill-intentioned men, abusing the prince's confidence, were using the Orléans name to stir up trouble, and his departure from the capital would make it easier to preserve order.

At first, Orléans seemed unpersuaded, and so Lafayette resorted to threat. He painted a grim picture of the tide of dissatisfaction with the prince in Paris and foresaw danger for him personally if he remained in the capital. Moreover, Lafayette declared, he in-

[52] *Mémoires*, II, 357 and n. 2. For Mirabeau's words see *AP*, XIX, 402 (Oct. 2, 1790).

[53] "Exposé d'Orléans," *AP*, XVI, 733–34; Orléans to National Assembly, July 3, 1790, *ibid.*, p. 720; *Mémoires*, II, 357; Conde de Fernan Nuñez to Conde de Floridablanca, Oct. 18, Albert Mousset, *Un témoin ignoré de la Révolution, le Comte de Fernan Nuñez* (Paris, 1924), pp. 94–46; Baillard Huber to Lord Auckland, Oct. 15, *The Journal and Correspondence of William, Lord Auckland* (London, 1861–62), II, 365; and Baron de Staël-Holstein, *Correspondance diplomatique*, ed. L. Léouzon le Duc, Oct. 15, p. 136.

tended to defend the king with his life, if necessary. If he remembered his exact words ten years later, he told the prince: "I have contributed more than anyone to upsetting the steps to the throne; the nation has placed the king on the last one; I will defend him there against you, and before you take his place there, you will have to pass over my body, and that will not be easy."[54]

Orléans was now apparently impressed, and Lafayette pushed his advantage. He told Orléans that the king wished him to undertake a special diplomatic mission to London and that he himself believed Orléans, because of his many friends in England, capable of rendering his country useful service there. Since the people of the Austrian Netherlands (the Belgians) were threatening to revolt against France's ally Austria, Orléans' assignment would appear as a conspicuous mark of royal confidence at a time of international crisis.[55] By thus appealing at once to patriotism and ambition, Lafayette succeeded in winning the prince over, and before the interview ended Orléans consented to accept the mission. The two men parted on good terms.[56]

If the king should decide to create a new ministry, Lafayette was generally expected to have a decisive voice in selecting the new ministers,[57] and he obviously intended to use his influence to surround the throne with men he could trust, most of them old friends —and perhaps also Mirabeau, who, in spite of a notorious reputation in personal affairs, was greatly respected in the National Assembly for his insight and eloquence in affairs of state.[58] Although Lafayette had long considered Mirabeau a stalwart in the Orleanist faction, he could now afford to overlook that unfortunate association since Orléans was on his way to England. The morning after his confrontation with Orléans, however, Lafayette received

[54] *Mémoires,* III, 201. This part of the conversation in substance is reported also by Fernan Nuñez (Mousset, pp. 94–96), who says he learned it from an intimate friend of Lafayette, and by Huber (Auckland, II, 365).

[55] On the Belgian insurrection see below, pp. 21 and 271–97.

[56] "Exposé d'Orléans," *AP,* XVI, 733; Orléans to the National Assembly, July 3, 1790, *ibid.,* pp. 719–20; *Mémoires,* II, 357; and Grace Dalrymple Elliot (mistress of Orléans), *Journal . . . sur sa vie pendant la Révolution française,* ed. Fs. Barrière (Paris, 1862), p. 279.

[57] See below, pp. 26–45.

[58] Short to John Jay, Oct. 25, Boyd (ed.), XVI, 6 n.

a bad jolt. Shortly after their meeting, Orléans had discussed Lafayette's proposal with some of his friends, and they advised him not to go to England, since Lafayette could prove nothing against him.[59] Orléans decided to accept their advice, and in the evening after his interview with Lafayette he so informed Lafayette. It was obvious that if Orléans stayed in France, not only would the danger of plotting continue but also Lafayette's scheme for an understanding with Mirabeau would go a-glimmering. Lafayette immediately proposed that Orléans meet him again at Mme de Coigny's the next day.[60]

When Lafayette went to Mme de Coigny's on October 12, his trump card was his certainty of Louis XVI's confidence in him. Indicating that he would arrange an interview for Orléans with His Majesty so that the proposed mission to London would publicly be recognized as having been undertaken at the royal behest, he extracted a promise from Orléans to leave within twenty-four hours. A greatly astonished king did consent to see them, and his astonishment increased as the interview progressed, especially when, Orléans having indicated that he would try in London to discover who was causing the trouble in Paris, Lafayette interposed: "You are more interested in that than anyone else, because no one is so much implicated in it as you." The matter seemed settled once more. It remained only for Orléans to receive his formal instructions from the minister of foreign affairs, and he consented to pick them up early the next morning at Montmorin's office.[61]

That night, however, Orléans underwent another change of heart. The Duc de Biron, although he had been associated with Lafayette in the War of American Independence (under his earlier title, Duc de Lauzun), was now devoted to Orléans and indignant

[59] A. de Bacourt (ed.), *Correspondance entre le comte de Mirabeau et le comte de La Marck* . . . (Paris, 1854), I, 126–27, and Marquis de Clermont-Gallerande, *Mémoires particulièrs pour servir à l'histoire de la révolution qui s'est operée en France en 1789* (Paris, 1826), I, 232 n.

[60] *Mémoires*, II, 357.

[61] *Ibid.*, pp. 357–58; Fernan Nuñez to Floridablanca, Oct. 18, Mousset, pp. 95–96. Cf. M. de Simolin, Russian ambassador, to Comte d'Osterman, Russian chancellor, Oct. 19, F.-S. Feuillet de Conches (ed.), *Louis XVI, Marie-Antoinette et Madame Elisabeth, lettres et documents inédits* (Paris, 1865), I, 266–67; Comte de Quélen to President de Saint-Luc, Oct. 18, Vaissière (ed.), p. 27; and Bacourt (ed.), I, 127.

at his friend's meek compliance with Lafayette's demands, and so he sought a way out. Orléans had committed himself to the royal court, but, Biron figured, a higher authority might intervene and authorize him again to decline the assignment to London. The rules of the National Assembly required a deputy to get its consent before absenting himself, but if Orléans were to appeal to his fellow deputies at Versailles, they probably would consent to a leave of absence unless some colleague were to present a good case for not granting it. Mirabeau was just the man to present that case.

With Orléans' approval Biron went to see Mirabeau, who, although the National Assembly was in session, was in Paris, nursing a temporary illness. When Biron told Mirabeau how Lafayette had prevailed on the prince to agree to leave the country,[62] Mirabeau, who only a few days earlier had given Lafayette the impression that he would "abandon M. le duc d'Orléans to his turpitude,"[63] now grasped the chance to join the group that aimed to pluck the growing feathers from a soaring Caesar's wings. He agreed, with real or feigned indignation, that Orléans' proposed absence from his post as deputy should be publicly debated,[64] believing (or at least so he declared later) that the manner by which Lafayette had coerced a representative of the people "would alarm the friends of liberty, scatter doubts upon the causes of the Revolution, furnish a new pretext to the malcontents, isolate the king more and more, and sow new seeds of distrust both inside and outside the kingdom."[65] Whether Mirabeau cared much for the principle of justice involved or, as one of Mirabeau's intimates claimed, feared Lafayette's republican proclivities,[66] he was keen enough to put his finger on the major issue at stake in Lafayette's banishment of a prince of the blood: "Above all, it left without rival the man to whom the hazard of events had just given a new dictatorship, the man, who at that moment disposed, in the midst of liberty, of a police more active than that of the old regime, the man who, by

---

[62] Bacourt (ed.), I, 127–28. Cf. speech of Biron, Oct. 2, 1790, *AP*, XIX, 403.

[63] Lafayette to [Mme Simiane], [Oct. 9], *Mémoires*, II, 413.

[64] Bacourt (ed.), I, 127–28.

[65] Speech of Mirabeau, Oct. 2, 1790, *AP*, XIX, 402. Cf. *Mémoires*, II, 358.

[66] Bacourt (ed.), I, 127.

means of that police, had just assembled a bill of indictments without indicting, who, in imposing on M. d'Orléans the obligation to leave instead of having him tried and condemned if guilty, patently eluded in that way alone the inviolability of the members of the Assembly."[67]

Lafayette seemed to have played into his opponents' hands. Despite all his good intentions to establish personal liberty, he had laid himself open to the charge of having confused executive power with judicial power, usurped the authority of the courts, and arbitrarily assumed that a man was guilty before he was put on trial, giving Mirabeau the opportunity to play the role of champion of justice, defender of the National Assembly's dignity, and enemy of incipient tyranny. Mirabeau told Biron that if Orléans would attend the session of the National Assembly two days later (October 14), he expected to attend too, and he would defend the prince and denounce Lafayette, who was assuming the airs of a "mayor of the palace." Biron promised that Orléans would be there.[68] The next day (October 13) Mirabeau's colleague and confidant, Comte de Frochot, tried to dissuade him from breaking with Lafayette but succeeded only in inducing him to soften his denunciation.[69]

When Biron reported his conversation with Mirabeau to Orléans, it was already late at night on October 12. Persuaded that the cards were again in his favor, at daylight on October 13 Orléans once more let Lafayette know that he intended to stay in France. Upon receiving that news, Lafayette, determined to persist, asked Orléans to meet him at Montmorin's office, and whether out of fear, politeness, or overconfidence Orléans agreed. Bright and early on October 14[70] the three men met. Orléans at first was stubborn. He stated that only his enemies could claim that Lafayette had proofs against him—to which Lafayette retorted (if his memory did not deceive him): "It is, rather, my enemies who say so. If I were in a position to produce proofs against you, I would al-

---

[67] Mirabeau's speech, Oct. 2, *AP*, XIX, 402.

[68] Bacourt (ed.), I, 127–28.

[69] Louis Passy, *Frochot, préfet de la Seine* (Evreux, 1867), pp. 20–22.

[70] Fernan Nuñez to Floridablanca, Oct. 18, Mousset, p. 96.

ready have had you arrested," and he frankly admitted he had looked for them everywhere.[71]

Montmorin had already drawn up Orléans' instructions, and at this point he produced them. He had made them as high-sounding as credibility permitted. Not only was Orléans to try to discover the means by which the British government was trying to foment disorder in Paris and the military preparations the British were making to take advantage of France's domestic schisms but he was also to explore Britain's intentions with regard to the Austrian Netherlands. If the British proposed to promote an independent Belgian monarchy, he was to attempt to find out who was the monarch they proposed to give to the new state (and "it is possible that the outcome may prove to be to the personal advantage of M. le D. d'Orléans").[72] The prospect of advancing cooperation among France, Britain, Prussia, and the United Provinces (the Dutch Netherlands) by himself becoming the ruling prince of the Austrian Netherlands was extremely attractive to the ambitious Orléans.[73]

Besides, Orléans could hardy have failed to realize that Lafayette held the better cards. While Mirabeau might or might not win support in the National Assembly, Lafayette had the certain backing of the king and the foreign minister. For a third time Orléans capitulated. Since the mission to London would appear a genuine diplomatic maneuver undertaken at royal behest and not a mere pretext, he need no longer fear that his departure would look like a confession of guilt, and he perhaps sincerely thought he was making a personal sacrifice in order to quiet public effervescence.[74] But what about his duty as a deputy in the National Assembly? He would have to ask the National Assembly for a passport.

Lafayette and Montmorin, whether or not they knew that Mira-

---

[71] *Mémoires*, II, 358.

[72] Montmorin's instructions to Orléans, Oct. 13, Comte Carton de Wiart, *La Candidature de Philippe d'Orléans à la souveraineté des provinces belgiques en 1789* ("Mémoires de l'Académie royal belgique, Lettres," ser. 2, Vol. XVIII [Brussels, 1923]), pp. 15–19. Cf. Fernan Nuñez to Floridablanca, Oct. 18, Mousset, p. 96.

[73] Mirabeau to La Marck, Oct. 14, Bacourt (ed.), I. 363.

[74] "Exposé d'Orléans," *AP*, XVI, 733.

beau had promised to speak in the prince's behalf if he appeared
in the National Assembly, wanted no public debate of the question.
They prevailed upon Orléans to ask the National Assembly in
writing instead of in person for a passport.[75] Montmorin sent a covering letter saying that he was extremely anxious to expedite the
prince's departure on an important mission for the king.[76] One
of Lafayette's aides was instructed to deliver the letters, wait for a
reply, and bring it back to Paris.[77] Lafayette had already obtained
from the Hôtel de Ville a passport for Orléans, his secretary (the
novelist and artillery officer Choderlos de Laclos), and their suite,
signed by members of the Police Committee and countersigned
by himself,[78] and that day (October 14) Louis XVI also signed a
passport, which Montmorin countersigned.[79]

On the morning of the fourteenth Mirabeau, as he had agreed,
returned to Versailles from Paris. On the bridge at Sèvres, he met
Lafayette's aide, going in the opposite direction, carrying the National Assembly's passport for Orléans.[80] The prince's papers were
now completely in order, duly endorsed by all the proper authorities, and upon the request not merely of Lafayette but also of the
minister of foreign affairs. A charge of arbitrary action by the
"mayor of the palace," Mirabeau recognized, would hardly carry
conviction.[81] Moreover, despite Biron's solemn pledge, Orléans
was not in the National Assembly that day, and by afternoon he
and his secretary had left for London.

After learning from Biron the details of what had happened,
Mirabeau was unwilling to acknowledge defeat. He still claimed
that Orléans could not be proven guilty even if he were, and he
hoped that the prince might yet be kept from actually leaving.[82]

[75] Ibid., and Fernan Nuñez to Floridablanca, Oct. 18, Mousset, p. 96.

[76] Passy, p. 22, and Mémoires, II, 358, 363.

[77] Inferred from AP, IX, 441; Mémoires, II, 363; and Passy, p. 22.

[78] Listed in "Note de quelques papiers deposés au Bureau" in a collection of the papers
of the Duc d'Orléans, Bibliothèque de la Ville de Paris (hereafter cited as BVP), 29411,
folio, p. 1. This passport was dated Oct. 13.

[79] Ibid. See also Mousset, p. 96.

[80] BVP, 29411, folio, p. 1; Mémoires, II, 363; and Passy, p. 22.

[81] Passy, p. 22.

[82] Mirabeau to La Marck, Oct. 14, Bacourt (ed.), I, 363.

As expected, the Orléans affair had created a sensation, giving Lafayette's enemies hope for a political maneuver against him. It
happened that when the prince reached Boulogne, the municipality
there, perhaps disingenuously, detained him and sent to Paris to
inquire about the validity of his passports. On Saturday evening
(October 17) Paris knew that Orléans had been stopped at Boulogne by a demonstration which Lafayette's sympathizers regarded
as a job contrived to give the Orleanists a pretext for recalling their
man and reopening the attack. Lafayette's entourage surmised that
Orléans' friends were planning to denounce the prince in the National Assembly, thus providing a pretext for his return, in the
belief that once he arrived in Paris, where the National Assembly
would soon be meeting, his popularity would enable him to "triumph over his enemies."[83]

As part of this maneuver, Biron tried to find out how strong Lafayette's case against Orléans really was. The story had circulated
that Lafayette had said in the presence of Mme de Simiane and
others that Orléans' "letters of credence" from Louis XVI assign-
ing him to his post in England were actually "letters of pardon"
for his crimes.[84] Enemies of Orléans, hearing this tale, condemned
Lafayette for failure to bring the duke to justice; friends of Orléans
replied that the prince was innocent regardless of what Lafayette
might say. Biron wrote to Lafayette repeating the slur and stating
that, though he himself did not believe it, many others did. Lafayette replied that in refusing to believe gossip to the effect that he
had proof of the prince's guilt but was unwilling to denounce
him Biron had acted with justice. Biron seems to have been satisfied with this response.[85]

At Boulogne Orléans protested that his duty required him to
carry on,[86] and since all the official agencies concerned testified to

[83] Morris diary, Oct. 17–18, Davenport (ed.), I, 262–63. See also Lacroix, II, 328,
332–33, and *AP,* IX, 457.

[84] Morris diary, Oct. 22, Davenport (ed.), I, 267–68.

[85] Copy of Lafayette to Biron, Oct. 18, BVP: 29411, folio, Correspondance du duc
d'Orléans, Part II, p. 2; speech of Biron, Oct. 2, *AP,* XIX, 403; and Charles Nauroy,
"Lauzun," *Le Curieux,* II (1896), 36. Morris (I, 268) gives Lafayette's letter at second
hand and misquotes it but gives its import correctly.

[86] "Exposé d'Orléans," *AP,* XVI, 733.

the genuineness of his passports,[87] he was allowed to continue on his way to England. Lafayette's friends took his unreadiness to return to Paris as an admission that he and his supporters did not dare to take the risk that "no proof existed" of his guilt.[88] Dismayed by Orléans' refusal to see the issue through, Mirabeau made no secret of his chagrin. "They claim that I am in his party," he declared; "I wouldn't have him for my valet."[89]

For the time being, the Orleanists' ardor was decisively dampened, and it did not escape notice that Mirabeau, though "known to have been the soul of the party," refrained from taking any open part in their frustrated tactics.[90] Lafayette had outmaneuvered Orléans and his would-be champion, the man who by general repute had the sharpest mind in French politics.

The royal family was prominent among those who had good reason to feel pleased. Probably without knowing the ins and outs of the Orléans-Lafayette controversy, the king's sister, Mme Elisabeth, made no secret of her satisfaction at being in Paris: "I like it here much better than among the Versailles people. M. de La Fayette has behaved perfectly; the National Guard too. All is quiet. Bread is abundant. The court goes on as before."[91]

BIBLIOGRAPHICAL NOTES

Some secondary sources assume that Lafayette instigated the demonstrations friendly to the royal family on October 7 and subsequently. We have found no contemporary evidence that substantiates that view.

Salmour (pp. 271–72) portrays Lafayette at the Tuileries on Oct. 9 as barging "all out of breath" into the royal presence and out again in five minutes to take charge of hundreds of heavily armed National Guardsmen. He also has one of Lafayette's aides inform Montmorin that if he did not want his carriage stopped outside the palace, he had better let it be known when he was coming. Salmour's account of panic and insolence on the part of Lafayette and his men betrays his anti-revolutionary bias, and probably Short's account of the same day (above, p. 7) of calm and a good supply of bread betrays

---

[87] See above, p. 22.

[88] Short to Jay, Oct. 25, Boyd (ed.), XII, 6, n. 5.

[89] Bacourt (ed.), I, 128. See also [Chevalier de l'Aigle?], Les Forfaits du 6 octobre, ou examen approfondi du rapport de la procédure du Châtelet sur les faits des 5 et 6 octobre 1789 (Paris, 1790), p. 159, n. 47.

[90] Short to Jay, Oct. 25, Boyd (ed.), XVI, 6, n. 5.

[91] Mme Elisabeth to Mme de Bombelles, Oct. 13, Feuillet de Conches (ed.), I, 263.

his pro-revolutionary bias. We have found enough evidence of a general outward calm despite specific incidents of disorder to explain the contradiction between the report of the pro-Lafayette American envoy and that of the anti-Lafayette Saxon envoy.

André Maurois, *Adrienne, ou la vie de Madame de La Fayette* (Paris, 1960), p. 213, implies that one reason for the hostility of Lafayette to Orléans was their former rivalry for the favor of Aglaé de Hunolstein, but he seems to push the *cherchez-la-femme* thesis somewhat too far. His book is nevertheless the best biography of Lafayette's admirable wife.

The Lafayette-Orléans controversy became a *cause-célèbre* again in July 1790 (see below, chap. XX), and a plethora of pamphlets appeared both in October 1789 and July 1790 which discussed the relevant issues with more or less partisan fervor and corresponding inaccuracies. The unpublished doctoral dissertation of C. A. McClelland, "The Lameths and Lafayette: The Politics of Moderation in the French Revolution, 1789–1791" (University of California, 1942), pp. 116–18, discusses a number of the pamphlets, indicating which favored Lafayette and which Orléans.

Emile Dard, *Le Général Choderlos de Laclos, auteur des* Liaisons dangereuses (*1741–1802*) (Paris, 1936) gives a good, extensive account of the Lafayette-Orléans controversy (pp. 193–204), though we would differ on some points, particularly on the chronology of events.

Joseph Droz, *Histoire du règne de Louis XVI pendant les années ou l'on pouvait prévenir ou diriger la Révolution française* (Paris, 1860) gives (III, 39–41) several details which seem fictitious. We doubt his statement, for example, that Lafayette sent the Marquis de Sémonville to engage Mirabeau in a conversation so as to delay his departure until after the National Assembly could vote on Orléans' passport.

Lafayette's account of his relations with Orléans and Mirabeau was published in essays entitled "Sur le duc d'Orléans après le 6 octobre" (*Mémoires,* II, 355–58) and "Mirabeau" (*ibid.,* pp. 359–68). Before his *Mémoires* appeared, J. Sarrans, one of his aides in 1830, published from these articles the passages dealing with Orléans in his *Louis-Philippe et la contre-révolution de 1830* (Paris, 1834), I, 350–55.

The attacks upon Bacourt for his mangled editing (see Gottschalk and Maddox, p. 256) lead to suspicion of the exact wording of the letters he has published in his *Correspondance* of Mirabeau. Nevertheless, the charges against him are generally about his rewording of phrases and sentences rather than of content and thought, and we have felt justified in some instances to quote his wording, especially where they do little or no credit to Mirabeau or La Marck, whose reputation he would be likely to try to shield. J. P. Städtler (ed.), *Briefwechsel zwischen dem Grafen von Mirabeau und dem Fürsten A. von Arenberg, Grafen von der Mark* . . . (Brussels and Leipzig, 1854) is a German translation of Bacourt's work with occasional supplementary notes. Since Städtler was La Marck's secretary and admirer, his translations add credence to the passages which reveal La Marck's relations with Mirabeau. Incidentally the few facsimiles that Städtler gives at the end of Vol. I correspond exactly with Bacourt's printed texts.

CHAPTER II

A Lafayette-Mirabeau Coalition?

THE REMOVAL of Louis XVI to Paris meant something more to Lafayette than the mere presence of the royal family and the consequent difficulties of guarding them. It meant also that as long as His Majesty remained, Paris would once more become the center of political activity in France, and sooner or later the National Assembly and the king's ministers would join him there. The removal of the royal government to Paris, however, would create a serious hazard. One of the motives openly voiced by the Parisians who had forced Louis to leave Versailles was that they wished to take their trusted monarch away from the influence of his distrusted advisers. Anyone who remembered the lynching of two royal officials after the capture of the Bastille the preceding July (and no one had better cause to remember it than Lafayette, who had tried in vain to save them)[1] had good reason to wonder what the outcome might be if some of the incumbent ministers took up residence among a resentful and still excited populace. Considerations not merely for their own safety but, more persuasively, for the future progress of the Revolution suggested that perhaps they should be replaced. Had Lafayette been obtuse enough not to speculate upon the advisability of getting more acceptable ministers, other leaders of the Revolution would not have lost much time in pointing it out to him.[2]

Mirabeau was prominent among those who showed a keen interest in forming a new ministry. He had earned a reputation as a pamphleteer before the Revolution, he was taking a conspicuous

[1] Gottschalk and Maddox, pp. 148–50.

[2] Cf. (among others) Morris diary, Sept. 24, 25, 29, and Oct. 2, 4, Davenport (ed.), I, 227, 229, 235, 240, 241.

part in the debates of the National Assembly, and he had considerable justification for thinking of himself as an astute political observer. But he also had the reputation of being an ambitious man, weighed down by debt, unscrupulous, and of flexible loyalties. Lafayette was only one of many who did not trust him. The two had been fellow members of the pre-Revolutionary Societé de Trente, but their paths had begun to diverge when in July Lafayette had found out that Mirabeau was one of the more active supporters of the Orleanist faction.[3] Nevertheless, after the restoration of order on October 6 Mirabeau sent his constituents a well-balanced account of the Versailles riot, making comments favorable to Lafayette.[4] Whether or not that account indicated a change of heart, Mirabeau was an obvious person to consult regarding a possible reshuffling of the ministry, and Lafayette proceeded—perhaps on his own initiative, perhaps on that of Mirabeau's friend Étienne Dumont, who recognized that Lafayette was the man of the hour —to sound him out.[5]

On October 8 the two men conferred on the issue. Mirabeau, as was his wont, spoke frankly, even brutally, of his preferences, which were to steer clear of both the Scylla of the "aristocrats" and the Charybdis of the "republicans." He was particularly vehement, on the one hand, about one of the royal entourage, Comte de Saint-Priest, minister of the king's household, and on the other hand, about the more liberal Patriots in the National Assembly, the ones who were most insistent upon further reduction of royal and aristocratic power—Adrien Duport, Alexandre de Lameth, and Joseph Barnave. Lafayette was not persuaded on either score, and the two agreed only that the time had not yet come for a decisive change of ministers, although Mirabeau made plain that when that time came, he expected to become one. Lafayette was convinced that in any case Mirabeau would abandon the Duc d'Orléans.[6]

[3] Étienne Dumont, *Souvenirs sur Mirabeau et sur les deux premières assemblées législatives,* ed. J. Benetruy (Paris, 1951), p. 112. See also Gottschalk and Maddox, pp. 78–79, 91–92, and *Mémoires,* II, 361.

[4] *Courrier de Provence,* Oct. 5–6, pp. 239–57.

[5] Dumont, pp. 122, 283.

[6] Lafayette to [Mme de Simiane], [Oct. 9], *Mémoires,* II, 413. See also Morris diary, Oct. 8, Davenport (ed.), I, 248.

Later that day the American statesman and merchant Gouverneur Morris visited Lafayette's home. In keeping with the role that he had gratuitously assumed as adviser to Lafayette, Morris undertook "to tell La Fayette what appears necessary as to a Change of Adm[inistratio]n."[7] He and his friend Mme de Flahaut had decided that she, with her influence upon the queen, and he, with his on Lafayette, could play a winning hand at the game of minister-making. Their candidate was Talleyrand, bishop of Autun and a leading member of the National Assembly. Talleyrand had a distinct advantage over Mirabeau in Morris' eye in that he did not yet share Mirabeau's general reputation for unscrupulousness. In a hurried conversation Morris learned that his host was thinking of a sort of coalition ministry, "taking one Minister from each Party" in the National Assembly—which, Morris thought, would be a mistake; what Lafayette should have were "Men of Talents and Firmness and for the Rest it is no Matter."

At dinner the next afternoon (October 9) Lafayette, as usual, entertained a large company, and Morris was there again in his capacity of self-appointed adviser,[8] and again he and Lafayette talked about the proposed ministry. With less discretion than perhaps was appropriate in speaking to a foreigner without official capacity, Lafayette discussed several of the candidates. This time Morris was more specific about Talleyrand, urging him for the ministry of finance. Lafayette demurred, on the ground that Talleyrand was "a bad man—false," but Morris defended his nominee and pointed out that if Lafayette took Talleyrand, he would also get Mirabeau. Lafayette showed surprise at this statement, being convinced that the two men were enemies, but Morris denied that. In addition, Morris asserted, the bishop believed that Louis XVI should have bestowed a distinguished decoration upon the commandant general in recognition of his services[9] (and Morris suspected that this remark did more to convince Lafayette of Talley-

---

[7] Morris diary, Oct. 8, Davenport (ed.), I, 248. See also *ibid.*, pp. 235–36 (Sept.29).

[8] *Ibid.*, pp. 248–49.

[9] The false impression had already gone around that the king had in fact done so: see M. de Lescure (ed.), *Correspondance secrète inédite sur Louis XVI, Marie Antoinette, la cour et la ville de 1777 à 1792* (Paris, 1866), II, 390.

rand's merit than a record of "many good actions" would have done). The conversation turned to possible candidates for other ministerial posts and led Morris to conclude that "the great Question was how to get rid of [Jacques] Necker," the incumbent minister of finance, who, he had to admit, was popular but who lacked the "Talents equal to the Situation" and was "already frightened and sick of the Business."[10]

Conversations like these permitted Lafayette to recognize that although the events of October 5 and 6 had made him appear to be the man of the hour, they had left him somewhat cut off from the political groups that had been taking shape since the first meeting of the Estates General. At the beginning of the Revolution he had shared the political views and had counted on the friendship of a group of fairly united leaders of the Patriots—especially Lameth, Barnave, Duport, Mounier, La Rochefoucauld, and the Comte de Latour-Maubourg. The first three (soon to be known as "the Triumvirate") had begun to break away from him in September, when they had won constitutional provisions for a unicameral legislature and a royal suspensive veto, and despite Lafayette's efforts to keep all six working together, Mounier had felt much more thwarted by the anti-aristocratic success of Lameth, Barnave, and Duport than Lafayette had and now, fearful and angry over the violence of October 5 and 6, was planning to withdraw from the National Assembly and carry his protest to the provinces. That left Lafayette with only two of this once united group, La Rochefoucauld and Latour-Maubourg, to agree with him that the revolution so far accomplished was enough. In short, the old Patriots had begun to split in two (not counting Mounier), and the two splinters now faced each other in relative hostility despite the hope on both sides that they might again cooperate. Lameth assisted by Duport and Barnave was the leader of the group that, in Duport's phrase, wanted to "plow deep."[11] Lafayette, assisted by La Rochefoucauld and Latour-Maubourg, was the leader of the group that opposed the conservative royalists on one side and the "deep-plowing"

---

[10] Morris diary, Oct. 9, Davenport (ed.), I, 250.
[11] Duport quoted in Lafayette's *Mémoires*, II, 370.

reformers on the other. The gap between them seemed to widen as each tried to secure a ministry to its liking.

The Lameth group was prepared to accept some men for the new ministry who might be acceptable to Lafayette, but they also insisted that Necker should not be retained, and Lafayette, while no longer so friendly to Necker as he once had been, still was inclined to consider him useful as a popular figure. Lafayette learned of their preferences from one of their number, the deputy J.-L.-A. Emmery, who did not approve of their opposition to Necker and urged Lafayette not to associate himself with the ministerial changes they proposed.[12]

Morris again went to Lafayette's home on October 11. Although his host seemed reluctant to talk about the proposed ministry, Morris proceeded to deliver a lecture on "the present Situation of France and the Necessity of combining Men of Talents who have Principles favorable to Liberty." Lafayette himself, he contended, could not be both minister and soldier, still less minister of every department; he must have colleagues whom he could trust. When Lafayette objected to some possible candidates because of their morals, Morris was cynical: "Men do not go into Administration as the direct Road to Heaven"; they are "prompted by ambition or avarice."[13] When Lafayette indicated that he had some old friends in mind for the council of ministers, Morris questioned their talents, and when Lafayette responded that he would give them chief clerks who would supply whatever they lacked and would himself as a member of the council "take Care to manage everything there," Morris reflected, but did not say, that that was small consolation since "he himself wants both Talents and Information." When Lafayette indicated that he was considering Mirabeau for the ministry, Morris protested that Mirabeau was so profligate as to disgrace any administration and had too little principle to be trusted. But he refrained from expanding on the subject, for, he later confided to his diary: "I know pretty well the Man I am speaking to and therefore can estimate his Reasons"[14] (leaving the implication that they

[12] *Ibid.*, p. 370 and n. Lafayette gives the name as "Emery," but he obviously meant Emmery, comte de Grozyeulx, member of the National Assembly.

[13] Morris diary, Oct. 11, Davenport (ed.), I, 252–53.

[14] *Ibid.*, p. 253.

were based upon what he had previously called Lafayette's *besoin de briller*).[15] Lafayette also indicated, to Morris' displeasure, that he intended to keep Necker, "whose talents he despises," because he considered him an honest and trustworthy minister.[16]

Other political figures than Morris and the Triumvirate had begun to entertain the desirability of replacing Necker and some of his colleagues. La Marck, as a friend of the queen, satisfied that the Revolution had already gone far enough, conceived of a ministry of which Mirabeau would be the dominant member but which would be under at least the nominal leadership of Monsieur, the Comte de Provence, the elder of the king's brothers. Lafayette soon learned of a proposed alliance of Mirabeau, La Marck, and Provence.[17] Independently, the incumbent keeper of the king's seals, Archbishop Champion de Cicé of Bordeaux, was seeking to oust Necker as *premier ministre* and take his place. Every one of the interested groups was now courting Lafayette, meaning to exploit his influence to win the king's approval for its own slate of ministers.

Lafayette himself was beginning to lose confidence in Necker and some of his colleagues in the old ministry. Not only were they believed to have been responsible for painful errors in the past in Versailles but they also seemed inadequate for what would need to be done in the future in Paris, such as to provide food, restore the stability of the military forces, keep the provinces quiet, and work with the National Assembly for a viable constitution. Some of Lafayette's friends also wished to avoid incurring Mirabeau's displeasure, for they shared the universal regard for his political insight and oratorical ability despite their distrust of his brutal frankness, patent ambitions, and potential venality. And Mirabeau, opportunist that he was, was prepared to shift his position toward Orléans, Provence, Lafayette, or any combination among them.

So a Lafayette-Mirabeau coalition did not seem unlikely. For a short while the Orléans scandal had threatened to create an un-

[15] *Ibid.*, p. 223 (Sept. 18).

[16] *Ibid.*, p. 253.

[17] *Mémoires*, II, 363, and Bacourt (ed.), I, 97–99, 106, 119, 123–26, 352–53. See also Passy, pp. 22–24. Morris (I, 256) heard of a meeting of Mirabeau with Provence on Oct. 12.

bridgeable gap between the two men, but even while preparing to denounce the commandant general for high-handed behavior in that episode, the versatile Mirabeau had not cut all his ties with him. On October 13, the eve of the date fixed for that ultimately canceled denunciation, he sought out Lafayette and, not finding him, sent him what he described as "an obliging but severe letter."[18] The contents of that letter may be judged from a memoir that Mirabeau wrote about (and probably for) Lafayette at this time. It was itself obliging but severe: "There is one man in the state, who, by his position, is exposed to every hazard, who cannot even compensate for his reverses by his successes, but who, in some manner, is the guarantor of peace, one might even say of public safety, which involves at the same time the food supply, finances, army discipline and peace in the provinces. . . . That man . . . is Lafayette," who had behind him both armed force and extensive influence upon the executive authorities. Nevertheless, if the supply of provisions should fail, Lafayette's army would be powerless and might even turn against him; therefore, he must constantly feel responsible for an adequate bread supply. For that purpose, the power of the Commune of Paris and his own military authority were not enough; he must have the cooperation of a larger force and of all governmental agents. In short, "in the new situation Lafayette must have a ministry that is in perfect accord with him." Otherwise, his influence would fade before the people's hunger and the government's shortage of funds: "Eloquence, virtue, public esteem do not provide bread without flour and do not create money without a finance program."

Mirabeau went on to urge that Lafayette throw his weight where it would count the most—in creating a ministry that, faithful to the popular cause as well as to the king's interests, and to political unity as well as to personal friendship, would either mount a triumphal dais or go to the scaffold with him. Immediate action was imperative, for within a fortnight, bread riots, financial ineptitude, and provincial rebellion might bring conflagration. Even three days might give the numerous intrigues already afoot enough leeway.

[18] Mirabeau to La Marck, Oct. 13, Bacourt (ed.), I, 360.

Some people thought that "the man whom it is useful to keep [Necker]" would resign within two months, but then he would be quitting at a time when the mischief he had done would be irreparable, and it would be better if he quit sooner. If he remained, he would "add to his glory that he never paid any heed to his own preference [for retirement] when the public good was at stake. Moreover, if M. de Lafayette becomes the chief, will it not be considered his doing?"[19]

Mirabeau, in short, was pleading that Lafayette become the real chief minister immediately, though retaining Necker in nominal control. In fact, he already had or was soon to have in mind a ministerial slate in which Necker would be retained as first minister ("because he must be rendered powerless as he is incompetent, and yet his popularity preserved for the king") with La Rochefoucauld replacing Saint-Priest in the ministry of the king's household, Champion de Cicé retained as chancellor, Duc de Liancourt replacing Comte de Latour du Pin as minister of war, La Marck in Comte de La Luzerne's place as minister of the navy, Talleyrand in Necker's as minister of finance, Mirabeau as a member of the king's council without portfolio, Mounier as king's librarian, Montmorin as governor of the dauphin but replaced in the ministry of foreign affairs by the Comte de Ségur, ambassador to Russia, who was Adrienne de Lafayette's uncle (by marriage to her mother's half-sister) and one of Lafayette's oldest friends, and Lafayette in the council as marshal of France and generalissimo "for a term in order to rebuild the army." It would have been difficult to concoct a slate more likely to be acceptable to Lafayette and at the same time to Mirabeau. And to this list Lafayette apparently took few significant exceptions, resting content to suggest La Rochefoucauld instead of Champion de Cicé as chancellor, any of three experienced financiers instead of Talleyrand as minister of finance, and Talleyrand in foreign affairs instead of Ségur.[20]

[19] Dated between Oct. 10 and 20 in *Mémoires*, II, 491–94, and Mirabeau, *Mémoires,* VI, 364–69. The editors of both these works call this document a "note." Since it refers to Lafayette in the third person, perhaps it is not a letter, but it may well itself be the "obliging but severe letter" that Mirabeau mentioned.

[20] Bacourt (ed.), 411–12.

After the showdown with Orléans an unnamed friend of Lafayette, probably La Rochefoucauld,[21] kept trying to persuade Mirabeau "to rally to our party." He warned Lafayette, however, that Mirabeau was "extremely angry" over Orléans' forced departure, and it would not be easy to win him over. When the Assembly moved to Paris, Lafayette's correspondent anticipated a new crisis. Lafayette must therefore be prepared to "use his political influences still better" by putting his own trusted men in key diplomatic posts and in the ministry. The slate of ministers this adviser recommended differed in one important regard from Mirabeau's. He proposed making Lafayette's old friend Lamoignon de Malesherbes keeper of the seals and sending Champion de Cicé away. "If you have any other ministry than ours," he wrote, "if the Revolution fails, we are slaves after waves of blood, the rest of us dishonored, and you a rebel, hanged, without glory, without honor, and almost without talent. If you succeed, for unfortunately people judge after the outcome, we are free as Frenchmen, honored as your friends, and you the outstanding man of the world and of the century; and you assure yourself the finest and happiest old age, which you will be permitted to enjoy at age forty if you wish." In this adviser's opinion "the Rubicon has been crossed," and by sending the Duc d'Orléans away, "you are obliged to be popular to excess and especially very thoroughly in favor of the government, for you will soon need it despite your presence in the council." But Lafayette himself should take no rank higher than commandant general of the National Guard: "That is the most modest title but it is necessary."[22]

For their part, Duport, Barnave, and Lameth, while disliking Mirabeau and disapproving Lafayette's having sent Orléans away, felt it imperative at this juncture to make an effort to conciliate

[21] We think he was La Rochefoucauld because almost all who were at this time the most likely to write to Lafayette calling him "mon cher ami" three times and speaking as if the writer saw him often and on a most friendly basis, who might mention "our party" and "our ministry" and what the king might consent to do, and who were in a position to deal frankly with Lafayette on the Orléans affair and on what posts he should or should not take are named in the letter–e.g., Maubourg and Montmorin–except La Rochefoucauld.

[22] [La Rochefoucauld?] to Lafayette, [Oct. 15?], Mémoires, II, 411–13.

the strongest elements in the old Patriot party. They therefore arranged for Lafayette to meet with them and Mirabeau on October 15 at the home of the latter's niece, Mme d'Aragon, at Passy. Lafayette attended with Maubourg.[23] Mirabeau started off on the wrong foot by speaking with characteristic bluntness. Narrating his experiences in the election campaign of the previous spring, he told of having hired a man to watch one of his professed followers, with orders to kill him if he failed to keep his promises. His listeners expressed shock, but Mirabeau brushed it off with a Machiavellian flourish: "In revolutions the petty moral kills the grand one."[24] Since Mirabeau had recently advocated publicly that only the person of the king should be regarded as inviolable, Lafayette feared he had meant to imply that the queen was not to be so regarded, and he wanted Mirabeau to understand that he would be no party to a policy of hostility to the queen. Mirabeau made another bluff retort (in keeping, Lafayette thought, with his pose of appearing tougher than he really was): "Very well, General, since you wish it, let her live; a humiliated queen can be useful, but a queen with her throat cut would be good only as a subject for a bad tragedy."[25]

When the assembled deputies turned to the subject of the royal government's competence, the Triumvirate maintained that the king's current ministers, while not partisans of absolutism, were not wholly "detached from the old regime," and consequently they wanted new men. Considering members of the National Assembly logical candidates for the ministry, the group gathered at Passy set about to choose a slate from among their fellow-deputies. They agreed that none of those present were to be included, even Mirabeau (eager for office though he was) admitting that the prejudice against him made it discreet to wait for time to improve his reputation.[26] They agreed also that to purge the ministry merely of men unenthusiastic about the Revolution would hardly suffice to insure the success of the new order, since the holders of other offices—am-

---

[23] Alex[andre de] Lameth, *Histoire de l'Assemblée constituante* (Paris, 1828), I, 180–82; *Mémoires*, II, 363–64; and Bacourt (ed.), I, 128 n., 361–62 n.

[24] Lameth, I, 181–82 n.

[25] *Mémoires*, II, 364.

[26] Lameth, I, 184.

bassadors, provincial governors, intendants, in fact the whole old bureaucracy—could be counted upon no more than ministers not to sabotage the Revolution. Furthermore, a general purge would reveal where Louis XVI stood, for as chief executive he filled all the posts in the royal service, and so the creation of a new bureaucracy would reveal his willingness or unwillingness to "name to all offices men devoted to the public interest." Hence his response to a call for a purge would provide a measure of his commitment to the Revolution. Only one man in the Passy caucus had the king's ear, and Lameth came away from it with the impression that Lafayette had accepted a mandate to present to the king "that expression of opinion, which was [also] that of the majority in the [National] Assembly."[27]

Despite the attempt to form a united front at Passy, the Patriot leaders failed to remove some stubborn obstacles in the way of a lasting accord. For one thing, there still was Necker's popularity. Although Lameth and his friends insisted that Necker must go, Lafayette had determined not to get rid of him. Then there was Mirabeau's opportunism. He hesitated, although badly in debt, to consider any royal post less than a ministry even if it would keep him in the limelight until he might become a minister, for he thought of himself as "the only man capable of maintaining the social edifice which was ready to collapse."[28]

About the same time that Mirabeau was giving Lafayette advice and meeting with him and the Triumvirate[29] he likewise was trying to win the confidence of the royal court. He prepared a lengthy memoir to submit to the Comte de Provence which proposed that the king immediately prepare to withdraw to a place from which he would be in a better position to guide the Revolution.[30] Mirabeau's scheme was simply to have Louis get ready secretly to withdraw to Rouen, in the heart of loyal Normandy but far enough from the frontiers to rouse no suspicions of foreign meddling in his plans; when all was ready, to proclaim that he ac-

[27] *Ibid.,* pp. 184–85.

[28] Bacourt (ed.), I, 130.

[29] See above, pp. 27–29 and 35–36.

[30] Bacourt (ed.), I, 364–82. The memoir is dated Oct. 15.

cepted certain parts of the work of the National Assembly; to call upon it to join him in Rouen and to continue its work, subject to revision by a subsequent convention; and to announce further reforms he wished considered. This memoir was presented to Provence by La Marck, who asked him to submit it to the queen.[31] Mirabeau, it would seem, had persuaded himself that Lafayette and Provence could work together in a ministry under his silent leadership for the preservation of the monarchy.[32]

Some of Lafayette's friends, whether they were aware of Mirabeau's tactics or not, were working at cross purposes to those tactics. On the Comtesse de Ségur's insistence Gouverneur Morris promised to write to Lafayette urging him to stay out of the ministry,[33] and Talleyrand decided not to accept a place in it since the time was not yet ripe for a new ministry. "The present Circumstances have sufficient Force," the bishop reckoned, "to consume another Administration before Things are entirely fixed,"[34] and Lafayette too "must be preserved, because he is useful."[35]

Even before Morris sent his letter to Lafayette, he was told that Lafayette had decided not to enter the king's council himself.[36] Nevertheless, he sent his letter.[37] He allowed himself, it declared, "the folly of offering opinions which bear the appearance of advice" because his regard for Lafayette and his "sincerest wishes for the prosperity of this kingdom" had pushed him "beyond the line which caution would have drawn." The proposed constitution, Morris prognosticated, would prove ineffective and the National Assembly would soon fall into disrepute, rendering it "indispensable to increase the royal authority." The freedom and happiness of France would then depend upon the quality of His Majesty's advisers, and consequently "the ablest and best men should be added

---

[31] *Ibid.*, pp. 222–25.

[32] *Ibid.*, pp. 129–30, 352, and *Mémoires*, II, 363. Cf. La Marck to Mirabeau, Oct. 13, Bacourt (ed.), I, 361.

[33] Morris diary, Oct. 14, Davenport (ed.), I, 259.

[34] *Ibid.*, p. 255 (Oct. 11).

[35] *Ibid.*, p. 259 (Oct. 15).

[36] *Ibid.*, p. 260 (Oct. 16).

[37] *Ibid.*, pp. 259 (Oct. 15), 261 (Oct. 16).

to the present administration." Morris then relayed several reasons why some of Lafayette's friends entreated him not to go into the king's council himself. Among them were that he would perhaps have less weight inside than outside the council, since "it is not always that the wisest man is the most eloquent"; that if his opinions prevailed, he would be called upon as a general to execute his own orders as councillor and run the risk of public hostility to such a concentration of power; that "the retreat of the Duke of Orléans" would be coupled with Lafayette's entering the council "in a manner particularly disadvantageous and disagreeable"; and that if Mirabeau also entered the ministry about the same time "every honest Frenchman will ask himself the cause of what he will call a very strange coalition." Morris minced no words regarding Mirabeau, who, in his opinion, was one of those "men who are to be employed, not trusted."[38]

By the time Lafayette received Morris' well-reasoned letter, at least one criterion for the selection of the proposed ministry must have seemed to him absolute. That was that candidates should be advocates of the Revolution as thus far accomplished. The application of that criterion would probably mean the sacrifice of the support of the Lameth group, which proposed to go still further in diminishing the king's power, and it might also mean the alienation of Mirabeau if his commitment to Provence and, through him, to a counterrevolutionary effort were to appear more productive of the ends he desired than his commitment to Lafayette.

Yet if Mirabeau's scheme to save the monarchy by withdrawal to Rouen were to work, the king would need all the support he could muster, and particularly Lafayette's. Thus, at the very moment that Lafayette's friends were urging him not to enter the king's council and to have nothing to do with Mirabeau, Mirabeau and La Marck found Lafayette's presence in the council practically indispensable; and at the very time that Lameth and his friends wanted Lafayette to join them in order to "plow deep," Mirabeau and his friends were anxious to win him to a plan to restore royal leadership. Hence Lafayette was in a key position; whether the

---

[38] Oct. 16, Jared Sparks, *The Life of Gouverneur Morris* (Boston, 1832), I, 330–33.

Mirabeau program or the Lameth program or neither would win seemed to depend in large part upon his decision.

Two far from playful tugs-of-war soon developed. One pair of adversaries, the Triumvirate and Mirabeau, sought Lafayette's support as their prize. The other pair of adversaries, Lafayette and Provence, wanted Mirabeau as their prize, meaning not so much to win him over as to keep him from joining the other side. Whichever side won, Necker was likely to lose unless Lafayette could prevail upon the victors to retain him. Having decided not to join the council himself, Lafayette seems to have wanted Mirabeau to make a similar decision—to keep himself on ice for some opportune future occasion—meanwhile taking care not to commit himself too far to the court party. Mirabeau, on the other hand, though he wanted Lafayette to join the ministry with him, needed money and wanted prestige. In Lafayette's opinion at least, Mirabeau was "not inaccessible to money," even though "for no sum would he have supported an opinion that would have destroyed liberty or dishonored his intellect."[39] So Lafayette, without insult to Mirabeau's liberalism or intellect, tried to buy him with money and prestige at the very time that he was trying to buy Lafayette with appeals to glory and virtue.

Lafayette thought the government might give Mirabeau a diplomatic post, which would pay him a handsome emolument, take him away from Provence, and put him under Montmorin. He took Mirabeau to see Montmorin on the morning of October 17, and perhaps also to see Necker that afternoon.[40] But though Lafayette had intended that it should be they who would win Mirabeau over, Mirabeau reported to La Marck that "the affair is hot, and La Fayette won over as far as he can be." According to Mirabeau, while Necker realized that he was under heavy fire, Lafayette, although dismayed by the shortage of provisions and concerned over unrest in the provinces, was hesitant to see Necker go. Mirabeau urged La

---

[39] *Mémoires*, II, 367–68. Bacourt (II, 24) thinks La Marck never said the words that Lafayette attributed to him—that Mirabeau "permitted himself to be paid only to be of his own opinion."

[40] Two letters of Mirabeau to La Marck, Oct. 17, Bacourt (ed.), I, 385–87. See "Bibliographical Notes" below, pp. 45–46.

Marck to get exact details on the bread supply and other needs of Paris, as well as on the discontent of the people: "You deal [me] a winning hand if you get this information for me."[41]

Mirabeau was playing a losing hand, nevertheless. On that very day, La Marck was also busily negotiating with Lafayette, who indicated that he was ready to get Mirabeau an advance of 50,000 francs and a definite promise of an embassy in Holland, England, or Turkey. La Marck rejected the offer, however, because he wanted Mirabeau to be untrammeled by Lafayette's patronage. Lafayette, he thought, still had "petty views" on the subject of "his ministry." "Oh, what a man!" he exclaimed. "But you know him."[42]

The next day, Lafayette had an interview with Antoine-Omer Talon, civil lieutenant of the Châtelet, one of the principal law courts of Paris. Talon was acting as an intermediary for Archbishop Champion de Cicé, who was still trying to keep some of the current ministry in power under his own leadership. Talon seems to have preferred that Mirabeau should not become a minister but that La Marck should, within a ministry dominated by the archbishop,[43] but Lafayette was of the opinion that "to choose a Fleury [i.e., an old ecclesiastic like Louis XV's minister—meaning the archbishop] or some man of that type would be pretty unfortunate."[44] After his interview with Lafayette, Talon was convinced that Mirabeau had outwitted only himself, for everyone else was alienated by his "smartness." Lafayette continued friendly toward Mirabeau, however, and Talon believed that if Mirabeau wished, Lafayette would still propose him for the ambassadorship to Constantinople with the desired remuneration.[45]

[41] Bacourt (ed.), I, 385. Mirabeau's opinion was expressed before the interview with Necker: see "Bibliographical Notes," below, pp. 45–46.

[42] La Marck to Mirabeau, Oct. 17, Bacourt (ed.), I, 386–87. La Marck says (*ibid.,* p. 130) that the 50,000 francs were probably to be taken from the royal funds at Lafayette's disposal but Mirabeau never received them. Theodore de Lameth, Alexandre's brother, says (Bibliothèque nationale [hereafter cited as BN], nouvelles acquisitions françaises, fol. 125 vo.–126 vo.) that Lafayette sent 25,000 francs, but his account seems implausible. Duquesnoy believed (II, 370) that Mirabeau manipulated so as to "borrow" from both Talon and Lafayette; cf. Theodore de Lameth, *Notes et souvenirs* (Paris, 1914), pp. 198–99.

[43] Oct. 13, Bacourt (ed.), I, 359.

[44] Lafayette to Maubourg, [Oct. 18], AN: F[7] 4767.

[45] Talon to La Marck, Oct. 18, Bacourt (ed.), I, 387–88.

On October 18, the eve of the National Assembly's first meeting in Paris, the ministerial contingencies were, if anything, more confused than before. Two things, to be sure, had become clarified—that for the time being at least Provence no longer was in the puzzle and that Lafayette also had withdrawn. But whether, if the old ministry stayed on, Necker or Champion de Cicé would be its leading light or whether an entirely new ministry would be named, whether Mirabeau was still a likely candidate, and whether agreement could be reached on other candidates were all unsettled questions. Morris, although he had now decided not to trouble Lafayette with advice "unless he asks for it, and perhaps not then," nevertheless was still expressing his opinion, and it still was that Mirabeau should not be taken into any council: "Lafayette has committed a great blunder in opening himself to Mirabeau. If he employs him it will be disgraceful, and if he neglects him, it will be dangerous, because every Conversation gives him Rights and Means."[46] Mirabeau's friends, on the other hand, could not afford, politically or financially, to alienate Lafayette. On the eve of the transfer of the National Assembly from Versailles to Paris they could well expect—in fact, intend—that Lafayette's prestige as guardian of the capital's peace be enhanced.

The National Assembly had held no meetings between Thursday, October 15, and Monday, the nineteenth, but that long weekend passed without untoward event. Still Lafayette took no chances. He ordered the National Guard to report for special duty early on the morning the National Assembly was to open in Paris. Special patrols policed the heart of the city near the Hôtel de Ville, the Palais Royal, and the Tuileries. Other detachments, lining all approaches to the Archbishop's Palace, near the Cathedral of Notre Dame, where the National Assembly was to sit, held back the crowds and cleared a passage for the deputies' carriages. National Guardsmen manned artillery pieces at strategic points, and five hundred cavalry patrolled the cathedral square. On the terrace of the Tuileries Palace, fifty men from each division assembled to

[46] Morris diary, Oct. 18, Davenport (ed.), I, 263.

join their commander-in-chief in an oath of special allegiance to the National Assembly on behalf of all their comrades.[47]

The National Assembly began its sitting at ten o'clock and proceeded in its customary fashion. About midday Bailly, Lafayette, and a deputation from the Assembly of Representatives, escorted by the Garde de la Ville and a select detachment of the National Guard, left the Hôtel de Ville to pay the nation's deputies a courtesy visit. Lafayette, after some hesitation, had decided to go as the commandant general, wearing the shining epaulets, the royal blue coat with standing red collar, and the white underdress of the Paris National Guard.[48] Mirabeau had suggested that he wear his uniform, and Lafayette had consented, persuading himself that to go as a civilian member of the National Assembly, as Duport preferred, would look too affected and might displease his men.[49] That simple decision gave Mirabeau an advantage in the tug-of-war with the Triumvirate, for he had prepared a pleasant surprise for Bailly and Lafayette.[50]

As the dignitaries of the Commune passed along the sunny streets, Lafayette saw orderly crowds packed behind the National Guards who lined the way. The National Assembly suspended its debate to receive the Representatives of the Commune and joined the spectators in applause as they entered the Archbishop's Palace.[51] As soon as the applause died down, Bailly presented the homage of the Commune, and he engaged "your National Guard" and every inhabitant of the capital "to shed the last drop of blood for your safety, the inviolability of your persons, and the freedom of your deliberations." The president of the National Assembly thanked

[47] *Nouvelles de Paris*, Oct. 18, pp. 4–5; *Journal de Paris*, Oct. 21, p. 1351; Marquis de Ferrières, *Mémoires*, ed. M. M. Berville and Barrière (Paris, 1822), I, 340; Comte de Montlosier, *Mémoires* (Paris, 1830), I, 318; and Short to Jay, Oct. 21, Boyd (ed.), XVI, 5, n. 4.

[48] *Mémoires*, II, 372.

[49] Lafayette to Maubourg, [ca. Oct. 19?], AN: F[7] 4767. Nauroy in *Le Curieux*, I, 96, places this letter, for no good reason, in 1790, but it fits better here.

[50] Étienne Dumont, *Recollections of Mirabeau and the Two First Legislative Assemblies of France* (London, 1832), p. 158.

[51] See, among others, *AP*, IX, 568–60; Lacroix, II, 345–47, 360–62; *Mémoires*, II, 372–75; *Point du jour*, Oct. 20, pp. 371–76; *Journal de Paris*, Oct. 21, pp. 1351–53; *Courier national*, Oct. 20, pp. 4–5; *Courrier de Provence*, Oct. 19–20, pp. 340–47; and Montlosier, I, 316–17.

the Commune for its respectful welcome and for the pains it was taking, under the leadership of two members of the National Assembly, its modest and learned mayor and the "hero whose arm defends" the Commune: "This hero is a sage, whom only an interest in humanity called to the fields of glory and who, under the banner of a forever illustrious warrior [George Washington], seems, like him, to take his lessons from a new Lycurgus [Benjamin Franklin]."[52]

The ceremony might have ended at that point but for Mirabeau's little surprise. He ascended the tribune—to take advantage, he announced, of "the first of our sessions in the capital" to "pay an obligation of justice" and "a debt of sentiment" to "two of our colleagues" who "have been called by public vote to occupy the two highest offices in Paris." He did not like eulogies, he asserted, but he wanted to present some familiar facts: "You know the difficulties, truly impossible to describe, in which these virtuous citizens found themselves. Discretion does not permit me to reveal all the delicate circumstances, all the perilous crises, all the personal dangers, all the threats, all the hardships of their position in a city of 700,000 inhabitants, kept in continual ferment as a consequence of a Revolution that overthrew all the old bonds, in a period of trouble and terror when invisible hands were diminishing abundance and secretly resisting all the care, all the efforts of their chiefs to feed that great multitude of people." They had had to "fear everything and to dare everything" when the very measures taken to prevent an uprising served to produce one, when moderation appeared timidity and force tyranny, when distrust, unrest, and excess made even well-intentioned citizens almost as suspect as conspirators, when discretion made it desirable to take charge of disorder in the hope of restraining it. Rebuking "a certain number of men who, imbued with falsely republican notions, become jealous of authority at the very moment they confer it" (an unmistakable allusion to the Lameth group), Mirabeau called for a vote of thanks "to our two colleagues" as an invitation to all good citizens to respect legitimate authority, to facilitate the work of their chiefs, and to inculcate obedience to law and to "all the virtues of liberty."[53]

[52] *AP*, IX, 358–59, and Lacroix, II, 345–47.
[53] *AP*, IX, 459–60, and Lacroix, II, 360–61.

"Universal applause" filled the hall, and the National Assembly passed unanimously the vote of thanks Mirabeau had requested.[54] His angling for victory in the contest with the Triumvirate for an alliance with Lafayette thus passed into the public arena for everyone to see.

Bailly, in reply to Mirabeau's panegyric, expressed his own deep appreciation, but, he added: "It belongs more to M. de Lafayette than to me." Whereupon Lafayette took the floor. With tears in his eyes and a trembling voice he spoke with "noble simplicity":[55] "Excuse me, Gentlemen, for my emotion. It is a true measure of my profound gratitude." Then, loyally and tactfully he paid tribute to Bailly: "It is truly glorious to have earned the esteem of the National Assembly under the orders of the chief who has directed my work." He also remembered the thousands of National Guardsmen who for three months had fought the battle for order at his side and even now stood on duty from one end of Paris to the other: "I grasp this occasion to do the National Guard the justice of stating that it has always used its force in a manner befitting the purposes which induced it to take up arms." Then, as Mirabeau had also proposed, the National Assembly passed a vote of gratitude to the Commune as well as to the National Guard of Paris.[56]

Despite some effort to persuade Bailly and Lafayette as members of the National Assembly to remain, Bailly decided rather to act as head of the deputation of the Commune, and so he and Lafayette led their companions out of the hall.[57] The National Assembly now seemed allied with the mayor and the commandant general of Paris in a bond that tied nation and capital together. In praising the Commune and the National Guard of Paris and in applauding Mirabeau's implication that on October 5 Lafayette had had to lead his men to Versailles in order to restrain them, the National Assembly had gone far to wipe out the tension which had existed

---

[54] *Point du jour*, Oct. 20, p. 376. Montlosier says (I, 317) that there was some opposition from royalist deputies, but no other source known to us confirms that impression.

[55] *Patriote français*, Oct. 20, p. 2. See also *Journal de Paris*, Oct. 21, p. 1353; Duquesnoy, I, 451; and Dumont, *Recollections*, p. 158.

[56] *AP*, IX, 460.

[57] Lacroix, II, 347. See also *Point du jour*, Oct. 20, p. 376; *Courrier de Provence*, Oct. 19–20, pp. 346–47; and *Gazette de Paris*, Oct. 21, p. 174.

between the city and the nation's deputies since the October Days. But whether Mirabeau's maneuver succeeded in tying Lafayette to his wagon remained to be seen.

Nor was it clear that all the members of the National Assembly shared the good will that prevailed. Some outstanding deputies had ceased to attend, convinced that good citizens were helpless in the face of intimidation, and the belief went around in the provinces that the king was not free to move about as he wished.[58] Nevertheless some diplomats in Paris reported to their home offices that tranquility seemed restored.[59] Baron de Staël-Holstein, the Swedish ambassador and Necker's son-in-law, even went so far as to declare that peace in Paris depended largely upon Lafayette, who "has great qualities," although "his status . . . has carried him beyond his stature" and "those who praise him govern him." If he could establish better control over the National Guard, show still greater ardor in searching out conspirators, and break with the Lameth faction, he would inspire more confidence in those who were suspicious of his democratic predilections. "Nevertheless, he alone is able to save France or at least to preserve it from total ruin, having in his power the only semblance of force which still exists." Necker's ability combined with Lafayette's integrity and the king's popularity, Staël-Holstein calculated, might yet prove equal to the occasion.[60]

BIBLIOGRAPHICAL NOTES

Except insofar as their reports help to fix events in time, the testimony of Fernan Nuñez, Huber, Simolin, Staël-Holstein, Fitzgerald, and other diplomatic agents in Paris is often second hand. In some instances, however, these diplomats seem to be relaying the testimony of principal witnesses. Fernan Nuñez, for example, apparently had the confidence of Montmorin, Staël-Holstein that of Necker, and Short that of Lafayette.

One of the letters of Mirabeau to La Marck of Oct. 17 (see above, nn. 40 and 41) presents a puzzle. It was written that morning and indicates that later that day Mirabeau was to see Necker. It infers that perhaps Lafayette,

[58] Mounier, "Exposé," *AP*, IX, 587; "Lettre de M. le Comte de Lally-Tollendal à ses commettants," Oct. 17, *ibid.*, pp. 651–52; and Staël-Holstein to Gustavus III, Oct. 22, Staël-Holstein, pp. 145–46.

[59] Fernan Nuñez to Floridablanca, Oct. 13, Mousset, p. 93; Staël-Holstein to Gustavus III, Oct. 22, Staël-Holstein, pp. 145–46; and Short to Jay, Oct. 20, Boyd (ed.), XVI, p. 5 n.

[60] Staël-Holstein, pp. 145–46.

perhaps Montmorin, or perhaps both were to accompany him there, Alfred Stern's *Das Leben Mirabeaus* (Berlin, 1889), II, 107, states that both men accompanied him to Necker's office right after Lafayette had brought him to see Montmorin and that the four spent "several hours" together. And J. Benetruy, as editor of the *Souvenirs de Dumont* (p. 283), apparently following Stern, even assumes that the interview lasted "five hours."

We think, however, that Mirabeau's letter does not bear this interpretation. It says (Bacourt [ed.] I, 385): "Necker n'a voulu me voir, d'abord, que seul; c'est pour cinq heures." This appears to mean that Mirabeau went (and probably alone), if he went at all, at five o'clock that afternoon to see Necker. The *Souvenirs et portraits* (Paris, 1882) of the Duc de Lévis (p. 378) would seem to support Stern's version, since he speaks of meeting Mirabeau immediately after the latter had an interview with Necker "qui ne dura pas de moins de cinq heures." But Levis does not mention Lafayette or Montmorin as accompanying Mirabeau. Neither does Mme de Staël in a rather lengthy narrative of an interview of Mirabeau with Necker "vers la fin de 1789 pour l'engager à le faire nommer ministre" in her *Memoirs of the Private Life of My Father* (London, 1818), pp. 28–30; see also Mme Necker de Saussure (ed.), *Oeuvres complètes de Mme la baronne de Staël* (Paris, 1821), XVII, pp. 24–25.

In short, it would appear that Mirabeau went to see Necker, if at all, on October 17 for a five o'clock appointment, and probably alone. The comments about Necker in Mirabeau's letter of that date apparently pertain not to that appointment but rather to Mirabeau's expectation that Necker could be persuaded either to resign or to accept Mirabeau as a colleague. Mme de Staël claimed (*loc. cit.*) that Necker, far from being intimidated, flatly refused to accept Mirabeau as a ministerial colleague.

CHAPTER III

Orderly Revolution?

WHILE, as deputy in the National Assembly and a leader of the Patriot group, Lafayette was immersed in the issues of the Revolution at the highest levels, he was also, as "Commandant General of the Paris National Guard and of all the regular troops in the Generality of Paris,"[1] obliged to deal at the local level with the less exalted details of preserving order in an urban society racked by the uncertainties of a collapsing regime. The anomalous position of the commandant general could have escaped few practiced eyes these October days. He was the idol of the city's populace; he had the tens of thousands of its police force at his disposal; and in addition he commanded the king's forces for several thousand square miles centered upon Paris. As a general of royal troops he was responsible to a king who in a sense was his ward, and while as a general he was subject to civilian control, yet those who controlled him made no secret of their deference to him. A soldier in that position could become a dictator if he chose. But did he choose? With the American example in mind, he constantly insisted that the military should be subordinate to the civil authority. Ten years later, while ready to admit that he had perhaps been powerful enough in 1789 to have imposed a good system of laws upon France, he claimed that his scruples in favor of liberty had not permitted him to do so: "The very character that would have diminished the risk in the violation of those scruples carried with it an inability to violate them."[2]

Even if Lafayette had been less scrupulous as a watchman for

---

[1] Assembly of Representatives to the Municipality of Estampes, Oct. 14, Lacroix, II, 289. See also *ibid.*, p. 274, n. 1.

[2] *Mémoires*, III, 241.

liberty, he could hardly have succeeded in violating it as a dictator, for others were jealously watching him. Among the most watchful were the sixty districts of Paris—"sixty different republics,"[3] Short called them—each, with its own assembly of citizens, feeling that it represented the will of its constituents more directly than the deputies it had delegated to the Assembly of Representatives at the Hôtel de Ville. Each district had raised one of the battalions of the Paris National Guard, and the assemblies of some districts on occasion challenged Lafayette's authority over their battalions, issuing independent orders and insisting upon their priority, particularly in regard to the companies of unpaid volunteers. On October 9 the Assembly of Representatives, recognizing that the presence of the king and the unsettled state of the capital would sometimes require speedy, well-coordinated police measures, attempted to obviate the districts' interference and to resolve doubts about the obligations of the unpaid militia by vesting the commandant general with exclusive responsibility for the orders to all National Guard personnel, paid or unpaid.[4] But in some districts jealousy of his influence and suspicion of his purposes remained undiminished.

One of the Paris National Guard's most pressing needs at the moment was for a formally authorized cavalry. Thus far the Assembly of Representatives had approved a mounted unit only provisionally, and Lafayette had been using horsemen borrowed from local police units. He now requested the Commune's Military Committee, of which he was the chairman, to make formal recommendations for appointing officers to the cavalry corps. Since in keeping with his practice, Lafayette had prepared dossiers on the prospective officers, a choice was readily made, and he submitted the selected names to the Representatives at the evening session of October 9. Threatened by a bread riot that day,[5] the Assembly of Representatives unhesitatingly accepted the list he submitted,[6] thereby giving definitive sanction to a cavalry unit. He informed the Military Committee, besides, that the king's service now re-

---

[3] Short to Jay, Oct. 20, Boyd (ed.), XVI, 6, n. 4.

[4] Lacroix, II, 226–27.

[5] See above, pp. 11–12.

[6] Lacroix, II, 235, and see below, n. 7.

quired, and he proposed to name, additional aides, some of whom would serve as unpaid volunteers and some as supernumeraries, also unpaid. The committee promptly approved his recommendations.[7]

In some ways nonpaid officers were easier to get than nonpaid men. Long before the October Days Lafayette and his Military Committee had tried to persuade the Assembly of Representatives to issue an ordinance obliging all qualified citizens to join the National Guard. Not only were some qualified citizens failing to enroll but others already enrolled were sending substitutes, sometimes paid Guardsmen or, more often, their servants, to take their turns at guard duty, a practice that was contrary to the spirit of the *Règlement* and indeed threatened to destroy the character of National Guard service as a voluntary sacrifice by willing, cooperative citizens. Lafayette proposed that the committee make the regulations on enrollment and substitution more explicit. Accordingly it drew up a new section (Title X) of the *Règlement,* which proposed that no civil or military post at the disposal of the Paris municipality should ever go to any Parisian qualified for the National Guard who without good reason failed to enroll within a fortnight of the promulgation of the proposed decree or, thereafter, of attaining age twenty. The committee, in addition, recommended a tax from which only those who had served four years in the National Guard before reaching the age of fifty should be exempt, and it defined its previous regulations so as to prohibit substitutions explicitly.[8]

The removal of the King's Bodyguard from Paris placed a fresh burden on Lafayette's already overworked troops, who had been on continuous emergency duty since October 5. In the absence of the Bodyguard, he estimated, one hundred Paris Guardsmen would be needed in constant attendance at the Tuileries. So he proposed to make the grenadiers, the company of picked paid men in the first battalion of each of the six divisions of the Paris National Guard, responsible for routine palace duty. They were mostly former French Guards, who, having in the Old Regime shared with the

---

[7] *Procès-verbal de la formation et des opérations du Comité militaire de la Ville de Paris* (Paris, 1790) (hereafter cited as *Procès-verbal du Comité militaire*), Part II, pp. 9–12.

[8] *Ibid.,* pp. 12–17.

King's Bodyguard in patrolling Versailles, would not be complete strangers to the new service. In order to restore a paid company to the six divisions furnishing these grenadiers, he must raise six more paid companies.[9]

Since the addition of six paid companies would increase the cost of the military establishment, Lafayette recognized that he would have to try to increase the city's income. One way to do so was to improve the collection of taxes. The protection of the collectors of taxes upon goods entering the city gates was assigned to the *chasseurs des barrières,* but this corps, also not yet complete, operated on a somewhat impromptu and informal basis pending the Commune's appointment of its officers. According to a plan already under consideration the chasseurs were to consist of six paid companies each of which was to be attached directly to one of the six divisions of the Paris National Guard but kept distinct from that division's ten district battalions (each raised by a Paris district and bearing its name). Hence the chasseurs would be neither explicitly identified with nor responsible to any of the districts. The Paris officials, and the king's ministers as well,[10] wished to improve the collection of taxes at the city gates and to run down smugglers, but at the same time they recognized that the proposed organization of chasseurs might incur the resentment of the districts. At least some districts might be expected to protest the expense involved in supporting them, and, perhaps even more vehemently, their independence of the district authorities. To bridge the gap between the chasseurs and the districts, Lafayette laid before the Military Committee a scheme whereby each division chief would name the officers of the new company but communicate their names to the presidents of the ten districts that provided his battalions. The Military Committee, taking occasion "to laud the wisdom and delicacy which guided him in all his undertakings," submitted Lafayette's recommendations to the Assembly of Representatives, adding to them a request for two new companies of paid cavalry.[11]

On October 12, Lafayette took up a number of his military problems with the Assembly of Representatives. Among other things

[9] *Ibid.,* p. 18.

[10] Saint-Priest to Bailly and Lafayette, Oct. 10, Tuetey, III, 273, No. 2819.

[11] *Procès-verbal du Comité militaire,* Part II, p. 19 (Oct. 12, 13).

he announced that having been commissioned to assume command of all the royal forces in the generality of Paris, he had asked Louis XVI to appoint Mathieu Dumas his adjutant quartermaster general (*aide maréchal-général des logis*), and the king had consented. Dumas, already a National Guard officer, had previously served with General de Rochambeau's expeditionary army in America, had the confidence of Minister of War Latour du Pin, and had long been a personal friend of Lafayette. The Representatives recognized in the king's appointment of an officer friendly to the Revolution another victory for national solidarity and adopted a resolution indicating their satisfaction.[12] The appointment meant that Dumas would share the command, under Lafayette's orders, of the royal troops stationed within a fifteen-league radius of Paris. These troops, once a potential menace to the revolutionary city, could now be expected to be an ally.

Lafayette next took up the recurrent embarrassment regarding deserters from the royal army. After the insurrection of October 5–6 a number of soldiers of the Flanders Regiment had come to Paris from Versailles without orders, food, quarters, or officers. The Flanders Regiment was the one that Saint-Priest had summoned to Versailles before October 5 in expectation of an attack from Paris, but upon the approach of the National Guard that night it had, without its officers' consent, put itself at Lafayette's disposal. Were they merely deserters or were they loyal revolutionaries? In any event, their presence in Paris without proper logistic arrangements could be expected to cause complications. Some Representatives suggested that the Flanders soldiers be incorporated in the National Guard, others pointed out that such a procedure would seem a reward for desertion and might encourage further desertion. The Representatives agreed that desertion must not be encouraged and left the matter of preserving both good discipline and good will in the Flanders Regiment "to the prudence and sagacity of M. le Commandant-général."[13]

At that point a battalion commander of the National Guard in-

[12] Lacroix, II, 268, 274, and Mathieu Dumas, *Mémoirs of His Own Time* (Philadelphia 1839), I, 113. Dumas speaks of a twenty-mile radius as the extent of Lafayette's military jurisdiction, but the other sources speak of fifteen leagues.

[13] Lacroix, II, 210, 269.

terrupted. He had been instructed by the municipal Subsistence Committee to march with a detachment to nearby Saint-Denis, presumably to escort a shipment of food to Paris, and he had come to consult his general about these instructions. The interruption gave Lafayette an opportunity to point out again that overlapping authority sometimes handicapped his control of his troops. He had difficulty, he complained, in maintaining the public peace because some other authority, without informing him, disposed of units he was counting on for police duty.[14] This sort of interference was a delicate matter, for not only the Commune's committees but also the more sensitive district assemblies assumed the right to issue orders to units of the National Guard.

Here again the Representatives took no action, for they hesitated to consider themselves authorized to act independently of the district assemblies that had elected them. That evening, in fact, while they accepted almost all the regulations recommended by the Military Committee for maintaining discipline, punishing infraction, and prohibiting substitutions in the National Guard, they put them into operation only provisionally, pending approval by the districts.[15] The next day they adopted in principle the Military Committee's recommendations for the additional paid companies of infantry and cavalry.[16] Although the commandant general was authorized to put the tentative provisions into effect at once, the Representatives ordered them sent to the districts for final approval.[17] He was authorized also to name twelve new aides-de-camp, six with pay and six without pay.[18]

Added to Lafayette's complications were the responsibilities thrust upon him by the National Guards of neighboring communities. Even while the Military Committee was worrying about the disappearance of the arms issued to his own unpaid Guards,[19] he was receiving requests from several Paris districts and communities

14 *Ibid.*, p. 270.

15 *Ibid.*, pp. 270–71.

16 *Ibid.*, p. 279 (Oct. 13).

17 *Ibid.*, pp. 280–81.

18 *Ibid.*, p. 281.

19 *Procès-verbal du Comité militaire*, Part II, p. 20.

of the *banlieue* for more and more equipment. When he informed the Representatives of this predicament, they decided that he should ask the king if the royal arsenals could fill the need,[20] and when he accordingly asked His Majesty's ministers for arms, he received their promise to comply. Anxious to speed up delivery, he shortly afterward requested and obtained permission to approach the king directly. Louis XVI proved most generous.[21]

Lafayette was also sometimes called upon to arbitrate disputes among the personnel of nearby National Guard units. A good part of his time, for example, went to the rivalry of the officers of the Versailles National Guard. In the outburst of pro-royalist sentiment since the October Days, the Versailles National Guard had been the butt of severe criticism for having fired upon the King's Bodyguard on October 5. Lieutenant Colonel Laurent Lecointre, commander of the First Division of Versailles, and some fellow officers had drawn up a memorial vindicating the Guard but accusing the Comte d'Estaing, its commandant, of having deserted his command. The Comte de Gouvernet, Estaing's second in command, disapproved of these recriminations, but Lecointre insisted on publishing them. The disagreement of the Versailles officers was already profound when, on October 12, Lafayette recalled the Paris troops on duty at Versailles. The municipality of Versailles, long anxious about the capacity of its Guard alone to protect the palace, was further distressed upon finding that two of its cannon had been taken off by the Flanders Regiment, and they sent Lecointre to see Lafayette about regaining them.

On October 13 Lecointre went to the Hôtel de Ville in Paris, but Lafayette was very busy at the time and invited him to his home later that afternoon. When Lecointre arrived, he found Gouvernet, who had come to see Lafayette about the proposed denunciation of Estaing. Both Versailles officers asked Lafayette to return Versailles' cannon, and he promised to bring the matter before the Assembly of Representatives and to inform Gouvernet, the senior officer, of its decision. Lafayette then retired to his study, leaving

---

[20] *Ibid.*, and Lacroix, II, 279 (Oct. 13).

[21] Lacroix, II, 383 (Oct. 22), and cf. Gottschalk and Maddox, pp. 259, 267.

the two men with Adrienne in the salon, where they engaged in a heated argument. While they were still arguing, Lafayette left his house to return to the Hôtel de Ville. The upshot of their dispute was that although the Paris Commune returned the two pieces, Estaing and Gouvernet resigned their posts, leaving Alexandre Berthier, a veteran of the War of American Independence and a future marshal of France, temporarily in command at Versailles.[22]

Another of Lafayette's predicaments came from the hostility outside of Paris to the King's Bodyguard. The municipality of Estampes, through which a detachment of the Bodyguard had passed, impounded their arms and horses and asked the Commune of Paris to approve its action. The request created a touchy situation, for if the Paris Commune, which, in fact, had no legal authority in such extramural affairs, supported the people of Estampes, its decision might alienate the King's Bodyguard, and vice versa. As was becoming customary in delicate matters, the Assembly of Representatives referred this case to Lafayette, who recommended a course that he hoped would inspire in the people of Estampes the devoutly wished "sentiments of peace and union." Accordingly, the Representatives sent two delegates to Estampes with a reminder that the Bodyguard had now "taken the oath prescribed by the National Assembly" and so were no longer to be regarded as enemies.[23] The appeal had the desired effect, and the procedure adopted for Estampes later established a precedent for a similar instance at Melun.[24]

Several other incidents demonstrated both the increasing interdependence of the Representatives and Lafayette and the tightening of his authority over Paris and the *banlieue*. When a deputation from Montmartre asked for a paid company of the National Guard, the Representatives referred the matter to the commandant general.[25] When the militia of Charonne refused to obey their

[22] *Procédure au Châtelet,* III, 38 (testimony of J.-E. Jouanne); "Déclaration par M. Lecointre" in "Pièces justificatives du Rapport de la Procédure au Châtelet . . . par M. Charles Chabroud," *Procès-verbal de l'Assemblée nationale,* L, 25–33; and Lacroix, II, 316 (Oct. 16). Cf. J.-J.-R. Calmon-Maison, *L'amiral d'Estaing* (Paris, 1910), p. 393.

[23] Lacroix, II, 288–90 (Oct. 14). See also *ibid.,* pp. 281–82 (Oct. 13), 313–15 (Oct. 16).

[24] *Ibid.,* pp. 321, 322 (Oct. 17).

[25] *Ibid.,* p. 288 (Oct. 14).

commander because he had been named by Lafayette's predecessor and not by Lafayette, the Representatives reconfirmed his status on condition that the Charonne militia first affiliate with the Paris National Guard by taking the civic oath to be administered by Lafayette.[26] When Saint-Ouen asked for the affiliation of its National Guard with that of Paris, the request was granted on condition that the Saint-Ouen Guard take orders from the Paris commandant general.[27] When the election of the captain of the District of Bonne-Nouvelle's paid company was contested, the Representatives decided in his favor only after consulting with Lafayette.[28] When a law official, pursuant to a court order, attempted to put seals upon the effects of a National Guard lieutenant and his fellow-officers resisted, Lafayette was called upon to countermand their resistance.[29] When the illustrious chemist Antoine-Laurent Lavoisier, as one of the "directors of the powder supply," advised that more gunpowder be stored in the Arsénal for the winter, the Representatives ordered the commandant general to provide a convoy for a shipment of 15,000 hundredweight from Nancy.[30] When the Châtelet delayed in adopting the new code of criminal procedure, Lafayette urged the Representatives to request that it be put into effect quickly and thus hasten the trial of hitherto suspended cases, and the Representatives did as he had suggested.[31]

The clamor of soldiers from the royal army to be admitted into the National Guard was another of the vexing problems which were regularly referred to Lafayette. In consequence, one of his aides prepared a statement making clear that the Guard no longer would accept "deserters," and the Assembly of Representatives authorized him to arrest all such "deserters." It not only asked the minister of war to make its intention known throughout the army but also announced to all the other municipalities of the realm that since "our National Guard, thanks to the generous efforts of

[26] *Ibid.*, pp. 290–91 (Oct. 14).

[27] *Ibid.*, p. 295 (Oct. 14).

[28] *Ibid.*, pp. 305 (Oct. 15), 311–12 (Oct. 16), 323–24 (Oct. 17).

[29] *Ibid.*, p. 311 (Oct. 16).

[30] *Ibid.*, p. 337 (Oct. 19).

[31] *Ibid.*, pp. 292, 296–97 (Oct. 14).

our fellow citizens and the tireless zeal of the commandant general, who so well justifies our choice, is perfecting itself day by day," it had ordered that no soldier from another service should be enrolled in the Paris National Guard unless he had an unconditional honorable discharge.[32]

Upon the transfer of the National Assembly from Versailles to Paris, the Assembly of Representatives left the mayor and the commandant general to take such precautions as might be needed to make that ceremony orderly and fitting.[33] Lafayette, anticipating that the interval between the adjournment of the National Assembly's meetings at Versailles on October 15 and their resumption in Paris on the nineteenth might be "stormy," ordered special patrols to go on duty on the eve of the National Assembly's transfer.[34] As we have seen, they did their job well.

By mid-October, therefore, Lafayette had good reason to feel proud of his command. On past Sundays he had sometimes reviewed National Guard units on the Champs-Elysées, and for the second Sunday of Louis XVI's residence in Paris (October 18) he prevailed upon the king to participate in the review. In getting Louis to leave the Tuileries for the first time in his twelve days of residence there, Lafayette expected to counteract the persistent rumor that the king was his prisoner. Although the weather was rainy, the king walked from the palace, wearing a broad hat to keep off the rain, and some of the spectators took offense at the lack of dash in the king's appearance. Lafayette had provided him with a National Guard escort of five hundred unpaid troops, who made a smart appearance despite the bad weather.[35] The pleasure of the king as he watched the unpaid citizen-soldiers of the National Guard drill was unmistakable, and the satisfaction he openly expressed to Lafayette was appreciatively reported in the newspapers.[36] Lafayette's own confidence in the Guard was somewhat

[32] *Ibid.*, p. 339 (Oct. 19). See also *ibid.*, pp. 323 (Oct. 17), 338 (Oct. 18).

[33] *Ibid.*, p. 295 (Oct. 14).

[34] *Journal général de la cour*, Oct. 16, p. 221. Cf. *ibid.*, Oct. 21, p. 260, and Morris diary, Oct. 17, Davenport (ed.), I, 262.

[35] Duquesnoy, I, 456, and *Journal général de l'Europe, supplément*, Oct. 19, p. 137.

[36] *Gazette de Paris*, Oct. 20, p. 167. Cf. *Chronique de Paris*, Oct. 20, p. 232; *Révolutions de Paris*, No. 15, Oct. 17–24, p. 12; and *Journal général de la cour*, Oct. 20, pp. 247–48.

shaken by a complaint from another quarter that day. He learned that those who were temporarily acting as the patrol at the city's toll gates were living at the expense of the tax collectors, and he took steps to stop that abuse.[37]

Skeptics soon had a good reason to question the competence or willingness of the Paris authorities to cope with continued unruliness. The supply of bread, abundant immediately after the king's removal to Paris, quickly diminished, and hunger again became widespread. On the morning of the nineteenth three flour wagons were stopped on their way to the Halles, and when the chairman of the local district committee urged their release, the people resisted until the National Guard intervened to defend him.[38] During the rest of that day and all of the next, however, quiet prevailed, for those were the days of the National Assembly's first sessions in Paris with its display of general good will and Mirabeau's eloquent tribute to Bailly and Lafayette.

The atmosphere suddenly changed, however, early in the morning of October 21. A woman outside the baker's shop of Denis François, a member of the National Guard Battalion of the District of Notre-Dame, the neighborhood of the Archbishop's Palace, accused him of refusing to put his full stock on sale. He denied the charge and allowed her to inspect his bakery. Unfortunately for him she found some loaves—reserved, it would appear, for the National Assembly—and carrying a loaf outside, she convinced the gathering crowd that François was hoarding. Overpowering the guard at the shop door, the crowd seized the baker and threatened to hang him. With the help of the National Guard the district authorities interceded and took him to the Police Committee at the Hôtel de Ville. It was about 8:30 in the morning, and only three of the committee were on duty. They put the baker in the custody of the available National Guardsmen and went into the city hall square, the Place de Grève, to try to quiet the crowd, which rapidly became an angry mob. At the door of the building the Guardsmen put up no real resistance, and the mob broke through, dragged François to the square, and hanged him. A man in a National

[37] Lafayette to M. le Comte [de Saint-Priest?], Oct. 18, AN: AA65, plaq. 1, dr. 474, pièce 25.

[38] See below, n. 39.

Guard uniform cut off his head, someone mounted it on a pike, and a jubilant crowd paraded it through the streets.[39]

However great the violence at Versailles during the October Days, Paris itself had not seen such lawlessness since the lynching of two royal officials in July, when the National Guard was new and green. On that occasion, Lafayette, having been unable to prevent the outrage, had resigned in sorrow and disgust[40] and had resumed his post only on the pledge of loyal cooperation of district and city officials in the preservation of order. This time the outbreak caught him unawares, but experience had taught him that he must act sternly. Apprised of what had happened, he called up the district battalions, put extra guards at the Tuileries, posted cavalry in the court of the Louvre, and threw special detachments around the Archbishop's Palace and the Hôtel de Ville. When the mayor and some members of the Assembly of Representatives arrived, they deputed one of Lafayette's aides, the Chevalier de La Colombe, and two of the Police Committee to hasten to the National Assembly and ask for both prompt aid in obtaining food and the immediate passage of a *loi martiale* (riot act).[41] After a long discussion the National Assembly accepted a set of emergency resolutions. Among other measures, it authorized its Constitution Committee to draft a bill against riots and to present a plan for a special tribunal to judge cases of *lèse-nation,* and it instructed its Investigations Committee in cooperation with the Paris Police Committee to find out the causes of the current unrest.[42]

When Lafayette arrived at the Assembly of Representatives, he reported that he had already taken steps to guard the king, the National Assembly, and the municipality. The Representatives

---

[39] *AP,* IX, 472; Lacroix, II, 396–97 (Oct. 23); *Patriote français,* Oct. 22, pp. 3–4; *Courrier de Provence,* Oct. 21–22, pp. 340–41; Ferrières, I, 341–42; Duquesnoy, I, 455–58; *Courrier de Paris,* Oct. 21, pp. 35–36, Oct. 22, pp. 46–50; and *Révolutions de Paris,* No. 13, Oct. 17–24, pp. 26–28.

[40] See Gottschalk and Maddox, pp. 145–58.

[41] Morris diary, Oct. 21, Davenport (ed.), I, 266; Ferrières, I, 342; and Lacroix, II, 363–64 (Oct. 21).

[42] *AP,* IX, 472. See also *Point du jour,* Oct. 22, pp. 397, 402; Lacroix, II, 396–97 (Oct. 23); *Courier national,* Oct. 22, pp. 2–3; *Journal de Paris,* Oct. 22, p. 1357; Ferrières, I, 342; Duquesnoy, I, 460; and A. Lameth, I, 189–90.

commended his foresight and ordered that he recover the head of François, arrest those who were carrying it about the town, break up all assemblages, and repress disturbers of the peace by every possible means. Armed with this mandate, he ordered one of his aides, Pierre-Auguste Lajard, to quiet the disturbances around François' shop, and Lajard's force, with bayonets fixed, broke up the crowds there and elsewhere in the neighborhood. Before many hours passed, the National Guard arrested the leaders of the ring that had lynched François. In the meantime, however, another dangerous crowd had gathered in the Faubourg Saint-Antoine, proposing to march to the District of Saint-Marcel, gather recruits there, attack the monasteries to get the arms believed stored in them, and proceed to the Hôtel de Ville to force a reduction in the price of bread. So Lafayette had to deploy a considerable force in the Faubourg Saint-Antoine. It was able to disperse the crowd promptly, arrest its leaders, and maintain order.[43]

Unwilling, as usual, to act without civil authorization, Lafayette nevertheless went so far as to insist that he must speedily be authorized to use military force if he were to be held responsible for order,[44] and the Representatives, now fully assembled, dispatched a second deputation to the National Assembly to urge speedy action on a *loi martiale*. The National Assembly answered by giving the deputation a copy of the resolutions passed in response to the Commune's first deputation, adding that it intended not to adjourn until it had passed the desired riot act. When the deputation returned, the Representatives decided not only to comply with the National Assembly's request for the cooperation of the city's police in investigating the causes of the current disorders but proceeded immediately to create a municipal Comité des Recherches. In addition, it drafted for prompt publication a resolution inviting citizens to report to the new committee whatever information they might have about plots to disturb public order and offering high monetary rewards to any who would provide evidence leading to the

[43] Lacroix, II, 364, 369; *Patriote français,* Oct. 23, p. 4; and *Mémoires,* II, 375–76.

[44] Lacroix, II, 379, n. 2; *Courrier de Paris,* Oct. 23, pp. 57–58; and *Gazette de Paris,* Oct. 22, p. 184. Cf. Victor Barrucand (ed.), *Mémoires et notes de Choudieu* (Paris, 1897), pp. 452–53.

arrest of the guilty. To encourage informers further, the mayor was instructed to request the king to grant immunity to anyone who exposed a conspiracy with which he might have been connected; Bailly immediately went to the Tuileries and got Louis XVI's written consent to do so.[45]

The Constitution Committee had meanwhile prepared a draft of a *loi martiale*. It proposed that upon the outbreak of a riot the local authorities should display a red flag, summon the crowd three times to disperse, and if it failed to do so after the third summons, use force to quell the rioters. One of the Triumvirate, Adrien Duport, warning against too rapid resort to military power, proposed an amendment stipulating that first a municipal official should ask potential rioters to choose a committee to present their grievances and then quietly disperse, and that only if they failed to do so, should the authorities proceed with the three warning summonses. The bill was passed with Duport's amendment and went to Louis XVI at once for his sanction.[46]

At the request of the king's keeper of the seals, Lafayette once more enjoined the inhabitants of Paris to place lights at the entrances and first floors of their houses so as to dispel the usual darkness of the streets and thus discourage disorder.[47] At ten o'clock that night (October 21) Lafayette went to the Assembly of Representatives to consider the best way to give publicity to the new riot act and to get approval of the steps he proposed to take in case the men already on trial at the Châtelet for François' murder were sentenced to death. He had of his own accord taken measures to back justice with sufficient force, but always deferring to the civil arm, he wanted definitive orders from the Assembly. The Representatives thought that Lafayette's precautions showed "that breadth of enlightenment, that wisdom in planning, and that consistent devotion to the general welfare which characterized him in such a special manner." For the final details of the law to be made clear, the king's keeper of the seals and the officers of the Parle-

[45] *AP*, IX, 472–73, and Lacroix, II, 365–67, 369 (Oct. 21), 389 (Oct. 22).

[46] *AP*, IX, 474–76, and A. Lameth, I, 191–94.

[47] *Journal général de la cour*, Oct. 24, p. 285, and *Mémoires*, II, 376.

ment of Paris had to be consulted, and so aides of Lafayette were sent to get their opinions. When they returned, the Representatives completed their plans for the announcement of the *loi martiale* and commissioned Lafayette to make the military arrangements for this ceremony, which was to be carried out "with all possible solemnity."[48]

That night the Châtelet sentenced the man who was chiefly responsible for lynching François, and on the following morning he was hanged on the Place de Grève. The man who had incited the Saint-Antoine riot was likewise executed on October 22, and the man who had cut off the already dead François' head was banished for nine years.[49] On the day of the executions the *loi martiale* was announced in various parts of the city by selected police officers, dressed in official costume, preceded by city drummers and trumpeters, and escorted by a police guard of five men and a National Guard detachment of foot and horse.[50] It was also published with explanatory comments in the newspapers.[51] A few days later François was given a military funeral as a citizen-soldier and "innocent victim of the people's error."[52]

The phase of the lynching that was particularly painful to the commandant general was the reluctance that the National Guardsmen on duty at the Hôtel de Ville had shown to obey their captain's orders to protect François.[53] On October 22 his order of the day indicated his displeasure over this breach of discipline.[54] As authorized by the proposed regulations on discipline that were still awaiting the districts' approval,[55] he decided that a military court should investigate the matter, and he appointed a court martial to meet

[48] Lacroix, II, 373. See also *ibid.*, pp. 369–70.

[49] *Ibid.*, pp. 375–76.

[50] *Ibid.*, pp. 383–85 (Oct. 22).

[51] E.g., *Révolutions de Paris*, No. 15, Oct. 17–24, p. 27; *Chronique de Paris*, Oct. 23, pp. 242–43; and *Journal de Paris*, Oct. 22, p. 1359.

[52] Lacroix, II, 439 (Oct. 27).

[53] Duquesnoy, I, 457, 462–63; *Patriote français*, Oct. 24, p. 4; and *Chronique de Paris*, Oct. 24, p. 247.

[54] *Journal général de l'Europe*, Nov. 3, pp. 5–6, and *Gazette de Leide*, Nov. 3.

[55] See above, p. 52.

that afternoon.[56] In due course the court found 10 officers and 180 men guilty of disobedience, and acting on its advice, Lafayette cashiered all of them.[57]

As was perhaps to have been expected, this action provoked some opposition among the districts of Paris. The District of the Cordeliers, under the presidency of Georges-Jacques Danton, who on several previous occasions had disapproved of Lafayette,[58] protested that the findings of the military court must be considered invalid until the majority of the districts had approved the establishment of military councils. Although the Cordeliers' own National Guard battalion protested against this protest,[59] other districts endorsed the Cordeliers' reproof of the commandant general's actions, some of them taking issue also with the new *loi martiale* as a potential source of military excess. Several districts defended it, and the controversy became heated in the course of the next few days.[60]

A few other measures that Lafayette took encountered similar opposition. When the Military Committee presented to the Assembly of Representatives its list of officers for the new cavalry companies, some districts immediately found fault with it. Similar protests reproved the independence of the new infantry companies, describing them as a paid corps attached to the divisions, with officers chosen by the division chiefs.[61] This hostility was doubtless due in part to the jealousy with which some districts eyed the Hôtel de Ville but also to the apprehension of the centralization of military power in the hands of some of Lafayette's subordinates. For example, the District of Saint-Victor alleged that the commander of its battalion, P.-A. Guillotte de Saint-Valerin, who was also vice president of Lafayette's Military Committee, was acting in a high-handed manner and contrary to the wishes of the district. Guillotte

---

[56] Lacroix, II, 382, 390–91, and *Chronique de Paris*, Oct. 24, p. 247.

[57] See above, n. 39, and Duquesnoy, I, 469.

[58] Gottschalk and Maddox, pp. 115–16, 146–47, 160, 319.

[59] *Chronique de Paris*, Oct. 24, p. 247, and Lacroix, II, 389, n. 2, 390–91.

[60] Lacroix, II, 422–23, 430–36 (Oct. 26), 439–40 (Oct. 27), 447–48 (Oct. 28); *Révolutions de Paris*, No. 16, Oct. 24–31, p. 3; *Chronique de Paris*, Oct. 27, pp. 258–59; *Journal de Paris*, Oct. 29, p. 1393; and *Patriote français*, Oct. 26, p. 3.

[61] Lacroix, II, 382 (Oct. 22), 391–92 (Oct. 23), 404–8, 413–15 (Oct. 24).

felt called upon to make a public explanation of his behavior.[62]

Among those who sometimes felt that the commandant general or his staff were not sufficiently responsive to the civil authorities was Bailly. Having sent notes which had not been promptly answered, he at one point begged Lafayette to instruct his staff to remedy that negligence. Besides, the mayor expected the commander-in-chief to furnish him with a list of the names of every guardsman sent out of the city on duty, indicating whether he was a paid or unpaid soldier. Lafayette's answer was formal and correct: he had given the desired order and the list would soon be forthcoming.[63] Nor did the mayor hesitate to ask favors of the commander-in-chief. He wanted commissions—now for a man who had distinguished himself in defending the Hôtel de Ville against the mob on October 5, again for "the son of one of my friends," and again for another whose family Bailly wished to oblige.[64] Despite a steady stream of sometimes *ex cathedra* communications from the mayor to the commandant general,[65] Lafayette regularly deferred to Bailly. "Our perfect harmony in these difficult times," he afterward recollected, "was never troubled."[66] He made a conscious effort to show the mayor every deference "even beyond what he could expect," because he wished not merely to show his personal regard but also "to introduce in France the subordination of the armed force to the civil authority."[67]

Whether genuine or feigned for political purposes, the fear in some quarters of a military dictatorship was not allayed when the public learned of a meeting of National Guard officers at Lafayette's house. With the François lynching fresh in mind, he had called them together to consult upon improvement of the service. "We," he told them, "are the only soldiers of the Revolution; we

[62] P.-A. Guillotte de Saint-Valerin, *Mémoire justicatif* [Paris, 1789], p. 20.

[63] Bailly to Lafayette and Lafayette to Bailly, Oct. 20, BN: Fr. 11697, p. 4. See also Tuetey, II, 417, No. 3959.

[64] Bailly to Lafayette, Oct. 22, BN: Fr. 11697, pp. 5–6, 8–9. See also Tuetey, I, 101, No. 955.

[65] See below, "Bibliographical Notes," p. 69.

[66] *Mémoires*, IV, 321.

[67] *Ibid.*, II, 301.

are the only defenders of the royal family from attack; we are the only ones obliged to preserve the freedom of the representatives of the nation; we are the only guardians of the public treasury." Any harm to those sacred trusts through the negligence of the National Guards, he said, would dishonor them forever and bring down upon them the hatred of the provinces as well. "I beg therefore, Gentlemen, in the name of the *patrie,* that your citizen-soldiers associate themselves more solemnly than ever with me by an oath to sacrifice even their personal interests for the proficient and exacting service that we so sorely need under existing circumstances." If, after careful reflection, only part of their battalions were willing to make that sacrifice, they were to try to form of that part a company of grenadiers and a company of chasseurs—i.e., picked men—in each battalion. These men were to bind themselves for four more months (apparently all Lafayette thought would be necessary to complete the constitution) to be ready at any hour day or night if need should arise. But he stressed that this special service was to be entirely voluntary: "I prescribe nothing. I leave it all to your discretion." He asked only that they let him know within three or four days the result of their deliberations so that he could make his own decision. He then, with perhaps pardonable exaggeration, compared the few brief months so far served by the Paris National Guard with the prolonged "hardship that the Americans had endured to ensure their liberty." The Americans, he asserted, "had for seven years left their homes, their wives, their children, deprived of shelter, lacking clothes and food," and "I, who had the honor to be their general, went several months without an écu, living solely on the soldier's ration, and I swear on my honor that during seven years of misery, I never heard a real complaint from an American." Finally came his peroration: "Please bear in mind that our situation is truly alarming because of the unreliability in the performance of duty of which, I am sorry to say, I accuse a number of citizen-soldiers. I place no value on my own head but I swear to defend the French constitution for which we are striving, and I value my word more than my life."[68]

[68] *Ibid.,* pp. 376–77, which, however, omits the passage about the hardships of the Americans. We have followed the text given in *Discours adressé par M. le Marquis de La*

Lafayette must have been aware that since he had already been compared to Cromwell,[69] his words might easily have sounded like a bid for a dictator's crown. In 1792 two of his most bitter opponents, Maximilien Robespierre and Camille Desmoulins, were to go so far as to accuse him of having instigated the murder of François in order to get greater military authority through a *loi martiale*.[70] Yet the possibility that his speech might be interpreted as an attempt to organize a corps bound by a special oath of personal loyalty to himself apparently had not dawned upon Lafayette. For he had completely identified himself with the Revolution as he saw it, the Revolution with France, and France with Paris. The man who had placed resistance to oppression among the rights of man[71] was now in a position to be attacked for wanting to use force to muzzle the people. His rationale was that he believed in forcing obedience to a *free* government, and the government that he foresaw emerging from the Revolution under his leadership would, of course, be free.[72]

After speaking in this stern fashion about a corps that he knew had worked hard and had sacrificed much, Lafayette might have wondered whether he was asking more than his men would accept. He did not have to wait long for an answer. On October 24 the commander of the Battalion of the District of Saint-Roch, one of the better residential areas, came at the head of a large deputation to present him with an address signed by four hundred volunteers, possibly all the volunteers in the battalion. They pledged themselves to perform their services with precision and not to lay down their arms until the general himself would order them to do so or told them "that the great work of our liberty is completed."

Fayette aux officiers de la Garde nationale assemblés chez lui (Paris, 1789), which apparently was published in December 1789. Cf. *Chronique de Paris*, June 2, 1790, pp. 5–6, and Camille Desmoulins, *Révolutions de France et de Brabant*, No. 7, p. 304.

[69] Gottschalk and Maddox, pp. 356–57.

[70] *Défenseur de la constitution*, No. 6 [ca. June 22, 1792], p. 173, and No. 10 [ca. July 25, 1792], p. 300 and n., in *Oeuvres complètes de Robespierre*, ed. Gustave Laurent (Nancy, 1939), and *Vieux Cordeliers*, ed. Albert Mathiez (Paris, 1936), p. 166.

[71] Gottschalk and Maddox, pp. 86, 95–97.

[72] Cf. *Mémoires*, II, 383–87.

Soon this pledge of the Saint-Roch battalion was repeated by all the other fifty-nine.[73] The address of the District of Saint-Nicolas-du-Chardonnet declared: "Our fate is linked to yours. . . . The peace of the present generation, the happiness of future generations have been placed in your hands. Command, and you will find citizens ready to obey."[74] Nevertheless, it quickly became clear that these unanimous expressions of loyalty subtly indicated opposition to specially pledged companies. As the Battalion of Saint-Roch put it, they wanted no such distinctions in their ranks: "All the citizen-soldiers of the battalion . . . would have liked to conform to their general's wishes," for "they all have the spirit of grenadiers and chasseurs."[75]

If the assassination of François had indeed been engineered by a conspiracy to subvert the Revolution as Lafayette envisioned it, the conspirators had failed, and if he had indeed engineered it to strengthen his own hand, he had succeeded, for he was stronger than ever, and the danger in Paris to his vision of the Revolution seemed at least temporarily averted. But the danger still loomed large in the provinces. Disaffection grew as the news of the Paris riot of October 21 reached more distant parts. It was especially ominous in Dauphiny, where Mounier, having left the National Assembly in disgust, was received with favor and openly engaged in building opposition to the National Assembly. Anxious to forestall civil war, Lafayette wrote to Mounier on October 23 in a pleading, yet self-confident tone. He admitted that after the October Days Mounier had been justified in fearing that some party in Paris was opposed to "the reigning branch" of the Bourbons (a reference to an Orleanist "plot") and that ill-intentioned men were fomenting riots. Since that time, however, those dangers had passed. He had induced the Duc d'Orléans to indulge "his natural taste for travel." The prince's party, attempting to make an issue out of Lafayette's action, had only embarrassed themselves, but if

---

[73] *Ibid.*, pp. 377–78.

[74] Oct. 27, BVP: Collection Liésville, Rev. papiers divers, 1–7 avril 1794.

[75] Battalion of Saint-Roch to Lafayette, Nov. 30, in Lafayette's *Discours aux officiers de la garde nationale,* pp. 7–8. See also below, p. 98, for the reaction in the District of Saint-André-des-Arts.

the issue had been joined, "Would my eyes have searched in vain for Mounier to defend me?"

Lafayette admitted to Mounier that the menace of riots, which he labeled "subsidized," continued, some persons being particularly intent upon assassinating him himself. Yet he believed he had better control of the public now than ever before: "If our bread lasts I answer for everything." Speedy justice had been meted out to François' murderers, and a military court was soon to try the National Guardsmen who had failed to protect him. Spectators disturbed the deliberations of the National Assembly, he claimed, less in Paris than they had in Versailles; the people greeted the king with affection when he appeared among them; and His Majesty was expected soon to resume his favorite sport of hunting. Although he had sent his Bodyguard away, their service would be arranged in a manner that would fully satisfy Mounier, while leaving to the National Guard the privilege which even the court and the aristocrats conceded their performance merited.

As for his own position, Lafayette went on, "I am astounded by my immense responsibility, but it does not discourage me." Dedicated by affection and duty to the people's cause, he intended to combat aristocracy, despotism, and political faction with equal ardor. He was ready to admit the weakness of the National Assembly, but, he bluntly admonished, to discredit it would be dangerous and truly blameworthy. Obviously meaning to allay apprehension of his own ambition, he assured Mounier that he hated the idea of excessive influence for a single person and was far more convinced than Mounier thought he was of the need to rebuild the monarch's executive authority. The only way he could see to avoid civil war and to accomplish something desirable was to work with the National Assembly and the king resident in the capital: "I consider this great work possible, I believe it certain, if great citizens and great talents do not abandon the public service." He was ready to guarantee success if the provinces would cooperate for the general interest rather than start a civil war, which would lead to dismemberment of the realm, possibly a change of dynasty, and, much worse, the enslavement and misery of present and future generations.

Having thus given Mounier a sanguine picture of the current circumstances, Lafayette then made an *ad hominem* appeal: "I entreat you not to produce the evil that you fear and that would be the inevitable result of a collapse, which you can prevent. . . . You recognize me as a man of honor, someday you will recognize that I am neither ambitious nor even extreme in my program, and if your friendship and your confidence in me do not bring about your prompt return, if you abandon me in the midst of the difficulties, dangers, and faction that I am fighting against, at least spare the public, spare yourself regrets—nay more, remorse." He begged Mounier, instead of obstructing his efforts, to let him know what ought to be done: "If I perish in my efforts to save our country, at least don't give me reason to put the ultimate blame upon the desertions of those whose adherence would have saved us and whose opposition will spoil everything."[76]

The proud and somewhat self-righteous rhetoric behind the appeal to Mounier was not unjustifiable, for when it was written, as several contemporaries observed, Lafayette had accomplished much and had good reason to feel proud. His enemies, in the opinion of his Italian-American friend and frequent visitor, Filippo Mazzei, found him the only stalwart obstacle to their designs.[77] And the English historian Catharine Macaulay wrote to George Washington: "Your friend and *élève*, the Marquis de la Fayette, has acted a part in this revolution which has raised him above his former exploits . . . and shows him far above those base and narrow selfishnesses with which particular privileges are so apt to taint the human mind."[78] Mounier apparently did not altogether share this admiration, but he did not succeed in stirring up Dauphiny, and rebellion, though continually dreaded, did not yet mar Lafayette's version of the Revolution.[79]

---

[76] *Mémoires,* II, 415–20.

[77] Filippo Mazzei to Stanislaus Poniatowski, Oct. 23, Raffaeli Ciampini (ed.), *Lettere de Filippo Mazzei alla corte di Polonia (1788–1792)* (Bologne, 1937), I, 218–19.

[78] Catharine Macaulay to Washington, [ca. Oct. 23], Jared Sparks (ed.), *The Correspondence of the American Revolution, being letters of eminent men to George Washington* (Boston, 1853), IV, 285.

[79] Cf. *Mémoires,* III, 238.

The best, though still inadequate, study of the Paris National Guard for this period is Gordon B. Ringgold's unpublished Ph.D. dissertation, "The French National Guard," submitted at Georgetown University in 1951.

The letters of Bailly to Lafayette are largely available in Paul Robiquet, "La Correspondance de Bailly et de Lafayette," *La Révolution française,* XIX (1890), 54–76. The originals are in the Bibliothèque Nationale, Fr. 11697.

The lengthy attack on Lafayette by Robespierre in the *Défenseur de la Constitution,* No. 6, ca. June 22, 1792, must be discounted as testimony for the events of October 1789. When it was written, Robespierre was considerably more suspicious of and hostile to Lafayette than he probably was in October 1789.

A pamphlet attributed to Antoine Estienne and entitled *Interrogatoire de Monsieur Marie-Paul-Joseph-Roch-Yves-Gilbert de La Fayette, commandant général de la Garde nationale parisienne . . . pardevant les grands-jurés du Palais-Royal et de la terrasse des Feuillans . . .* (Paris, [1790]) pretends to be a set of questions to and answers by Lafayette. It is composed skillfully enough to raise the question whether it was not indeed written with Lafayette's collusion. In answer to the query whether he did not conspire to get a *loi martiale* the pamphlet has him say (pp. 11–13) that the situation was such that all good citizens could see the need for a *loi martiale.*

Mounier's activities after leaving Versailles on October 10 are detailed in Jean Égret, *La Révolution des notables: Mounier et les monarchiens* (Paris, 1950).

The *Mémoires de Condorcet sur la Révolution française,* ed. Marquis de La Rochefoucauld-Liancourt (Paris, 1824) say (II, 329) that Mounier answered Lafayette's appeal of October 23 with the retort: "If you are no longer the accomplice of the Revolution, you are still its courtesan." While this retort is not implausible, these so-called *Mémoires* are not by the Marquis de Condorcet and are otherwise spurious, and so we doubt the authenticity of the words attributed to Mounier. More authentic is the letter said to be by Mounier to the Comte de Virieu, July 10, 1790, given in Maurice Irisson d'Herrison, *Autour d'une révolution* (1788–1799) (Paris, 1888), pp. 124–25, which says (among other things): "I am not sufficiently pleased with M. de La Fayette to consent to be his protégé."

CHAPTER IV

Mirabeau Overreaches

LAFAYETTE rarely was introspective. Had he been more curious about his own motives, he might have pondered to what extent he identified his personal advantage with his country's welfare and both of them with his humanitarian ideals. But that sort of self-analysis was alien to him. In the still heated ministerial crisis, intensified by the exile of the Duc d'Orléans, the defection of Mounier, and the lynching of François, he assumed that his ideals of liberty coincided with France's welfare, and while to achieve them he was ready to sacrifice his personal advantage, he felt confident that all three could be advanced at once. Since he had been born rich and had already become one of France's most powerful men, his personal quest was to serve like his model Washington as the symbol and architect of unity among conflicting factions in a revolutionary crisis.

Mirabeau was a different sort of person. He had huge debts, exercised only the power that eloquence gave, and otherwise enjoyed little esteem among his peers. Whereas Lafayette was ready to give up personal advantage to promote his ideals, Mirabeau was not averse to letting it be known confidentially that he needed money and was for hire, even if his opinions might not be. Whereas Lafayette was modest or, at least, anxious not to appear immodest in public, Mirabeau did not hesitate to claim superiority to others —Lafayette among them. Whereas Lafayette sometimes seemed coy about being self-sacrificing, Mirabeau, with a frankness that often shocked his hearers, admitted that he was self-seeking. He thought of himself as a hard-headed, decisive realist and of Lafayette as an indecisive, sentimental idealist. Since they agreed, however, that France had to avoid chaos and could best reach order and prosperity through a limited constitutional monarchy with a strong executive, he was ready to work with Lafayette toward that end; he would provide direction, he assumed, and Lafayette a popular following.

Sometimes the relations between the two men, each immersed in other affairs besides, had to be carried on through intermediaries. For Lafayette the Marquis de Sémonville, an alternate deputy in the National Assembly, sometimes acted in that capacity, and for Mirabeau the Comte de La Marck. The last days of October and the early days of November were filled with much coming and going of principals and intermediaries. "Lafayette takes half my nights," Mirabeau complained.[1]

By this time Lafayette had determined that while he might perhaps try to influence the choice of new ministers privately, he would take no public stand and would accept no portfolio himself if there were to be a new ministry at all. On the other hand, Champion de Cicé and Necker meant to remain in power if they could, while Mirabeau sought to form an opposition alliance with Lafayette— an alliance which Mirabeau seemed to have publicly proclaimed on October 19 by his eulogy of the commandant general but to which Lafayette was not yet committed. In the several days that followed that eulogy Mirabeau made it his business to keep in frequent touch with Lafayette. He was to find Lafayette frustrating and, he thought, irresolute.

Having lost interest in Orléans, Mirabeau now meant, preferably with Lafayette but, if necessary, without him, to save the throne from further indignity while preserving the achievements of the Revolution. His objective was an alliance of the throne with the Revolution, and he had some reason to suppose that the throne might be aiming at the same objective. On October 18 he received what he called an *adresse* (a subtle proposal) from a man who appeared to him to be "one of the leaders of the intrigues"[2] and whom he afterward designated to La Marck as Montmorin. He saw in this bid from one minister a chance to undermine another, Necker,

---

[1] Mirabeau to La Marck, Oct. 22, Bacourt (ed.), I, 400.

[2] Mirabeau to Lafayette, Oct. 19, *ibid.,* pp. 389–90.

and he decided to use it for what it was worth with "the dictator" (Lafayette).[3] He believed he had made the most of it by giving his interlocutor the impression that he was "indispensably necessary" to the intrigue.[4]

One of Mirabeau's weapons was sheer blandishment. After telling Sémonville about the *adresse,* he wrote to Lafayette: "Whatever may come, I shall be yours to the end, because your great qualities have impressed me immensely and because it is impossible for me not to take a very lively interest in a career that is so splendid and so closely linked to the revolution that is leading our country to liberty." Intrigues were getting worse all the time, he asserted, but he had no intention of becoming an accessory to the treacherous collusion of the other ministers with "the crude or, rather, the truly frenzied arrogance" of Necker, "the contemptible charlatan who has brought the throne and France to within two fingers' breadth of ruin." The incumbent ministers had deliberately insulted him, he protested; they had intended to denounce him as an ambitious man who created difficulties; they had treated the National Assembly's decrees with contempt; they were trying to discredit Lafayette's most loyal friends and most useful agents. Hence, he announced, he intended to force a showdown in the National Assembly and give the nation "a chance to judge whether the incumbent ministry is the right one to save the state." Having long recognized that the inadequacy of the food supply was one of the ministry's most vulnerable points, he urged Lafayette to investigate some sources of foodstuffs in England that he had already called to his attention: "I well understand your policy of not wanting to be responsible for the food supply, but nevertheless you are in fact."[5]

This letter thus made a blunt proposal that the two of them combine forces in order to get rid of the incumbent ministry and create a new one under their control. Lafayette, however, still was not convinced that Necker was expendable, and his reply was circumspect. Regarding the mysterious *adresse,* since he knew little about it, he preferred to postpone discussion until the two could

[3] Mirabeau to La Marck, Oct. 19, *ibid.,* p. 392.

[4] *Ibid.*

[5] *Ibid.,* pp. 389–90.

meet personally. Yet, "without requesting the sacrifice of a reply that you owe to yourself, I will beg you not to abandon a plan that we owe to the public welfare." He was concerned apparently to fend off suspicion that he was either temporizing or compromising: "Do not believe that I am avoiding any responsibility, and since dishonor does not enter into my calculations, I consider as alternatives only the Revolution or my head."[6]

On the day after this exchange of letters (October 20), the attack upon the ministry began. It started out with a complaint that Champion de Cicé's office had not properly circulated the National Assembly's decrees of August 4–5, intended to abolish the privileges of nobles, clergy, gilds, provinces, and cities. Mirabeau intervened with the intention of widening the debate to propose an investigation of the food supply, which was under Necker's jurisdiction. The National Assembly, however, was content with requiring its decrees to be henceforth circulated promptly and with summoning the keeper of the seals to explain why the August Decrees had not received proper attention.[7]

That morning a conference at the office of the minister of war, Comte de Latour du Pin, decided in favor of some major changes in the ministry. The participants decided to work for the resignation of Champion de Cicé and offer his place to Talon. Informed of this offer during the early afternoon, Talon immediately wrote to La Marck, ridiculing the idea and asking for advice on how to proceed. He was confident that the minister-makers who had talked to him had no intention of making Mirabeau a minister, and "it appears that they have projects" even against Lafayette. "Thus, to judge by what has been revealed to me," Talon advised, "the general must join with men in a position to support him."[8]

If Lafayette did not learn from Talon or La Marck about Latour du Pin's activity, he quickly found out about it more directly. The unnamed gentlemen who had approached Talon were from the Lameth-Duport group, as Alexandre de Lameth soon let La-

[6] Lafayette to Mirabeau, Oct. 19, *ibid.*, p. 391.

[7] *AP*, IX, 468–69.

[8] Talon to La Marck, Oct. 20, Bacourt (ed.), I, 392–94.

fayette know.[9] He asked openly whether Lafayette would like to have command of the Army of Flanders, leaving him to guess that he spoke for the minister of war. Of all the offers recently intimated to Lafayette—constable, generalissimo, marshal[10]—this one seemed the most attractive, for the Army of Flanders would be the one that would move into the Low Countries if the diplomatic pot were to boil over. "It is obvious," he confided to Mme de Simiane, "that at this juncture everyone who feels kindly toward me or who wants to find a spot close to the place where I shall be concerns himself about my future status." Some well-wishers, he conceded, might even be motivated by a desire to promote the public good. Nevertheless, he would consider their offers only when he had ceased to be useful where he was, and, he remarked, with a cynicism revealing that he was neither self-seeking nor politically naïve: "I guess, *entre nous,* that ingratitude will save me by that time from the embarrassment of compensation."[11]

So now there seemed to be at least three groups within the incumbent ministry that were attempting to determine its future. Montmorin was obviously engaged in an effort to preserve most of it and to that end had made advances to Mirabeau. Champion de Cicé appeared to be endeavoring to bring about a new ministry. Latour du Pin was in collusion with Alexandre de Lameth and his followers to oust both Necker and Champion de Cicé and to circumvent Mirabeau. Each of the three groups was trying to win Lafayette's support by arguments and blandishments of some kind —to which his reaction was to let well enough alone and to urge all Patriots to unite for the good of the country.

On the evening of October 20 Mirabeau called on Lafayette again. In order to coordinate the administrative departments of the city and settle their disputes the Assembly of Representatives had recently required the mayor to create a Bureau de Ville, consisting mostly of city officials,[12] and since the commandant general had to attend the Bureau's first meeting, he took Mirabeau with him in his

[9] Lafayette to [Mme de Simiane], [ca. Oct. 20], *Mémoires,* II, 414.

[10] See Gottschalk and Maddox, pp. 316–18.

[11] *Mémoires,* II, 414.

[12] Lacroix, II, 353–55.

carriage. As they jogged along the city streets, Lafayette once more urged his companion to accept an embassy, but Mirabeau was not responsive. Although he was willing to admit to—even to impress upon—La Marck that he was gravely hampered by lack of funds, he was determined to hold out for an office high enough to justify payment of the large sum he needed; a lesser one would only compromise him without helping him out of his financial embarrassment.[13]

The conversation in Lafayette's carriage, Mirabeau thought, went off well, but the next day La Marck received a different impression from Sémonville: Lafayette apparently had given Sémonville to understand that, for his part, he was somewhat annoyed by Mirabeau's tough dickering, although La Marck thought that Sémonville himself was beginning to favor an alliance of Lafayette and Mirabeau.[14] How much of each of these countervailing impressions was genuine and how much pretended on both sides for bargaining purposes would be difficult to tell.

Late the next day Lafayette saw Mirabeau again. The commandant general, still concerned that the Duc d'Orléans' partisans might succeed in their maneuver to bring him back to Paris, seemed to Mirabeau unduly eager for news on that score (perhaps believing that Mirabeau might have private channels of information). Mirabeau afterward told La Marck that Lafayette was more interested in "gossip than in good advice." For all that, the two men resumed serious talk about a remunerative post for Mirabeau, and this time Lafayette was ready with a concrete offer—the embassy at Constantinople. Mirabeau again declined, although he expressed willingness to consider an ambassadorial assignment at some more important capital and to accept an advance payment of salary. His purpose, as he and La Marck had previously agreed, was to secure an appointment distinguished enough to serve as a springboard to a ministerial post.[15] So Mirabeau's future remained in doubt, largely dependent upon Lafayette's ability to find him a

[13] Mirabeau to La Marck, Oct. 21, Bacourt (ed.), I, 395–96.
[14] La Marck to Mirabeau, Oct. 21, *ibid.*, p. 397.
[15] Mirabeau to La Marck, Oct. 22, *ibid.*, p. 398.

position that he would deem acceptable. But he had another string to his bow, for meanwhile La Marck kept prodding Champion de Cicé to come to an agreement with Mirabeau.[16]

The incumbent ministers proved to be less sharply divided and vulnerable than Mirabeau expected them to be. On October 21, the day on which François was lynched and the *loi martiale* was passed, Champion de Cicé, in answer to the summons of the National Assembly, gave a lengthy explanation of the conduct of his office, and the Assembly postponed action upon it.[17] That day too the National Assembly demanded that the ministry render an account of what it had done to better the food supply. In response, the ministry closed ranks and exhibited a unity of purpose that strengthened its position considerably. On October 24 it sent a memorial to the National Assembly signed by all eight of its members. It pointed out the formidable difficulties, foreign and domestic, that impeded the free circulation of grain, placed the main responsibility for the food supply on the officials of the Paris Commune, pleaded that the general disorganization made law enforcement difficult, and announced their willingness to resign if others were ready to do better than they. But they warned against "the rash men who would make such promises" and asked for the National Assembly's confidence if they were to remain in office. The Assembly made no immediate reply to this show of ministerial solidarity, leaving the victory at least temporarily with Necker and his colleagues.[18] Mirabeau was angry, detecting in their memorial a personal attack, and he prepared to reply at the next session.[19]

Lafayette was likewise angered by the ministerial maneuver. The intimation of inadequacy on the part of the Commune, of which he was a member, in meeting the food crisis reflected upon him. He felt embarrassed, too, that he had not been informed in advance that the ministers intended to send their memorial. It looked as if, while he had been trying to convert the brutality

---

[16] La Marck to Mirabeau, Oct. 22, *ibid.*, pp. 398–99.

[17] *AP*, IX, 472–74.

[18] *Ibid.*, pp. 519–21.

[19] Duquesnoy, I, 475, and Dumont to Samuel Romilly, Oct. 26, Dumont, *Souvenirs*, pp. 283–84.

toward François into an object lesson on the need for order, to respond to Mounier's resentment with a plea for cooperation, and to channel Mirabeau's ambition into a harmless venality, his assumed friends, Necker and Montmorin, had been preparing a coup that rebuked the Revolution and threatened to wipe out his efforts for unity among the advocates of a moderate constitution. Although in July he had looked for evidence in defense of Necker against Mirabeau's charge that Necker had not pressed the matter of provisions as hard as he should have,[20] now he felt obliged to look for evidence against Necker on a similar charge.[21]

He did not have to look far. He had long been familiar with the futile efforts to bring American foods to France. The ministers' memorial, while pointing out the difficulty of securing grain from practically every country in western Europe, had failed to mention the United States. Yet Lafayette knew of a plan by Jefferson, while American minister to France, for importing salt meat from the United States.[22] In fact, William Short, as Jefferson's secretary, had personally delivered Jefferson's letter on the subject to Necker's porter at the end of September but had received no reply and, as chargé d'affaires since Jefferson's departure, had written (October 14) to ask the minister for an interview. Ten days having passed since then without word from Necker, Short undertook another method to find out what the French government intended to do regarding Jefferson's suggestion. Whether by chance or design, he called on Lafayette the very day the ministers claimed they were doing all they could to alleviate food shortages, and on Lafayette's suggestion he wrote to him the next day, describing Jefferson's proposal as a good means of achieving both relief and economy.[23]

This was exactly the kind of information Lafayette was looking for. La Marck, who visited the commandant general later that day, left with the impression that if Mirabeau would challenge the ministers' claim to having loyally cooperated with the Paris Com-

---

[20] See Gottschalk and Maddox, pp. 73–76.

[21] La Marck to Mirabeau, Oct. 24, Bacourt (ed.), I, 402–3.

[22] Gottschalk and Maddox, pp. 311–12.

[23] Short to Lafayette, Oct. 25, Library of Congress (hereafter cited as LC), William Short papers.

mune, Lafayette would be ready to go to the National Assembly's tribune and back him up. All Lafayette now needed to join Mirabeau's camp definitively, La Marck inferred, was the strength of his conviction, and he urged Mirabeau to set his sails accordingly.[24]

Mirabeau was pleased. The new turn of affairs seemed to clear the way for the course he had originally planned—to work with Lafayette so far as his own interests and policy dictated. Like Lafayette he wanted order; order was not possible without food; the ministry had made their handling of the food supply an issue of confidence. Good, then! He would challenge them on that issue. He proposed to speak in the Assembly at the next session, and he asked La Marck to line up supporters. "By God," he wrote, "don't consider me beaten, for I am not and I shall not be." He counted on La Marck and Sémonville to convince Lafayette that in "whipping" him, his attackers were whipping Lafayette's "page."[25]

It was now Lafayette's turn to seek out Mirabeau. He asked Maubourg to bring him to a meeting and when Maubourg was unable to find him, Lafayette sent an aide to ask for a conference the next Sunday (October 25), when the National Assembly would not meet. Mirabeau's expectations grew. He had promising lines out in all directions. La Marck seemed to be winning Lafayette over; Talon was working on Champion de Cicé; and so Mirabeau ventured to hope that things might yet so turn out that he would have to be beholden to no one. "You recognize," he wrote cryptically to La Marck, "that for a certain arrangement there is no need to knock on any door."[26] He probably meant that if Champion de Cicé would cooperate, they could force Necker's resignation, with or without Lafayette's approval, and they could then form a new ministry.

Lafayette, who was now beginning to have a numerous, well-paid system of intelligence,[27] soon was informed of what Mirabeau

---

[24] La Marck to Mirabeau, Oct. 24, Bacourt (ed.), I, 402–3.

[25] Mirabeau to La Marck, Oct. 24, *ibid.,* p. 403.

[26] Mirabeau to La Marck, Oct. 25, *ibid..* p. 404. See also Talon to La Marck, Oct. 25, *ibid.,* p. 405.

[27] Papiers du Comité des Recherches, AN: Dxxix[bis] 34, dossier 357, pp. 2, 8. See also Appendix I below.

was up to. Besides, the Duc de Liancourt, perhaps intentionally, let fall a remark that came to Mme de Simiane's ear, and thence to Lafayette's, leading him to surmise that Liancourt was conniving with Mirabeau and Talleyrand to confront him with a plan to oust Necker. The plan was to form a new ministry including Champion de Cicé and Saint-Priest of the old ministry, with Liancourt and Talleyrand as new members, and with Mirabeau as an influence in it though not necessarily a member. Lafayette guessed that he had been deliberately if indirectly informed of this design in order to sound him out upon it.[28] Such a slate could hardly have won his wholehearted approval, for Montmorin and La Rochefoucauld were not in it and Saint-Priest and Talleyrand were. Lafayette had perhaps begun to change his mind in Talleyrand's favor when he had last talked to Morris about him, [29] but toward Saint-Priest he had begun to feel a keen resentment ever since that minister's display of ill will toward him during the October Days.[30] He was once more inclined to wonder whether he ought to have anything at all to do with the whole ministerial business, even at the risk, if he remained linked with no party in the National Assembly, of losing all influence there.[31]

Little time was left for politics before Mirabeau's expected challenge of the ministry, fixed for Monday, when the Assembly would resume its sessions. Sunday, October 25, was filled with correspondence and meetings by La Marck and Talon, seeking to win the support of Chancellor Champion de Cicé and the court for their ministerial candidate.[32] Lafayette seems to have been busy too. Montmorin, it was now clear, was ready to buy off Mirabeau. He informed Lafayette that the court was ready to offer Mirabeau an embassy at either The Hague or London, with the added inducement that he might enjoy the attached honor and income

---

[28] Lafayette to [Mme de Simiane], [post Oct. 25], *Mémoires*, II, 432. The reference to Corsica in this letter suggested a later date to the editors of the *Mémoires*, but Lafayette began to be interested in Corsica toward the end of October: see below, pp. 378–79.

[29] See above, pp. 28–29.

[30] Lafayette to unknown, "ce mardi," *Mémoires,* II, 420.

[31] Lafayette to [Mme de Simiane], [*post* Oct. 25], *ibid.,* p. 432.

[32] Cf. Bacourt (ed.), I, 404–6.

while remaining in Paris and in the National Assembly. Although Montmorin was not prepared to accept Mirabeau as a colleague in the ministry at the moment, he was ready to place him in reserve until the next May (when presumably the revolutionary crisis would be over).

Lafayette informed Mirabeau, when they met that Sunday, of Montmorin's offer and promised to see the queen about it himself. Although Mirabeau thought Montmorin's offer a "pompous proposition," Lafayette seemed to him to be "less decided than ever and succumbing to the fatality of his indecision." Gathering that now Montmorin thought his cooperation indispensable, he decided to "re-enter the lists determined not to lose the least scrap of ground." He expected not to have long to wait, "since everything will collapse between now and the end of the next month, at the very latest."[33]

Upon learning of Mirabeau's interview with Lafayette, La Marck advised him to accept Montmorin's offer. He himself went to call upon the commandant general in order to give him "a dose of decision."[34] Lafayette, he learned, was still willing to get a 50,000-franc advance for Mirabeau as ambassador and to show him a draft of a royal letter promising an eventual ministerial appointment. Since Mirabeau could not count upon entering the ministry immediately, La Marck favored his accepting Lafayette's proposition, which would at least relieve him of incurring further "subordinate difficulties[35] [i.e., debts]," but Mirabeau decided to hang back. Since Montmorin was willing to make a high bid for his silence, for the time being at least silence seemed golden.

Things did not work out smoothly, however. Despite the attractiveness of a sinecure embassy Mirabeau's supporters kept trying to put him into the projected ministry, while his opponents were equally determined to keep him out. Talon, who was in Champion de Cicé's confidence, was one of the most hopeful that Lafayette yet would ally with the chancellor against Necker and

---

[33] Mirabeau to La Marck, Oct. 26, *ibid.,* pp. 406–7.

[34] La Marck to Mirabeau, Oct. 26, *ibid.,* p. 407.

[35] La Marck to Mirabeau, Oct. 26 (a later letter), *ibid.,* pp. 408–9. Cf. Duquesnoy, I, 483–84.

that Mirabeau would profit by such an alliance. Lafayette counted upon Talon, in turn, to "continue the surveillance" of the incumbent ministry[36] and keep him informed of Champion de Cicé's intentions.[37] To help Mirabeau out of his financial straits meanwhile, Lafayette sent him a sum of money—23,000 francs— which Mirabeau considered "a ridiculous shipment."[38]

Mirabeau's own efforts to see Lafayette were not always successful; Lafayette was sometimes too busy. He did get to see him, however, on the twenty-eighth. He found the commandant general "careworn, unhappy, and discouraged" and began to doubt Lafayette's influence: "He is crossed on everything . . . and there is no one, down to the animalcule Montmorin, who backs him." Not realizing that until recently Lafayette had been eager not to weaken the incumbent ministry, he attributed Lafayette's failure to be decisive to incompetence and weakness: "What a man! What an outlook! I am afraid . . . he will pretty soon ball things up."[39]

Perhaps (as Talon thought) because of Mirabeau's promptings, Lafayette nevertheless did move. Late on the twenty-eighth he urged Talon to keep up his vigilance, since "the wheel will turn." Talon, thinking that the tone of Lafayette's note meant that he had dropped Necker, pressed upon Champion de Cicé as well as Lafayette the desirability of placing Mirabeau in the government. Sémonville was also pushing Lafayette and Champion de Cicé to bring matters to a head.[40]

By this time Lafayette had apparently begun to speculate whether Necker and Mirabeau might not be brought to sit in the royal council together. But would Necker accept Mirabeau, and vice versa? He raised that question with Mirabeau: "What would you say if M. Necker threatens to resign in case Mirabeau comes in?" And far from avoiding Mirabeau, he now asked to speak with him for a moment at the National Assembly and to go home with

[36] Talon to La Marck, Oct. 29, Bacourt (ed.), I, 413.

[37] Talon to La Marck, Oct. 26, 29, 30, *ibid.,* pp. 408, 413–14.

[38] Mirabeau to La Marck, Oct. 28, *ibid.,* p. 409. That the sum Lafayette sent to Mirabeau was 23,000 francs is shown by La Marck's letter to Mirabeau, Oct. 28, *ibid.,* p. 410.

[39] Mirabeau to La Marck, Oct. 28, *ibid.,* p. 409.

[40] Talon to La Marck, Oct. 29, 30, *ibid.,* pp. 413–14.

him after the session: "Mutual confidence and friendship is what I give and hope for."[41] Thus Mirabeau seemed about to find a place, along with Necker, in the ministry that Lafayette now envisaged.[42]

This arrangement of the influential commandant general with the eloquent deputy, however, was not to materialize. Champion de Cicé had other plans. Until recently he had been enthusiastic about a coalition with Lafayette and Mirabeau whereby nothing was to be done except in concert and he was to keep the other two informed on the attitude of the other ministers. As La Marck shortly afterward contended, Lafayette's power and Necker's powerlessness made it appear for a while that "nothing was easier for the coalition than the prompt destruction, although not all at once, of that ministry," which was "as incompetent as it was disunited," but Lafayette kept postponing a decision, and finally the archbishop changed his mind. La Marck's guess was that the archbishop's defection was due to the ministry's having become jealous of the power that Lafayette was acquiring over the king and queen; that was why they had decided either to remain ministers together or to resign as a single body, counting on the dread of the confusion that their offer of joint resignation would create to keep them in power. "If that is so," La Marck concluded, soon after it was all over, "Lafayette has been fooled, [and] the archbishop is disloyal."[43] Lafayette himself had already divined that the ministers "wanted to free themselves of 'my despotism',"[44] and years later, when defending himself against the charge of having deceived Mirabeau, he contended that it was Champion de Cicé, and not he, who had been responsible for Mirabeau's disappointment, although he considered the archbishop's behavior justifiable in view of Mirabeau's indiscretions and untrustworthiness.[45]

At any rate, just as Mirabeau's friends were beginning to congratulate themselves on the apparent success of their politics, he was

[41] Lafayette to Mirabeau, Oct. 29, *ibid.,* p. 413.

[42] This is inferred from Mirabeau's letter to La Marck, Nov. 5, *ibid.,* p. 417.

[43] La Marck to Mirabeau, Nov. 10, *ibid.,* pp. 420–21.

[44] Lafayette to [Mme de Simiane], [ca. Oct. 25], *Mémoires,* II, 432.

[45] *Ibid.,* pp. 370–71.

subjected to attack both inside and outside the National Assembly. A pamphlet entitled *Domine salvum fac regem* ("God save the king") appeared in which he was accused, along with Orléans, of having plotted the events of October 5–6. Nor did Mirabeau's enemies hesitate to insult him in public. Morris reported that one such insult "was so pointedly affrontive as to ruin him," and "he cannot be now placed in the Ministry and is lost in the Opinion of the Assembly."[46] Mirabeau, still hoping to retain Lafayette's support, claimed that Le Pelletier, the author of the pamphlet had been "inspired, informed, hired, etc., etc." by the keeper of the seals, who was "a slippery old customer."[47]

Others rejoiced at Mirabeau's discomfiture. When Morris next saw Lafayette (November 1) he congratulated him upon having got rid of an embarrassing ally, expressing the opinion that Mirabeau's stock now had declined among his colleagues in the National Assembly. Lafayette asked "with Eagerness" if Morris really believed that, and Morris replied that Talleyrand had said so. Thereupon Lafayette expressed a desire to become better acquainted with Talleyrand, and Morris, grasping the opportunity, invited him to dinner with the bishop. Lafayette, however, thinking that he could not dine away from home without "an *histoire*"—i.e., without arousing unfriendly speculation—suggested instead that Talleyrand come to breakfast at the Rue de Bourbon.[48]

The next Tuesday morning (November 3), when Morris and Talleyrand arrived, they found their host closeted with Adrienne's cousin, the Prince de Poix, who had come early "to make terms for Mirabeau."[49] Lafayette welcomed Talleyrand with expressions of esteem and of hope for frequent visits. Another bread riot had broken out in the Faubourg Saint-Antoine, and so the food shortage became the principal subject of conversation. In due course Lafayette asked what the bishop thought about providing a new ministry, and he replied that, since famine and bankruptcy seemed

---

[46] Morris diary, Nov. 1, Davenport (ed.), I, 279–80. The editor's explanation of this passage (p. 280, n. 1) is obviously mistaken.

[47] Mirabeau to La Marck, Nov. 3, Bacourt (ed.), I, 415.

[48] Morris diary, Nov. 1, Davenport (ed.), I, 279–80.

[49] *Ibid.*, p. 282 (Nov. 3). "Prieur de Poix" is an obvious error for "Prince de Poix."

inevitable, Necker should be allowed to remain in office and bear the brunt of the dissatisfaction. He agreed, however, that another ministry should be got ready to take office "some Months hence," and they talked about who might be included. When Lafayette, as if casually, asked whether Mirabeau did not have great influence in the National Assembly, Talleyrand answered that it was "not enormous."[50]

The conversation then veered back to the food problem, and they discussed remedies without agreeing upon any. When they turned to the ministry again, Lafayette brought up the name of La Rochefoucauld, who, he was willing to admit, might lack ability but whose reputation and integrity were "important." Talleyrand insisted only that the change of ministers must be complete, and Lafayette agreed, adding finally, that "the Friends of Liberty ought to unite and to understand each other."

For Lafayette that plea went to the heart of the matter; if all friends of liberty would unite, France's other problems would be easier to solve. To Morris and Talleyrand, as they compared notes on their way to the Palais Royal, this attitude implied only that Lafayette had "no fixed Plan" and that although he had "a great Deal of the *Intriguant* in his Character," he "must be used by others because he has not Talents enough to make Use of them." Morris himself thought that Lafayette would insist only upon La Rochefoucauld and would accept "any Person we please" in return.[51] And so, though perhaps too certain of their own greater wisdom, they had good reason to congratulate themselves that in Lafayette's political calculus Talleyrand had gained magnitude while Mirabeau had declined.

Mirabeau, however, was far from ready to give up. He begged La Marck to go see Lafayette, remind him that he had "disarmed" Mirabeau without giving any guaranty in return, and warn him that "the perfidy of others" might compromise him too. If La Marck could find out what Lafayette "had in his soul," Mirabeau

[50] *Ibid.*
[51] *Ibid.*, pp. 282–83.

hoped yet to benefit from Champion de Cicé's maneuvers.[52] So on the morning of November 4 La Marck visited Lafayette, talked to him for two hours, and got an appointment for Mirabeau that evening.[53]

Accordingly Mirabeau went to see Lafayette. At first, the general seemed reticent, but after Mirabeau showed considerable awareness of what was going on, he talked more freely. He agreed that they might have to ward off still further hostile moves. When, however, Lafayette again proposed to get for Mirabeau a promise of an embassy, Mirabeau refused categorically. As he recognized, his refusal meant that he now either had to become a minister or remain simply a deputy. He still felt certain that if Necker were not amenable, he could outwit the ministry, not seeing "what miracle will permit them to survive."[54] If only Lafayette would take a stand, Mirabeau felt sure of his support because he was "furious against the ministers."[55] Yet he considered the general "equally incapable of breaking his word and of keeping it at the right time," as well as ineffectual "except in case of an explosion, when he could and to a certain extent would do everything."[56]

Mirabeau's decision not to accept an embassy proved a rash one. He needed money and he wanted prestige, but his only chance of getting either depended more than ever upon Necker's consent to his entering the ministry. His plan now, therefore, was to get Necker's consent, and he counted on La Marck to persuade Lafayette to threaten that if Necker did not respond favorably, the king would receive undeniable charges of the minister's incompetence. He also planned to move in the National Assembly that the ministers sit with it in a consultative capacity, subject to questioning. If his motion passed, as he expected it would, the ministry would be obliged to choose between sitting with the legislature or

[52] Mirabeau to La Marck, Nov. 3, Bacourt (ed.), I, 415.

[53] La Marck to Mirabeau, Nov. 4, *ibid.,* pp. 415–16.

[54] Mirabeau to La Marck, Nov. 5, *ibid.,* p. 417.

[55] Mirabeau to La Marck, Nov. 6, *ibid.,* p. 418.

[56] Mirabeau to La Marck, Nov. 5, *ibid.,* p. 417.

refusing to do so, and he felt sure that in either case it would not long survive. La Marck must therefore "try to get something finished by Monday" (November 9), when, Mirabeau anticipated, his enemies would make a major move and "the treasury will not have a single écu."[57]

Meanwhile Mirabeau himself fired the opening gun in his final campaign to finish off the ministry. On November 5 he denounced the keeper of the seals in the National Assembly for not yet having informed the provincial courts of the new criminal procedure, and the Assembly required the accused minister to produce evidence that he had in fact done so.[58] Open warfare like this no longer permitted Mirabeau to believe that he could manage without rapping on Lafayette's door, and he tried to see him that midnight, but the commandant general had "not yet returned."[59] The next morning Mirabeau learned why: the ministers had had a meeting with Lafayette, and dejectedly Mirabeau complained: "It is impossible to be more completely duped than he is."[60] Obviously Mirabeau thought that a man in the general's position who did not want to overthrow the incumbent ministry in order to dominate its successor must be a dupe. He did not understand, any more than Talleyrand or Morris, that as a military man who scrupulously sought to promote civil authority and national unity Lafayette was reluctant to engage in conflict with the government or that he might for tenable reasons prefer Necker to either Mirabeau or Talleyrand.

Mirabeau now felt forced, with or without Lafayette's support, to intensify the attack. Meaning to anticipate his opponents and not wait for the expected blow to fall on Monday, he undertook to propose the admission of ministers to the National Assembly right away. Early on the preceding Friday, November 6, he asked La Marck to urge Lafayette to support his move: "Tell him that now he has left as his only recourse a ministry of first-rate power, . . . that this ministry must be ready for the commotion which will

[57] *Ibid.*

[58] *AP*, IX, 696–97.

[59] Mirabeau to La Marck, Nov. 6, Bacourt (ed.), I, 418.

[60] *Ibid.*

come from Necker's dismissal, that if I present him with one whose talents and stability he will concede and which will undertake the responsibility, he ought to give me carte blanche to create it." Lafayette should be told, too, that the weakness of the treasury and the impending censure would probably lead to a new ministry even without his collaboration but that, thanks to Mirabeau's "PERSONAL LOYALTY" (his capitals), he would be in a position to "take credit for proposing such a ministry."[61]

Once more Mirabeau outreached himself. Lafayette, having less reason to deceive himself or others about the sentiment of the ministry and that of the National Assembly, probably being better informed on both scores, and perhaps also being prepared to believe that Mirabeau's loyalties were for sale if the price was right, refused to take a stand in his favor—or, perhaps more accurately, took the stand that he must take no stand. Champion de Cicé meanwhile (if Lafayette was not mistaken)[62] induced the highly respected deputy Jean-Denis Lanjuinais to oppose Mirabeau. Lameth and his supporters also lined up against him.[63] So when on November 6 Mirabeau proposed his set of resolutions, indirectly rebuking the ministry for the shortage of food and the emptiness of the treasury and directly proposing that ministers be admitted to the National Assembly, he did not get the support he had anticipated.[64] The debate was resumed the next day, and Lanjuinais warned that if the ministers were given a consultative voice in the Assembly, "we would expose them to becoming the playthings of ambitious men if there are any such in this Assembly." Thereupon he moved that *no* deputy might become a minister for three years after his term of office as deputy had expired. Indignantly Mirabeau proposed that the motion apply only to himself and to no other deputies, but a motion passed that no deputy might become a minister for the duration of the National Assembly.[65] So Mirabeau never became a minister, nor an ambassador either.

[61] *Ibid.*, pp. 418–19.

[62] *Mémoires*, II, 370.

[63] A. Lameth, I, 241 n.

[64] *AP*, IX, 703–14.

[65] *Ibid.*, pp. 705–18.

Some historians, looking back upon the events that followed and beholding the increasing weakness of the throne and the gradual deterioration of authority in France, have lamented the failure of Lafayette to form an alliance with Mirabeau. They have thought of it as the failure of the most popular and powerful man at that juncture in France's history to join with the best brains in the National Assembly and create an effective, enduring constitutional monarchy. But Lafayette did not know (nor can anyone now be certain) that without his alliance with Mirabeau the monarchy was doomed and that with it it would be saved. Lafayette did know, on the other hand, that Mirabeau was personally distrusted (by others besides himself), that his influence in the National Assembly was debatable (as indeed his defeat well demonstrated), that he was opposed politically by the Lameth group, the Talleyrand group, and others,[66] and that he was courting the royal family in a fashion that might prove dangerous to the kind of constitution Lafayette wanted.[67] Those considerations would have been reason enough, even if Lafayette had chosen to be a minister-maker, to hesitate to select Mirabeau as an ally. But he did not choose to be a minister-maker. On the contrary, his principles, like those of Washington, dictated that the military should be subordinate to the civil authority and that he do what would divide the Patriots least, and so he chose to remain silent—at any rate, in public. Since he did remain publicly silent, Mirabeau's defeat was not his defeat.

Yet, had Lafayette planned to betray Mirabeau to his own advantage, he could hardly have planned better. Mirabeau perhaps thought that Lafayette had betrayed him by intention;[68] he certainly thought Lafayette had been weak, indecisive, and naïve. But who knows whether the alliance of Lafayette and Mirabeau would have won enough support to name a ministry or, even if it had, whether it would have changed the course of history in any other way than by mutual stultification of the two allies to the advantage of third parties? Certainly Mirabeau's estimate of his ability to con-

[66] Cf. Théodore Lameth papers, BN, n.a.f. 1388, fols. 52–52vo. and Ferrières, I, 362–64.

[67] Mémoires, II, 363. See above, pp. 29–30, and below, pp. 115–17.

[68] Mémoires, II, 370–71.

trol the political situation had lacked foundation, but if he was stultified, for the time being at least Lafayette was not.

BIBLIOGRAPHICAL NOTES

If Bacourt's edition of Mirabeau's correspondence has been guilty of tampering with the original texts, as has sometimes been maintained (see above, p. 25), such tampering would have been biased in Mirabeau's favor. Even so, Bacourt's versions reveal Mirabeau, we think, as unworthy of personal confidence, no matter how astute as a political observer. The biographers of Mirabeau (the best of whom for this period still is Stern) have usually made this point, but with greater emphasis on his political astuteness than on his untrustworthiness. To explain Lafayette's relations with him, however, the emphasis has to be on Mirabeau's lack of personal integrity. Among the more recent biographies of Mirabeau are J. J. Chevallier, *Mirabeau: Un grand destin manqué* (Paris, 1947) and Duc de Castries, *Mirabeau, ou l'échec du destin* (Paris, 1960). They add little to the understanding of the Lafayette-Mirabeau relationship.

CHAPTER V

Rumors, Plots, and Counterplots

A MID THE scheming on ministerial posts Lafayette as chief police officer of the capital and the surrounding area had to maintain a ceaseless vigil. The chronic fear of counter-revolutionary activity incubated a double danger—not merely that counterrevolution might succeed but also that the fear of counter-revolution might lead to violent reaction among the populace, all too ready to attribute every misfortune to conspirators. Lafayette himself was prone to feel that conspiracy was rife, but his roseate recollection of American revolutionary behavior led him to believe that if conspiracy encountered calm vigilance by the authorities and unity of purpose among the people, liberty might be achieved by order and not by violence.

Sometimes the suspicions of conspiracy were largely imaginary, but who could tell? His intelligence agents were busy,[1] and it was part of their business to hunt for plots. On October 24, the city's police committee was informed that one of the queen's secretaries, Jacques-Mathieu Augeard, was engaged in a scheme to enable the royal family to flee to Metz. He was arrested and eventually acquitted, but that some royalists would feel bound to get the king out of his "prison" in Paris seemed logical to assume, and since the National Guard would oppose such a move, elimination of its commander would be a likely preliminary step. Lafayette and others were convinced that he was marked for assassination. Although they had so far uncovered no convincing evidence of a murder plot, he and his aides kept looking for it.[2] An angry coachman was

[1] Papers of the Comité des Recherches, AN: D xxix^bis 34, dosier 357, pp. 2, 3, 8.

[2] Gottschalk and Maddox, pp. 296–97, 315; *Révolutions de Paris* (Prudhomme), No. 17, Oct. 31–Nov. 7, p. 31, No. 19, Nov. 14–21, pp. 3, 6; and *Courrier de Paris*, Nov. 13, pp. 389–90.

reported to have shouted on the day that François was lynched: "The baker's not the one who should be hanged but the wretch Lafayette and the wretch Bailly."[3] Rumors that the commandant general was in danger led a provincial National Guard to offer "to fly to his aid upon the first word."[4]

Not all the danger was concentrated in Paris. In the town of Vernon, about fifty miles down the Seine River in Normandy, a riot broke out in protest against the removal of flour to Paris, and the Paris Assembly of Representatives learned on October 28 that its agent, Jean-Michel Planter, was liable to be lynched. The episode had all the potential of a counterrevolutionary protest against governmental centralization, and if other dissident areas were not to catch fire from it, strenuous measures were called for.

Vernon was outside the jurisdiction of the Assembly of Representatives, and so the Representatives appealed to the National Assembly and the king for cooperation. Recognizing the possibility of a national upheaval, Louis XVI called together a council of his ministers, the commandant general, the mayor, some Representatives of the Commune, and the president of the National Assembly, who instructed Lafayette to send a detachment of the Paris National Guard there to be joined by a contingent of the royal army. Lafayette designated a National Guard officer, A.-C.-A. Dières, to command the entire expedition (about five hundred men).[5]

This was the first expedition to go from Paris into the provinces with instructions not only from king and royal ministers but also from Commune and commandant general. In his orders to Dières, Lafayette stressed that the expedition was setting a precedent: "It is of the utmost importance that, on this first occasion since the king and the National Assembly took up residence in Paris, their authority should be respected and all disobedience to that authority be punished in the most striking manner." He promised to send whatever force might be needed, "and I will neglect nothing to support an expedition of this importance." He warned Dières against

---

[3] *Courrier de Paris,* Oct. 22, p. 50.

[4] The officers of the National Guard of St. Gal to Lafayette, [ca. Nov. 9], Cornell University Library, Rare Book Room, Lafayette Archives (hereafter cited as CU: Lafayette Archives), Carton IV, envelope 2447–50.

[5] Lacroix, II, 451–57 (Oct. 28), 457, 461–62, 464 (Oct. 29).

appeasement: "It will be extremely dangerous to negotiate or to betray the slightest weakness. By showing no indulgence this time, we shall avoid much greater misfortunes. The people of Paris . . . believe their safety dependent upon providing very telling examples to discourage other towns from following a similar line of conduct."[6]

By the time the expedition reached Vernon, it found that Planter had been placed in hiding in another town and that the provisions for Paris were safely stored in Vernon's magazines. Nevertheless, Dières took steps to restore Planter's prestige and to bring the instigators of disorder to justice.[7] Two days later, a convoy of heavy wagons rolled out of Vernon under escort carrying breadstuffs to Paris. By November 6 Vernon was reported to be quiet, and the Paris Representatives ordered Lafayette to recall most of his troops.[8] Nevertheless, a complaint lodged with the Paris Commune by some of Vernon's citizens was to demand his attention for several weeks to come, providing a foretaste of the recriminations that might follow attempts to preserve provincial order by a show of force from Paris.[9]

For its part the Commune resented the rumor that on its demand Louis XVI had sent the King's Bodyguard away, and it tried to get him personally to repudiate that charge.[10] This appeal for the monarch's intercession led to the erroneous inference that since the king had not sent the Bodyguard away, Lafayette intended to restore it to its service in Paris. The District of the Cordeliers, hostile to the Bodyguard and fearful of Lafayette's potential military power, undertook to mobilize the districts against that alleged purpose and prepared a circular to the districts, signed by D'Anton (*sic*) as president, advocating that only the Paris National Guard should do guard duty at the Tuileries.[11] The issue became suffi-

---

[6] Lafayette to Dières, [prior to Oct. 30], Henri Leclercq, *Les journées d'Octobre et la fin de l'année 1789* (Paris, 1924), pp. 503–4.

[7] *Ibid.*, p. 504, and Lacroix, II, 490–92, 496 (Oct. 31).

[8] Lacroix, II, 575.

[9] *Ibid.*, III, 51, 55–56 (Nov. 26), 62–63, 69–70 (Nov. 28). See also below, pp. 163 and 182–83.

[10] *Ibid.* II, 543–44 (Nov. 4), 619 (Nov. 13), 628–29 (Nov. 14), 641–42 (Nov. 16).

[11] LC: Thatcher Collection, French Revolution autographs, No. 431, and Lacroix, II, 543–44 (Nov. 4), 619 (Nov. 13), 628–29 (Nov. 14), 641–42 (Nov. 16).

ciently touchy to make Mme de Simiane uneasy, and Lafayette had to reassure her that it would turn out well.[12] Acting upon the Representatives' request, Louis XVI finally quieted uneasiness by stating that he had sent the Bodyguard to the provinces of his own accord and now preferred to depend on the Paris National Guard for guard duty until he could reorganize the service.[13]

Despite the animosity of the District of the Cordeliers and its supporters, the Assembly of Representatives continued to express its confidence in Lafayette. For example, it did not accede to his request to be relieved of the privilege of nominating the officers of the new companies in the Paris National Guard.[14] The Assembly of Representatives, considering this a good occasion to support him against the opposing district, begged him "on the contrary, to make nominations whenever the situation requires it."[15] Accordingly, seeking to avoid the charge of being arbitrary in his selections, he asked the division chiefs, the general staff, and the Military Committee for their recommendations and then proceeded to draw up a list of the new officers. The Assembly of Representatives approved the resulting list,[16] and no district is recorded as having made a complaint against this procedure.

Relations with some of the districts, however, remained delicate. The Guillotte affair revived with an embarrassing memoir sent to Lafayette and the Representatives by the District of Saint-Victor protesting against Guillotte's conduct as its battalion commander and as its delegate to the Assembly of Representatives. Accusing him of having secured the election of his relatives as officers, the district demanded not only his recall from the Assembly of Representatives but also his and their dismissal as officers of the National Guard.[17]

The Assembly of Representatives investigated the case and declared the district's action null and void,[18] and when the Saint-

[12] [ca. Oct. 25], *Mémoires*, II, 432.

[13] Lacroix, II, 634 (Nov. 16).

[14] *Ibid.*, pp. 501–2 (Nov. 2).

[15] *Ibid.*, pp. 489–90 (Oct. 31).

[16] *Ibid.*, pp. 502–3 (Nov. 2).

[17] Guillotte, pp. 22–23, and Lacroix, II, 465 (Oct. 29), 537 (Nov. 3), 560, 566–67 (Nov. 5).

[18] Lacroix, II, 574, 587–88 (Nov. 6), and Guillotte, pp. 24–27.

Victor assembly defied the Representatives' resolution, they ordered Lafayette to carry out their wishes so far as they pertained to Guillotte's military status.[19] The commandant general turned the problem over to Jean Charton, the division chief in whose jurisdiction the Battalion of Saint-Victor fell, and Charton summoned the battalion officers, read the decisions of the Representatives, and explained that an officer could be removed only by a court martial.[20] But Lafayette's enemies were not easily silenced. In an anonymous pamphlet that pretended to be a manuscript found in the papers of Lafayette's secretary, they reproached the National Guard for its antidemocratic spirit.[21]

As yet, however, unfriendly literature was scarce. Comforting messages came from towns outside Paris approving the transfer of the seat of government to Paris.[22] Some of them were addressed directly or indirectly to Lafayette, and in his replies he emphasized his hope for national unity, his respect for Louis XVI as monarch and for monarchial authority within the limits set by a liberal constitution, and his intention to subordinate himself and his position to legitimate authority. Words like *fraternal* and *fraternity* occurred frequently in his letters. For example, to an address of the National Guard of Besançon thanking the Paris National Guard for protecting the king and the deputies of the National Assembly,[23] he replied: "To continue to defend the National Assembly against public enemies, to assure the inviolability of the Representatives of the Nation and the freedom of their debates as well as the rights of a beloved monarch whose personal happiness is a necessity as well as an obligation for us, and to maintain with firmness the decrees of the National Assembly and particularly those that unite by every tie of fraternal equality all parts and all citizens of

[19] Lacroix, II, 590 (Nov. 9).

[20] Guillotte, pp. 26–27.

[21] *L'Espion patriote à Paris; manuscrit trouvé dans les papiers du secrétaire de M. de la Fayette (signé: H.J.). S'imprime à la Samaritaine aux dépens de la Milice bourgeoise. Se distribue sur le Pont Neuf et dans tous les districts. Octobre 1789.*

[22] Lacroix, II, 394–95 (Oct. 23), 449–50 (Oct. 28), and *Journal de Paris*, Oct. 29, p. 1393.

[23] *L'Observateur*, Oct. 31, p. 289. A slightly variant version of this address and of Lafayette's response (see below, n. 24) is contained in [L.-P. Bérenger (ed.)], *Mémoires historiques et pièces authentiques sur M. de da Fayette . . .* (Paris, [1790]), pp. 222–24.

the Empire are the principles to which our honor mutually binds us and for which we are ready to shed the last drop of blood."[24]

To those who looked to him as a leader, Lafayette always responded as a dutiful servant of the new government. To a provincial National Guard commandant who asked for information on how to organize and regulate his command, he replied that he must be guided by his own judgment until the National Assembly drew up definitive regulations for the National Guard units of the entire realm.[25] To another he answered that he did not have authority to decide such questions: "I can only urge upon your fellow-citizens ... perfect agreement on matters of public welfare.... I hope that ... calm and harmony will reign in your city until the National Assembly and our virtuous monarch have definitely decided upon the organization and service of the bourgeois guards throughout the realm."[26]

A letter from the German-speaking city of Strasbourg was especially welcome because of its strategic importance and the counterrevolutionary influences reputedly rampant there. In his response Lafayette once more appealed for national unity. Assuring the Strasbourg commander of "the most fraternal feelings" of the Paris National Guard, he wrote: "The attachment of your compatriots to the name *French,* Sir, cannot be better expressed than at a moment when that name is becoming the pledge of liberty and happiness. In vain do prejudice, selfishness, or ambition seek to deceive the people regarding their imprescriptible rights and their true interests; they will be forever consecrated in that constitution with which the Representatives of the Nation, together with the best of kings, occupy themselves unremittingly."[27]

Despite Lafayette's avowed policy of nonintervention in local

---

[24] *Journal de Paris,* Oct. 29, pp. 1396–97, and *Révolutions de Paris* (Prudhomme), No. 16, Oct. 24–31, p. 44. See also above, n. 23.

[25] Lafayette to M. Marasse (commandant at Epernay), Oct. 29, Archives Départementales de la Marne, E 530, and *Annales historiques de la Révolution française* (hereafter called *AHRF*), VII (1930), 71–72.

[26] Lafayette to MM de la Garde nle de Provins, Oct. 31, Bibliothèque de Troyes, Ms. 2770 (recueil).

[27] *Lettre de M. le Marquis de la Fayette à M. . . . . de la Garde nationale strasbourgeoise, datée de Paris le 8 novembre 1789.* The French version is available in several libraries. The German version is in BN: Lb^{39} 8133. Cf. *Annales patriotiques et littéraires,* Dec. 21, p. 2.

affairs outside Paris he did interfere in the dispute at Versailles. Lecointre had hoped to succeed Estaing and Gouvernet when both resigned their posts in the Versailles National Guard,[28] but he was disappointed.[29] Despite Lafayette's previously avowed unwillingness to accept appointment as commandant of the Versailles National Guard,[30] the municipality of Versailles elected him to that post, and the exceptional circumstances induced him to accept. He first consulted the Commune of Paris and then conveyed its decision to the Versailles municipal authorities: "It has seen in this partiality for its commandant general a new mark of the fraternity which unites it to you, and it has thought that I could hardly fulfill its intentions better than by carrying out your orders"; so he accepted the new "duties dear to my heart," promising soon to go to Versailles and place himself under their orders.[31] Despite Lafayette's assumption of jurisdiction, the relations of Lecointre and his partisans with the civil authorities became so tense that at one point a heavy contingent of the Paris National Guard, reinforced by regulars, had to remain on duty all night. For Lafayette to attempt to direct the required police action from Paris was obviously unwise, and he later instructed Berthier, now his second in command at Versailles, to learn the wishes of the municipality there and to carry them out without delay.[32] Lecointre was thus once more kept in check.

Sometimes even when Lafayette did nothing regarding the friendly gestures that came his way, they took printed form and were published by their authors, obviously meaning to bask in the reflection of his glory. The National Guard of Fontainebleau, for instance, published an address expressing friendly feelings for him

[28] See above, pp. 53–54.

[29] *Procédure au Châtelet*, III, 38; "Déclaration par M. Lecointre" in "Pièces justicatives," *Procès-verbal de l'Assemblée nationale*, L, 25–33; and Lacroix, II, 316. Cf. Calmon-Maison, p. 393. Lecointre set forth his side of the controversy in Versailles in *A Monsieur le Marquis de La Fayette, généralissime des Troupes du Roi, Commandant général des Gardes nationales de Paris et de Versailles*, Nov. 21 (Versailles, 1789).

[30] Gottschalk and Maddox, p. 216.

[31] Lafayette to Messieurs, Oct. 29, Bibliothèque de Versailles, and *Mémoires de la Société des sciences morales, des lettres, et des arts de Seine et Oise*, X (1874), 368.

[32] Lafayette to Berthier, Nov. 14, Bibliothèque de Versailles (kindness of M. Bréchin). Cf. *Courrier de Paris*, Nov. 13, p. 406. See also, n. 29 above.

and their Paris colleagues.[33] A Paris fusilier put out a pamphlet urging every eligible citizen to join the National Guard, and he dedicated it to Lafayette. In it he quoted Lafayette (probably apocryphally): "The Frenchman is all agog for change. I have always heard it said that he cools off quickly, but he will not do so on this occasion, I hope."[34] Another soldier in the Paris National Guard in a brochure dedicated to his commander-in-chief proposed a "standard of Liberty" as a symbol of French union and therefore an "object of terror" to all enemies of the *patrie* and public felicity.[35] An appeal for a truly national army which all male citizens at the age of seventeen would enter and whose cost would be borne by the municipalities was printed with Lafayette's letter of approval as an appendix.[36]

Some observers could not help feeling uneasy about the heaping of popular affection upon the leader of a citizen army, particularly when other military forces were melting away in the high revolutionary temperature. Moreover, Lafayette was accumulating enormous political influence as well. National Guard affairs were now nominally under the supervision of a municipal committee known as the Department of the National Guard, but its chairman was Guillotte, who could be expected to run that department in accordance with Lafayette's policies. Bailly being continually engrossed in executive duties, the Representatives had decided to choose a president and had elected Lafayette's old friend the Marquis de Condorcet to that office. The chairman of the municipal Comité des Recherches was another friend, Brissot de Warville. And the leading member of the Police Committee was the Abbé Claude Fauchet, an eloquent preacher who from time to time effusively praised Lafayette in public remarks.[37] So by November

---

[33] *Lettre à M. le Marquis de la Fayette du 9 novembre, 1789* [Fontainbleau? 1789].

[34] A fusilier of the District of the Mathurins, *Hommage à M. le Marquis de Lafayette, ou le recruteur patriote aux citoyens soldats de la Garde nationale parisienne* [Paris, 1789].

[35] La Neuville, *Projet de l'étandard de la liberté,* reviewed in *Courrier de Paris,* Nov. 5, pp. 275–76.

[36] M. le Prince, *Observations d'un citoyen du District Saint-Louis de la Culture.* Lafayette's letter was dated Oct. 28.

[37] Gottschalk and Maddox, pp. 302–5, and J. Charrier, *Claude Fauchet, évêque constitutionnel du Calvados, député à l'Assemblée législative et à la Convention* (1744–1793) (Paris, 1909), I, 103, 110, 112–13.

some of the commander-in-chief's close associates were in key positions at the Hôtel de Ville, augmenting his hold upon those whom he preferred to think of as his masters.

The commandant general's staff soon had to be increased, thus increasing his following, for the burden of its work was enormous.[38] On top of routine military and police problems, he had to deal with sometimes jealous or fearful local authorities. For example, on the complaint of the District of Saint-Louis-de-la-Culture he transferred the privately organized association of the Volunteers of the Bastille from the Bastille to the École Militaire.[39] The Hôtel-Dieu complained to him that the District of Notre Dame had appropriated some of its space as barracks for its paid company, and he sent the complaint to the civil authorities with an alternative suggestion that he said would "accord with the good of the service."[40] For all his influence, however, some of the Paris districts protested against the formation of the special companies of grenadiers and chasseurs that he had asked his officers to create, and the Representatives asked his staff to help draw up a circular justifying them.[41] In the District of Saint-André-des-Arts some of the volunteer Guards expressed a desire to form a company of grenadiers, and Lafayette at first encouraged them, but after the district assembly and most of the volunteer Guards disapproved of the inequalities that would thus be created within the battalion, he yielded.[42]

Along with such local dissatisfactions complications were thrust upon Lafayette from outside of Paris. One of the most complicated, though flattering, problems arose from the frequent requests for affiliation (some used the word *fédération*) with the Paris National Guard. For a time they came at the rate of one every other day, and from remote cities as well as from nearby villages.[43] The Na-

[38] Lacroix, III, 2–3 (Nov. 20), and *Procès-verbal du Comité militaire,* Part II, pp. 36–37.

[39] Lacroix, III, 4, 11–12 (Nov. 20), 14, 19–22 (Nov. 21).

[40] Lafayette to the Bureau of the Hôtel-Dieu, Nov. 16, *ibid.,* p. 26.

[41] *Ibid.,* pp. 14–15 (Nov. 21), 49 (Nov. 25).

[42] *Mémoire sur la formation d'une compagnie de grenadiers et de chasseurs dans la Bataillon de Saint-André des Arcs* [Paris, *post* Dec. 16, 1789].

[43] Lacroix, II, xviii–xix.

tional Guard of Grandpré in the Ardennes offered Lafayette the post of commander,[44] and the Breton town of Landivisiau not only elected him commander of its militia but asked the National Assembly to approve his election,[45] thus making it an event of national import. In addition, some communities expected him to arbitrate their domestic troubles. The assembly of Bourg-la-Reine brought to him a complaint against two officers of its militia.[46] A similar controversy developed at Vaugirard, and when he reported events of this nature, the Representatives generally counted upon him to investigate and report back.[47]

"I am astonished by my immense responsibility," Lafayette had confessed to Mounier,[48] and well he might be. His hard work in behalf of the Revolution, his sincerity, his affability, his genuine respect for his men, his spirited defense of his troops whenever outsiders questioned their zeal or competence, his firm insistence upon discipline,[49] and his honest conviction of the importance of the National Guard made a profound appeal to officers and common soldiers alike. The battalions organized assemblies where they discussed matters of interest to them both as soldiers and as citizens, and from those assemblies flowed a political influence rivaling that of the district assemblies.[50] The esteem in which the National Guard held their commander was so great as to lead sometimes to acts of violence against those who spoke against him. To discourage such misguided displays of loyalty, he once proclaimed in an order of the day that "the commandant general . . . recognizes as friends only the friends of liberty and order."[51] By this time the coupling of "liberty" with "order" was neither accident nor habit; he fully recognized that it was not going to be easy to attain them

---

[44] *Patriote français*, Nov. 24, p. 3.

[45] *AP*, X, 252 (Nov. 25).

[46] Lacroix, III, 53 (Nov. 26).

[47] *Ibid.*, II, 477 (Oct. 30), 576–77 (Nov. 6), 607 (Nov. 11), and III, 60 (Nov. 27).

[48] Oct. 23, *Mémoires*, II, 418.

[49] Cf. *Journal général de la cour*, Nov. 10, pp. 421–22.

[50] *Révolutions de Paris* (Prudhomme), No. 18, Nov. 8–14, p. 15, and *Révolutions de Paris* (Tournon), No. 17, Nov. 1, pp. 6–7.

[51] *Mémoires*, II, 378.

both at the same time though both could easily be lost at the same time, menaced as they were, on the one hand, by those who preferred order to liberty and, on the other, by those who preferred liberty to order.

Despite all the eventful changes of recent months, the financial plight of the monarchy had not improved. As a mark of their patriotism a number of wealthy persons had sent their silver to the mint in September as *dons patriotiques,* and in October ladies gave their jewels and gentlemen their silver shoe-buckles to the treasury. Few of those who gave *dons patriotiques* had made a larger contribution than Lafayette, and he now made another. The regular tax system having broken down, the government had recently required taxpayers to make a *contribution directe,* a fourth of their yearly incomes, to the treasury. Lafayette's income was estimated by his intendant at about 80,000 livres, and so his share of this "direct contribution" was 20,000 livres, which the regulations would have permitted him to pay in two installments. But "habituated," so his intendant wrote, "to going beyond the call of duty and to giving an example in everything that may be in the nature of civic spirit and generosity,"[52] he made his declaration on November 12 and promised to pay the entire sum due, which he declared to be not 20,000 but 25,000 livres.[53]

Pro-revolutionary gestures like Lafayette's were counterbalanced by others' anti-revolutionary actions, particularly by those who had recently left France out of animosity or fear. At this stage these émigrés were mostly royalists who had gone abroad after the fall of the Bastille and the October Days. Many of them had gathered in London, and Lafayette thought it conceivable that they might combine with the Duc d'Orléans against the Revolution. To offset them, he counted upon the French ambassador, the Marquis de La Luzerne, and with the approval of Bailly and Montmorin and from the funds put at his disposal by the National Assembly's Comité

[52] Jacques-Philippe Grattepain-Morizot, quoted in André Girodie, *Exposition du centenaire de La Fayette, 1757–1834 catalogue* (Paris, 1934) (hereafter cited as Girodie catalogue), p. 35, item 35.

[53] Certificate issued to Lafayette by the municipality of Paris, Nov. 12, thanking him for his willingness to pay his *contribution directe,* Huntington Library, HM 9441.

des Recherches, he sent his aide-de-camp Chastel de Boinville to
London to keep an eye on Orléans and to act as a special intelligence agent.[54]

Boinville, moreover, had an especially dramatic duty to perform. He was to warn Orléans that Lafayette considered it inappropriate for him to return to France before the Revolution was
over; if he did return, he would do so only as Lafayette's enemy;
hence, upon his arrival in Paris Lafayette proposed to challenge
him to a duel, fight him the very next morning, and then go before
the National Assembly to justify his action.[55] For a chief police
officer to kill a suspected conspirator in a duel because he could
not prove his case in court would hardly have looked to the National Assembly like good revolutionary practice. Yet, confident in
his own integrity, Lafayette committed these instructions to writing so that they might be communicated to La Luzerne.[56] When
Boinville arrived in London and showed the ambassador his instructions, La Luzerne was impressed. He praised Lafayette for
having done an "extremely noble, loyal, and decisive" thing but
guessed that it would not be necessary to resort to extremes because Orléans would prudently spend the winter in England.[57]

La Luzerne sent a fuller report a month after Orléans' arrival.
He took the occasion to congratulate the general upon his recent
achievements, assuring him that not only the English people but
also their king respected and admired him and that even the
émigrés spoke with more consideration of him than of other men
in high position in France. The prince, on the other hand, was not
popular with either the French or the English in London, La Luzerne believed, but had so far shown no signs of wishing to return
to France. The ambassador promised to watch him and, should he
seem about to leave, to inform Lafayette.[58]

[54] Papers of the Comité des Recherches, AN: D xxix[bis] 34, dossier 357, pièce 1.

[55] "Instruction pour M. de Boinville, mon aide-de-camp," *Mémoirs*, II, 429–31. See
also Bacourt (ed.), I, 390–91.

[56] A.-F. Bertrand de Moleville, *Histoire de la Révolution de France* (Paris, 1801–3),
III, 333–34 n.

[57] La Luzerne to Lafayette, [end of Oct.?], *Mémoires*, II, 431–32.

[58] La Luzerne to Lafayette, Nov. 25, *ibid.*, pp. 427–29.

Boinville's intelligence in London soon enabled Lafayette to discover that some sort of "parlementary coalition" was afoot with the intention of opposing the Revolution.[59] As the highest courts of France the parlements had long had the right to "verify" the royal decrees and thus to delay their execution. When the National Assembly turned its attention to reform of the judiciary, some of the parlementarians were quick to perceive that their ancient right provided a possible way to block enforcement of the Assembly's program even when approved by the king. Early in September the parlements, according to custom, had recessed, leaving Chambres de Vacations to carry on their work in the interim. On November 3 the National Assembly decreed that the Chambres de Vacations were to stay on—in other words, it prolonged the "vacation," from which, as later developed, the parlements were never to return. On the sixth the recess chamber of the Parlement of Normandy, sitting at Rouen, provisionally registered this decree of the third but drew up a vehement protest, which it forwarded to the royal ministers for Louis' attention, declaring that the chamber had registered the National Assembly's decree only out of loyalty to a maltreated monarch. This denunciation looked like an attempt to defy the National Assembly and to split it from the king, who, it implied, was not free.[60]

Having been warned by Boinville, Lafayette was not caught wholly unawares by this parlementary maneuver. When the Rouen chamber's declaration reached the ministers (November 8), Champion de Cicé consulted Lafayette, who insisted that the chancellor inform the National Assembly and that the king promptly disapprove of the defiant declaration, thus affirming the solidarity of royal court and National Assembly.[61] When subsequently Champion de Cicé on the king's behalf submitted to the Assembly the chamber's declaration, the outraged deputies charged the law court

[59] Papers of the Comité des Recherches, *loc. cit.*

[60] *Mémoires*, IV, 179. For the acts of the National Assembly regarding the parlements, see *AP*, IX, 664–66 (Nov. 3), 729–30 (Nov. 9), 741–43 (Nov. 10), and X, 7–9 (Nov. 12), 129 (Nov. 20).

[61] *AP*, X, 70 (Nov. 16), 86 (Nov. 17), 115 (Nov. 19), 254–56 (Nov. 25).

of the Châtelet in Paris to try the authors of the offending document for *lèse-nation* and requested Louis to name other members of
the Rouen Parlement to a different chamber, which would be required to register the decree without protest. The king did as he
was asked but pleaded for clemency to the offending parlementarians, and after a stormy debate the National Assembly consented
to drop the charge of *lèse-nation*.

The entire episode thus seemed to betoken an alliance of king
and nation against the enemies of the Revolution, as Lafayette had
intended that it should. It also betokened an alliance of Lafayette
and Champion de Cicé. When, a few days later, the Parlement of
Metz also resolved to give only provisional registration to the new
decrees on the ground that the king and the National Assembly had
acted under duress, Louis XVI immediately considered its resolution null, the National Assembly suggested a reorganization of the
Metz Parlement, and the Parlement yielded.[62] Thus two of the most
venerable courts of France, its highest legal authorities, were frustrated in a maneuver that might have prevented reform, and the
portrayal of the king and the National Assembly as the unwilling hostages of the armed citizenry of Paris lost some of its
persuasiveness.

Nevertheless, the resistance of the parlements to the decrees of
the National Assembly continued. The next January the Parlement
of Rennes proved recalcitrant. Summoned before the National Assembly, these Breton magistrates refused to submit.[63] Morris
warned Lafayette that great tact must be employed in dealing with
the Bretons; their protest seemed to him to carry conviction that
they had popular support. Lafayette, however, felt confident that
nine-tenths of the people of Brittany were on the side of the Assembly,[64] and he apparently was right. On January 15, as if to counter-
balance the Rennes Parlement and the aristocrats, three hundred
representatives of the National Guards of Brittany and Anjou met
in the Breton town of Pontivy and swore to fight all enemies of the

---

[62] Morris diary, Nov. 18, Davenport (ed.), I, 305. Cf. *ibid.*, p. 298. (Nov. 12).

[63] *AP*, XI, 125–27 (Jan. 8).

[64] Morris diary, Jan. 10, Davenport (ed.), I, 363.

Revolution and to maintain the rights of man and the new constitution.[65] The parlements of France were doomed to extinction.

Despite Lafayette's mounting prestige and power, most observers still took his word that all he wanted was, after the king
and the National Assembly had reached whatever solution of the
country's ills they could, to retire, as had the American Cincinnatus,
to his own vine and fig tree. But some thought they caught a
glimpse of a more complicated design hatching in Lafayette's
brain, and among them was Gouverneur Morris.

On November 18 Morris dined at Lafayette's house.[66] A much
discussed matter of the moment was a proposal by Necker to create
a national bank—a plan that Morris believed would not work and
Lafayette conceded was widely regarded as unacceptable. When
Lafayette suggested that Talleyrand should come forward with a
better plan, Morris contended that only a minister ought to do so
and deputies were now excluded from the ministry. Thereupon
Lafayette admitted that he was not pleased with the decree forbidding deputies to become ministers; he would "*for once* take a
Ministry out of the Assemblee," if Mirabeau and one or two others
were excluded. Morris, however, doubted that Talleyrand would
in any event accept office in the "present wild Situation of Affairs."[67]

Lafayette seemed to agree. He had recently taken Mirabeau to
see Montmorin, and on that occasion Mirabeau had called the National Assembly "a wild ass, which could be mounted only with
a great deal of maneuvering."[68] Lafayette thought that Mirabeau's
words well described the National Assembly, but he went on to
intimate that the situation would soon change; the Assembly would
"be obliged to give him Authority" although he had theretofore
declined it. Morris thought that the expression on Lafayette's face
clearly betrayed that such authority was "the Wish of his Heart."
When he inquired what the nature of that authority would be,
Lafayette defined it as "a Kind of Dictatorship such as Generalis-

[65] J. Bellec, "Les deux fédérations bretonne-angevines," *La Révolution française*, XXVIII
(1895), 22–25.

[66] Morris diary, Nov. 18, Davenport (ed.), I, 306.

[67] *Ibid.*

[68] *Mémoires*, II, 366.

simo," though he did not know what the exact title would be. Morris reiterated his old doubts: Could he count on the National Guard to obey him? Lafayette replied that they would obey, but, apparently annoyed, he turned to another guest. Later that day Morris confided to his diary: "Here is vaulting Ambition which o'erleaps itself. This Man's Mind is so elated by Power, already too great for the Measure of his Abilities, that he looks into the Clouds and grasps at the Supreme. From this Moment every Step in his Ascent will I think accelerate his Fall."[69]

Eventually Morris was to prove right about Lafayette's fall, but not immediately, and not for the reason he indicated. Lafayette's major complications came not from his "vaulting ambition" so much as from his scrupulous hesitation to "grasp at the supreme." Before the day was over, Morris learned from Mme de Chastellux, widow of a writer-general who had been one of Lafayette's old friends, that he intended "to imitate Washington and retire from the public Service as soon as the Constitution is established." But Morris remained cynical: "He may believe this himself," he wrote in his diary, "but nothing is more common than to deceive ourselves."[70]

Others too, though for different reasons, remained cynical. The Committees of Police and Investigations (Recherches) continued to receive reports of plots to stir up the populace by spreading false rumors and seditious sentiments.[71] Morris himself nearly got mixed up in one such plot. The young Comte de Luxembourg, a prince of the blood, continually courted him, dropping broad hints about a plan to begin a counterrevolution in the provinces.[72] It involved some kind of a royalist coup by the King's Bodyguard, but if what Luxembourg told Morris was correct, the objections of some of the Paris districts to the return of the Bodyguard had ruined the "plan." Lafayette, the count added, had denied "in the

---

[69] Morris diary, Nov. 18, Davenport (ed.), I, 305–6.

[70] *Ibid.*, pp. 306–7.

[71] *AP*, X, 339–42 (Nov. 30): B.-J.-B. Buchez and P.-C Roux, *Histoire parlementaire de la Révolution française* (Paris, 1834–38), III, 256, 418; and *Gazette de Leide*, Nov. 17.

[72] Morris diary, Nov. 2, 5, 6, 9, 11, 17, Davenport (ed.), I, 282, 286, 289–90, 291, 293–94, 305.

Hearing of many Persons" that he had prevented the return of the Bodyguard—a public declaration that Luxembourg thought a great imprudence. Morris saw in Luxembourg's tale, however, nothing significant except that there was "much latent Animosity" against Lafayette and that "while he is building his Castle others are employed in mining the Foundation."[73]

If Lafayette did not know of Luxembourg's project, he already was informed about other alleged conspirators (and it turned out that they were all parts of the same scheme). Before the October Days he had received a vague report of a counterrevolutionary plot in which a Lieutenant Morel had become somewhat involved and which he had betrayed to Lafayette. Considering the evidence at that time too meager, Lafayette had employed Morel to collect more precise information.[74] Morel had continued his investigation since then and sometime about November 1 reported that the Marquis de Favras, who seemed to be attached to the household of the Comte de Provence, was engaged in a plan to carry off the king. Lafayette charged Morel to continue his investigation, and Morel, acting as a sort of agent-provocateur, cultivated the acquaintance of Favras.[75] Since the alleged plot seemed to incur some large money transactions, Lafayette also tried, apparently unsuccessfully, to induce the Amsterdam banker Jacob van Staphorst "to act as a Spy for Discovery of Intrigues of the Aristocratic Party."[76] One of Lafayette's aides, besides, was put on Favras' trail.[77] For a time, however, none of Lafayette's agents learned anything concrete about Favras.[78]

No matter how confident Lafayette felt about the loyalty of his officers, he was not equally ready to depend on the rank and file of his Guards, for they sometimes paid less heed to their officers than to their district assemblies. Determined to make to the men the same sort of appeal he had made to their officers, he visited several companies, both paid and unpaid, and addressed them on

[73] *Ibid.*, Nov. 18, p. 307.

[74] See Gottschalk and Maddox, pp. 296–97, 315.

[75] Edmond Cleray, *L'affaire Favras, 1789–90* (n.p., [1932]), pp. 56–58, 62.

[76] Morris diary, Nov. 27, Davenport (ed.), I, 315.

[77] Cleray, pp. 56–58, 63.

[78] See below, pp. 119–21.

"their duty to the *patrie*."[79] He urged them to guard against gossip, to volunteer for more duty than required in the *Règlement,* suggesting one full day a week, to throw their weight on the side of "concord and peace," and to maintain the vigilance that alone would accomplish the Revolution.[80]

In the course of these rounds, on November 20 Lafayette went directly to the Battalion of the Cordeliers, the district that was the leader of opposition to the Assembly of Representatives. He pleaded for harmony between the National Guardsmen, the districts, and the municipality, pointing out that the chief aim of the enemies of the Revolution was to sow discord among its friends. He assured his soldiers that good feeling reigned between the king and the National Assembly. Not only would the friends of liberty bring freedom to France but they would also have "the glory of making all Europe free," for the entire continent would soon follow France's "beautiful example."[81] Camille Desmoulins, who had been and would be again among his critics, thought that some of Lafayette's words were "worthy of a Roman."[82]

The appeal had the desired effect on some districts. The entire Battalion of the Petits-Pères marched to Lafayette's home to inform him that they had taken an oath "to maintain with all their power the greatest unity and most perfect accord among all companies of the National Guard and to render their service with the most careful precision."[83] Many soldiers took a special pledge to serve one full day out of every six during the next four months wherever in Paris their general might wish. The unpaid troops of another battalion promised the utmost care and devotion in maintaining order.[84] From the Faubourg Saint-Antoine, frequently a center of discord, he received a promise that upon the first alarm hundreds

---

[79] *Révolutions de Paris* (Prudhomme), No. 19, Nov. 14–21, p. 13. See also *Révolutions de Paris* (Tournon), No. 19, Nov. 20, p. 23, and No. 26, Nov. 22, p. 7; Comte de Seneffe to M. de Bellanger, Nov. 29, Vaissière, p. 161; *Journal général de la cour*, Nov. 22, p. 517, and Nov. 24, p. 533; *Gazette de Leide, supplément,* Dec. 4; and *Courier national*, Nov. 22, p. 7.

[80] *Courrier de Paris,* Nov. 25, p. 171.

[81] *Chronique de Paris,* Nov. 22, p. 363.

[82] *Révolutions de France et de Brabant*, Dec. 7, p. 100.

[83] *Journal de Paris,* Nov. 22, p. 1522.

[84] *Chronique de Paris,* Nov. 18, pp. 346–47.

of men would rise to defend the liberty of the capital with "the last drop of their blood."[85]

Meanwhile tension mounted. A common rumor had it that a great counterrevolutionary uprising would come on November 25. Some considered this tale doubtful,[86] but Lafayette, working with the Comité des Recherches of Paris, that of the National Assembly, and volunteer informers,[87] probably had more dependable information. At any rate, he took no chances. He ordered an artillery emplacement constructed in the little park around Henry IV's statue on the Pont-Neuf, where his guns could not only command the Seine River but would also serve as an alarm to call out the National Guard. Three successive volleys from the Pont-Neuf battery would be a signal for every guardsman to scurry to his post.[88]

As November 25 approached, Lafayette took perhaps exaggerated precautions.[89] He required division and battalion commanders to take special pains to build up esprit de corps. He went himself to review the posts. He ordered his men to work night and day to get the artillery in place at the Pont-Neuf. On the day before the aristocratic coup was expected, he asked the Guard to wear their uniforms for the next eight days, so that even if the anticipated blow came only later in the week, they would be ready to report at once.[90] He doubled the guard at the Tuileries and called out all his cavalry. To a grateful Assembly of Representatives, he explained that the approach of winter required "particular precautions to assure the public tranquility."[91]

[85] *Journal général de la cour*, Nov. 7, pp. 396–97, and *Révolutions de Paris* (Tournon), No. 20, Nov. 20, pp. 7–8.

[86] Duquesnoy, II, 67; *Révolutions de Paris* (Prudhomme), No. 19, Nov. 14–19, pp. 6–13; *Courier national*, Nov. 22, p. 7; and *Chronique de Paris*, Nov. 24, p. 370.

[87] Cf. AN:D xxix^bis 2, dossier 23, pièce 14, and *ibid.*, 34, dossier 357, pièce 1.

[88] Lacroix, III, 42 (Nov. 24); *Révolutions de Paris* (Prudhomme), No. 19, Nov. 14–21, pp. 6–13, and No. 21, Nov. 28–Dec. 5, pp. 26–27; and *Journal général de la cour*, Nov. 22, p. 517.

[89] *Journal général de l'Europe*, Nov. 28, pp. 184–85; *Gazette de Paris*, Dec. 6, p. 3; *Courier national*, Nov. 22, p. 7; *Chronique de Paris*, Nov. 24, p. 370; and *Journal général de la cour*, Nov. 24, p. 533.

[90] *Annales patriotiques et littéraires*, Nov. 23, pp. 2–3; *Courier national*, Nov. 22, p. 7; Lacroix, III, 42–43 (Nov. 24); Seneffe to Bellanger, Nov. 29, Vaissière, p. 161; *Gazette de Leide, supplément*, Dec. 3; and *Journal général de l'Europe, supplément*, Dec. 3, pp. 73–74.

[91] Lacroix, III, 42–43 (Nov. 24).

For the time being, no coup came. Whether the report of a projected rising had originated with Lafayette for his own purposes, or the commandant general's measures disconcerted the plans of the conspirators, or they were half-baked attempts that never should have been taken seriously, Paris did not know. At any rate, order prevailed on November 25, and the aristocrats "determined to be quiet."[92] But rumors of plots continued.

Every Paris district now had its own police committee, and along with the numerous other police authorities some of them worked with occasionally excessive zeal to track down persons suspected of hostility to Lafayette. In addition, threatening letters sometimes came to Lafayette's personal attention. One anonymous letter, for example, warned him that if he did not restore Louis XVI to power, others would do so and he would cease to be the first man in the state.[93] He questioned an Abbé de Lasteray on this matter and learned that the abbé had merely overheard a suspicious conversation.[94] Lafayette contented himself with submitting Lasteray's testimony and the anonymous letter to the Paris Comité des Recherches.[95] About the same time one Baudry de La Richardière was accused of having called Lafayette several abusive names such as "aristocrat," "villain," and "fool." The National Guard of Sables d'Olonne imprisoned La Richardière, and from prison he appealed to the National Assembly.[96] The National Assembly decided that La Richardière had been punished enough and asked the king to pardon him, which he did.[97] A few days later another such case arose when the Paris Comité des Recherches sent a Mlle Regnaud de Bissy to the Châtelet for having publicly denounced Lafayette and the National Guard,[98] but she denied the charges and apparently the case was dropped.

[92] Morris diary, Nov. 25, Davenport (ed.), I, 312.

[93] Letter, n.d., unsigned, endorsed by Joseph-Léonard Poirey, Lafayette's secretary, AN: D xxix[bis] 3, dossier 28, pièce 13.

[94] *Ibid.*, pièces 11-12.

[95] Minutes of the Comité des Recherches of Paris, Dec. 18, *ibid.*, pièce 11.

[96] *AP*, X, 499-500 (Dec. 10); *Journal des États généraux*, VI, 282; *Courier national*, Dec. 10, p. 4; *Courrier de Paris*, Dec. 12, p. 8.

[97] *AP*, X, 500 (Dec. 11), 571 (Dec. 14).

[98] *Révolutions de Paris* (Tournon), No. 23, Dec. 13-20, pp. 31-32.

One of the charges of anti-Lafayette activity took a grimly humorous turn. On December 19 the police committee of the District of Saint-Germain-l'Auxerrois summoned a man who was accused of having admitted that a group of conspirators had chosen him to assassinate Lafayette. The accused turned out to be none other than Lieutenant Morel, whom Lafayette had commissioned to spy upon alleged conspirators. Morel, confessing that he had pretended to agree to murder Lafayette, claimed to have done so only in order to make a genuine plot miscarry and that Lafayette himself knew all about his doings. So the committee sent two of its members to Lafayette to find out if he was telling the truth. Lafayette assured them that he did in fact know of Morel's plan and requested them to arrange Morel's release so that he might renew his espionage upon the conspirators.[99] In times when a police authority could arrest a man accused of plotting to assassinate the one who had hired him to spy on other suspects, how much credence could be placed in future reports of assassination plots?

Nevertheless, as rumor followed upon rumor, the fear would not down that the lives of Lafayette and Bailly were in danger. The Assembly of Representatives received a letter from the Commune of Saint-Claud-en-Angoumois, almost three hundred miles away, begging the Commune of Paris to give "these respected and precious citizens" a special bodyguard and offering "fifty men ready to sacrifice their lives for the safety of two men so essential to the cause of liberty." Since Paris had long provided both of them with an adequate guard, the Representatives instructed their president to explain that the two men were protected by "the love, gratitude, and veneration of their own fellow townsmen."[100] They should have added that a band of eager police agents was also on guard.

BIBLIOGRAPHICAL NOTES

In October 1789, a second *Révolutions de Paris* began to appear, put out by M. Tournon, one of the two original publishers who had put out Nos. 1–15 in cooperation. After their rupture it became necessary to distinguish between the two journals of the same title—which we have done by indicating parenthetically the name of the respective publishers, Prudhomme and

[99] Cleray, pp. 60–61.

[100] Lacroix, III, 183–84 (Dec. 14). Cf. *Annales patriotiques et littéraires,* Mar. 11, p. 3.

Tournon. With No. 35 Tournon's journal changed its title to *Révolutions de l'Europe*.

The story of the parlements' futile effort to block reform of the judicial system is told in considerable detail in Henri Carré, *La fin des Parlements* (*1788-1790*) (Paris, 1912), pp. 135-46.

Cleray's study of the Favras affair is badly organized, but it contains useful information, carefully researched, and for the role of others than Lafayette we have generally depended upon it.

We have already said about Dom Leclercq's detailed study of the October Days that it is unconvincing in several regards but provides a number of details not otherwise available to us; see Gottschalk and Maddox, pp. 306, 328, 386-87.

CHAPTER VI

The Favras Plot

THE retiring minister of France in the United States, the Comte de Moustier, reached Paris in mid-November, bringing with him letters from President George Washington, Lafayette's "adoptive father," and Alexander Hamilton, a former companion-in-arms, who was now the American secretary of the treasury. The letters had been written in New York over a month earlier, before Washington or Hamilton could have known about the October Days. For one usually so reserved as Washington his was a warm letter. Lamenting the "interval of silence between two persons whose habits of correspondence have been so uninterruptedly kept as ours," he found the excuse for it in "the new and arduous scenes in which we have both been lately engaged." He expressed special concern over the revolution in France, which "is of such magnitude and of so momentous a nature that we hardly yet dare to form a conjecture about it." Nevertheless, he fervently prayed "that its consequences may prove happy to a nation in whose fate we have so much cause to be interested and that its influence may be felt with pleasure in future generations."[1] The president offered no advice; yet by recalling that he too was playing a stellar role in the inauguration of a new government, his letter could hardly have failed to suggest that Lafayette occupied in France a position similar to that of his avowed model in America.

Hamilton, while requesting aid in the settlement of the American financial debt to France, expressed satisfaction with the French Revolution so far. Less sanguine than his president, however, he acknowledged some doubt that the French would achieve a good

[1] Oct. 14, J. C. Fitzpatrick (ed.), *The Writings of George Washington* (Washington, 1931–40), XXX, 448–49.

constitution because of "disagreements among those who are now united," "the vehement character of your people," "the reveries of your Philosophic politicians," and "the refractoriness of your nobles." Yet, with "wishes for your personal success and that of the cause of liberty," he urged Lafayette to be "virtuous amidst the seductions of ambitions, and you can hardly in any event be unhappy."[2]

Two other friends joined Lafayette in Paris about this time. One was the Anglo-American writer Thomas Paine, who returned to Paris about mid-November and upon occasional visits to Lafayette's house[3] learned the details that he afterward recorded in his *Rights of Man*.[4] The other was one of Lafayette's oldest and dearest associates, the Comte de Ségur, who had left his post as ambassador to Russia in October and had now reached Paris.[5] Lafayette called upon him shortly after his arrival. The count had already found his father, a marshal of France and a former royal minister, bitterly critical of the Revolution, and many others in the higher circles of society of like opinion. He felt, however, that such old-time dignitaries were unjust to the revolutionary leaders. In that frame of mind Ségur greeted Lafayette, and the two friends talked for hours about the political situation. While Lafayette narrated the story of the Revolution since its inception, his listener reflected that the narrator had worked ceaselessly to promote the idea of liberty. As Ségur years later reconstructed their conversation, Lafayette was confident that a reign of law ultimately would replace France's arbitrary rule. At the same time, he seemed profoundly unhappy over popular excesses, which, he was persuaded, had been the work of conspirators and not of the people: "A certain number of brigands have appeared—where from, I do not know—hired by unknown hands and who, despite our efforts, have committed deplorable crimes, profiting from every excitement created by the imprudent resistance of the court and the privileged orders to the re-

---

[2] Hamilton to Lafayette, Oct. 6, H. C. Syrett and Jacob Cooke (eds.), *The Papers of Alexander Hamilton* (New York, 1964), V, 425–26.

[3] Morris diary, Nov. 27, Dec. 11, Davenport (ed), I, 315, 330.

[4] See Gottschalk and Maddox, pp. 82, 252, 342.

[5] Morris diary, Nov. 20, Davenport (ed.), I, 308.

forms favored by the public. We hunt them out, we punish them, we disperse them, but in vain; they always return." The general himself, however, was ready to let bygones be bygones, Ségur inferred; his aim for the future was, as a soldier, to maintain public order and, as a deputy, to contribute to the establishment of liberty.

Ségur confessed to being less hopeful. As he saw the situation, Lafayette was faced with a dilemma: As a Patriot deputy he depended on one set of supporters, while as commander of the National Guard and protector of the king he must retain the support of quite another. Thus, in trying to moderate the ardor of the revolutionaries and, at the same time, to get the court to accept a liberal constitution, he ran the risk of alienating both. Lafayette replied that he recognized his awkward position, but "having done my duty, I shall have nothing to reproach myself for."[6]

Ségur soon had a chance to present Lafayette's views at court. Conceding that the general had rendered the royal family signal service, Marie Antoinette begged the count to keep reminding him of his duty as commander of Paris to see that the king's dignity and safety suffered no loss. Ségur ventured the opinion that the plight of the royal family was the result of its own unwise acts and urged the queen to accept the Revolution as an inescapable reality, which could be tempered, however, by good faith at court.[7]

Perhaps as a result of Lafayette's conversation with Ségur and Ségur's with the queen, shortly afterward the king requested Lafayette to set forth his ideas regarding what the king's council could do to advance the Revolution, while preserving as much royal authority as was consistent with the national interest.[8] In reply Lafayette wrote a *Mémoire adressé au roi,* which outlined a program based upon the premise that a good constitution which would leave the king a strong executive was still possible if Louis would take the lead and guide the Revolution in a liberal direction.[9]

---

[6] Comte de Ségur, *Mémoires ou souvenirs et anecdotes* (Paris, 1827), III, 447–54.

[7] *Ibid.,* pp. 455–60.

[8] *Mémoires,* II, 436 n.

[9] "Mémoire adressé au roi, et imprimé par l'ordre de la Convention nationale," *ibid.,* pp. 436–39 and AN: C184, dossier 117, p. 72 (armoire de fer). The document in the Archives Nationales is signed by Lafayette though written in another hand. It is dated in

The document's first words identified national with monarchial interests: "No matter how difficult our situation may be, we must and can[10] triumph over it, but we have no time to lose or opportunities to neglect. The establishment of a free constitution in which every [other] interest yields to the interest of the people is the only chance of welfare for the nation and for the king as well as the only system in which I can cooperate." The king must, therefore, firmly decide which course to take; on the one hand was "the debris of a powerless aristocracy, always taking and never giving," and on the other the whole nation, the source of his glory, happiness, and power. The only appropriate procedure would be to rally to the national (in Lafayette's vocabulary this meant *popular*) standard. The king should support the constitution and let his court know that he intended to be the man of the people. The king's ministers, rather than competing with the National Assembly for popular support, should respect and serve it—which they could do without either losing their own dignity or refusing to take part in its deliberations.

Having thus rebuked the government for its failure to collaborate with the National Assembly, Lafayette turned to the shortcomings of the Assembly. Through personal and party rivalries and through preciosity (*le bel esprit*), he stated, it had lost standing and wasted time. It should realize that the good citizens of France would not tolerate anything like the English Long Parliament of Charles I's time (a sinister parallel drawn perhaps for the king's instruction no less than for the Assembly's) and should zealously complete the task of a constitutional convention, leaving ordinary acts of legislation to the forthcoming and better composed legislature.

Having thus blamed both court and Assembly for the prolongation of the constituent process, Lafayette made specific proposals for their future guidance. The court should avoid appearing reluctant or constrained in reaching decisions and should take such

---

still another hand (probably a later investigator's) "9bre 1789," but the date is undoubtedly *post* Dec. 14, 1789: see *Mémoires*, II, 438 n. The two versions do not differ in any essential regard. The National Convention ordered its printing: *AP*, LIV, 517–18 (Dec. 5, 1792).

[10] The manuscript version says *peut;* the printed version (p. 436) *doit.*

military, diplomatic, and household measures, including some cases of exemplary punishment for conspiracy, as would remove hope not only from the enemies of liberty but also from the Orléans faction, which must be carefully watched and rigorously pursued. A committee of the principal ministers should meet at least twice a week to deal with ways to enforce the laws, guarantee internal and external security, give unity and strength to the executive power, and follow a vigorous but popular policy. The ministry's first task should be to establish a bureau of provisions for the realm.

For its part the National Assembly should name a committee of influential members to guide and expedite its work. The Assembly's goals should be specific: the reorganization of municipalities and provincial assemblies so as to put local administrative bodies into operation at once and under the royal government's direction, leaving France divided (in accordance with a plan recently adopted by the Assembly) into local subdivisions (the departments);[11] the adoption of immediate[12] measures to reestablish order and shore up finances; the disposal of the church's property and the regulation of the clergy; the statement of principles affecting the military forces, placing all their operations under the king's control; the definition of the executive power so as to vest the king with the necessary authority, especially the power to conduct foreign negotiations; the fixing of an appropriate civil list and the tentative appropriation of funds for the other departments of government; the reform of the judicial system and the creation of a supreme court or an elective senate;[13] the enunciation of the basic principles of commerce and a basic plan of education; and the regulations of finances so as to provide sufficient means (even to carry on a war) until the first legislature should meet.

When all this was done, Lafayette continued, the decrees of constitutional import should be combined into one general document, thus facilitating the changes that then might be recognized

[11] The written document says *d'après les nouvelles divisions du 15 décembre*. The printed text (p. 438) has corrected the date to *du 14 decembre*.

[12] The printed text (p. 438) has changed this to *provisoires*.

[13] The printed text (p. 438) italicizes *la création d'un tribunal suprême ou d'un sénat électif*.

as necessary. The proclamation of the constitution should be the National Assembly's last act, a signal for the obliteration of all dissensions and factions and for the return of the émigrés. The king should then take an oath to maintain the constitution and call a new legislature. By that time he should have strengthened his council by filling the important posts with citizens who by their talents and patriotism had contributed the most to the successful completion of the plan Lafayette proposed. To disarm any suspicion that he himself might be making a bid for a ministerial post Lafayette asserted that the confidence of the public had given him the only power that he wanted, that of being useful: "My scruples and my reputation make it important that the close of the revolution should mark my complete withdrawal from all political activity."

This memoir brought together a number of ideas which Lafayette had previously advanced, and they had undergone little change in his mind since the Revolution began. He still wanted a constitution for France that in some significant regards was modeled upon the Constitution of the United States, though in others adapted to the French political tradition. The major difference in his proposal from the American constitution was that France would have a hereditary and not an elective executive. Yet, as in the American constitution, the executive was to retain considerable power—to appoint the ministers, to conduct foreign relations, to command the armed forces, to influence local affairs, and to spend an adequate appropriation voted by the legislature. As in the American constitution, the legislature was to be bicameral, with an upper house known as a Senate (presumably with significant judicial authority, since Lafayette was willing to accept it in place of a supreme court).[14]

Most of Lafayette's proposals were eventually to become part of the constitution that the National Assembly drew up and that the king accepted, although reluctantly. But Lafayette's timetable was to prove overoptimistic. He estimated that all that his *Mémoire*

---

[14] In *Mémoires*, II, 346 n. (apparently written somewhere between 1795 and 1799) Lafayette made clear that he did not mean each of the two institutions to be a complete substitute for the other, since by *sénat électif* he meant an upper house such as that of the United States or of France of the Directory period, and by *tribunal suprême* he meant a high court such as the Court of Cassation of France was to be.

adressé au roi proposed could be accomplished by the next August or September.[15] He underestimated the amount of work the Assembly would have to do, the opposition to change by vested interests, the more or less justifiable divisions of opinion in the public and the National Assembly engendered by untried reforms, and the recurrent conviction of the French court, clergy, and aristocracy, and of foreign rulers that concession had reached the point of diminishing returns. Optimism, however, was characteristic of Lafayette and a source of both his weakness and his strength—weakness because he held that, once the objective was clear, only the ill-intentioned or the short-sighted would block the way toward it; strength because it emboldened him to persist against the obstacles that blocked the way toward the consummation he devoutly wished.

The opposition came also, however, from those, no matter how well or ill intentioned and no matter how far or short sighted, who were earnestly persuaded that change had already done more harm than good and must be stopped. Since the royal censorship had collapsed, a flood of pamphlets and journals now poured in upon the reading public. Among them were a number that a fearful community suspected of being seditious. As the year 1789 drew to a close, the pamphlet warfare became more acrimonious, stooping even to forgery. A brochure, *Étrennes à la nation,* claiming that George Washington was really a friend of the Old Regime, published what it claimed to be a letter from him to Lafayette. The letter was, however, soon denounced as spurious.[16] The municipal authorities of Paris had tried to limit the number and activity of news hawkers and journalists, but on December 12 a member of the Assembly of Representatives complained that numerous tracts indecently calumniating religion and the king were being sold even in the lobbies of the National Assembly's meeting hall. Thereupon the Representatives requested the commandant general to give greater attention to enforcing the regulations on the circulation of printed matter.[17]

[15] *Ibid.,* p. 439.

[16] *Patriote français,* Dec. 31, p. 5. See also Buchez and Roux, IV, 32–42, and *Révolutions de Paris,* No. 25, Dec. 26, 1789—Jan. 2, 1790, p. 5.

[17] Lacroix, III, 174, 179–81.

It was perhaps no coincidence, therefore, that that very day the police committee of Marat's district, Saint-Nicolas-du-Chardonnet, obviously shocked by his intemperate criticism of certain conspicuous persons and policies, arrested him and took him to the Comité des Recherches at the Hôtel de Ville. As the committee was questioning him, Lafayette came in, and Marat put his case before him. Protesting that he had been misunderstood and unjustly treated, he denied that he had ever attacked Lafayette himself or his principles. "You fought to break the irons of the Americans," Marat later claimed to have said. "Can anyone believe that you wish to put them on your compatriots?" Marat did not, however, think equally well of some members of the general's staff. When Lafayette asked who they were, he replied that he would name them later in the columns of the *Ami du peuple*.[18] In the end Marat was released and given a guard to escort him home. In his next issue, while expressing opposition to Lafayette's proposal to create special companies of grenadiers and chasseurs, he did so in a relatively gentle manner.[19]

In the long conversation which, according to Marat, he and Lafayette had at the Hôtel de Ville, perhaps they talked about the counterrevolution, for the *Ami du peuple* later warned that the aristocrats planned to suborn all the militia of the realm—a charge that might well have come from Lafayette.[20] From whatever sources Marat derived his suspicions, they were not without foundation. Morel, still serving Lafayette,[21] was now also in the confidence of Favras and acting perhaps as a double spy. Late in November Favras sent him to a local banker, Pomaret, to borrow 2,000,000 livres.[22] The banker naturally asked for security, and as instructed by Favras, Morel offered an assignment on property that Pomaret knew belonged to the Comte de Provence. Pomaret replied that he must consult the banking firm of Cottin and Girardot. Now, these were Lafayette's own bankers, and Cottin *fils* and T. Jauge

---

[18] *Ami du peuple,* Dec. 19, pp. 4–5.

[19] *Ibid.*

[20] *Ibid.,* Dec. 20, pp. 5–7.

[21] Testimony of Gouvion and Masson de Neuville at the trial of Favras, Feb. 9, 1790, as reported in *Gazette universelle,* Feb. 15, pp. 307–8.

[22] Cleray, p. 37.

of that firm were among his aides-de-camp.[23] Although Favras himself went to see Pomaret and told him that the loan would be secured by the property of a very important person, Pomaret did not go through with the deal. Favras' effort to negotiate a loan was known to Provence at least by December 18, on which date he consented that his treasurer confer with Favras about security for such a loan.[24] Probably other members of Provence's entourage knew about Favras' plan, and they may have told Lafayette.[25]

In the meantime, because of Pomaret's hesitation Favras had approached other bankers. On December 6 he began negotiations with Chomel, a Dutchman, who recognized at the outset that the loan was for the Comte de Provence.[26] Lafayette learned a good deal about what Favras was up to, and the probable source of his information was Chomel. On December 23, Chomel asked Favras to furnish notes signed by the important person who he had asserted was to give security for the loan.[27] Meanwhile an agent of the Paris Comité des Recherches had been shadowing Favras for weeks, and having learned that Favras would go to the quarters of Provence's treasurer on the evening of December 24, he and several National Guard officers posted themselves at the appointed hour where they could observe the treasurer's door.[28] Paris was brightly lighted that night, for it was Christmas eve and Lafayette had asked householders to place lights at their doors to provide greater safety to people going to midnight mass, and he had also ordered the National Guard to stay on duty all night.[29] At six o'clock in the evening Favras and Chomel came to the house under surveillance, along with Chedeville, one of Provence's intendants. After much coming and going of several involved in the negotiation, they left. An officer of Lafayette's staff followed Chedeville's carriage, arrested him,

---

[23] Cf. Gottschalk and Maddox, p. 289.

[24] Cleray, pp. 37–38, 42–43.

[25] La Marck to Mirabeau, Dec. 1, Bacourt (ed.), I, 426, and Mirabeau to La Marck, Dec. 26, *ibid.*, p. 439. Cf. *Mémoires*, II, 363.

[26] Cleray, pp. 40–41.

[27] *Ibid.*, pp. 40–50, and see below, Appendix II.

[28] Cleray, p. 62.

[29] *Journal général de la cour*, Oct. 24, p. 285, Dec. 25, p. 778, and *Révolutions de Paris* (Tournon), No. 24, Dec. 19–24, p. 23.

and took him to the Comité des Recherches at the Hôtel de Ville.[30]
Another National Guard officer arrested Favras and took him also
to the Hôtel de Ville. Masson de Neuville, an aide of Lafayette,
visited Favras' home, confiscated those of his papers he could find,
and arrested his wife.[31]

Lafayette and the Comité des Recherches were waiting at the
Hôtel de Ville. Chedeville was quickly released. When the arresting officer brought in Favras, Lafayette saw him for the first and
only time. He had become convinced, and remained convinced all
his life, that part of Favras' purpose had been to murder him and
Bailly,[32] and he already had lived with that threat for weeks. Some
time later, when he had ceased to be friendly to Lafayette, Marat
claimed that once during those weeks, when Lafayette had found
himself unexpectedly surrounded by a crowd, he had betrayed
marked fright, which Marat regarded as a betrayal of cowardice.[33]
Upon Favras' arrival Lafayette had him searched and took charge
of his papers. The Comité des Recherches, after questioning the
prisoner for a long time on the alleged plot, concluded that his
purpose had been to raise troops, make off with the king, and kill
Necker, Bailly, and Lafayette,[34] and it sent him to the Abbaye
prison. They later questioned his wife[35] and sent her to the Abbaye
also.

When the Comité des Recherches adjourned at five o'clock on
Christmas morning, it had no convincing proof of Provence's complicity in Favras' affairs. Perhaps Lafayette hoped to find none. At
any rate, he had already given Provence a chance to deny his guilt
or, if he were guilty, to destroy such evidence as he could. Even
before the arrest of Favras, he had sent his aide-de-camp Boinville,
recently returned from England, to Provence to warn him of the
impending event.[36] At a moment when he was trying to get the
king to act as the major symbol of the Revolution, he wanted

[30] Cleray, pp. 51–53, 62–63.

[31] *Ibid.*, pp. 68–69, 74–75.

[32] *Mémoires*, II, 392.

[33] *Ami du peuple*, July 22, 1790, p. 6.

[34] Cleray, pp. 63–64, 74, and *Mémoires*, II, 391–92.

[35] Statement by the Marquise de Favras, *Gazette de Paris*, Aug. 10, 1790, p. 1.

[36] *Mémoires*, II, 392; VI, 19.

neither to disgrace the king's brother, second only to the Dauphin in line to the throne, nor to force him into open opposition to the Revolution. When Boinville told Provence his errand, the prince denied being in the plot although he admitted that he had begun to suspect it.[37]

If Lafayette had meant to save Provence for his own political motives, his plan was nearly upset when on Favras' person a letter was found that in his judgment clearly incriminated Provence. Bailly also learned the contents of that letter, since the two had examined Favras' papers together.[38] Doubtless with Bailly's consent, Lafayette went personally to see Provence at his residence, the Palais de Luxembourg, and returned the letter to him, assuring him that he was not yet publicly compromised, since he and Bailly could be trusted with the secret. Provence seemed greatly relieved.[39]

But that was not the end of the prince's worries. That day a handbill appeared stating that Favras, in addition to planning to raise 30,000 men and assassinate Lafayette and Bailly, had intended to cut off the food supply of Paris; and the handbill, after giving other details of the alleged plot, ended with a point-blank accusation: "Monsieur, the king's brother, was at the head of it."[40]

Provence consulted with his friends about his predicament, and Mirabeau, still balancing between Lafayette and Provence,[41] was among them. Like Favras, Mirabeau believed that the king should leave Paris, and he had recently expressed the opinion that if Louis did so, the National Assembly would collapse and if Lafayette, trying to "play Washington," called out the National Guard to oppose such a step, he would soon meet, and would well deserve, his doom.[42] His contempt for Lafayette had not diminished. In his opinion, everything at the "Rue de Bourbon" continued "to be lost

[37] *Ibid.*

[38] Morris diary, Dec. 27, Davenport (ed.), I, 346.

[39] *Ibid.*

[40] Lacroix, III, 284 (Dec. 26); *Journal général de la cour*, Dec. 28, p. 803; and *Ami du peuple*, Dec. 29, p. 5.

[41] See below, pp. 135–38.

[42] Dumont, *Souvenirs*, p. 127.

in the sublimity of details,"[43] and the general was "the luckiest and most inactive crapshooter [*joueur de krebs*] in the world."[44] When he learned of the "subterranean events" of recent days, he was astonished that Lafayette had shown "an intelligence and a capacity which he surely does not have" and attributed this extraordinary display to Sémonville, who he suspected was a double spy.[45]

To Mirabeau the case of the Comte de Provence seemed to parallel that of the Duc d'Orléans, in which Lafayette had made accusations without sufficient evidence, and he saw a fresh opportunity to humiliate Lafayette and further his own ends. He joined the Duc de Lévis, first gentleman of Provence's chamber, in persuading Provence to take the offensive against his accuser.[46] Accordingly, on the morning of December 26 Lafayette received a request to call again at Provence's residence, and when he did so, he found Provence surrounded by his household, adopting the tone of complainant rather than defendant. He showed Lafayette the pamphlet that charged him with having headed the Favras conspiracy, and he said (in Mirabeau's words): "You have great influence in Paris, Monsieur de La Fayette. I have no doubt that you are taking some action to counteract a malicious rumor from which the ill-intentioned say you derive advantage."[47] If Lafayette was caught unawares by Provence's "high terms," he nevertheless responded dryly and officially. He knew of no way, he stated, to discover the pamphlet's author except to offer a reward for information leading to his identification, and that would be done. Provence then announced his further plan: "I shall go to the Commune of Paris to give my side of the story. I hope you will be there."[48]

---

[43] Mirabeau to La Marck, Dec. 22, Bacourt (ed.), I, 434.

[44] Dec. 23, *ibid.*, p. 436.

[45] Dec. 26, *ibid.*, pp. 437, 439.

[46] Mirabeau to La Marck, Dec. 26, *ibid.*, p. 438.

[47] *Ibid.*

[48] Morris' diary (I, 346–47) gives Lafayette's version of this episode. It corresponds with Mirabeau's (*loc cit.*) in every essential except that Mirabeau gives the two remarks of Provence quoted above as a single speech while Lafayette's version interjects the comment of Lafayette, thus breaking Provence's speech in two. Although Mirabeau's account was earlier, we follow Lafayette's (though available only at second hand) since Mirabeau probably was not present and possibly was describing the speech as he had planned it rather than

Later that day the Assembly of Representatives received a formal request from Provence for permission to appear before them in an extraordinary session, and they made preparations to receive him in a manner befitting a brother of the king. Meanwhile Bailly and the Police Committee published a bulletin forbidding vendors to circulate the libelous handbill and offering a reward for the identification of its author.[49]

The Assembly of Representatives now held its meeting in the Grande Salle of the Hôtel de Ville. That evening the mayor sat in the president's seat, and on his left a large armchair had been placed parallel to that of the president, according to the custom of the law courts for princes of the blood.[50] A deputation of twelve Representatives was appointed to receive Provence.[51] When he arrived, he came without guards, trusting to the Garde de la Ville, which that night did the honors at the Hôtel de Ville. The reception committee conducted him to his chair beside the mayor, and when he had taken his seat, the room reverberated with applause, followed by a respectful silence.

Then the prince read a prepared speech.[52] It declared that he came before them as a "citizen of the city of Paris" to explain his relations with Favras and to refute a slanderous broadside. He had needed funds, he owned, to meet his obligations, but rather than place an additional burden on the public treasury, he had de-

---

as it actually was delivered. We doubt that Mirabeau was present because if he had been, he or Lafayette would most likely have said so in at least one of their several later comments on the Favras affair. He perhaps was at the National Assembly: see *AP*, XI, 22–23. Nevertheless, that day Mirabeau sent to La Marck, as a direct quotation, the words here given, and he probably knew them precisely because he had, as he implied, prepared them. He also sent La Marck a copy of the speech which Provence was later to read before the Commune and which Lafayette thought Mirabeau had likewise written: see Morris diary, Dec. 27, Davenport (ed.), I. 347, and *Mémoires*, II, 391–92.

[49] Lacroix, III, 285, 294.

[50] *Gazette national ou le Moniteur universel* (hereafter cited as *Moniteur*), Dec. 29, p. 572.

[51] Lacroix, III, 282. The story told in his old age by a then hostile Sémonville (see Irisson d'Herisson, pp. 52–53, and Cleray, p. 96) that Lafayette carefully put on a blond wig for the occasion because he thought it would make him look young is not totally implausible, but Lafayette was only 32 years old at the time and would probably have been more concerned, if anything, that he did not look old enough.

[52] Lacroix, II, 283–84, and *Moniteur*, Dec. 29, p. 522.

cided to borrow; when Favras had let him know that the money was available, he had given instructions to his treasurer to make a loan but he had neither seen Favras nor communicated with him since 1775 and knew nothing of his activities otherwise.[53] He himself, he went on, had been friendly toward the Revolution since the Assembly of Notables (in 1788, when he had voted in favor of doubling the Third Estate), and he still believed in the great Revolution, of which the virtuous king should be the leader. He concluded with assurances that the happiness of the king and of his people was the sole object of his thought and prayers, and he would never change them.

Despite the Representatives' rules, Provence was interrupted several times by applause. His story might have been nothing but the truth; in any event, he had read the speech convincingly, and the effect was all that he could have hoped for. Whether Bailly considered the count's exculpation satisfactory or not, he answered him with more than the usual polite phrases. He also read the proclamation of the Department of Police offering a reward for identification of the handbill's author, and he mentioned the prompt efforts of the commandant general to stop its sale, whereupon Lafayette reported the arrest of three persons involved in copying it.

Provence then scored another point; he asked for pardon of the offenders. Shouts of approval greeted this sign of royal grace, although amid the joyful din could be heard cries of "No pardon!" Provence then left, the reception committee escorting him to his carriage.[54] And so Provence, instead of appearing as a disloyal coward who had saved himself by sacrificing Favras, as Lafayette continued to think (even after the prince as Louis XVIII sat on the throne of France),[55] seemed to be an innocent and generous leader of the Revolution falsely accused by irresponsible men.

So far as Lafayette knew, the king and the queen were not implicated in the Favras affair. When Marie Antoinette learned of Provence's action, she was astonished and in a long interview[56]

[53] See below, Appendix II.

[54] Lacroix, III, 248–86 .

[55] *Mémoires*, II, 391.

[56] *Chronique de Paris*, Dec. 29, p. 510.

spoke to Lafayette about it. She believed that Provence would not have made his dramatic appearance before the municipality unless Lafayette had advised him to do so, but he assured her that he had not; on the contrary, he considered it a mean performance (*une grande platitude*). The queen seemed to be pleased by this information and told him, on that occasion or soon after, that, far from favoring the elevation of her brother-in-law, she regarded him as her personal enemy.[57]

On first learning of the Count of Provence's reaction to the slanderous handbill, Gouverneur Morris wrote in his diary: "This touches Lafayette who has too many of these little Matters on the Anvil."[58] The next Sunday (December 27) he and Short again were guests at the Rue de Bourbon, and after dinner Lafayette gave them his version of the Favras plot. He recalled that a letter found on Favras "seemed to show" that the Comte de Provence was "but too deeply concerned in it" though only he and Bailly knew of that letter and he had personally returned it to Provence. (Perhaps Lafayette overlooked the likelihood, now that Morris and Short knew of it, that its existence might no longer remain a secret.) Lafayette asserted that Provence's speech had been written by Mirabeau, whom he now called "an abandoned Rascal." Morris, reminding his host that he had long been warning him against Mirabeau, delivered a message that the Comte de Luxembourg had asked him to convey: "Mirabeau had sworn that he would ruin Lafayette." But, Morris went on, Provence had "thrown the Cards" into Lafayette's hands. Since the prince had publicly declared himself a revolutionary, Lafayette should keep him at the head of the Revolution, for, should a counterrevolution occur, its leaders would never dare to touch a brother of the king, and he would act as a shield for those below him; and in case the Revolution succeeded, he would be no liability since his weakness would prevent him from acquiring any real weight. Morris gathered that Lafayette appreciated this idea, and he went on to insist that the future administration must be made up of men of good character. His host acceded,

[57] *Mémoires*, II, 391, 393.
[58] Morris diary, Dec. 26, Davenport (ed.), I, 345.

but Morris doubted that his conviction would last, since "his Temper is turned toward Intrigue and must unite itself to Men of similar Disposition."

Almost immediately, however, the marquis showed that if he were indeed an intrigant, he was a naïve one. As Short and he were leaving, Morris asked if Lafayette had seen much of "the Gentleman" (meaning Talleyrand) Morris had recently brought to him for an interview. Morris (apparently forgetting whose temper was turned toward intrigue) was disconcerted when the general, making no effort to hide the gentleman's identity, replied that he would like to put Talleyrand in charge of the king's library as a step toward appointment as head of national education, and he asked Morris to sound out Talleyrand on this plan[59] (which Morris did the next day).[60] Clearly Lafayette still felt that he could help determine who would be minister of what.

Paris was deeply agitated by the arrest of Favras. The newspapers carried accounts that showed no doubt regarding Favras' guilt, though he was still to be tried. They cast Favras in the role of a villain who had been foiled by the ever watchful Lafayette: while himself under the shadow of the assassin's knife, the heroic commandant general had saved Paris from the catastrophes hatched by counterrevolutionaries. Revolutionary Paris was beginning to feel that two main defenders stood between it and failure, and of the two, Bailly seemed a far less impregnable bulwark than Lafayette.[61]

Then another outrage shocked the people, especially the National Guard, of Paris. Early in the morning of December 28, an unpaid National Guardsman named Trudon came off sentry duty displaying a stab wound, which, he claimed, had been inflicted by an unknown assailant.[62] Near his sentry box Guards found a bloody

[59] *Ibid.*, pp. 346–47 (Dec. 27).

[60] *Ibid.*, p. 349 (Dec. 28).

[61] *Ami du peuple*, Dec. 29, pp. 3–5; *Journal général de la cour*, Dec. 27, pp. 796–97; *Révolutions de Paris* (Tournon), No. 24, Dec. 19–26, pp. 23–24, and No. 25, Dec. 27–Jan. 2, 1790, pp. 10–13; *Courier français*, Dec. 28; and Desmoulins, *Révolutions*, No. 6, pp. 260, 261.

[62] Lacroix, III, 294.

stiletto with a slip of paper attached bearing the words: "Go on ahead and wait for Lafayette."[63] Snatched up by the newspapers, the episode appeared a terrifying sequel to the Favras plot.[64] Some implied that Trudon had not been seriously hurt, if indeed he had not inflicted a slight wound on himself in order to win Lafayette's favor;[65] at least one commentator hazarded that Lafayette had himself contrived the whole affair in order to bind his followers more closely;[66] but the doubters were few.

The reaction of Paris was prompt. The District of Saint-Leu voted to offer the mayor and the commander-in-chief a bodyguard of thirty men each and appealed to the other districts to do the same, so that the city's sixty battalions might perform this service in rotation. The District of Saint-Jacques-L'Hôpital evinced lively alarm over the dangers menacing "the heroic protector" of "nascent liberty" and pledged to forestall any plot against "the illustrious defender of national liberty."[67] Before the year closed, six hundred National Guardsmen bound themselves by oath to avenge any insult to or attack upon their general.[68] The district where the assault had taken place sent a full report to the municipal Comité des Recherches, which since Lafayette was a member of the National Assembly,[69] sent it on to that body. Though "profoundly affected," the deputies were content to rely on the Paris committee "to discover and punish the perpetrator."[70]

It was now Mirabeau's turn to be annoyed. He was prepared to

---

[63] "Va devant et attends Lafayette" was the wording in a report by the Comité des Recherches, but other sources gave other wordings: *ibid.*, pp. 294–95; *Ami du peuple*, Dec. 31, p. 4; and *Gazette de Paris*, Dec. 31, p. 4.

[64] *Patriote français*, Dec. 29, p. 3; *Chronique de Paris*, Dec. 29, p. 511; *Ami du peuple*, Dec. 29, p. 8; and *Courrier de Paris*, Dec. 29.

[65] Duquesnoy, II, 224; Mirabeau to La Marck, Dec. 29, Bacourt (ed.), I, 440; and *Lettres à Monsieur le Comte de B**** (Paris, 1789–90), V, 150.

[66] Marquis de Vaudreuil to Comte d'Artois, Dec. 25, Léonce Pingaud (ed.), *Correspondance intime du Comte de Vaudreuil et du Comte d'Artois pendant l'émigration (1789–1815)* (Paris, 1889), I, 75.

[67] Lacroix, III, 295–96 (Dec. 26). See also *Journal général de la cour*, Jan. 2, p. 12, and *Chronique de Paris*, Jan. 1, p. 3.

[68] *Journal général de la cour*, Jan. 6, p. 44.

[69] *AP*, XI, 37–38, and *Journal des débats*, Dec. 29, pp. 4–7.

[70] *Journal des débats*, Dec. 29, p. 7.

believe that the Trudon incident was one of the many intrigues contrived to keep Provence from achieving his ambition to become prime minister. "Hell has unloosed all kinds of slander . . . upon Monsieur," he wrote to La Marck, now in the Austrian Netherlands, "and upon everyone who seems attached to him"; left to his own feeble devices, Provence would end up like the Duc d'Orléans. The queen, Mirabeau surmised, was merely wheedling Provence, while the king would do nothing.[71] In history's previous uprisings "the hero of the day was far from being so much master of Paris as La Fayette," whose "national gangs" were openly threatening that "if their general suffered any harm whatsoever" they would make a hecatomb of nobles and prelates in revenge. Reluctantly Mirabeau admitted that Lafayette had "at least the talent to keep his men in shape" and "knew how to get for himself many captains of the guard." The year 1789 thus seemed about to end with Mirabeau still frustrated and Lafayette still the "hero of the day."[72]

On December 28 the Paris Comité des Recherches indicted Favras for planning to take the king away from Paris, corrupt the National Guard, and assassinate Necker, Lafayette, and Bailly. The Châtelet, which tried him, still followed the old procedure— no jury, and conviction on the testimony of no fewer than two witnesses. Lafayette and Bailly, wishing to annul the charge of murder, wrote the trial court that one of the so-called witnesses (Morel) was the informer who had betrayed the plot and thus should not serve as both accuser and witness. The court in this instance, however, preferred to consider the Comité des Recherches as the formal accuser.[73]

The National Guard was under strict orders to police the Châte-

[71] Dec. 29, Bacourt (ed.), I, 440–41. See also Dec. 31, *ibid.,* p. 442.

[72] Dec. 31, *ibid.,* p. 442.

[73] *Mémoires,* II, 393. See also *Révolutions de Paris* (Prudhomme), No. 25, Dec. 26– Jan. 2, p. 5; *Chronique de Paris,* Dec. 28, p. 507, Dec. 29, p. 510, and Dec. 30, p. 515; *Journal général de la cour,* Dec. 27, pp. 796–97; *Courrier de Paris,* Dec. 29, pp. 269, 271; and *Ami du peuple,* Dec. 29, p. 5. J.-M. Augeard, *Mémoires secrets,* ed. Evariste Bavoux (Paris, 1866), pp. 228–29, claims that Lafayette tried hard to get another witness, but we have found no evidence to substantiate his story. See also below, Bibliographical Notes, p. 134.

let, and it performed its duty well. A few demonstrations against the accused took place around the prison (and Lafayette thought that they were instigated by Favras' accomplices, fearful of his revelations), but the National Guard contained them. When Talon, as an officer (*lieutenant civil*) of the Châtelet, accompanied by the king's attorney (*procureur*), came to consult him on some details in the case, the commandant general took the occasion to assure them that while no doubt the Châtelet would take no action out of cowardice, it could count upon the National Guard to carry out whatever the court decided.[74]

Throughout the ensuing weeks, though Lafayette considered the judges "well-known counterrevolutionaries"[75] and suspected Talon of secretly urging Favras not to mention his accomplices, on the ground that it would do him no good and could only do them harm, the commandant general and his colleagues at the Hôtel de Ville studiously stayed out of the trial. He had done his duty, he thought, in making the arrest and in notifying the Châtelet that one of its witnesses was also the informer;[76] now the courts should entirely independently decide the question of Favras' guilt.

Yet, no matter how hard he tried, Lafayette could not avoid indirect implication in the trial. The accused claimed that his intention had been not to harm Lafayette or others but only to aid the Belgians in their war of independence,[77] and he called upon Mirabeau to corroborate his claim. Mirabeau testified that while he had seen Favras several times in connection with some financial matters, he denied ever having had a conversation of more than two minutes with him. He admitted that he had once heard Favras say something about Brabant but could remember no mention of Lafayette.[78] Lafayette was left, however, with the impression that Mirabeau had had a direct hand in Favras' plot in its early stages though not in its final form.[79]

[74] *Mémoires*, II, 390, and III, 246–47.

[75] *Ibid.*, II, 390.

[76] See above, p. 129.

[77] See below, pp. 276–88.

[78] *Moniteur*, Feb. 8, p. 154.

[79] *Mémoires*, II, 391–92.

Lafayette was further implicated in the trial when the accused's counsel charged that Morel, the principal accuser, had made his accusation merely to collect a reward offered by the Paris Commune for evidence against conspirators. Since Morel was an officer in the Paris National Guard, the court summoned Gouvion and Masson de Neuville as witnesses. Both officers testified that Morel had made damaging charges against Favras even before the Commune had offered such a reward.[80] In addition, the *Révolutions de Paris* published the authorization which Lafayette had given to Morel the previous September "to investigate all conspiracies against the nation, the law, the king, and the Commune of Paris as prescribed by his oath as a member of the Paris National Guard."[81] The respectability of Morel as a witness was thus confirmed, and that of Favras impugned, without Lafayette's being called to testify.

In the midst of the tragedy unfolding behind the Châtelet's door a moment of farce occurred outside. On the final day of the trial a sizable group of unemployed workmen, with a few musicians at their head, marched along the street, carrying clubs on their shoulders like guns. At the Châtelet they halted and "presented arms" to the National Guardsmen patrolling Favras' trial. The soldiers were amused, but their commanding officer saw fit to question the workers' leaders. They declared that they were on their way to Lafayette's home to ask him to find them jobs. The officer, fearful that frolic might lead to demonstration, and demonstration to riot, hustled them off.[82] The incident, otherwise a meaningless bit of byplay, showed the confidence of the unfortunate in Lafayette, the carefulness of the Châtelet's patrol, and the pitiable if good-natured helplessness of the unemployed.

On February 17 the judges of the Châtelet deliberated all day and far into the night on Favras' fate. An enemy of Lafayette subsequently charged that the commandant general, "servile slave of

[80] *Moniteur*, Feb. 14, 21, pp. 177, 208.

[81] *Révolutions de Paris* (Prudhomme), No. 31, Feb. 6–14, pp. 34–35. See also Gottschalk and Maddox, pp. 296–97, 315.

[82] *Courrier de Paris*, Feb. 18, p. 231, and *Révolutions de Paris* (Tournon), No. 32, Feb. 14–21, p. 24.

the factions," went to the Châtelet and told the judges that if they did not condemn Favras, he could not answer for their lives, since he would then be master neither of the people nor of his militia.[83] Though frequently repeated, that charge is uncorroborated, it is uncharacteristic of Lafayette (if for no other reason than that he would not readily have admitted inability to control his men), and it is contradicted by his own more circumstantiated statement that he assured officials of the court that the judges need have no fears in rendering their verdict.[84] Shortly before midnight the Châtelet declared Favras guilty of counterrevolutionary conspiracy and condemned him to be hanged in the Place de Grève.

Up to the last minute Favras asserted his innocence of conspiracy either against the state or against persons like Lafayette, Bailly, and Necker, and he steadfastly refused to bargain for his life by naming the "great lord" at whose bidding, some believed, he had acted. About eight o'clock at night on February 19 the Châtelet police brought the prisoner into the square, and National Guardsmen surrounded him. Lafayette was not there.[85] Still unflinching, Favras was hanged, the first counterrevolutionary victim of formal "revolutionary justice" to suffer the extreme penalty. (Other victims so far had been unceremoniously lynched.) Lafayette was shocked by the "fierce applause" which, he learned, arose from the spectators at the moment of execution, and perhaps too apologetically, he suggested that it might have come from "the accomplices, rather than the enemies, of Favras, who thus betrayed their impatience to see the holder of their secrets die."[86] Although he never doubted that the accused man was guilty as charged, he respected him as "a hero of loyalty and courage," while "his august accomplice [the Comte de Provence] lacked both the one and the other."[87] He

---

[83] Clermont-Gallerande, I, 307, 310. See also Marquis de Maleissye, *Mémoires d'un officier aux Gardes françaises (1789-1793)*, ed. M.-G. Roberti (Paris, 1897), p. 124; Augeard, pp. 228-29; *Mémoires du comte de Paroy: souvenirs d'un défenseur de la famille royale pendant la Révolution (1789-1797)*, ed. Étienne Charavay (Paris, 1895), p. 143; and *Gazette de Paris*, June 20, 1792, p. 4.

[84] *Mémoires*, II, 393-94, III, 246-47.

[85] Lafayette said that he saw Favras only once, at the time of his arrest: *ibid.*, II, 391.

[86] *Ibid.*, p. 394.

[87] *Ibid.*, p. 391.

was proud that the National Guard had protected the prisoner throughout his ordeal against mob violence with a zeal for which Favras himself publicly thanked them.[88]

As he often did at trying moments, Lafayette that night penned a note to Mme de Simiane. "I was . . . touched this evening by the courageous death of that man, guilty though he is. The public fury hurt me also." Although he still thought he was right to have suggested that Morel as accuser of Favras ought to have had corroboration from two other witnesses rather than one, nevertheless "the death of M. de Favras appears to me to be just." But the day had been a hard one. It had brought a crisis in the National Assembly[89] and his peremptory refusal to come to an understanding with Mirabeau,[90] in addition to the execution of a brave man for whose arrest he had been responsible, and he wanted sympathy: "Adieu until tomorrow. I am much in need of the solace of your friendship, for I am tired of men. . . ."[91]

Some months afterward one of Favras' brothers asked Lafayette for permission to publish a justification of the dead man and was invited to do so. Lafayette saw him several times after that and received from him the impression that those who on Christmas eve 1789 had confiscated Favras' papers had overlooked a number of pieces which would have revealed a different conspiracy from that for which he had paid the extreme penalty. These papers, Lafayette believed, eventually fell into the hands of Talon. They were inherited by his daughter, who gave them to Provence after he became King Louis XVIII, and they were burned.[92]

All during January and February 1790, as the Favras trial proceeded from revelation to revelation, it remained prominent in the press and in the national malaise. Again and again, even after the condemned man was hanged, Lafayette would have to deal with him as both a reality and a myth,[93] and he will appear and reappear in the following pages.

[88] *Ibid.*, p. 393.

[89] See below, pp. 234–35.

[90] See below, pp. 235–36.

[91] *Mémoires*, II, 443–44.

[92] *Ibid.*, p. 394–95.

[93] See below, Appendix II.

Ségur's *Mémoires* (III, 447–60) put his conversations with Lafayette and Marie Antoinette in quotation marks, implying that he is reporting their exact words, but more likely he quoted from notes subsequently made or from memory. The circumstantial evidence, however, corroborates their main purport.

Leclercq's *Vers la fédération,* like Cleray's study of the Favras case, compiles numerous details without being careful about the relative credibility of his sources. For example, he believes both that Lafayette and Bailly wrote to the Châtelet that Morel was the accuser (p. 45) and that they refused to name Favras' accuser because he was "un homme trop considérable" (pp. 48–49). The first statement he takes verbatim from Alexis de Valon, "Le Marquis de Favras," *Revue des deux mondes,* II (1851), 1122. The second he borrows (almost verbatim) from Augeard (pp. 228–29). Valon apparently saw Lafayette's letter on this subject to Talon as *lieutenant civil* of the Châtelet, but he does not refer to Lafayette's *Mémoires,* which tell the same story. Thus Valon's account, on the basis of a document not available to us, corroborates Lafayette's (*Mémoires,* II, 393), which is our major source for this detail. Short's letter to Jefferson, Mar. 9, in Boyd (ed.), XVI, 222, gives much the same story and, though probably also derived from Lafayette, is a much earlier record.

Gérard Walter, *Le comte de Provence* (Paris, 1950) discusses the Favras case at length (pp. 127–55 and 417–22) but says little about Lafayette's part in it.

See also Appendix II below.

CHAPTER VII

The "Nonpartisans"

MIRABEAU had only slowly, and perhaps even reluctantly, moved into the orbit of the Comte de Provence. After the National Assembly had decreed (November 7) that a deputy might not become a royal minister, La Marck concluded that those who were attempting to unseat the incumbent ministry must adopt a new strategy, and he undertook to "animate" and "scare" Lafayette by playing up the danger of the "total loss of his glory" and at the same time to give him "complete confidence" in Mirabeau. Meanwhile he asked Mirabeau to be patient: "It is fairly certain that if Lafayette is undecided and loses more times, he will become nothing."[1]

Presumably La Marck (and possibly Mirabeau too) saw Lafayette on November 10 with the intention of initiating the outlined course of action.[2] Shortly afterward, apparently with a view toward becoming an ambassador, since he could no longer expect to be named minister, the disappointed deputy asked Lafayette to take him to see Montmorin, and Lafayette did so. It was on this occasion that Mirabeau displayed his animosity toward the National Assembly by denouncing it as "a wild ass that could be mounted only with a great deal of maneuvering."[3]

Then for a period of twenty days Lafayette had little, if anything, to do with Mirabeau. He heard a great deal about him, however, and what he heard was worrisome. Among others, Sénac de Meilhan, a mutual friend of his and the Comte de Provence, informed him that Mirabeau was concocting some sort of arrangement for a

[1] La Marck to Mirabeau, Nov. 10, Bacourt (ed.), I, 420–22.

[2] *Ibid.*

[3] *Mémoires,* II, 366. See above, p. 104.

new ministry with the prince at its head.[4] Respecting Mirabeau's talents even if he despised his character, Lafayette wanted to keep him, as one of the Assembly's abler orators, on his side and away from the ambitious prince. On or about December 1[5] he spoke to Sémonville about Mirabeau, intending that Sémonville should carry back to Mirabeau what he said.[6] In that way the would-be ambassador found out that Lafayette had three major complaints to make against him: (1) he seemed to have been avoiding Lafayette recently, and so (2) the general feared that he had formed other political associations, and in addition (3) Lafayette had found in a trunkful of Mirabeau's papers, then under investigation, some intimations that Mirabeau had been accessory to the insurrection of October 5–6.[7]

After Sémonville had relayed these complaints, Mirabeau carefully composed an exculpation,[8] which he first submitted for La Marck's perusal before sending it to Lafayette.[9] His relationship to Lafayette, he wrote (and La Marck read), was for Lafayette to determine, "and I accept your answer, whatever it may be." His own attitude, "barring some wrong of which I consider you incapable," would always be one of "loyalty and personal devotion." He promised to keep away from faction (meaning the Orleanists), whose existence as a cohesive group he doubted and whose chances of success he considered negligible in any event; he would nevertheless continue to disapprove of useless or perilous measures of repression that tended irresistibly "toward a reef on which, in my opinion at least, you will be the first one wrecked." As to his alleged new political associations, he asserted that Lafayette was deceived. Such associations as he had (he here meant Provence)[10] were, he claimed, merely of a friendly, conversational nature. Since,

---

[4] *Mémoires*, II, 363, 366. Cf. La Marck to Mirabeau, Dec. 1, Bacourt (ed.), I, 426, and La Marck's explanation, *ibid.*, p. 129.

[5] This we take to be the meaning of *d'aujourd'hui*: Bacourt (ed.), I, 424.

[6] *Ibid.*, p. 423. Cf. *ibid.*, p. 129.

[7] Dec. 1, *ibid.*, pp. 423–25.

[8] *Ibid.*

[9] *Ibid.*, p. 426.

[10] Cf. La Marck's explanation, *ibid.*, p. 129.

though the times were great, men were petty, he saw less and less of those whom he wanted to associate with, and if he had not seen Lafayette of late, wasn't he justified, since Lafayette had only now noticed his absence and had kept none of his promises? Lafayette in fact, he argued, ought to feel grateful to him for having ceased to make observations that, though designed to serve him, risked his displeasure. He had declared a hundred times (but only to Lafayette and a few personal friends) that the commandant general's dizzy position and personal indecision were blinding him to the unsteadiness of his situation, that preference for mediocre men would ruin his most beautiful career, and with it the public welfare.

As for the imputations of criminal activity on his part, Mirabeau remonstrated, some of them had no foundation whatsoever, others were among "the thousand minor calumnies" intended to try "the sensitiveness of my talent," and still others he just did not understand. He admitted that he had many debts, but they were in themselves "the best response ... to the confabulations of calumniators" (meaning those who accused him of venality). Even his mistakes, he claimed, could be explained to the shame of his enemies, and he did not intend to be stopped by such maneuvers. And so would Lafayette please return his papers, which must by that time have been inventoried and, in any case, "will produce nothing more against me than so many sterile flutterings with which you have been worn out in this connection for several months."

When La Marck examined Mirabeau's proposed letter, he had already decided to see Lafayette again, intending to talk about the affairs of his own country, the Austrian Netherlands, but he expected Mirabeau's name to come up. "Your letter is strong and may humiliate him," he warned. "But if a rupture with you results [it is] the truth [that] will have caused your break. It is he who will be in the wrong. Keep a copy of this letter."[11] He soon satisfied himself that Lafayette had indeed learned about Mirabeau's budding relations with Provence and so probably would not react to Mirabeau's blandishments as they hoped.[12]

[11] La Marck to Mirabeau, Dec. 1, *ibid.*, p. 426.

[12] Cf. *Mémoires*, II, 366. Another letter, which Lafayette (*ibid.*, n. 1) learned from the *Mémoires de Mirabeau* [ed. Montigny] (of which we have used the Paris, 1841 ver-

On the contrary, Lafayette was still trying to bolster Necker's position in the royal ministry. Necker's several efforts to strengthen the French treasury had failed so far to raise enough cash or credit to reduce the danger of royal bankruptcy, and, pressed for money, he now counted upon the part payment of the United States debt to France which was due in January. Short, however, had been requested by Hamilton to see if France would be content with only the interest due,[13] and Morris hoped to avoid the international embarrassment that would result if Necker brought the matter up for debate in the National Assembly. He therefore came forward with a proposal that might provide France with the much needed funds, save his own country's face, and make some profit for himself and his associates. He suggested that a "Society of Friends to America" buy the forthcoming obligation of the United States to France, paying for it with French perpetual *rentes*.[14] Short approved of Morris' plan; so did Lafayette, who perhaps saw in it a coup for Necker. He told Morris that Necker "must be kept for the Sake of his Name,"[15] and he persuaded the finance minister to promise not to dispose of the claim upon the American payment without first communicating with Short.[16]

Because of their own desire to make a profit, the Dutch bankers, instead of cooperating with Morris, competed with him, and so his scheme failed.[17] Meanwhile, however, the American debt was not debated in the National Assembly, and Necker remained in power. Hence Mirabeau, more hostile to Necker than ever, moved farther away from Lafayette and closer to Provence, and that was how it happened that at the time of Provence's involvement in the Favras scandal, he was one of the prince's major advisers.[18]

---

sion), VII, 282, is not of Dec. 1, as the editor, who apparently cited it from memory, thought, but of Apr. 28, 1790: see Bacourt (ed.), II, 6–7; Louis de Loménie, *Les Mirabeaus* (Paris, 1891), V, 59 n.; and below, pp. 340–42.

[13] Hamilton to Short, Oct. 7, Syrett and Cooke (eds.), V, 429–30.

[14] Morris to Hamilton, Jan. 31, Davenport (ed.), pp. 396–97.

[15] Morris diary, Dec. 2, *ibid.*, p. 320.

[16] *Ibid.*, pp. 319, 320 (Dec. 1, 2), 329–30 (Dec. 11).

[17] Morris to Robert Morris, Feb. 1, *ibid.*, p. 401.

[18] See above, pp. 122–24 and n. 48.

In the National Assembly continual debate on finances and other moot issues created controversies that became increasingly vehement, and after the Assembly moved from the Archbishop's Palace to the Salle du Manège (November 9), the division into at least three separate groups became more conspicuous. Because of the tendency of deputies of like views to cluster in different parts of the meeting hall—to the left, to the right, or in front of the presiding officer—they soon were commonly known as the Left, the Right, and the Center. The deputies of the Left were prominent members of a recently formed association, the Amis de la Constitution, which was to become famous as the Jacobin Club, or the Jacobins, so-called because they met at the monastery of the Jacobin monks. The Jacobins generally followed the leadership of the Triumvirate—Barnave, Duport, and Alexandre de Lameth—whose intention to continue the reform movement until royal absolutism and hereditary privilege were thoroughly obliterated had intensified almost with each debate. The Right, in contrast, had tended to harden in opposition to further diminution of the royal prerogative, aristocratic privilege, and the Catholic establishment. The adherents of the Center balanced between these two programs, subject to rhetorical persuasion, to popular pressure, or to their own independent judgment regarding the measures under consideration.

The royalist-inclined Paris correspondent of the *Mercure de France* called the three groupings the Enragés, the Aristocrats, and the Moderates and named Lafayette as the leader of the Moderates.[19] Lafayette himself, however, was opposed to faction and was striving to achieve a consensus among the deputies. While he recognized that distinct and possibly antagonistic groupings had crystallized among his colleagues, he preferred to think of those who sympathized with his moderate views not as a faction or a party but rather as "the friends of liberty, equality, public order, and therefore the true constitutionals."[20]

To counteract the influence of the Left, about forty moderate-royalist deputies proposed to form a club of nonpartisans or, as they

---

[19] *Mercure historique et politique de Bruxelles* (bound with the *Mercure de France*), Jan. 9, p. 164.

[20] *Mémoires*, IV, 91. Cf. *ibid.*, III, 239.

were eventually to be called, Impartiaux. Their aim was to avoid the extreme policies of both the Left and the Right—in other words, to preserve the constitutional reforms already achieved and to oppose further revision in the direction of either aristocratic reaction or democratic reform. The Revolution, they held, had already gone far enough and should now come to a halt. They asked the deputy Pierre-Victor Malouet to become one of their fifteen "commissioners," or executive committee. Apprehensive that an organization of "non-partisans" might be attacked as a coalition "against the constitution," Malouet proposed that he first approach "a large number of deputies who have always followed the line of reason and moderation between aristocracy and democracy." His "nonpartisan" colleagues agreed not to have a large-scale meeting until they had made their conciliatory purpose known, and they decided that "the commandant general of the Paris militia would be the first one informed of it."[21]

Accordingly, on December 29 Malouet called on Lafayette. As usual, other guests were being entertained at the Rue de Bourbon, and so Lafayette took him into his private study. Malouet proceeded to explain that his friends, though slandered as obstructionists, actually were honest men and good citizens. Although they did not approve of everything that had been done and did disapprove of dangerous innovations, they were determined to oppose any resistance to the laws already adopted, and they wished to unite all those who would support the constitution as now achieved. The Assembly's immediate attention should go to the preservation of royal power—in conformity, however, with constitutional principles. If disorder persisted, government credit would decline, taxes would drop off, the army would disintegrate, and hunger, grievances, and unhappiness would be the only fruits of the Revolution. Without a strong central, constitutional executive, Malouet predicted, anarchy would be the outcome: "Therefore I invite you to attend our meetings and to put yourself at the head of the moderate men who want liberty, peace, and justice for all."[22]

---

[21] Baron Malouet (ed.), *Mémoires de Malouet* (Paris, 1868), I, 389, 391.

[22] *Ibid.*, p. 392.

Since it appeared that Malouet and his friends were resolved to uphold the Declaration of Rights and a liberal constitution, Lafayette could well assume that their views might fairly coincide with those he had but recently detailed for Louis XVI as his own. So he received the overture favorably; he too, he said, felt convinced of the need to re-establish peace and confidence and to leave the executive authority strong. Latour-Maubourg and Jacques-Guillaume Thouret, both liberal deputies, happened to be visiting with Adrienne at the moment, and Lafayette suggested that they should also be told of Malouet's proposal. They were invited into the study, and Malouet restated his views for their benefit. Like Lafayette, they were pleased at the prospect of establishing moderation in the National Assembly and peace throughout the country.[23] So the four men decided that Malouet should confer with his friends, and Lafayette, Maubourg, and Thouret with theirs, and they would meet together on December 31[24] at the home of the Duc de La Rochefoucauld.[25] "In all ways," wrote the deputy Duquesnoy, upon hearing of Lafayette's effort to unite the political parties, "France will owe to Lafayette more than it is possible to say; the friends of liberty cannot pronounce his name without respect and admiration."[26]

The meeting took place at La Rochefoucauld's house as arranged.[27] Thouret failed to attend, but La Rochefoucauld, Latour-Maubourg, Liancourt, and the Marquis de Lacoste, another of the small band of nobles who had consistently shown liberal tendencies, accompanied Lafayette as his political friends. Malouet brought with him a selected group of deputies who usually sat with the Right but had given some indication of readiness to accept reform. They had been chosen at a meeting called immediately after

[23] *Ibid.*, p. 393. Cf. *Journal des Impartiaux*, quoted *ibid.*, pp. 389–90 n.

[24] Malouet's dating. La Rochefoucauld says Jan. 3. See "Bibliographical Notes" below, p. 153.

[25] Malouet, I, 392–94; *Mercure historique et politique de Bruxelles*, Jan. 9, p. 164, Mar. 6, pp. 78–81; and Lafayette to M. d'Hennings, Jan. 15, 1799, *Mémoires*, III, 239 (of which the manuscript original in the Huntington Library, HM 21654, is more complete).

[26] Duquesnoy, II, 230 (Dec. 30).

[27] See above, n. 24.

his previous conference with Lafayette to represent the "non-partisans" on this occasion.[28]

It did not take long for Lafayette and his associates to perceive that they were dealing with a formal committee from a fairly well organized group of deputies who had committed themselves to explicit policies and were now engaged in winning adherents. This impression was quite different from that which Lafayette and Maubourg had received from Malouet two days earlier, when they had inferred that a group of uncommitted individuals would engage in a free discussion of matters of mutual concern. One of Lafayette's friends pointed out that their side spoke for no organization, that each of them had come purely on his own responsibility, and that they were not yet ready to admit that the National Assembly was divided into two distinct parties, even if regrettably it often split on heated issues. Malouet's side answered that nevertheless two parties did exist in the National Assembly and they hoped to draw the two together.[29]

As was now clear, Malouet and his companions were proposing that Lafayette and his friends join with them in organizing a relatively formal affiliation of moderate Rightists. Doubtless Lafayette and his associates listened to Malouet's committee politely, but they were hardly ready to commit themselves definitively to any one group of deputies. On the other hand, they certainly wanted good order and hoped for a working majority of men of Patriotic principles in the National Assembly. Consequently they thought it worth while to explore further what substance Malouet and his "nonpartisans" actually intended to give to their words. So, agreeing to talk in the interim with some of their own friends, they consented to meet with Malouet's group again on January 3.[30]

Meanwhile, the year 1789, which came to be known as "the first year of French liberty," was ushered out with fitting ceremony. On

[28] Malouet, I, 394–97; "Lettre de M. le duc de La Rochefoucauld . . . ," *Mercure de France*, Mar. 6, pp. 78–81; *Moniteur*, Mar. 10, p. 569; Augustin Challamel, *Les Clubs contre-révolutionaires* (Paris, 1895), pp. 105–7; and *Mémoires*, IV, 91–92. See also "Bibliographical Notes" below, pp. 152–53.

[29] See above, n. 28.

[30] Malouet's dating. La Rochefoucauld says Jan. 6. See "Bibliographical Notes" below, p. 153.

the last day of the year the Assembly of Representatives sent to Lafayette and the mayor a deputation "to carry . . . the sentiments of esteem and admiration with which it will always be imbued for the founders of liberty." When Lafayette in turn went to the Assembly of Representatives to express his "respectful devotion," the applause that greeted him gave "the most appreciative proof of its satisfaction."[31]

Despite growing criticism the fading year had enhanced Lafayette's glory and given him a foremost place in the hearts of millions of Frenchmen. Probably no man in Paris—not even the king, whose glory of late had lost much of its luster—was a serious competitor in popularity, although Bailly had until recently kept abreast.[32] Medals, engravings, songs, pamphlets, journal articles, public orations, official citations, and private letters testified to the esteem in which contemporaries held the commandant general. The royal engraver, P.-S.-B. Duvivier, publicly asked the Assembly of Representatives for permission to make a medal that would preserve Lafayette's features for posterity.[33] Smart hostesses seeking busts of Bailly and Lafayette to adorn their salons could find handsome ones in terracotta for six livres.[34] Portraits of the National Guard's commander were numerous. One of them bore as an inscription a quatrain of which the first line read: "Mars and Minerva together have applauded his selection."[35] As commandant general Lafayette granted one publishing firm's request to publish an almanac of the Paris National Guard,[36] and he permitted another to put out a *Manuel militaire* "upon the invitation of M. de la Fayette."[37] A colored map of Paris showing the areas patrolled by each of the National Guard divisions was likewise dedicated to him.[38] His heroic role in the

---

[31] Lacroix, III, 321, 323–24, 328 (Dec. 31).

[32] Mme de Corny to Jefferson, Nov. 25, Gilbert Chinard, *Trois amitiés françaises de Jefferson* (Paris, 1927), p. 192.

[33] Lacroix, II, 457–58, 459–60, 467 (Oct. 29).

[34] *Journal général de la cour,* Nov. 9, p. 416, Nov. 10, p. 424.

[35] *Mercure de France,* Nov. 7, p. 3.

[36] Lafayette to Bailly, Dec. 19, Tuetey, III, No. 2521.

[37] *Chronique de Paris,* Dec. 15, p. 456.

[38] *Ibid.,* Dec. 4, p. 412.

American Revolution was continually recalled. The *Gazette de Paris* printed a twelve-line paean which ended: "And the Bayard of America is the Wasingthon [*sic*] of the French."[39] The dramatist Marie-Joseph Chénier described him as:

> Du sage Washington le vertueux rival,
> Son élève autrefois, maintenant son égal.[40]

Late in 1789 appeared *Les principaux événemens de la Révolution de Paris* by the novelist F.-G. Ducray-Dumesnil, dedicated to "M. le Marquis de La Fayette, Restorer of Liberty in America, and Defender of Her Rights in France."[41] When both Virginia and Pennsylvania named new counties in his honor, a Paris journal suggested that Paris should rename a street for Lafayette and another for Bailly.[42] When the former "Rue de Calonne" was in fact renamed the "Rue de Lafayette," Desmoulins suggested that other cities follow that example and then recorded the paradox that Lafayette had removed his armorial bearings from his carriage and substituted the initials "L" and "F" while the mayor had changed his servants' dress from plain coats to livery. "I have blushed for the honor of letters," Desmoulins commented. "The *philosophe* has become a marquis of dandies, and the marquis a *philosophe*."[43]

If, as Lafayette insisted, he sought neither glory nor power but only the success of the Revolution, he could take pleasure in the progress it had made in 1789. The France of only a year earlier seemed remote indeed. Although the aristocracy had resisted, it had not succeeded in halting the Revolution; although the king had balked, he had made concessions; although the counterrevolutionaries had plotted, they had been frustrated; although the Patriots had splintered, they had abolished many privileges, adopted the Declaration of Rights, and made some headway in nationalizing the church's property and in drafting a constitution that provided

---

[39] Nov. 9, p. 23.

[40] "Epitre au roy," *Chronique de Paris*, Nov. 7, p. 301.

[41] Boyd (ed.), XV, xxxii–xxxiv, and the illustrations between pp. 280 and 281.

[42] *Chronique de Paris*, Nov. 1, p. 277.

[43] *Révolutions de France et de Brabant*, No. 3, pp. 100–101.

a system of governmental checks and balances. Writs now ran in the name of "Louis XVI, by the grace of god and the constitutional law of the state, king of the French" in recognition of the principle of the sovereignty of the people.

Less hopeful men might fret over the resultant weakness of the executive arm, but Lafayette counted upon the constitution in the end to provide the king with adequate power to guarantee order in a free and happy France, and he expected the constitution to be completed before the next summer was over. He recognized, however, perhaps better than others, that civic order within a system of liberty would be no easy goal to attain. As if to remind him of the difficulty, a rumor spread abroad that an attempt on the life of "the illustrious Washington of France" had been made on New Year's Eve, a bullet knocking his hat off as he was leaving the Tuileries.[44] This rumor, though probably untrue, reinforced the popular conviction that Favras and his accomplices had really meant to assassinate him and the mayor. It brought patriotic indignation to a boiling point.

National Guards had already resorted to reprisal on several occasions in defense of their commander's good name.[45] Swearing to die in his defense, the District of Petit-Saint-Antoine now implored him to increase his bodyguard, begging for its battalion the honor of being included.[46] On New Year's Eve hundreds of National Guards signed an oath to avenge every insult to their general and to spare no priest or noble if any further attempts were made upon his life, and bills, conspicuously posted on Paris walls, broadcast warnings to that effect.[47] Lafayette felt called upon to put a stop to such threats of violence from men who wore the uniform of custodians of the peace. In one of his orders of the day, he declared: "I recognize as friends only the friends of liberty and order."[48]

[44] *Journal général de la cour*, Jan. 1, p. 7. See also *Courrier de Paris*, Jan. 2, p. 330.

[45] *Journal général de l'Europe*, supplément, No. 3, pp. 33, 125.

[46] *Chronique de Paris*, Jan. 3, p. 12, Jan. 4, p. 16.

[47] *Journal général de la cour*, Jan. 6, p. 44, Jan. 10, p. 78, and *Journal général de l'Europe*, No. 1, p. 33.

[48] *Mémoires*, II, 378.

Some patriotic journalist announced that they were ready to defend "our mayor and our general" against calumniators and assassins but agreed also to obey his orders and the law.[49]

On New Year's Day Morris was one of the dinner guests at Lafayette's house, where conversation ranged over the current political scene. The marquis flatly asserted that Mirabeau and the Comte de Provence were "closely allied," that Provence was "a weak and indolent Creature," and that Mirabeau was "an active and artful Rascal." The conversation then touched upon the case of General Pierre de Besenval, accused of resisting the people at the time of the attack on the Bastille. After months of imprisonment in Brie-Comte-Robert he had been transferred to Paris and was undergoing a protracted trial in the same court, the Châtelet, that was soon to begin to try Favras. Morris urged Lafayette to speed up Besenval's trial because not only the prisoner's old friends but also humbler Parisians were showing sympathy for the former commander of the Swiss and the "violent Torrent" which once had been directed against him might now break out against his prosecutors. This warning of popular fickleness, Morris assumed, affected Lafayette. When the conversation turned to the National Assembly, Lafayette presupposed that his American visitor, despite his criticisms of it, would acknowledge that the constitution it was drawing up would be better than England's, but Morris quickly denied that such was his opinion.[50]

The New Year's festivities continued on January 2. Several members of the Military Committee came to present to the commander-in-chief, their president, their good wishes for the new year.[51] The officers of the mounted constabulary (maréchaussée) of the Île de France, which was part of the royal force under Lafayette's command, upon offering their respects to the Assembly of Representatives, requested permission to take the civic oath at some future time in his presence.[52] Lafayette also presented a deputation of the Na-

[49] Chronique de Paris, Jan. 2, p. 6. See also Desmoulins, Révolutions, No. 6, pp. 279, 282.

[50] Morris diary, Jan. 1, Davenport (ed.), I, 355.

[51] Procès-verbal du Comité militaire, Part II, p. 51.

[52] Lacroix, III, 343–44 (Jan. 2).

tional Guard and, according to the Representatives' official minutes, "expressed the sentiments of these brave military men with his
characteristic noble simplicity." The president, thanking the National Guard as well as "the hero whom it had the honor to have as
its chief," declared that "the Assembly congratulated itself on having confided its defense to warriors commanded by a general
whose discretion equaled his valor."[53]

That afternoon Lafayette with a deputation of National Guards
joined Bailly and a committee of Representatives to carry New
Year's greetings to the National Assembly.[54] At the Salle du Manège
Bailly, speaking for both the Commune and the National Guard,
urged the deputies to hasten to complete the constitution, and the
National Assembly's president invited Lafayette and Bailly to resume their places as deputies in the Assembly.[55] The next day Lafayette was one of a deputation that represented the Commune at a
service in the still unfinished Church of Sainte-Geneviève. Gene-
viève was the patron saint of Paris; her fete day was January 3, and
a solemn mass was said that day in the church. Lafayette occupied a
place of honor beside the mayor.[56] Despite the recent (December
19) secularization of church property, the good relations of the
National Guard with the city's churches[57] were thus once again
symbolized.

January 3[58] was also the day fixed for the second meeting of the
Malouet committee with Lafayette and his associates at the home
of the Duc de La Rochefoucauld. Since Lafayette had agreed that
his group would try to interest other colleagues, they had previously
talked with a few other members of the National Assembly about
Malouet's proposals, but none of the others had been willing to
join in the conversations.[59]

So the men who attended the conference on January 3 were

[53] *Ibid.*, p. 345.
[54] *AP*, XI, 64–65.
[55] *Ibid.*, p. 65, and Duquesnoy, II, 244. See below, p. 150.
[56] Lacroix, III, 359–61.
[57] Gottschalk and Maddox, pp. 297–97, 301–6.
[58] See above, n. 24.
[59] See above, n. 28.

the same ones who had gathered for the same purpose on December 31. But the atmosphere was less friendly.[60] Malouet had no new proposals; he again dwelt on the need to reestablish executive power. The Duc de La Rochefoucauld and his friends agreed that the executive power should be strong, as the safety of a great state demanded, and they believed that the French people generally thought likewise. But, as the duke put it with his friends' approval, the royal power could not be strengthened or defined by a few isolated decrees. Since the constitution was only partly ready and since certain governmental bodies were still to be organized, it was not yet possible to mesh the royal executive power explicitly with that of other bodies. When, however, the constitution was about to be finished, the Assembly should then write a definitive set of articles delimiting the king's power and its relations with all other parts of the government. In La Rochefoucauld's opinion, the executive power was "the keystone of the arch which could be put in place only after all the other parts of the edifice had been formed and disposed."[61]

Malouet was given to feel that while his hosts were friendly to him and his associates personally, La Rochefoucauld and his colleagues were much cooler toward collaboration than they had been three days earlier.[62] Malouet and his associates were not prepared to postpone strengthening the executive authority until all the rest of the constitution was drawn up. Perhaps they feared their bargaining power would wither away while their opponents filled the constitution with measures they disapproved.[63] The conference ended without achieving further agreement and without arranging for another meeting. Before he left, Malouet made clear that he and his associates intended to issue a public report of what had occurred; they would also publish a declaration of "principes im-

---

[60] Malouet, I, 397.

[61] *Ibid.*, p. 407 n. The version there given of the "Lettre de M. le duc de la Rochefoucauld" (see above, n. 28) elides part of the account given in the *Journal des Impartiaux*, No. 7, [*post* Feb. 24], pp. 18–22.

[62] Malouet, I, 397.

[63] See the editor's note, *ibid.*, pp. 405–6.

partiaux" and form a club that would be open to anyone who would
subscribe to those principles.[64] This announcement was practically
an admission that Malouet's hope of collaboration with Lafayette
had failed and that he must look elsewhere for support of his
"impartial principles."

As had generally been expected, the debates that now rent the
National Assembly most violently were on the issue of how much
executive authority to vest in the king. Lafayette felt that he had to
try to hold the balance, perhaps even effect a compromise, between
the Impartiaux, who would give Louis XVI more authority than
some moderates thought he ought to have, and those deputies
who would grant him less. One of the considerations that reduced
confidence in the monarch was the unpopularity of his wife, Marie
Antoinette. Her chief adviser ever since she had come to France had
been the Comte de Mercy-Argenteau, the Austrian ambassador,
and Lafayette arranged a long conversation with him concerning
the queen. Both men recognized that a great deal depended upon
her discretion and that her Habsburg pride, her exalted concept
of royalty, and her ambiguous role as an Austrian princess though
queen of France would make it difficult for her to pick her way
discreetly. The ambassador believed that Marie Antoinette would
be well advised not to hold formal audiences, and Lafayette agreed.
Mercy communicated the gist of that conversation to the queen,[65]
but his private inclination (and therefore presumably the queen's)
was far from cooperative. He wrote to the Austrian chancellor,
Prince von Kaunitz,[66] that while Lafayette was firmly resolved to
guard the personal safety of the king and the queen, he obviously
was completely under the influence of "the republican spirit of liberty" and his major aim was to have a king over whom he could
be "lord and master," but since he had "more ambition than ability," it was doubtful that he could stay on the "slippery path he has
taken." This judgment of Lafayette was a serious error; by under-
estimating his ability and his patriotism and overestimating his re-

[64] *Ibid.*, p. 397, and see above, n. 30.

[65] Mercy to Marie Antoinette, Jan. 4, Feuillet de Conches (ed.), I, 283.

[66] Copy of letter of Mercy to Kaunitz. Jan. 4, BN: n.a.f. 6963, p. 21.

publicanism and ambition, Mercy strengthened Marie Antoinette's aversion to him and, with him, the more moderate revolutionary leaders.

At the next meeting of the National Assembly (January 4) the Abbé de Montesquiou, elected with the support of the Impartiaux, for the first time took the fauteuil of the presiding officer. In his inaugural remarks he "exhorted all the deputies to observe harmony and peace in the bosom of the Assembly."[67] Hardly had he finished than Lafayette and Bailly entered and, amid ringing cheers of welcome, took their places as members.[68] At least one observer noted that only one side of the Assembly applauded.[69]

One of the important items on the day's agenda was the question of the civil list. It was decided that a deputation be sent to the king to ask what sum he wanted and that the president, as its spokesman, "beg His Majesty to consult his spirit of economy less than the dignity of the nation." This motion passed with only two dissenting votes. The deputation was immediately chosen, and of its fifty-seven members Lafayette was the second elected.[70] When the deputation waited upon the king and the president urged him to consider his subjects' desire to surround the throne with pomp and splendor, Louis XVI replied that he preferred that adequate funds first be made available to pay the interest on the public debt, to maintain the operating expenses of the government, and to insure the defense of the realm. "What concerns me personally," he concluded, "is, in the present circumstances, my least anxiety."[71] When the president reported the king's reply to an applauding Assembly the next day, confidence and good-will still seemed to bind king and National Assembly together in mutual respect.

If, however, as Lafayette contended, there had been no recognizable parties in the National Assembly when the negotiations with Malouet began, those very negotiations had gone far toward making them more easily recognizable. The Impartiaux now for-

---

[67] *AP*, XI, 67–68.

[68] *Ibid.; Courier français,* Jan. 5, p. 33; and *Point du jour,* Jan. 5, p. 357.

[69] *L'Observateur,* Jan. 7, p. 561.

[70] *AP*, XI, 68.

[71] *Ibid.,* p. 107.

mally organized as a political club, meeting at the Monastery of the Grands-Augustins, and soon began to publish a *Journal des Impartiaux*. The Left carried on at the Jacobins. And Lafayette and his friends came to refer to themselves semi-facetiously as the "Comité de La Rochefoucauld." Before long the name *Impartiaux* gave way in popular usage to the more accurate *Monarchiens*.

As promised, a declaration of the principles of the Impartiaux soon appeared in print.[72] They constituted a frank proposal to call the Revolution to a halt, stressing that while counterrevolution would be an absurdity, a return to peace and order was overdue. While pleading for loyalty to the constitution that would be adopted (subject to future amendment), they affirmed that peaceful respect for the law could best be achieved by giving the king the principal executive authority, by making the Roman Catholic Church the only public cult, by guaranteeing freedom of the press but with proper precautions against license, by putting "the union of this vast empire" under the protection of the law and the king, and by placing the royal army and the National Guard also under the monarch.

Lafayette and his friends could hardly have subscribed to that program without reservations. Their openly avowed program, jointly and severally, stood in clear opposition to the contention of the self-styled "Impartiaux" that the Revolution had now gone far enough. Lacoste, for one, was in favor of using still more of the church's property to meet the national deficit. Lafayette, already a conspicuous champion of the Protestants and mildly interested in the Jews,[73] could hardly have accepted exclusive establishment of the Catholic Church. Besides, as a champion of freedom of thought he might well hesitate to sanction the return of censorship in the guise of undefined precautions against "license of the press." Nor, advocate of a strong executive though he was, was he likely, without a more definite commitment to the program he had recently submitted for His Majesty's consideration, to encourage a reversal

---

[72] "Principes impartiaux," bound with *Journal des Impartiaux* [*post* Jan. 3], pp. 1–7. See also Challamel, pp. 102–5, 108–14, and Malouet, I, 375–79, 397–405.

[73] See Louis Gottschalk, *Lafayette and the Close of the American Revolution* (Chicago, 1942), p. 184.

of the recent municipal revolution by giving the king loosely qualified control of local government and the nation's armed forces. The crucial issue still was not that the executive power be considerable (on that he could easily agree with the Impartiaux), but what the king intended to do with it if he got it, and neither Lafayette nor the Impartiaux yet knew to what extent Louis XVI was ready to advance or to oppose the Revolution.

A report of the meeting of Lafayette, La Rochefoucauld, and other Fayettists with Malouet and his associates soon appeared in the *Mercure de France*,[74] and Lafayette indignantly assumed that Malouet had made their discussion public in order to compromise him and his supporters. Besides, he suspected that "the club of pretended impartials has been established under auspices that do not smack of impartiality," since he considered several of Malouet's collaborators confirmed aristocrats or royalists. "I wish that club no harm," he wrote Mme de Simiane,[75] ". . . but this self-styled impartial party will be nothing but dull, and if the ministers join forces with it, they will destroy the royal authority because they will link its destiny to all the abuses that the others [the Impartiaux] want to preserve and with all the selfish interests that they mean to satisfy." So Malouet had to continue his efforts to brake the Revolution without Lafayette's cooperation.

BIBLIOGRAPHICAL NOTES

Louis and Charles de Loménie's five volumes on the Mirabeaus (1889–91) are still the fullest (but not, we think, the best) study of the Comte de Mirabeau during the French Revolution, although several one-volume biographies have since appeared (see above, p. 89). The eight volumes of the so-called *Mémoires de Mirabeau* edited by Lucas de Montigny are in fact a biography.

Malouet's *Mémoires* were published by his grandson, and the editor added lengthy and useful footnotes to them. Since they were published in 1868, which, according to the editor, was sixty years after they were written, they must have been completed in 1808, or almost twenty years after the events here narrated. In writing his account, Malouet apparently referred to the publications of the Club des Impartiaux, among them the "Exposé des motifs qui ont porté les Impartiaux à se reunir . . ." (bound with the *Journal des Impartiaux*), pp. 6–11. At any rate, the account they gave of those events

[74] See above, n. 19.

[75] [Ca. Jan. 18], *Mémoires*, II, 445–46. The editors (*ibid.*, p. 445, n. 2) date this letter "du mois de mars," but the contents make clear that it is of mid-January.

coincides in all but trivial details with the account that La Rochefoucauld gave of them (Feb. 17) within weeks of their occurrence in a letter to the editor of the *Mercure historique et politique de Bruxelles,* No. 10 [Mar. 6], pp. 78–81. La Rochefoucauld's letter was republished in other contemporary journals, including the *Journal des Impartiaux,* No. 7 [*post* Feb. 24], pp. 18–22. Rarely have political opponents agreed so largely in their accounts of a joint meeting at which they disagreed. The major points of difference are on the dates of the two meetings at La Rochefoucauld's home. Malouet puts them on Dec. 31 and Jan. 3, while La Rochefoucauld puts them on Jan. 3 and 6. We have adopted Malouet's datings because while La Rochefoucauld admitted in his account that he was relying upon his memory, Malouet claimed to have depended upon "des notes très-exactes" in replying to La Rochefoucauld (*loc. cit.,* pp. 21–23).

The early volumes of Feuillet de Conches' collection of documents were severely criticized for carelessness of editorial apparatus, but the texts they present seem essentially reliable. See [Lord Acton?] in the *North British Review,* LII (1870), 259–62.

CHAPTER VIII

Fraternity or Disloyalty in the National Guard?

THOUGH extensive on paper and impressive on parade, the Paris National Guard was not yet equal to its numerous obligations. On paper on November 1 Lafayette had under his command as paid troops 6,000 infantry, 800 cavalry, 600 grenadiers, 700 chasseurs, and 100 guards for the river, quays, and islands of the Seine—8,200 hired, professional soldiers altogether. The *Règlement* provided that when the unpaid companies were completed, he should also have 500 unpaid Guards available daily, but he did not want to depend on unpaid troops for routine service, for citizen-soldiers, though they might show up well in emergencies, often failed to report when all was quiet. Lafayette, the Military Committee, and the Representatives worked out a plan to create a seventh company of chasseurs to guard the grain market, and by November 18 the new corps was, in fact, set up.[1]

The recruitment of paid soldiers created a special problem. The Paris Commune had announced a higher rate of pay for the National Guard than that of the regular army. As this discrepancy became known, as the prestige of the Paris National Guard soared, and as the news spread that additional paid companies were being recruited, royal soldiers thronged to the capital to enlist. Scores of them had honorable discharges and consequently were acceptable, but some of them had not been honorably discharged. A number of such soldiers petitioned the Assembly of Representatives to enroll them in the paid companies of the National Guard, and the Representatives gave Lafayette authority to do so provided the king would not regard their enrollment as encouraging further

[1] Lacroix, II, 476 (Oct. 30), 591 (Nov. 9), 657–58 (Nov. 18), and *Procès-verbal du Comité militaire*, Part II, pp. 38–40.

desertion from the royal army. Louis gave permission to incorporate such recruits in the National Guard up to December 1.[2] Thus it appeared by the end of November that enough trained men would be available to meet any emergency.[3]

Lafayette and the civil authorities of Paris realized that their critics both at the royal court and in the district assemblies would regard their diligence in discouraging desertion from the royal forces as a test of their sincerity—the court because it wanted co-operation with the king's attempts to preserve discipline in his army, the districts because, jealous for their own authority, they wanted to restrict the number of paid troops in the Paris National Guard. Lafayette asked the battalion commanders and the division chiefs to screen their units regularly every Monday and Wednesday in order to identify possible deserters and assigned two of his aides to assist in this process and report after each survey.[4] When a deserter was identified, Lafayette gave him a safe-conduct certifying not only that the king's pardon granted him immunity if he returned to his post by December 1 but also that he was entitled to draw three sous per league on the way.[5] Despite this leniency, on one occasion a group of migrant soldiers insisted upon being admitted into the Paris National Guard at once, and when Lafayette refused, they sent to the Tuileries and demanded to see the king, but Lafayette sent them to jail instead.[6]

A fresh complication arose when foreign migrant soldiers, deserters from the Austrian ruler Leopold II's forces in his restless Belgian provinces, sought to enter the Paris National Guard. Apprehensive that they might become a greater menace to order and a more susceptible tool of counterrevolutionaries than French deserters, Lafayette determined to keep them away. He instructed his commanders to stop the Belgian deserters outside Paris and to bring those arrested inside the city to the Police Committee at the

[2] Lacroix, II, 558, 566 (Nov. 5), and *Chronique de Paris,* Nov. 15, p. 355.

[3] Lafayette to Marquis de Bouillé, Nov. 14, *Mémoires,* II, 422–23.

[4] *Ibid.*

[5] Certificate signed by Lafayette, countersigned by Gouvion, Nov. 18, BVP: Collection Liésville, Révolution divers, Série 21.

[6] *Journal général de la cour,* Dec. 8, p. 648.

Hôtel de Ville, and he asked that committee to take whatever steps might be required to get them out of Paris.[7]

Neither the National Guard's courts-martial nor the Paris police courts, however, had jurisdiction in cases of desertion from the royal army; such cases rested with the prévôt-général of the Maréchaussée of the Île de France. Lafayette and Bailly consulted the king's minister of war and the city's Police Committee, and on January 9, after many hours' work, they presented a feasible plan to the Assembly of Representatives. It provided that two commissioners be attached to the general staff of the National Guard and be made responsible for the surveillance of military personnel in Paris. They were required to furnish Bailly and Lafayette with lists of soldiers in Paris on furlough or as deserters, abettors of desertion, and prisoners. Deserters from the king's troops would continue to be accountable to the prévôt-général of the Maréchaussée of the Île de France, but the new commissioners were empowered to arrest military offenders, take prescribed action on those who were not deserters, and turn deserters over to the prévôt for judgment, reporting to Lafayette (among others) the names of all military personnel arrested. Every soldier upon arrival in Paris on furlough was required to surrender his papers to a commissioner and receive in exchange a certificate confirming his leave, which he was to return when it expired, getting his papers back and then quitting the city. The Assembly of Representatives accepted this plan provisionally, ordered it printed, and sent it to the districts for their approval.[8]

Meanwhile the police duties of the National Guard piled up. For one thing, the commandant general continually received requests for detachments for special services. He had to supply contingents to guard the city treasury[9] and to escort additional muskets and powder for the Paris National Guard.[10] In addition to policing the boulevards, rounding up deserters, and arresting smugglers and

---

[7] Lajard to the Department of Police, n.d., *Moniteur,* Jan. 7, p. 26.

[8] Lacroix, III, 389–90 (Jan. 9), and "Règlement de l'Assemblée des Représentants de la Commune de Paris, concernant la police militaire des recrues pour l'armée et soldats de toutes armes, en semestre dans la Ville de Paris," *Moniteur,* Jan. 24, pp. 94–95.

[9] Lacroix, II, 549 (Nov. 4).

[10] *Ibid.,* pp. 629–31 (Nov. 14), and III, 67 (Nov. 28).

debtors, National Guards had to patrol the Opéra, where young dandies came to show their disapproval of actors loyal to the Revolution or to make sarcastic remarks about Lafayette or other popular idols.[11] All day long and often until late at night Guards also stood before the doors of the Châtelet, while an angry people gathered in the street to hear the latest news about the Besenval trial.[12]

The mayor made numerous additional demands upon the commandant general. He too called for special detachments—to guard provisions,[13] to escort prisoners,[14] to watch over endangered persons,[15] to patrol important buildings,[16] and to protect some woods adjacent to Paris from pillage.[17] On the complaint of the author that a popular play was being performed against his wishes, the mayor gave orders to stop the performance at the Théâtre Français and asked the general to send an additional force there.[18] Since some Parisians, expecting tax reform, tried to avoid paying the old taxes, he called upon the commandant general to defend the tax collectors. Expecting protests at financial centers like the Caisse d'Escompte or the Trésor Royal, he also asked for an increase of the guard there. And he wanted the town criers arrested for advertising unauthorized or seditious pamphlets.[19]

At times Lafayette made plain that he believed Bailly importunate. On one occasion he had to indicate that his Guards were needed for other services in the city.[20] On another occasion, obviously annoyed, he remonstrated that the subject of Bailly's letters

[11] Bailly to Lafayette, Nov. 28, Tuetey, I, 115, No. 1074.

[12] *Journal de Paris,* Jan. 11, p. 44; *Moniteur,* Jan. 11, p. 88; *Courrier de Paris,* Jan. 11, 12, 15, pp. 60, 66, 113–14; and *Journal général de la cour,* Jan. 17, 18, pp. 131–34, 139.

[13] Bailly to Lafayette, Nov. 5, Tuetey, I, 362, No. 3261, and Nov. 19, *ibid.,* p. 364, No. 3278.

[14] Nov. 15, *ibid.,* II, 319, No. 2934; Nov. 17, AN:AF[11] 48, liasse 375, p. 4; and Nov. 28, Tuetey, I, 115, No. 1074.

[15] Nov. 2, Tuetey, I, 114, No. 1064.

[16] Nov. 8, *ibid.,* II, 394, No. 3715; Lafayette to Bailly, Nov. 11, *ibid.,* p. 395, No. 3720, and BN: Fr. 11697, pp. 7–8; and Bailly to Lafayette, Nov. 17, AN: AF[11] 48, liasse 375, p. 4.

[17] Nov. 13, Tuetey, I, 115, No. 1070, and Lafayette to Bailly, Nov. 15, BN: Fr. 11697, pp. 11–12.

[18] Dec. 16, BN: Fr. 11697, p. 17. See also Lacroix, III, 278 and 288–89 (Dec. 26).

[19] Jan. 2, Robiquet, p. 56, and Tuetey, I, 264, No. 3288.

[20] Bailly to Lafayette, Nov. 15, BN: Fr. 11697, pp. 11–12.

was "a lot of commotion for slight reason."[21] He must have been particularly annoyed by the implied reprimand in the mayor's request that every post commander make a daily report of arrests directly to him.[22] When Bailly complained, now that a cavalry troop had been provided, that fewer patrols were encountered on the city streets than before, Lafayette had to admit that repeated rebukes on that subject had so far had little effect. Besides, he explained, the cavalry had so much to do in guarding the royal family, the National Assembly, and the Commune and in policing emergencies that often no mounted men were otherwise available. He promised, however, to issue orders that as many cavalry as possible be sent on patrol.[23] When the mayor pointed out that the absence of patrols made the streets especially unsafe during the long winter nights,[24] Lafayette immediately set up additional guard-houses,[25] but he in turn complained that his night patrols were impeded because the street lamps were not carefully tended.[26] When Bailly requested a heavier guard for the king's magazine in Saint-Denis, Lafayette in fact sent a company of pensioners (Invalides) there, but when Bailly then asked that he also send forty paid soldiers to guard some prisoners to be transferred from the overcrowded cells at the Châtelet, Lafayette balked. At a time when emergency followed emergency and the unpaid companies were rendering far more service than the *Règlement* demanded, he protested that he could not spare almost half a paid company for prolonged duty outside of Paris. Enumerating the many things his men were called upon to do, he expostulated: "Although up to the present moment the Paris National Guard has borne itself with the greatest zeal wherever its assistance has been deemed necessary," the Guards would object to acting as custodians of prisoners

---

[21] Lacroix, III, 321–23 and 335–36 (Dec. 31).

[22] Bailly to Lafayette, Nov. 15, Tuetey, II, 319, No. 2934.

[23] Bailly to Lafayette, Oct. 30, BN: Fr 11697, p. 9, and Lafayette to Bailly, Oct. 31, *ibid.*, p. 10.

[24] Dec. 11, 28, *ibid.*, pp. 14–15, 18.

[25] Dec. 12, 15, *ibid.*, pp. 15–17.

[26] Lafayette to Bailly, Dec. 19, and Bailly to Cellerier, Dec. 22, Tuetey, III, 240–41, Nos. 2521–22.

in Saint-Denis. His letter was polite and restrained, but it betrayed a harried man.[27]

Numerous petty details also required Lafayette's formal approval or, at least, cognizance. The abundance of documents he had to produce led Condorcet to remark that Lafayette's secretary's handwriting was the most familiar one in Paris.[28] He had to sign leaves of absence for members of his command,[29] endorse commissions for newly appointed officers,[30] and make decisions regarding questions of property that arose in the course of the destruction of the Bastille.[31] He kept up a steady correspondence with the Military Committee and the Assembly of Representatives on routine Guard affairs.[32] A soldier requesting the Assembly of Representatives for a commission,[33] another who, though nominated for a commission, had not been allowed to serve,[34] influential persons asking for commissions for friends[35]—all eventually addressed themselves to the commandant general, although, as he reminded the mayor, he had given up making nominations for commissions in the National Guard except for staff members.[36]

The National Guard, despite its increasing duties, performed its daily rounds with considerable precision. Troops drilled almost every day on the Champs-Elysées, and Lafayette often reviewed a division there or on the Place Vendôme,[37] making an impressive show of the police power available for the preservation of order.

---

[27] Jan. 10, Robiquet, p. 56.

[28] Condorcet to Lafayette, [May 1 or 8], Charavay, p. 568.

[29] See, e.g., a Lieutenant Schneider's petition to Monsieur le Commandant de la Garde nationale parisienne, Nov. 6, LC: Thatcher Collection, French Revolution autographs, No. 144.

[30] E.g., Brevet de chef d'escadron of J.C. de Verdière, Nov. 6, American Library Service Catalogue, sale of Aug. 1951.

[31] Lafayette to Cellerier, Nov. 18, 1789, BVP: 10441, dossier Palloy, and Cellerier to demolishers of the Bastille, Nov. 23, Tuetey, I, 51, No. 491.

[32] *Procès-verbal du Comité militaire,* Part II, p. 49–53, and Lacroix, III, 364–72.

[33] Lacroix, III, 184 (Dec. 14).

[34] *Ibid.,* p. 199 (Dec. 17).

[35] Bailly to Lafayette, n.d., BN: Fr 11697, pp. 5–6, and Dec. 1, p.13.

[36] Lafayette to Bailly, Dec. 8, *ibid.,* p. 14.

[37] *Journal général de la cour,* Dec. 25, p. 780, and *Révolutions de Paris* (Tournon), No. 24, Dec. 20–26, p. 13.

The very uniform of the National Guard, nevertheless, created complications. Since counterrevolutionaries were believed to be infiltrating the Paris National Guard patrols, Lafayette required his men to wear their uniforms when on duty, but uniforms could easily be acquired by aristocrats, and so the public remained anxious on that score.[38]

Lafayette leaned heavily on Gouvion to supervise the daily work of the staff and the division chiefs. Gouvion had at first consented to act as chief of staff for only three months,[39] but, that term having expired, he proved willing to stay on. When Lafayette informed the Assembly of Representatives of Gouvion's decision, the Assembly, "enthusiastically" endorsing a proposal "made on behalf of an officer whom it loves and esteems by a general who every day renders himself more worthy of its admiration and its gratitude," voted unanimously to send a deputation to thank the chief of staff and to offer the salary which thitherto Gouvion had declined. When Gouvion came to the Assembly to thank it in his turn for its "confidence and esteem," the Representatives again offered to pay his salary and again he declined, asking them to apply the funds to other purposes.[40]

Lesser officers could not afford to be equally generous, but Lafayette understood that rewards—at least in honors where money was hard to find—would help to build up esprit de corps. So when the cavalry officers appealed to him against a proposed reduction of the salaries promised when their corps was originally planned, he and the Military Committee urged the Representatives to pay the promised amount.[41] When the Comte de Saint Genois, who had acted as major of the Battalion of the Petits-Augustins until the reorganization of the Paris National Guard and then as a volunteer, requested permission to wear a major's insignia, Lafayette supported his request, and the Representatives granted it.[42] Lafayette likewise thought the commander of the troops who had guarded

[38] *Journal général de la cour*, Dec. 8, p. 648.

[39] Gottschalk and Maddox, p. 189.

[40] Lacroix, II, 636–37 (Nov. 16).

[41] *Ibid.*, III, 37 (Nov. 23), and *Procès-verbal du Comité militaire*, Part II, pp. 37–38.

[42] Lacroix, III, 53 (Nov. 26), 63–64 (Nov. 28).

Besenval at Brie-Comte-Robert deserved special recognition. That commander was François-Louis Bourdon, who as a deputy in the National Convention was to become known as Bourdon de l'Oise. Taking him to the Assembly of Representatives, Lafayette reminded them of his bravery in storming the Bastille and of the distinguished manner in which at Brie-Comte-Robert he had combined vigilant supervision with consideration for his prisoner's comfort. The Assembly listened with approval and voted to give Bourdon a laudatory citation.[43]

A rather special case was that of a simple fusilier named Joseph Arné, who Lafayette was told was the one who had captured the governor of the Bastille on July 14.[44] Lafayette sent for Arné and received him kindly, promising him a promotion upon the next vacancy. Elisée Loustalot, of the *Révolutions de Paris,* was pleased,[45] and Desmoulins in his *Révolutions de France et de Brabant* praised Lafayette as one who showed gratitude toward patriots.[46]

Since the National Assembly still had under advisement the definitive organization of France's armed forces, some of the Paris National Guard's problems could be only tentatively resolved. Private companies, such as the Basoche of the Palais de Justice and the Volunteers of the Bastille, persisted despite the Commune's efforts to disband them;[47] the disbanded Basoche of the Châtelet had reorganized, and the Citoyens Arquebusiers Royaux had taken the place of the former Chevaliers de l'Arquebuse. Some districts tried to delay action upon these reorganized units until the National Assembly made up its mind about them, and Bailly, though under pressure to break them up, deferred to Lafayette.[48] The Citoyens Arquebusiers Royaux finally forced the issue by asking permission to take an oath of loyalty to the municipality. The Garde de la Ville then asked for the same privilege, and the Assembly,

---

[43] *Ibid.,* II, 408 (Oct. 24), and III, 42 (Nov. 24).

[44] *Chronique de Paris,* Dec. 17, p. 402.

[45] *Révolutions de Paris* (Prudhomme), No. 23, Dec. 13–19, pp. 27–28.

[46] *Révolutions de France et de Brabant,* No. 5, [*ca.* Dec. 19], p. 200. Arné actually was named an officer in July: see *Annales patriotiques et littéraires,* July 11, 1790, p. 127.

[47] Gottschalk and Maddox, pp. 137, 188, 282, 303, 365.

[48] Lafayette to Bailly, Dec. 7, Tuetey, III, 200, No. 5173.

despite the opposition of some districts, decided to allow both groups to do so.[49] To add luster to their oath-taking Lafayette ordered a number of mounted and foot contingents of the National Guard to assist. On December 22, he, Bailly, and the Representatives went into the Place de Grève to find not only the Garde de la Ville, the Paris Arquebusiers, and the National Guard contingents but also representatives from thirteen neighboring communities, who had come to lend further dignity to the ceremony. While the commander-in-chief and the Representatives looked on, the mayor administered the oath.[50]

The Paris National Guard differed from that of most other cities in that it had paid troops. The core of the paid troops was the former French Guard, regularly on duty as the center company of each district battalion and the grenadier company of each division. The approximately 600 grenadiers were thus the *crème de la crème*. They performed the responsible service of guarding the Tuileries and the Salle du Manège. Some of the districts opposed special favors for the grenadiers, but the grenadiers were determined to preserve their prestige. Besides the original center companies and the grenadiers Lafayette now had other paid troops, including the chasseurs. Since the chasseurs often were not Parisians, some districts were reluctant to accept them, and some of the old French Guards charged that the chasseurs, though jealous of the special decoration which former French Guards were authorized to wear, were really not true friends of liberty. Incensed, the chasseurs sent a committee of their officers to Lafayette to protest that they were incapable of unfriendly feelings toward comrades, were honored to belong to the National Guard, and stood ready to protect all citizens. They asked permission to post a statement to that effect, and Lafayette agreed, countersigning it himself.[51] This public avowal of loyalty helped to calm the dispute among the paid troops temporarily.

Among the unpaid troops disputes were harder to settle, for they

[49] Lacroix, III, 176–77 (Dec. 12).

[50] *Ibid.*, pp. 246–47.

[51] *Journal général de la cour,* Dec. 28, pp. 802–3, and *Chronique de Paris,* Dec. 26, pp. 499–500.

more distinctly involved the prerogatives of the districts. Quarrels between battalion commanders and district assemblies practically immobilized two National Guard companies. One of these quarrels centered upon Dières' expedition to Vernon,[52] which had so incensed part of the Vernon citizenry as to induce his district, the Petits-Augustins, to remove him from his command. But then another group in Vernon interceded in his behalf, and the Representatives undertook a full investigation, ordering Lafayette to reinstate him pending their decision. Thereupon, backed by leftist journalists like Loustalot and Marat, the District of the Petits-Augustins denied the Representatives' right to annul the order of a district assembly and appealed to the other fifty-nine districts for support.[53]

The other quarrel was the old one centering upon Guillotte, who was still repudiated by the District of Saint-Victor.[54] Upon Lafayette's request the Assembly of Representatives consented also to hear his case. He wholly denied the charges brought against him—refusal to obey Lafayette's orders, nepotism, fraud, and incompetence. Charton and members of Lafayette's staff appeared and testified in his favor, but finally Guillotte felt obliged to resign as vice-president of the Military Committee.[55]

The committee had meanwhile been spending a great deal of time drafting a plan for an artillery corps. Back in August Lafayette had assembled for that purpose about 240 men, whom he had placed under the command of Chevalier Adrien Poissonnier Desperrières, formerly an officer of the royal artillery. They had acquired a few cannon, and Lafayette had also obtained muskets for them, but they still were in need of clothing, and he urged the Representatives to make provision for their equipment and support. Gouvion drafted a project that proposed at little cost[56] to provide

---

[52] See above, pp. 91–92.

[53] *Révolutions de Paris* (Prudhomme), No. 23, Dec. 12–19, pp. 22–23, No. 24, Dec. 19–26, pp. 27–29, and No. 25, Dec. 26–Jan. 2, pp. 29–30; *Ami du peuple,* Dec. 23, pp. 6–8; and Lacroix, III, 123–24 (Dec. 5), 158–59 and 162–63 (Dec. 10), 174–75 (Dec. 12).

[54] See above, pp. 62–63.

[55] Lacroix, III, 117 (Dec. 4), 139–40 (Dec. 7), 151 (Dec. 9), and Guillotte, pp. 33–52.

[56] Lacroix, III, 321–23, 334–36 (Dec. 31).

three artillery companies. The Military Committee approved of his plan and sent it to Lafayette for presentation to the Assembly of Representatives.[57] The committee sent along with it a recommendation to pay the sum fixed in the *Règlement* for each paid infantryman in two installments—upon recruitment 56 livres for his uniform and arms, and later 24 for lesser items of wearing apparel and equipment.[58]

On December 21 Lafayette went to present these recommendations, together with another regulating the daily service of troops on duty. When he entered the meeting room of the Assembly, it was discussing a constitution for the Paris Commune, and so, apologizing for the interruption, he deposited his documents with the secretary and started to leave. The Assembly burst into cheers, demonstrating, as its minutes reported, that "there was never a time when the Assembly did not consider itself happy to receive in its midst the hero of French liberty." The Assembly decided to postpone his recommendations to an early meeting.[59]

Since other business seemed more urgent, the Assembly was able to consider Lafayette's proposals only ten days later. The Marquis de La Salle, who had briefly preceded Lafayette as commandant of the Paris militia,[60] was now hoping to get command of the proposed artillery. Probably to avoid becoming personally involved, Lafayette reminded the Assembly that if it decided to establish an artillery corps, he did not want to take part in naming its officers since he preferred to nominate only staff officers. In the end the Representatives ordered that not only the Military Committee's plan but also another proposed by La Salle, which was less costly and so had won some support in the districts, be printed and sent to the district assemblies, with a request for prompt attention. The Assembly agreed to finance the most urgent expenses of some of the cannoneers in the meantime. The matter remained a delicate one, however, giving rise to further recriminations in the districts.[61]

[57] *Procès-verbal du Comité militaire,* Part II, pp. 41–42 (Dec. 14), 43 (Dec. 15), 45 (Dec. 17).

[58] See below, p. 173.

[59] Lacroix, III, 238–39. See also the note *ibid.,* pp. 242–43.

[60] *Ibid.,* pp. 321–23, 335–36 (Dec. 31).

[61] See below, pp. 261–63.

The approach of winter meant an increased demand for fuel. With the passage in August of decrees that suppressed the hunting privileges of nobles, common people felt that they had the right not only to hunt but also to chop down trees in woods and forests, and hordes armed with saws and axes thronged to the wooded spots near Paris. Lafayette decided the National Guard must intervene. The Assembly of Representatives on December 4 empowered him to enforce the old laws against pillage of the woods and in case of resistance to instruct his officers to "meet force with force."[62] When, on the following day, a strong National Guard detachment ordered wood cutters in the Bois de Boulogne to desist, a fair number refused, and the Guard took fifty-six of them to the Conciergerie to await trial.[63] Shortly, the National Assembly placed the public forests, woods, and trees under the protection of government officials and the National Guard.[64]

As the population sought to keep warm, fires became more frequent. Responsibility for police duty in case of fire fell upon Gouvion and the commander of the National Guard division in whose jurisdiction the fire occurred. Upon the outbreak of a fire, the commander of the district National Guard was to call the district battalion to the scene and report to the mounted watch, who in turn would notify the mayor, the commandant general, various other National Guard officers, and the local fire station. The general staff and the division officers were to take charge of the district battalion and do whatever they could to protect life and property, calling up other units if necessary. The division staff was to keep Bailly and Lafayette informed as long as the fire lasted.[65]

Despite a commendable desire to eschew authority over other areas, the Paris Commune, by its very prestige as the municipality of the capital city, was unable to avoid acting as a leader or a model for nearby communities. A few instances of this nature concerned trivial matters that involved Lafayette. For example, the National Guard of Belleville asked for brevets like those of Paris, and the

[62] Lacroix, III, 119–20, 121–22 (Dec. 4).

[63] *Journal général de la cour*, Dec. 6, p. 632, Dec. 8, pp. 646–47; *Moniteur*, Dec. 10, p. 347; and Lacroix, III, 121–22.

[64] *AP*, X, 502–3.

[65] *Moniteur*, Dec. 11, pp. 449–50.

Representatives instructed Lafayette to handle the request.[66] The National Guard of Petit-Montrouge asked his aid in solving a problem[67] which he knew only too well in his own command—how to get all eligible citizens to do their militia service. When the commander of the National Guard of Vaugirard quarreled with his municipality, Lafayette sent an aide to mediate, but he thought it only fair that the municipality of Paris also should participate, which it did.[68]

The growing spirit of cooperation among communities near Paris suggested the publication of a sort of house organ for the country's National Guards. A group of unpaid Paris Guardsmen banded together to form a Society of Soldier-Citizens with the patent intention of promoting National Guard solidarity. They proposed to publish the *Cocarde nationale: journal de correspondance entre tous les milices du royaume,* whose main purpose would be to provide National Guard units a channel of communication throughout the country. On December 1 they circulated a prospectus describing the journal and inviting their comrades, especially those of Paris, to subscribe and to contribute items of interest. If Lafayette did not instigate the project, he obviously gave it his approval, for the circular ended: "Our best friend, the brave and loyal Lafayette, sends all of you his warm greetings."[69] The first number of the *Cocarde nationale* appeared on January 4, and it was dedicated to "Joseph-Gilbert La Fayette by six volunteer soldiers who honor and love you." It ran to sixteen numbers, until April 17.

More and more the militia of the provincial cities turned to that of Paris for leadership, as a long letter from Toulouse strikingly illustrated. The writers were two officers who had read Lafayette's appeal to his Paris command to devote four more months to the Revolution.[70] Their letter began by querying how Lafayette, who had found in remote America a heroism that excited his ad-

---

[66] Lacroix, III, 118 (Dec. 4).

[67] *Ibid.,* p. 92 (Dec. 2).

[68] *Ibid.,* pp. 60 (Nov. 27), 95 (Dec. 2).

[69] Lamare to "Nos chers camarades," Dec. 1, *La Cocarde nationale,* prospectus.

[70] See above, pp. 63–64.

miration, could believe that only Parisians were worthy of being soldiers of the Revolution; the provinces too had shared the benefits of the Revolution and were prepared to share its burdens. Every good citizen, the Toulouse officers asserted, was animated by the desire to forestall aristocrats, protect "the Restorer of French Liberty," and defend the Revolution. Therefore they proposed that provincial National Guard contingents share the honor of guarding Louis XVI, each canton sending a small number of men to serve with the Paris National Guard. In that way Frenchmen would be knitted together in a closer union, and all France would join in securing the national well-being.

Despite the eager patriotism and provincial jealousy of these Toulouse officers, Lafayette did not consider their proposal to distribute guard duty at the Tuileries a practical one. When he replied, he nevertheless tactfully agreed that the Revolution in fact was the work of all Frenchmen—a "happy concert which guarantees the welfare of our country"; all Frenchmen should consider themselves companions in arms, sharing equally in the victories of liberty. The king too, he added, wished to preserve equality among his subjects and so intended to confer upon all the provinces, in the course of time, the "benefit of his presence," thereby providing good citizens, lawfully armed, the honor of guarding his sacred person in the places he would visit.[71]

Lafayette soon had a good occasion to call the Paris Commune's attention to the spontaneous drift toward this "happy concert" of the National Guard throughout the realm. Early in November a Captain Brichard, of the Battalion of the Cordeliers, had visited Montpellier, and its National Guard, upon learning that he was a Paris officer, invited him to affiliate with them. About a month afterward the officers of the Montpellier National Guard, having voiced a desire "to unite with those citizen legions [of the Paris Guard] by the most direct relations,"[72] sent a committee to Paris to

---

[71] J.-M. Rouzet and M. Lacène to Lafayette, Dec. 15, and Lafayette's reply, Dec. 29, Bibliothèque municipale de Toulouse, Recueil factice "Elections-Garde Nationale," pp. 599–606 (courtesy of M. P.-H. Thore). See also the "Bibliographical Notes" below, p. 179.

[72] Register of the officers of the Montpellier National Guard, Nov. 17, Lacroix, III, 221.

seek Brichard's good offices. He took them to see his commandant general, whom they presented with a resolution declaring their "just admiration for their brothers of Paris" and their "respect for the hero citizen on whom the nation and the sovereign have conferred the command of the Paris National Guard" and attesting their conviction that only through "the most intimate union . . . among all good bourgeois" could the state be regenerated. The resolution asked for the closest bonds of affiliation with the Paris National Guard. Replying that only the Assembly of Representatives could grant the affiliation they sought, Lafayette undertook to present them to that body, and on December 19, accompanied by two Montpellier deputies in the National Assembly and five officers of the Cordeliers Battalion, he brought them to the Hôtel de Ville. The Montpellier colonel general presented their petition, vowing that his men, at a word from Paris, would rush to defend the common cause. The president of the Assembly answered that both the Commune and the National Guard of Paris reciprocated their feelings of fraternity, and the Representatives by acclamation granted the request for affiliation.[73] On the next day, the Battalion of the Cordeliers paraded in honor of the Montpellier committee, and the Cordeliers' officers entertained it at a banquet, where the diners drank to the health of the nation, the king, Lafayette, the Montpellier officers, and others, ending with a toast to "the liberty of the whole world."[74] Three days later the National Assembly received an address from 6,000 National Guardsmen of eighty-seven communities in Dauphiny, Provence, and Vivarais who had formed a "federation" (*acte fédératif*) in support of the National Assembly's decrees.[75]

By the time the Revolution neared the close of its first year, the requests from the provinces for some kind of associations with the Paris National Guard were so numerous that Lafayette decided to make a special announcement about them. He assembled representatives from each of his battalions at the Hôtel de Ville and told them that he had received 140 letters from the principal National

[73] *Ibid.,* pp. 219–22 (Dec. 19).

[74] *Ibid.,* pp. 229–30.

[75] *AP,* X, 753.

Guard units of the realm, every one of which evinced gratitude to
the National Assembly for its work and for its close cooperation
with the king. Furthermore, these National Guards promised a
fraternal loyalty to their common principles and stood ready to give
their lives, if necessary, for the prospective constitution. Some at
least of Lafayette's listeners must have recognized that the idea of
the fraternity of Frenchmen had come a long way since the begin-
ing of the year 1789. A reporter of the event was moved to comment: "That pledge of fraternal confederation by more than 300,000
well-armed citizens clearly proves that the Revolution is irrevoca-
ble and the constitution fixed, and that the aristocrats have no recourse but to submit and even to become patriots."[76]

A less energetic and self-confident man might have been overwhelmed alone by the details that confronted Lafayette as commandant general of the Paris National Guard, but his command of
the royal forces in the generality of Paris presented him with additional complications. It involved him in the affairs of communities fairly distant from Paris and kept him in frequent consultation
with the king's ministers over troop movements.[77] When a village
on the road to Rouen seized a shipment of swords to Paris merchants, they appealed to him as commander in the generality and
to the Assembly of Representatives, who left it to him to take whatever measures "his wisdom should suggest."[78] When some of the
inhabitants of Houdan, complaining to the royal minister that their
village was disorderly, requested a detachment of dragoons while
others, denying disorder before the Assembly of Representatives,
petitioned that no dragoons be stationed among them, the Representatives again left the decision to Lafayette "not in his capacity
of commandant general . . . but as commander-in-chief of all the
troops within a radius of fifteen leagues of Paris."[79] When the

[76] *Annales patriotiques et littéraires,* Dec. 21, p. 1. Cf. *Journal de Paris,* Dec. 20, p.
1660, and *Gazette de Paris,* Dec. 22, p. 4.

[77] Latour du Pin to Lafayette, Oct. 28, Tuetey, II, 428, No. 4055; Nov. 13, *ibid.,* p.
395, No. 3722; and Nov. 15, *ibid.,* p. 428, No. 4058; and Lafayette to Saint-Priest, Nov.
19, Indiana University Library, Ball Collection. Cf. minister of war to Lafayette, Dec. 4,
6, 9, Tuetey, I, 116, Nos. 1077, 1080, 1081.

[78] Lacroix, III, 126–27 (Dec. 4).

[79] *Ibid.,* pp. 222–23 (Dec. 19).

colonel of a regiment stationed at Vernon believed his troops were no longer needed there, the minister of war asked Lafayette if the regiment might be withdrawn. But if Vernon seemed quiet, Saint-Denis continued to be troubled, and the minister consulted Lafayette about sending soldiers there.[80]

Disturbances like those in Rouen, Vernon, and Saint-Denis paled in comparison with the continual uproar in Versailles, where Lafayette was also commandant general. The people of that town had made their living largely as purveyors to the court and to those attracted by the royal residence, but after the departure of the king on October 6, the palace and the great houses having closed, their business had slowed down. Employers laid off workmen, and hundreds of families faced mid-winter without money for fuel or bread. On January 7, in the course of a disagreeable, foggy afternoon, a crowd assembled in the Place d'Armes. Berthier tried to persuade them to go home, but, instead, they took him with them and descended upon the Hôtel de Ville to demand that the price of bread be reduced. With some 2,500 persons clamoring outside the city hall, the municipality lowered the price of bread to two sous per pound, two-thirds of what it still cost in Paris and elsewhere in the generality. By that time Berthier had brought up the National Guard, and the crowd, satisfied now, went home without further trouble.[81] When Lafayette heard of the turmoil in Versailles, he was prepared to regard it as a conspiracy of "ill-disposed persons."[82]

The municipality of Versailles decided the next morning that it could not afford to subsidize the sale of bread unless the national government helped, and it sent a deputation to Paris to appeal for that help. The officials of the capital city advised the deputation not to present its case to the National Assembly because of the excite-

[80] Latour du Pin to Lafayette, Jan. 7, and Lafayette to Latour du Pin, Jan. 10, and Latour du Pin to Lafayette, Jan. 14, Archives du Ministère de la Guerre, Archives Historiques (hereafter cited as AMG: AH), carton LX, chemise Minutes janvier et 1ere quinzaine de fevrier.

[81] "Procès-verbal des troubles rédigé par la municipalité de Versailles," A. Defresne and F. Evrard, Les subsistances dans le district de Versailles de 1788 à l'An V (Rennes, 1921), I, 249–60; Patriote français, Jan. 11, p. 1; Journal général de la cour, Jan. 9, pp. 71–72; Révolutions de Paris (Prudhomme), No. 27, Jan. 9–16, pp. 5, 8–9; and Révolutions de Paris (Tournon), No. 27, Jan. 9–16, pp. 14–15.

[82] Lacroix, III, 418 (Jan. 9).

ment that might follow. Instead, it conferred with several prominent deputies, the minister of the king's household, and Lafayette. They advised the Versailles authorities to restore the price of bread to three sous, and the king asked Lafayette to send reinforcements to Versailles.[83] Once reinforced, the Versailles authorities met the threat of riot by declaring martial law, at the same time raising the price of bread, though this time to only two and one-half sous the pound. On January 12 Lafayette was able to assure the Paris Commune that calm had been completely restored in Versailles.[84]

Still Lafayette could not help feeling disturbed when he placed the Versailles uprising in the broader pattern of unrest. In Toulon an ugly dispute had arisen between the commander of the naval base and the local "patriots."[85] In Paris itself the workers engaged in demolishing the Bastille were refusing to take orders from their foreman and were behaving in a way that seemed to Jacques Cellerier, the mayor's deputy in charge of public works, to be instigated by counterrevolutionaries. He was concerned also about the grumbling of the unemployed in the Faubourgs Saint-Antoine and Saint-Marcel and in other poor residential sections. At a conference with Necker, in which Bailly and Lafayette also took part, he was permitted to increase the number of Parisians employed on public projects while hastening the return of out-of-town workers to their homes.[86] Disaffection among the laborers lent impetus to the steps Lafayette had already initiated to install a guardhouse for an emergency reserve close by the Hôtel de Ville. The Bureau de Ville was sufficiently apprehensive of new insurrections to vote that the orphans in the nearby Hôpital du Saint-Esprit be moved elsewhere so that it might speedily be made ready for the National Guard.[87]

---

[83] Defresne and Evrard, I, 253.

[84] *Ibid.*, p. 252, n. 3. See also Lacroix, III, 398–99 and 418–19 (Jan. 9); Lafayette to the municipality of Versailles, Jan. 10, Bibliothèque de Versailles; *Patriote français*, Jan. 11, p. 1; and *Mémoires*, II, 378–79.

[85] See below, pp. 186–90.

[86] Cellerier to Necker, Jan. 19, 30, A. Tuetey, *L'assistance publique à Paris pendant la Révolution* (Paris, 1895–97), III, 113, 117 (hereafter references to Tuetey, unless otherwise indicated, continue to be to his *Répertoire*); Lacroix, III, 153–55, 333, 400–403, VI, 697 and n. 2.

[87] Lacroix, III, 403–4 (Jan. 9), VI, 697 (Aug. 12).

On January 9 the trial of Favras began, and fifty grenadiers were assigned to regular guard duty in the courtroom. On January 11, when Favras himself was called upon to testify, great crowds assembled outside the Châtelet, and Lafayette ordered up cannon, had them loaded with grapeshot, and sent detachments of cavalry, grenadiers, and chasseurs to police the adjacent streets. For a time the officers on duty thought they might have to ask the municipality to proclaim martial law, but no crisis flared up.[88]

Fear of an aristocratic plot revived as the Paris populace learned of new angles in the Favras case. The National Assembly was told that the lives of certain most respectable citizens were no longer safe and that Lafayette and Bailly had advised the Archbishop of Paris to leave France because they could no longer answer for his safety, although Bailly later informed the National Assembly that neither he nor Lafayette had ever made such a statement.[89] Another ugly story had it that Lafayette's house was mined, and to still popular indignation he had his house and neighboring residences searched, but the searchers found no mines.[90] The alleged threats upon his life aggravated the uneasiness of the people of Saint-Antoine already exercised by the bread shortage and unemployment. They insisted that he move to their quarter, where, they reasoned, he would be safer than among "the aristocrats" of the

[88] The account of the events of Jan. 11–12 above and below is derived chiefly from the following (but see the "Bibliographical Notes," p. 179): Duquesnoy, II, 276–77; *Gazette de Leide*, Jan. 26, pp. 1–2; *Mémoires*, II, 393; Buchez and Roux, IV, 289–90; *Moniteur*, Jan. 16, pp. 58–59; *Courrier de Paris*, Jan. 13, 14, pp. 86–88, 99–101; *Chronique de Paris*, Jan. 13, 14, pp. 51–52, 54; *Révolutions de France et de Brabant*, No. 8, pp. 350–53; *Journal général de la cour*, Jan. 12–15, pp. 89, 99, 101–2, 109, 115, 118–19; *Révolutions de Paris* (Tournon), No. 27, Jan. 9–16, pp. 23–27; *Annales patriotiques et littéraires*, Jan. 13, p. 3; *Journal de Paris*, Jan. 15, 16, pp. 58, 63–64; *Patriote français*, Jan. 13, p. 3; *Courier national*, Jan. 13, pp. 7–8; *Gazette de Paris*, Jan. 14, p. 2; *Lettres à Monsieur le comte de B****, V, 429–30; Victor du Pont to E. I. du Pont, Jan. 12, 1790, B. G. du Pont (ed.), *Life of Eleuthère Irenée du Pont from Contemporary Correspondence* (Newark, 1926), I, 127–28; Lacroix, III, 429–30, 436; and Ségur, III, 471.

[89] *AP*, XI, 114. See also *Journal de Paris*, Jan. 9, pp. 34–35; *Point du jour*, Jan. 8, p. 366; *Moniteur*, Jan. 9, p. 75; *Courier français*, Jan. 8, pp. 66–67; *Journal général de l'Europe*, No. 10, pp. 162–64; *Journal général de la cour*, Jan. 11, p. 86; Duquesnoy, II, 257–58, 268; and *Révolutions de Paris* (Tournon), No. 27, Jan. 9–16, pp. 15–16.

[90] *Gazette universelle*, No. 10, p. 162; A. Young, *Travels in France during the Year 1787, 1788 and 1789* (London, 1890), p. 294; *Correspondance de Thomas Lindet pendant la Constituante et la Législative (1789–1792)*, ed. A. Montier (Paris, 1899), p. 49; and Mirabeau to La Marck, Jan. 10, Bacourt (ed.), I, 448–49.

Faubourg Saint-Germain. Unable to "resist these considerations of the public welfare," he decided to establish a foothold in the Faubourg Saint-Antoine, and on Sunday morning, January 10, he went there to attend mass. On his way a large crowd milled about him, muttering their discontent. He made a little speech praising their patriotism, commiserating with them on their privations, and urging them to pay less heed to the enemies of the Revolution. They were touched, but when he offered them money a voice cried out: "We want no money. Lower the price of bread!" Lafayette explained that he was not in charge of the food supply but promised to do everything he could. Murmurs changed to cheers: "Vive Lafayette!" "His horse," Camille Desmoulins reported, "was almost smothered by the pats and kisses of the faubourg, exulting in the honor of guarding our Washington."[91]

Though recurrent demonstrations, suspicions, accusations, and threats made the loyalty of the hard-working National Guard all the more imperative, yet the payments to the *gardes soldés* were now in arrears. The daily wage of 4 livres that cavalrymen were to receive[92] had not been paid since October 1. To make matters worse, Lafayette had come to the conclusion that an enlistment bounty was no longer necessary. He realized that the city's revenue hardly sufficed for other routine operating costs, he was aware of the stern opposition of many districts to the accumulating expenditures for the National Guard, and he also recognized that several hundred royal soldiers clamoring to enlist provided a reservoir of gratuitously available recruits. So he had proposed that a bounty of only 26 livres be given to new recruits upon enlistment to buy articles of small equipment, saving the remainder for the city treasury. On January 7 Gouvion had taken these recommendations to the Representatives, who adopted them gladly.[93]

Reports of disloyalty in the ranks of the Paris National Guard,

---

[91] *Révolutions de France et de Brabant*, No. 8, pp. 349–50. See also *Courier national*, Jan. 14, pp. 7–8; *Journal général de la cour*, Jan. 11, 12, pp. 87, 93–95; *Révolutions de Paris* (Tournon), No. 27, Jan. 9–16, pp. 15–17; *Annales patriotiques et littéraires*, Jan. 15, p. 2; and *L'Observateur*, Jan. 16, pp. 586–87.

[92] Gottschalk and Maddox, p. 204.

[93] Lacroix, III, 379–80.

always a source of dread, became particularly frightening at this juncture. A few such reports suggested that some Guardsmen's grievances centered upon the inadequacy of their pay, others that they meant to free Favras, and most that they had been suborned by counterrevolutionaries. For several days Lafayette investigated such reports, and plausible testimony led him to believe that among the paid Guardsmen there were a number who planned some kind of mutinous action. They intended, he was told, to proceed on the morning of January 12 from a rendezvous on the Champs Elysées to the Hôtel de Ville, hoping to pick up popular support en route and perhaps to join forces with dissident troops from nearby Neuilly and Versailles. Although Lafayette's information led him to infer that former French Guards were not involved, he instructed the captains of the paid companies to keep their men in barracks. Any man who disobeyed that order was to be stripped of his arms and placed under guard.[94]

To be ready for any mutineers who might keep the rendezvous in the Champs-Elysées, Lafayette made secret preparations. Around midnight on January 11 he dispatched orders to the battalion commanders to put their unpaid men under arms at once and stand by, and he also alerted the cavalry. In order to allay suspicion of his objective he referred in his orders only to the demonstration that day outside the Châtelet. His plan was to assemble the unpaid infantry in the morning in a centrally located square, the Place Vendôme; the grenadiers and the chasseurs, the select among the paid Guardsmen, would join them at the last moment. From the square the infantry would march to the Champs-Elysées in two columns; he would himself lead one to the north and west of the Champs-Elysées; the Duc d'Aumont, chief of the Sixth Division, would take the rest of the infantry to the east and south of the parkway; Jean-Augustin de Ruhlières, commanding the cavalry, would intercept any aid that Neuilly or Versailles might send the insurgents. In that fashion Lafayette's loyal Guards would encircle the disaffected men.[95]

With this general plan in mind, the commandant general con-

[94] Gouvion to the captains of the paid companies, Jan. 11, *Courrier de Paris*, Jan. 14, pp. 97–99.

[95] *Ibid.*, pp. 99–100.

sulted the minister of war and sought the king's approval. He asked permission also to send any troops he might arrest to Saint-Denis, for the Paris prisons were filled and, besides, it seemed advisable to keep these prisoners outside the capital. The king approved the commandant's plan. Though usually a stickler for military responsibility to the civic authorities, in this crisis Lafayette seems not to have consulted the Assembly of Representatives and to have moved with formal royal consent alone, preferring to expose his secret to as few as possible.

At two o'clock in the morning of January 12 the call to arms began in the district barracks. Soon after daybreak the battalions started for their posts. A number marched to the Place Vendôme to be ready for further instructions at nine o'clock; over a thousand men reported to the Châtelet and its neighborhood to contain the crowds outside Favras' prison; others reported to their assigned posts at the Tuileries, the Manège, the Place de Grève, the Halles, and the barriers; still others patrolled the Palais Royal and the faubourgs.

According to Lafayette's intelligence, the insurgents intended to assemble in the morning, but when morning came, he learned that the rendezvous had been set for mid-afternoon. His men, however, were already on their way to the Place Vendôme, and so he let them assemble and wait, despite the worsening January weather. Scouts sent to the Champs-Elysées reported that by one o'clock a considerable band had collected and others were constantly straggling in. Impelled by the threat of a storm Lafayette decided to act at once. Ordering Ruhlières and Aumont to move out as planned, he went to the head of his column and waited for his horse. When it was brought, a shabby man dashed up and seized the bridle. A soldier nabbed him, but he claimed that he merely wanted to hold the general's stirrup. Lafayette mounted, gave the command to march, and led his column to the Champs-Elysées. In the center of the parkway he saw about two hundred men in uniform; they were the mutineers his scouts had been watching. Stationing his battalions at their appointed places, he waited for Aumont's detachment to take its post and for Ruhlières' to strengthen the infantry on the west. All went off as planned.

When the insurgents were completely surrounded, Lafayette

rode out to them and denounced them as unworthy to wear their country's uniform. Some fell on their knees to implore mercy, but he ordered the Guards to close in. Before they could do so, four of the culprits broke through the line and ran toward the Seine, where, according to several reports, one of them jumped in and was drowned. Lafayette then ordered a detachment to strip the malcontents of their uniforms and arms. The Guards promptly did so, tossing the paraphernalia into a cart. Then, following Lafayette's orders, they sent the captives, bound and under heavy escort, to the military depot at Saint-Denis.[96]

As soon as he could, Lafayette reported to his superiors. Accompanied by a number of his officers, he went first to the Tuileries, where the king engaged them a long time. From the palace he moved on to the Hôtel de Ville. Paris was dark now, it was raining, and a stiff breeze was blowing. He could well feel pleased that he had rounded up the insurgents before they could find cover in a long, dark, wintry night. When he entered the Grande Salle, the Assembly of Representatives and the spectators greeted him with loud applause. Free now to give details, he described at some length the disorders that had marked the last few days and eulogized the part taken by the National Guard in suppressing them. They had arrested over 200 troops of the center companies, but, he claimed, not one of them was a former French Guard.[97] The Representatives voted their thanks to the commandant general and to "the soldier citizens under his orders," whose "courage and patriotism" paralleled "the talents and virtues of their general." The Assembly also instructed its Comité des Recherches to inquire into the whole scheme to subvert the paid troops, asking the districts, the National Guard, and other good citizens to aid in the inquiry; it summoned a court martial to convene at once to try the prisoners; and it or-

[96] See above, n. 88. Mazzei in a letter to King Stanislaus Poniatowski, Jan. 15, Ciampini (ed.), I, 262, says three of the mutineers jumped into the river and two drowned.

[97] There is considerable discrepancy among observers upon these numbers. Ségur (III, 471) recollected in his memoirs that all the arrested men were former French Guards, but though he was an eyewitness, he was not in a position to know. The report of the effects confiscated from the arrested men accounted for only 197 uniforms: Lacroix, III, 426 (Jan. 12). The French Guard sent a deputation to the Assembly of Representatives to repledge its loyalty, and this deputation admitted that two (of two thousand former French Guards) were among the culprits: *ibid.*, p. 448 (Jan. 14), and see below, p. 193.

dered its eulogy of Lafayette and the National Guard printed and dispatched not only to the sixty district assemblies but to the sixty battalions as well.[98]

Not everyone shared the general enthusiasm for the National Guard's victory over mutiny. Lafayette's brother-in-law, the Vicomte de Noailles, a cavalry officer, who had witnessed the occasion, was reported to have said of the National Guard cavalry that it "manoeuvred as well as men can who know nothing about it."[99] And no doubt some were amused by a poem in the royalist newspaper *Actes des apôtres*[100] which asked why the "immortal Lafayette" should have thought he must mobilize 10,000 Guards merely to undress about 150. Otherwise, comments on the affair were more complimentary. Morris, who had taken no pains to conceal his doubts about the Paris militia, recorded that in this instance "all agree that La Fayette has acted with great Prudence and Decision."[101] Even Mirabeau was hardly critical: "You can well imagine that Lafayette did not fail to parade many troops and much activity."[102] For days after the great event the domestic press and foreign observers sang the commandant general's praises.[103]

Before the day of the mutiny ended, Lafayette learned that a letter could still make a packet sailing to the United States; so he dashed off a short message to George Washington.[104] This was the first time since the preceding May that he had written to the man he regarded as a father. He could not let the packet sail, he wrote, "without a line from your filial friend, who . . . wants to express to

[98] Lacroix, III, 429–30, 436, and *Assemblée des Représentans de la Commune de Paris. Extrait des délibérations . . . du mardi 12 janvier 1790* (Paris, 1790).

[99] Victor du Pont to E. I. du Pont, Jan. 12, B. G. du Pont (ed.), I, 127–28.

[100] "Epigramme sur l'expédition de M. de la Fayette aux Champs-Elysées, le 12 janvier, 1790," *Actes des apôtres*, No. 25, pp. 10–11. Cf. *ibid.*, [No. 39], pp. 3–12.

[101] Morris diary, Jan. 12, Davenport (ed.), I, 365.

[102] Mirabeau to La Marck, Jan. 15, Bacourt (ed.), I, 451.

[103] See above, n. 88. See also *L'Observateur*, Jan. 14, pp. 578–79; F.-L. Bruel (ed.), *Un siècle d'histoire de France par l'estampe, 1770–1871. Collection de Vinck* (Paris, 1914), II, 1367, Nos. 1790, 1793, 1794. For the foreign observers see Short to Jefferson, Jan. 12, Boyd (ed.), XVI, 108; Morris diary, Jan. 12, Davenport (ed.), I, 365; Young, p. 294; and Mazzei to King Stanislaus, Jan. 15, Ciampini (ed.), I, 262–63.

[104] Louis Gottschalk (ed.), *Letters of Lafayette to Washington* (New York, 1944), p. 346.

you those affectionate and respectful sentiments that are never so well felt as in uncommon circumstances." He counted on Short and Paine to furnish the details of those "uncommon circumstances" (and they did),[105] but he hastened to acknowledge his need as a disciple for the master's approval: "How often, my beloved General, have I wanted your wise advices and friendly support!" Fresh from his victory in the Champs-Elysées, he expressed the hope (in his Gallic English) that the enemies of the Revolution would be frustrated: "We have come thus far in the Revolution without breaking the ship either on the shoal of aristocracy or that of faction, and amidst the ever reviving efforts of the mourners [i.e., for the Old Regime] and the ambitious [i.e., for power in the new regime] we are stirring towards a tolerable conclusion. Now that everything that was is no more, a new building is erecting, not perfect by far, but sufficient to insure freedom and prepare the Nation for a Convention in about ten years, where the defects may be mended." He trusted that his "adventures" would turn to the advantage not only of France but also of "mankind in general," for "Liberty is sprouting about in the other parts of Europe, and I am encouraging it by all means in my power." He signed this brief note "Your most devoted and filial friend, Lafayette."

Only a few days earlier, Washington had communicated to a mutual acquaintance a less modest estimate of the "adventures" of his "devoted and filial friend": "I shall sincerely rejoice to see that the American Revolution has been productive of happy consequences on both sides of the Atlantic. The renovation of the French Constitution is indeed one of the most wonderful events in the history of mankind; and the agency of the Marquis de la Fayette in a high degree honorable to his character. My greatest fear has been that the nation would not be sufficiently cool and moderate in making arrangements for the security of that liberty of which it seems to be fully possessed."[106]

[105] Short in a letter to Jefferson, Jan. 12, Boyd (ed.), XVI, pp. 106–8, and Paine in *The Rights of Man* (1791), of which Lafayette said in this letter: "Common sense is writing a book for you."

[106] To Catharine Macaulay Graham, Jan. 9, Fitzpatrick (ed.), XXX, 497–98.

BIBLIOGRAPHICAL NOTES

The originals of the correspondence of Lafayette and Bailly are now to be found in large part in the Bibliothèque Nationale and the Archives Nationales. They have been not only analyzed by Robiquet (see above, p. 69) but also calendared by Tuetey. We have from time to time, however, found it desirable to refer in the footnotes above to the originals, since both Robiquet and Tuetey sometimes failed to provide the information we cite.

The friendly relations of Lafayette and Berthier during this period are described (with some slight inaccuracy) in General Derrécagaix, *Le Maréchal Berthier, prince de Wagram & de Neuchâtel* (Paris, 1904–5), 1, 17–18.

Pierre Henri Thore, "Fédération et projets de fédérations dans la région toulousaine," *AHRF,* XXI (1949), 346–68, examines the claims of various National Guard units to having originated the idea of federation and then argues that Rouzet (see above, p. 167 and n. 71) and the Toulouse National Guard were among the earliest to suggest it. It is obvious from the above pages, however, that the Montpellier National Guard was earlier, and it would appear that Paris (see below, pp. 435–36) and perhaps other communities (pp. 94–97, 98–99, 434–35) were earlier still.

For dramatic events like the frustrated mutiny of January 12 many newspapers give extensive accounts, as indicated in n. 88 above. They are rarely independent eyewitness accounts, however, for they frequently borrowed from each other. For that reason we have leaned heavily upon the minutes of the Assembly of Representatives carefully edited by Lacroix, with footnotes and appendixes.

CHAPTER IX

Growing Popularity

AFTER THE arrest of the mutineers on January 12, tension relaxed for a short time, not because plotting had ceased but because the friends of the Revolution became more confident. When the émigré Prince de Conti asked if he could return to France without danger, Lafayette unhesitatingly assured him that the National Guard would protect him as it did other members of the royal family.[1] The preservation of order at the trial of Favras enhanced popular self-confidence, and although the schemes ascribed to him sounded extravagant and in parts even fantastic, his presumed victims became more precious in the public's esteem. Although the aristocratic press did not cease to hold the commandant general up to ridicule or censure,[2] the popular newspapers usually reflected general admiration for Lafayette, Bailly, and Necker.[3] Still, there were exceptions. When National Guard detachments swooped down on debtors and other pitiable offenders, their conduct seemed questionable, even arbitrary, to some. On December 30, the District of the Prémontrés asked Lafayette to instruct the National Guard not to arrest those accused of debt. On the following day, the District of the Pères-de-Nazareth threat-

---

[1] *Révolutions de Paris* (Tournon), No. 28, Jan. 16–23, p. 6, and *Journal général de la cour*, Jan. 22, p. 175.

[2] Cf. Short to Jefferson, Jan. 12, Boyd (ed.), XVI, 107, and Vicomte de Grouchy and A. Guillois (eds.), *La Révolution française racontée par un diplomate étranger, correspondance du Bailli de Virieu, ministre plénipotentiaire de Parme, 1788–1793* (Paris, [1902]), pp. 166–67.

[3] E.g., *Journal de Paris*, Jan. 15, p. 59; *Moniteur*, Jan. 18, p. 146, Jan. 21, p. 166; Desmoulins, *Révolutions*, No. 7, pp. 301–4, No. 8, p. 384; *Mercure de France*, Jan. 16, pp. 134–35; and *Révolutions de Paris* (Tournon), No. 27, Jan. 9–16, p. 9 n., No. 28, Jan. 16–23, pp. 11–17, 32.

ened, if the offending orders were not revoked, to withdraw its battalion from the National Guard.[4]

Marat led the chorus of those who declared that imprisonment for debt was an abuse that the Revolution should abolish.[5] On January 7 he accused the Guards of being "contemptible fellows" and "mere machines" in the hands of their commanders, who were "valets of the court." In retaliation, on January 9 the Châtelet revived the unserved warrant of October 8 and sent its officers, with a National Guard detachment, to arrest the provocative journalist. Again he escaped, sought refuge in the friendly District of the Cordeliers, and under the protection of Danton, now the district's recognized leader, continued to publish his paper. The district assembly decided that the writ of October 8 was invalid, having been issued before the National Assembly's reform of criminal law procedure, and on January 12 the *Ami du peuple* carried an appeal to Lafayette,[6] who, though jealous for the reputation of his troops, in this instance had allowed "a shadow of doubt to fall upon their patriotism." The Châtelet had sent the detachment that had tried to arrest him, Marat asserted, without Lafayette's approval. If the court could make soldiers march without their general's orders, "what will the Nation, who regards you as its avenger, think?" Claiming that such a "usurpation of power" would bring the destruction of public liberty by the very ones who should defend it, Marat urged Lafayette to forbid his Guards to march without his explicit orders. The *Ami du peuple* particularly blasted a battalion commander of the National Guard, Boucher d'Argis,[7] first for having arrested a vendor of the *Ami du peuple* and then for having ordered Marat's own arrest.[8]

The National Assembly's Comité des Rapports (Communications Committee) took cognizance of the case and asked Lafayette

---

[4] *Révolutions de Paris* (Tournon), No. 28, Jan. 16–23, pp. 24–26, and Lacroix, III, 509–10 (Jan. 21), 700–701 (Feb. 4), IV, 54–55 (Feb. 9).

[5] *Ami du peuple*, Jan. 7, pp. 3–5, Jan. 10, pp. 3–4, Jan. 12, p. 6.

[6] *Ami du peuple*, Jan. 12, pp. 3–5.

[7] *Ibid.*, p. 8.

[8] *Ibid.*, Jan. 14, pp. 4–8.

for further information. Perhaps intending to prevent a prolonged debate on Marat's charges on the floor of the Assembly, he sent his reply to Latour-Maubourg, requesting him to read and deliver it to the committee.[9] For the time being, the National Assembly took no action, preferring to leave Marat to the courts.[10] The Paris Assembly of Representatives, however, on Boucher d'Argis' complaint, exonerated him, branded the *Ami du peuple* as incendiary and seditious, and also ordered its editor's arrest.[11] But Marat eluded arrest.

Where popular uneasiness existed, it was not due to the rhetoric of journalists alone. Although the winter had so far been mild and the bread shortage had been less disastrous than had been feared, the exodus of émigrés, the flight of capital, and the chronic national deficit created economic uncertainty, and unemployment mounted. A large number of former domestics in the Faubourg Saint-Germain begged to be admitted to the paid companies of the National Guard in order to earn some money, and Lafayette told them he would gladly welcome honest domestics as soon as vacancies permitted. A letter from a writer claiming to be representative of over a hundred unemployed servants appeared in the press expressing the gratitude of the "poor and unfortunate" to Lafayette, whose "goodness and humanity" earned their "respectful zeal."[12]

While Paris was still exercised by the Marat affair and by the hardships of winter, the controversy over Dières, who had commanded the expedition to Vernon, revived. On January 14, a deputation that claimed to represent a majority of Vernon's citizens appeared before the Assembly of Representatives, declared the charges against Dières false, and asked that their National Guard be permitted to affiliate with that of the capital. They also extolled a young Englishman for having saved the life of the agent of the Paris Subsistence Committee during the recent disorders in Vernon,

---

[9] Lafayette to Maubourg, [*ca*, Jan. 14, 1790], AN: F7 4757. The version of this letter by Nauroy in *Le Curieux*, I (1884), 95–96, misreads *Favras* as *preuves*.

[10] Cf. *AP*, XI, 261–64 (Jan. 20).

[11] Lacroix, III, 458–59, 462–63 (Jan. 15).

[12] *Journal général de la cour*, Jan. 25, pp. 196–97.

and a few days later Bailly awarded him a civic crown and Lafayette an appropriately engraved sword.[13]

Meanwhile, however, another delegation of Vernon citizens, accompanied by one from the District of the Cordeliers, presented a memoir condemning Dières. They maintained that that officer had first exceeded his orders and only afterward had received from Lafayette *ex post facto* instructions authorizing the actions he had already taken. A majority of the Representatives were indignant that a charge of collusion with arbitrary behavior should be brought against Lafayette. The Cordeliers' deputation then challenged the right of the Paris Assembly to pass judgment in a case involving another commune, but the Representatives decided that they had such jurisdiction. Thereupon, the Vernon deputation, recognizing that in implicating Lafayette it had made a tactical error, repudiated its entire memoir. The Assembly of Representatives then resolved that Dières' conduct had been irreproachable, the opposing Vernon delegations composed their differences, and the Assembly ordered the disavowal of the offending memoir printed, posted in Paris, and dispatched to Vernon with an appeal for a return to peace and union. Lafayette thus won another bout with the Cordeliers, but Robespierre, rising to prominence in the National Assembly as one of the deputies most devoted to the popular cause, continued to believe that Lafayette and the National Guard had acted beyond their authority[14] and might become a menace to freedom.

The Cordeliers did not take long to renew the fight. Shortly after the Châtelet's futile attempt to capture the Friend of the People, its district assembly adopted a resolution that no citizen of the district might be arrested without the commandant general's explicit order, and then only if the order were given to the district's own battalion.[15] Other districts, though not equally emphatic, also condemned the indiscriminate use of the National Guard.[16] The

---

[13] Lacroix, III, 441–42 (Jan. 13), 459–61 (Jan. 15).

[14] *Ibid.*, pp. 445–47, 450–56 (Jan. 14), 501 (Jan. 21), and Laurent (ed.), *Défenseur de la constitution* in *Oeuvres complètes de Robespierre* IV, 179 and n. 22.

[15] Lacroix, III, 522–23 (Jan. 20).

[16] *Ibid.*, pp. 502 (Jan. 21), 700–701 (Feb. 4), IV, 50–55 (Feb. 9).

issue came to a head when, on January 16, an outraged member of the Assembly of Representatives called attention to No. 99 of the *Ami du peuple,* which again attacked Necker, Bailly, and other prominent officials. The Representatives, incensed that Marat was goading his readers to violence, ordered the National Guard to use the greatest severity against vendors of the *Ami du peuple* and other incendiary publications and instructed the Châtelet to execute the earlier warrant against Marat.[17]

Although some districts and journalists approved of the Representatives' action,[18] the District of the Cordeliers took the position that no citizen should be arrested without the consent of the district in which he lived. By the procedure it now prescribed the officer commanding any detachment that Lafayette might send was first to report to the Cordeliers' National Guard, from which an officer then would conduct the visiting officer to the district's committee (of which Danton was the chief), and if that committee approved, the district's guard would aid the visiting detachment to make an arrest; otherwise, Lafayette's detachment must withdraw.[19]

The police authority of the Commune soon collided head on with the Cordeliers' resistance. On January 21 Lafayette received instructions from Mayor Bailly to provide the Châtelet with sufficient force to arrest Marat. The next morning Lafayette ordered Raphael Carle, commander of the Battalion of the Barnabites, to assist two Châtelet bailiffs armed with the old writ for Marat's arrest. Both the bailiffs and Carle acted prudently. They reported first to the district committee, but the committee refused to honor the writ on the old ground that it antedated the National Assembly's decree reforming criminal procedure. The bailiffs returned to the Châtelet for instructions, while Carle kept his detachment under arms, though carefully avoiding any provocative action. In the interval the Cordeliers' assembly convened, drew up an address presenting its view, and sent Danton with a deputation to deliver the address to the National Assembly. The National Assembly de-

[17] *Ibid.,* III, 465, 471 (Jan. 16).

[18] *Ibid.,* pp. 520–21 (Jan. 22); *Courrier de Paris,* Jan. 13, p. 86, Jan. 19, pp. 162–63; and *Moniteur,* Jan. 23, pp. 90–91.

[19] Lacroix, III, 522–25 (Jan. 22).

cided that the law reforming the criminal procedure could not be
retroactive and that therefore the writ of October 8 was still valid.
Upon learning of this decision, the assembly of the Cordeliers notified Carle that it was willing to let him arrest Marat, but by that
time the wanted man had escaped. Carle withdrew his frustrated
battalion and reported his failure to Lafayette.[20] Yet the fuss had
not been entirely futile; Marat decided he had had enough of Paris
for a while and fled to England. When Lafayette in turn reported
to the Representatives what had happened, they joined the commandant general in praise of the "zeal and prudence" of the National Guard in handling a "delicate situation."[21]

The Marat affair provoked considerable comment in the press.[22]
The aristocratic *Journal général de la cour* claimed that Marat had
climbed up a flue and escaped over the rooftops and that Louis XVI,
when Lafayette reported the episode to him, burst out laughing at
the picture of a soot-covered Marat peering out of a chimney.[23]
Loustalot, hitherto one of Lafayette's admirers, defended Marat for
his courage, commended the "wise and vigorous resolutions" of the
Cordeliers, and warned that a coalition of the paid staff of the
National Guard with the Châtelet "will be the end of the Revolution and liberty." Declaring that while he did not approve of Marat's
views, he was prepared to defend Marat's rights, Loustalot, addressing Lafayette, reviewed his revolutionary career unfavor-
ably: "Every day you are called the French Washington and
the guardian angel of France. . . . [But] ask yourself whether
you have been more useful to the Revolution than it has been
to you. We armed ourselves without you, . . . and took the
Bastille. . . . You have moved from inactivity . . . to almost absolute
power." You have been able, he continued, to place friends in
lucrative posts; the court dares not oppose you, men flatter you, the
aristocrats fear you, and patriots applaud you and march under your
banner. Yet there was room for doubt about Lafayette's heroism

[20] *Ibid.*, p. 525 (Jan. 22), 543–48 (Jan. 23); Duquesnoy, II, 308–9; and *AP*, XI, 287–
88 (Jan. 22).

[21] Lacroix, III, 517–18 (Jan. 22).

[22] *Courier national*, Jan. 23, p. 8, Feb. 4, p. 7; *Courier français*, No. 24, p. 197.

[23] *Journal général de la cour*, Jan. 23, pp. 178–79, Jan. 25, p. 195.

during the insurrection of October 5–6 and about his prudence
in defending Dières; and his use of arbitrary force against Marat
might have been worse than imprudent; a single shot in the District of the Cordeliers might have started a civil war.[24] Desmoulins
too cited Marat's eloquence as evidence of "courage, heart, and
great character" and shortly announced that he himself had moved
into the District of the Cordeliers so as to be among the patriots who
lived there and to enjoy the protection it afforded to honest men.[25]
A formidable opposition seemed to be coalescing against the potential abuse of police authority by Lafayette—the journalists
Marat, Loustalot, and Desmoulins, the left-most districts, led by
the Cordeliers and Danton, and the left-most deputies, of whom
Robespierre was the most conspicuous.

Since November a crisis had been brewing in Toulon that was
to test the strength of the opposition to Lafayette. Toulon was
France's most important Mediterranean naval base, accommodat-
ing about one-quarter of France's entire marine force. Comte
d'Albert de Rioms, commanding officer at Toulon and veteran of
the War of American Independence, feared that the new revolutionary notions would place power in the hands of the masses there
and destroy discipline among the workers in his yards. When some
employees of the Toulon arsenal expressed a wish to join the National Guard, the commander disapproved. Nevertheless a few
workers enrolled, arousing bad feelings on both sides.

On December 1, the expected eruption had come. Albert and
four of his officers were arrested and imprisoned in the Hôtel de
Ville. They suffered no worse fate only because the local National
Guard protected them from an angry crowd. On December 7 the
king notified the National Assembly what had happened, and in
the ensuing debates the major issue was not the release of the naval
officers (which was assumed) but the degree of censure for the
Toulon authorities.[26] On the eleventh a deputation from Toulon
appeared before the Paris Assembly of Representatives to solicit

[24] *Révolutions de Paris* (Prudhomme), No. 28, Jan. 16–23, pp. 29–31, No. 29, Jan.
23–30, pp. 10–16.

[25] Desmoulins, *Révolutions*, No. 9, pp. 426–28, No. 10, pp. 464–66.

[26] *AP*, X, 416–20.

its intercession in the National Assembly on behalf of their city.[27] Upon his release Albert too came to Paris to present his case.[28] Lafayette listened to his story and assured him that he would try to get justice in the National Assembly also for him.[29]

Once more Lafayette was caught in an old dilemma—how to harmonize civic authority with military discipline. As a soldier he understood Albert's concern for discipline, and as a general he could envisage a future tour of duty that might require friendly relations with naval officers of Albert's rank.[30] On the other hand, he realized that the municipality and the National Guard of Toulon might have difficulty controlling the people if an aristocratic naval commander employed the manner of the quarterdeck in dealing with the workers' leaders. To condemn the officials of Toulon might alienate a large and strategically important city; to censure Albert might disgust veterans in the French army and navy.[31] Some deputies wished to drop the Albert matter altogether. He insisted, however, that the National Assembly clear his name, while Ricard de Séalt, a deputy from Toulon, maintained that nothing must be done that would reflect on the municipality of Toulon. A debate was scheduled in the National Assembly for January 15.

On the eve of the debate Lafayette informed Maubourg, his right-hand man in the National Assembly, that he "set a most high value on M. Albert's being freed from blame and complimented." He had learned that Ricard proposed to introduce a resolution expressing the Assembly's satisfaction with the count's behavior "up to the month of December,"[32] but Lafayette wanted to eliminate the words "up to the month of December," thus clearing Albert unconditionally. At the same time he was eager, without explicitly rebuking the Toulon municipality, to shield the Toulon National

---

[27] Lacroix, III, 165, 169.

[28] *Chronique de Paris*, Dec. 13, p. 447, Dec. 22, p. 483, and *AP*, X, 529–49, 572–73, 588–89, 692, XI, 30.

[29] Lafayette to Maubourg, [Jan. 17?], *Le Curieux*, I (1884), 95–96.

[30] *Ibid.*

[31] Cf. Duquesnoy, II, 283.

[32] Lafayette to Maubourg, [Jan. 14?], *Le Curieux*, I (1884), 95–96.

Guard and thought that the National Assembly could do so by "praising the National Guard for having protected Albert." He was willing, if necessary, to go himself to the Assembly, but hoping that the affair might be adjusted without his direct participation, he requested Latour-Maubourg to seek the support of Duport, Lameth, Barnave, and others of Jacobin leanings in heading off Ricard, for if anyone spoke disparagingly of Albert, the settlement that he wanted would be hard to get. "M. d'Albert has great confidence in my ability to bring his affair to a successful conclusion," Lafayette wrote. "He is the man with whom I shall perhaps serve next spring; I should very much like to have him in my debt." Maubourg, of course, understood the reference to "next spring." It indicated that Lafayette expected the French to intervene openly in the current insurrection in the Austrian Netherlands,[33] with himself as commander of land forces and Albert of naval forces.

On January 15 Ricard delivered what a colleague described as "a violent and very exaggerated diatribe against M. d'Albert,"[34] but the National Assembly the following day agreed to a general, impersonal resolution stating that the motives of Albert, his officers, the National Guard, and the municipal officials of Toulon had presumably all been good and guilt rested on none of them.[35] That resolution, however, did not satisfy Albert and his friends, who insisted that he and his officers deserved explicit vindication and formal recognition of their services as naval officers. Lafayette now decided that he must enter into the controversy openly, and the best way to begin was with the Jacobins. All he asked for, he maintained, was mere courtesy for Albert.[36] He arranged a meeting with Duport, requesting Maubourg to join them somewhat later, preferably without Ricard but with him if Ricard would not come alone

---

[33] Morris to Washington, Jan. 22, Davenport (ed.), I, 377; Lafayette to M. d'Hennings, Jan. 15, 1799, *Mémoires*, III, 264–65; S. Tassier, *Les démocrates belges de 1789* in *Mémoires de l'Académie royale de Belgique*, XXVIII (1931), 280; and Jules Garsou, "La Fayette et la Belgique," *Le Flambeau*, XVII (1934), 300–301. See also below, pp. 276–96.

[34] Duquesnoy, II, 289. See also *AP*, XI, 190–91.

[35] *AP*, XI, 210–22.

[36] Lafayette to Maubourg, [Jan. 17], *Le Curieux*, I (1884), p. 95, but see the original in AN: F⁷ 4767. The original differs from the printed version only in one significant regard: in the printed version *sans retard* is wrong; it should be *sans Ricard*.

still later. Thus Lafayette apparently expected to reach an understanding first with Duport, then with Maubourg, and finally to
bring their joint influence to bear on Ricard.[37] As subsequent developments seem to indicate, he succeeded—partly, in any case.

On January 18 Lafayette took his place in the National Assembly. A deputy named Goupil de Préfeln ascended the tribune to
point out that the decree already passed might dim the luster of the
Comte d'Albert's reputation: "I call as witness the hero who is
listening to me (M. de Lafayette), the companion of his noble
work; he is in a better position than anyone else to do justice to M.
d'Albert." And then he moved that the president write to Albert
that the "Assembly had never ceased to hold him in the esteeem
merited by his glorious services." Ricard then asked that the same
testimonial be sent to the other officers at Toulon, and C.-F. Bouche,
a deputy from Aix-en-Provence, opposed sending such a letter to
Albert unless a similar one were sent also to the municipality and
the National Guard of Toulon.

The time had come for Lafayette to speak. "It is not as a com-
rade in arms of M. d'Albert," he said; "it is not in the name of a free
nation, France's best ally; it is as a *National soldier* that I support
the motion of M. Goupil de Préfeln, and I think that the National
Guard of Toulon will applaud it." Nevertheless, after some debate
the National Assembly decided that a testimonial of approval go
not only to Albert but also to the other naval officers, the municipal
officials, and the National Guard involved in the affair[38] Albert
promptly replied, thanking the National Assembly for its esteem,
"no less precious to me because it seeks to honor with the same
sentiment" the other persons involved. The deputies applauded his
sentiments heartily.[39] Thus Lafayette, having counted upon the
Jacobins for support, had won another point. Military honor and
discipline had been vindicated without visible derogation of civil
authority. Lafayette's presence in the National Assembly on the
eighteenth had obliged him to forgo seeing Mme de Simiane that
day. He sent her a tender note of apology, expressing the intention

[37] *Ibid.*

[38] *AP,* XI, 227–28, 230 (Jan. 18).

[39] *Ibid.,* p. 288 (Jan. 23).

to see her later. He explained that he had championed "M. d'Albert, whose affair would have turned out badly if I had not got myself involved in it, but I hope to have calmed some spirits."[40]

Lafayette's resumption of attendance at the National Assembly piled fresh burdens upon his willing shoulders. Not only was he named an alternate member of the Naval Committee[41] but he was frequently consulted also by the National Assembly's Military Committee, which was engaged in drafting a bill regulating the National Guards of the realm, and he in turn kept the Paris Military Committee busy with requests for advice, although he was not always able to attend its meetings and was sometimes forced to send apologies instead.[42] At one of his Sunday dinners, Lafayette asked Morris what he thought the French should do about their militia. Morris replied that the National Guard should not be "fixed by the Constitution" but, rather, provided for by readily changeable statute. Lafayette agreed that in general it would be a mistake to make a too detailed constitution. He and some others, he said, were determined to select such articles from the constitutional legislation as would form "a Constitution properly so called," considering the rest mere statutes alterable by the ordinary process of legislation. Morris approved, but his example of legislation that should not be considered part of the constitution probably did not impress Lafayette: he advised that the National Assembly regard the Declaration of Rights as masons would scaffolding, knocking it down upon finishing the structure they were building.[43]

Lafayette soon had occasion to show that for him at least the natural rights of man were something more substantive than scaffolding. Two brothers of the prominent Agasse family had recently been condemned to death for counterfeiting. Their uncle was president of the fashionable District of Saint-Honoré, and his son and a nephew, a younger brother of the two condemned men, were volunteers in that district's National Guard. Both the assem-

[40] [Ca. Jan. 18, 1790], Mémoires, II, 445–46. See above, p. 152, n. 75.

[41] AP, XXXII, 559 (Jan. 15).

[42] Procès-verbal du Comité militaire, Part II, pp. 55 (Jan. 26), 57 (Feb. 12). See also Lacroix, VII, 355.

[43] Morris diary, Jan. 17, Davenport (ed.), I, 369.

bly and the battalion of the district held all three of these guiltless Agasses in high regard, and a lieutenant of one of the battalion's companies offered to resign in favor of the condemned men's brother. The district assembly, unwilling to permit this sacrifice, decided instead to create the office of provisional lieutenant-en-second in the grenadier company, and the Saint-Honoré battalion asked its division chief, the Duc d'Aumont, and Lafayette to approve that decision.[44]

The National Assembly had just passed (January 21) a law that repudiated the old practice of attainder, or "corruption of blood," by which the kin of a condemned man were deemed also punishable for his crime. Seizing the opportunity to publicize the significance of criminal law reform which he had so long championed,[45] Lafayette deliberately made a point of showing his sympathy with the Agasses. Upon consultation with Gouvion and Aumont he suggested not only that the brother of the condemned men be accepted as a lieutenant of the grenadiers but also that the cousin be named lieutenant in a volunteer company. The district and its National Guard approved, and together with Lafayette and Aumont they arranged a ceremony to install the two new officers.

On Sunday morning, January 24, Lafayette with Gouvion and others of his staff joined Aumont and the Battalion of Saint-Honoré on the lawn of the Palais du Louvre. A detachment of the battalion and the district assembly escorted the president of the district, his son, and his nephew there. After the battalion commander conferred their commissions on the two cousins, Lafayette, with appropriate comments and military pomp, presented a National Guard sword to each of the new officers and put them in a place of honor at the head of the battalion. Lafayette and Aumont then reviewed the battalion as it marched to mass in its parish church.

The following day upon Lafayette's request the Assembly of Representatives confirmed the commissions granted provisionally to the two young men of the Agasse family. That morning a deputation from the Battalion of Saint-Honoré reported the ceremony

---

[44] See below, n. 46.

[45] See Gottschalk and Maddox, pp. 247–48, 299, 319–21.

of the preceding day to the National Assembly, which ordered the report printed and dispatched to all the districts of the realm. The press also gave the Agasse affair wide, enthusiastic publicity, of which Lafayette received his share.[46] A few days later Aumont gave a dinner in honor of Lafayette and the officers of the Saint-Honoré battalion.[47]

For the same morning that he gave swords to the young Agasses, Lafayette had scheduled another ceremony, and he went to the Hôtel de Ville as soon as the Saint-Honoré battalion marched off to church. The charge of counterrevolutionary sympathy was common at the time, and the *plumets-porteurs de charbon*—the men who delivered coal under the supervision of officers responsible for collecting the *octroi* on coal—was one of the organizations thus accused. To repudiate the accusation they asked the municipality to let them take the civic oath of loyalty. Upon the request of the Representatives, Lafayette and Rocquain de Vienne, the city coal inspector, had arranged that the oath-taking should be surrounded with the proper solomnity; that the men were poor laborers was in no way to detract from—in fact was to stress—the honor due them as loyal citizens.

Shortly after Lafayette arrived at the Hôtel de Ville a detachment of the Battalion of Saint-Louis-en-l'Île marched into the Place de Grève, followed by Rocquain de Vienne and a long formation—812, in fact—of coal porters. They massed in front of the perron, and their leader came forward to ask if they might send some of their number to take the oath before the Assembly of Representatives. Lafayette carried that request to the Representatives, who, in order to demonstrate "that precious equality which ought to exist among citizens and which ought to be the founda-

[46] Lacroix, III, 533–36, 551–56, 565–67, 590–92; *Moniteur*, Jan. 31, p. 123; *Gazette de Leide, supplément*, Feb. 5; *Courier français*, Jan. 26, pp. 201–3; *Journal de Paris*, Jan. 26, pp. 102–3, Jan. 27, pp. 106–7, Jan. 28, p. 112; *Révolutions de Paris* (Tournon), No. 29, Jan. 23–30, pp. 11–13; *Révolutions de Paris* (Prudhomme) No. 29, Jan. 23–30, pp. 27–30; Desmoulins, *Révolutions*, No. 10, pp. 453–55; *Point du jour*, Jan. 26, pp. 176–78; *AP*, XI, 315–16; *Journal général de la cour*, Jan. 26, p. 207; *Courrier de Paris*, Jan. 25, pp. 257–69; Mazzei to King Stanislaus, Jan. 25, Ciampini (ed.), I, 268; and Short to Jefferson, Jan. 28, Boyd (ed.), XVI, 131–32. See also below n. 47.

[47] *Courier national*, Jan. 25, pp. 7–8.

tions of our liberty," decided to invite all 812 into the Grande Salle. On his way to deliver this invitation Lafayette requested all those on duty in his staff office to accompany him and then, with some top-ranking officers of the Paris National Guard, went into the square again to invite the coal carriers to a reception by the mayor and the Representatives of the Commune. Inside the Grande Salle, the porters, with right hands raised, swore loyalty to the nation, the law, the king, and the Commune of Paris. The mayor shouted: "Vive le roi! Blessings on the Revolution, which has made us brothers!" There followed cries of "Vive la Nation!" and "Vive le maire! Vive le commandant général!" Lafayette and Bailly acknowledged the cheers, and the coal porters marched out proudly.[48] The Revolution seemed to have made many hitherto underprivileged men brothers of the more privileged.

Meanwhile, the trial of Favras went on, and one of his accusers implied that counterrevolutionaries were counting upon support from the former French Guards, the core of the paid companies of the Paris National Guard.[49] The lingering nostalgia of some of these Guards for their old regiment lent color to that imputation. They had so far failed to surrender their old regimental cannon and banners and, to make matters worse, it now turned out that two former French Guards had been among the mutineers on the Champs-Elysées. The resentment of the paid troops at recriminations like these came to a head when a rightist journal reported that some former French Guards had been arrested on suspicion of preparing some "very dangerous designs."[50] Indignant, the paid troops sent a deputation to their commander to deny the accusation. He invited them to present their case to the Assembly of Representatives, and he himself introduced them to the Assembly. Their spokesman, earnestly affirming the devotion of his comrades to the Revolution, the Commune, and their general, asked the Representatives to set a date for the presentation of their old regimental colors to the city. The president of the Representatives responded

[48] Lacroix, III, 533, 561–63, and *Journal de Paris*, Jan. 27, pp. 106–7.

[49] *Moniteur*, Jan. 21, pp. 81–82.

[50] *Journal général de la cour*, Jan. 20, quoted in Lacroix, III, 496 (Jan. 20). Cf. above, p. 176, n. 97.

that the Commune would gladly receive the flags as an additional token of homage from the "first apostles" of liberty: "You testify to a most inviolable love for your general; a thousand times your general has declared to this Assembly his love for you; a thousand times he has solemnly rendered justice to your zeal and your patriotism." The Assembly agreed to publish a denial of the offending newspaper's allegation and to order the public prosecutor to start proceedings against its author.[51]

Lafayette and the council of the former French Guard set January 26 for the ceremony of depositing the regimental standards. That morning some 2,000 former French Guards massed in the Place de Grève—under the sixty-six banners of their quondam regiment but wearing the National Guard uniform (not conspicuously different from their old regimentals). When all was ready, a detachment led by Captain de Beyssac entered the Hôtel de Ville to report to Lafayette, who, with his staff and some other National Guard officers, marched with Beyssac and his comrades into the Grand Salle. As the present commander of the erstwhile French Guards, Lafayette addressed Bailly, who presided: "I come at their head to swear in your presence to live, and to die if necessary, to maintain the constitution that is due in large part to their bravery."[52] Beyssac then fervently vouched for their wholehearted loyalty to the Revolution and the Commune, and the mayor graciously acknowledged their past services, accepted their flags, and urged them always to strive to be citizens no less than warriors.

The speeches finished, the Representatives, with the mayor at their head and followed by the National Guard officers, Beyssac, and his detachment, joined the soldiers waiting in the square below. Then, led by the National Guard band and the color guards, they advanced in procession to the Cathedral of Notre Dame. At the doors of Notre Dame the dean, in full canonicals, met them and preceded them into the cathedral. Before an altar at the entrance to the choir, the dean, Bailly, Lafayette, and Beyssac took their places, while the Representatives seated themselves in the transept

[51] Lacroix, III, 495–97 (Jan. 20).
[52] Ibid., p. 575 (Jan. 26).

and the soldiers stood with their banners in the nave. Bailly then announced that they had come to confide to the church the "standards that had conquered liberty," and each color guard, coming forward in turn, presented his banner to the dean. Beyssac spoke in conclusion: "We received our standards in the name of the king from the hands of the church; the nation has given us others; we hasten to return the old ones to the church that has blessed them."

Then, leaving their venerable flags with the dean, the soldiers marched out of the cathedral, their color guards picked up the flags of their respective districts, and the procession marched back to the Hôtel de Ville under their new flags.[53] Now only the glorious tradition of their historic regiment and the medals granted to them by the revolutionary Commune for their services to the nation remained to distinguish the old French Guards. A few days later they asked their general to approve their bestowal of that medal upon his aides. Seeing in this liberality a genuine effort to identify the old French Guards with other National Guards, Lafayette listed thirteen aides who had served since the beginning to receive the medals.[54]

In the Second Year of Liberty just begun, some aristocratic pamphlets and satires mocked Lafayette's heroics, but the "patriot" press continued to offset them with laudatory engravings, songs, verses, and prose eulogies. A play entitled *La Journée de Louis XII* had an enormous success largely because Louis XII, who in his day had called together the Estates General, reminded the audience of Louis XVI, and one of the play's characters was named La Fayette.[55] When fear was expressed over the way "the dearest hero of the day" exposed himself to admirers, beggars, and petitioners alike, even the aristocratic *Journal général de la cour* reassured its readers that his person was sacred: "The impious are struck with fear upon nearing it; the innocent kiss it, and everyone respects

[53] *Ibid.*, pp. 564 and 573 (Jan. 25), 575-77 and 579–80 (Jan. 26). See also *Moniteur*, Jan. 29, p. 114; *Révolutions de Paris* (Tournon), No. 29, Jan. 23–30, p. 18; *Courier français*, Jan. 25, p. 197, Jan. 27, pp. 225–26; and *Courier national*, Jan. 30, p. 7.

[54] Lafayette to [Committee of the former French Guards], Jan. 26, copy provided through the courtesy of the late S. W. Jackson.

[55] *Annales patriotiques et littéraires*, Jan. 17, p. 4, and *Chronique de Paris*, Jan. 21, p. 83. Cf. *Lettres à Monsieur le comte de B****, V, 500.

it."[56] The Chevalier d'Anterroches, whom he had once befriended and who was now settled in America, sought and obtained from the Lafayettes permission to name his children after them, Gilbert and Adrienne.[57] His Italo-American admirer Mazzei sang his praises to the king of Poland.[58]

The pride of Paris in its citizen army and its commandant general was echoed in other parts of France. The National Guard of Lyon sent a high-sounding address to their Paris comrades expressing gratitude to the "hero" who commanded them. The National Guard of Lower Dauphiny, 12,000 strong, appointed a committee to correspond with other National Guard units. Montpellier's National Guard, recently affiliated with that of Paris, invited the 30,000 guardsmen of its vicinity to "federate" in support of the National Assembly. Despite Morris' candid opinion that the loose plan for France's local administration would not work and that too much talk about liberty made it too late to change it,[59] the evidence steadily mounted that the National Guard units of France were spontaneously forming "federations" to draw the realm together tightly behind the Revolution.[60]

Lafayette quickly came face to face with this grass-roots movement. A deputation from Clermont called upon him, a fellow Auvergnat, to request affiliation with the Paris National Guard. He gladly presented them to the Assembly of Representatives, and their spokesman, mentioning the satisfaction Auvergne derived from being the commandant general's birthplace, expressed the attachment of Clermont's National Guard for that of Paris: "We are brothers in feeling, we wish to be brothers in arms." Amid applause Bailly welcomed the request as an especially meritorious

---

[56] Jan. 19, p. 150.

[57] Lafayette to d'Anterroches, Jan. 21, Sparks MSS., Harvard College Library. Cf. Louis Gottschalk, *Lafayette between the American and the French Revolution (1783–1789)* (hereafter cited as *Between*), (Chicago, 1950), p. 261.

[58] Jan. 25 and 29, Ciampini (ed.), I, 268–69.

[59] Morris diary, Jan. 10, Davenport (ed.), I, 362.

[60] *Chronique de Paris*, Jan. 14, p. 56, Jan. 15, p. 60, Jan. 16, pp. 63–64; Desmoulins, *Révolutions*, No. 5, pp. 198–99, No. 11, pp. 500–503; and *AP*, XI, 271 (Jan. 21), 293–95 (Jan. 23).

"link in the chain of citizens united for the defense of liberty" because the sentiments of Clermont were seconded by Paris' own commandant general. A Representative who had recently been in Auvergne on the Commune's business then described the assistance given him by the officials and the National Guard of Clermont. Thereupon Abbé Fauchet moved that the Representatives invite the municipalities of the kingdom to name Lafayette the generalissimo of all the country's National Guards.[61]

The idea was not new; it had been proposed by several provinces the previous August.[62] When, on one such occasion, a suggestion that he assume a sort of dictatorship had been made, he had quietly responded: "Do you think that that will improve our patrols?"[63] This time his response had to be more explicit. He thanked the abbé but reminded the gathering that the National Assembly was the proper body to regulate the affairs of the National Guard. Moreover, he continued: "I have always believed that it would not be good policy to place in the hands of one man so extensive a command of citizen soldiers. Such an extensive power could cause very great harm. I intend, when the National Assembly undertakes to consider the important subject of National Guard organization, to explain in a precise statement all the reasons why no one man should receive command of more than the National Guards of one department. . . . I shall congratulate myself then to find myself at the head of those of the department of the capital of the realm."[64] That should have settled the matter. Though courted by both sides, Lafayette persisted in declining to be either the royal lieutenant general or the popular generalissimo.

Lafayette's speech did no harm to his popularity. The *Moniteur* and the *Courier national* in identical reports gave him great credit for opposing Fauchet's motion: "Good citizens, though distressed

[61] Lacroix, III, 516 (Jan. 22).

[62] See Gottschalk and Maddox, pp. 262–65.

[63] *Mémoires*, II, 380–81 n. See also *Journal de Paris*, Jan. 29, p. 116.

[64] Lacroix, III, 517, *Moniteur*, Jan. 28, p. 109, *Mémoires*, II, 380–81, and Mazzei in Ciampini (ed.), I, 269, give different versions of Lafayette's speech, but they agree essentially on its purport.

by the restlessness of a new-born liberty, remain calm, for a true friend of liberty watches over you."[65] The *Journal de Paris* declared that this "virtuous citizen" would never accept honors unless they made him more useful to the cause of liberty.[66] Desmoulins, who had been among the spectators in the Grande Salle that day, admitted that he had at first feared that the general might welcome the abbé's proposal, but, he now reported, Lafayette had spoken "not softly or with the feeble gesture with which Caesar thrust aside a crown" but "with a convincing tone." Although you now enjoy an unprecedented popularity, Desmoulins warned, apostrophizing Lafayette, the people are quick to change their minds; most patriots look with suspicion upon your frequent visits to the now less popular minister Necker and your long, frequent conferences with the king's wife. "I answer," Desmoulins said, "that your purpose is to convert them. . . . What other object could you have? . . . Are you not our Washington? What need have you with the vain titles of generalissimo, of dictator? . . . Be only Lafayette, a name that belongs to you alone."[67]

Adrienne too recognized that her husband's model was no Roman dictator. In a letter to Washington on January 14 she wrote: "In the midst of the disturbances of our revolution I have always shared the pleasure that M. de La Fayette found in following in your footsteps, in being beholden to your example and instruction for his ways of serving his country, and in picturing your satisfaction upon learning of his success."[68]

The skeptical Morris was less inclined to think that Washington would or should find satisfaction in Lafayette's achievements. Only a few days after Adrienne he also wrote to the American president about Lafayette: "He acts now a splendid but dangerous Part. Unluckily he has given in to Measures as to the Constitution which he does not heartily approve, and he heartily approves many Things which Experience will demonstrate to be injurious. He left Amer-

---

[65] *Moniteur,* Jan. 28, p. 109, and *Courier national,* Jan. 29, p. 8.

[66] Jan. 29, p. 116 .

[67] Desmoulins, *Révolutions,* No. 12, pp. 565–70.

[68] Maurois, p. 219.

ica, you know, when his Education was but half-finished. What he learned there he knows well, but he did not learn to be a Government Maker."[69]

On the other hand, La Luzerne, who had formerly been the minister of France in Philadelphia, thought that Lafayette's education had been more than "half-finished" in America. A letter of his to Washington from London read: "Your friend, the Marquis de Lafayette, finds himself at the head of the revolution, and it is indeed a very fortunate circumstance for the state that he is, but very little so for himself. . . . He has need for all aid of that wisdom and prudence which he acquired under your tuition, and assuredly he has hitherto proved himself worthy of his master."[70]

In France, in any case, no one could any longer rival Lafayette in popularity—not the king, not Bailly, and certainly no other member of the National Assembly. The Battalion of Saint-Germain-l'Auxerrois gathered for a dinner at the Archbishop's Palace on the last day of January, and (as a member of the battalion described the affair, with perhaps pardonable hyperbole) after the toast to the king, "with what impatience the next toast was awaited!" No one proposed it, everyone knew what it would be and cried: "To our General!" Five hundred arms were raised ("with what ardor!"), and five hundred glasses were drained amid shouts of "Long live our General!"[71]

BIBLIOGRAPHICAL NOTES

The most recent biography of Marat is the revised edition (Chicago, 1967) of Louis Gottschalk, *Marat, a Study in Radicalism*. On the *affaire de Marat* of January, 1790, however, it is meager, and we have relied above largely on the detailed accounts in the notes in Lacroix, III, esp. 520–25, 540–48, 613–15.

The *Mémoires* of Lafayette, while nearly always made up of his own writings, were posthumously published, having been compiled and edited by members of his family. They sometimes depart from the exact wording of the originals. The original of the letter to M. d'Hennings, Jan. 15, 1799 (*Mémoires*, III, 219–69), now in the Huntington Library, San Marino, California (HM 21654), differs, for example, from the printed version because of a number of relatively unimportant editorial corrections and usually

[69] Morris to Washington, Jan. 22, Davenport (ed.), I, 377.

[70] Jan. 17, Sparks, *Correspondence of the American Revolution*, IV, 310–11.

[71] *Supplément au Journal de Paris*, No. 10, Feb. 11, p. 1.

negligible omissions. Only where we have found variant readings that seem to matter have we indicated them.

André Maurois was able in his *Adrienne* to use some letters of Mme de Lafayette in the Château La Grange-Blénau that were not available to us when we worked among the papers there in 1929–30. Maurois' biography of Mme de Lafayette is more complete than any other, but for this period it contains new sources only rarely, probably because La Grange-Blénau did not pass into the hands of the Lafayettes until 1800. When we quote from versions of the documents he uses, we have preferred to make our own translations rather than to borrow those of the translation of *Adrienne* by Gerard Hopkins (New York, 1961).

CHAPTER X

Renewal of the Patriotic Oath

A T THE beginning of February 1790 the debates of the National Assembly became inflamed by the danger of France's involvement in a war over "the United States of Belgium."[1] Combined with misgivings about the agitation of émigrés abroad and of aristocrats at home, it impelled the friends of a monarchical constitution to wish for a clear-cut decision on the distribution of authority in the conduct of foreign affairs. If the king could not be trusted to deal candidly with foreign affairs, then obviously his authority over the diplomatic corps and the armed forces ought to be curtailed—obviously, at least, for those who identified France with the Revolution. By the same token, if he could be trusted to support the Revolution abroad as well as at home, the diminution of his once decisive power in the conduct of foreign affairs might be less imperative. On the other hand, the Right insisted that the National Assembly should take steps to strengthen the executive authority to a degree that would enable the monarch to restore prestige abroad and order at home.

Some of the king's partisans claimed that the king had so far given his consent to the decrees of the National Assembly only because he was under duress as Lafayette's prisoner. Lafayette tried to counteract that claim by repeatedly requesting Louis to leave the Tuileries and move freely about the city and into the surrounding country, but Louis remained aloof from the Parisians' demonstration of affection and only rarely and briefly left the Tuileries, while the queen made even less effort to reconcile herself to a position she

---

[1] See below, pp. 274–81.

considered humiliating.[2] Apparently Louis XVI had placed Lafayette's moderate political analysis, submitted in December,[3] into his strongbox without formally indicating any reaction to it. For his part, however, in his dealings with the royal family Lafayette persisted in making no secret of his own attitude. In later years he remembered having once warned them: "If I have to choose between liberty and royalty, between people and king, you may rest assured that I shall be against you, but so long as you remain faithful to your civic duties, I shall sincerely support constitutional royalty." On another occasion, he recalled, he had declared to the king: "You know that I of course am republican, but in the present situation my very principles make me royalist; I would not feel bound by honor to defend the authority which has been delegated to you if I were not already so bound by my principles." And in restrospect he claimed to have said to the queen: "You ought to have all the more confidence in me, Madame, because I have no royalist superstition. If I believed that the destruction of royalty would benefit my country, I would not hesitate, for what are called the rights of a family to the throne do not exist for me. But I have become convinced that in the present circumstances, the abolition of constitutional royalty would be a public misfortune. More reliance is to be placed upon a friend of liberty who acts out of duty, patriotism, and conviction than upon an aristocrat impelled by prejudice."[4]

[2] *Mémoires*, II, 417–18, III, 207–8. For anecdotes, sometimes doubtful, of ill-will at court toward Lafayette and his frends see [Jeanne-Louise] Campan, *Mémoires sur la vie de Marie-Antoinette reine de France et de Navarre*, ed. Fs. Barrière (Paris, 1886), p. 283; Comte de Saint-Priest, *Mémoires*, ed. Baron de Barante (Paris, 1929), II, 29; *Mémoires de Weber, frère du lait de Marie-Antoinette, reine de France*, ed. Fs. Barrière (Paris, 1885), p. 290; B.-H.-R. Capefigue, *Louis XVI, son administration et ses relations diplomatiques avec l'Europe* (Paris, 1844) IV, 229; and Ernest Daudet, *Histoire de l'émigration pendant la Révolution française* (Paris, 1904), I, 24.

[3] See above, pp. 114–17.

[4] The quotations in this paragraph come from *Mémoires*, III, 212. They are given there as direct quotations and are so treated here. The fragment from which they are taken is entitled "Sur la démocratie royale de 1789 et le republicanisme des vrais constitutionnels," which was written by Lafayette about 1799. Since he was probably quoting from memory and his memory might well have deceived him as to both time and wording, these quotations must be regarded as expressing his lifetime views though perhaps the verbatim content and the occasions he here ascribes to them may be mistaken. For what is said to be Condorcet's version of Lafayette's relations with the court (which largely confirms Lafayette's own statements on this subject) see the so-called *Mémoires de Condorcet*, II, 151–52.

Lafayette's recollection of these sentiments was probably correct in spirit if not in letter; so long as the king's policy was equivocal, Lafayette could not give him wholehearted support, but if the king would again make public his willingness to accept the Revolution, Lafayette was ready to serve him as a constitutional monarch. As yet, however, Louis was prepared neither to accept the Revolution wholly nor to reject it wholly.[5]

Paris was quiet for a time after the mutiny of January 12, but the fear of counterrevolutionary plots did not abate. On January 29 Besenval was finally acquitted after an orderly procedure (and the next day he paid his respects to Lafayette, to whose men he openly expressed his gratitude for their soldierly conduct),[6] but the protracted Favras trial kept public opinion in turmoil. Lafayette remained convinced that the Comte de Provence had been in the plot with Favras, and the behavior of some others in the king's household also roused suspicion and resentment. Although Bailly and Lafayette received courteous treatment at the Tuileries, several other leading members of the National Assembly did not, and the National Guard officers on duty sometimes avoided unpleasant scenes only by their own prudence. Gouvion, who was directly in charge of the palace guard, informed Lafayette of an undercurrent of bitterness at the Tuileries toward revolutionaries.[7] Moreover, National Guard officers from Hainault came to Paris to tell Lafayette that their men had seized enough munitions stored up by aristocrats to equip 80,000 men.[8]

That report might have seemed fantastic, but the Comte d'Artois, King Louis' brother, gave more plausible cause for alarm. Having emigrated to the court of his father-in-law, the king of Sardinia, he kept busy at Turin with French affairs. Near the end of January, a circular addressed by the émigrés to the princes of the Holy Ro-

---

[5] Staël-Holstein to Gustavus III, Feb. 7, Staël-Holstein, III, 210–11; Morris diary, Jan. 26, 29, 31, Davenport (ed.), I, 389, 391, 393; Young, pp. 320–24; and Desmoulins, *Révolutions,* No. 8, p. 358.

[6] *Moniteur,* Jan. 25, p. 199; *Révolutions de Paris* (Prudhomme), No. 29, Jan. 23–30, p. 32; and Ciampini (ed.), I, 265. See also [Montjoie], *Histoire de la conspiration de L.-P.-J. d'Orleans* (Paris, 1800), IV, 155–56.

[7] *Mémoires,* II, 417–18 n., III, 207–8, IV, 407–8, VI, 8–10.

[8] *Journal général de la cour,* Jan. 26, pp. 207–8.

man Empire fell into Lafayette's hands. It was an appeal to the German princes for some kind of action against the revolutionary government of France.[9] It appeared to provide indubitable proof of the king's brother's enmity to the Revolution—enmity to the point of enlisting foreign intervention in behalf of counterrevolution. If Louis XVI was privy to such plans, no friend of the Revolution could trust him, but if he was not, then ought he not repudiate them publicly and forcibly? Despite Morris' advice to the contrary, Lafayette decided to let the people know the danger that confronted them. Before publishing the émigrés' circular, however, he showed it to Montmorin, who as foreign minister was especially concerned with agitation abroad.[10]

The news that the émigrés were seeking to encourage foreign intervention exacerbated the political tension, and whether the king should take a public stand as leader of the Revolution became a subject of social conversation. Morris, though a private American citizen, went so far as to prepare a note on the subject for the eyes of the queen, and (as he admitted) he "very imprudently" aired the opinion at the foreign minister's home that the king should make no public declaration. He was uncertain whether the plan to make such a declaration had originated with Necker or with Lafayette but reflected that in any case Montmorin had "probably agreed to it."[11]

Tension changed to genuine alarm as the international crisis worsened. The king of Sardinia was rumored to be ready to attack France in behalf of the émigrés,[12] and a Prussian army intervened in the Belgian imbroglio by occupying Liège, thus raising the possibility of a war on two fronts. How was the army to be put in a state of readiness without running the risk that the king would use it against the Revolution? Lafayette talked with several liberal deputies who as members of the National Assembly's Military Committee and as army officers could speak with some authority. He

[9] Morris diary, Jan. 26, Davenport (ed.), I, 389.

[10] Jan. 26–31, *ibid.,* pp. 389–93; Morris to Montmorin, Jan. 26, *ibid.,* pp. 393–95.

[11] Jan. 29–31, *ibid.,* pp. 392–93. Cf. *ibid.,* Feb. 1, p. 403.

[12] *Courier national,* Jan. 30, p. 8.

turned also to William Short as one who was familiar with British parliamentary control over the British army. In his letter to Short he frankly outlined the dilemma: "Standing armies have always been regarded as one of the great obstacles to the establishment of a free constitution; it is necessary, nevertheless, in France to maintain a very large one," and if the army was to be effective, strict discipline was required and the king must have recognized authority to enforce it. Confronted by this dilemma Lafayette listed eight points upon which he asked Short's opinion: (1) the number of men and officers that should compose each branch of the service—horse, foot, and artillery, (2) a method of recruitment that would permit strengthening the army in time of war, (3) the pay of officers and men, (4) a principle guiding promotions while leaving to the king the right to make half of them from the rank of captain up, (5) the annual grant of subsidies for the payment of troops, (6) the oath the troops should take, (7) the use of soldiers for tax collection or other domestic purposes and under what conditions, and (8) the penal code and courts martial. The proper answers to these debatable matters seemed important as steps toward reestablishing military discipline, but Lafayette made clear that he wanted to leave the king "everything that it is possible to give to the executive power without compromising public liberty," especially since "the [foreign] powers that would trouble the revolution will be decided by the greater or the lesser energy that we put into the constitution on this point."[13] What Short said in reply to Lafayette's request is unknown, but it enlisted the young American chargé d'affaires, along with Washington, Franklin, and Jefferson, among the American advisers to the foremost leader of the French Revolution. On this issue Morris apparently was not consulted—perhaps, as Lafayette reflected long afterward, because he had begun to suspect the value of Morris' advice: "It was an unfortunate circumstance that his British constitutional prejudices led him to become a bad adviser."[14]

Meanwhile the ministry continued to discuss how to counter the worsening international tension. Necker, supported by Champion

[13] Lafayette to Short, Jan. 31, LC: Short papers, Vol. V (where it is erroneously dated 1789).

[14] Lafayette to Jared Sparks, June 17, 1832, Harvard College Library.

de Cicé and Montmorin, undertook to urge the king to repudiate the émigrés and place himself at the head of the Revolution. The queen and others at court seemed to believe that Lafayette and his friends, if gingerly handled, could be won over to the king's side, thus affording an opportunity to widen the split between moderates and radicals in the National Assembly and prevent further attrition of the royal prerogative.[15] Although probably loath to rebuke the Comte d'Artois and to seem to consent in advance to reform, Louis XVI finally yielded to the advice of his liberal ministers and set about to draft an address for him to deliver directly to the National Assembly.[16] This was to be the first time since July 15, upon news of the capture of the Bastille, that Louis would appear in person before the National Assembly.

The proposed maneuver pleased the friends of Lafayette among the moderates, but some leading figures at the Jacobin Club questioned the desirability of a step that would probably increase the king's popularity. Among them was Alexandre de Lameth, who reasoned that to make the king more popular without gaining control of his policy was dangerous, for Lafayette's influence over him might not last. They voiced their doubts to Lafayette, but he adhered to his belief that if Louis XVI publicly assumed the role of advocate of reform, whatever popularity accrued to him would help rather than hurt the Revolution. Besides, Lafayette expected the announcement of royal support for a written constitution to foster greater unity within the National Assembly.[17] He would have liked Louis without unnecessary delay to make a simple statement, but Necker and Montmorin preferred an elaborate one, and so Necker prepared the kind of speech he believed appropriate. The final draft was not approved until a council meeting on February 3, and no evidence indicates that Lafayette saw it before Louis delivered it.

[15] Fersen to his father, Feb. 1, P. Wormeley (ed.), *Diary and Correspondence of Count Axel Fersen* (Boston, 1902), p. 81.

[16] Mme de Staël, *Considérations sur les principaux événemens de la Révolution française* (Paris, 1818), I, 373–74; Morris diary, Jan. 29, Davenport (ed.), I, 391; Vandreuil to Artois, Mar. 6, Pingaud (ed.), I, 134; Duquesnoy, II, 351; Staël-Holstein to Gustavus III, Feb. 7, Staël-Holstein, pp. 154–55; and Ferrières, I, 366, 385.

[17] *Mémoires*, III, 210–11, and A. Lameth, I, 315–16, 325.

The delay, however, allowed the king's intention to address the Assembly to become widely known.[18] On February 4 an air of expectancy hovered over the Salle du Manège. As the king's speech was to avow, he wanted "this day on which your monarch comes to join you in the freest and most intimate manner to mark a memorable turning-point in the history of this empire."[19] The deputies' seats, many of which had often been vacant, now were filled, and ambassadors, eminent Frenchmen, and fashionable ladies crowded into the galleries. Lafayette and Bailly were in their places as deputies when the president, Bureau de Pusy, called the meeting to order. About eleven o'clock an aide brought Lafayette a note from Louis XVI to give to the president,[20] who read it aloud; it said that the king would come about midday and wanted to be received without ceremony. When the applause that greeted this announcement died down, the president suggested that a deputation escort the king to the hall, and accordingly he was instructed to appoint thirty deputies for that purpose. He chose them from the various groupings in the Assembly, and among them was Lafayette.[21]

The deputation went immediately to the Tuileries. Wearing a simple black suit, accompanied only by his ministers, the two National Guard officers on duty, and his pages, and escorted by the thirty deputies, Louis XVI walked from the palace to the Salle du Manège. They all entered by the nearest door, which happened to open on the president's left,[22] and the aristocratic party was later to reproach Lafayette for favoring the Left by taking the king through that door.[23]

As Louis XVI entered, deputies and visitors rose and shouted

---

[18] *Mémoires*, III, 211; Duquesnoy, II, 346–47, 354–55; *Courier national*, Feb. 5, p. 1; *Gazette de Leide*, Feb. 12, p. 2; *AP*, XI, 429; and *Journal de Paris*, Feb. 5, p. 141.

[19] *AP*, XI, 431.

[20] *Courrier de Paris*, Feb. 8, p. 66, and J.-B. Poncet-Delpech, *La première année de la Révolution vue par un temoin (1789–1790)*, ed. Daniel Ligou (Paris, 1961), p. 231.

[21] Duquesnoy, II, 347–48, 355; *Journal de Paris*, Feb. 5, p. 141; *Courrier de Paris*, Feb. 7, pp. 65–66; *AP*, XI, 428; *Courier national*, Feb. 5, p. 2; and *Gazette de Leide*, Feb. 12, p. 3.

[22] *Gazette de Leide*, Feb. 12, p. 3; Desmoulins, *Révolutions*, No. 12, p. 535; and Duquesnoy, II, 355.

[23] *Mémoires*, III, 211 n.

"Vive le roi!" The president ushered the king to a chair draped with royal purple velvet embroidered with golden fleurs de lys. The ministers followed and placed themselves behind the king. The seating arrangement appeared to have been intended to symbolize the equality of the legislative with the executive branch of the government,[24] but the king (whether by design or inadvertence) did not sit down. Instead, standing before his chair (and thus obliging his hearers to stand) and with his hat off, he began at once to read his lengthy address.

The king's coming personally to the Assembly without display and hesitantly beginning his speech[25] was disarming, and most of the deputies were disposed to be generous.[26] Although he pleaded for greater executive power to deal with widespread disorders, threats of foreign war, bread shortage, and fiscal deficit, the tenor of his address was studiously conciliatory. His own objective, he declared, was the same as that of the deputies—the welfare of France—and he begged them to unite toward that end. The new constitution, he supposed, would require the sacrifice of privileges from clergy and nobility and would require a similar sacrifice for himself, but "I will defend, I will maintain, constitutional liberty, whose principles the general will, in accord with my own, has sanctioned." He even promised that he and the queen would bring up the dauphin as heir to a constitutional throne. He implored those who did not share the "spirit of concord, which has now become so necessary," to "relinquish all the memories afflicting them" in return for his gratitude and affection.

As the king read on, he was interrupted more and more frequently by cheers. Most of the approval came from the Center, the Left, and the galleries, for the Right found some of the royal concessions disturbing.[27] When the speech was done, the applause was loud and prolonged. President Bureau de Pusy expressed the Assembly's heartfelt gratitude to the king for binding himself "to

---

[24] Desmoulins, *Révolutions*, No. 12, p. 535.

[25] Morris diary, Feb. 4, Davenport (ed.), I, 405.

[26] Duquesnoy, II, 349–54.

[27] *Courier français*, Feb. 5, pp. 281, 283–84; *Courier national*, Feb. 5, p. 2; Desmoulins, *Révolutions*, No. 12, p. 546; and Duquesnoy, II, 348, 349.

defend the constitution and the laws." Then, amid continuing rounds of approval, Louis XVI and his ministers left, escorted by the thirty deputies. At the palace, Marie Antoinette and the dauphin met them. Declaring that she entertained the same opinions as her husband, she too promised to educate her son to respect liberty and maintain the law.[28] Lafayette might well have felt pleased; king, queen, and dauphin were now committed to a constitutional monarchy.

By the time Lafayette returned to the Salle du Manège with the rest of the king's escort the Assembly had decided to match Louis' solemn pledge: every deputy would take the civic oath, adding a vow to defend the new constitution; any deputy who refused would be barred from the Assembly.[29] One by one the deputies took the oath. Marked applause echoed through the chamber when Champion de Cicé, Bailly, and Lafayette, each in his proper turn, swore "to be faithful to the nation, to the law, to the king, and to maintain with all my might the constitution decreed by the National Assembly and accepted by the king."[30] According to the *Courrier de Paris,* Lafayette, who had gone to the tribune from the left, walked from the tribune on the right and took his seat with the Moderate Right. Many other deputies followed suit, and seats on the Right often empty before were now occupied. The *Courrier de Paris* interpreted this act as a gesture of conciliation from the Moderate Left to the Moderate Right.[31] Although the Extreme Right remained aloof, angry, or uncertain, the general feeling ran that the thing to do was to accept the king's avowed intention as sincere while remaining vigilant.[32]

When Lafayette went home to dinner that afternoon, he found a number of visitors gathered to celebrate the morning's triumph. Among them was a popular actor, Jean Maudit de Larive, who

[28] Duquesnoy, II, 349–50; Ferrières, I, 588; and Montlosier, I, 342, 432.

[29] Montlosier, I, 431–32, and Desmoulins, *Révolutions,* No. 12, p. 549.

[30] *AP,* XI, 432. Poncet-Delpech, p. 233, says that "les dames Lafayette . . . et les externes qui occupaient les tribuns" also took the oath.

[31] Feb. 8, p. 66.

[32] Duquesnoy, II, 349–52, 354–56; *Mémoires,* III, 211; A. Lameth, I, 323–26; and Lindet to the municipal officers of Bernay, Feb. 4, Montier, pp. 63–64.

had once played the role of Bayard and had received from a descendant of Bayard a gold chain that that hero was said to have worn. With Lafayette's friends gathered round him, the actor gave the chain to "the new Bayard" and recited a poem composed for the occasion. Who better than you, it asked, has the right to the armour of the *chevalier sans peur et sans reproche*. Despite the grandiloquence, everybody applauded—the actor for his gesture, the general because he "so richly deserved it."[33]

Not all of Lafayette's guests were so flattering, however. Morris called just after the dinner hour. He had already learned of the morning's doings from Montmorin and was unhappy about them. He thought that they showed how feeble the king's ministers were and that the Assembly's oath to support a constitution not yet made was "a strange Oath." To the jubilant Lafayette Morris remarked that His Majesty's act "can do no Good and must therefore do Harm." This answer visibly surprised Lafayette, who explained that now he would be able to "advocate the royal Authority" in the Assembly. Morris changed the subject.[34]

When dinner was over, Lafayette returned to the Hôtel de Ville for the evening session of the Assembly of Representatives. It was long past five on a winter evening, and as he rode across the river to the Place de Grève, he saw candles gleaming in windows, and he found the Hôtel de Ville a blaze of light. The people had spontaneously made this illumination to celebrate the union of the king and the Revolution.[35] Before Lafayette reached the Hôtel de Ville, Bailly had given the Representatives a glowing account of Louis

---

[33] *Moniteur*, Feb. 12, p. 170:

> D'un order chéri des guerriers
> Cette antique et simple parure,
> Dans les combats ornait l'armure
> Du plus brave des chevaliers.
> Qui mieux que vous aurait des droits sur elle?
> Comme Bayard, sans reproche et sans peur,
> Sage, vaillant, à vos devoirs fidèle,
> Chaque jour vous obtient une gloire nouvelle;
> Et malgré les complots et l'envie en fureur,
> Vous sortez des dangers toujours calme et vainqueur.

See also *Journal de Paris*, Feb. 18, p. 196.

[34] Morris diary, Feb. 4, Davenport (ed.), I, 404–5.

[35] *Mémoires*, III, 211; *Moniteur*, Feb. 8, p. 153; and *Courier national*, Feb. 6, pp. 6–7.

XVI's speech and of the National Assembly's oath-taking, and the Representatives had decided that they too would take the new oath, whereupon Bailly had administered it to the Representatives as well as to the other city officials and to the spectators present in the Grande Salle. And since a great crowd in the square below also wished to take the oath, the mayor with a number of Representatives had gone down and administered it to them too.[36] When Lafayette arrived, the mayor interrupted the Assembly's business in order to administer the oath to him, and Lafayette once more swore to be faithful to the nation, the law, and the king, and to maintain the constitution. The officers of his staff and of the National Guard on duty at the Hôtel de Ville then did likewise.[37]

The Abbé Fauchet, who a few weeks before had proposed that Lafayette be named commander of the National Guards of the entire realm, saw in the prevailing mood an opportunity to bind at least some of the towns of France together in defense of the constitution under the leaders of Paris, "the first city of liberty." He now proposed that all the affiliated municipalities and National Guards be invited to confer on the mayor of Paris the title of "First Municipium of the Affiliated Communes" and on Lafayette that of "First Brother-in-Arms of the Affiliated National Guards." While the Representatives agreed with his sentiments, they hesitated, out of concern that the provinces might look upon the plan as an attempt of the metropolis to dominate the country, and so they took no action on his motion.[38]

The business that had especially brought Lafayette to the Assembly that evening was a promise to honor one of the Volunteers of the Bastille. Mlle de Monsigny, daughter of an officer in the Bastille garrison, had informed the Representatives that Auben Bonnemer, a member of the Volunteers, had saved her life during the attack on the Bastille, and she had requested that her defender receive some civic recognition of his gallantry. The Assembly had complied, and the young lady and Bonnemer, with a detachment of his comrades, were now present, prepared to participate in a

[36] *Révolutions de Paris* (Tournon), No. 30, Jan. 30–Feb. 7, p. 13.

[37] Lacroix, III, 692–94.

[38] *Ibid.*, p. 709.

public ceremony. Bailly handed Mlle de Monsigny a civic crown, which she placed upon her protector's head. Then Bailly took up a handsome, suitably engraved sabre, provided by the girl's father, and gave it to Lafayette, who in turn presented it to Bonnemer with a few words of praise and embraced him "with that affection," the secretary of the Assembly recorded, "which evokes reciprocal feelings from all the army he commands and all the citizens he protects."[39] The *Moniteur* considered the soldier's "simple and touching gratitude" for Lafayette's kindness "more flattering to the hero of America than Abbé Fauchet's tedious panegyric."[40]

When Lafayette finally left the Hôtel de Ville, he had every reason to share the "hard to describe" but "delightful and charming state of excitement that pervaded Paris that evening."[41] The National Assembly seemed more united in purpose than ever before, the king had committed himself in advance to accept whatever they might decide, and Lafayette could confidently anticipate that an acceptable monarchical constitution soon would ensue.

For the ten days that followed Paris was jubilant over the stirring events of February 4.[42] One of the newspapers to which Lafayette subscribed, the *Journal de Paris*,[43] devoted several issues to Louis' address and to the oath taken by the deputies of the National Assembly and the Paris Assembly of Representatives.[44] The *Mercure de France* published a poem that compared Lafayette with the greatest captains of France's history, calling him not merely "Héros de l'Amérique et de la Liberté" but also "Héros de l'Univers."[45] Even the journalists who had recently denounced him for

[39] *Ibid.*, pp. 675, 695–96.

[40] *Moniteur*, Feb. 6, p. 146.

[41] *Courrier de Paris*, Feb. 6, p. 33.

[42] See, e.g., *Courier français*, Feb. 5, p. 281; *Point de jour*, Feb. 5, 6, pp. 295–96, 298–306, 309; *Courier national*, Feb. 5, pp. 2–8; *Courrier de Paris*, Feb. 5, 27, pp. 27–31, 65–66; *Patriote français*, Feb. 5, p. 4; *Chronique de Paris*, Feb. 5, pp. 143–44; *Moniteur*, Feb. 6, pp. 147–48; and *Gazette de Leide*, Feb. 12, pp. 2–4.

[43] The Lafayette College Library, Easton, Pa., owns Lafayette's copies of the *Journal de Paris* from Oct. 23 to Dec. 30, 1789.

[44] *Journal de Paris*, Feb. 5–7, pp. 141–48, 151–52.

[45] Feb. 6, p. 37.

his part in the pursuit of Marat were gratified. Loustalot praised
him for refusing command of the National Guards of the realm
and printed letters from members of the National Guard proclaiming their devotion to their general.[46] Desmoulins published a correspondent's eulogy of "the virtues and talents of this young hero of
liberty" and himself praised the general for his civic virtues.[47]

Within several hours of the king's address, nevertheless, Lafayette had reason to wonder whether the victory of the Revolution
was decisive. The Patriot deputies who waited upon His Majesty
that evening were disappointed in their reception. The king gave
his entire attention to some resentful aristocrats who had gathered
at the palace while he seemed to ignore Lafayette's friends. When
Lafayette learned of this disillusioning incident, he feared that
perhaps Louis was once more vacillating.[48] Since the king had,
however, formally given his word to support the Revolution, Lafayette lost no time in making the most of that gesture. "The Commandant General hastens to congratulate the National Guard," he
wrote in his orders of the day for February 5; yesterday's events had
rallied the "true friends of liberty" more closely than ever around
"the best of kings" and "ought to redouble the sentiments of love,
loyalty, and trust that unite the Nation to its chief"—sentiments
that Louis XVI would find "especially in the hearts of the generous
soldiers who bear arms for the constitution"; and the king's promise
to defend that constitution "ought to become the signal for tranquility and order throughout the realm."[49] The *Journal de Paris,*
upon publishing this order of the day, attributed it "to that young
Hero whose life, talents, and character must be counted among the
things that for several years have been preparing the great revolution which is taking place."[50]

Lafayette was not the only one persuaded that the king's speech
had produced the good results he so devoutly sought. Necker's son-

[46]*Révolutions de Paris* (Prudhomme), No. 30, Jan. 30–Feb. 6, pp. 1–8, 31–32, and
No. 31, Feb. 6–13, p. 32.

[47] *Révolutions,* No. 12, pp. 563–70.

[48] *Mémoires,* III, 211–12.

[49] *Journal de Paris,* Feb. 8, p. 154.

[50] *Ibid.*

in-law, Staël-Holstein, soon reported that although the royal conciliation had displeased both the aristocrats and the "Enragés," who
feared it would increase enthusiasm for the court's program, Lafayette's influence had never been greater. Necker and Lafayette, he
believed, were now fairly well united and could be regarded as the
sole sources of strength behind the government. Probably reflecting Necker's views, his son-in-law prophesied that the fate of
France would rest on the degree of power the constitution would
leave to the executive, Necker's ability to recoup the country's finances, and the king's readiness to make trips in the city, and even
outside, in order to show that he was free to do so.[51]

Among contemporary Englishmen opinions of Lafayette var-
ied. Traveling in France, a young Englishman wrote to his father:
"The Marquis de la Fayette is the only one whose reputation has
been continually increasing, and it must be owned that he has acted
with wonderful temper and good sense."[52] About the same time
more influential men in England were passing judgment on Lafayette's work. Edmund Burke, who was already putting down on
paper the diatribe that was to appear later that year as *Reflections
on the French Revolution,* with an unfriendly remark on Lafayette,[53] attacked the French in the British Parliament as "the ablest
architects of ruin that had hitherto existed" and denounced "the
assumption of citizenship by the army" as "the very worst part" of
the French example. In reply Richard B. Sheridan joined Charles
James Fox in defense of the revolution in France, Sheridan paying
"high compliments" to Lafayette "and others of the French
patriots."[54]

On the day after Louis XVI's speech, the commander of the National Guard accompanied the mayor and a deputation consisting
of one Representative per district to the Tuileries to express the
Commune's gratitude. They rode to the palace through lanes of
"admiring citizens of all orders."[55] Bailly's address stressed the

---

[51] Staël-Holstein to Gustavus III, Feb. 7, Staël-Holstein, pp. 154–57.

[52] Lt. Robert Arbuthnot to Sir William Arbuthnot, Feb. 7, privately communicated.

[53] Everyman's Library edition (New York, 1953), p. 217.

[54] *The Parliamentary History of England from the Earliest Period to the Year 1803,*
XXVIII (London, 1816), 354–69 (Feb. 9).

[55] *Courrier de Paris,* Feb. 7, p. 49.

confidence of the capital: "You will be Louis the Just, Louis the Good, Louis the Wise; you will be truly Louis the Great," and Louis, thanking the mayor, promised to visit the city's institutions, especially those that served the people, hoping that the Parisians' demonstration of respect for law would provide a wholesome example to other cities of the realm.[56] On the following day the same deputation waited upon the queen, who repeated her pledge to adhere to her husband's principles.[57]

A number of the Paris districts felt that they should express their gratitude not through their Representatives alone but more directly. Several districts proposed that all of the district presidents and battalion commanders should wait upon the king and assure him of the respect and loyalty of the whole commune. The District des Filles-Saint-Thomas proposed, besides, that the division chiefs and the commander of the cavalry should be invited to join the deputation, with the mayor and the commandant general at its head. Lafayette and the other city officials readily agreed, and February 12 was set as the date for the ceremony.[58]

National Guard units were sometimes too impatient, however, to wait for the appointed day. Some detachments went to their district churches to take or, in some cases, to repeat the civic vow, the parish priests officiating; others came to the Hôtel de Ville to bind themselves to the new oath in the presence of the Representatives.[59] On February 11 eight battalions marched into the Place de Grève at one time. Since they numbered between three and four thousand men, they decided to take their oath outdoors, drawn up in front of the Hôtel de Ville. Accordingly, Lafayette and the Representatives went down to the square,[60] where he briefly addressed the assemblage: "French patriots, citizens, and soldiers, you who unite under these titles have come to promise to defend the Law, the Nation, the King, and Liberty. This is the most beautiful day of

---

[56] Lacroix, IV, 1, 3–4 (Feb. 5). See also *Journal général de la cour*, Feb. 7, p. 299; Desmoulins, *Révolutions*, No. 12, pp. 557–60; and *Patriote français*, Feb. 8, p. 3.

[57] Lacroix, IV, 9, 12–13 (Feb. 6), and *Journal général de la cour*, Feb. 7, pp. 299–301.

[58] Lacroix, IV, 1, 5–6 (Feb. 5), 9 (Feb. 6), and the note on pp. 83–88.

[59] *Ibid.*, IV, 1 (Feb. 5), 17–18 (Feb. 6), 26 (Feb. 8), 45–46 (Feb. 9), 65 (Feb. 11), 77–78 (Feb. 12), 95–100 (Feb. 13), and the note on pp. 120–24. See also *Révolutions de Paris* (Tournon), No. 30, Jan. 30–Feb. 5, p. 14.

[60] Lacroix, IV, 63 and n. 1.

our lives. Let us swear then to be faithful forever to our oaths. Let us swear to die in defense of the Laws of the Nation." The soldiers answered: "We so swear!" Then they shouted "Long live the Nation, the King, Liberty, and M. the Commandant."[61]

As the news of the king's speech and the National Assembly's oath spread to the provinces, citizens and National Guards assembled in squares and churches to take the pledge. For a fortnight the words "I so swear" solemnly echoed and re-echoed throughout the realm.[62] In the provinces the desire to keep up with the mainstream of the Revolution fostered the desire for a generalissimo for a nationwide citizen militia. On February 5, the National Guard units of the Vivarais, gathered at Puy-en-Vélay (now Le Puy), not far from Lafayette's birthplace (Chavaniac), took the oath, and by "universal acclamation" elected him "Generalissimo of the National Troops of Velay and Vivarais."[63] From Brittany, where he owned large estates, came a petition entreating the Paris Assembly of Representatives to urge him to accept command of the Rennes National Guard. While acknowledging their pleasure over the honor thus bestowed upon their commandant general, the Representatives replied that their own principles as well as Lafayette's forbade his acceptance of any National Guard command other than those of Paris and its vicinity.[64]

Meanwhile Lafayette continued his other serious duties, among which was the discussion of proposed provisions of the new constitution with his fellow deputies. In response to the request of the National Assembly's Constitution Committee for advice on the organization of the National Guards of the realm, he was now able to provide a draft of the regulations that the Paris Military Committee had drawn up. On February 11 he invited a deputation of his Military Committee to his home to meet I.-R.-G. Le Chapelier, a member of the National Assembly's Constitution Committee,

---

[61] *Journal général de la cour*, Feb. 12, p. 341.

[62] *Moniteur*, Feb. 12, p. 169; *Révolutions de Paris* (Tournon), No. 30, Jan. 30–Feb. 5, pp. 16, 23; *Gazette de Leide, supplément*, Feb. 19; and *Courier français*, Feb. 11, pp. 335–36.

[63] *Journal général de la cour*, Feb. 13, pp. 347–48.

[64] Lacroix, IV, 24–25 (Feb. 8).

and Le Chapelier asked him and his colleagues to meet with the
Constitution Committee when it should take up the reorganization
of the National Guard. On the following day the Paris committee
elected four members to accompany its president, Lafayette, whenever such a meeting should take place.[65]

Decisions on these matters, however, were delayed by sharp
dissensions over the king's authority in foreign and military affairs. The shadow of war lengthened[66] even as the king was trying
to save his prerogatives by an alliance with the deputies of Lafayette's persuasion. To complicate the situation further, not all high
French military officers shared Lafayette's enthusiasm for the Revolution. He hoped, however, to be able to use Louis XVI's declaration in favor of the constitution to rally wavering military commanders to support the National Assembly.

As early as the previous November, when reports had circulated
that the counterrevolutionaries were planning to take the king
to Metz,[67] Lafayette had cautiously encouraged an effort to win
the hesitant military to the support of the Revolution. The initiative on that occasion apparently had been taken by the Marquis
Achille de Châtelet, who had come to know Lafayette well only
recently but was better known to Lafayette's cousin the Marquis de
Bouillé. Shortly after the October Days, Châtelet had decided that
the country would profit from a liaison of Lafayette with Bouillé,
who was commander of one of the best disciplined forces in the
royal army, with headquarters at Metz. Bouillé had so far hesitated
to take the new civic oath, and his hesitation had roused considerable animosity among the inhabitants of Metz.[68] Châtelet and Lafayette spoke seriously about Bouillé, and Lafayette got the impression that Bouillé had instructed Châtelet to sound him out,
while Châtelet got the impression (or pretended he had) that Lafayette wanted him to take steps to bring about an understanding
with Bouillé. If a war were to break out, Lafayette would prefer,

---

[65] Procès-verbal du Comité militaire, Part II, pp. 56–58.

[66] See below, pp. 280–83.

[67] See above, p. 90.

[68] Marquis de Bouillé, Mémoires, ed. MM. Berville and Barrière (Paris, 1822), pp.
96–97.

Châtelet gathered, to push Bouillé rather than Rochambeau for commanding general if Bouillé could be won to the popular cause.[69] Shortly after the October Days Châtelet had made his first move to bring about an understanding toward that end. He wrote a letter to Bouillé, implying that he did so upon Lafayette's suggestion[70] (which Lafayette later denied).[71] The commandant general, he stated, felt that "all well-intentioned men should unite to defend the king and the constitution," and Châtelet himself considered "the safety of public affairs absolutely dependent upon the close cooperation of you two."[72]

Bouillé had known Lafayette for years as a younger cousin, and more recently as a public figure. He believed him to be more ambitious than able but not dishonest, and since at the moment Lafayette held great power while Bouillé was discouraged, he was willing that the two of them cooperate, provided their views did not clash. So, after some hesitation, Bouillé wrote Châtelet that if Lafayette would tell him his principles and if they proved satisfactory, he would "join with him to save the *patrie*," warning, however, that, though he did not want the return of arbitrary power, he wanted the prevailing disorder even less: he hoped for a government strong enough to defend the country from outside attack and to maintain order and a reasonable amount of freedom within.[73] Châtelet sent this letter to Lafayette, who wrote to Bouillé that day, but his letter apparently went astray.[74] After some time had passed, Bouillé, having received no reaction, took occasion, in a formal communication regarding such military matters as the return of deserters in Paris and of army equipment seized during the July uprising, to raise the political issue again. If the Paris com-

---

[69] Châtelet to Bouillé, Nov. 20, *ibid.*, pp. 89–93. Lafayette denied (*Mémoires*, IV, 99–100, 163) that Châtelet ever was his aide, as Bouillé alleged.

[70] Châtelet to Bouillé, [*post* Oct. 6], Bouillé, pp. 84–86.

[71] *Mémoires*, IV, 99.

[72] See above, n. 70.

[73] Bouillé to Châtelet, Oct. 30 [?], Bouillé, pp. 86–88. The original of this letter in CU: Lafayette Archives, Carton V (microfilm) is dated Oct. 23.

[74] Châtelet to Bouillé, Nov. 20, Bouillé, p. 92, which is corroborated by Lafayette to Bouillé, Nov. 14, *Mémoires*, II, 424.

mander could rally honest and courageous men around him to save the country, Bouillé promised his cooperation: "May the troubles that surround you soon end, . . . and I will gladly join with all those who have correct, pure intentions and are of the same mind."[75]

After another wait of over two weeks for a reply, Bouillé wrote again about deserters, this time protesting also against the calumnies that were spreading in Paris about him and which he was certain were due to his efforts to preserve discipline among his troops: "I take pleasure in the thought that my principles are yours as well as all true citizens'."[76] He wrote again on November 19, but only to ask for favors for two of his officers.[77]

Weeks having passed without an answer from Lafayette, Bouillé, chagrined, wrote to Châtelet reproaching him for having encouraged him to believe that Lafayette would receive his overture favorably. Châtelet's reply explained that Lafayette had in fact written to Bouillé and was concerned that his letter either had gone astray or had been intercepted in the mails, and he gave his reasons for feeling convinced that Lafayette really wanted to cooperate: "He has struck me as a man devoured by the desire to put his name at the head of the revolution of this country as Washington has put his at the head of that in America." Although lacking the genius to command events, Lafayette was, Châtelet judged, at least an honest and deserving man, and what was needed, he implied, was an alliance of a man of Bouillé's principles with Lafayette's indecision.[78]

Even before Châtelet sent that letter, Lafayette had, in fact, responded to Bouillé's direct approach. He did so in a long, outspoken epistle detailing the difficulties of his situation. He lamented the complications created by deserters but declared that it would be unjust to believe him guilty of negligence in his attempts to send them back to their regiments. At one time, he confessed, he had been glad to have soldiers who might have been used against him desert and join his forces, but that time had passed, and now he re-

---

[75] Bouillé to Lafayette, Oct. 31, CU: Lafayette Archives, Carton V (microfilm). See also Bouillé, pp. 88–89.

[76] Nov. 18, CU: Lafayette Archives, Carton V (microfilm).

[77] Nov. 19, *ibid.*

[78] Châtelet to Bouillé, Nov. 20, Bouillé, pp. 89–93.

garded desertions as "one of the most dangerous plagues afflict-ing the realm." The government of Paris honestly was sending back all who had come in violation of the king's orders as soon as they were discovered. To prove his point, he offered to send Bouillé a copy of his twice-weekly inspection sheets. He was equally frank, though briefer, regarding the confiscated military property, indicat-ing that he favored replacement for royal property and compensa-tion for private property.

The rest of Lafayette's letter carefully analyzed the political situation at the time (November 1789). "We both have loved lib-erty," he declared. "I have considered necessary a heavier dose of it than you, and I wanted it for the people and by the people." But the kind of revolution he wanted had already been accomplished, and "today we fear the same evils—anarchy, civil dissensions, and the breakdown of all public authority; we hope for the same good things—the restoration of credit, the consolidation of constitutional liberty, the return of order, and a strong measure of executive power." He believed a counterrevolution now "happily impossible" and, moreover, criminal, since it would bring civil war and the massacre of the weaker party. The king was convinced of the truth of this view, he continued, and all good men should be. "The National Assembly, after having destroyed at Versailles, begins to build in Paris," and as confidence grew, it would become more con-structive. "And the more you, my dear cousin, rally to the new con-stitution, the greater chance you will have to serve the public wel-fare." As for himself, circumstances and the people's confidence, he modestly claimed, had placed on him a degree of responsibility far superior to his talents, but he had proved that he despised faction as much as he loved liberty, and he eagerly awaited the day when he could show that no personal ambition motivated his action. Mean-while he hoped to meet with his "dear cousin's" approbation.[79]

Bouillé was not wholly satisfied with this response. He hated despotism as much as Lafayette did, he rejoined, but he was con-

[79] *Mémoires*, II, 421–24, gives the full text of this letter under date of Nov. 14. Bouillé, pp. 93–94, gives only that part of it which pertains to the political situation and assigns it the date of Nov. 15. Some slight differences of emphasis occur in the two versions. We have followed Lafayette's, which is exactly the same as the copy in CU: Lafayette Archives, Carton V (microfilm).

vinced that excessively liberal measures would not endure whereas "reasonable and moderate liberty would last for a long time." Still, he was ready to second the quest of all good Frenchmen for the happiness of the nation and the destruction of arbitrary power.[80] This brief reply to Lafayette's screed, as Bouillé afterward confessed, was intended to be noncommittal in the hope of finding out more about Lafayette's purposes.[81] In December Bouillé wrote at least twice more to Lafayette, once merely about some soldiers[82] but the other time to inform him that his son was going to Paris and he had asked him to see Lafayette often.[83]

Lafayette did not reply to any of Bouillé's letters for weeks. In the meantime the general at Metz maintained his hold upon his army, waiting for a favorable moment to serve the king. Upon Latour du Pin's request, however, he took the new oath of loyalty to the nation, law, and king, thus lessening his unpopularity with the townspeople of Metz.[84] For a time complaints against him subsided, but in February reports again came to the National Assembly alleging that Bouillé opposed fraternization between his soldiers and the National Guards and refused to provide arms for the Guard from the king's stores at Metz. The Metz National Guard also asked the Paris commander to intervene in their behalf.

This was a delicate matter, however, for Bouillé must not be alienated. His military talents were generally recognized, and his garrison at Metz would be a principle bulwark in case of war if he remained loyal to the revolutionary cause. But would he? Shortly after Louis XVI's speech in the National Assembly Lafayette learned that Bouillé, overwhelmed that the king "had surrendered without reservation to madmen and criminals," spoke of resigning his post and leaving France.[85] Apologizing for his delay in answer-

---

[80] Bouillé to Lafayette, Nov. 20, Bouillé, pp. 95–96. The original in CU: Lafayette Archives, Carton V (microfilm), differs in wording but not essentially except in the omission of the salutation *mon cher cousin*.

[81] Bouillé, pp. 94–95.

[82] Dec. 17, CU: Lafayette Archives, Carton V (microfilm).

[83] Dec. 25, *ibid*.

[84] Bouillé, pp. 96–97.

[85] *Ibid*., pp. 104–5.

ing his cousin's letters, Lafayette wrote to Bouillé, hoping to dissuade him: "Today, all of us ought to rally around the king to confirm a constitution which you like less than I do, which may have some defects, but which assures public liberty and which has taken too firm a hold on the minds of Frenchmen to permit its enemies to attack it without upsetting the monarchy." All honest men now belonged to the same party, of which the king had declared himself to be the head: "Let us give him the reward due his virtue, all of us joining with him to restore order."

Then, alluding to the troubles at Metz, Lafayette begged his cousin "to arrange matters to the general satisfaction." Unlike some other generals, Bouillé was in a good position to restore cordial feelings without weakening military discipline. The best way to secure for the king the desired constitutional authority was "to convince the friends of liberty of the perfect accord of all agents of the executive power with the king's principles." He had heard, Lafayette admitted, that the general had thought of quitting his *patrie,* "as if your talents do not belong to it, as if even some private injuries could give you the right to rob us of the battles you will win for us and in which I hope you will allow me to fight under your orders." As for himself, he did not, he repeated, expect to benefit from the Revolution personally. The king's recent speech presented a good reason for him to renew his engagement not to profit from his extraordinary position, and he urged his "dear cousin" to seize the same occasion to make his peace with the friends of the constitution. "When someone says: 'M. de Bouillé has the greatest talents and the confidence of his troops,' I would like it if no one would add: 'He is the enemy of our principles.'" Lafayette apologized for his bluntness, but, "I have recounted to you only what has been said to me twenty times in the last three days, and I would like not to hear this reproach against you again."[86]

In a postscript added the next day Lafayette suggested how Bouillé could make a show of conciliation. Bouillé had insisted on keeping his royal command aloof from the citizen army of

---

[86] Lafayette to Bouillé, Feb. 10, *Mémoires,* II, 441–43. Bouillé's version (pp. 105–7) omits the significant sentence: "La démarche du roi est une occasion." Bouillé replied to this letter on Feb. 19; see below, p. 358.

Metz, but Metz had chosen as commander of its National Guard a Lieutenant-Colonel Duteil of Bouillé's artillery. Lafayette, as requested by the Metz National Guard, had obtained Louis XVI's approval of that choice, but the Metz National Guard had asked him, besides, to get the king's permission for Duteil to continue to hold his rank in Bouillé's artillery as well. Lafayette believed that Bouillé ought to grasp this opportunity to assuage local public opinion.[87] Whatever became of that suggestion, for a while at least Bouillé reluctantly reconciled himself to the king's new revolutionary posture.

Others fell in more readily with the prevalent spirit of national reconciliation. The Comte de Provence and the Duc d'Orléans (the latter from London by affidavit) took the new oath. On February 9, Bailly invited the National Assembly to attend a *Te Deum* the next Sunday at which the Paris National Guard proposed to pledge allegiance to the forthcoming constitution.[88] On February 10 Louis XVI, true to his word, giving up seclusion in the Tuileries, went with Marie Antoinette and their children to the Cathedral of Notre Dame, and Lafayette accompanied them. Escorted without ceremony by only a small guard, they drove to the cathedral and attended mass. After the service, they visited the Enfants Trouvés, where Marie Antoinette took her son to see some seventy abandoned babies and enjoined him to remember that someday it would be his duty to protect poor orphans like them. The queen herself took a newly arrived foundling in her arms and kissed it. The newspapers waxed eloquent about this touching evidence of the queen's *sensibilité*. By the time the king's party was ready to leave, the neighboring streets had filled with people, and the little procession made its way back to the palace through crowds of happy Parisians shouting, "Long live the king, the queen, and the dauphin!"[89]

That day Morris again dined at the Lafayettes'. Among the

---

[87] Lafayette to Bouillé, Feb. 10, *Mémoires*, II, 443.

[88] *Patriote français*, Feb. 16, p. 4, and *AP*, IX, 535 (Feb. 9), 548–51 (Feb. 11), 638 (Feb. 18).

[89] *Journal général de la cour*, Feb. 11, pp. 334–35; *Moniteur*, Feb. 20, p. 204; *Courier national*, Feb. 11, p. 8; *Courier français*, Feb. 11, p. 335; and *Journal de Paris*, Feb. 13, p. 176.

papers he had recently received from America was a copy of an address Washington had made on January 8 to the Congress, and he read it to Lafayette.[90] Presumably Lafayette rejoiced to hear Washington's description of the "present favorable prospects" of American affairs and at least silently appreciated how pat for the moment were such sentiments as "A free people ought not only to be armed but disciplined" and "Every valuable end of government is best answered by the enlightened confidence of the people."[91]

Lafayette had reason to believe that the government of France at last had won "the enlightened confidence of the people." All the districts of Paris but Danton's Cordeliers and seven others accepted the proposal of the District des Filles-Saint-Thomas to choose representatives to pay their respects to their ruler. On February 12 the other fifty-two sent the presidents of their assemblies to wait on the king, thirty-five sent their battalion commanders as well, and Lafayette, Bailly, and the chiefs of three National Guard divisions accompanied them.[92] After Saint-Priest had led them into the king's presence and Bailly had presented the district representatives and division chiefs to His Majesty, the spokesman for the presidents pledged the loyalty of the districts, and the spokesman for the battalion commanders declared that the Paris National Guards had sworn "to pour out the last drop of their blood to maintain your constitutional authority and the safety of your sacred person." In response, Louis XVI expressed his satisfaction with the districts and the National Guard. The deputations then waited upon the queen, who received them in the company of her daughter and the dauphin. The spokesman expressed gratitude for her interest in the unfortunate and for her pledge to rear the dauphin in the principles of his virtuous father, "the best of kings" and "the restorer of liberty." Marie Antoinette affirmed her deep appreciation of these sentiments: "The zeal shown by the National Guards during our sojourn here proves their loyalty and assures them of our good will."[93]

---

[90] Morris diary, Feb. 10, Davenport (ed.), I, 408.

[91] Fitzpatrick (ed.), XXX, 491–94.

[92] Lacroix, IV, 87–88 n. 2, 91–93.

[93] Ibid., pp. 80, 89; Journal général de la cour, Feb. 14, p. 355; Chronique de Paris, Feb. 13, p. 174; Journal de Paris, Feb. 14, pp. 177–79; and Moniteur, Feb. 16, p. 184.

This and similar ceremonies following upon the king's gracious address of February 4 were but preliminary to the pageant planned for Sunday, February 14. For that occasion the dean of the Cathedral of Notre Dame had increased the seating capacity with new benches. In addition to the officers and men representing each battalion and to the members of the National Assembly, so many ministerial, city, military, and other dignitaries had been invited that others could be admitted by ticket only, and more asked for tickets than could be accommodated.[94] Lafayette chose to identify himself with his men rather than with the municipal officers or the deputies of the National Assembly and as the National Guard commander, to ride at the head of the escort of the National Assembly.[95]

On February 14, shortly after booming cannon announced the dawn, the National Guard was on foot, some marching out to line the route of the National Assembly from the Manège to Notre Dame, others clearing the streets for the municipal officers' procession from the Place de Grève to the cathedral. With battalion flags flying, the color guards of the sixty districts fell into line on the cathedral parvis. The Dames de la Halle, who traditionally marched ahead of the city's processions dressed in ceremonial white, gathered on the Rue Saint-Honoré outside the National Assembly's hall, and in the streets behind them cavalry, grenadiers, chasseurs, fusiliers, and volunteer companies took their places. Thousands of people packed themselves at the windows on the lines of march and on every street and square that the rows of guards had not blocked off.

Shortly before eleven o'clock, Lafayette ordered the procession to start from the Manège. The Dames de la Halle, carrying baskets filled with flowers and wearing blue-white-and-red cockades, moved out ahead, followed by the National Guard. When the last detachment of the Guards had passed, Lafayette, mounted on a handsome white prancer and accompanied by his staff and division chiefs also on horseback, joined the procession. Behind them came

---

[94] Lacroix, IV, 27–28 (Feb. 8), 63 (Feb. 11), 96, 106 (Feb. 13), 115–16 (Feb. 15); *Journal général de la cour*, Feb. 14, p. 358; *Courier français*, Feb. 15, p. 367; and *AP*, XI, 584 (Feb. 13).

[95] *AP*, XI, 596 (Feb. 14), and Lacroix, IV, 116 (Feb. 15).

the deputies of the National Assembly, flanked on both sides by uniformed men. As they passed, the National Guards lining the streets presented arms. The air of quiet dignity was broken only by the sound of drums, the footfall of the marchers, and the hoof-beats of the horses.[96] Paris had seen many magnificent parades, but never before had it seen the deputies of a sovereign people proceed as a body through its streets.

An artillery salute greeted the National Assembly as it entered the cathedral square and continued toward the portal through a lane formed by the color guards of the sixty battalions and their escorts. The Guards presented arms as their general rode past, followed by the long line of deputies. Only then did the crowd break its silence, and resounding applause mingled with the music of the band, the ringing of bells, and the salvos of artillery. At the portal Lafayette, his staff, and the division chiefs dismounted and joined the mayor, the dean, and the cathedral chapter. It took about an hour for deputies, Representatives, and ministers to reach their assigned places. The dean and the cathedral chapter meanwhile stood before the nave altar, with Lafayette and Bailly at opposite ends of the altar steps. On the front of the altar were emblazoned the words "God, the Law, and the King." At last Gouvion led a long line of National Guard officers, detachments, and color guards into the cathedral nave. Spectators filled the galleries. Outside, the skies were overcast, giving only a dull, gray light, but the altar tapers created circles of brightness inside.

The ceremony began with the celebration of mass at the nave altar. Then came a sermon on the text of the story of Asa the king (II Chron. 15), who found his people without the true God and without law but turned them again to Jehovah. After elaborating on the righteousness of an alliance of king and people, the preacher reminded the assembled troops that in swearing to be loyal to their

---

[96] *Courrier de Paris*, Feb. 15, pp. 177–79, gave the fullest account of the celebration. See also Lacroix, IV, 115–19; *AP*, XI, 596–600; *Chronique de Paris*, Feb. 15, pp. 182–83; *Journal général de la cour*, Feb. 15, pp. 364–66; *Moniteur*, Feb. 21, p. 210; *Courier national*, Feb. 15, pp. 2–5; *Courier français*, Feb. 16, pp. 366–67; *Gazette de Leide, supplément*, Feb. 23, 26; *Révolutions de Paris* (Tournon), No. 32, Feb. 13–20, pp. 3–4, 20–22, and engraving facing p. 31; *Patriote français*, Feb. 16, pp. 3–4; Ferrières, I, 390; and *Courrier de Provence*, Feb. 14–19, pp. 181–84.

country they were pledging themselves to conquer liberty, that in repressing license while maintaining liberty and in protecting the king while upholding the constitution they would banish tyranny and slavery and establish the rule of law and freedom.[97] Bailly then walked to the front of the altar, bowed to the National Assembly, and recited the patriotic oath: "I swear to be faithful to the nation, the law, and the king, and to defend the constitution unto death." Instantly the color guards dipped their flags; the officers drew their swords, crossed them, and formed an archway of interlocking steel down the center passage of the long nave; and once more the deputies, with hands upraised, swore to defend the constitution "unto death." The Assembly of Representatives, the royal ministers, the military, and the others inside the cathedral repeated the words "unto death"; and as those words rang out from hundreds of throats, the people outside heard them and also shouted "unto death." Once again bells tolled, drums rolled, and cannon thundered; and at that moment, the skies cleared, and sunshine streamed through the stained glass windows, bathing the National Guards and their standards in a warming light.[98]

Lafayette's cause seemed triumphant. He was the commandant general of the country's most reliable military force, which had just sworn to defend a set of laws that he anticipated would be worthy of their confidence. He was a general in the army of a once absolute monarch who had consented to be the leader of his revolutionary people and defender of their forthcoming constitution. He was an influential figure in the constituent body that was bringing forth that constitution. Truly, he had much to be thankful for as the cathedral choir began to chant the *Te Deum*.

The service ended, the National Guard marched out of the cathedral. Lafayette, the mayor, the city's representatives, and the nation's deputies followed. In the square the military waited in the wide avenue formed by the sixty battalions. Lafayette and his officers mounted and headed the procession of the deputies back to the Manège, while other officers and National Guard units escorted

---

[97] *AP*, XI, 597–600. See "Bibliographical Note" below, p. 228.

[98] See above, n. 96.

the mayor and the Representatives to the Hôtel de Ville, past crowds that greeted them with shouts of "Long live the nation!" "Long live the king!" "Long live the National Assembly!" It was mid-afternoon before the last units of National Guards ended the parade. After nightfall, hundreds of Parisians gathered in the Place de Grève to see the illuminations in the windows of the Hôtel de Ville. Great transparencies shone in the darkness, flashing patriotic sentiments—among them a paraphrase of a sentence in the king's speech to the National Assembly: "I shall maintain liberty, and my wishes are in accord with your principles."[99]

BIBLIOGRAPHICAL NOTES

Lafayette's letters to Jared Sparks in the Harvard College Library, though of a much later date than 1789–90, sometimes contain, as befits correspondence with a historian, reflections on the past not otherwise available.

The notes by Lacroix on the events of February 12 and 14 (IV, 83–94, 115–19) are full, and they cite or quote at length a number of contemporary sources. The *Archives parlementaires* (XI, 596–600) treats the events of the fourteenth as a session of the National Assembly but gives nearly all its space to Abbé Mulot's sermon (without indicating its source). In general the two accounts jibe. We have pieced in details from other sources; see n. 96 above.

Somewhere between 1797 and 1800 Lafayette wrote a lengthy comment (*Mémoires*, IV, 98–117) on Bouillé's memoirs, which were first published in English although the editors of Lafayette's *Mémoires* (IV, 98 n.) changed the page references to those in the French edition (1821). Neither Bouillé nor Lafayette published the correspondence between them in full, but a more complete set of their letters is now available in the originals in the Cornell University Library on microfilm and in the Archives Nationales (not the Bibliothèque Nationale, as incorrectly stated in Gottschalk and Maddox, p. 391, and at various points in the revised [1965] edition of the earlier volumes by Gottschalk on Lafayette). The complete set makes clear that the correspondence was appreciably more friendly, less businesslike on Bouillé's part than the versions in his memoirs would lead one to infer, although insofar as he quotes them, he does so accurately enough.

[99] See above n. 96, and esp. *Courier national*, Feb. 15, p. 5.

CHAPTER XI

Police Power or Agrarian Reform?

THE émigrés, the Comte d'Artois in Turin foremost among them, were perhaps the most frustrated that the king had decided to play the role of leader of the Revolution. Many of them saw in the new turn of affairs a victory for Lafayette. But the Marquis de Vaudreuil, who, though himself an émigré in Rome, was well informed of what went on at the Tuileries, assumed that despite appearances to the contrary, Lafayette was not yet entirely the master of France.[1]

Yet the idea of a master for France—of a dictatorship—was in the air. Notwithstanding the confidence engendered by the king's gracious surrender to the Revolution, new crises seemed to call for a strong hand to preserve order. Urban discontent abided for several all too familiar reasons—unemployment, rising prices, tax rebellion, war scare, food shortages, religious disputes, political agitation. In addition, in the rural areas payment was still sometimes demanded of seignorial obligations that the peasants believed to have been canceled by the famous August Decrees, which presumably had abolished "feudalism," and they felt betrayed. Recurrent alarm was brought to a head by the lynching of five collectors of the hated salt tax in Beziers.[2]

In the expectation of a thoroughgoing debate on that tragedy Lafayette once more turned to others for advice. Short had lately become Jefferson's surrogate both as representative of the United States and as adviser to Lafayette. When Lafayette and La Rochefoucauld joined with some others to form a new club, dedicated to

---

[1] Vaudreuil to Artois, Feb. 13, Pingaud (ed.), I, 102. See also same to same, Feb. 27, Mar. 13, 20, *ibid.*, pp. 123–24, 138–39, 143, 149.

[2] *AP*, XI, 613–16 (Feb. 16).

the moderate revolutionary principles of 1789 (the Société de Quatre-Vingt-Neuf), they had proposed (without consulting those they honored) the names of Washington, Franklin, Jefferson, and Short (but not Morris) for membership.[3] When the proposals of the Judiciary Committee for the reorganization of the French law courts came up for consideration, Lafayette had sent copies of the committee's report to Short (and also to Morris) asking for comment.[4] Now that the issue of rural disorder had become critical, Lafayette asked the American chargé d'affaires to go with him to talk about it with Thouret, who was a member of the Constitution Committee. Early on February 15 the three men held a consultation "about the Means of quelling Riots." They apparently agreed that in the event that municipal officers failed to act in an emergency, the National Guard commanders be given power to act on their own initiative.[5]

Lafayette still had this problem on his mind later that day, when both Short and Morris came to call. Taking them into his study, he spoke freely on the political situation. When he told of the suggested plan to authorize local military commanders to act on their own authority Morris was shocked, and he warned Lafayette that it would have "evil Consequences personal and political." But, Lafayette countered, what are we to do if the civil authorities fail to use the powers committed to them for law enforcement? Morris answered that the decentralization brought about by the "Institution of the [elective] Municipalities is radically wrong" and would bring on "endless Confusion and great Debility," but the people had been "flattered . . . with such extravagant Notions of Liberty" that the system could not be altered "untill Experience shall have made them wiser" and that meanwhile the king should appoint a commissioner for each district to act as guardian of the peace. Lafayette feared that the Assembly would not give the king the power to name such commissioners but might be willing to allow commissioners already appointed for other purposes to exercise

---

[3] Short to Jefferson, Jan. 28, Boyd (ed.), XVI, 133. For a fuller discussion of the Société de 1789 see below, pp. 317–19.

[4] Morris diary, Jan. 26, Davenport (ed.), I, 389.

[5] *Ibid.*, Feb. 15, pp. 411, 413.

such authority until the new municipalities were organized.[6] This conversation made clear, and subsequent debates made clearer, that there seemed to be three alternative solutions of the local disorders—greater responsibility with strict accountability for municipal officials including the National Guard officers, greater authority for the local royal officials, or significant concessions to the demands of rioting crowds. Lafayette and Short evidently thought the Assembly would prefer the first of these, even though Morris considered it a disastrous course.

As the conversation continued, Lafayette candidly stated that he "must give the King a Sugar Plum for his Speech to the Assembly." Morris replied with a smile that there was no sugar plum to give, for the Assembly had "already parcelled out the executive Authority in such a Way that they cannot restore it to the Monarch." Lafayette indicated certain changes of the royal ministry that might be tried, but Morris did not approve of them. France's finances, he added, "are in the High Road to Destruction" and "Anarchy seems to menace and even already to attack on every Quarter."[7] He departed for England shortly after this conversation, not to return to France until the next November, leaving the thirty-year-old Short, in whom he apparently had no great confidence, to act as the principal American consultant to the thirty-two-year-old Lafayette, in whom he had little more.

The next morning Lafayette rode out to the Champs-Elysées with his staff on a bright, sunshiny day to hold a divisional review. Some 4,000 men of the Fourth Division were drawn up in formation, and almost as many spectators had gathered to watch. When the commandant general appeared, the crowd welcomed him with shouts of "Vive Lafayette!"[8] Some of them had been beguiled there by the hope that the king would appear, but he did not come, giving as his reason that his public appearances created too much in-

---

[6] *Ibid.*, 411–12.

[7] *Ibid.*

[8] *Courier français,* Feb. 17, p. 384; *Révolutions de Paris* (Tournon), No. 32, Feb. 13–20, p. 24; and *Journal général de la cour,* Feb. 16, p. 374, Feb. 17, p. 381; *Chronique de Paris,* Feb. 7, p. 151; *Courrier de Paris,* Feb. 17, pp. 215–16; and *Révolutions de Paris* (Prudhomme), No. 32, Feb. 13–20, p. 6.

convenience for those who guarded him.[9] For over an hour the troops performed their drill with élan as spectators cheered. After inspection, Lafayette administered the patriotic oath to the division, the soldiers responded with "I so swear!" and the bystanders also took up the cry. When at last the Guards marched off, the crowds gathered around Lafayette and followed him as he rode from the field.

Thus escorted, the commander of the Paris National Guard arrived at the Manège some time after the day's session had opened.[10] He entered the Assembly in time to participate in a solemn debate on provincial disorders. Talleyrand, the newly chosen president of the National Assembly, had read a letter from Champion de Cicé describing the lynching at Béziers and pointing out that the local authorities had not helped the local royal soldiery to preserve order. The deputies were horrified. Emmery proposed that the Constitution Committee bring in by the following day a bill designed to deal with future events of a similar nature. Another deputy advocated that cavalry be stationed in the villages. Still another proposed that the local authorities use persuasion and enlightenment to counteract the exploitation of ignorance by agitators.[11]

Lafayette now went to the tribune. Prolonged applause welcomed him, and then silence as his colleagues listened. Several times already, he began, the National Assembly had expressed its indignation at excesses such as those just denounced, but the excesses had not ceased. On the contrary, they had multiplied. "The people, above all, want liberty, but they also want justice and peace; they expect them not only from the end product of our work but also from our provisional decrees; they expect them from the zeal of civil and municipal officers, who, if they set greater store by their popularity than their duties, thereby become unworthy. The people expect them also from a vigorous executive authority, which must no longer be sought among ruins but where it actually is, in the constitution." The executive authority ought to be vested "by and for" the constitution with sufficient energy to restore pub-

---

[9] Lescure (ed.), II, 408 (Dec. 16), 424 (Feb. 16).

[10] See above, n. 8.

[11] *AP*, XI, 613-15 (Feb. 16).

lic order, "without which liberty is never either sweet or assured." Lafayette thus formally committed himself to a policy of cooperation of king, Assembly, and local officials to assuage popular discontent by both repression of disorder and concession to the demands for reform. Before he concluded, he joined Emmery in stressing the urgent need for action by the Constitution Committee. Applause again broke out as he left the tribune.

In a brief speech Mirabeau then asked that the Communications Committee concert with the Constitution Committee to bring in a bill covering instances when the civil authorities might fail to use the means at their disposal to preserve order.[12] The Assembly instructed its committees accordingly. Mirabeau thus once more supported Lafayette publicly, yet privately he still was captious. That day (February 16) he expressed to La Marck, now in Belgium, the fear that the Revolution had reached a critical point where the nation's impatience and its penchant for enthusiasm would make every event an occasion or a pretext to reinforce the royal authority with provisional powers, to the point where the king would be strong enough to forestall a constitution. "Lafayette conspires for royalism by his gallantry," he alleged; "our virtuosi conspire for royalism by their corruption; our democrats conspire for royalism by their divisions and their petty deals to their private advantage," while the country seethed with conflicts, and no one could tell what the outcome would be.[13]

On February 18, as spokesman for the Constitution Committee, Le Chapelier presented a bill to the National Assembly. While intending to safeguard the civil authority against encroachments by the military, the committee sought also to give to officers of the National Guard and the royal army sufficient power to suppress violence in case of negligence or sabotage by civil authorities. Hence, the bill proposed that whenever life, property, or tax collection was threatened by violence, municipal officers be required to declare

---

[12] *Ibid.*, p. 615; *Moniteur*, Feb. 17, p. 192; *Journal de Paris*, Feb. 17, pp. 191–92; *Courier national*, Feb. 17, pp. 4–5; *Courrier de Provence*, Feb. 14–19, pp. 198–99; *Patriote français*, Feb. 17, p. 2; *Point de jour*, Feb. 17, pp. 79–80; *Gazette de Leide*, Feb. 26; and *Mémoires*, II, 381–82.

[13] Bacourt (ed.), I, 465.

martial law and to enforce it or face criminal prosecution for breach of trust; that in their default the officers of justice or, in their default, any four notables of the communal council or, in their default, any eight active citizens be empowered to call out the constabulary, the National Guard, and, if necessary, the regular troops; but that the municipal authorities be permitted to intervene at any point, and the military be required to retire upon their order.

Despite his intense interest in the preservation of order Lafayette did not attend the National Assembly's session that day, for his presence was required elsewhere. On February 18 Paris itself was once more the scene of a serious show of violence. That day several wagons of military supplies moved through the streets of the Faubourg Saint-Antoine toward the city gates, and always suspicious of counterrevolutionary plots and embezzling officials, the people stopped three wagons, not knowing that the mayor's office had given the royal army permission to move them. The National Guardsmen on duty, equally suspicious, sent to the staff for orders, but when an officer arrived to rescue the equipment, he was almost too late. A crowd had gathered, and a riot impended. As soon as word reached Lafayette, he set off to the scene with as many mounted troops as he could muster. He found an excited multitude clustered around a smoking bonfire of tents and stakes, and men busily feeding the flames with additional materials from the wagons. When spectators rushed up to tell him of the plot they had intercepted, he explained that the equipment had originally been intended for soldiers who no longer were stationed in Paris and was now needed by troops at the frontier. The people heeded. Shouting "Long live the commandant general," they gave up the wagons, put out the fire, and dispersed. Upon returning to the Hôtel de Ville Lafayette reported the episode to the Assembly of Representatives.[14] Deputy Lindet described the disturbance to his constituents: "Lafayette, always detested by the party of the opposition, is always the object of the confidence of the Parisians, and he merits their admiration. . . . He gives orders at his home and goes to pay his

---

[14] *Révolutions de Paris* (Tournon), No. 32, Feb. 13–20, illustration facing p. 28, incorrectly dates this episode as of Feb. 19, but see Lacroix, IV, 144 (Feb. 18) and n. 1.

respects to the king, he comes to the National Assembly, he attends the Assembly of the Commune, he holds a review, he is everywhere, he knows everything, he circumvents every [plot]; firm, affable, active, moderate, his ever serene countenance proclaims the impassivity of his soul."[15]

On February 19 Lafayette attended the session of the National Assembly, even though that day Favras was hanged. The Assembly debated not the proposed decree on local disorders, however, but the allowances to be granted to monastics who, the church having been nationalized, would leave their monasteries, and Lafayette took no part in the day's debate. The delay it brought in the consideration of the proposed decree on local disorders made him impatient. He confided later to Mme de Simiane that he was not altogether satisfied with the bill on local disorders; it was "pretty mediocre," he thought, but "it will suffice to establish order anew if provided with some changes that are being made in it." The aristocracy did not want the proposed law, he understood, although Saint-Priest thought that it might do.[16]

As Lafayette left the meeting of the National Assembly that day, someone confidentially proposed to him that he come to an understanding with Mirabeau. Mirabeau's policy and his at this juncture were known to coincide in some respects: both were striving to achieve—and rapidly—a constitution that would be both liberal and acceptable to the king and the moderate royalists in the Assembly; both favored an executive authority strong enough to prevent chaos in the provinces without being strong enough to block constitutional reform. Several colleagues doubtless wanted them to cooperate, but who made this particular proposal of an alliance is unknown; Lafayette did not indicate the go-between's name even to his most trusted confidante. But nothing came of the proposal. Lafayette replied to it (as he himself admitted) a little tartly: "I do not like him, nor do I admire him, nor do I fear him. I see no reason why I should come to an understanding with him."[17] Mirabeau's opinion of Lafayette was hardly more complimentary. He

[15] Montier (ed.), pp. 83–84.

[16] Lafayette to [Mme de Simiane], Feb. 19, *Mémoires*, II, 443–44.

[17] *Ibid.*, p. 444.

privately accused Lafayette of "preferring intrigue to revolution" and of being prepared to run the risk of civil war: "If he acquires some addition to his popularity and command over Paris by contrived eulogies, I am convinced that he loses thereby in power."[18]

As some historians have maintained, again a great opportunity was lost that day to stabilize the Revolution and bring to France the blessings of a moderate monarchical constitution. Those who accept that view, however, are inclined to think of Lafayette as more naïve politically and of Mirabeau as less opportunistic morally than the evidence warrants. The deputy Adrien Duquesnoy, who kept a private diary of events and so wrote neither with an eye for popular appeal nor with the advantage of hindsight, reflected the opinion of contemporary moderates. Mirabeau, he thought, was not only a political intriguer but a cheat in money matters,[19] while Lafayette, "joined to virtue, to a great virtue, a genuine love of the public welfare, the love of true glory, of that pure glory that remorse does not trouble and public hatred does not pursue." Although Mirabeau was more gifted, Duquesnoy believed, he was without marked influence in the National Assembly. He was "impetuous, hasty, threatening, and dominated not by love of good but by hatred, vengeance, and all the violent passions." Lafayette, on the other hand, had an imperturbable sangfroid, never yielded to petty passions or to short-term calculations, and pursued his purpose with candor and directness: "He is truly the man of the Revolution, whom posterity will recognize as the true creator of French liberty. Think what he could have done if he had not had an honest soul, and say if you know many men in history to compare with him. Absolute master of an immense army that obeys him blindly and disciplines itself every day, strong in the enthusiasm of the people and the esteem of the public, what could he not have done if he had been wicked?"[20] To have assumed in 1790 that two such unlike men as Lafayette and Mirabeau could work well together and turn the Revolution into peaceful, wholesome monarchical channels would have been to assume that Mirabeau would

---

[18] Mirabeau to La Marck, Feb. 6, Bacourt (ed.), I, 464.

[19] Duquesnoy, II, 369–70 (Feb. 10). Cf. above, pp. 88–89.

[20] *Ibid.*, pp. 402–4 (Feb. 19).

be guided chiefly by patriotic motives and would succeed where Lafayette was bound to fail. In February 1790 few would have made
such an assumption.

The Constitution Committee, as Lafayette had anticipated, altered its bill on local disorders, but the change had not yet been announced to the National Assembly when on February 20 the debate
reopened. Lafayette was present, having asked to be placed on the
list of speakers.[21] Barnave objected to the provision in the original
bill giving judicial officers, holdovers from the Old Regime, the
power to quell disorder if the municipal authorities failed to do so.
What the committee should have done, Barnave asserted, was to
put pressure on the municipal authorities to do their duty by laying
down specific penalties for their failure to do so.[22] Le Chapelier
then read the committee's revised draft of the bill, and it seemed
to meet Barnave's objections. It stipulated that if any municipal
authorities did not take all necessary steps to protect life, property,
and tax collections and if damage resulted, they would be barred
from public office and held financially liable, and if found guilty of
conniving at disorder, they would be subject to criminal prosecution. The revised bill proposed to give no independent power to
officers of the National Guard, constabulary, or royal army, who
were to remain subject to the civil authorities. Thereupon Mirabeau
asked for time to study the committee's new draft, but since it was
intended to provide merely provisional measures,[23] the Assembly
decided to debate it at once.

Lafayette then took the floor.[24] "The troubles that have occurred and still occur in the provinces," he began, "have shocked
... your sense of justice. You have felt that nothing is more opposed

[21] Lafayette to [Mme de Simiane], Feb. 19, *Mémoires*, II, 444. Note 2, *ibid.*, says that
this letter is about the *loi martiale*, but this note is corrected *ibid.*, III, 516.

[22] *AP*, XI, 652–53.

[23] *Ibid.*, p. 654.

[24] The quotations from Lafayette's speech given below are based on the versions in
AP, XI, 654; *Mémoires*, II, 383; Montlosier, I, 347–48; *Moniteur*, Feb. 22, p. 213; *Point
du jour*, Feb. 21, p. 128; *Journal de Paris*, Feb. 21, pp. 207–8; *Courier français*, Feb. 21, p.
414; *Courrier national*, Feb. 21, p. 6; *Courrier de Provence*, Feb. 20–22, p. 234; *Gazette
de Paris*, Feb. 22, p. 2; *Patriote français*, Feb. 22, p. 2; *Courrier de Paris*, Feb. 22, 23, pp.
314–16; and *Révolutions de Paris* (Tournon), No. 31, Feb. 21–28, p. 42. These sources
do not all agree, but the variants are generally nonessential differences in wording.

to liberty than license, you have thought it necessary not only to establish a new constitution but to provide one that would also be beloved and respected by everyone." He had prepared, he confessed, to speak on the previous draft of the bill, but since the committee had now substituted another that he had not been able to study, he would content himself with a few general observations: "The revolution being over, the only problem that remains is to lay down the constitution. For the revolution disorders were necessary; the old order was only servitude, and in such cases insurrection is the most sacred of duties."

Although Lafayette's words were but an emphatic restatement of those in the Declaration of Rights affirming that resistance to oppression was a natural right, the deputies on the Extreme Right here burst into vehement heckling.[25] Ignoring the outburst (possibly because he knew—what the Right did not know—that he was heading where they might follow), Lafayette hurried on: "But . . . the new order must grow firm, personal safety must be assured, the new constitution must be made an object of love, public power must take on strength and energy." With a constitution that was the "product of a unanimous will," citizens no longer had good reason to rebel and therefore "all insurrection" was "criminal"; consequently insurrection must be opposed at once "with a sufficient repressive force." He urged, however, that the Feudalism Committee (which dealt with agrarian grievances) confer with the Constitition Committee and that any deputy who had any relevant proposals publish them or submit them to the latter committee so that the Assembly might end its debates on the subject, it was hoped not later than the next session.[26]

Montlosier, who was often at odds with Lafayette, later affirmed that he was the wisest person to discuss the provincial disorders.[27] The Moderates and the Leftists among the deputies heard Lafayette with approval, but the Extreme Right disliked his effort to

[25] A. Lameth, I, 352, and *Courrier de Paris*, Feb. 23, p. 316.

[26] See above, n. 24. Full accounts of Lafayette's speech are given in *Courrier de Paris*, Feb. 22, p. 314, and *Patriote français*, Feb. 22, p. 2. The part of the speech in which he denounced insurrection, is largely corroborated by the brief reference to it in *Mémoires*, II, 383, and *AP*, XI, 667, n. 1. See also *Journal de Paris*, Feb. 21, p. 207, and *Point du jour*, Feb. 21, p. 128. The version in *AP*, XI, 654, is incomplete.

[27] Montlosier, I, 347–48.

preserve the Revolution so far achieved—or so, at least, Lafayette thought.[28] He was left to wonder why "those who had the greatest interest in seconding our zeal for the safety of persons and of property" should so often have sought to thwart "the constitutional enemies of anarchy," and he came to the conclusion that it was because they did not want a revolution that stopped at abolishing privilege, for such a revolution might achieve a stable and enduring structure; they preferred revolutionary excesses that might result in a backlash.[29] His suggestion that the Feudalism Committee should be consulted regarding steps to quiet the rural districts apparently was an acceptable compromise to those who preferred appeasement of present unrest to police repression, but not to those who wanted to enhance the royal authority. Speaking from the Right, J.-A.-M. de Cazalès moved that the Assembly confer special emergency power on the king to handle the disorders.[30] Mirabeau protested that Cazalès' plan would make the king a dictator, and Malouet proposed instead that all local officers be made immediately responsible to the king, military commanders being empowered, in case the civil authorities failed to act, to declare martial law. The Assembly then adjourned the debate until the next session.[31]

Lafayette's *obiter dictum* that against depotism "insurrection was the most sacred of duties" was to be long remembered. Years afterward he complained that, taking his words out of context, traducers made him say that insurrection was unconditionally "the most sacred of duties." During the later course of the Revolution, their unqualified formulation was quoted from time to time to harass him, his enemies accusing him as its author of being insincere in the enforcement of law and order and at heart an advocate of anarchy.[32] They failed to mention that he had decried insurrection against a constitutional regime.

The day after Lafayette's speech on "the most sacred of duties"

---

[28] *Mémoires*, II, 384.

[29] *Ibid.*, pp. 384–85, n. 1.

[30] *AP*, XI, 655.

[31] *Ibid.*, p. 658.

[32] *Mémoires*, II, 385–87. See also Vaudreuil to Artois, Mar. 13, Pingaud (ed.), I, 138–39, and A. Lameth, I, 352–56.

was a Sunday. He and his cavalry commander, Ruhlières, had planned that the National Guard cavalry that day have their standards blessed and take the patriotic oath. Again admiring crowds assembled in the streets—this time to watch Ruhlières' men file by on their freshly curried horses to the Cathedral of Notre Dame. As the commandant general passed, cheers rang out: "Long live our General!" and "Long live French liberty!" and he responded with a salute, smiling and bowing to right and left. At the cathedral portal the dean and the mayor greeted them and led the way into the cathedral, while Representatives and other spectators watched from transepts and galleries. The cavalry, having dismounted, marched down the center aisle and took their places in the nave. Ruhlières presented their banners, and as the color guards brought them to the altar, the dean blessed them. Lafayette then made a short talk, appealing reverentially for unity: "The God who comes to bless our arms binds us from this day forth to act only as one family of this august empire."

The ceremony over, Lafayette, his staff, and the cavalry remounted and, taking their places in the procession as before, rode toward the Place de Grève. As they passed, cheers again followed them: "Long live the Nation!" "Long live the King!" "Long live the Commandant General!" Upon reaching the Hôtel de Ville, Lafayette and his staff and all the cavalry went to the Grande Salle, where the Assembly of Representatives, having preceded them, received them and the mayor administered to the cavalry the oath to be faithful to the nation, the law, the king, and the commune, and to defend the constitution unto death.[33]

On Monday, February 22, the National Assembly turned its attention again to the bill for calming the provinces.[34] The debate centered upon whether police power or agrarian reform should receive prior consideration as the means of meeting provincial insurgency. Lafayette's friend La Rochefoucauld opened it with re-

[33] Lacroix, II, 141 (Feb. 18), 176 (Feb. 22); *Journal général de la cour*, Feb. 22, p. 419; and *Courier national*, Feb. 22, p. 8.

[34] The account of the debate that follows depends chiefly on *AP*, XI, 658–740. See also *Moniteur*, Feb. 23, pp. 217–18; *Journal de Paris*, Feb. 23, pp. 214–16; *Point du jour*, Feb. 23, pp. 154–55; *Courier français*, Feb. 23, pp. 427–28; and *Courier national*, Feb. 23, pp. 7–8.

marks supporting the view that to quiet disorder it was necessary both to fill the gaps in the still unfinished work of reform and to tighten the demands on local authorities for the preservation of order. On the other hand, Robespierre, maintaining that the reports of disorder were exaggerated, spoke against the use of force and in favor of more clearly understandable reform measures. Comte de Clermont-Tonnerre, a leader of the Impartiaux, pleaded for a strengthening of the king's hand until the people learned how to use their new-found liberty. "The revolution is over," he declared, "and if you remain in doubt, remember that yesterday you heard those words from the mouth of an honorable member [meaning Lafayette], of the man for whom it is especially appropriate to speak of liberty and revolution."[35] In response, Dupont de Nemours, prominent among the group of economists known as the Physiocrats, stated that the best way to protect life and property would be to hold negligent local authorities financially liable for injury to persons or property resulting from disorder unless the liability could be fixed upon the fomenters of violence.

Then Duport, now generally recognized as a leader of the Jacobin Club, went to the tribune. Arguing that repression was not called for at the moment, he cited the words that Richard Sheridan recently had pronounced in the British House of Commons in praise of France's achievement of liberty under the leadership of Lafayette and other French patriots.[36] Instead of resorting to repression, Duport thought, municipal officers faced with an uprising should move among the people and enlighten them: "Isn't that the method, Gentlemen, most often and most successfully used by the commandant of Paris? How many incipient riots and even riots already under way has he not quieted, not with bayonets but by his sheer presence and by that so moving power which his virtues impart to his appeals."[37] If irony was intended, it escaped contemporary observers.[38] At these words applause filled the hall and "cov-

[35] *AP*, XI, 667, and *Journal de Paris*, Feb. 23, p. 214.

[36] See above, p. 214.

[37] The quotation above is from the version of Duport's speech in *Journal de Paris*, Feb. 23, p. 215. See also *Courier national*, Feb. 23, p. 8.

[38] Georges Michon, *Essai sur l'histoire du parti feuillant. Adrien Duport. Correspon-

ered both him who received and him who had rendered this hom-age."[39] Duport had thus used his forensic skill to turn his opponent's reputation into an argument for his own point of view, which was similar to Robespierre's: Leave the preservation of local order to the new municipalities without augmenting royal authority in local affairs. The Jacobin point of view temporarily seemed to triumph. Prieur de la Marne, destined to become a member of the Jacobin Committee of Public Safety under the Terror, contended that the disorders were the work of counterrevolutionary agents. And Pétion de Villeneuve, destined to become the Jacobin mayor of Paris in 1791, reiterated Robespierre's argument: The accounts of rural lawlessness were exaggerated and the existing *loi martiale* would suffice to maintain order.

Then Mirabeau presented his analysis of the emergency. He scathingly rebuked both those of the Right who proposed a royal dictatorship and those of the Left who opposed putting new vigor into the law. He proposed an alternative set of resolutions that would place heavy penalties on local authorities who failed to apply martial law at times of disorder and that also authorized the con-stabulary, the National Guards, and the royal troops to intervene on their own initiative to keep order unless stopped by command of the local municipality. After Mirabeau, the rich but liberal Duc d'Aiguillon reiterated the Jacobin argument that the local disorders were due to disappointment with the inadequacy of agrarian re-form, and he advocated that a new law on manorial dues, dis-tinguishing those forthwith abolished from those abolished with compensation, be sent to the provinces simultaneously with a new law on local disorders.[40]

---

dance inédite de Barnave in 1792 (Paris, 1924), p. 72, thinks Duport here spoke "not without irony." The *Gazette de Paris* (Feb. 24, p. 4), while eulogizing Lafayette, questioned the wisdom of Duport's reference to him, for a popular demand might arise to give him dictatorial powers and "un éloge maladroit paroit une satyre." See also *ibid.*, Feb. 25, p. 1, repeating the warning: "Every citizen [should] speak to him [Lafayette], even to praise him, only with that respect that is due to the modesty of any man whom adulation causes to blush." Obviously the *Gazette de Paris* thought Duport was *maladroit* rather than *satiri-cal*. See also the "Bibliographical Notes" below, p. 248.

[39] *Journal de Paris*, Feb. 23, p. 215. See also *Gazette de Paris*, Feb. 24, p. 3.

[40] *AP*, XI, 670–72; *Courier national*, Feb. 24, pp. 1–2; and *Journal de Paris*, Feb. 24, pp. 217–19.

The lines of division by this time had sharpened. When Aiguillon left the tribune, Lafayette took his turn, obviously intending to reconcile the opposing factions. "Gentlemen," he pleaded, "in all the arguments I have heard, one great truth impresses me. The people are deceived. We need to correct their error. We need to tell them just how far the promises that have been made go and to show them the limits of their expectations."[41] Once again, agreeing with Aiguillon, he called for a prompt consideration of a report of the Feudalism Committee on those seignorial dues which had not yet been abolished. But the creation of the new government must also go forward: "We need to accelerate the work on the constitution. That is the way to end the troubles, to spread peace and contentment; it is the only way to respond to the urgent desire of the people and to satisfy all its concerns." The pending bill to calm the provinces was in his opinion only a provisional measure and should be accepted as such, leaving the Assembly free to turn its attention to a report of the Feudalism Committee on steps to restore calm. He concluded by moving that Le Chapelier's project to make municipal authorities financially and criminally responsible for local riots be voted into law, that vote to be followed by consideration of a report on "feudalism."[42]

The *Journal de Paris,* always ready to take Lafayette's side, reported: "These words, fully reflecting the sentiment of one who wished to establish order in, for, and by liberty, seemed to bring all spirits instantly into calm agreement with that view."[43] But calm did not last long. Deputies of the Extreme Right persisted in prolonging the debate to speak in favor of a royal police authority. Finally, Le Chapelier and others tried to bring the discussion to an end by postponing the vote until the next day. By this time the Assembly had been sitting for eight hours, and nerves were so frayed that no decision could be reached. Lafayette again went to the

[41] This part of the speech is taken from *AP*, XI, 672, which derived it from *Moniteur*, Feb. 24, p. 220.

[42] The speech is not given in full in *AP*, XI, 672. We have pieced it out by adding passages from *Mémoires*, II, 383–84, whose version is apparently taken from *Journal de Paris*, Feb. 24, p. 219.

[43] *Journal de Paris*, Feb. 24, p. 219.

tribune. He could see no reason, he said, why the Assembly should take no action before considering the report of the Feudalism Committee. Therefore he seconded the suggestion that the Assembly vote the next day, first on Le Chapelier's bill and the amendments to it, immediately after which the Assembly should hear the Feudalism Committee's report. The deputies accepted his suggestion, and the session closed at five-thirty.[44]

Lafayette had intended to go that afternoon to the Archbishop's Palace to attend a meeting of the men who had governed Paris during the Bastille crisis, the former Electors of Paris,[45] who were planning to publish a record of their work. At a meeting in December they had been able to examine the minutes of only a few of their early sessions, and they had called a second meeting for February 22, to which they had invited Bailly and Lafayette. That meeting having been scheduled for five o'clock, Lafayette was late, but when he arrived, the Electors greeted him with a round of applause, and he briefly expressed his pleasure at being among them once more. The Electors then proceeded with their business, deciding to celebrate every year on July 14 at the Hôtel de Ville and to march from there to Notre Dame for a service of thanksgiving for the "conquest of liberty." They then corrected and approved their minutes down to the account of the events of July 14. Since Lafayette and Bailly were associated with the affairs of the Commune after July 15, the Electors invited them to come to their next session (February 26) and assist in preparing the rest of their report. It was eleven o'clock before the meeting broke up and Lafayette's day ended.[46]

The next day (October 23) the National Assembly continued its debate on the ways to calm the provinces. At this session a new bill was provisionally adopted and debated article by article. When finally passed, the decree provided: (1) that a false claim that an

[44] *Ibid.*, pp. 219–20, Feb. 25, pp. 221–22; *Courier national*, Feb. 24, pp. 5–7; *Courier français*, Feb. 23, pp. 428–29; *Point du jour*, Feb. 23, pp. 156–58; *Moniteur*, Feb. 24, p. 220; *AP*, XI, 672–73; and Duquesnoy, II, 420.

[45] Gottschalk and Maddox, pp. 98–130 *passim*.

[46] J.-S. Bailly and H.-N.-M. Duveyrier (eds.), *Procès-verbal des séances et délibérations de l'Assemblée générale des Electeurs de Paris* (Paris, 1790), III, 1, 6–21.

act had emanated from the National Assembly and the king be punishable as a disturbance of the peace; (2) that the king send to all municipalities his speech of February 4, a conciliatory appeal of the National Assembly entitled "To the French,"[47] and the hitherto approved decrees, with instructions to publish all of them and to have them read from every pulpit; (3) that municipal officers employ every means in their power to protect persons, property, and the collection of taxes and, in case of riot, proclaim martial law; (4) that municipalities aid each other if requested to do so or be held answerable for consequent damages; and (5) that local officials, if they could have prevented disorder, be held financially liable for resultant damage.[48]

Lafayette took no part in this debate, nor did others who were known to be closely identified with him, but presumably he was satisfied with the law that finally was enacted. It provided that municipalities that were derelict out of fear or counterrevolutionary persuasion might be severely punished, but if they wanted to do their duty, they were encouraged to use all the means that publicity, martial law, neighboring municipalities, and the local courts could provide. No additional powers, however, were granted to the king or to his ministers, nor did the National Assembly countenance the view of the Jacobins that no real emergency existed and all that was needed was to assure the rural population of the end of seignorial privileges. Lafayette later claimed that it would have been improper for him to have taken too prominent a part in the debate on the final act; yet he assumed a large share of the responsibility for it. "My redoubled insistence . . . and the good will with which I was heard permit me to think that I had some influence on the measures taken on the occasion of the disorders."[49] Further agrarian reform, however, had less influential advocates and long remained a knotty issue.

The esteem in which most of Lafayette's compatriots continued to hold him was not impaired by the delay in manorial reform.

[47] *AP*, XI, 548–51 (Feb. 11).

[48] *Ibid.*, pp. 677–85, and *Mémoires*, II, 384–85.

[49] *Mémoires*, II, 384, n. 1. Michon (p. 72) claims that the law as finally enacted was contrary to Lafayette's wishes, but we know no evidence that supports that contention.

Once again the matter of granting him some financial compensation, first aired the preceding August,[50] occupied the attention of the municipality and the citizens of Paris. On February 23, the District of the Oratoire voted to approve the earlier decision of the Assembly of Representatives to grant the commandant general 100,000 livres. A few days later—and surprisingly enough—the District of the Cordeliers, which had defied the National Assembly and defended the now self-exiled Marat, not only suggested a larger compensation—120,000 livres—but also requested the Representatives and the other fifty-nine districts to join in beseeching Lafayette to accept it. It had been earned, they declared, "not by right of payment but as a testimonial of gratitude and a feeble compensation for the expenses that his patriotism and his devotion to the public welfare have brought upon him in his work for the benefit of the Commune and the success of the Revolution." During the next few days other districts endorsed the Cordeliers' suggestion.[51] Accordingly, on February 27, the president of the Assembly of Representatives waited upon Lafayette and asked him not to refuse the honorarium again. The commandant general was loath to accept but gave the president a letter formally recording his appreciation. The letter recalled that he had declined an earlier offer of the same nature, and since the same situation still prevailed, he renewed his request not to be compensated.[52] Since money was not acceptable, some admirers thought that perhaps some other substantial token of appreciation would be. The District of Saint-Jacques-L'Hôpital asked the other districts to join in presenting the commandant general a gold sword to be embellished with the arms of Paris and a cap of liberty set in diamonds and to be inscribed: "Given by the inhabitants of Paris to their defender, 1790." This proposal, however, was to materialize only a year and a half later, when he retired as commandant general.[53]

On February 28 the National Assembly turned its attention to

[50] See Gottschalk and Maddox, pp. 277–81.

[51] Lacroix, IV, 177 (Feb. 22), 197 (Feb. 24), 220 (Feb. 26), 227 (Feb. 27).

[52] *Ibid.*, p. 224.

[53] *Ibid.*, p. 237, n. 2.

the military establishment. It decreed, among other things, that military appropriations were to be voted annually by the legislature and that the legislative branch had the power to make all regulations concerning recruitment, pay, and discipline. It ordered, further, that every year on July 14 the officers take an oath before the authorities of the municipalities where they were stationed to remain faithful to the nation, the law, the king, and the constitution decreed by the National Assembly and accepted by the king, to give whatever assistance was required by the civil authorities, and never to employ force against any citizen except upon the order of the civil authorities. Soldiers were required to take a similar oath of loyalty at the hands of their officers and also to swear never to desert their flags and always to observe military regulations.[54] Although the new law began by declaring that the king was "the supreme head of the army," it failed to vest in him control of military affairs. Yet Lafayette probably found things in these provisions to approve both as soldier and as statesman, for they were not only a decisive step toward subordinating military to civil authority but also a necessary prelude to military reorganization for the effective defense of the realm.

On the day the army bill passed, Lafayette felt called upon to write a letter declaring his loyalty to Louis XVI. It was perhaps intended only to give the king a sort of "sugar plum," the small satisfaction that, as Lafayette had told Morris, Louis XVI had earned, but it may also have been Lafayette's way of apologizing for not having won for the monarch the kind of military control he had promised. It ran: "I place at your Majesty's feet the gratitude of a heart that knows how to appreciate his kindnesses and respond to his confidence. Let us believe, Sire, that your benevolent intentions will be fulfilled. When the people and the king make common cause, what can prevail against them? I swear at least to Your Majesty that, if my hope were deceived, the last drop of my blood would bear witness of my loyalty to him." The king placed this letter in his iron box, whence, in a darker day, it would be

[54] *AP*, XI, 741–42.

withdrawn and submitted as evidence that the then captive Lafayette had joined forces with the then helpless king against the
Revolution.[55]

But that tragic day was far off and unportended, while Lafayette's endeavor to promote both order and reform were recent and
clear. An unnamed admirer of Lafayette in Paris wrote on February 25 to an English journal an enthusiastically laudatory letter
which was subsequently reprinted in the *Gazette of the United
States*. The writer stated that he had frequent opportunities to see
and talk with "that truly great young man." "I did not think he
could be so popular as I find he is. He is almost idolized by his
countrymen." Nor was this admiration confined to "persons of
mean condition," for the Comte d'Estaing had recently told the
writer that Lafayette had consistently shown "courage, skill, and
virtue" in most trying and critical situations. When the writer had
asked how old this idol was, Estaing replied: "Were we to calcu-
late his years by his works, it might be asserted that he has lived
centuries, but, in fact, he is but three and thirty."[56] Morris and
many of the young hero's countrymen would not have joined in
this encomium, but perhaps at this point in time they would have
concurred in the estimate of his success and popularity.

BIBLIOGRAPHICAL NOTES

The *Archives parlementaires* do not indicate the sources of the debates for
the period covered in Volume XI (Dec. 24, 1789–March 1, 1790). We have
found that sometimes the speeches as recorded in that volume are less complete than as recorded in one or more contemporary journals and memoirs.
See below, Bibliographical Notes, chap. XIV, 336.

Michon's biography of Adrien Duport quite naturally is more friendly
to Duport than to Lafayette. Nevertheless, we consider his assumption of
palpable hostility between the two men as early as February 1790 to be premature. A. Lameth, I, 352–56, indicates that he and his friends were largely of
the same opinion as Lafayette on the bill to deal with provincial disorders.

[55] *Mémoires*, II, 444–45, dates this letter Feb. 20, but the date on the original (AN:
C184, pl. 117, no. 71 [armoire de fer]) is unmistakably Feb. 28. See also *AP*, LV, 688.
As stated in the *Mémoires* (II, 445, n. 1), at the time of preparing the letter as a historical
record Lafayette had forgotten why he wrote it and thought it was a letter of thanks for
the king's address of Feb. 4.

[56] Quoted in Boyd (ed.), XVI, 256 n. Actually Lafayette would not be thirty-three
until Sept. 6.

CHAPTER XII

"Adored . . . But What a Burden!"

EVEN before the Revolution Lafayette had acquired a well-earned reputation as a philanthropist. He had frequently given generously to charitable causes; he had been among the foremost in winning freedom of worship for France's Protestants; he had invested not only time and energy but also good hard cash in the effort to win emancipation for Negro slaves in France's colonies.[1] He continued to be a leader in the quest for human rights during the Revolution and in the struggle to abolish social distinctions that could not be justified as based upon general utility. He had made a special point of honoring members of the Agasse family because he felt that attainder should not devolve upon the innocent merely because of kinship with the guilty.[2] He was prepared to defy the convention that frowned upon actors and to let them serve in the National Guard.[3] He held that even domestics were entitled to serve in the National Guard.[4] Believing in freedom of conscience as "the foremost of rights" and opposed to "every kind of superstitious or philosophic intolerance," he wanted a decree on the freedom of religious cults that "would favor none of them and, after the example of the United States, would allow each society to maintain its own temple and ministers."[5]

The status of the Jews in France had been debated in the National Assembly on several occasions, and on December 24, the As-

---

[1] See index of Gottschalk, *Between,* under "Humanitarianism," "Philanthropy," "Protestants," "Slavery," etc.

[2] See above, pp. 190–92.

[3] Gottschalk and Maddox, p. 199.

[4] See above, p. 182, and *Journal général de la cour,* Jan. 25, p. 196.

[5] Lafayette to Hennings, Jan. 15, 1799, *Mémoires,* III, 244–45.

sembly decided that while Protestants were eligible to hold office in the French government, by implication at least Jews were not. The Jews of France numbered about 40,000 and were distinguishable as three separate groups. Those of the Midi—Bordeaux and Bayonne—had inhabited France for generations, were generally of Spanish origin (Sephardim), and were usually tolerated by their neighbors. Those of the Three Bishoprics, Lorraine, and especially Alsace—areas that had become parts of France only in recent centuries—were German Jews (Ashkenazim) and were commonly regarded as more foreign and less acceptable to their neighbors. Those of Paris were either Sephardim or Ashkenazim. The Jews of southern France—a few thousand in all—had commonly been considered Frenchmen, but the decree of December 24 seemed to deny that they were. The Jews of Bordeaux petitioned the National Assembly to confirm that they retained the full rights of active citizenship, while the friends of the Jews of Paris pleaded their cause in the city's Assembly of Representatives. Their champions pointed out that on several previous occasions the Jews of Bordeaux had not been discriminated against and had voted for members of the Estates General, that the Jews of Paris had supported the Revolution from the outset, more than one hundred of them being enrolled in the Paris National Guard.[6]

On January 28 Talleyrand, reporting for the Constitution Committee, introduced a motion providing that Jews who had previously enjoyed the status of voter should be accorded the rights of active (i.e., voting) citizens. The motion provoked a bitter debate, which went on all afternoon, until finally, at five o'clock, the presiding officer ordered a roll call upon a motion that would grant the rights of active citizenship to the Jews of the Midi. When Bishop Talleyrand voted "Yes," the Right hissed and the Left applauded. When Lafayette answered "Yes," the Left and the galleries cheered. The motion passed with 374 votes to 224.[7]

The bill recognized only the Jews of Bordeaux and Bayonne as active citizens. Some of the Ashkenazic Jews of Alsace, prefer-

---

[6] Lacroix, III, 604–7 and 625–36 (Jan. 28).

[7] *AP*, XI, 364–65, and Duquesnoy, II, 324–30.

ring or feeling obliged to consider themselves foreign, had petitioned to be excused from the duties of active citizenship, but some
of the Ashkenazic Jews of Paris did not approve of that petition.
Lalkind Hourwitz, a translator of Hebrew in the Bibliothèque du
Roi and author of a work entitled *Apologie des Juifs,* which had
been crowned by the Academy of Metz, came to consult Lafayette
on the issue. He was troubled, he said, about taking the civic oath to
defend the constitution because, although the Declaration of Rights
applied to all men, the new law seemed to deny the rights of active
citizenship to some of those "who pray to the Supreme Being in
Hebrew." He could not, he told Lafayette, swear to such contradic-
tory statements or defend a law directed against his fellow Jews.
Lafayette permitted his visitor to announce publicly that the commandant general believed the Jews of Paris and elsewhere in the
realm "merited approbation." Thereupon Hourwitz presented his
case in the *Chronique de Paris,* making clear that Lafayette supported it.[8] Nevertheless, full citizenship for eastern Jews was not
granted for some time to come.

Lafayette also advocated the abolition of the slave trade and the
eventual emancipation of the slaves in the French colonies. He was
a member of the abolitionist Société des Amis des Noirs, and he
and Adrienne owned and supervised by correspondence a plantation known as "La Belle Gabrielle" in Cayenne, where they were
carrying on an experiment intended to serve as an example of the
humane treatment and gradual emancipation of slaves.[9] He and
La Rochefoucauld drew Short into the Société des Amis des Noirs,[10]
and he had made the acquaintance of William Wilberforce, a
leader of the movement to abolish the British slave trade.[11] In
August Wilberforce, hoping that the French National Assembly
would favor abolition, had encouraged Thomas Clarkson to go to
France to promote that cause, and Lafayette and other members of
the Society of the Friends of the Negroes received him cordially.

---

[8] Hourwitz to the editor, Feb. 18, *Chronique de Paris,* Feb. 22, p. 210.

[9] Gottschalk, *Between,* pp. 244, 262–63.

[10] G. G. Shackelford, "William Short: Diplomat in Revolutionary France, 1785–1793," *Proceedings of the American Philosophical Society,* CII (1958), 601.

[11] Gottschalk, *Between,* pp. 34–35, 37, 52.

Although meetings of the society were hard to arrange because, as Clarkson recorded, Lafayette "has not time to attend"[12] and missed meetings when they were arranged,[13] nevertheless a conference of the Friends of the Negroes agreed to advocate a bill whereby free blacks and mulattoes should qualify for the same political and civil rights as whites.[14] Soon rumor labeled Clarkson as a British spy engaged in inciting insurrection among the West Indies slaves, and Lafayette, volunteering to vouch for him to the municipal authorities, advised him to make a public denial of the charge and to change his hotel so as to be nearer the Lafayettes and the police of the quarter "should there be any appearance of a collection of people about the hotel."[15]

Having gained the impression that Lafayette might be willing to take the lead in proposing abolition in the National Assembly, Clarkson was encouraged to hope for a speedy success, but he was quickly disillusioned. The West Indian planters, usually buyers, sellers, and owners of slaves, had organized the Société des Colons Français Résidant à Paris, generally known as the Club Massiac, and the merchants and manufacturers of the port cities had organized the Comité des Deputés Extraordinaires to fight interference with the colonies, and Barnave associated himself with their policy. An anonymous writer, obviously intending to undermine Lafayette's reputation as an opponent of slavery, wrote a make-believe letter to the Club Massiac pretending that Lafayette must no longer be a member of the Amis des Noirs since he had recently offered to sell fifty-seven slaves from his Cayenne plantation. A pamphlet soon appeared, apparently in response, upholding Lafayette's reputation as a champion of the Negro slave.[16]

---

[12] Thomas Clarkson, *History of the Rise, Progress, and Accomplishment of the Abolition of the African Slave-Trade by the British Parliament* (London, 1808), II, 134. See also *ibid.*, pp. 123–24.

[13] *Ibid.*, p. 143.

[14] Henri Grégoire, *Mémoires* (Paris, 1857), I, 390.

[15] Clarkson, II, 129–31.

[16] The anonymous letter was of Dec. 28, 1789, AN: D xxv 86, dossier 825, pièces 36–37. This document is quoted almost in full in H. Guilhamon, *Journal des voyages en Haute-Guienne de J.-F. Henry de Richeprey* (Rodez, 1952), pp. xxvi–xxvii, n. 1. The defense of Lafayette was contained in M. Degouge, *Réponse au champion americain, ou colon très aisé à connaitre* [Paris, Jan. 18, 1790], which is described in Parke-Bernet Galleries catalogue No. 731, sale of Jan. 28, 1946, p. 41.

Nothing daunted by this controversy, Clarkson carried on. His propaganda campaign led him to import thousands of pamphlets and illustrations revealing the horrors of the slave trade, and Lafayette and Adrienne were among those who helped distribute them among the members of the National Assembly.[17] Clarkson begged Wilberforce (for whom, he said, Lafayette had "absolutely a greater respect . . . than for any other person in the English nation") to urge the commandant general to put the plight of the blacks before the National Assembly: "A speech from him will make the difference of four hundred votes."[18] Clarkson had meanwhile been in touch also with Mirabeau, who early in November had agreed to take the initiative in proposing the suppression of the slave trade in French territories. Lafayette was suspicious of Mirabeau's motives when Clarkson apprised him of this arrangement. "Mirabeau," he remarked, "is a host in himself, and I should not be surprised if by his eloquence and popularity only he were to carry it; and yet I regret that he has taken the lead in it. The cause is so lovely that even ambition, abstractedly considered, is too impure to take it under its protection and not to sully it. It should have been placed in the hands of the most virtuous man in France. This man is the Duc de la Rochefoucauld. But you cannot alter things now. You cannot take it out of his hands."[19]

When Clarkson was called back to England, early in 1790, Mirabeau had not yet made a move in the National Assembly on the Negro question. Before leaving France, Clarkson called upon Lafayette in order to discuss with him the prospects of the abolition movement in France. Lafayette afterward confessed that he carefully avoided telling his visitor the whole truth, for the opposition was greater than he was willing to admit to a foreigner, and he foresaw that procrastination would prove necessary.[20] It was probably on this occasion that Clarkson was pleased to encounter mulatto

[17] Clarkson, II, 151–52.

[18] Quoted (without date) in R. I. Wilberforce and S. Wilberforce, *Life of William Wilberforce* (London, 1838), I, 229–30.

[19] Clarkson, II, 145–46.

[20] Lafayette to Clarkson, Jan. 27, 1798, M. M. Kennedy, *Lafayette and Slavery* (Easton, Pa., 1950), p. 30. The version of this letter in *Mémoires*, III, 402, is incomplete. The original is in the Jackson Collection, Yale University Library. See also *Mémoires*, III, 71 n.

officers from the National Guard of San Domingo at Lafayette's home. Though hesitant to accept command of National Guard units outside of the vicinity of Paris, Lafayette had made a point of accepting the honorary commandership of a unit formed by the "free men of color" in the colony.[21] He spoke on the subject of emancipation with feeling, blaming the white colonists for the anticipated defeat and foreseeing "nothing but desolation" in San Domingo. "He hoped," Clarkson reported, "the day was near at hand when the two great nations, which had been hitherto distinguished only for their hostility, one toward the other, would unite in so sublime a measure [as abolition]; and that they would follow up their union by another, still more lovely, for the preservation of eternal and universal peace." Thus the Revolution in France "through the mighty aid of England might become the source of civilization, of freedom, and of happiness to the whole world." According to Clarkson, Lafayette said: "No other nations were sufficiently enlightened for such a union, but all other nations might be benefited by it."[22]

The slave trade found a number of its most influential backers among the merchants of the coastal cities of France who engaged in commerce with the French West Indies. In consequence, Lafayette had also discussed with Morris, before he left for England, the relevance of the slave trade to the wider opening of the French West Indies to American traders. As Morris well knew, the French merchants engaged in trade with the islands would resist any move to permit readier access to the island ports for American merchants and thus weaken their own monopoly. So a three-cornered fight was going on, the issue in one corner being the abolition of the slave trade, in another the emancipation of slaves, and in the third the removal of restrictions upon American trade with the French West Indies. The fight so embittered relations among the combattants that Lafayette was doubtful much could be done; the best suggestion he could make was a conference of the Amis des Noirs, the white colonists, and the merchants, in the hope that they might

[21] Clarkson, I, 388, and *Mémoires*, III, 71.

[22] Clarkson, II, 164–65.

be able to agree on a program. Morris thought such an agreement a "mere Utopia."[23]

Morris' cynicism again appeared justified. The Chamber of Commerce of Bordeaux, supported by the city's National Guard, in February sent a deputation to Paris to oppose abolition and the opening of French West Indies ports to foreigners. This deputation, calling itself the Armée Patriotique Bordelaise, called on the king, the queen, the Jacobin Club, the National Assembly, the Commune of Paris, and others as well as Lafayette. He tried to induce them not to press the National Assembly, asserting that the best they could hope for was an adjournment of the question to a subsequent legislature. Undeterred by Lafayette's views, their spokesman appeared at the National Assembly on February 25 and told the deputies that prohibiting the importation of slaves would ruin the French colonies and consequently the French merchants trading with the West Indies. On the following day, the Assembly learned that dangerous unrest had indeed developed in San Domingo between the blacks and their masters.[24]

The course Lafayette and his friends now adopted was to try to prevent the passage of a law expressly guaranteeing the continuation of the slave trade. Protagonists and opponents of the slave trade mobilized their forces. On February 26, at the Jacobin Club a merchant of Nantes presented the case for the slave trade, and on February 28, Mirabeau presented the case for its abolition.[25] A letter to the editor of the *Gazette de Paris,* predicting that the Amis de Noirs would ruin the colonies if not checked, asked if Lafayette would support the attacks on slavery and thus expose Louis XVI to the loss of "millions of useful, rich, and hardworking subjects."[26] Lafayette not only did not yield to anti-abolitionist pressure; on March 1 he made a donation of 192 livres to the Société des Amis des Noirs.[27]

[23] Morris diary, Jan. 10, Davenport (ed.), I, 362.

[24] *AP,* XI, 698–99, 710, and Michel Lhéritier, *Liberté (1789–1790): les Girondins, Bordeaux et la Révolution française* (Paris, 1947), pp. 133–38.

[25] F.-A. Aulard, *La Société des Jacobins* (Paris, 1889–97), I, 9–17.

[26] Mar. 2, p. 2.

[27] Girodie catalogue, p. 90, item 128.

The debate waxed bitter and alienated old friends. Four years earlier Lafayette had brought Condorcet into the Friends of the Negroes, and Condorcet in turn had introduced Alexandre and Charles de Lameth.[28] But the Lameths had drifted away, and it was now rumored that their alienation was attributable to Charles's wife's proprietary interest in large plantations in San Domingo, and Charles de Lameth was reported to have said about this time: "Lafayette is the smallest general and the biggest intriguer I have ever known."[29] But Condorcet remained a staunch advocate of the cause. Lafayette, he said, in reply apparently to a query from another scientist, had been a champion of liberty long before the Revolution, and while they had worked together on liberal projects, others had sought personal advancement: "If you have been told that I consider M. de La Fayette the most certain prop of our liberty, you have been told the truth."[30]

Continual unrest in the colonies constrained the National Assembly to name a special Colonies Committee to examine the problems relating to the colonies, slavery, and the slave trade. Alexandre de Lameth and Barnave were named to the committee,[31] and on March 8 Barnave presented the committee's report. It proposed that local decisions be left largely to the colonial assemblies, that the National Assembly make no innovations in colonial commerce, that the colonists and their property be put under the special protection of the nation, and that inciting insurrection be condemned as criminal.[32] Thereby Barnave's committee asked the Assembly to bind itself not to interfere with the slave trade. If Lafayette found any consolation in the report, it could have been only that noninterference with colonial commerce would mean that the French West Indies were to remain no less open to United States

---

[28] J.-P. Brissot, *Mémoires* (*1754–1793*) (Paris, [1911]), ed. C. Perroud, II, 86, n. 3.

[29] Letter to Mme Galitzen, Mar. 20, O. Staroselskaya-Nikitina (ed.), *Zapiski Otdyela Roukopisey,* No. 7 (1941), pp. 77–79.

[30] Condorcet to Jean-Claude de La Métherie, [Feb–Mar, 1790?], Etienne Charavay (ed.), *Lettres autographes composant la collection de M. Alfred Bovet* (Paris, 1887), II, 105, pièce 288. See also A. C. O'Connor and M. F. Arago (eds.), *Oeuvres de Condorcet* (Paris, 1847–49), I, 328–29, and *La Révolution française,* VI (1884), 727.

[31] *AP,* XII, 2–6 and 19 (Mar. 2).

[32] *Ibid.,* pp. 72–73.

shipping than before.[33] As he had warned Clarkson, Mirabeau's bad reputation did not help the Negro cause,[34] and at this point Mirabeau's reputation was worse than ever because it was noised abroad that Lafayette had learned by special courier from England that the Duc d'Orléans had deposited 60,000 louis d'or to Mirabeau's account in a Paris bank.[35] Mirabeau tried to oppose the Colonies Committee's suggestions, but he was shouted down, and trembling with wrath, he left the tribune. The Assembly passed the committee's recommendations by a vast majority.[36]

Whether or not Wilberforce ever sent the letter which Clarkson had begged for and whether or not Lafayette shared Clarkson's view that a speech from him would make a tremendous difference, he did not speak in the Assembly that day. Although he wanted the shamefulness of the slave trade aired,[37] he had apparently decided that for the moment the cause was lost, and he was not so quixotic as to play a conspicuous role in a hopeless endeavor. Possibly, too, he just did not find the time. When in the midst of this political crisis a friend requested a favor, Lafayette did not even acknowledge the request until an embarrassing interval had passed. Then he apologized: "The little time that my duties as deputy leaves me, and other circumstances relative to my personal situation have been the cause of this apparent neglect."[38] The slaves of the French colonies were not to owe their liberation to Lafayette. Nevertheless, after the vacillating policy of successive French governments led to insurrection and massacres in the colonies, the Lafayette family was persuaded that at Cayenne the horrors of civil war had been mitigated by their humanitarian experiment.[39]

Many "other circumstances" relative to Lafayette's "personal

<hr>

[33] Lafayette to Washington, Mar. 17, Gottschalk (ed.), *Letters.* pp. 347–48.

[34] See above, p. 253, n. 19.

[35] Duquesnoy, II, 444–45. Presumably the rumor was false, for otherwise Lafayette's *Mémoires* probably would have mentioned it.

[36] *AP*, XII, 73 (Mar. 8).

[37] *Mémoires*, III, 71 n.

[38] Lafayette to Brissot, Feb. 15, Indiana University, Ball Collection, XI, No. 23.

[39] Lafayette to Clarkson, Jan. 27, 1798, *Mémoires*, IV, 403, and Virginie de Lasteyrie (ed.), *La vie de Madame de Lafayette* (Paris, 1869), p. 209.

situation" kept him occupied when he was not attending to his "duties as a deputy." As commandant general of the Paris National Guard he continued to be burdened with bureaucratic details—commissions, identification papers, letters of recommendation, committee meetings, and steady correspondence with those members of the Paris Commune and of the National Assembly who even on petty matters preferred to complain directly to him. Bailly, at least partly because complaints were likely to come first to the mayor's attention, continued to be one of the chief complainants. After Ambassador Mercy-Argenteau had been forced at the city barrier to get out of his carriage and explain who he was, foreign envoys, fearing that their diplomatic immunity might be jeopardized, appealed to Montmorin, who appealed to Bailly, who appealed to Lafayette.[40] Bailly was personally piqued by the negligence of the National Guards on duty at his own home, who failed to regard that post as one of honor, as he thought they should.[41] Lafayette also had to appease the solicitous mayor regarding several routine matters, such as overlapping responsibilities in cases of fire (which were arranged satisfactorily by an understanding that firemen should direct the putting-out of fires while the National Guard gave them police support),[42] the time for putting out the street lights (which they fixed between three and four o'clock in the morning, although Lafayette and Gouvion preferred that they be kept on until daybreak),[43] and special precautions for the pre-Lenten carnival.[44]

The Assembly of Representatives customarily counted upon Lafayette to deal with any personal matters pertaining to the Paris National Guard. When a sixty-year-old man complained that the fusiliers of his district had tried to oblige him to mount guard,[45] or

[40] Bailly to Lafayette, Mar. 1, Robiquet, p. 60, and BN: Fr 11697, pp. 44–46, and Bailly to Messieurs, Mar. 8, BVP: Collection Etienne Charavay, fols. 19–20.

[41] Bailly to Lafayette, Mar. 4, Robiquet, pp. 61–62.

[42] Bailly to Lafayette, Mar. 3, Robiquet, p. 61, and Tuetey, II, p. 378, No. 3571, and Lafayette to Bailly, Feb. 5, BN: Fr. 11697, p. 189.

[43] Gouvion to Bailly, Feb. 7, cited in Lacroix, III, 560.

[44] Bailly to Lafayette, Feb. 10, Robiquet, p. 58.

[45] Lacroix, IV, 96–97 (Feb. 13).

when a woman asked for news of her husband who she believed
was enrolled in the Paris National Guard,[46] or when some question
of pay arose in the National Guard,[47] the Representatives passed
the problem on to Lafayette or his colleagues. When unauthorized
persons were seen wearing the French Guard medal, the Representatives appointed a committee to work with him on keeping that
prized decoration from unauthorized individuals.[48] The National
Assembly also got involved because some of his soldiers took insignia they thought inappropriate from a man who happened to be
a deputy, and he reported the affair to the president of the National Assembly, who thereupon complained directly to Lafayette.[49]

In cases involving the cashiering of an officer, imprisonment of a
guardsman, expulsion from the corps, and even capital punishment, Article 13 of the *Règlement* made the commandant general
sole judge. Lafayette never used this authority, however, without
consulting Bailly. He at first adopted the practice of turning those
accused of crimes or misdemeanors over directly to either the
Châtelet or the Bureau de Ville. But, he soon found, the court was
too lenient, and the Bureau too dilatory, and neither seemed to provide an effective deterrent to continued offenses. So he determined
that the National Guard could itself weed out offenders more
zealously. In consequence, he adopted a system that had once prevailed in the former French Guard. As now modified, it provided
a supervisory committee in each company, and another for the
division as a whole. The company committee reported breaches
of discipline to the division committee, which passed on to the
commandant general those cases deemed worthy of his attention,
together with its recommendation. Lafayette either decided such
cases himself or referred them to a court-martial, whose decision
was then presented to him and the mayor for acceptance or rejection. He maintained that the authority of the supervisory committees was limited to reporting offenses and advising on penalties,
but he found that they sometimes exceeded their authority and

[46] *Ibid.*, p. 103.
[47] E.g., *ibid.*, p. 102.
[48] *Ibid.*, pp. 75–76 (Feb. 12).
[49] Bureau de Pusy to Lafayette, Feb. 13, AN: AF[11] 48, liasse 375, p. 11.

sought to make final judgments. In several instances he mitigated the sentences recommended by a court-martial, and if a supervisory committee recommended imprisonment, he referred such cases sometimes to the Bureau de Ville or more often to the mayor, suggesting a milder sentence if he thought such punishment excessive.[50] Thus he had created a system whereby the supervisory committee was a kind of investigating jury, the court-martial a trial jury, and either the Bureau de Ville or preferably the mayor with the commandant general's concurrence the final judges.

The system worked well in simple cases. When, for example, the supervisory committee of the National Guard cavalry cashiered two troopers for insubordination, thereby inciting dissatisfaction among their comrades, Lafayette sent the committee's report to Bailly, approving of the decision as in the best interests of the corps,[51] and that seems to have settled the matter. But at times the mayor feared that the supervisory committees had claimed arbitrary power. In one instance he protested to Lafayette against sentencing a National Guardsman to six months' imprisonment, pointing out that the supervisory committees had no authority to pass sentence.[52] Lafayette's reply indicated that he had never considered the opinion of a supervisory committee to be a definitive judgment; moreover, he regarded proper disciplinary measures as compatible with humanitarian principles. Recalling that Bailly had frequently been asked to review the decisions of courts-martial, he explained that he had recently ceased sending cases to the Bureau de Ville because it had left a case unsettled for a long time, and he cited his softening of the penalty of one man sentenced to have his hair cut off and of another ordered to leave Paris and not return under penalty of life imprisonment: "A citizen should be exposed to the loss of his honor, his estate, and his liberty only by the decision of competent judges."[53]

Lafayette indeed acted on that principle consistently. When he

[50] Lafayette to Bailly, Feb. 23, BN: Fr. 11697, pp. 41–43.

[51] Lafayette to Bailly, Feb. 5, *ibid.*, p. 36.

[52] Bailly to Lafayette, Feb. 21, *ibid.,* pp. 39–41, and Robiquet, p. 59.

[53] Lafayette to Bailly, Feb. 23, BN: Fr 11697, pp. 41–43. The criticism of Lafayette's procedure by Paul Robiquet on the ground that Bailly had to act as "the defender of the freedom of the individual" requires more evidence than Robiquet (pp. 59–60) advances.

had occasion to review three sentences for theft, two of them seemed to him beyond either his own competence or the mayor's to approve, since one recommended banishment from Paris, and the other imprisonment, in addition to expulsion from the Guard. Upon referring these cases to Bailly, he expressed doubt that they should either banish or lock a man up, even if the *Règlement* gave them authority to do so, for the *Règlement,* he thought, could be only provisional until it had been sanctioned by "the executive power." Consequently he had reduced the two sentences, expelling the accused from the National Guard as recommended but turning them over to the Châtelet for trial. Since thievery on the part of National Guardsmen seemed all too common and since mere expulsion from the corps was not a sufficient penalty for it, he proposed as a regular practice thereafter not merely to expel all convicted Guardsmen from the ranks but likewise to send them to the Châtelet for trial.[54]

Despite his desire to avoid conflict with the civil authorities, Lafayette was inevitably involved in the power conflict of the jealous district assemblies with the Assembly of Representatives. One of the principal complaints of the districts was that the National Guard operated under a *Règlement* which they had not yet formally approved. After an accumulation of "difficulties" Lafayette placed the matter before the Assembly of Representatives, which then urged the districts to abide by the *Règlement,* even though it was only provisional, until the National Assembly should pass a definitive law governing National Guards. Battalion commanders continued, nevertheless, to grumble to the commandant general that they received orders from their district assemblies which contradicted those of their division chiefs or required them to police areas assigned by the National Guard staff to others. Districts went so far as to question the brevets given to battalion officers,[55] and in the plan of Lafayette's Military Committee for an independent artillery corps within the Paris Guard[56] the districts saw only another threat to their independence. On January 31 the District of

[54] Lafayette to Bailly, Mar. 3, BN: Fr 11697, p. 46.

[55] Lacroix, IV, 13 (Feb. 6), 27–29 (Feb. 8), and Gouvion to Monsieur le Président [of a district], Feb. 2, BVP: Collection Etienne Charavay, fols. 333–34.

[56] See above, pp. 163–64.

Notre-Dame expressed a preference, in view of the expense of a separate corps and the excellence of the cannoneers already available, that each of the sixty districts have its own artillery detachment.[57] By mid-February, six other districts had endorsed this preference.[58]

The District of Saint-Lazare went further, protesting in a vigorous resolution against any new military units whatsoever: "We do not intend to cast the slightest shadow on the confidence merited by our brave general, but he is mortal. Is it not possible that he may be succeeded by two or three aristocrats who will forge chains to oppress us?" Copies of this protest went to Lafayette and the Assembly of Representatives.[59] Then the District des Enfants-Rouges carried the districts' demands to a logical conclusion. It passed a resolution attacking the Representatives' military policy in toto, pointing out that the Assembly had enlarged authorized paid units, had created new ones not authorized in the *Règlement,* and had incurred expenditures beyond those approved by the districts. This resolution was printed, and copies were sent to the National Assembly, the mayor, the commandant general, and the other fifty-nine districts.[60] Since the Representatives' policy usually was based upon the commandant general's military recommendations, the attack was also an indictment of him.

The Cordeliers now took the initiative in attempting to organize a deputation from all the districts to demonstrate to the Representatives their solidarity against an independent municipal artillery. On February 27 a delegation from twenty districts, claiming to represent forty in all, presented the Assembly of Representatives with their protest. The Assembly received the deputation with marked courtesy and promised to consider its views carefully.[61] On March 4, the District des Enfants-Rouges, thus emboldened, protested against the creation of any new corps or any increase in the present corps without the consent of the districts and condemned military

[57] Lacroix, II, 614, III, 19–21, 227–28, 703–4.

[58] *Ibid.,* III, 240–43.

[59] *Ibid.,* IV, 27 (Feb. 7), 39 (Feb. 8).

[60] *Ibid.,* pp. 243–44 (Feb. 27).

[61] *Ibid.,* pp. 227–32, 244–45 (Feb. 27).

expenditures beyond the limit provided in the *Règlement*. The president of the Assembly replied that the Representatives would be guided by the will of the majority of the districts, that the District des Enfants-Rouges was not warranted in implying that the specified limit of expenditures had been exceeded, and that no one district had the right to reproach the Representatives of all the districts. The Assembly thereupon cut short the discussion.[62]

That peremptory action did not end the conflict. Forty-three districts banded together to oppose an independent municipal artillery corps, and on March 8 they sent a deputation to the Assembly of Representatives to protest against the creation not only of an artillery corps but of any corps not provided for in detail in the National Guard *Règlement*. After some altercation between the Assembly's president and the deputation's spokesman regarding the authority of the Representatives as the elected deputies of the districts, the Assembly agreed to create no further corps without the consent of the districts.[63] The districts thus won that round, and the effect of their victory soon became evident.

During the past summer, when they had lived in dread of a royalist coup, many National Guard companies had seized cannon wherever they could find them, and about 200 men, expecting to form the nucleus of an artillery corps, were already serving as gunners on a provisional basis. Now the districts, no longer fearing a royalist attack, were neglecting their guns and even objected when the municipal Department of the National Guard carried on inspections.[64] Lafayette appealed to the Bureau de Ville to decide what was to happen to these artillerymen, and the Bureau came to the conclusion that it would be "a grave injustice suddenly to stop the pay of two hundred brave soldiers who had sacrificed all their hopes in defense of liberty."[65] So they continued to be paid and to serve as before, but no municipal artillery corps was formally created.

[62] *Ibid.*, pp. 243–44 (Feb. 27), 297–98 (Mar. 4).

[63] *Ibid.*, pp. 323–28 (Mar. 8).

[64] *Moniteur*, Mar. 19, p. 318, and Lacroix, IV, 302–4, 310–11 (Mar. 5), 317–18 (Mar. 6).

[65] Lacroix, IV, 401–2 (Mar. 13).

A project to increase the cavalry corps presented to the Bureau de Ville on February 27 had no better fate. The Bureau invited Lafayette to consult with it on "this important request,"[66] and on March 2 it entertained the report of a committee charged to investigate the petition of some young men to form a volunteer company of *chasseurs à cheval,* furnishing their own horses, uniforms, and equipment. Lafayette was not present, however, and so the Bureau invited him to consider the matter with them on March 6. He attended the session on that date, but the Bureau's minutes make no further mention of a project to organize a volunteer cavalry unit.[67]

Lafayette's Military Committee, nevertheless, continued to engage in drawing up regulations for the volunteer companies of chasseurs and grenadiers which he still apparently hoped to create. He also hoped to add dash to the Guard's reviews and parades with a full-fledged military band for each division, but the Bureau de Ville decided that the *Règlement* did not authorize it to create a paid band corps. Nor was the Garde de la Ville granted its petition, addressed to Lafayette, to be retained, since the Military Committee, to which Lafayette submitted its memoir, felt bound by the *Règlement* to suppress all former guard and police units in the city. The best the committee would do was to advise Lafayette to send their memoir to the National Assembly for consideration.[68]

In the same vein, despite the shortage of man power in the Paris National Guard, the Assembly of Representatives persisted in its policy of discountenancing private paramilitary organizations.[69] On February 25 the Company of the Chevaliers de l'Arc asked permission to take the new civic oath, presenting testimonials (signed by Lafayette, Gouvion, and other members of the National Guard staff) of the "zeal and distinction" with which they had served the Revolution. The Representatives consented to administer the oath but only with the understanding that their consent did not imply

[66] *Ibid.,* pp. 235–36 (Feb. 27).

[67] *Ibid.,* pp. 264 and n. 7 (Mar. 2), 318–19 (Mar. 6).

[68] *Procès-verbal du Comité militaire,* Part II, 60–61 (Mar. 16), and Lacroix, IV, 402 (Mar. 13).

[69] Gottschalk and Maddox, pp. 188, 233, 287.

that the company would be a permanent organization.[70] And all the Representatives would do for the Basochiens, who made a similar request, was to permit their taking the patriotic oath only as an *ad hoc* group to be called the Volunteers of the Basoche and to give each of them individually a certificate to show his children "as a testimonial of the gratitude of a vast people."[71]

While the Military Committee and the Assembly of Representatives thus tried to avoid conflict over new military units, the districts did not end their competition with the Hôtel de Ville with mere expressions of indignation over unauthorized corps. In the name of liberty they protested against the police order, reaffirmed on January 12,[72] requiring the National Guard to assist in the arrest of debtors, and they obliged the Department of Police to act discreetly and avoid conflict with the district assemblies on that score.[73] The districts' zealous defense of freedom of the press provided an added cause for conflict with the Commune's police authority. Hardly had the attack from districts on the Left in the Affaire de Marat died down, if only temporarily, when districts on the Right began an attack in the Affaire de Laizer. Marat had offended the city authorities because he considered them too moderate; the new offender considered them too extreme. Early in 1790 an anonymous satire had appeared under the title *Confession générale de M. Necker et de l'Assemblée nationale,* in which Lafayette was portrayed as usurping Louis' authority, keeping him a prisoner, and only feigning to renounce his ambition to "imitate Cromwell." In the final days of February there appeared another brochure, entitled *Protestations de Messieurs de Mirabeau, Chapelier, Clermont-Tonnerre, sur quelques arrêtés de l'Assemblée nationale,* which pretended to be a denunciation of the *Confession générale de Necker* but which alleged that the Châtelet had been bribed and described Lafayette, Bailly, and Necker as "brigands"

[70] Lacroix, IV, 208 (Feb. 25), 225 (Feb. 27).

[71] *Ibid.,* pp. 290–97 (Mar. 4), 396–97 (Mar. 13), and *Journal de la municipalité,* Mar. 9. pp. 501–2.

[72] Note in Lacroix, IV, 50–55 (Jan. 13).

[73] *Ibid.,* III, 502, 509–10 (Jan. 21), 689, 700–701 (Feb. 4), IV, 43–44, 55–56 (Feb. 9).

who were holding the king prisoner and which in an appended appeal urged the French people to cleanse the earth of these "monsters" and "*enragés*." On February 25 the patrol of the District des Petits-Pères seized the *Protestations* from a bookseller, and the Department of Police on February 27 arrested the Chevalier Laizer, a former lieutenant of the French Guard, as its author. Laizer protested that he had written no pamphlet, and the District des Minimes, in which he lived, rose to his defense, demanding that he be examined and, if found innocent, released within twenty-four hours. It also demanded the suppression of the municipality's Comité des Recherches, which Lafayette had helped to establish the preceding autumn. These demands went unheeded, and Laizer remained in jail awaiting trial.[74] But other pamphlets of a defamatory nature continued to appear.[75]

Other districts and their National Guard battalions supported the District des Minimes, demanding the suppression of the Châtelet as well as the Commune's Comité des Recherches and attacking the Assembly of Representatives. On the other hand, the Battalion of the Minimes took issue with its district assembly's demand for the suppression of the committee. It not only submitted a resolution to that effect to the commandant general, the districts, and all the other battalions of the National Guard but also sent a deputation to the National Assembly and to the Assembly of Representatives to announce its approval of the committee and its condemnation of the recent attack upon the Paris regime.[76] Chiefly because of the loyalty of the Battalion des Minimes, Laizer's defenders did not immediately win their demands, but compliance was not long delayed.[77]

[74] *Ibid.*, IV, 270, 272–75 (Mar. 3); *Courrier de Paris*, Feb. 26, pp. 371–72; and George Coquard (ed.), *Le général La Fayette, Catalogue des . . . autographes . . . de la collection de M. Blancheteau . . .* (Paris, 1934), (hereafter cited as Blancheteau catalogue), p. 55, item 189.

[75] Lacroix, IV, 331 (Mar. 8), 372 (Mar. 10), and Comte de Combourg to Comtesse de Calan, Mar. 9, Granges de Surgères, "Lettres anecdotiques de Jean-Baptiste de Chateaubriand, 1789–1790," *Revue de la Révolution*, XIV (1889), Part 2, pp. 1–14.

[76] Lacroix, IV, 320–21, 331–32 (Mar. 8), 366–68, 371–73 (Mar. 10). See also *AP*, XII, 98, and Clermont-Gallerande, I, 352.

[77] Laizer was acquitted only on Mar. 12, his publishers on Apr. 22: Lacroix, IV, 281–82.

The shortage of food and other necessities was always worse in Paris in the winter months, and widespread need helped the disorder that spread through the city to infect the Île de France as well. Renewed disturbances in Montmartre led the mayor to ask Lafayette to station a special guard at the gate to that area, and reports of rioting and the hoarding of breadstuffs in nearby communities prompted Bailly to request adequate measures to insure the uninterrupted transportation of provisions.[78] Clashes occurred at the city gates between the chasseurs attempting to stop salt-smuggling and groups of people abetting the smugglers,[79] the excise on salt and tobacco being particularly hateful. The chasseurs went so far as to hunt out persons believed guilty of receiving contraband goods. On March 16 Lafayette heard a complaint to the Assembly of Representatives that the chasseurs, in their zeal to seize contraband, were searching homes without proper warrants from the civil authorities, and he immediately undertook to investigate the charges. Reports from his officers, however, led him to believe, as he was always prone to believe, that the crowds at the barriers, though they gathered ostensibly in behalf of smugglers, actually were instigated by persons bent upon stirring up trouble. Genuinely apprehensive of plots by enemies of the Revolution, he kept the cavalry alert to gallop to any point at the first alarm. But an old difficulty arose. No matter how quickly reports of trouble might come to the Hôtel de Ville, sending orders consumed time, for no cavalry were stationed near the Hôtel de Ville. Even though the Bureau de Ville had several times ordered the immediate establishment of nearby barracks for three hundred men, nothing had been done. Lafayette again confronted the Bureau de Ville with the danger, and the Bureau expressed astonishment that weeks should have elapsed without its orders having been carried out and again ordered that the barracks be set up forthwith.[80] But still nothing happened.

The Hôtel de Ville's anxiety, however, about the evasion of the

---

[78] Mar. 3, 5, Tuetey, I, 365, No. 3293, III, 275, No. 2843.

[79] *Courrier de Paris,* Mar. 4, p. 467.

[80] Lacroix, III, 403–4 (Jan. 9), 484–85 (Jan. 19), IV, 317–19 (Mar. 6), 507 (Mar. 26).

excises did not abate. On March 3 the Representatives selected a committee to consult with the administration and the commandant general on the problem and report back to the Assembly.[81] That day the chasseurs attempted to catch a smuggler, and a small riot resulted. Three days later the Department of Police placed the agents of the tax-farmers under the protection of the Commune and instructed the National Guard to take the firmest measures to prevent the smuggling and sale of contraband in the city.[82]

The scarcity that made smuggling profitable also provoked the waylaying of foodstuffs. On March 8 Lafayette received a call for help from Meaux, where the people had seized two boatloads of flour, in violation of the laws forbidding the hampering of grain shipments. By the National Assembly's act of February 23 a municipality was required to send military support upon appeal from a nearby town, and so Lafayette applied to the Bureau de Ville for authority to dispatch a detachment of the Paris National Guard to Meaux, and the Bureau instructed him to do so at once.[83] Rumor had it that the Meaux officials had proclaimed martial law, that the people had beaten off the National Guard, hanged the mayor, and pillaged the homes of "aristocrats," and that two thousand foot soldiers had been sent from Paris to Meaux along with a detachment of cavalry and "many cannon." But the next day the Assembly of Representatives learned that no deaths had occurred at Meaux and that Lafayette had thought it necessary to send no more than three hundred men. The Assembly approved "the sagacious measures taken by M. the Commandant General."[84]

As if to demonstrate again that the love of civic order knew no social barriers, shortly afterward another group of Paris workers took the patriotic oath. These were the laborers who had been pulling down the Bastille ever since July 16, when Lafayette had given

[81] *Ibid.*, IV, 271–72, 282–86 (Mar. 3), and *Journal de la municipalité*, Mar. 5, pp. 499–500.

[82] *Courrier de Paris*, Mar. 4, p. 467; *Moniteur*, Mar. 12, pp. 189–90; Lacroix, IV, 284–86 (Mar. 3); Bailly to Lafayette, Mar. 11, Tuetey, II, 418, No. 3973; and *AP*, XII, 98.

[83] Lacroix, IV, 329 (Mar. 8).

[84] *Ibid.*, p. 459 (Mar. 9). See also *Courrier de Paris*, Mar. 10, p. 65, Mar. 13, pp. 118–20; *Journal général de la cour*, Mar. 10, pp. 447–49, Mar. 11, pp. 557–58; and *Moniteur*, Mar. 17, p. 310.

the contract for its demolition to Palloy's house-wrecking firm.[85] Lafayette had visited the site on one occasion, and after Palloy had shown him the pathetic souvenirs of the once proud fortress, he himself picked up a hammer to help in the work of demolition. Before leaving, he asked Palloy to give each of the workingmen a glass of wine as his treat. The wrecking of the Bastille proceeded until the beginning of March, when Palloy's workers celebrated the completion of their task in a formal ceremony. Gathered at the site of the Bastille, with hands upraised they repeated the patriotic oath and then shouted in unison: "I so swear." On the following day, over a thousand of them paraded in the Hôtel de Ville, where the president administered the oath again. According to Palloy, the cost of Lafayette's complimentary wine had so far been paid only in part, and he asked the Bureau de Ville and Lafayette's secretary to provide the sum he calculated still due him.[86]

As commander of the king's troops within a radius of fifteen leagues of Paris, Lafayette's concern with military esprit de corps extended beyond the walls of Paris. Having found the pay of royal soldiers on special assignment inadequate, he recommended various pay adjustments to meet the cost of moving to and from or of living in the Paris area. Minister of War Latour du Pin granted increases of a few sous in the daily wage of specified detachments and in the sums allowed for wood and fodder. Early in March, when Lafayette had to send a detachment of the Flanders Regiment to Houdan, he sent along a quartermaster to see that the soldiers received the same pay they had received at Versailles. These men therefore got four sous per day, but the quartermaster found that other soldiers on the same mission were receiving only two sous and undertook to equalize the pay of all of them. Accordingly Lafayette requested that the pay of all be raised to four sous (though he recognized that the extraordinary expense might be burdensome), and the minister granted that request likewise.[87]

[85] Gottschalk and Maddox, p. 117.

[86] BVP: Collection Lièsville, carton relatif à M. Palloy, No. IV, pp. 989–90, 1000; *Courrier de Paris,* Mar. 4, 5, pp. 467, 483–88; and Girodie catalogue, pp. 95–96, item 136.

[87] Feb. 5, AMG: AH, carton LX, chemise fev. 1–15, 1790, pièce 28 (on which marginal notes indicate that approval was sent on Feb. 13); "Observations sur la lettre du ministre à

Saint-Priest as minister of the interior kept Lafayette informed about the forces of the provost-general of the Île de France,[88] and the movements of Lafayette's own troops from one place to another were a frequent source of communications with Latour du Pin. If the municipality of Dreux asked for reinforcements[89] or the commander at Versailles and Rambouillet claimed that his command was too small to protect the châteaux and other royal properties against armed looters,[90] letters went back and forth. Tax collection broke down at Verneuil-au-Perche, but when the ministry of war asked him to transfer the troops recently sent to Houdan, Lafayette stated that he could not spare them.[91] When the Invalides stationed at Saint-Denis complained that their muskets were too heavy, Lafayette suggested, and the minister approved, that they be armed with halberds, preferably marked with a device that would appeal to "the pride of the brave veterans."[92] Latour du Pin approved Lafayette's rebuke of an officer at Clermont-en-Beauvaisis for withdrawing his men without permission after a fight between a soldier and a citizen, endorsed his having ordered another detachment to that town, and then, when its municipal authorities requested the withdrawal of that detachment, left the answer to him. The minister seemed to be making a special effort to comply with Lafayette's wishes, and if there was any basis for the gossip at court that Lafayette and Latour du Pin had had a falling out because the minister was reluctant to grant the Cross of Saint Louis to National Guard officers,[93] their extant correspondence does not provide it.

Lafayette en date du 13 février 1790," *ibid.*, pièce 70; *ibid.*, carton LXI, chemise Intérieur (mars 1790), pièces 29, 30.

[88] Latour du Pin to Lafayette, Feb. 2, *ibid.*, carton LX, minutes de jan. et première quinzaine de fev.; same to same, Feb. 20, *ibid.*, carton LXI, chemise Minutes, 16–28 fev. 1790; and Tuetey, II, 323, No. 3981.

[89] AMG: AH, carton LX, chemise Minutes, jan. et fev. première quinzaine, 1790, Feb. 6.

[90] Lafayette to Latour du Pin, Feb. 10, *ibid.*, pièce 59; and Lafayette to Chevalier de Langlois, commander of the Chasseurs des Evechés, Feb. 12, Bibliothèque de Versailles (kindness of M. Bréchin).

[91] Latour du Pin to Lafayette, AMG: AH, carton LX, Feb. 9, chemise fev. 1–15, 1790, pièce 56, and Lafayette to Latour du Pin, Feb. 10, *ibid.*, pièce 59.

[92] An officer at the Hôtel des Invalides to [Latour du Pin], Feb. 12, *ibid.*, pièce 68, and *ibid.*, carton LXI, chemise Intérieur (mars 1790), pièce 23.

[93] Vaudreuil to Artois, Mar. 20, Pingaud (ed.), I, 149; Mme de Vatre à M. de Givray,

In the meantime the movement to "federate" with the National Guard of Paris had gained momentum from the king's pledge of February 4 to support the Revolution. Lafayette encouraged the incipient spirit of fraternity. When the National Guard of Senecy in Burgundy asked his support for a memoir they were sending to the National Assembly, he urged upon them, with a "moderation compatible with their patriotism," to make "every reasonable sacrifice" for public concord.[94] When a "plan de confédération générale," which had been presented to the National Guard of Besançon as early as the preceding December, was brought to his attention in February, he graciously acknowledged its receipt.[95] Among the requests for affiliation with the Paris National Guard was one from Tours, delivered by a deputation of its National Guard. When Lafayette introduced them to the Assembly of Representatives, the spokesman read a resolution pledging his corps' devotion to the Revolution, with assurances of "the most fraternal feelings" for the National Guard of Paris, who, he said, had set an example of the civic spirit that should animate all Frenchmen. As presiding officer of the Representatives Abbé Fauchet expressed his colleagues' pleasure with the visitor's words: "The commendation that you give to M. the Commandant General and the Parisian National Guard finds the same sentiments in the hearts of all the Representatives, together with a fitting eagerness to realize that union and fraternity which the Assembly adopts with enthusiasm."[96]

Despite the anonymous pamphlets attacking the Paris commandant general, evidence accumulated that the devotion to him of the largely middle and upper class National Guard units of the realm was gaining support. Artists and journalists still welcomed the opportunity to do him honor. Among the artists who had most recently done so were the engraver Romin Girard, who offered

---

Mar. 23, Vaissière (ed.), pp. 213–14; and Lescure (ed.), II, 436 (Apr. 2). See also below, p. 307.

[94] E.g., Lafayette to the staff of the National Guard of Senecy in Burgundy, Mar. 6, Collection of Dr. Max Thorek, Chicago, Ill. See also S. W. Jackson, *Lafayette: A Bibliography* (New York, 1930), pp. 160–61; *Moniteur,* Mar. 3, p. 251, Mar. 19, p. 318; and nn. 95 and 96 below. (After Dr. Thorek died, his collection was dispersed.)

[95] Tuetey, XI, 227, No. 725.

[96] Lacroix, IV, 313–16 (Mar. 6).

a *Collection complète des drapeaux faits dans les soixante districts,*
which he had dedicated to Lafayette,[97] and a pupil of the illustrious
Jacques-Louis David named Godefroy, who proposed to sell sets
of drawings of deputies including Lafayette.[98] When Jean-François
de Carteaux, artist and lieutenant in the National Guard cavalry,
destined within a few years to become famous as a general, presented to the Assembly of Representatives a painting of his commander with the intention of collecting subscriptions to engravings
of it, the *Journal de la municipalité et des districts de Paris,* seconding the Representatives' applause, commented: "Our descendants,
no doubt, will regret not having witnessed the virtues of our commandant general in order to imitate them; too much cannot be
done, therefore, to depict the model of them."[99]

The popularity of that model in Paris was displayed when on
Sunday, March 7, he reviewed the Second Division, about five
thousand strong, on the Champs-Elysées. The *Courrier de Paris*
reported that the troops made a "very brilliant" showing, which
was "much applauded" and that the commandant general received
from the spectators ample testimony of "the public's satisfaction."[100] The *Journal général de la cour* also noted that a "pro-
digious crowd" gathered both in carriages and on foot to watch
the review, although it implied that what had brought them there
was the hope of seeing the king (and, to be sure, when Lafayette
arrived alone, while they greeted him with cheers, their cheers
were mingled with cries of "Long live the king").[101] But, as the
same journal had earlier indicated, some persons made no such in-
vidious comparisons. One morning, it reported, the officers on duty
at the Tuileries informed Lafayette that a "young woman of the
people" insisted upon presenting a petition to His Majesty in person and refused to allow anyone else to take it. Lafayette went to
see her and asked if she would like him to take her petition to the
king. She replied: "I can refuse you nothing. Whether I place my

[97] *Journal de Paris,* Mar. 5, p. 256.

[98] *Moniteur,* Mar. 17, p. 310.

[99] Mar. 3, p. 490, and Lacroix, IV, 251 (Mar. 1).

[100] Mar. 8, p. 36. See also J. G. Wille, *Mémoires et journal* (Paris, 1857), II, 228.

[101] Mar. 8, p. 534. See also *Gazette universelle,* Mar. 8, p. 392.

petition in your hands or in those of the king, is it not the same thing?"[102] The *Gazette universelle* editorialized that Lafayette's zeal for the public welfare was exposing him to ruin. General Washington had set the precedent for such disinterestedness, the editorial conceded, but Washington had no children as his disciple had; Lafayette's delicacy would be intelligible if he were to hold his post for only a few months, but the Commune wanted him to stay on for a long time.[103] The Francophile Chevalier de Pio, formerly Neapolitan chargé d'affaires in Paris, after having dined at the Rue de Bourbon, neatly summed up Lafayette's situation: "How he is adored, that man, but also what a burden he has!"[104]

BIBLIOGRAPHICAL NOTES

Clarkson's *History . . . of the Abolition of the African Slave Trade* is largely autobiographical. Though published almost thirty years after his visit to France in 1789–90, its account of that visit seems to be corroborated by the parts of his correspondence with the Neckers and Mirabeau once owned by Stuart W. Jackson and now in the Yale University Library.

Albert Krebs, "La Fayette et l'abolition de l'esclavage," *Les Cahiers français: documents d'actualité,* No. 24 (Dec. 1957), p. 26, says that the slaves of "La Belle Gabrielle" were sold by the National Convention in 1794 as the property of an émigré (which Lafayette was at the time), and this statement is borne out by *Mémoires,* III, 72, 401, n. 1, IV, 224, n. 1. See also Albert Krebs, "La Fayette et le problème de l'esclavage," *Annuaire-Bulletin de la Société de l'histoire de France* (1956–57), pp. 54–55, and J. Letanconnoux, "Le Comité des Deputés extraordinaires des manufactures et du commerce de France et l'oeuvre économique de l'Assemblée constitutante (1789–1791)," *Annales révolutionnaires,* VI (1913), 176, 187, 189–90. Kennedy, p. 6, says that Lafayette liberated his slaves toward the end of 1789, but we have found no evidence for that statement. A number of as yet unexploited documents related to "La Belle Gabrielle" are in CU: Lafayette Archives, Carton III.

The background of the controversies over San Domingo is told by Gabriel Debien in *Les colons de Saint-Domingue et la Révolution: Essais sur le Club Massaic (août 1789-août 1792)* [Paris, 1953] and "Les colons des Antilles et leur main d'oeuvre à la fin du XVIII⁰ siècle," *AHRF,* XXVII (1955), 259–83.

[102] Feb. 9, p. 314.

[103] Mar. 10, p. 399. See also *Chronique de Paris,* Mar. 8, p. 267.

[104] Pio to Jefferson, Mar. 14, Boyd (ed.), XVI, 231.

CHAPTER XIII

"Missionary of Liberty"

THE AREA known to the Old Regime as the Austrian Netherlands embraced the countries now named Luxembourg and Belgium (except for the Bishopric of Liège, which was a separate principality within the Holy Roman Empire). The provinces of the Austrian Netherlands were largely independent of each other and, particularly Brabant and Flanders, jealous of their traditional rights and prerogatives. In defense of those rights and prerogatives they had been threatening since 1787 to revolt against the centralizing reforms that their Habsburg ruler, the Holy Roman Emperor Joseph II, tried to institute. Belgian resistance to Joseph's reforms was led at first in the separate provinces by their several estates, representing the clergy, nobles, and chief cities. Although supported by the Belgian people, the estates wished to retain firm control of their provincial institutions regardless of any advantages that Joseph's centralizing tendencies might provide. Louis XVI, reluctant to aid the rebels against the emperor, his ally and brother-in-law, hoped to find a basis for a peaceful settlement, especially since the rival alliance of Prussia, Britain, and the United (Dutch) Provinces favored the insurgents. In August 1789, with the example of successful revolution in France before them, the Belgians seemed ready to explode, and in September Lafayette received a memoir counseling French intervention on their behalf.[1] The imminence of international conflict over

---

[1] In CU: Lafayette Archives, Carton IV, there is a two-page memoir entitled "Considérations Politiques concernant les Pays-Bas Autrichiens, copie remise à l'Administration le 12-7bre [September] 1789, envisage la coopération de la France à la révolution prète à éclater dans les Pays-Bas Autrichiens."

the dispute in Belgium served as a pretext early in October for sending the Duc d'Orléans on a "special mission" to England, perchance to promote his own ambitions for a Belgian crown.[2]

By late October the Belgian revolt took a new turn. A popular party in several Belgian cities demanded a change similar to that advocated by the "Patriots" in France—popular sovereignty—against the opposition of the estates dominated by the clergy and the nobility. Early in the conflict Lafayette had expressed sympathy with the Belgian patriots, envisaging the possibility that the emperor and the conflicting parties of rebels might be brought together in a settlement that would provide autonomy for the Austrian Netherlands while leaving them under the Habsburg crown. Such a settlement would frustrate the Anglo-Dutch-Prussian alliance and strengthen France's supporters not only in the Austrian but also in the Dutch Netherlands and at the same time serve the cause of liberty.[3] In October Mirabeau,[4] and in December the king of Prussia,[5] learned of Lafayette's involvement in Belgian affairs. By that time the insurrection had spread to the Bishopric of Liège, and Prussia had sent troops into the bishopric. These complications explain why Lafayette presumed that he might be engaged in a military campaign in the spring.[6] As early as October 1789 the Chevalier de Ternant, whom Lafayette had known in America, who was now colonel of the infantry Regiment of Royal-Liègeois, and who was spoken of as the next French minister to the United States,[7] had begun to busy himself with lining up secret military forces, and since he had once been Lafayette's agent in an earlier effort to promote the republican cause in Holland,[8] an astute ob-

---

[2] See above, pp. 17–18.

[3] CU: Lafayette Archives: "Mémoire sur la necessité de rétablir à main armée la liberté belgique," probably of October 1789, and a set of letters to Lafayette in October and December 1789, mostly from the Belgian patriot Tort de La Sonde.

[4] Mirabeau to La Marck, Oct. 28, Bacourt (ed.), I, 409.

[5] Frederick William II to Comte von der Goltz, Dec. 3, E. E. Hubert (ed.), *Correspondance des ministres de France accredités à Bruxelles de 1780 à 1790* (Brussels, 1920–24), II, 481–82.

[6] See above, pp. 74, 188.

[7] Morris to Washington, July 31, 1789, Davenport (ed.), I, 170.

[8] Gottschalk, *Between,* pp. 338–40.

server like Morris was led to surmise that Ternant, with Lafayette's knowledge, was now similarly engaged.[9]

In December Lafayette received permission to assemble troops near the Belgian border but delayed doing so openly, pending the National Assembly's passage of an army bill that would determine how control of the army was to be divided. Meanwhile he treated with two Belgian patriot emissaries in Paris, M. Torfs, agent of the Brabant estates in France, and Tort de La Sonde, and they, in turn, informed the leaders in Brussels what was going on. In January, with Montmorin's cognizance, Lafayette sent Sémonville to Brussels as his personal agent.[10] Sémonville was to encourage the popular party (led by J. F. Vonck) and to try to persuade the members of the estates party to join in a representative assembly like that of France in order to make a constitution like that being drafted in France; if the Belgian leaders could reach such an agreement, then the French government might present it to Joseph II as a solution that promised to end the rebellion, leave the emperor in possession, and eliminate Anglo-Dutch-Prussian influence.[11]

When on January 12 Lafayette wrote to President Washington: "Liberty is sprouting about in the other parts of Europe, and I am encouraging it by all means in my power,"[12] what he had in mind particularly as "the other parts of Europe" were the Austrian Netherlands.[13] On January 22 Morris wrote to Washington: "Our friend Lafayette (who by the bye is trying to stir up a Revolution in the King of Prussia's [sic] Dominion) burns with Desire to be at the Head of an Army in Flanders and drive the Stadholder [William of Orange] into a Ditch."[14]

[9] Morris diary, Oct. 9, Nov. 1, Davenport (ed.), I, 250–51, 280, and Lafayette to Montmorin, Feb. 1, *Mémoires,* III, 21.

[10] M. van der Noot to Lafayette, Jan. 2, CU: Lafayette Archives, Carton IV, folder 2820–2821.

[11] *Journal général de l'Europe,* No. 15, p. 267; Lafayette to Hennings, Jan. 15, 1799, *Mémoires,* III, 265; and *ibid.,* pp. 13–14, 16–18.

[12] Gottschalk (ed.), p. 246.

[13] He perhaps did not have Corsica in mind as one of "the other parts of Europe" since Corsica was a French possession. But see below, pp. 378–79. In 1799 he claimed that except for the United States and the Dutch Netherlands he concerned himself at this time only with Belgium: *Mémoires,* III, 264–65.

[14] Davenport (ed.), I, 377.

Arrived in Brussels, Sémonville saw the Belgian leaders and soon notified Montmorin and Lafayette that a peaceful solution of the Belgian crisis seemed unlikely.[15] Early in January the deputies of the several estates assembled in a "national" congress and proclaimed "the United States of Belgium." Sémonville, feeling that the presence of Prussian soldiers near the Austrian Netherlands would place France at a marked disadvantage, suggested to Lafayette that France make a show of force but at the same time announce its peaceful intentions: that it had no designs upon the liberty of other peoples, and only if the Belgian people as a whole (not merely the deputies of the estates) explicitly proclaimed their rights, could they be treated as a sovereign nation, but meanwhile France would maintain friendly contact with those who were engaged in the dispute with the emperor.[16] Sémonville's letter led Lafayette to urge Montmorin to assemble troops on the Belgian frontier at once; in the expectation that the National Assembly would soon pass the projected army bill, "the king can prepare troop movements before that and announce them afterward, and speak out as the chief of a great, proud, and free nation."[17]

Meanwhile Ternant had made considerable progress with the Belgian emissaries in Paris, and they signed an agreement to push the program that Lafayette advocated. It contemplated that the Belgians, assembled in a national convention, would draw up a liberal constitution, which Joseph II would then be asked to accept. Lafayette considered such a convention "a *sine qua non* to which the European sovereigns will in their turn be willing to accede,"[18] and he proposed, if Montmorin agreed, to submit the arrangement to the emperor as a basis for French mediation. A special emissary, he suggested, should go to Vienna to confer with Joseph II upon the future of the Austrian Netherlands. A delicate mission of that

[15] Van der Noot to Lafayette, Jan. 2, CU: Lafayette Archives, Carton IV, folder 2820–2821; "Considérations sur l'état actuel des Provinces belgiques," *ibid.*, envelope 2472–2488; "Note de M le Cte de Mont . . . sur les dépèche [*sic*] de Mr. de Sémonville," *ibid.*, folder 2643–2763; and Lafayette to Montmorin, Feb. 2, *Mémoires*, III, 21.

[16] Sémonville to Lafayette, Jan. 27, *Mémoires*, III, 22–24.

[17] Lafayette to Montmorin, Feb. 1, *ibid.*, p. 22.

[18] *Ibid.*, p. 21.

sort would require sympathetic management, and so the then ambassador, the Marquis de Noailles (who, incidentally, was Adrienne's uncle), should be replaced by the Comte de Ségur, and Lafayette advised the foreign minister to clear the way promptly for Ségur to take up his mission. "Our affair is going well both to the advantage of liberty, which ought always to take precedence, and to that of our policy," Lafayette wrote Montmorin on February 1. "Only decision and promptness are needed." Ternant's understanding with the Belgian agents "should be the objective of our efforts, the end of M. de Sémonville's negotiations, after which we become masters of the situation and protectors of Belgian liberty." Since Torfs and La Sonde planned to depart soon for the Netherlands, Lafayette desired to send Montmorin's reactions that very evening to Sémonville.[19]

Montmorin replied by means of marginal comments on Lafayette's letter and seemed to fall in with Lafayette's proposals, but in fact he discouraged and delayed them. He obviously did not share the opinion that foreign policy should take second place to the promotion of liberty, but he consented to discuss the proposed program with the Austrian ambassador in Paris, even though he doubted that the ambassador had any significant authority in Belgian matters. He also agreed to send Ségur to Vienna "as soon as possible, but circumstances must permit it and arrangements relative to his predecessor must be settled." To Lafayette's proposal that the king, even before an army bill was passed, should plan a show of force on the Belgian border Montmorin gave his approval with the proviso that "we get mixed up in nothing in order not to provoke the storm that this arrangement is designed to prevent."[20]

Negotiations with Necker, Mercy-Argenteau, and other interested persons caused further delay. Not until February 8, a full week after he had submitted his plan for a settlement of the Belgian crisis, did Lafayette relay to Sémonville the decisions that had tentatively been reached. He counted on Mssrs. Torfs and La Sonde,

[19] We follow here the original in CU: Lafayette Archives, Carton IV, which reads *après lequel nous devons* instead of (as printed in *Mémoires,* III, 20) *Nous serons alors.* The original contains several passages that are omitted from the published text. They deal mostly with monetary allowances to Sémonville and La Sonde that Lafayette asked for and Montmorin hesitated to approve.

[20] Marginalia of Montmorin, *Mémoires,* III, 19–22. See also *ibid.,* p. 20 n.

he said, when they should reach Brussels, to inform Sémonville of the plan concocted in Paris[21] for an autonomous Belgium within the Habsburg empire.[22] Sémonville was to determine whether such a plan had a chance of success in Brussels; everyone who had been consulted in Paris—including Montmorin, Ternant, Ségur, and Mercy-Argenteau—had approved of it, although the last-named thought the emperor might think it extravagant. Montmorin, however, still wanted some precise answers to some questions about its feasibility: Should Torf's plan be presented to the Austrian government through the Belgian leaders or directly? In either case, what support would it receive in the Netherlands? Montmorin wished to talk these matters over with Sémonville or, if Sémonville preferred not to leave Brussels, Ternant could go to confer with him there.

Troop movements on the Belgian frontier, Lafayette informed Sémonville, would already have taken place had not Necker "quibbled" over the cost. Nevertheless, "I am pushing this move with all my power," he wrote. He had urged that 25,000 men be placed under General de Rochambeau's command in Flanders and that reinforcements be sent to Alsace as well. He also informed Sémonville (and presumably Sémonville was to inform his Belgian contacts) that the French Revolution was now entering a quieter stage; since the king's gesture of February 4, "parties still exist in the Assembly, but their conduct is much more moderate." In short, "all my affairs . . . are going very well," and "I leave to your efforts, to whatever resources you command, the outcome of the present negotiations, whose success will ensure our revolution and prepare others."[23]

But all did not go as planned. When La Sonde reached Brussels he found that although the "enlightened" Belgians proposed to organize a provisional federal republic, modeled on the Swiss cantons, they were not in control and, unless their position improved rapidly, the privileged estates, with Prussian and Dutch support,

---

[21] Lafayette to Sémonville, Feb. 8, *ibid.*, p. 30. This letter is placed by the editors out of chronological order. It obviously went out before Torfs and La Sonde left Paris. See also Mme de Lafayette to Mme d'Hénin, July 25, 1796, *ibid.*, IV, 291.

[22] See above, p. 277. Cf. *Mémoires*, III, pp. 20 n., 21.

[23] Lafayette to Sémonville, Feb. 8, *ibid.*, pp. 28–31.

would take charge.[24] Sémonville gave much the same intelligence. Calling a national assembly that would be representative of the Belgian people, he said, would present great difficulties, because of differences in language, rivalries among the provinces, and disputes between partisans of the estates and of the emperor. Furthermore, the princess of Orange, wife of the stadholder and sister of the Prussian king, was working hard to get Britain and Prussia to join the Dutch Republic in a prompt recognition of Belgian independence designed to swing a grateful Belgium into the orbit of their alliance while destroying the chances of the popular party. New Belgian emissaries were being sent to France, but Sémonville did not consider them friendly and advised Lafayette not to reveal his wishes to them. Instead, he counseled a concentration of troops on the Belgian frontier, convinced that then a simple explanation of French tactics would make France the logical choice as mediator of Belgium's party conflicts.[25]

The situation, never simple, became more complex even as Sémonville wrote. In the first place, the Prussians learned early about Sémonville's mission and guessed that he was Lafayette's agent rather than a fully accredited agent of the French foreign office.[26] Moreover, Sémonville doubted that the plan of Torfs and Ternant would be acceptable to either party in the Belgian civil conflict, since neither of them seemed to want Habsburg sovereignty to continue. Apparently without letting Lafayette know, Montmorin also distrusted Torfs's judgment. At least, when he informed the French ambassador in Vienna of Torfs's scheme for a constitutional monarchy in Belgium under a Habsburg scion and instructed him to get the Austrian court's reactions, Montmorin did not hide his lack of enthusiasm.[27] Thus Lafayette was weakened on two fronts: the Prussians knew more about his manipulations than he wished them to know, while his own government had less confidence in

---

[24] La Sonde to Lafayette, Feb. [no day given], *ibid.,* pp. 26–28.

[25] Sémonville to Lafayette, Feb. [no day given], *ibid.,* pp. 24–26. Cf. below, p. 283 and n. 41.

[26] Von de Goltz to Frederick William II, Feb. 12, Hubert (ed.), II, 488. See also Tassier, p. 312; Théodore Juste, *La république belge (1790)* (Brussels, 1884), pp. 87–91; and Ludwig Sevin, *Das system der preussichen Geheimpolitik vom August 1790 bis zum Mai 1791* (Berlin, 1903), p. 30 n.

[27] Montmorin to Noailles, Feb. 13, Hubert (ed.), II, 476–78.

his projects than he assumed it had. He revealed his discontent to Morris and Short but put the blame largely on Minister of War Latour du Pin rather than on Montmorin. Morris thought war imminent enough to give Lafayette, a mere general, the benefit of his advice on the strategy by which it should be conducted.[28]

The popular movement in the United Dutch Provinces could not easily be separated from that in Belgium, since they had a common enemy in the House of Orange, and some of the Dutch too took their cause directly to Lafayette. Two "Dutch patriots" (as they called themselves) pointedly outlined the need for a leader in the common cause: "The command will be confided to a single chief who should unite all the parties. It is useless, Monsieur le marquis, to give you the name of that chief, upon whom all eyes are fixed and who already has won the liberty of America and France."[29] Whatever Lafayette's response was to that overture, made early in 1790, the "Dutch patriots" who made it believed until mid-March that he approved. They came to Paris to see him, only to find that he would not give them an audience or even answer the letter they sent.[30]

If the impression the letters of these "Dutch patriots" convey is correct, Lafayette's change of heart toward them is probably ascribable to Montmorin's circumspect attitude toward the Belgian insurrection. France's domestic complications dictated prudence in foreign policy. When questioned by the Prussian ambassador about Sémonville's presence in Brussels, Montmorin repudiated responsibility although he admitted that Sémonville might be Lafayette's personal agent. While he acceded to Lafayette's request for a stipend to Sémonville,[31] he took the precaution to sound out not only the Austrian ambassador in Paris but also the French ambassador in Vienna on Austria's reaction to Torfs's proposal.[32]

In the end the fuss over that proposal proved a waste of effort.

[28] Morris diary, Feb. 15, Davenport (ed.), I, 411–12.

[29] Van Hoey and Huber to Lafayette, Jan. 24, CU: Lafayette Archives, Carton IV, folder 2822–2834.

[30] Same to same, Mar. 14, *ibid.*

[31] "Note concernant l'existence de M. de Sémonville à Bruxelles," Feb. 1790, *ibid.*, folder 2772–2788.

[32] Montmorin to Noailles, Feb. 13, *ibid.*, folder 2456–2465; *Mémoires*, III, 20 n.; and Hubert (ed.), II, 272 n.

When Torfs arrived in Brussels and presented it to the leaders of the aristocratic clerical party,[33] they were not favorably impressed. Sémonville, convinced that little could be done at the moment to promote popular sovereignty in Belgium, returned to Paris. In the meantime the Prussian ambassador in Paris had formally reported that while both Mirabeau and Lafayette would rejoice if Austria lost Belgium, their policy was no less unfriendly to Prussia; they hoped not only that the Belgian revolt would result in a popular government which would ally with France but also that the spirit of revolt would spread to the United Provinces.[34] A Prussian agent in Brussels lent color to the Paris ambassador's fears when he reported that Lafayette's emissary had promised the Belgians 20,000 men and recognition of their independence.[35]

Lafayette thus became a focal point of Prussian diplomatic concern. General Martin Ernst Schlieffen was the commander of the Prussian forces in Liège. In 1785, when Lafayette was on his way to inspect Prussian army maneuvers,[36] he had met Schlieffen in Hesse, and recalling that brief encounter, Schlieffen now took the liberty of discussing the situation in Belgium with him "as one soldier to another." "My country," he wrote, "wishes the redoubtable Austria to be less powerful in that province; yours . . . ought to desire it likewise." Prussia was indifferent regarding the form of Belgian government, he asserted, and so perhaps the two nations would not find themselves at odds in that regard; he and his army were in Liège merely to keep order, for his king had no ulterior designs on that principality.[37]

Some time was to elapse before Lafayette would answer Schlieffen's letter. By the end of February the contest in Belgium had ceased to be merely a fight between the Belgian provinces seeking autonomy and a high-handed ruler who had swept away certain of their outworn but venerable privileges, and it had become an openly three-cornered struggle instead. The aristocratic-controlled

[33] Torfs to Lafayette, Feb. 26, CU: Lafayette Archives, Carton IV, folder 2813–2819.

[34] Feb. 2, Sevin, pp. 28n, 30.

[35] Hubert (ed.), II, 270 n.

[36] Gottschalk, Between, p. 182.

[37] Schlieffen to Lafayette, Feb. 22, Mémoires, III, 31–32.

Congress of the Belgian Estates, cautiously encouraged by British-Prussian-Dutch support, demanded independence; the Habsburg prince, allied to the French Bourbons, refused to grant it; and the Belgian liberals, who had the sympathy of some French liberals, including Lafayette, sought a constitutional regime providing local autonomy within the Habsburg empire. In this uneven struggle the Belgian liberals had the least strength.

The situation changed when Joseph II died (February 20). In due course the new Habsburg ruler, Leopold II, rescinded his predecessor's decrees, confirmed the privileges of the Belgian estates and provinces, made concessions to Belgian autonomy that amounted almost to independence, and opened the door to further reform. The Belgian Congress, however, rejected Leopold's offer, although some leaders of the popular party favored it. As Sémonville had indicated, the Congress sent Comte de Thiennes, accompanied by Torfs, to Paris to solicit recognition of Belgian independence,[38] with appeals for support addressed not only to Louis XVI but also to the National Assembly and to Lafayette. The Belgian popular party, however, disavowed Thiennes and begged Lafayette to "oppose his mission as coming from a body who have usurped the sovereignty of their country in violation of the rights of the people."[39] Thiennes carried a letter of the Belgian Congress to Lafayette appealing to his love of liberty, and Thiennes thought, when he presented it, that his host was flattered. Yet, while Lafayette was pleased that "the spirit of liberty was making so much progress in all the countries of the world," he delayed making any commitment to any of the parties in the Belgian crisis.[40] It seemed clear that he wished first to consult with Montmorin, and (what Thiennes probably did not know) Sémonville had also warned him that the Congress' agents did not sympathize with the pro-French popular party.[41]

On March 11 Thiennes and Torfs informed Montmorin that they had been commissioned to deliver to him a document which,

[38] *Courier national,* Mar. 15, pp. 6–7, and Tassier, pp. 313–18.

[39] Short to Jefferson, Mar. 9, Boyd (ed.), XVI, 220.

[40] Von der Goltz to Frederick William II, Mar. 12, Hubert (ed.), II, 491.

[41] *Mémoires,* III, 24. Cf. above, p. 280 and n. 25.

it was easy to guess, was the Belgian Congress' declaration of independence along with a request for French recognition. Montmorin postponed answering until he could consult Louis XVI.[42] The king, who had so far refused to receive communications from the Belgian Congress, once more adhered to that policy and instructed Montmorin to so inform the National Assembly. Montmorin thereupon told Thiennes that since the principles of the Belgian Congress were not consistent with popular sovereignty and since Leopold's conciliatory program appeared quite acceptable, France at that juncture in its affairs could remain only passive in the Belgian complications.[43]

Montmorin then informed the National Assembly of his policy. The Assembly, however, having independently received the Belgian agents' communication, had to decide whether to take a position with regard to the Belgian crisis in particular and thus perhaps to create a precedent with regard to international relations in general. By implication at least, the issue involved was not alone the recognition of Belgian independence; it was also the power to carry on correspondence with foreign nations: Should it rest in the future with the National Assembly, with the king as the chief executive, or with both?

The National Assembly was expected to bring up the Belgian matter in the morning session of March 17, and Lafayette prepared a resolution which he intended to present on that occasion advocating that the decision be left to the king. He composed it carefully. First he wrote out a rough draft; it was redrafted (with stylistic modifications) by another hand; and he then corrected the second draft.[44]

On March 17, after the discussion of some routine matters, Rabaut-St.-Étienne, the current president of the National Assembly, read Montmorin's letter, which informed the Assembly that in the king's opinion justice, prudence, and dignity required him not to

---

[42] *AP*, XII, 205–6.

[43] Von der Goltz to Frederick William II, Mar. 12, 19, quoted in Hubert (ed.), II, 277, nn. 3 and 4.

[44] See n. 46 below. The redrafting might have been done with Montmorin's assistance: see below, pp. 286 and n. 48, 287 and n. 52.

correspond with the Belgian Congress and so he had returned unopened a communication presumed to contain a declaration of
Belgian independence and had instructed his minister to report his
action to the Assembly.[45] Rabaut added that letters similar to the
one addressed to the king had been sent to himself and to the Assembly but likewise remained unopened.

Lafayette was the first to go to the tribune, where he read his
prepared speech. "There is no friend of liberty, Gentlemen," he
began, "there is no Frenchman but owes to the Belgian people his
approval and good wishes." Nevertheless, the letter Rabaut had referred to raised two questions: To whom was it addressed? And
from whom did it come? "It was written to the constituent assembly of France, whose lofty duties were irrelevant to that purpose;
it was written by a congress whose members no one respects
more than I but which, in keeping with the present composition of
the Belgian estates, does not yet show signs of emanating from the
sovereignty of the people." Every consideration, therefore, pointed
to the desirability of leaving the matter to the king. Lafayette expressed confidence that "the king of the French . . . will not mislead
us on the way to act toward a people who long to be free and who
are beginning to recognize their rights." Therefore he formally
proposed that "the National Assembly, having given due attention
both to a letter of M. de Montmorin in which that minister in-
forms it of the king's intention not to open a communication from
the Belgian estates and to the domestic situation of the Low Countries, . . . is of the opinion that it can do no better than to leave
the matter entirely to the wisdom and the known sentiments of
the king."[46]

When Lafayette stopped speaking, applause and cries of "Vote"
came from both the Left and the Right.[47] But Lafayette's resolu-

[45] Montmorin to Rabaut-St.-Etienne, Mar. 15, *AP*, XII, 205–6.

[46] A number of contemporary journals reported this speech between Mar. 18 and 26,
and it was separately printed: See André Martin and Gérard Walter, *Catalogue de l'histoire
de la Révolution française*, II (Paris, 1938), 614, No. 18364. Some slight differences occur
in the several versions, but they agree on the main points. The version in *Moniteur*, Mar.
18, p. 315, was copied in *AP*, XII, 206. See also Short to Jay, Mar. 25, Boyd (ed.), XVI,
267–68.

[47] *Mercure historique et politique de Bruxelles*, Mar. 27, pp. 299–300; *Gazette de*

tion was not to pass without discussion. Two deputies rushed to the tribune. Pétion de Villeneuve, already recognized as a leader of the more radical Jacobins, was unable to make himself clearly heard above the cries of "Vote." Coming up behind him, however, was Dupont de Nemours, who, having seen Lafayette read from a manuscript, had concluded that he was acting in collusion with Montmorin; he shouted out a warning not to adopt a measure presented by a single deputy on the basis of a single letter from a minister—a step that would take from the Assembly any voice in declaring war and making peace and would leave them no more than slaves![48] Immediately recriminations flew back and forth until the Vicomte de Noailles reminded his colleagues that their agenda for the day concerned the constitution and finances, and "for the present," he insisted, "we cannot take up any extraneous matter."[49] The Assembly agreed and turned to the order of the day. So Lafayette's resolution was not acted upon. Yet he had won a moral victory, for the Assembly had expressed no disapproval of the king's action and had given no recognition to the Belgian Congress. The royal prerogative in foreign affairs remained an open question, subject to later consideration.

The Vicomte de Noailles may have wished only to proceed, as he said, to the main business of the Assembly, but his motive was suspect in at least one quarter. The French ambassador in London, La Luzerne, implied that the Noailles, Adrienne's family, were ill disposed toward Lafayette and for some time, La Luzerne believed, the Vicomte de Noailles had been "doing his utmost to ruin" him.[50] Lafayette himself gave no indication that he considered the Noailles unfriendly, but his having spoken disparagingly of a Congress that was trying to win independence for Belgium brought astonished

---

Leide, supplément, Mar. 26; and *Journal de Paris*, Mar. 18, p. 305. The statement sometimes encountered that Lafayette was a poor public speaker is not confirmed by the contemporary evidence, which frequently indicates that he received an enthusiastic response from his audience. Cf. Gottschalk, *Between*, p. 297.

[48] Desmoulins (*Révolutions*, No. 18, p. 102) gives the fullest text of Dupont's words. It is supplemented by the *Courrier de Provence*, Mar. 17–19, p. 27. See also *Courrier français*, Mar. 18, p. 140, and *Journal des Impartiaux*, No. 10, pp. 7–8.

[49] *AP*, XII, 206.

[50] Morris diary, Apr. 6, Davenport (ed.), I, 476.

criticism from some of his admirers. Brissot's *Patriote français,* while agreeing that the Belgian Congress did not emanate from a sovereign people, voiced the opinion that the National Assembly should at least have opened the letter from the Belgians.[51] Desmoulins delivered a more vigorous rebuke: "I ask M. de la Fayette's pardon, for I am infinitely honored to have him as one of my subscribers, but I shall not conceal from him that his motion brought sorrow to all patriots." He, like Dupont, presumed that someone else had written the speech Lafayette read: "I heard you speak more than an hour one day before the Commune. You expressed yourself with more clarity, more purity, more dignity. This is not your style, and even less is it the doctrine that I have heard you profess." The proper answer to have made to the Belgian appeal, in Desmoulins' opinion, would have been that when the Belgian Congress showed that its powers did in fact emanate from the people, the National Assembly would recognize it.[52] S.-N.-H. Linguet, once an outstanding critic of the *philosophes,* now editor of the *Annales politiques* and a champion of Belgian independence, went directly to Lafayette to deliver his complaint. His argument was a practical one—the disadvantage to France if the British succeeded in establishing their control of the Belgian provinces.[53] The Russian ambassador at London soon advised his government that Leopold's overtures seemed likely to fail because the people of Belgium were divided: those of the province of Brabant apparently wanted a theocratic government while those of Flanders "governed by the amiable French and the vigorous Lafayette, Mirabeau, Barnave, and all the rest of those great men, want a democratic government founded on the rights of man, that sublime discovery of the generalissimo of the Parisians, which, as all the world knows, has made France the happiest country of the universe."[54] Although the ambassador was obviously being sardonic about France, he reflected a point of view about French influence

[51] Mar. 19, p. 1.

[52] *Révolutions,* No. 18, pp. 195–204.

[53] *Annales politiques,* XVI, 140–41, quoted in Hubert (ed.), II, 277, n. 1.

[54] S. R. Vorontzov to Comte de Nesselrode, Mar. 19, A. de Nesselrode (ed.), *Lettres et papiers du chancelier comte de Nesselrode, 1760–1850* (Paris, 1904), I, 17–78.

in the Belgian situation that was widely held and essentially correct.

The Belgian Congress decided not to accept the olive branch that Leopold proffered, and not at all averse to a dispute in the Habsburg possessions, the Prussians approved its rejection of Leopold's terms. Lafayette's intended resolution actually played into the Prussians' hands. When the Belgian Congress learned of Montmorin's and Lafayette's maneuvers, it expressed "very strong displeasure"; some members proposed that all Frenchmen be expelled from Belgium, and the Congress' agents with its army actually discharged all French officers as well as all Dutch officers not pledged to the House of Orange.[55] But the Flemings and other liberal, pro-French elements of the population did not give up.

Thomas Paine had been in Paris since October, and in mid-March, when he wrote to Dr. Benjamin Rush of Philadelphia, his comment on events in Paris, probably reflecting Lafayette's opinion, was optimistic: everything was "going on right" despite "little inconveniences, the necessary consequences of pulling down and building up," and "our friend the Marquis is, like his great patron and master General Washington, acting a great part."[56] When Paine decided to return to England, Lafayette, having recently learned that Washington had received none of his letters for the past year, sent with him a letter for Paine to forward from England. It was dated March 17, the day of the debate in the National Assembly on the Belgian issue. "In these times of troubles," Lafayette apologized, it had become increasingly difficult to find dependable means of communicating with America.[57] This letter, therefore, gave a full account of events, one that was reassuring but not unrealistic: "Our revolution is getting on as well as it can with a Nation that has swallowed up liberty all at once, and is still liable to mistake licentiousness for freedom." Hence the National Assembly had

[55] Ruelle to Montmorin, Mar. 25, 31, Hubert (ed.), II, 297, 299, and La Luzerne to Montmorin, Apr. 30, *ibid.*, p. 289 n.

[56] Mar. 16, LC, courtesy of Mr. Sidney Kramer. See also *Quarterly Journal of the Library of Congress* (July–Sept. 1943), p. 22, and P. S. Foner (ed.), *The Complete Writings of Thomas Paine* (New York, 1945), II, 1285–86.

[57] Mar. 17, Gottschalk (ed.), pp. 347–48. Washington did, however, receive Lafayette's letter of Jan. 12, 1790: see above, pp. 177–78.

been destructive rather than constructive, revealing "more hatred to the ancient system than experience on the proper organization of a new and constitutional government," and so "everything has been destroyed and not much new building is yet above ground." In addition, "we still are pestered by two parties, the Aristocratic that is panting for a counter revolution, and the factious [i.e., the Jacobins], which aims at the division of the Empire, and destruction of all authority and perhaps of the lives of the reigning branch, both of which parties are fomenting troubles."[58]

Yet, while admitting that "there is much room for critics and calumnies," Lafayette turned to the brighter side of the picture: "We have brought about an admirable and almost incredible destruction of all abuses. . . . Everything not directly useful to, or coming from the people has been levelled. . . . We have made more changes in ten months than the most sanguine patriot could have imagined." To offset reports of French disorder he attested that "our internal troubles and anarchy are much exaggerated." In fact, the contemporary French scene, he thought, was analogous to that of the United States before the Philadelphia Convention drew up the new American constitution: "Upon the whole this Revolution, in which nothing will be wanting but energy of government just as it was in America, will implant liberty and make it flourish throughout the world, while we must wait for a Convention in a few years to mend some defects which are not now perceived by men just escaped from aristocracy and despotism."[59] In brief, "the Washington of France," reporting to his American archetype, took the position that, while all was not for the best in France, the worst had been eliminated, some good had been done, mistakes could be corrected in the future, and the idea of liberty thus would spread abroad.

A tradition in his family has it that at an art exhibition in 1790 Lafayette saw a painting of the wrecking of the Bastille and exclaimed, "Lucky man, whoever owns it!" Whereupon a voice behind him said, "General, it is yours." The voice was that of the

[58] Gottschalk (ed.), p. 347. In the interest of smoother reading we have here corrected Lafayette's frequent little errors in English spelling.

[59] Ibid.

painter Hubert Robert.[60] One of the gifts that Lafayette now
begged leave to present to his "dear General' was another picture
of the Bastille "just as it looked a few days after I had ordered its
demolition."[61] It was a pen-and-ink drawing inscribed at the bottom "Cathala, Architecte Inspecteur de la Bastille, fait le 7 Aoust
1789."[62] Along with the painting went one of the enormous keys to
the Bastille which Palloy had preserved and presented to Lafayette
—"the main kea [sic] of that fortress of despotism," 7½ inches
long and weighing well over a pound.[63] Lafayette sent these gifts
to Washington as "a tribute which I owe as a son to my adoptive
father, as an aid de camp to my General, as a Missionary of Liberty
to its Patriarch."[64]

A few days later a mutual friend, the Comte d'Estaing, wrote to
the "Patriarch" a glowing account of his disciple's successes: "The
health of M. le Marquis de la Fayette stands up despite his labors,
[and] his popularity keeps right on growing. I would shed my
blood to cement it; by contributing to it I would serve my country
and friendship. It seems to me that I esteem him still more every
day, and that used to seem to me impossible to imagine."[65]

When Thomas Paine finally went back to London, he was
charged with seeing that the Bastille key and the picture, with Lafayette's accompanying letter, reached Washington, but not until
the end of May did he find a good opportunity to forward them.
They went by a young American returning from England, with
whom Paine sent along a letter of his own that reconfirmed Lafayette's devotion to his adoptive father: "I feel myself happy in
being the person through which the Marquis has conveyed this
early trophy of the spoils of despotism, and the first ripe fruits of

[60] Henry Mosnier, *Le Château de Chavaniac-Lafayette: description, histoire, souvenirs*
(Le Puy, 1883), p. 31, and Maurois, p. 443.

[61] Gottschalk (ed.), p. 348.

[62] Courtesy of the Mount Vernon Ladies Association of the Union, letter of Oct. 15,
1964.

[63] *Ibid.* The size and weight of this key make it highly unlikely that Washington
tossed it in his hand and put it in his pocket, as is said in Bernard Fay, *George Washington,
Republican Aristocrat* (Boston, 1931), p. 256.

[64] Gottschalk (ed.), p. 348.

[65] Mar. 20, Boyd (ed.), XVI, 559.

American principles transplanted into Europe, to his master and patron. . . . That the principles of America opened the Bastille is not to be doubted; and therefore the key comes to the right place."[66] When Paine reported his arrangements to Short, he complained that although he had written five letters to Lafayette, he had received not a line in reply. But he was not discouraged. He sent Short "some soft reproaches" of Lafayette as well as a paper which he wanted Short to have published as a pamphlet in France and which he requested Short and Lafayette to discuss together. It recommended an offensive in the English Channel by the combined fleets of France and Spain.[67] Short eventually found that Lafayette had indeed received the letters from Paine but had not found time to answer them.[68]

For a short time it looked as if the Belgian imbroglio might yet constrain Lafayette and Mirabeau to join forces.[69] Although they acted for different, even conflicting reasons, they pulled in the same general direction, both favoring a dominant voice for the king in international diplomacy. Each felt not only that royal control of foreign policy was in itself a desirable constitutional principle but also that his own special purpose would be best served that way. Mirabeau's special purpose was to advance the interests of his friend and patron La Marck, a member of an old Belgian noble family, the Arenbergs, hoping to make him a leader among the rival forces there, and Lafayette's was to promote the Belgian popular party's aims.

In March the conflict between the Statists, advocates of the Congress, strong particularly in Brabant, and the Vonckists, the popular party, strong particularly in Flanders, became a veritable civil war.

[66] Paine to Washington, May 1, Foner (ed.), II, 1302–3. See also same to same, May 31, *ibid.*, p. 1304, and Paine to Short, June 1, *ibid.*, pp. 1306–7. Washington received the key on Aug. 10: William M. Van der Wyte, "The Story of the Key to the Bastille," *Americana*, VI (1911), 627–28.

[67] Paine to Short, June 1, 22, H. W. Landin, "Some letters of Thomas Paine and William Short on the Nootka Sound Crisis," *Journal of Modern History*, XII (1941), 364, 369–70, and Foner (ed.), II, 1307, 1309–10. Morris diary, Aug. 15, Davenport (ed.), I, 572–73, indicates that Lafayette did have the pamphlet translated and published, apparently anonymously.

[68] Short to Paine, June 8, Landin, pp. 366–67.

[69] See below, p. 361–66.

Count Cornet des Grez, who had emerged as a powerful figure in Flanders, had mobilized the Flemish estates behind a program of reconciliation with Austria and had entered into correspondence with the Habsburg court for that purpose. When the Vonckist leaders were put to flight by defeat at the hands of the Congress, he retired to French territory at Lille, where other Belgian exiles also gathered and where rumors ran that La Marck and Mirabeau were expected. La Sonde wrote to Lafayette from the French city of Douai, not far from Lille, that Cornet des Grez, hoping to win over the powerful Arenberg family, had arranged for La Marck to be made second in command of the army under General van der Mersch which was supporting the Flemish cause against the party of clergy and nobility in Brussels.[70] According to La Sonde, the National Guard of Douai were not "well disposed to give a favorable reception" to La Marck and Mirabeau.

Lafayette sent Ternant to confer with Cornet des Grez, who about the same time wrote Lafayette a sixteen-page letter detailing his ideas on how France could best cooperate with the cause he represented. Indicating that the purpose of the Prussian-born princess of Orange was to sow dissension in Belgium, thereby promoting the ambitions of the House of Orange, he argued that the diplomacy of France ought to center upon an effort to counteract her policy; hence he advocated that "insinuations" be made in Berlin, The Hague, London, and other interested capitals intended to persuade them to follow the example of France in refraining from intervention in the domestic disputes of the Belgian provinces and agreeing to meet in a general conference to iron out their cross-purposes there. If Leopold would be lenient in his treatment of the insurgent Belgian provinces, Cornet des Grez prophesied that within a few years the Belgians would turn again to him or to some other member of the Habsburg family as their ruler.[71]

Ternant brought back to Lafayette a detailed account of Cornet des Grez's views that confirmed this letter. The Flemish leader, it was clear, looked upon the Belgian revolution as a part of the

[70] La Sonde to Lafayette, Apr. 4, 6, *Mémoires,* III, 33–34.
[71] Apr. 7, CU: Lafayette Archives, Carton IV, envelope 2489–2531.

entire European diplomatic situation and thought that a general congress of the powers concerned (Britain, Prussia, the United Provinces, Austria, and France) might settle Belgian affairs without recourse to war while at the same time strengthening the forces of liberty and defeating the ambitious Dutch or French pretenders and the aristocratic program of the Congress at Brussels. The count had actually received overtures from Leopold, lending some substance to the hope that the Habsburg ruler might be persuaded to deal leniently with the Belgians.

Now that he had a hopeful picture of the Belgian situation, Lafayette, favorably impressed by the good record Leopold had compiled when he had been grand duke of Tuscany, anticipated a peaceful reconciliation that would discourage the ambition of the House of Orange or of any individual Frenchmen in Belgium. Two alternatives appeared the most likely now: either the Belgians would achieve independence or some Habsburg prince would be placed at their head,[72] and an international conference seemed the best way to choose between those alternatives peacefully. With that choice in mind, on April 7 Lafayette wrote to General Schlieffen the long overdue answer to his letter of February 22. He stated his views on Belgium candidly: "Believe, Sir, that the French people know too well the price they have paid for liberty ever to seek to interfere with that of other people or to watch with indifference while other powers try in any way to interfere with its exercise among their neighbors." He assured Schlieffen that King Frederick William II of Prussia would find King Louis XVI of France prompted by principles of liberty, justice, and moderation consistent with his personal character as well as the national will and with the frank and straightforward policy that befitted the role of a citizen-king supported by a free and vigorous nation.[73]

Convinced of the strength of the popular movement and the loyalty of Van der Mersch's army, Lafayette decided to make his views clear also to the Belgians. On the same day he took occasion to reply politely to the overtures that the "Sovereign Congress of the

[72] Lafayette to Cornet des Grez, Apr. 7, *Mémoires*, III, 36–41.

[73] Lafayette to Schlieffen, Apr. 7, *ibid.*, pp. 34–36. The copy of this letter in CU: Lafayette Archives, Carton IV, envelope 2489–2531, dates it Apr. 8.

Belgian Estates" had made to him through Thiennes and Torfs. Here too, and in almost the same words as he had used to Schlieffen, he stressed that "the French nation knows too well the price of that foremost of good things [liberty] ever to be able to interfere with its exercise among their neighbors or to watch with indifference while other powers interfere with it in any way." His personal preference, he added, "has always been to see all the peoples of the world enjoy their rights, too long usurped, and to give themselves a constitution that, in keeping with these principles, best suits their situation." Consequently he could "view only with lively pleasure the step that the Estates of Flanders had taken."[74]

Lafayette then sent his personal approval and encouragement to Cornet des Grez. As a mark of his complete confidence in his correspondent he enclosed copies of the letters he had written to Schlieffen and to the Belgian Congress. The Belgian count's views on the diplomatic situation were interesting and significant, he affirmed, but "multiple occupations" prevented him from making detailed comments except on the most essential points. He agreed that every effort should be made to reduce the influence of the House of Orange in Belgium and to quiet any Belgian fears of "an excess of zeal" on the part of Frenchmen; like Cornet des Grez he thought that the presence of a French agent at Brussels would be undesirable, and he would oppose sending any until the count should approve. Despite the many difficulties that he foresaw in the way of an international conference to consider the Belgian situation, he promised to pass the proposal on to Foreign Minister Montmorin, especially since such a conference might lead to liberal constitutional reforms among the various peoples of Europe (and "I would like my country to have the honor of the earliest overtures"), while a general war might be detrimental to "our happy revolution."

Meanwhile Leopold would do well, Lafayette held, to place confidence in Cornet des Grez: "It could not be better placed. As a friend of humanity and liberty, I am attached to monarchs who wish to become their advocates," and he trusted that the Austrian

---

[74] [Apr. 7], CU: Lafayette Archives, Carton IV. See also Tassier, p. 376, and Lafayette to Cornet des Grez, Apr. 7, *Mémoires*, III, 36.

ruler would win the confidence of Belgian patriots by supporting
a free government. Thus Lafayette committed himself to a policy
of Belgian reconciliation with Austria in the hope of preventing
war while promoting the liberal cause.[75] The French ministry,
he presumed, was prepared to second Leopold in such a policy,
but it could take no definite steps until Austria's attitude became
more clearly defined. Lafayette proposed that meanwhile he and
Cornet des Grez continue their correspondence, neither giving any
consideration to information otherwise obtained.[76]

The Belgian Patriot cause went from bad to worse in the late
spring of 1790. Van de Mersch was defeated and imprisoned.
Peasant uprisings took the form of crusades in favor of the clergy
and subjected the Patriots to a veritable terror. Some of the Vonckist leaders sought refuge in France, and they and their followers
at home began to look to Leopold as a possible liberator.

One of those who knew of Lafayette's dealings with the Belgians
and had kept himself otherwise informed about Belgian affairs was
Charles-François Dumouriez, *maréchal de camp* in the French
army and on occasion an agent of the foreign ministry. In May
Dumouriez, having heard that the Prussian ruler was willing to
support Leopold's policy in Belgium in the event of a general
agreement among European powers, decided that he ought to go to
Belgium. "It is time, my dear Marquis," he wrote Lafayette, "to
give serious attention to the Low Countries; I can deal with them
only through you." Recognizing that Lafayette was suspicious of
him because he was believed to be a supporter of the Duc d'Orléans' ambitions in Belgium, he insisted that he had never had any
close relations with the Orleanist faction, nor did he know anything
about its designs.[77]

Dumouriez thus betrayed that some presumably well-informed
Frenchmen believed one of Lafayette's aims in Belgium to be a desire to thwart—or, at least, not to assist—the ambitions of the Duc
d'Orléans there. In short, the issue of intervention in Belgium con-

---

[75] *Mémoires*, III, 35 n.

[76] *Ibid.*, pp. 36–40.

[77] Dumouriez to Lafayette, May 2, 1790, *ibid.*, p. 40. Charavay, *Lafayette*, p. 240, n. 1,
speaks of another letter of Dumouriez to Lafayette of the same tenor, May 13.

cerned not simply a conflict of international rivals; it involved also the relations of certain French personalities toward each other, the constitutional problem of control of France's foreign and military affairs, and the alignment of the nascent parties in the National Assembly with or against the monarch. The hope arose at the royal court that Lafayette's willingness to leave the resolution of the Belgian question to the king would alienate his popular following and force him into the "Austrian Cabal," as the queen's coterie was sometimes called.[78]

By this time Belgian affairs had become enmeshed with another international crisis. Conflict loomed between London and Madrid as a consequence of the seizure by the Spanish of an English settlement on Nootka Sound, off the west coast of Vancouver Island. The Spanish claimed a monopoly over that territory and consequently considered the English interlopers. The British government, however, demanded not only the release of the captives but also compensation from Spain. By early May, the British navy had begun to prepare for hostilities, and Parliament was ready to put pressure on Spain. If war followed, Spain was likely, invoking the Family Compact of the Bourbons, to call upon France to make common cause against Britain.

Gouverneur Morris, who had been speculating on these probabilities in England, wrote to the marquis early in May to tell him of British warlike preparations. France, he thought, must prepare not merely to return the British blow but to anticipate it, offering Leopold support against Prussia in return for the transfer of his rights in Belgium, and then France, with the cooperation of Belgian patriots, must occupy all Belgium.[79] Morris enclosed a letter to Ternant, leaving it unsealed so that Lafayette could read it, in which he expressed confidence that France could so conduct the impending war "as to change entirely all present appearances in Europe." He sent both letters to Lafayette by the French ambassador's courier.[80] When Lafayette's aide Boinville, still in London on

---

[78] Cf. Lescure (ed.), II, 438 (Apr. 10).

[79] Morris diary, May 5–7, Davenport (ed.), I, 504–5, and Morris to Lafayette, May 7, *ibid.*, pp. 506–7.

[80] Morris to Ternant, May 7, *ibid.*, p. 508. See also Morris to William Carmichael, May 7, *ibid.*, p. 509.

his special mission to keep an eye on the Duc d'Orléans, called on Morris, he learned of the strategy for a general European war that the American was recommending and offered to go home and advocate it.[81] Morris' agitation doubtless served to reinforce Lafayette's expectation that France was on the verge of war with Britain. He wrote to Cornet des Grez that the "political circumstances appear to be distinctly changed so far as England is concerned, perhaps even in relation to the Belgian provinces, since the date of your last letter."[82]

By mid-May the Nootka controversy seemed to be merging with the Belgian crisis to embroil France in alliance with Spain and Austria in a war with Britain in alliance with Prussia and the United Provinces.

BIBLIOGRAPHICAL NOTES

The study by Suzanne Tassier remains, despite its age, the best account of the Austrian Netherlands during the French Revolution. That by R. R. Palmer in *The Age of the Democratic Revolution: A Political History of Europe and America, . . . 1760–1800,* Vol. I: *The Challenge* (Princeton, 1959), pp. 341–57, is, despite its brevity, perhaps the best account in English, especially useful for its bibliographical references.

The Lafayette Archives at Cornell University contain an impressive collection of papers relevant to Lafayette's part in the Vonckist revolt. A note by Lafayette indicates that he gathered them to "rappeller de plus en plus à mes amis le but auquel je tendais, celui d'établir la liberté en Belgique." Some of them were published in *Mémoires,* III, 13–48.

G. Dansaert, *Le vrai visage de La Fayette* (Brussels, [1943]) is a spotty collection of essays on the several stages of Lafayette's career rather than a systematic biography. It quotes many printed works, both contemporary and subsequent, usually indicating only the author without precise references. As a Belgian, Dansaert is particularly interested in Lafayette's role in his country's affairs and gives a useful account (pp. 157–78) of Lafayette's relations to Belgium in 1789–92.

The memoirs of Sémonville as published by Irisson d'Herisson, mentions (p. 71) his mission to Belgium but sheds little light upon it.

[81] Morris diary, May 11 and 13, *ibid.,* p. 512–14.

[82] N.d. but *ca.* May 1790, CU: Lafayette Archives, Carton IV.

CHAPTER XIV

Monarchy, but of What Kind?

IN HIS speech of March 17 Lafayette was one of the first to call the National Assembly a "constituent assembly." Yet the constitution was far from completion, the Right had already made a demand for adjournment, and the hint had been dropped that ambitious deputies and others who profited from the Revolution were deliberately prolonging discussion. Some observers listed Lafayette among them. Mirabeau, anxious to belittle him, labeled him another Sir Charles Grandison, that hero of Samuel Richardson's novel whom a later critic, Hippolyte Taine, thought so pompous as to be fit only to be stuffed and placed in a museum. Hence Mirabeau called him *Grandisson [sic]-Cromwell,* "an ambitious impotent who wants to enjoy supreme power without daring to seize it."[1] Occasionally too Mirabeau and others ridiculed him as a clown, calling him *Gilles-César.*[2] The émigrés, with less humor than Mirabeau, accused him of playing the role of a Cromwell or of a mayor of the palace who, at the head of an army, held his king prisoner.

To the better disposed, Lafayette was more likely to call to mind

---

[1] Dumont, *Souvenirs,* p. 164.

[2] Notes of L.-J.-A. de Bouillé, *Souvenirs et fragments pour servir aux mémoires de ma vie et de mon temps, 1769–1812,* ed. P.-L. de Kermaingant (Paris, 1906), p. 136, n. 1, and La Marck, quoted in Bacourt (ed.), II, 125–26. See also Arthur Chuquet (ed.), *Souvenirs de baron de Frenilly, pair de France (1768–1828)* (Paris, 1909), p. 125. These works state that this sobriquet was originated by the Duc de Choiseul, Louis XV's famous minister, and that Choiseul first used it in protest against what he considered exaggerated praise for Lafayette upon his return from America. We have never, however, encountered it before 1790. M. F. A. de Lescure (ed.), *Rivarol et la société française pendant la Révolution et l'émigration (1753–1801)* (Paris, 1883), p. 197, adds to these nicknames *le général Morphée,* referring to the allegation that Lafayette slept while the Château of Versailles was under attack on Oct. 6, but that accusation was not yet common in early 1790.

a Plutarchian figure. To some he recalled the patriot-general Cincinnatus, recently personified by the universally admired commander-in-chief of the American army during the American Revolution. When Desmoulins heard Lafayette speak on March 17, he was reminded, besides, of Pompey addressing a patrician Senate. He considered, too, whether, if all were known, Lafayette might not appear more like a Fabius the Cunctator, risking his glorious reputation out of love for his country.[3] When Jacob-Job Élie, hero of the capture of the Bastille, came to receive a sword voted to him by the Electors and Lafayette joined them in congratulating him, Élie declared in his address of thanks that his sword was a symbol of loyalty to the nation, the law, and the king under the command of Lafayette, the "Scipio of America and hero of French liberty."[4]

How much of Lafayette's popular acclaim went to him unsolicited and how much he carefully cultivated would be hard to tell. He continually performed acts of charity, and he occasionally attended baptisms.[5] From time to time he went to the populous faubourgs, where he generally was received as a hero. On one such occasion the chaplain of the Battalion of the District of Popincourt welcomed him as "the best of brothers, the best of citizens," and the "liberator of America," who was now the French workingman's liberator.[6] The accounts of the moneys he and Bailly spent from the sums put at their disposal by the National Assembly's Comité des Recherches give no clear indication of subsidies to journalists, but sometimes payments to his aides and others were made for unspecified reasons, and while, when the reason is specified, it is usually reimbursement of travel expenses for some kind of investigative mission, on at least one occasion it was "for divers operations in Paris," and the possibility that those "divers operations" included propaganda may not be ruled out (or, for that matter, ruled in).[7]

[3] See above, p. 287 and n. 52.

[4] Bailly and Duveyrier, III, 33–39. See Lacroix, III, 36 (Nov. 23), 39 (Mar. 19). See also *ibid.*, IV, 722.

[5] *Moniteur*, Feb. 28, p. 239.

[6] *Courrier de Paris*, Mar. 20, pp. 228–29. Cf. [R.-F.] Lebois, *Générosité de Monsieur frère du Roi envers son district, et arrivé de M. le marquis de La Fayette à Saint-Sulpice* [Paris, 1790].

[7] AN: D xxix[bis], dossier 357, p. 6 (Feb. 12). See below, Appendix I. The *Journal du*

Military reviews, too, provided public occasions for the inculca-
tion of personal loyalty to the commandant general. One of the
most fervent displays took place on March 21, when he reviewed
the cavalry on the Champ-de-Mars. When it was over and Lafayette rode off, a portion of the crowd followed him with "cries of
affection and devotion." They escorted him all the way back to the
door of the Manège, causing some uneasy deputies, upon hearing
the shouts, to go out to see what was going on.[8] He reached the
meeting room in time to hear the Baron de Menou call upon the
National Assembly to devote its main sessions four days a week exclusively to completing the constitution and the other three to putting order into the national finances, all other matters being rele-
gated to evening sessions.[9]

Lafayette immediately went to the tribune to support Menou. He
favored any motion, he declared, that would "assure our progress,
calm unrest, and refute slanders." What would the Assembly's detractors be able to say if the National Assembly, shunning fruitless
or tumultuous debate on minor questions, decided that its task
could be summed up in two words: *constitution* and *finances?* Attention to finances was imperative, for the Revolution ought not
only to restore to the people its rights but also to assure its happiness, and yet the plain truth was that the people were still suffer-
ing hardship, commerce was languishing, workers were unemployed. Attention to the constitution was imperative "because with
it we get everything: a representative legislature where law is made
with wisdom; judicial order based upon juries; administrative bodies that are elective but subordinated on a graduated scale to the
supreme head; an army that is disciplined without potential for
abuse; a system of education that imparts all essentials and culti-
vates all talents; a nation that is peaceful but ready to take arms

---

diable, No. 24, p. 2, No. 42, pp. 2–3, expressly denied being paid by Lafayette, but the
satirical tone of this journal makes it hard to know how its words are to be taken. In any
case, it was hostile to him.

[8] *Journal de Paris,* Mar. 21, p. 319; *Courrier de Paris,* Mar. 23, p. 274; and *Mémoires,* II,
396.

[9] *AP,* XII, 289–92.

for liberty; a king vested with all the power that a great monarchy requires and with the prestige that befits the majesty of a great people; in short, a firm and complete organization of government, and that distinct definition of every power which by itself excludes all tyranny." These were principles of government that Lafayette had learned not from books (though a literate man, he had had small time for book learning) but from active participation in two great revolutions, and they were principles that even as late as 1830 he was loyally to advance for France—a strong monarchical executive limited by good republican institutions.

Having thus spoken as a legislator, Lafayette continued, now speaking as head of the police. He reminded his hearers that "the National Guards, whose zeal is as enduring as it is energetic, long to find in our decrees their constitutional role and there to learn of their duties." Yet the need for judicial reform seemed to him even more pressing, for (and here he probably had the resistance of the parlements in mind) "too often the law finds adversaries in its principal agencies, and every kind of faction can still try, in its misguided guilt, to raise obstacles or pretexts against the establishment of public order." Aware that some deputies still believed he wanted change for ulterior motives, he closed his speech with a simple repetition of his intent: "Perhaps some impatience may be permitted to one who, having promised the people not to flatter them but to defend them, has promised himself that the end of the Revolution, while replacing him exactly where he was when it began, will leave him wholly and completely to the purity of his memories."[10] Thus, once again, Lafayette announced his intention to seek no power for himself but to retire when the French had completed their Revolution. He was "vigorously and justly applauded."[11]

Other deputies spoke for or against Menou's motion, and finally, the Assembly voted not to divide the morning sessions into two exclusive series, one for constitutional matters and the other for

[10] Our text here follows *Mémoires*, II, 396–97. See below, Bibliographical Note, p. 336. See also, among numerous other sources, *AP*, XII, 292; *Journal de Paris*, Mar. 22, p. 323; *Moniteur*, Mar. 22, pp. 331–32; and *Point du jour*, Mar. 22, pp. 119–20, Mar. 23, p. 121.

[11] *Journal des Impartiaux*, No. 10, pp. 8–9.

finances, but otherwise to adopt Menou's motion.[12] Now Lafayette could expect that at least in the sessions devoted to the making of the constitution it would move forward with fewer interruptions than before.

Lafayette's speech on the subject met with enthusiastic approval. Later that day his steadfast admirer Duquesnoy was moved to confide in his journal: "We do not yet know what France owes to the Marquis de Lafayette; he is the man of the Revolution, he is perhaps the saviour of the empire. I know that even the best informed men are ignorant of much that he has done and of much that he does every day." Lafayette was now financially ruined, Duquesnoy (mistakenly) declared, and "France will be eternally disgraced if she does not restore his fortune."[13] And the *Journal de Paris* said that all ambitious men might profit from the example presented "when a man . . . who has seen open before him the paths to grandeur and ambition . . . declares so solemnly that the end of the Revolution will put him back in the ranks of simple citizens and leave him the purity of his memories."[14]

Yet the approval of Lafayette's speech was strained. Loustalot analyzed it in a six-page special article. He described Lafayette's political position as unenviable: On the one hand, the aristocrats attacked him as ungrateful for royal benefits and as ambitious in a way that was equally dangerous to crown and to people; on the other hand, zealous patriots condemned him for building up the people's confidence in himself to a point where he could abuse it. Thereupon, Loustalot again[15] listed several acts of the commandant general which he looked upon with suspicion—among them the commandant general's choice of obscure men for his staff, his recruitment of paid companies in the National Guard, his conduct in the Marat affair, his project for an artillery corps that would have put all the city's cannon at his disposal. Now, however, the journalist conceded, Lafayette had replied effectively to all his detractors, and he extolled Lafayette for intending, like

---

[12] *AP*, XII, 292–93.

[13] Duquesnoy, II, 482–83.

[14] Mar. 22, pp. 323–24.

[15] See above, pp. 185–86.

Cincinnatus, to be not the idol but the protector of his people.[16]

Desmoulins took this occasion to comment again on the modern "Fabius the Cunctator," whom he proposed to look upon "as the object of our dearest hopes" and was ready to defend with his life, even though the general had accused him of being one of his detractors. Yet Desmoulins did not conceal his misgivings about the dispute between the Commune and the district assemblies over military affairs, for if the districts were to decline, military committees would fill their place and the National Guard would become a praetorian guard. The National Guard uniform, he therefore feared, would divide citizens into those in uniform and those not in uniform, and it was not the uniform but the cockade that would unite Frenchmen. He hoped, however, that once the constitution was completed, Frenchmen would put aside their uniforms as the American soldiers, following Washington's example, had done, returning like Cincinnatus as civilians to their farms.[17]

Loustalot and Desmoulins must have known, for it was no secret, that Lafayette was a leading member of the French branch of the Society of the Cincinnati, made up of selected veterans of the War of American Independence. In fact, Lafayette had recently paid out considerable sums to provide badges for the order—between 1787 and 1789 over 27,000 livres, presumably to be repaid by the society.[18] Lafayette admired the role of both the Plutarchian and the American Cincinnatus at least as much as these reprehensive journalists did.

Lafayette's burdens increased as he endeavored not only to assuage the growing suspicion of the districts and the popular press but also to persuade the royal court to reconcile itself fully with the Revolution. After February 4 Louis undertook to move more freely among his people, but his retinue persisted in retaining the old etiquette. Lafayette once tried to introduce at court some

[16] *Révolutions de Paris*, No. 37, Mar. 20–30, pp. 17–23.

[17] *Révolutions*, No. 19, pp. 279, 297–98, 303. Other journals that commented more or less favorably include *Gazette de Leide*, Apr. 6, and *Journal des Impartiaux*, No. 10, pp. 8–9. Mirabeau's *Courrier de Provence*, Mar. 20–21, p. 63, noted merely that Lafayette had "vigorously supported" Menou's motion, of which it approved, and the *Moniteur*, Mar. 22, pp. 331–32, offering (as usual) no comment, printed Lafayette's speech in full.

[18] Girodie catalogue, pp. 48–49, item 70.

women who had not previously been presented but failed, and moreover, he found that the courtiers treated with coolness or disdain deputies and other "patriots" who presented themselves at the Tuileries, although the royal couple (but not the courtiers) always showed a proper regard for Bailly and Lafayette.[19] Louis rejected a particularly fitting occasion to appear in public on March 22, the anniversary of the entry of Henry IV, the first Bourbon king, into Paris in 1594. The city had traditionally celebrated that event with a solemn procession and thanksgiving service. For the first time the anniversary had rolled around in revolutionary times, and the mayor and the commandant general went to the Tuileries Palace to receive the king's orders concerning the ceremony, but the king had no suggestions to make.

The mayor and the commandant general therefore proceeded to make arrangements of their own. On the anniversary morning Lafayette joined Bailly and the Representatives in the Grande Salle of the Hôtel de Ville, where they welcomed the presidents of the districts. They all then descended into the Place de Grève, where the Garde de la Ville and a detachment of National Guards waited to escort them to the cathedral. At Notre Dame the dean and the cathedral chapter joined them, and they moved on to the Church of the Grands-Augustins for a high mass.[20] Paris might have been worth a mass to Henry IV, but Louis XVI seemed as yet unwilling to pay that price for it.

The next opportunity for the royal couple to go among the people came late in March when Lafayette accompanied them on a visit to a plate glass factory in the Faubourg Saint-Antoine. Some of the courtiers professed to believe that the lives of the monarchs would be in danger in that neighborhood, but Lafayette, while taking the precaution to provide a National Guard escort, was ready to gamble on the loyalty of his worker-friends.[21] On this and other similar occasions the royal couple, unwilling to relax the court etiquette of the Old Regime, would allow in their carriage as

---

[19] *Mémoires*, III, 207–9.

[20] Bailly to Lafayette, Mar. 20, Tuetey, II, 30, No. 285, and Lacroix, IV, 423–24 (Mar. 16), 466 (Mar. 20), 481–82 (Mar. 22).

[21] *Mémoires*, III, 20 n.

commanders of their escort only those rare division chiefs of the
National Guard who had had the privilege of riding with them in
the old days, and so Lafayette, persuaded that if such discrimination were known, it would play into the hands of the Jacobin opposition, undertook to ride with them himself as the commanding
officer.[22]

On another occasion—this time a visit on March 30 to the Gobe-
lins' tapestry works in the District of Saint-Marcel—the news of
the royal family's excursion was allowed to leak out beforehand,
and many people turned up to see them ride through the streets.
Lafayette and Saint-Priest accompanied them. The crowds were
enthusiastic and welcomed their visitors' appearance with shouts:
"Long live the king!" "Long live Lafayette!" Marie Antoinette
was also acclaimed, much to her surprise. At the tapestry works
the district president made a speech of welcome, to which the king
replied with "touching simplicity," and he gave the president 8,200
livres to distribute among Saint-Marcel's poor and the factory
workers. The women of the Halles, always conspicuous on ceremonial occasions, sang songs addressed mostly to "Mon Général,"
but they included verses about the king and the queen. When
the royal party left, the cheers that followed them were long and
loud.[23] A story soon went the rounds that the queen, obviously
thinking of the catastrophe of the preceding October, pointedly
remarked: "One must admit that these people are far gentler when
one comes to them than when they are brought."[24]

Lafayette afterward recorded two incidents that took place at
the tapestry establishment. One occurred when the king asked a
workman whether he had served in the army and in what regiment.
"Sire," the man replied, "in your regiment of guards, but I left
sometime before the capture of the Bastille, and the general [mean-

---

[22] *Ibid.*, pp. 209–10.

[23] Fernan Nuñez to Floridablanca, May 14, Mousset, pp. 232–33; *Mémoires*, III, 209 n.;
Journal de Paris, Apr. 25, p. 464; and *Journal général de la cour*, Apr. 23, p. 181.

[24] Fernan Nuñez to Floridablanca, May 14, Mousset, p. 233, says these words were
addressed to Lafayette. According to an earlier report (Vaudreuil to Artois, Apr. 17, Pingaud [ed.], p. 168) Marie Antoinette said to Bailly: "Yes, the people are good, when their
masters come to visit them; but they are barbarous when one sends them to visit their
masters."

ing Lafayette] refuses me the medal [awarded to the former French Guards]. That's not fair, because if I had been there, I would have acted like the others." Lafayette, recalling the remark about ten years later, thought the man naïve to have believed that the king "had become patriotic and would approve of the July 14 insurrection."[25]

Lafayette's account of the other incident perhaps merely illustrates that his hindsight was, as everyone's, better than his contemporary understanding of events. About 1799 he remembered that during this visit he, moving in one direction along the tapestries on display, met the king and Saint-Priest, moving in another, just in front of a Gobelin depicting the assault upon the Huguenot leader Admiral de Coligny by a Catholic assassin in the Massacre of Saint Bartholomew in 1572. To Lafayette, who knew his country's history well, the meeting at that spot of that trio—a reformer, a king, and a royal minister—suggested an ironic parallel to the picture in the tapestry and, so he afterward narrated, he smiled, and he thought the witnesses of the episode understood why.[26]

Hindsight or no, these were recollections of soul-trying times. The Marquis de Lally-Tollendal, a deputy who had emigrated to Switzerland after the October Days but apparently had retained friendly feelings for Lafayette up to this time, now broke off all relations with him.[27] M. Labenette's *Journal du diable* had already joined in the sniping at Lafayette from the left while Jacques Peltier's *Actes des apôtres* had joined the journals that sniped at him from the right. The numerous pamphlets that attacked or ridiculed popular leaders became increasingly incendiary, and although the police assiduously confiscated and destroyed them, some were described or quoted for amusement, derision, or refutation in the growing revolutionary press.[28] A caricature entitled "La

[25] *Mémoires*, III, 209 n. This note was written about 1799: see *ibid.*, p. 191 n.

[26] *Ibid.*, p. 209 n.

[27] Lally-Tollendal to Louis XVI, July 9, 1972, *Mémoire de Lally-Tolendal [sic] au roi de Prusse pour réclamer la liberté de Lafayette* (Paris, 1795), p. 37.

[28] For such reports of counterrevolutionary literature see Desmoulins, *Révolutions*, No. 20, pp. 321–29; *Chronique de Paris*, Mar. 28, p. 348; *Courrier de Paris*, Apr. 2, pp. 433–35; and *Moniteur*, Apr. 2, p. 378.

Passion de Louis XVI" portrayed the monarch on a crucifix being tortured by Lafayette as Caiaphas the high priest, Bailly as Pontius Pilate, and the Duc d'Orléans as Judas Iscariot.[29] Marat, who returned from England in April, commissioned a caricature that would show Lafayette wearing a duke's coronet, and Bailly wearing a count's, both trampling on the Declaration of Rights while distributing daggers and the newly created paper money (*assignats*) to a cluster of Chevaliers of Saint Louis, uniformed officers, and sullen poor who were thus being suborned to stab in the back a figure representing the *patrie*, while decent women, children, and old men, stood by terrified.[30]

By the middle of March restlessness, temporarily allayed by the king's gesture of February 4, had begun to threaten once more, primarily because of the presumed manipulation of the money supply and the all too real scarcity of specie.[31] The problem of bad money driving out good was not new to Lafayette. Early in February he had received a letter from a man who described himself as the spokesman for a society of foreign capitalists "extremely enthusiastic for the French Revolution," proposing to provide France with specie and asking him as a man they trusted to put them in direct contact with the king and his ministers.[32]

There is no evidence that Lafayette complied with the request. On the contrary, he met the rising unrest in his usual manner, strengthening the forces at the Hôtel de Ville, drilling the National Guard daily, and dispatching contingents to help police neighboring towns.[33] As anxiety grew in Paris that the unemployed might be stirred to violence, he and Bailly were urged to create workshops to provide employment,[34] and the mayor instructed him to place a guard at the enclosure of Saint-Martin-des-Champs

---

[29] *Courrier de Paris*, Apr. 2, pp. 433–35.

[30] Marat to "mon cher concitoyen," undated, Indiana University, Ball Collection, X, Nos. 20–22.

[31] *AP*, XII, 98–101 (Mar. 9).

[32] M. de Seneffe to Lafayette, undated, CU: Lafayette Archives, Carton IV, folder 2789–2806. See also below, Appendix III.

[33] *Courrier de Paris*, Mar. 16, pp. 161–62, Mar. 17, pp. 178–79.

[34] Tuetey (ed.), *Assistance publique*, II, 496.

and to send a detachment to maintain order in Montmartre during the organization of a new municipality there.[35]

Meanwhile recurrent administrative details must at times have bored or exasperated even the patient commandant general—verifying identification papers, affirming brevets, commissions, promotions, furloughs, requisitions, pay vouchers, and pensions, entertaining visitors, and even acting as complaint adjuster for his men.[36] One of the less routine duties that filled the commandant general's long waking hours was that of rectifying injustices to men previously under his command. A chance to right a wrong came at the meeting of the former Electors of Paris on March 19, when they considered the claims of the Marquis de La Salle, who had taken command of the Paris bourgeois militia on July 13, the eve of the capture of the Bastille, and of the Chevalier de Saudray, who had been his second in command. Lafayette had retained La Salle as his own second in command until the day La Salle was accused of ordering powder to be shipped out of Paris. He had saved La Salle from lynching that day but had not been able to protect his home from pillage or to retain him in the National Guard. Lafayette now spoke in his behalf, undertaking, if the Electors wished, to secure some pecuniary compensation for him. The Electors authorized the commandant general and the mayor to present to the municipality La Salle's claims to public gratitude. As for Saudray, Lafayette favored him as inspector of the National Guard units under his command outside the city, and a resolution instructing the mayor as well as Lafayette to intercede for him

[35] Bailly to Lafayette, Mar. 25–28, Tuetey, II, 11, Nos. 105, 107, and *ibid.*, p. 419, No. 3975.

[36] Brevet, Mar. 24, Librairie Henri Sauffroy, *Catalogue,* of May 1933, item 69; identification papers, Mar. 14, collection of Dr. Max Thorek, Chicago; Latour du Pin to Lafayette, Mar. 27, AMG:AH, Carton LXI, chemise Minutes, mars 1790, pièce 138; Lafayette to Bonvallet, Mar. 25, Tuetey, II, 445, No. 4205; petition of the Baron de La Courtelle, Mar. 11, Pierpont Morgan Library, Lafayette Correspondence, I; Lafayette to Marquis de Cavalcatto [*sic*], Mar. 23, Archives de la Seine, facsimile made from document removed from D2 10, 521, No. 328. See also drafts of three letters by Marquis de Cavalcabo, evidently to Bailly, regarding a debt of M. Bauzée (*ibid.*); Lafayette to Latour du Pin, Jan. 24, described in Parke-Bernet Galleries catalogue No. 2280 (May 5, 1964), p. 32, item 108, requesting a commission as infantry major for his aide Jean-Louis Desmottes; Lacroix, IV, 306, 401–2, 509–10, 521, 531–39; *ibid.*, 2d series, VII, 102; and *Procès-verbal du Comité militaire,* Part II, p. 61.

also was passed. A few days later Bailly sent Lafayette his endorsement of the recommendation that the services of La Salle deserved monetary compensation from the Commune.[37]

On still another occasion Lafayette's ex officio duty was far from routine. For some time interest had been growing in Paris in a project to set up government-supported schools for blind children and for the deaf and dumb. When consulted by Mayor Bailly, Champion de Cicé as keeper of the royal seals proposed a school for the deaf and dumb with a board of supervisors including the mayor, the commandant general, and two members of the National Assembly. Accordingly a board of eleven, Lafayette among them, was created.[38] The District of Saint-Jacques-L'Hôpital sponsored a demonstration in the Grande Salle of the Hôtel de Ville of the methods for teaching the blind, and the commandant general graced the occasion.[39]

As reform upset more and more vested interests and violated more and more cherished conventions, "aristocratic plots" remained a threat on every side. The Comte de Maillebois was denounced as a counterrevolutionary by one of his servants and took flight on March 22. Reports about the émigrés in Turin soon lent plausibility to the fear that he was fomenting an uprising in southern France that would be supported by Spanish, Savoyard, and Neapolitan troops. Lafayette was inclined to believe the worst, but even if he had doubted the charges against Maillebois, duty required him to do all he could to forestall counterrevolution. The date anticipated by most Parisians for the uprising was Easter Sunday, which would fall on April 4. In the closing days of March Paris journals were filled with frightening accounts of the plans of the Turin émigrés under Maillebois' leadership. The aristocrats in Paris were said to be conniving with them to take the king to Lyon, where aristocratic forces would be prepared to place themselves under his leadership

[37] In March Lafayette attended the Electors' meetings on the 1st, 5th, 12th, and 19th: Bailly and Duveyrier, III, 25, 38–39, 33, 36, 41–45, and Bailly to Lafayette, Mar. 30, Tuetey, I, 22, No. 197. For the earlier history of La Salle, see Gottschalk and Maddox, pp. 110–11, 177–81.

[38] Lacroix, V, 3–4 and 13–20 (Apr. 15).

[39] *Journal de la municipalité,* Mar. 27, 1790, and Lacroix, IV, 466 and 477–80 (Mar. 20).

and suppress the Revolution. Some believed that the queen and her courtiers, "the Austrian Cabal," were pledged to do their utmost to assure the success of the plot,[40] and the enemies of the Revolution began to hope that in fact Lafayette's days were numbered. Artois was informed in Turin that the king's party was growing, since men were beginning to see through "the Hero Lafayette," that the impending retirement of Necker would weaken him further, that he "commences to be distrusted, and for a traitor, from distrust to insult, and from insult to death, the passage is rapid."[41]

In the uneasy atmosphere created by the alleged Maillebois conspiracy any combination of circumstances might have triggered an outbreak. The National Guard watched for every sign of disturbance. They arrested men putting up incendiary posters, selling provocative pamphlets, or speaking abusively of Lafayette or the National Assembly. They manned the battery in the Place Henri IV, patrolled the Palais Royal with particular care, kept a lookout at the Caisse d'Escompte, policed cafés frequented by aristocrats and districts where the unemployed and newcomers to Paris congregated, stood guard at the Tuileries and the Manège, and took special precautions to protect their commandant, periodically searching every corner of his house for would-be assassins.[42]

The prevailing uneasiness precipitated a number of delicate situations that involved Lafayette personally. The return to Paris of the émigré Prince de Conti might have aroused some apprehension, had he not immediately reported to his district assembly, taken the patriotic oath, and called upon Lafayette and Bailly even before he paid his respects to the king.[43] When the National Guard stopped a deputy of the National Assembly who had ventured forth without a tricolor cockade, he sent irate protests on the in-

---

[40] Details of the Easter plot are taken from *Courier national*, Mar. 29, p. 8, Apr. 2, pp. 5–8; *Chronique de Paris*, Mar. 28, p. 348, Mar. 30, pp. 354–55, Mar. 31, p. 359; *Courrier de Paris*, Mar. 26, p. 321, Mar. 29, pp. 369–70, Mar. 30, pp. 385–86, Mar. 31, pp. 407–10; *Gazette de Leide, supplément*, Apr. 9; Staël-Holstein to Gustavus III, Mar. 28, Staël-Holstein, pp. 159–60; and *Mémoires*, II, 456–59.

[41] Vaudreuil to Artois, Apr. 1, Pingaud (ed.), pp. 157–59.

[42] See n. 40 above, and *Journal général de la cour*, Apr. 2, 8, pp. 15, 63.

[43] *Journal de Paris*, Apr. 4, p. 376; *Moniteur*, Apr. 5, p. 387; *Courrier de Paris*, Apr. 4, p. 475; and *Journal général de la cour*, Apr. 4, p. 28, Apr. 5, p. 35, Apr. 7, pp. 54–55.

dignity he had suffered to their commander as well as to the press;[44] and when the District des Capucins-du-Marais, fearful of a rising by a large number of local unemployed, asked for an extra supply of arms, the Assembly of Representatives instructed him to provide it.[45] The Guards of Versailles arrested a man believed to be bent on stirring up disorder, and the municipal officials of Versailles asked him to come to Versailles to advise them what to do. "Just at present," he answered, "I think I cannot leave the capital."[46]

One reason Lafayette could not leave Paris was that on the morning of March 31 he went with Bailly and the head of the Paris Investigations Committee, Garran de Coulon, to confer with Louis XVI. The committee had been collecting evidence relating to the activities of Maillebois, the émigrés at Turin, and their alleged accessories among the courtiers in the Tuileries, and the city's officials wished to present that evidence to His Majesty. Some speculated that the king's younger brother, the Comte d'Artois, likewise was associated with Maillebois. Presumably, the king, upon hearing Coulon's report, agreed that the case should be investigated further; and the Châtelet soon summoned witnesses to testify regarding the plot.[47]

The tense atmosphere led to disturbing speculation about the future government of the realm. Rumor had it that at a dinner given by the Duc de Liancourt in his apartment at the Tuileries, after much imbibing, the conversation got around to the desirability of a regent or a lieutenant general to tide the country over the crisis; an informal ballot of the fifty-odd guests resulted in about three preferring the Comte de Provence, about thirteen the Duc d'Orléans, and all the rest Lafayette.[48] According to the

---

[44] Baron Guilhermy to Lafayette, Mar. 27, *Gazette de Paris*, Apr. 4, pp. 1–2. See also *Courrier de Paris*, Apr. 6, p. 28.

[45] Lacroix, IV, 590–91 (Apr. 1).

[46] Lafayette to the municipal officers of Versailles, Mar. 31, Bibliothèque de Versailles (courtesy of M. Bréchin).

[47] *Journal général de la cour*, Apr. 3, p. 23; *Gazette de Leide*, Apr. 13; *Courier national*, Apr. 5, p. 6; Lescure (ed.), II, 473 (Apr. 3); and *Moniteur*, Apr. 4, p. 383.

[48] Virieu to Comte Ventura, Apr. 5, Grouchy and Guillois (eds.), p. 186. Cf. Vaudreuil to Artois, Apr. 17, Pingaud (ed.), I, 167; Lescure (ed.), II, 436–37 (Apr. 2); and Clermont-Gallerande, I, 448–49.

report of the Parmesan envoy to his government Mirabeau, who
had been one of Liancourt's guests, disapproved of all the candidates: Provence was unreliable, Orléans cowardly, and Lafayette
insufficiently strong-minded to carry the weight of a regency.[49] It
was perhaps no coincidence that shortly afterward Lafayette revealed his awareness that Mirabeau had dubbed him Cromwell-
Grandison.[50] When the rumored balloting was bruited abroad,
some ventured to guess that aristocrats like Liancourt's guests had
chosen Lafayette leader with the ulterior motive of alienating
members of his own party from him.[51] The rumor was indeed
embarrassing, though for another reason, for it implied that since
Liancourt, and perhaps Lafayette, regarded Louis XVI as unfit to
rule, a lieutenant general was needed to rule in his name. Whether
or not the story was circulated to discredit Liancourt or Lafayette,
Liancourt formally issued a public denial of it and affirmed his fidelity to the king.[52]

Although Lafayette took seriously "the Maillebois counterrevolution which makes heads so hot," he was actually more distressed
by the strife among the political factions in Paris. On April 5,
having "only an hour for all the things I have to write," he once
more sent a letter of apology to Adelaïde de Simiane for not being
able to visit her. He nevertheless took the time to enumerate the
several vexations that currently troubled him. One of them was
that an unpleasant incident had caused him to lose confidence in a
previously trusted friend and supporter, the Baron de Menou.
Although Lafayette mentioned it to Mme de Simiane only in passing, Duquesnoy told the story at length. The Duc d'Orléans'
friends—Mirabeau and Biron foremost among them—were believed to be busily engaged in a secret correspondence involving
large sums of money. The correspondence was carried on through
Menou as intermediary so as to avoid openly inculpating Mirabeau,
who, Duquesnoy thought, was trying to serve both the Comte de

[49] Virieu to Ventura, Apr. 5, Grouchy and Guillois (eds.), p. 186.

[50] Lafayette to [Mme de Simiane], [Apr. 5?], Mémoires, II, 459.

[51] Lescure (ed.), II, 438 (Apr. 19); L'Observateur, Apr. 1, p. 726; and Journal général de la cour, Apr. 3, pp. 22–23.

[52] Journal de Paris, Apr. 2, p. 368, and Patriote français, Apr. 8, p. 3.

Provence and the Duc d'Orléans without either of them knowing about his relations with the other. When Lafayette learned about Menou's part in these transactions, he confronted him with it, but Menou claimed that while he had been allowing the couriers involved to travel with his endorsement, he was not himself engaged in correspondence with Orléans. He even forthwith demanded that Orléans announce publicly that he had never received any letters from him.[53] Whatever the basis of Duquesnoy's story, one of the troubles that Lafayette complained about to Adelaïde, was that the National Assembly, torn apart by "twelve or fifteen parties," was now presided over by the Baron de Menou, whom he referred to as an "Orléanist president."

In addition to his concern over Menou and Maillebois, Lafayette wrote Adelaïde, "I have for my Easter fortnight" the church question, "the parlementarians" in the districts, the possible pillage of the Caisse d'Escompte, the animus between districts and Commune, the rivalry of the civil and the military, the uncertainty about the royal army's future, the struggle over judicial reform, and "thirty thousand famished workers." Besides, he continued, he had fallen out with the Duport party, and Necker (whose health was bad) was preparing to resign. Mme de Simiane had recently pitied her friend because the king's indecision added to his trouble, and he thought she was right: the "two-horned" king and the queen were obsessed by aristocratic sentiments; their ministers delivered jeremiads, each trying to justify the others but meanwhile allowing what might be a most robust executive power to wither away.[54]

Adelaïde was not unreservedly Lafayette's partisan, for she was not only less committed to the Revolution than he but also, as one of the ladies of the court, in a position to know more than he about Marie Antoinette's preferences. She urged him to attend the Easter service at the Church of Saint-Germain-l'Auxerrois, where Her Majesty planned to hear Easter Mass. Lafayette did so, and he confided in Adelaïde that the queen seemed pleased. He had even spoken to the king about what he called "that plan"[55]—an unspeci-

---

[53] Duquesnoy, II, 480–82. Cf. above, p. 257.

[54] Lafayette to [Mme de Simiane], [ca Apr. 5?], Mémoires, II, 458.

[55] Ibid., p. 459.

fied project which Adelaïde was expected to recognize by that bare phrase alone. Subsequent developments suggest that "that plan" was to present to the king an outline of what in his own opinion the new constitution should contain.[56] In any case, he found that His Majesty considered "that plan" a good idea, and Lafayette proposed to see Saint-Priest and Montmorin about it the next day. He felt encouraged to persist on his course, avoiding all the conflicting parties: "I think I should occupy myself with the constitution and with order independently of club intrigues."[57]

Again Lafayette underestimated Marie Antoinette's ill will. A few days later he was ready to admit that he was getting nowhere, since the queen kept putting off conversations with him. He believed her "taken in by illusions" and able to twist the king to her point of view. Furthermore, he uncovered some reason to think that she actually hoped for the restoration of the monarchy of the Old Regime, if need be by flight. She seemed to him to be lending an ear to a counterrevolutionary group that was inviting the royal family to Bordeaux; the royal ambassador at Madrid was acting suspiciously; and the Maillebois "Easter" conspiracy (though Easter Sunday had come and gone) was still a threat: "In this situation it is only the complete surrender of the king that can save the commonwealth without civil war, of which the likelihood is greater today because the aristocrats keep up some hope and the factious profit from it to fish in troubled waters." Lafayette confidentially admitted that his own inclination would have compelled him to sympathize with the unhappy position of Louis XVI and Marie Antoinette even without Adelaïde's frequent pleading that he pay them the deference due their rank. But he was now persuaded that perhaps a sterner policy might have been better for them, and for the public welfare too. The king and the queen were behaving "like big children who take their medicine only if they are scared with tales of monsters." But, he wrote his confidante: "Don't get the idea that I am capable of frivolous behavior in order to gain control. We'll always be in agreement on what-

[56] *Ibid.* and see below, pp. 327–32.
[57] Lafayette to [Mme de Simiane], [*ca.* Apr. 5?], *Mémoires,* II, 459.

ever I shall do along that line." He was well pleased with her sentiments, he assured her, even though he implied that she might not
always approve of his: "I have a feeling that six months hence I
shall owe apologies to whoever has the misfortune to love me," and
when, after promising to see her the next day, he closed his letter
with his greetings "to all animate and inanimate beings that recall
to you the times so sweet that I yearn to see reborn," he did not
mean that, like Marie Antoinette, he wanted to see the Old Regime
restored.[58]

No one but Mme de Simiane seems to have learned of Lafayette's
temporary disillusionment. Publicly he continued to play the old
game of trying to unite the moderate parties in the Assembly, on
the one hand, and win over the king, on the other. Anyway,
whether the Easter conspiracy had been an illusion fondly harbored
by hopeful counterrevolutionaries or a specter conjured up by apprehensive revolutionaries, whether "real or supposed" (to use
William Short's phrase),[59] it did not actually take place. If fancy,
it had never materialized except for some anti-Protestant riots in
the Midi; if fact, it had been frustrated by the precautions that Lafayette and others had taken.

For the nonce counterrevolutionary designs seemed to imperil
systematic reform less than the activities of the radical revolutionaries. The more extreme deputies on the left of the National Assembly saw in the popular indignation against the aristocrats a
chance to swing many of the hitherto undecided to their side. They
were particularly successful in the Jacobin Club, which by this time
was the largest and most flourishing political club of France. Lafayette had never been an active member. He had known that
early in the career of the National Assembly a group of Breton
deputies had organized a Breton Club, but it was news to him when
it became the Club de la Révolution, with about fifteen or twenty

[58] Lafayette to [Mme de Simiane], [Apr. 9], *ibid.*, pp. 456–57. The letters of Lafayette
to [Mme de Simiane],[*ca.* Apr. 5?], *Mémoires*, II, 458–59, and *ce vendredi* [Apr. 9],
ibid., pp. 456–57, have been placed by the editors of the *Mémoires* in the wrong chronological order. The one they give first was written shortly after Pasquale Paoli was presented
at court (Apr. 8), not at the National Assembly (Apr. 22), and the one they give second
was written shortly after the queen's attendance at Easter Mass (Apr. 4).

[59] Short to Jay, Apr. 4, Boyd (ed.), XVI, 303.

members. When he learned that he was counted upon to be one of them, he was pleased.[60] Nevertheless, since he suspected that its leaders, such as Barnave, Duport, and Lameth, were friendly to Orléans and unfriendly to Necker,[61] the effort attempted at Passy, before the National Assembly moved to Paris, to unite his following with theirs failed.[62] After the move to Paris, the Club de la Révolution became the nucleus of an expanding and increasingly revolutionary Jacobin organization, which he attended rarely, and as time wore on, he became less and less sympathetic with their program for weakening the royal executive. By the end of October 1789 one of his colleagues in the National Assembly believed (though not altogether justifiably) that he had definitely broken with the Triumvirate.[63]

Then in March had come the debate whether to deal with the Belgian Congress during which Lafayette had delivered his carefully prepared address advocating that the whole matter be left to the king's decision.[64] After that address Duport and Lameth made remarks to Lafayette (apparently privately) that hurt his feelings.[65] Yet the moral victory Lafayette won that day had led him to revive his hope of restoring harmony among the advocates of limited constitutional monarchy. He did not know, he confessed to Latour-Maubourg, whether to attribute the possibility of a reconciliation to "the realization of our strength at the moment, or love of the Revolution, or that friendliness which they protest finding in the bottom of my heart, but the division of the popular party becomes ... harder for me to bear than ever. I have been tormented amid my successes by the thought that Duport got no joy out of them, that perhaps in that society [the Jacobin Club] they were blinded by hatred to the point of considering my popularity dangerous." But he now believed Duport and Lameth ready again for "the joys of friendship" and proposed to discuss with some trusted

---

[60] Lafayette to [Mme de Simiane?], [post Oct. 6], Mémoires, II, 415.

[61] See above, pp. 27–30.

[62] See above, pp. 34–36.

[63] Comte de Virieu to Mounier, Oct. 23, Irisson d'Herrison, p. 17.

[64] See above, pp. 284–86.

[65] See below, n. 66.

colleagues "the means of putting a stop . . . to this partisan rage, which has affected me since the day it began."[66]

That sweet dream of peace was soon disturbed, however. On March 31 the club chose Robespierre, already recognized as one of its most uncompromising reformers, its president for the first half of April. Robespierre, as his future attacks upon Lafayette were to show,[67] had already begun to entertain a set of suspicions about Lafayette, and perhaps Lafayette knew of his animosity. At any rate, early in April, once again lamenting his "falling-out with the Duport party," Lafayette confessed: "I have not been at the Jacobins and cannot go there alone."[68] From that time on, he became more and more convinced that the leaders of the Jacobin Club, particularly Alexandre de Lameth, proposed not merely to force Necker's resignation but also to weaken his own hold upon the Paris National Guard.[69]

Those who were now dissatisfied with the Jacobin program had meanwhile formed an opposing movement. For a time they rallied to the Society of 1789, which had been inaugurated at the beginning of the year 1790. The name "1789" was obviously meant to imply that the great reforms of 1789—such as the August Decrees intended to abolish privilege, the Declaration of Rights, the unicameral legislature, the suspensive royal veto, the nationalization of church property—were enough; they should now be confirmed and the Revolution ended, leaving the monarch with a considerable residue of his former power though far from absolutism. Among those who had once entertained Jacobin sympathies but who now joined with Lafayette to found this group were Bailly, Mirabeau, Sieyès, La Rochefoucauld, Dupont de Nemours, Talleyrand, and

[66] Lafayette to Maubourg, [Mar. 18], AN: F⁷4767. Mortimer-Ternaux, I, 433–34, and Charles Nauroy, in *Le Curieux*, I (1884), 123–24, give somewhat incomplete texts of this letter. Nauroy assigns to it the date 1791, possibly because it mentions "deux ans que j'ai cru que Duport m'aimait," but that phrase fits into 1790 better than 1791. The date Mar. 18, 1790, is obviously correct since the letter mentions the reaction of Alexandre de Lameth and Duport after Lafayette read a speech, as he did on Mar. 17, and was written the next day. See also Bibliographical Notes, chap. XV, p. 369.

[67] E.g., *Défenseur de la Constitution* (ed. Laurent), pp. 172, 177–78, 204–5. See also Gottschalk and Maddox, pp. 81 n., 111 and n., 122 and n., 250 n., 309 n.

[68] Lafayette to [Mme de Simiane], [Apr. 5], *Mémoires*, II, 459.

[69] *Ibid.*, II, 369–71, IV, 16.

Le Chapelier. Lafayette's eminence was such that men were prone to ascribe to him the leadership of any project in which he took part, but in this case, while he did not wholly repudiate responsibility,[70] at one point he attributed the initiative to Condorcet and Sieyès.[71] He was concerned enough, in any case, to want his most respected American friends to be selected as members of the society.[72] When Short announced this honor to Jefferson, he indicated that the founders comprised "some of the most respected characters of the [National] Assembly" but that some other deputies had been rejected—which, Short foresaw, was bound to "produce parties and discontent."[73]

Until early April Lafayette claimed that the Société de 1789 was not a political party,[74] and it seems, in fact, to have held its first politically significant meeting only on April 12, shortly after which it published its "Règlements."[75] In somewhat bombastic terms the society announced its intention to serve "as a center of communication for all general principles and not as a seat of collusion for particular opinions," to be "neither a sect nor a party but a *company* of the friends of man, and so to speak, *salesmen* of social truths." To "develop and spread the principles of a free constitution," the society proposed to correspond with other societies and to "promote all devices useful to the progress of the social art." Its founders thus registered not only their belief in the spirit of 1789 but also their faith in continual social betterment. Dues were 3 louis per year (60 livres, two and a half times those of the Jacobin Club and approximately equivalent to two months' wages of the ordinary workman), and so membership was hardly available to poor men. The published list of members, containing over four hundred

[70] *Ibid.*, II, 459 n. 1, IV, 155. Cf. Robespierre, *Défenseur de la Constitution* (ed. Laurent), pp. 177–78.

[71] Lafayette to Bureau de Pusy, Dec. 20, 1797, *Mémoires*, IV, 394.

[72] See above, pp. 229–30.

[73] Short to Jefferson, Jan. 28, Boyd (ed.), XVI, 133. Charles Perroud, "Quelques notes sur le Club de 1789," *Révolution française*, XXXIX (1900), 257, proves that the first meeting took place on Jan. 18.

[74] Lafayette to [Mme de Simiane], [Apr. 5?], *Mémoires*, II, 459.

[75] Challamel, pp. 391–414, gives the constitution and the list of members of the Société de 1789, but see above, n. 73.

names, included deputies, academicians, men of letters, financiers, and National Guard officers. Lafayette's primary concern in help-ing to create the Society of 1789 was to unite all men of good-will in an effort to complete the long-delayed constitution. He did not expect them to vote for all his program, only to keep disruptive motions from passing.[76] He hoped that deputies of the Left and the Center would cooperate to stabilize the revolution so far achieved rather than press on for more drastic changes. Some deputies, indeed, continued to be members of both the Jacobin Club and the Society of 1789.

The Society of 1789 published a weekly *Journal* (of which the first issue appeared on June 5 and the last—the fifteenth—on Sep-tember 15), intended to discuss not merely the issues currently be-fore the National Assembly but also matters of general interest such as law, international affairs, art, and the sciences. The mem-bers proposed to meet every Sunday evening. The Society of 1789 never became much more than a gentleman's social and debating society, and its journal acquired only a genteel influence. Some prominent members soon regretted having joined it and went back to the Jacobin Club,[77] but Lafayette was not one of them.[78]

The controversies that since the October Days had exacerbated the opposing factions in the National Assembly proved mild com-pared to the wrangling that arose over the relations of the church with the state. On April 12 Dom Gerle, who, though a cleric, fre-quented the Jacobin Club and looked to its leaders as his own, pro-posed what he apparently thought a relatively harmless motion—that the Catholic, Roman, Apostolic religion was and should re-main the religion of the nation and the sole authorized cult. The Right demanded an immediate vote, but Charles de Lameth spoke

[76] *Mémoires*, IV, 155.

[77] Lafayette to Bureau de Pusy, Dec. 20, 1797, *Mémoires*, IV, 394.

[78] Challamel, p. 417, seems to impute to Lafayette authorship of a *Projet de paix entre le Club de 1789 et la Société des Amis de la Constitution par un membre de l'Assemblée nationale* (Tourneux, II, 461, No. 9977), and [Estienne], *Interrogatoire de M. de la Fayette* has Lafayette explain that he quit the Société de 1789 to return to the Jacobins because he recognized that the schism was interfering with the work of the National Assembly. But Lafayette attributed the effort to rejoin the Jacobins to Sieyès and Condorcet, claiming that he and La Rochefoucauld did not accede: Lafayette to Bureau de Pusy, Dec. 20, 1797, *Mémoires*, IV, 394.

at some length in opposition, and when Mirabeau tried to support him, the Right started to walk out in protest. The president adjourned the session amid great excitement, which spread all over town, fanning the antipathy that many Parisians already felt for the "aristocrats."

Bailly had been warned that the deputies of the Extreme Right might be physically attacked, but he doubted that they were in real danger. Although Lafayette felt that the precautions he had already taken were ample, he offered to increase the guard if the mayor would order him to do so, and when Bailly thereupon gave the order, he called up enough detachments to double the guard at the Manège and on the streets leading to the Tuileries. Early the next morning (April 13) crowds appeared, bent upon getting seats in the National Assembly galleries or, failing that, upon hearing reports of the debates in the nearby streets. They found blue-coated National Guards on duty throughout the neighborhood, but were allowed to go where they liked provided that they went quietly.[79]

That morning when Lafayette came to the National Assembly, he found an unusually huge and excitable crowd gathered outside the Manège.[80] Inside, the attendance was large; about nine hundred deputies were in their places. Left, Right, and Center had brought out their full forces for a showdown on Dom Gerle's motion. Lafayette actually preferred the separation of church and state as in the United States, with each cult supporting its own churches and ministry, but he recognized that to go that far in the direction of religious liberty was impractical in the France of 1790.[81] At any rate, he took his seat far to the left, showing his disagreement with those who preferred a single established church.[82]

After some preliminary sparring, the Left proposed that the state should do no more than provide financial support for the Catholic Church. Dom Gerle was willing to accept this motion in lieu of his earlier one, but the Extreme Right opposed it. The Assembly soon seemed deadlocked, while tempers bristled. La

[79] Lafayette's speech of Apr. 13, *AP*, XII, 719. See also *Moniteur*, Apr. 14, p. 426.

[80] *Gazette de Paris*, Apr. 16, pp. 2–3.

[81] Lafayette to M. d'Hennings, Jan. 15, 1799, *Mémoires*, III, 244–45.

[82] *Journal de Paris*, Apr. 14, p. 417.

Rochefoucauld then introduced a resolution urging that whereas the majesty of religion elevated it above debate and the National Assembly could not regulate men's consciences, discussion of the issue was futile and should cease. The Moderates and the Left rose to his support, but the Right persisted, offering amendment after amendment and, with Mirabeau's younger brother as their spokesman, threatening to remain in their places until death, if necessary, unless the Catholic religion were declared the sole national religion.

Then a leader of the Right, the Marquis de Foucault, tried another tack. If the majority were to vote against the establishment of the Catholic faith as the one legal cult, he said, it would be because they were intimidated; the massing of troops outside the Manège demonstrated that the Assembly was not free. Shouting angrily across the chamber, he demanded that the commandant general withdraw his guards. Thus challenged, Lafayette asked to be heard, but Foucault remained standing at the tribune, and the president ruled that if Foucault were permitted to continue, Lafayette must then also have leave to speak. Thus appealed to, the Assembly voted to return to the day's agenda without further discussion, but Foucault, refusing to yield, went on: "My only amendment is that the Assembly is not free and cannot pass a decree." Nevertheless, the Assembly, deciding to disregard the several proposed amendments, accepted La Rochefoucauld's motion.

Then, as if by prearranged agreement, the deputies of the Extreme Right rose as a body and, standing in their places with hands upraised, began to swear an oath: "In the name of God and the religion we profess. . . ." But protests drowned them out, and the substance of their oath was lost. Lafayette now went to the tribune, followed by applause from Left and Center. Foucault, who still stood there, asked whether Lafayette meant to answer his charge. Lafayette said yes, whereupon Foucault proceeded to explain his behavior: "I was addressing myself to the mayor of Paris and to the commandant of the National Guard. I was saying to the former: 'Why don't you disperse the assembled citizens?' I was saying to the latter . . .: 'Withdraw your troops!' . . . The proof that danger has existed is that the commandant of the National Guard has had this hall surrounded with soldiers. I move, therefore, that in the future . . . troops shall never be permitted to come within more than three leagues of Paris." Whether he was in earnest or politicizing, the cards were stacked against him; he was interrupted three times by laughter.[83]

If Lafayette had been angered by Foucault's first attack, he no longer needed to be. Confident in the sympathy of most of his colleagues, he spoke as a responsible official explaining a justifiable police measure: "Gentlemen, some persons having told M. the Mayor of Paris of their misgivings about the safety of the capital, misgivings that neither he nor I believed to be well founded in any way, he thought nevertheless that it was his duty to order me to provide some reinforcement of the citizen guard with which the National Assembly has seen fit to surround itself." Thus, in a single sentence Lafayette made clear not only that he had done nothing uncalled for but, on the contrary, had acted in performance of his duty and in subordination to the civil authorities.

But one more sentence seemed indicated, for Foucault's insinuation that the National Guards were seeking to influence the Assembly's deliberations could not go unanswered. Lafayette could not have been insensitive to current accusations that he was aping Cromwell, although one of his chief concerns had been in contrast to Cromwell's to protect the legislature from insult and intimidation. "Permit me, Gentlemen," he now requested, "to take this opportunity to repeat to the Assembly, in the name of the National Guard, that there is not one of us who would not give the last drop of his blood to assure the execution of its decrees and the liberty of its deliberations and to preserve the inviolability of its members."[84]

As the speaker left the tribune, vigorous applause burst out from both deputies and visitors, and it continued even after he resumed his seat. Only the deputies of the Extreme Right did not applaud.[85] The Abbé Maury, one of the ablest of the Right, tried to get leave to speak, but the president called for a vote on whether to change the order of the day or to adjourn, and at four o'clock in

[83] *Ibid.*, and *AP*, XII, 718–19.

[84] *AP*, XII, 719; Tuetey, II, 431, No. 4091; and Poncet-Delpech, pp. 277–78.

[85] *Courier français*, Apr. 14, p. 359, and *Courier national*, Apr. 15, p. 8.

the afternoon, the session adjourned, the Left still jubilant and the Extreme Right defiant and distressed.[86]

The applause had reverberated in the streets, and so the assemblage outside the Manège was soon apprised of what had happened inside. As Lafayette and Mirabeau came out, the people met them with cheers and gathered around them.[87] Mirabeau started for his home, and Lafayette for the royal palace. A huge crowd accompanied the commandant general to his carriage, "men, women and children pressing on him to kiss his hands and the skirts of his coat," giving him "the air of a hero carried in triumph under the windows of the King and Queen and in their presence."[88] Even Desmoulins joined the crowd and shouted as lustily as he could: "Long live our general!"[89] Arriving at the palace, Lafayette told the king of the police precautions he had taken, adding that he would have given the king prompt warning of danger if he had thought necessary.[90]

The precautions quickly proved to have been more than idle histrionics. A short distance from the Manège several men insulted and threatened the younger Mirabeau and Cazalès, who had to draw their swords in self-defense, but some grenadiers came up in time and escorted them safely to their homes.[91] The Abbé Maury was rescued from an unfriendly crowd by some colleagues and later went off unmolested in an overcoat loaned him by a Jewish sergeant of the National Guard. A reporter of these events noted how ironical it was that a clerical deputy who had opposed decrees tending toward religious tolerance should seek safety in the cloak of a Jew and that deputies of the Extreme Right should find protection

---

[86] *AP*, XII, 719. Journals other than those already cited that carried accounts of the session on Apr. 13 include *Point du jour*, Apr. 14, p. 17; *Gazette de Leide*, Apr. 27; *Procès-verbal de l'Assemblée nationale*, Apr. 13, p. 7; *Chronique de Paris*, Apr. 14, p. 416; and *Patriote français*, Apr. 14, p. 3.

[87] *Gazette de Leide, supplément*, Apr. 27.

[88] Short to Jay, Apr. 23, Boyd (ed.), XVI, 373.

[89] Desmoulins, *Révolutions*, No. 21, pp. 352–53. See also Fernan Nuñez to Floridablanca, Apr. 15, Mousset, p. 119.

[90] *Journal général de la cour*, Apr. 17, p. 133.

[91] *AP*, XII, 719–20, 734; *Journal de Paris*, Apr. 16, pp. 427–28; *Gazette de Paris*, Apr. 16, pp. 2–3; and *Indécence inouie du vicomte de Mirabeau et de l'abbé Maury envers la nation, et justification de M. le marquis de La Fayette* (Paris, 1790).

in the very Guards whose withdrawal their colleagues had demanded.[92] The next day, when Cazalès and the Vicomte de Mirabeau tried to narrate their experience to the National Assembly and to record their thanks to the National Guard, the Left, clamoring to get on with the agenda, did not hear them out but passed to the order of the day.[93]

The victory of the Left and the Center over the delaying tactics of the Extreme Right held promise that the Assembly would proceed rapidly to complete the constitution. Perhaps the most vital question, however, remained as baffling as ever: What did the royal court really intend? So long as Louis XVI's position was vague and the court aristocrats influenced his policy, popular distrust of the king and "the Austrian Cabal" would embolden the Jacobin leaders to push for further change, and thus for instability and perhaps violence. On the other hand, Louis XVI could be expected to countenance the aristocrats who hoped to restore his quondam power unless he could be convinced that in the constitutional monarchy eventually provided, he, his church, and the officials of his choice would retain much of their erstwhile dignity and prerogatives. No one was in a better position to give that conviction than Lafayette, if even he could, and two court noblemen who had access to Lafayette undertook to sound him out.

One of them was Adelaïde de Simiane's youngest brother, Comte Roger de Damas, who had recently returned from service[94] in the armies of Tsarina Catherine of Russia, fighting the Turks. Finding Lafayette "the key to all the doors that led to anything" and remembering the "marked kindness" Lafayette had shown him as a boy and the marquis' "close friendship" with his family, Damas went to see him. The Hôtel Lafayette, he discovered, resembled a military headquarters. As he waited, he heard the general's

---

[92] *Journal de Paris*, Apr. 16, pp. 427–28. See also *Patriote français*, Apr. 15, p. 3; *Gazette de Paris*, Apr. 16, pp. 2–3; and Francisque Mège, *Gaultier de Biauzat, . . . sa vie et sa correspondance* (Paris, 1890), II, 315.

[93] *AP*, XII, 719–20, 734.

[94] Lafayette to [Mme de Simiane], [Apr. 9], which is only partly published in *Mémoires*, III, 456; it is given more completely in the manuscript copy in CU: Lafayette Archives, Box II. The published version omits the first sentence, which reads: "Ce bon Rog . . . [*sic*] part bien à propos pour que je puisse vous écrire."

aides-de-camp make remarks that he considered of "the most in-cendiary and alarming kind." Lafayette welcomed his visitor cordially, and Damas was impressed by his host's "simple and mod-erate conversation," but as Lafayette talked on, Damas became convinced that their political philosophies would no longer be compatible. He later found others of his old acquaintances and even his own family (probably his sister particularly) less royalist than himself, and in May he returned to the Russian army.[95]

The other nobleman who undertook to sound out Lafayette was Comte Valentin Esterhazy, a Hungarian noble attached to the queen's entourage and until the recent reorganization of local gov-ernment the commandant at Valenciennes. Impelled by popular unrest there and by fear for the safety of the queen in Paris, he had recently come to the capital.[96] According to his testimony, shortly after his arrival Lafayette took the initiative and invited him to his home. And, indeed, Lafayette was at this time likely to be seeking to communicate with someone close to the queen. At least two of his friends knew that he had in mind some sort of showdown with the royal family. He had already told Mme de Simiane that Louis XVI was willing to learn more about "that plan,"[97] and William Short informed his government that the king had asked Lafayette what his ideas were "with respect to the powers that would be left to the Monarch by the constitution."[98]

Why Lafayette should have thought he needed an intermediary can readily be surmised. As Short put it: "There are at court many people who wish really for a civil war. They will do all they can if they come to the knowledge of these conditions [of Lafayette] to prevent the king's adhering to them."[99] Frequent interviews be-tween king and commandant, Lafayette must have reasoned, could

---

[95] Jacques Rambaud (ed.), *Mémoires of the Comte Roger de Damas* (New York and London, 1913), pp. 114–18.

[96] Ernest Daudet (ed.), *Mémoires du cte Valentin Esterhazy* (Paris, 1905), p. 264. See also Feuillet de Conches (ed.), IV, 37 and below, Bibliographical Notes, p. 336. Esterhazy stated that he came to Paris "at the end of April," but the activities he narrates took place in mid-April.

[97] See above, p. 313–14.

[98] Short to Jay, Apr. 12, Boyd (ed.), XVI, 333.

[99] *Ibid.*, p. 334.

be expected to rouse curiosity in undesirable quarters, whereas interchanges through a third party would make negotiations not merely less obvious but also less formal and so more elastic, committing no one until he wanted to be. If the king were well advised, Short held (obviously reflecting Lafayette's opinion), he would not hesitate to accept Lafayette's conditions, which "would probably unite the well intentioned of all the parties" and without which "there seems no possibility of finishing the constitution and arranging the finances in peace."[100]

With the consent of the king and the queen, Esterhazy went to see Lafayette at the home of a mutual friend, Mme du Châtelet (who was related to the Duc du Châtelet, Adelaïde's uncle). Lafayette assured him of his personal friendliness toward the king but also of his unwillingness to show it until Louis had renounced all arbitrary authority. Do you intend then, the count asked, to play the role of a dictator such as Cromwell or of a renovator of monarchy such as General Monk? Lafayette replied that he wanted to establish order firmly but intended to do no more than to advise how that could be done. Esterhazy reported this conversation to the king, and the next day, with royal permission, returned to see Lafayette, who then presented him with a written proposal which Esterhazy described as "a sort of table of contents" of a scheme for dividing authority between the monarch and the people. It proposed, as Esterhazy later described it, to vest the monarch with extensive authority. He would have complete control of the army, appoint judges, and dispose of the funds for his personal use (*liste civile*) and of the appropriations for army, navy, and foreign affairs, which, however, would be voted by the legislature, to which his ministers would be accountable; he would also have the right to make peace and war (subject to the legislature's appropriation of funds for the conduct of war), but military officers would have no civil authority, and all civil and administrative officers (other than the royal ministry) would be elective. Lafayette asked that the king consent to these conditions and, according to Esterhazy,[101]

---

[100] *Ibid.*

[101] Feuillet de Conches (ed.), IV, 39.

also to the dismissal of certain ambassadors and of Bouillé as a general, although he was willing to keep Esterhazy at Valenciennes—a favor that the count claimed to have agreed to accept only when the king's authority should have been completely restored. Louis XVI, when his go-between again reported, found these proposals too ambiguous, and so Esterhazy went a third time to see Lafayette, this time at Lafayette's home.

That third discussion of the powers to be left to the king took place on or before April 12, for on that day Short, presumably with the consent of Lafayette, revealed to the American government that "the Marquis [had] reduced to writing his sentiments on this subject and put it into the King's hands" and "promises if the king will sign his consent to these conditions that he will support him against all parties." Short, believing that Lafayette's plan would result in a coalition strong enough to "prevent the continuation of present anarchy" and that "every day's delay renders the situation of public affairs more and more critical," expected Louis XVI to "come to a decision in a few days."[102]

Two days after their third interview Lafayette sent Esterhazy the written "sentiments" which Short had mentioned, and when Esterhazy still demurred, Lafayette (obviously having concluded that Esterhazy's usefulness as an intermediary had reached a point of diminishing returns) asked to see the queen personally. She received him that very day in the presence of the king.

As finally submitted for the king's examination, Lafayette's memoir was a lengthy document.[103] It began by describing his own political position. He was pleased, he said, to be engaged in combatting two factions bitterly opposing him—on the one side, the enemies of liberty and the constitution, who once had benefited from the old abuses and still retained their old prejudices, and, on the other, the enemies of monarchical unity (meaning the Extreme Left) and of the reigning branch of the royal family (meaning the Orleanists). Both of these factions, he continued, by their

[102] Short to Jay, Apr. 12, Boyd (ed.), XVI, 333–34.

[103] We have followed the text of the memoir and the king's autographed endorsement as given in the copy in the king's *armoire de fer* (AN: C187, dossier 133, pièce 8). It is given in full with slight variants in *Mémoires*, II, 449–56.

criminally excessive demands were fomenting disorder; in the center of this "double-headed and dangerous struggle," he found comfort in the thought that the interests of people and king were identical, and all his own sentiments in harmony with them. Harking back to the memoir he had submitted shortly after the court had moved to Paris,[104] he now assured His Majesty: "My principles, my opinions, my advice will be exactly the same."[105]

Then Lafayette presented a comprehensive outline of a constitution that he thought both feasible and desirable. He did so under eight major headings, which he entitled "Declaration of Rights," "Legislative Power," "Judicial Order," "Administration," "Army and Navy," "National Guards," "Public Education," and "Foreign Affairs."[106]

1. The Declaration of Rights, he thought, ought to enunciate general principles, one of which would provide for future constitutional conventions as the best way to correct abuses and avoid the risk that disagreement at any regular session of the legislature might precipitate a constitutional crisis.

2. In discussing the legislative authority, Lafayette candidly criticized the system of the Old Regime, by which ministers had issued decrees that compromised the king without consulting public need or public opinion. Under the new constitution, he pointed out, the suspensive veto permitted the king either to enjoy the fruits without the corresponding inconveniences of his sanction if he accepted a bill already debated by the deputies or to win support from the opposition and the right of appeal to public opinion if he vetoed it; thus "the suspensive veto is as effective as the English veto and may be used without danger." As for taxation, Lafayette considered it to the king's interest to proportion revenue to the needs of the state and to abolish abusive taxes, and so, "charged with the use of all funds," the king could not but prefer a fixed sum for the duration of his reign—without having to resort to ministers or

---

[104] "Mémoire adressé au roi," [ca. Dec. 15], Mémoires, II, 436–39. See also above, pp. 114–17.

[105] The printed text (Mémoires, II, 450) omits the word exactement from this sentence.

[106] Ibid., pp. 450–52. Each of the eight numbered paragraphs that here follow summarizes Lafayette's remarks under each heading in turn.

public funds. Despite the National Assembly's decree forbidding royal ministers to sit in the Assembly, Lafayette believed that ministers might be members of the legislative body but in that case with special precautions to assure that laws would pass only after careful deliberation.

3. Lafayette would make the king also "the supreme chief of justice," with the power to grant pardons. In the Old Regime, since judgeships had been hereditary properties, judges had been able, as in the parlements, to act in the king's name contrary to his wishes but with popular support. Under the new regime the courts would no longer be opponents of royal authority but would be its guardians because it would be established by the laws, whose application would be their only function.

4. The recently decreed abolition of the ancient provinces and the establishment of departments in their stead as administrative units would subordinate local government to the king. Lafayette envisaged a police system that would enable the king "to maintain the good order with which he is especially charged by the constitution."

5. Lafayette was not satisfied with the new army law, but it had, quite properly, made the executive the exclusive head of the defense forces, and it ought to make small difference to the king whether the domestic police was entrusted to the regular army, the constabulary, or the National Guards. What was imperative was that all land and sea forces be obedient to royal orders in a way that thitherto "the intrigues of generals and ministers, the pretensions of colonels, and all the military privileges have never permitted."

6. All citizens capable of bearing arms should be enrolled in the National Guard, but the Guard should be under the supervision of the administrative authorities, themselves responsible to the king. No citizen should have command of several National Guard units except when the legislative body authorizes larger combinations[107] to reinforce or to create armies under the king's command. "The armed nation ought always to have the king as supreme chief."

[107] The manuscript copy gives *rassemblement* in place of *commandement* in the printed text (p. 452).

7. The law on national education should afford the king the greatest opportunity to develop talents, to make himself dear to the people, and to enable the kingdom to flourish.

8. In diplomatic affairs, Lafayette still believed that whatever the rights of the representative assembly might be in principle, the geographical position of France and the current situation in Europe required that questions of war and peace should be left to the king's council. He realized that this opinion would meet opposition, yet considered it sufficient for the legislature to limit itself exclusively to making reservations at the time of registration of treaties, commercial regulations, or the acquisition or cession of territory.

In twelve numbered propositions Lafayette then recapitulated the royal functions and prerogatives that he wanted to have expressly stipulated in the constitution. (1) The French government is monarchical. (2) The throne is indivisible. (3) The crown is hereditary in the male line of the reigning family. (4) The king is the head of the nation, his person sacred and inviolable, and any criminal attack upon him a crime of *lèse-nation*. (5) The king shares in the legislative process by virtue of a suspensive veto that is binding upon three successive legislatures; laws are to be attested by his seal, proclaimed in his name, and sent by his orders to the local administrative bodies and the law courts. (6) Supreme executive power resides in the king's hands, and he chooses the ministers and their agents. (7) He is the source of justice, which is rendered in his name, and as such he inspects the courts to insure the maintenance of the constitution, the laws, and judicial discipline. (8) He dispenses the funds appropriated for the administrative service, of which he regulates the expenditure according to arrangements made by law. (9) Having charge of all the state's defense forces, he disposes of troops, ships,[108] fortifications, and munitions. (10) As protector of the kingdom's interests abroad, he is charged with the conduct of international negotiations and the selection of diplomatic agents. (11) As head of internal administration, he has authority over local administrative bodies and, through

---

[108] The printed text (p. 453) omits the words *des vaisseaux*.

them, over the National Guards on active duty; he authorizes every new administrative act; and he directs all levels of public instruction according to the provisions of the law. And (12) he is the source of honors and favors, and so distributes pardons, rewards, decorations, and extraordinary promotions; all hereditary titles and claims not established by him or by the people are abolished.

The rest of the memoir was devoted to an *ad hominem* argument in favor of a strong monarchy within a constitutional system: "It seems to me, Sire, that in this situation a king of the French, powerful abroad because of the full national force, vested at home with every means of doing good and checking evil, undisturbed and free in his personal activities, ought, when he is as virtuous as Your Majesty, not to regret having lost that appearance[109] of power which used to be exercised arbitrarily in his name and which the nation continuously begrudged him and challenged." But who would tell him truths like these? Ministers or secretaries frightened by responsibility, each bent on making an empire out of his department, which often was a mystery to both people and king? Courtiers and royal servants whose graft had become so much of a private property that they no longer felt any gratitude for royal favors? Judges who had acquired the right to judge by heredity? Financiers who had grown rich at the expense of the public treasury? Nobles who had so thoroughly distributed posts and pensions among themselves that they had achieved independence of the king? Yet these were the persons who now surrounded the king and the queen, seeking always to identify His Majesty's position with their own, veiling their prejudices or interests with a hypocritical pity for the people.

Lafayette advanced this program as the only road now open to the king, who before February 4 had risked merely his person and his throne but whose honor since then was at stake as well. He again pointed out two pitfalls that had to be avoided. On the one hand lay submission to the discontented aristocracy, which now could produce only massacres and bloody civil war, which must end either in victory for "the irresistible cause of the people" or

---

[109] The printed text (p. 453) says *opulence,* but as we read the manuscript, it says *apparence.*

in dismemberment of France for the aggrandizement of neighboring powers. On the other lay the victory of the Orleanist party, augmented by the personal enemies of the king and the queen and by those who sought to make France into a confederation of republics, rash men who, in his opinion, were misled and subsidized by foreign treasure. The union of people and king would dismay both the aristocrats, because without him they had no chance at all and with him only one chance in a thousand, and the Orleanists, because by separating the idea of liberty from the person of the king, they took from His Majesty the support of all good citizens.

Lafayette felt impelled to tell the king "that our circumstances are too difficult, too dangerous, too urgent for the public welfare and his own to be assured by half-measures and half-promises." He himself was willing to withdraw if Louis XVI preferred other counsels, but if the king decided to follow his advice, His Majesty should do so without reservations. Lafayette promised, in that case, to exert all his efforts to establish the principles he had outlined and to form an alliance of liberty, nation, and king. With such an arrangement "I have reason to count on success; at least I would not have to wonder whether someone else would have obtained more than I," and when the day came when the constitution was finished and a new government established, he would "with gratitude as well as respect" return "that precious token of His Majesty's confidence" and, as he had announced to both His Majesty and the National Assembly, retire to private life. If, however, he did not win the king's unreserved confidence, he did not intend to resign his post but he would find himself handicapped in every way. "I beg the king to recognize in this memoir," he concluded, "the frankness of a man who has never had a sentiment he was embarrassed to admit and who joins to a resolute constancy in his principles and an ardent love for his country the sentiments of the purest attachment to Your Majesty."

A cynic like Mirabeau might easily have felt justified in calling the author of this lengthy document "Cromwell-Grandison." It was high-sounding, chivalrous, patriotic, self-confident (overconfident as things turned out), and self-righteous at the same time that it was a bold, even brash bid for formal sanction of his already tremendous power. Yet the power that Lafayette sought was not his ultimate goal; to him it was but a means toward the accomplishment of a successful revolution, toward a constitutional prop for a tottering throne. But it is also easy to see why, when Lafayette was a refugee from France and a prisoner of her enemies and when the king was overthrown and on trial for his life, this letter, discovered in the Tuileries' safe, should also have been presented as evidence of their having conspired against the Revolution.[110] It was a frank bid for full royal confidence in return for an engagement to restore some of what had been lost and save what was left of monarchy. It was an explicit offer to form a third force between aristocrats who wished to restore the Old Regime and the anti-Bourbonists who wished a weak king or another king. It contained observations that, though impolitic, were plausible about the people who surrounded Louis and his queen, about the consequences that might follow if Louis failed to keep his promise of February 4. If "Cromwell" were to succeed in creating a constitutional monarchy with a strong royal prerogative, "Grandison" ran the risk of ruin at the hands of whichever side was victorious. Neither the king nor Lafayette could have been unaware of that danger.

At their interview Louis did not immediately agree to countersign Lafayette's memoir but promised to send him a note in his own hand later.[111] If Esterhazy's memory did not betray him, Lafayette in their conversations had demanded the recall of Bouillé and some ambassadors, but those conditions were not mentioned in Lafayette's written memoir, and Esterhazy believed that Louis' hesitation arose from these oral demands.[112] Short, however, although he confirmed that Louis XVI "had an aversion to several of the articles" in Lafayette's memoir, said nothing about unwritten conditions and indicated that Lafayette was out after much bigger game than a general and a few ambassadors. The king's acceptance of Lafayette's conditions, Short anticipated, would necessitate a distinct change in the ministry: "A new one will be formed of

[110] *AP*, LV, 440, 446–48, 688.

[111] The interview took place, we think, on April 14 and the king's autographed note was sent on April 16. See Bibliographical Notes below, p. 336.

[112] Feuillet de Conches (ed.), IV, 39.

some of those who are in the present administration and of such other persons as the Marquis de la fayette shall chuse." Short expected that then "an attempt will be made to separate the present assembly and call a new one—or at least to force them to confine themselves to the articles of the constitution and leave the framing of laws to the legislature which is to succeed them and which will be chosen under the constitution."[113]

Whether or not Louis XVI understood the implications that Short (probably with Lafayette's help) divined, after two days of deliberation[114] and in an autographed note on the last page of the memoir[115] Louis wrote that he was willing to adopt Lafayette's general principles although he considered the document vague in regard to the practical applications of some of them. The king added, however: "I believe I can be fully assured in that regard by his characteristic loyalty and by his attachment to my person. I therefore promise M. de Lafayette the most complete confidence in all matters that may concern the establishment of the constitution, my legitimate authority as set forth in his memoir, and the return of public tranquility."

Thus Lafayette could flatter himself that he had secured Louis XVI's commitment to his program of revolution in more binding terms than the king had given in his speech of February 4. But the king (or his advisers) must have recognized that he had provided himself with a loophole, in case he should ever wish to escape from that commitment, by allowing room to claim a misunderstanding on some specific practical point. Although Lafayette was given to believe that he had won the "most complete confidence" at court, its continuation was made contingent, in fact, not on the performance of precise contractual conditions but on the court's evaluation of his character and devotion. Lafayette had thus pledged himself anew, and in writing, to a set of monarchical principles and to personal fidelity to Louis XVI in return for a statement (also in writ-

---

[113] Short to Jay, April 23, Boyd (ed.), XVI, 375.

[114] See above, n. 111.

[115] In the manuscript the king's endorsement (despite Esterhazy's testimony to the contrary: Feuillet de Conches [ed.], IV, 40) is written at the bottom of the last page of Lafayette's memoir, but he sent Lafayette a separate copy of it. See below p. 335 and n. 116.

ing) that the king would trust him as long as in the royal judgment he was engaged in a course of action designed to ensure constitutional monarchy and restore public order.

Louis XVI sent Lafayette a duplicate of his endorsement and
put Lafayette's memoir with his own endorsement on it in his safe.
Lafayette, chivalrous, considerate, and self-confident, returned the
endorsement keeping only a copy, saying that no written contract
was necessary, the king's word would suffice.[116] Grandison thus triumphed over Cromwell.

Soon Esterhazy (and presumably the court, too) decided that
Lafayette in any case did not have enough following in the Assembly to carry through his program.[117] When the National Assembly
began to discuss the reorganization of the court system, Esterhazy
at least thought that Lafayette was committed to fight for the nomination of judges by the king (though the memoir does not say so).
As far as he could tell, however, Lafayette took no part in the debates on the issue, and when, on May 5, the National Assembly
adopted the principle (definitively decreed on July 5) that judges
should be elected by the people,[118] Esterhazy was convinced that
Lafayette had let the king down. When he expressed his chagrin
to some mutual friends, they arranged for him to see Lafayette
again, this time at Mme de Simiane's home. Esterhazy stated candidly that he thought Lafayette either wanted the king to have the
right to name judges—in which case he was obviously not influential enough to win his cause—or he had not wanted the king to have
that right—in which case his word was not to be trusted. The two
men parted without satisfaction on either side. Esterhazy claimed
that subsequently Lafayette invited him to a meeting at which
he and Minister Saint-Priest were to discuss some of the articles
in Lafayette's memoir, but he refused to go, giving as his excuse
that he had a previous engagement with the queen. Assuming that
since Lafayette did not in fact have majority support in the National Assembly, it was futile to deal with him, Esterhazy gave the
queen an account of what he had done. The queen, he implied,

[116] *Mémoires*, II, 449 n.
[117] Feuillet de Conches (ed.), IV, 40–41.
[118] *AP*, XV, 390, XVI, 701.

was of the same opinion.[119] And so nothing came of the whole labored interchange except evidence to use later against Lafayette and Louis XVI by their enemies.

BIBLIOGRAPHICAL NOTES

The reconstruction of Lafayette's speeches is difficult, more because they were variously rather than inadequately reported. In only rare instances do his available papers contain a draft in his handwriting which can reasonably be assumed to have been the version that he delivered. Even in such instances the possibility has to be faced that the draft in question was not strictly adhered to in the delivery or that it was a draft made after and not before delivery. In the more frequent instances where a speech is available only in printed versions, we have found that the contemporary newspapers gave either variant readings, since the stenography of the day was rudimentary, or readings that correspond so closely as to suggest that they copied from one another (as was frequently the case before publishers were protected by systematic copyright). For this period the versions of speeches in the *Archives parlementaires* are likely to be inadequate, being frequently derived from the reports in the *Moniteur*. Where Lafayette's *Mémoires* report a speech, it probably has been taken from the *Journal de Paris,* which, along with the *Moniteur,* was one of the best newspapers of the day. Wherever we could, we have checked the version given in the *Mémoires* against some contemporary version, and wherever we have found that Lafayette's memory gives corroboration to that contemporary version, we have tended to accept it. Occasionally we have tried to piece together what Lafayette or others actually said from a number of inadequate sources.

Confusion in the dating of the memoir Lafayette prepared for the king arises in part from an error in *AP,* which in one entry (LV, 440) dates it April 2, 1790, and in another (*ibid.,* p. 446) April 16, 1791, and in part from Lafayette's *Mémoires,* which gives both April 14 (II, 449) and April 16, 1790 (*ibid.,* p. 352). The dates April 2, 1790, and April 16, 1791, are obviously errors of transcription. The confusion between April 14 and 16, 1790, can be explained if one assumes (as we have) that Lafayette left with the king an undated autograph copy which the latter subsequently endorsed with his qualified acceptance of it, sending Lafayette only a copy of his endorsement. The manuscript of the memoir with the royal endorsement is dated April 16 at both the top of the page and the bottom of the last page, both times in the king's handwriting. Lafayette stated explicitly that the king's note was written on April 16 (*Mémoires,* II, 352). If he did not give that date also for his own memoir, it probably was because he remembered a lapse of time between his submission and the king's qualified acceptance of it. Hence we accept April 14 as the date of Lafayette's memoir and April 16 as the date of the king's endorsement of it.

Esterhazy's *Mémoires* were published in full by Ernest Daudet; Feuillet de Conches gave only extracts from them. We have concluded, however,

---

[119] Feuillet de Conches (ed.), IV, 40–41.

that the latter version sounded less "doctored" than Daudet's and have quoted from it, but the two versions differ only slightly in the passages that concern us. Esterhazy wrote his *Mémoires* between 1798 and 1800 (Daudet, p. i)— that is, almost a decade after the events dealt with in this chapter. Moreover, he quite naturally sees them in an egocentric fashion. Short, on the other hand, wrote his reports to Jay and Jefferson within only days after the events, and he probably derived his information directly from Lafayette. To a surprising extent the accounts of Esterhazy and Short dovetail, and both are corroborated by other contemporary sources, but wherever they disagree, we have depended upon the contemporary sources rather than Esterhazy's recollections.

CHAPTER XV

A Lafayette-Mirabeau-Bouillé Coalition?

SOME of the details of Lafayette's negotiations with the court were quickly though not always accurately noised abroad. Not only was Short aware of them but so were Esterhazy and several other persons at court, at least vaguely.[1] Besides, the Comte d'Artois in Turin, the Marquis de Vaudreuil in Rome,[2] and Necker's son-in-law, Staël-Holstein, had learned of them, and the last, as the Swedish ambassador, gave his king a confidential account of them. The principal rights that Louis XVI wished to retain, Staël-Holstein reported, were that of making peace and war and that of convoking the legislature, and Lafayette had agreed to support him (though Lafayette's written memoir had been silent regarding the right of convocation). The ministry was divided, the ambassador wrote, but had consented to an understanding with Lafayette provided that it remained secret, Necker and Montmorin approving and Champion de Cicé opposing the arrangement, and on that basis Louis XVI had agreed to give Lafayette direction of making a constitution; thus a "sort of dictatorship" had been created, making Lafayette "responsible for events."[3]

Whether or not Mirabeau was accurately informed of this arrangement (and it is possible that the court informed him of it), he began thinking of taking the initiative in bringing about a rapprochement with Lafayette. Since December his relations with Lafayette had not been close, even though they found themselves on the same side of such issues as bolstering the executive power

---

[1] See above p. 325; Lescure (ed.), II, 438 (Apr. 10), 445 (May 7); and Mme Elisabeth to Mme de Bombelles, Apr. 27, Feuillet de Conches (ed.), I, 360.

[2] Vaudreuil to Artois, Apr. 10, 30, Pingaud (ed.), I, 165.

[3] Staël-Holstein to Gustavus III, May 6, Staël-Holstein, p. 162.

of the king and opposing an established Catholic Church. The two deputies had seen each other from time to time at meetings of "the La Rochefoucauld Committee"[4] and perhaps also of the Society of 1789, but their encounters had been only casual.

Behind Lafayette's sometimes vague suspicions of Mirabeau there always lurked the shadow of the Duc d'Orléans. On April 27, the Châtelet, which had been investigating the insurrection of October 5–6 since December, finally summoned as a witness "Marie-Paul-Joseph-Roch-Yves-Gilbert de la Fayette, aged thirty-two years, major general in the armies of the United States of America, *maréchal-de-camp,* commandant general of the Paris National Guard, deputy of the National Assembly, living in Paris, Rue de Bourbon, Faubourg Saint-Germain." Omitting the events of October 5 in Paris, he began his testimony with his arrival in Versailles. In a straightforward, even terse, manner he recounted how he had tried to assure the safety of the palace before withdrawing to his lodgings at the Noailles home, only to rush back within less than an hour, clear the Château of intruders, stop a riot, and calm the rioters. Experience had taught him, he testified, "to distinguish the sentiments of the Parisian people, who might sometimes be misled but willingly listened to the voice of reason and of honor, from the efforts of some troublemakers, paid for or interested in disorder," and he recalled that he had warned the people against such troublemakers in his speeches from the balcony of the Château,[5] but he gave no troublemakers' names. Although he testified that his suspicions had been aroused by some talk about a "council of regency," he did not attribute that phrase to any Orleanist.

At least two contemporary observers subsequently accused the witness of having suppressed evidence in his testimony at the Châtelet, one attributing his discretion to an alleged promise made at the time of Orléans' departure for England that he would not reveal whatever evidence he had,[6] the other to an alleged desire to hide his

---

[4] J.-J. Pellenc to Lafayette, [May 28?], *Mémoires,* II, 460. See also *ibid.,* IV, 44. For other references to the La Rochefoucauld Committee see Bacourt (ed.), I, 409; A. de Lameth, II, 262; and L.-J.-A. de Bouillé, *Souvenirs,* I, 132.

[5] *Procédure au Châtelet,* II, 36–38.

[6] Bertrand de Moleville, II, 285–89, and III, 334–35 n.

own complicity.[7] But if Lafayette was thinking in political terms at all, he must have realized that it would be impolitic at this juncture in the Châtelet's history to impugn Orléans and Mirabeau any more than respect for the truth required. The Cordeliers had never ceased to attack the Châtelet over the Marat affair (which became the Danton affair when that court summoned Danton to appear before it for his interference with the arrest of Marat);[8] and its taking testimony which compromised Orléans and Mirabeau, both of whom the Cordeliers regarded as devoted friends of the Revolution, increased their animosity. Other districts joined the Cordeliers. On April 24 the District of the Petits-Augustins resolved that when the majority of the districts should have subscribed to the Cordeliers' complaint, the mayor should instruct the commandant general to give no assistance to the Châtelet in executing its decisions in cases of appeal or of *lèse-nation* until such cases had been communicated to the National Assembly. A pamphlet entitled *Lettres de Junius à M. de La Fayette* presented the need to supersede the Châtelet with a new court. Only a few districts seemed to disagree with the popular trend, among them being that of Saint-Philippe-du-Roule, which approved the court's investigation of the October Days and ultimately sent a copy of a resolution to that effect to the fifty-nine other districts and Lafayette, as well as Bailly, the National Assembly, and the Paris municipality.[9]

Whatever Mirabeau's reaction to Lafayette's testimony at the Châtelet, it did not impede, it perhaps even fortified, his intention to appeal to the commandant general for cooperation. The next day he sent Lafayette a lengthy letter. He began by frankly declaring that since the parlous state of public affairs could be remedied only by common action, anyone who shirked cooperation with "the one who alone is capable of determining its outcome" was behaving as a bad citizen. Hence he had determined to work with others for the public good and particularly not to separate himself

---

[7] Ferrières, II, 82. Cf. *Mémoires*, IV, 154, where Lafayette denies Ferrières charge.

[8] Combourg to Comtesse de Calan, Apr. 29, Granges de Surgères (ed.), p. 12; Perroud (ed.), I, 333; *Révolutions de Paris* (Prudhomme), No. 37, Mar. 20–30 pp. 7–23; and Desmoulins, *Révolutions*, No. 19, pp. 279, 297–98, 303.

[9] Lacroix, V, 134 and 139–47 (Apr. 26), 169 (Apr. 27), 294–97 (May 8).

from Lafayette. He had withdrawn from his earlier associations, he said, because Lafayette had erred in placing confidence in pygmies rather than in men of stature. Now, however, that the Barnaves, the Duports, and the Lameths were no longer wearing Lafayette out with their "active inaction," the situation had changed, and Lafayette had become "I do not say isolated but uniquely self-encircled." He should therefore ask himself what he was going to do, and Mirabeau owned that he was asking the same question of himself.

The safety of the state, Mirabeau reasoned in this letter, would depend especially upon the value that the people of the realm and of the rest of Europe would place upon a still uncertain constitution, and that uncertainty would be all the more dangerous because of the inaction of the only man who could ward off other dangers such as anarchy and administrative conflicts. "But certainly to do nothing is not the objective of the dictatorship conferred upon the only citizen in whose hands such power would be no novelty, who would appear only to continue in his accustomed place, who would find in his soul the only limits that such authority, in order to be beneficial, might convey. You will act then, Monsieur le Marquis, but what shall I do?" If he were not told Lafayette's intentions, he might have to remain inactive, lest in his ignorance he counteract them. But to be inactive, Mirabeau confessed, was contrary to his temperament and to his desire for glory. Besides, he was too thoroughly committed to remain neutral or silent.

Consequently, Mirabeau went on, he sought an understanding that would permit them and their friends to form a permanent and unconditional alliance. His esteem for Lafayette's private virtues, "happily in harmony with those unprecedented contingencies which have irrevocably linked you at so memorable a time to the destinies of France," induced him to seek such an alliance. No one realized better than himself, Mirabeau claimed, the fears and hopes that drew the sounder elements of the nation to Lafayette or attached more importance to Lafayette's serving as a rallying point for the divided nation. Although he too, he justifiably boasted, had won some laurels in his time, now, after long and systematic reflection, he had decided, putting the safety of the state above everything else, to give up every chance for any success that was not combined with Lafayette's. If Lafayette did not accept his bid, then Mirabeau requested that as a man of honor he say nothing to others about it and merely return his letter. If, however, Lafayette accepted his offer, then Mirabeau predicted: "We shall put together all the steps needed to succeed, everything for which, in an indissoluble political liaison, we can be mutually answerable to each other."

So far Mirabeau's weapon had been a bland appeal to Lafayette's patriotism and pride. Now, with characteristic bluffness, he admitted that his financial affairs were still in bad shape and asked for Lafayette's help. The burden of private mistakes and of his debts was so heavy, he confessed, that it weakened public confidence in him, and his anxiety interfered with his usefulness as a public figure. But why should his burden not be lightened so that he could devote his energies to public affairs? To be sure, he had once refused an ambassadorship, but the international scene had changed since then; Constantinople had now acquired an unprecedented importance, since affairs might there be so directed as to restore France, without resort to arms, to its high place among the European states.

In closing, Mirabeau pointed out that he had done something unusual by frankly presenting his view in writing, but he was not afraid to give Lafayette such a mark of confidence. In the event that he ever betrayed the alliance he was proposing, Lafayette would then have this written statement as evidence that its author had been unscrupulous. Except for that purpose, however, he trusted Lafayette to keep his overture secret.[10]

Lafayette's reactions to this letter could only have been mixed. He needed all the support he could get for the constitution he projected, and Mirabeau, no matter what his character and who his friends or enemies, was a persuasive debater. Yet Mirabeau had only a small following in the National Assembly and was widely distrusted as self-seeking and debt-ridden. Lafayette himself knew

---

[10] Mirabeau to Lafayette, Apr. 28, Bacourt (ed.), II, 1–6. Lafayette thought that this letter had been burned during the Terror (*Mémoires*, II, 366), but see Bacourt (ed.), II, 7.

of his having been linked at various times with the Duc d'Orléans, the Comte de Provence, and the Comte de La Marck and thought of him as meretricious.[11] In the present overture Lafayette eventually came to detect an ingenious trap: Mirabeau had placed him on his honor not to reveal his feeler while leaving himself free to join or to attack Lafayette, but that suspicion came only when Lafayette no longer had the letter before him and had an inaccurate recollection of its contents.[12] The letter itself makes plain that Mirabeau permitted him if he agreed to an alliance, to keep the letter and reveal its contents if its author ever acted contrary to the promises it avowed. Lafayette's very admiration of Mirabeau's slyness betrays his deep suspicion of Mirabeau—whether in 1790 or afterward.

At this juncture an alliance of Lafayette with Mirabeau, in any case, would have presented more complications than perhaps either of them realized. Within a few weeks of having extended to Lafayette his qualified autographed endorsement, the king wavered and began to think of other combinations. Louis XVI and Marie Antoinette had been considering engaging Mirabeau as an adviser with the understanding that his employment by the court should be known only to a few. La Marck, upon his return from the Austrian Netherlands in mid-March, had been secretly engaged as a friend of both parties in bringing about that understanding, but he had proceeded so slowly and carefully that Mirabeau at the time of his reapproaching Lafayette did not yet know about it.[13] Mirabeau seems meanwhile to have been trying to reach an agreement with the king through other intermediaries as well.[14]

Early in May the royal court decided to come to terms with Mirabeau, and within ten days or so of Mirabeau's overture to Lafayette, La Marck informed him of the arrangement Louis XVI was prepared to make. Mirabeau was delighted.[15] The king's offer

[11] See above, p. 39 and n. 39.

[12] *Mémoires*, II, 366, but see Bacourt (ed.), II, 7.

[13] Bacourt (ed.), I, 136–50.

[14] J. S. de Sacy, *Le comte d'Angiviller, dernier directeur général des bâtiments du roi* (Paris, 1953), pp. 249–50. See also below, Bibliographical Notes, pp. 368–69.

[15] Bacourt (ed.), I, 148–50.

meant royal favor, an escape from debts, and, for all its secrecy, the promise of a great career without having to curry Lafayette's favor. On May 10, Mirabeau, as La Marck was instructed to require of him, addressed a letter to Louis XVI. Moved, the letter said, by his fear of anarchy and of having any other ruler, Mirabeau engaged to try to serve the monarch's true interests, submitting in writing from time to time his opinions and advice. While considering counterrevolution dangerous and criminal, he promised, proceeding gradually, to try to bring about provisions in the constitution that would grant His Majesty full executive authority. The king was pleased with Mirabeau's project and engaged him on generous terms as a secret adviser.[16] As sketched in this project, Mirabeau's policy did not differ essentially from that outlined for Louis XVI by Lafayette on April 14, and it might well have been harmonized with Mirabeau's pledge of cooperation with Lafayette if all three men had acted together.

Lafayette seems to have known nothing about Mirabeau's arrangement with the court, but the rapprochement of Lafayette and the king was widely known. If the king, however, had ever really meant to give Lafayette a clear path, he soon lost confidence in him, as not only Esterhazy[17] but also Staël-Holstein testified. "Lafayette . . . is trying to win votes in the National Assembly to get the king more influence," the Swedish ambassador reported early in May, "but up to the present, no great success has crowned his efforts."[18] So when Mirabeau asked for two months in which to convert the country to his point of view, the court had no reason to fear that an alliance with him might work at cross-purposes to its alliance with Lafayette. Where Lafayette might not succeed, Mirabeau might, and in any event both men would be tied to the throne. Lafayette, in Staël-Holstein's opinion, was hoist on his own petard: "He is, . . . since his agreement, bound so closely to the

---

[16] Mirabeau to Louis XVI, May 10, *ibid.,* II, 11–13. For the financial terms of Mirabeau's deal see *ibid.,* I, 159–60, 163–65. A relevant contract is given in *Mémoires,* II, 496–97, which Loménie (V, 76–78) argues is not a formal contract but a draft. But if so, why should it bear the signatures of both Louis XVI and Mirabeau?

[17] See above, pp. 335–36.

[18] Staël-Holstein to Gustavus III, May 6, Staël-Holstein, p. 162.

king that this chief of liberty is obliged to sacrifice himself for the maintenance of the royal authority."[19] Whether or not Necker was the source of his son-in-law's information, in any case it discloses the kinds of rumor that were going around in court circles. Lafayette's commitment to preserve the remaining authority of the once absolute monarch was evidently at best semi-public, while Mirabeau's to both monarch and Lafayette was a better kept secret.

Apparently without directly replying to Mirabeau's feeler, Lafayette entered into closer relations with him—sometimes through their respective secretaries.[20] The combination of the international crises over Belgium and Nootka Sound with the new domestic tension over church affairs underscored the desirability of uniting the forces of the two leading proponents of orderly revolution. Convinced that the Catholic Church should have been formally recognized as the established church of France, some of the more defiant deputies of the Extreme Right coalesced into a political group that met at the monastery of the Capuchins on the Rue Saint-Honoré. They prepared a protest that appeared as a pamphlet, *Déclaration d'une partie de l'Assemblée nationale sur le décret rendu le 13 avril 1790 concernant la religion,* which, signed by nearly three hundred deputies, was widely distributed. Fearing to be compromised, the Capuchin monks closed their doors to the group, and it moved to rented premises in the Hôtel de l'Université. But not for long, for the district assembly of the Petits-Augustins soon complained that the signers were party to a conterrevolutionary plot. Thereupon, the accused appealed to the Assembly of Representatives, who referred the matter to the mayor, who asked Lafayette to provide them protection. By that time, however, they had again moved and reappeared as the "Salon Français" on the Rue Royale in the District of Saint-Roch, where, however, protests still followed them. The district battalion assigned a detachment to protect them, but in a short time the district assembly protested that members of he Salon Français had insulted the National Guards on that assignment, and the mayor felt obliged to go himself to calm

[19] *Ibid.*

[20] See below, pp. 402–3. See also p. 339 and n. 4.

an angry crowd and request the Salon Français to suspend its meetings. The Salon, claiming the right of assembly, refused, and the National Guard remained on duty to protect them.

The impatience of the people of the district did not abate, however, and on May 14 a crowd started for the building in which the Salon Français met, bent upon setting fire to it. But just as they reached it, Lafayette and Bailly arrived, and the would-be arsonists paused. The two officials found only a few deputies in the building, and nothing came of the outburst. When they left, things were just as they had been, the deputies standing on their rights, the people in constant fulmination, and the Guards patient and firm. The district assembly grew more and more unwilling to tolerate such a threat to the peace; the *procureur-syndic* of the Commune agreed; and on the following day he appealed to the Tribunal of Police, which forbade the Salon Français to continue its meetings in the Rue Royale, and the group moved once more.[21]

Although thus temporarily controlled in Paris, clericalism was fast uniting with aristocracy in irreconcilable militancy toward the Revolution. Outside of Paris the conflict between rights and order was sometimes more difficult to control. In the south of France dissident priests combined with nobles and officials to stir up hostility, and unrest was particularly marked in Marseilles, where dread of Savoyard and Spanish plans to attack the French frontiers joined with the unquenched fear of conspirators to keep the populace uneasy. In a burst of rioting on April 30 and May 1 a crowd, aided by some National Guardsmen, seized several of the royal strongholds in the Marseilles region and slew the commander of one of them. The municipality then arranged that the National Guard share with the king's regulars in garrisoning the forts, and quiet was restored.[22]

Upon learning of the riots in Marseilles the royal ministers decided to order the courts to bring the assassins to justice, to oblige the municipality to remove the National Guard from the forts, and

<hr/>

[21] Lacroix, V, 191–92 (Apr. 30), 207–8, 211–14 (May 1), 383–84, 389–96 (May 14); Challamel, pp. 369–78; Bailly to Lafayette, May 2, and Lafayette to Bailly, May 3, BN: Fr 11697, pièces 57, 58; and *Journal général de la cour*, May 15, p. 359.

[22] *Mémoires*, II, 399, n. 1, and AP, XV, 495–96 (May 12).

to ask the National Assembly to permit one of its number, the Marquis de Crillon, to go as the new commandant at Marseilles. While some of the National Assembly agreed that vigorous steps were desirable, they disagreed whether these were the right ones. In the ensuing negotiations among the deputies Mirabeau constituted himself an apologist for the people of Marseilles, who had elected him, noble though he was, to represent them in the Third Estate of 1789 (although he had chosen to sit for nearby Aix-en-Provence). Lafayette, on the other hand, felt constrained to uphold law and order.[23] He saw the Marseilles riots as a link, and an exceptionally dangerous one, in a chain of disorder that stretched into other cities of France, among them the naval base at Toulon, where the new commander was now having difficulties not very different from those of the old.[24] It looked to Lafayette (dubious, as police officers are wont to be, of the spontaneity of popular ferment) like a conspiracy directed by some malign hidden hand.

The Marseilles insurrection thus threatened to divide the Assembly three ways. Some, led by the Triumvirate, supported the popular party in the Marseilles municipality; some, led by Lafayette, supported the king's ministers' measures to restore royal authority, thus implying a lack of confidence in the Marseilles municipality; and some, led by Mirabeau, wished, while supporting the king's authority, to convey no rebuke at all or only a mild one to the Marseilles municipality. Although his view was closer to the Triumvirate's than was Lafayette's, Mirabeau was less willing to cooperate with them, and so Lafayette was able to get him to agree not to speak in apology for the Marseilles municipality, and Mirabeau had come to an understanding with some other concerned deputies that they would not speak either, all being satisfied with a simple, unrhetorical, general plea for order. Lafayette seems not to have known of Mirabeau's arrangement with other deputies (which he certainly learned later),[25] but in any case he arranged with La Rochefoucauld (apparently without Mirabeau's knowl-

[23] *Mémoires*, II, 459, n. 2. See also *ibid.*, VI, 9.

[24] *Ibid.*, II, 398–99, and *AP*, XV, 495–96 (May 12). See also above, pp. 186–90.

[25] *Mémoires*, IV, 43.

edge)[26] to introduce a motion requiring the municipality of Marseilles to send a deputation to account for its conduct to the National Assembly.[27]

The debates on domestic disorder reached a climax on May 12, when Saint-Priest reported the ministry's action regarding Marseilles to the National Assembly.[28] A heated discussion followed, in which Baron Antoine d'André, another deputy from Aix-en-Provence, blamed the disorder upon the Marseilles municipality, since it had conspicuously failed to prevent a murderous riot. La Rochefoucauld moved that the Assembly thank the king for the measures he had taken to repress excesses and to punish the guilty, particularly in Marseilles, but as yet he said nothing about requiring an accounting from Marseilles. His motion, with apparently deliberate care, avoided mentioning the word *municipality,* putting the blame on vagrants (*gens sans aveu*). The next speaker, Antoine Castellanet, a deputy from Marseilles, while supporting La Rochefoucauld's motion, emphatically maintained that the Marseilles municipality, being close to a hostile Spain and having been exposed to the insolence of the royal military, deserved no blame.[29]

Amid mounting excitement Lafayette next ascended the tribune. He started out boldly enough, by condemning the municipality of Marseilles and praising the ministry's actions:

When the king reminds a misguided municipality of its duty, seeks out the perpetrators of an assassination, watches over the security of ports and arsenals, when in various parts of the realm he suppresses disorder, I can see in such constitutional and indispensable exercise of authority only a guaranty of public safety.

Up to this point no intimation that the outbreak at Marseilles had been part of a broader pattern of domestic counterrevolution or foreign conspiracy, but now it came:

I do not overestimate either the counterrevolutionary movements, which it would be foolish to attempt and cowardly to fear and which it suffices to keep

---

[26] See below, p. 350.

[27] See below, pp. 349–50 and n. 31.

[28] *AP*, XV, 495–96 (May 12), and *Mémoires*, II, 399, n. 1.

[29] *AP*, XV, 496–97.

strictly under surveillance, or the influence of I know not what exalted or ambitious designs against the unity of the monarchy. And even if some jealous neighbors should wish to attack our new-born liberty, what can a nation, strong in its old qualities and its new virtues, united in liberty, thoroughly armed for its defence, confident of its chief's principles, what can it fail to do, I ask, to complete this great revolution, which will always be distinguishable by two principal characteristics, the energy of the people and the integrity of the king? But I must take this opportunity to call to the Assembly's attention this new and contrived ferment which reveals itself from Strasbourg to Nîmes and from Brest to Toulon, and which the enemies of the people vainly seek to blame them for, though it shows every sign of secret instigation.

Thus far Lafayette had identified the king with the people and the counterrevolution with the foreign enemies of France. Now, however, he went on to denounce not merely local governments that countenanced violence but also the delay in completing the constitution:

Let the just indignation of the Assembly against these illegal outbreaks hereafter protect both our commanders and our arsenals! Surely no one will discern in these excesses the designs or the advantage or the preferences of the people. But when municipalities and administrative bodies exceed their authority, when, still retaining the distrustfulness of the Old Regime after having eliminated its abuses, some will forget that it is confusion of powers that creates tyranny and that, once they are defined, the full exercise of each of them is needed for public vigor, let no vain quest for popularity keep any of us, Gentlemen, from laying down principles and bringing our fellow-citizens back to them.[30]

Lafayette then asked not only for approval of what the king had done but also for an almost explicit condemnation of the Marseilles municipality: "If the municipalities do not carry out their functions, we must sternly remind those municipalities of their duties." But (and here he revealed that he and La Rochefoucauld had previously agreed on the measure to be taken) "I reserve my remarks on the motion proposed to you until M. de La Rochefoucauld has indicated the amendment he will submit." Thereupon La Rochefoucauld proposed that two members of the municipality

[30] We have followed the version of this speech in *Journal de Paris,* May 14, pp. 539–40, which is also that given in *Mémoires,* II, 399–401. It is fuller than that given in *Moniteur,* May 13, 539–40, and *AP,* XV, 497. See also *Point du jour,* May 14, pp. 8–9.

of Marseilles be summoned to explain its conduct at the bar of the National Assembly.[31]

Mirabeau and the Jacobin leaders were outraged, the former because he had been given to understand that his colleagues would be content with an innocuous expression of disapproval of the municipality of Marseilles,[32] the latter because they preferred no expression of disapproval of the municipality at all. As Lafayette learned later, Mirabeau jumped to the conclusion that Castellenet and other Marseilles deputies had failed to keep their bargain to remain silent and that Lafayette and La Rochefoucauld were trying to make him lose face with the people of Marseilles if he kept his bargain and remained silent. Furthermore, knowing that he was widely imputed to have instigated the insurrection of the October Days in Versailles, he apprehended that he would be similarly charged with the insurrection in Marseilles. Egged on by Alexandre de Lameth, he now took his place in the tribune.[33] Neither the king nor the National Assembly, he argued, had enough facts to judge who had been responsible for the disorders at Marseilles, and to summon members of its municipality to the bar could be justified only upon the presumption of their guilt. If the actions of April 30 in Marseilles were criminal, he asked, were those of October 5–6 in Versailles any less so? He recommended, therefore, that the whole affair be referred for further examination to the National Assembly's Investigations Committee.[34]

The reference to the October Days was not wise. It gave Mirabeau's aristocratic brother the chance to propose tauntingly that the Marseilles affairs be sent to the same body, the Châtelet, that was investigating the earlier outrage.[35] The taunt was conceivably aimed not only at the elder Mirabeau but also at Lafayette, whose recent testimony in the Châtelet's investigation of the crimes of October 5–6 was suspected in some quarters of having tried to

[31] *AP*, XV, 497.

[32] See above, p. 347 and n. 25.

[33] *Mémoires*, IV, 43 (where this episode is erroneously dated May 2).

[34] *AP*, XV, 498.

[35] *Ibid*.

shield the Duc d'Orléans by revealing less than he knew.[36] Thus badgered, Lafayette went forward again, presumably to make his delayed remarks on La Rochefoucauld's amendment. When he reached the tribune and was about to speak, the Abbé de Villeneuve-Bargemont, another deputy from Marseilles, shouted from the middle of the hall: "They want to provoke the city of Marseilles. ... The idea is to get command of an army and drag the king off behind that army."[37]

So Lafayette now faced a double innuendo. The Mirabeau brothers, though for entirely different reasons, had equated the Marseilles affair with the affair of October 5–6, when Lafayette had escorted the king from Versailles to Paris, and the taunt from the floor had charged that a plan was afoot to provoke Marseilles into resistance so that an army could be sent there to take the king from Paris to Marseilles. "It is with the confidence befitting a pure conscience," Lafayette began, but at that point, the Right derisively interrupted. Lafayette turned to the deriding deputies and "with nobility and much firmness"[38] began again: "It is with the confidence befitting a pure conscience, it is with the confidence of a man who has never had to blush either for any action or any sentiment, it is with the most ardent desire that all the circumstances of the Revolution be clarified that I approve of M. de Mirabeau's motion to refer the details of the affair to the Investigations Committee."[39] Thus, whatever his original intention might have been, he openly seconded Mirabeau's tactics. Then, and only then, he went back to La Rochefoucauld's original motion (with no mention of the amendment to require an explanation from representatives of the Marseilles municipality): "With regard to the thanks that we owe the king, I am persuaded that the feeling of

[36] Lafayette's testimony is in *Procédure au Châtelet*, II, 36–39. For the suspicions about it see Bertrand de Moleville (1801 ed.), II, 284–89, III, 334–35 n. See also below, pp. 489–92.

[37] *AP*, XV, 498.

[38] *Point du jour*, May 14, p. 12. See also *AP*, XV, 498.

[39] *Journal de Paris*, May 14, p. 540, and *Mémoires*, II, 401. See also below, Bibliographical Notes, p. 369.

gratitude is unanimous and that that part of the motion will be voted unanimously."[40] There was a burst of applause.[41]

Further debate ensued before the Assembly voted. Some criticized the ministry; others defended it. Crillon announced that he would go nowhere except on the order of the Assembly. Mirabeau vehemently challenged anyone who had any charges to make against him in the Marseilles affair to put them before the Investigations Committee. Finally, after Alexandre de Lameth pointed out that La Rochefoucauld's motion particularly mentioned the municipality of Marseilles, a modified resolution finally was passed; it instructed the president of the Assembly to thank the king for the measures he had taken "in several places in the realm and notably at Marseilles," and it ordered the Investigations Committee to report upon the affair.[42]

The outcome of the session of May 12 was not a glorious victory for Lafayette. With his plea for order many heartily agreed, and to the king's desire to retain control of the country's fortifications there seemed to be no objection. But Lafayette had had to drop support of La Rochefoucauld's amendment to make the Marseilles municipality publicly accountable for its behavior and, falling in with Mirabeau and the Jacobin leaders, to content himself with a perhaps prolonged committee investigation. Lafayette's position seemed weaker when he left the Assembly that afternoon than when he had entered it that morning. He had crossed swords with Mirabeau, who only two weeks before had asked for an alliance and pledged loyalty, and had given ground. Could they still be allies?

Lafayette told some friends, who then told Mirabeau, that he regretted Mirabeau's having been personally offended by what had happened. Mirabeau quickly decided to act on that cue. On the day after the debate Lafayette received another letter from him. "Well! Monsier le Marquis," Lafayette read, "what I have dreaded so much has happened. By your amiable but fatal complacency toward your friends, you did me a great deal of harm

[40] *AP*, XV, 498.

[41] *Point du jour*, May 13, p. 470.

[42] *AP*, XV, 498–99.

yesterday, and, what displeases me most, you have done yourself some." Mirabeau went on to expound his point of view: the municipal officers of Marseilles did not merit rebuke and to summon them to the bar would have been to provoke a most dangerous outburst in Marseilles and destroy the good effect of the measures which the king had taken. That was why he had "pulverized the proposal of a summons." With typical bluntness he declared:

> You were converted; you gave up supporting it, and I have not given up opposing it. I remind you of these circumstances only to show you how indispensable trustworthiness is in political liaisons. You have had successes, why force me to win mine against you? That is to say, in some way, against myself. That's what has deeply disturbed me. That's what, if we do not take other steps, will bring ruin to the commonwealth.

Revealing that mutual friends had informed him that Lafayette appeared concerned about his feelings, Mirabeau assured him that he need feel no concern: "The lack of cohesion in our political liaison is the only ill effect that I have suffered." Success would elude them both unless they aimed for the same objective, and he would just as soon be wrong as right, he asserted, if they did not work together, for the outcome would be equally bad in either case. "Shall we together plan other steps on the Marseilles affair?" he asked. "Shall we keep an eye on the report that is to be made upon it in order to reconcile what principles demand with what necessity prescribes?" His purpose in writing was only to assure Lafayette and to be assured himself that neither of them felt any personal resentment. If Lafayette also felt that they should act together, Mirabeau asked him to say so to the bearer of his letter.[43]

Lafayette must have considered Mirabeau justified. In any event, he seems to have let Mirabeau know that he accepted the proffered olive branch.[44] In the debates on the Marseilles affair that followed he took no part,[45] and Mirabeau felt that he had temporarily triumphed.[46]

[43] May 13, Bacourt (ed.), II, 15–16.

[44] This assumption regarding Lafayette's reaction is based on their cooperation during the next two weeks and Mirabeau's letter to Lafayette, June 1, Bacourt (ed.), II, 19–22.

[45] [Estienne], *Interrogatoire de la Fayette*, pp. 13–14, however, gives so complete a defense of Lafayette's position as to suggest that he cooperated in preparing it.

[46] Mirabeau to La Marck, June 1, Bacourt (ed.), II, 24 and n.

The popular press shared Mirabeau's displeasure with Lafayette's performance. Loustalot damned Lafayette and La Rochefoucauld with faint praise: they were not "entirely sold to the ministry."[47] Desmoulins reminded Lafayette that he had once declared: "Insurrection is the most sacred of duties," and called Mirabeau "a good democrat" for having "thundered against the general."[48] The *Courier français* also maintained that Lafayette had been on the wrong side and only Mirabeau's eloquence had saved the citizens of Marseilles from humiliation.[49] And Robespierre was one day to charge that Lafayette "had provoked the anathemas of the National Assembly against Marseilles because, following the example of the destroyers of the Bastille, they had demolished an odious fortress."[50]

For all that, Lafayette's popularity remained virtually undiminished. On the evening of May 13, the day after his parliamentary concession to Mirabeau, he attended the inaugural banquet of the Society of 1789 in its elegantly furnished quarters at the Palais Royal. Though a member, Mirabeau seems not to have been present, but many other "excellent patriots" gathered at tables set for 124 covers. At the close, Sieyès, the president, proposed and the members drank the conventional thirteen toasts—to the Revolution, to the nation, the law, and the king, to the National Assembly, to the best of constitutions, to the liberty and fraternal union of all the peoples of the earth, to the writers who had prepared the way for the Revolution, and the like. The diners then took up a collection for the poor of Paris, which reached almost six hundred livres.[51]

It was a warm spring evening, and the windows facing the gardens of the Palais Royal were open. Promenaders, attracted by the bright lights, the sound of gaiety, and the clinking of glasses,

---

[47] *Révolutions de Paris,* No. 44, May 8–15, pp. 301–8.

[48] *Révolutions,* No. 25, pp. 564–68.

[49] May 13, p. 103.

[50] *Défenseur de la constitution,* No. 6, [June 1792], in *Oeuvres complètes* (ed. Laurent), IV, 172.

[51] *Chronique de Paris,* May 15, pp. 537–38, and *Courrier de Paris,* May 15, pp. 161–62, May 16, pp. 181–82. Challamel (pp. 417–18) mistakenly gives the date of this fete as May 18.

stopped beneath the windows. Word spread from mouth to mouth that Lafayette was inside. "That beloved name was no sooner pronounced than men wanted to see him at the door, and a thousand cries went up for 'the hero of the Revolution'."[52] Lafayette hesitated to show himself, but as the crowd redoubled its demand, his friends urged him to respond. Finally, glass in hand, he went out on the balcony and was greeted by a hearty cheer. Raising his glass, he drank a toast to the health of his "fellow-citizens." The crowd answered with: "Long live the Nation!" "Long live the King!" "Long live Lafayette and all the friends of Liberty!" Then they called for the mayor, and Bailly came to receive their applause. In an arcade below, a band was playing a new song, "Ça ira, ça ira," perhaps for the first time. It was a lilting lyric said to be based upon Benjamin Franklin's response when asked how things were going in the American Revolution: Ça ira ("getting along")! While not yet the fierce hymn of hate it was to become, in its earliest extant version it already bespoke the popular distrust of the privileged classes: "He who exalts himself will be humbled, and he who humbles himself will be exalted. . . . Through the prudent Lafayette all our troubles will abate, Ça ira! Ça ira."[53]

Despite the optimism at the Palais Royal, all were none the less aware how trying the times were. At the moment the leaders of all factions were anxiously scanning public reports of British naval preparations. The news that the British government was fitting out ships and sending out gangs to press sailors forced France to look to her own position, and, as Lafayette in his recent memoir had told Louis XVI, he was convinced that "our geographical position and the actual state of Europe" obliged the National Assembly to refer issues involving the possibility of war to the king's council.[54] That night (May 13) La Marck heard and informed Mirabeau that Lafayette intended to speak in the National Assembly the next day "in agreement with the ministry."[55]

[52] Courrier de Paris, May 15, p. 162. See also Chronique de Paris, May 15, p. 538.

[53] Courrier de Paris, May 15, pp. 162–63, and see below Bibliographical Notes, p. 369.

[54] Lafayette to Louis XVI, Apr. 14, Mémoires, II, 452–53.

[55] Bacourt (ed.), II, 16–17.

The morning after the banquet at the Palais Royal, as if to betoken their new understanding, Lafayette accompanied Louis XVI on a ride to the king's aunts' Château de Bellevue.[56] They did not stay long, however, and upon his return, Lafayette went to the meeting of the National Assembly. Montmorin reported to the National Assembly that the king had ordered France's warships and ports to be ready for action, and although the British government had given assurances that its naval measures concerned only its dispute with Spain, Louis XVI counted upon the nation's representatives to provide the wherewithal for necessary defensive measures.

Those who were not "in agreement with the ministry" were taken by surprise. When some members of the Assembly asked permission to speak, the president, Thouret, claimed that the list of speakers was already full. Charles de Lameth protested, and some deputies asked that the prepared list of speakers be read, whereupon Mirabeau objected that reading the list might prejudice the Assembly against those already listed; a specific rule might well provide that debate on the king's future messages be delayed for a day, but since no such rule yet existed, discussion of Montmorin's letter should take place at once. The Extreme Right, however, also apparently taken unawares, favored postponement of the debate. Lafayette, evidently seeking to conciliate all sides, supported Mirabeau's proposal about future debates but took issue with his contention that discussion proceed forthwith on Montmorin's communication: "In order that each of us may have time to reflect on this important letter, I move that the discussion be adjourned until tomorrow." After further remarks from other deputies, the Assembly agreed to postpone the debate as Lafayette had suggested.[57]

Accordingly, consideration of Montmorin's letter resumed on May 15, and it continued for a week. It had hardly begun when Alexandre de Lameth made clear that the principle involved was whether the sovereign people ought to delegate to the king the right to declare war and make peace. Jacobins like Alexandre and Charles de Lameth, Pétion, Barnave, and Robespierre expressed apprehen-

---

[56] *Journal général de la cour*, May 15, p. 340.

[57] *AP*, XV, 505–11, which follows *Moniteur*, May 15, p. 548.

sion that if the king exercised that right, the nation could be committed to aggressive wars in the interest of kings rather than of peoples. On the other hand, the right of the king to declare war and make peace and alliances was upheld by Clermont-Tonnerre, Malouet, and Maury, among others. They reasoned that foreign affairs could be safely left in his hands so long as the legislature controlled the purse strings. By May 20, the majority seemed to have reached agreement that France should never wage war against the liberty or for the possessions of other peoples, that the king should be responsible for the defense of the nation and for the conduct of diplomatic affairs though treaties and conventions with other nations would have to be ratified by the legislature, that ministers guilty of involving the country in an offensive war should be liable to punishment, and that no extraordinary funds should be spent for war without the prior consent of the legislature. But opinions were still divided on how, when, and by whom the country should be formally declared to be at war.

Lafayette undoubtedly, since he had so definitely committed himself, followed the debate carefully, but, contrary to La Marck's expectation,[58] took no open part in it until the final day (May 22). Meanwhile, multitudes filled the galleries of the National Assembly every day, and those unable to get into the Manège waited for news outside. Bailly and Lafayette called up additional detachments of the National Guard to keep order, and the crowds remained calm, though openly sympathetic with those who espoused the claim of the legislature to a decisive role in foreign affairs.

As a general in the royal army Lafayette was concerned with the growing threat of war as well as with the unceasing reports of counterrevolutionary plots. At Metz, whose garrison must provide the major resistance to an invasion from the Germanies, his cousin the Marquis de Bouillé was still in command, having changed his mind about emigrating. In reply to Lafayette's letter of February 9,[59] he proposed that they unite their efforts "for the sake of the general welfare and the strength of a monarchical con-

[58] See above, p. 355.
[59] See above, p. 222 and n. 86.

stitution that would assure the rights of the people and the power of the king."[60] Although Bouillé grew more and more perturbed over the rising revolutionary fervor in Metz, he held on. When his daughter got married and Lafayette wrote to congratulate him, his letter of thanks (dated March 14) contained, along with renewed expressions of alarm over the disorders in Paris and in Alsace, further assurances that he meant to stay at his post.[61]

In mid-April Lafayette, continuing to be anxious over the dissatisfaction of the people and the National Guard of Metz, persuaded Louis XVI to ask Bouillé to come to Paris, but the king's letter was so worded that Bouillé felt privileged to postpone his visit. Upon the persuasion of Latour du Pin, Bouillé subsequently participated in a federation of the National Guard units of Alsace and the royal garrison at Metz (May 4) and took the new loyalty oath, thereby regaining considerable good will and upsetting the émigrés' hopes that he might yet lead them to a victorious restoration. This gesture pleased both the king and his minister of war, who saw in Bouillé's ambivalence a possible means of clipping "the claws of the lion" (to use Latour du Pin's figure of speech), and they suggested that Bouillé stay in Metz and improve his potential as "a counterweight that could have great advantages." Bouillé, while holding in reserve his plan to resign and emigrate, sought to find out more about the intentions of those in power in Paris and especially Lafayette.[62]

Looking back in later years, the Metz commander wrote that Lafayette, had he been a truly great character instead of "a hero of romance who wanted, though heading the most criminal conspiracy, to preserve his probity, honor, and disinterestedness and to devote himself exclusively to the spirit of chivalry,"[63] would have boldly assumed all the authority, whether as lieutenant general or

---

[60] F. C. A. de Bouillé, *Mémoires*, p. 107. The letter there described is probably that of Bouillé to Lafayette, Feb. 19, CU: Lafayette Archives, Carton V (microfilm). See also below, Bibliographical Notes, p. 369.

[61] CU: Lafayette Archives, Carton V (microfilm).

[62] F. C. A. de Bouillé, *Mémoires*, pp. 112–18.

[63] *Ibid.*, p. 99.

constable, that the court offered; or if he preferred not to risk his popularity, he would have had himself named commander of all the National Guards of the realm and, by choosing his own subordinates, shrewdly built up his own force and weakened that of others; then he should have attracted to his side the most able, influential, and distinguished men of all classes and with their advice made France a constitutional monarchy with a solid base. Such was the wish, Bouillé believed, of the king and the great majority of the nation, and "favored by circumstances rather than by talent,"[64] Lafayette, in May 1790, had all the prestige necessary to be such a man on horseback. Probably without knowing it, Bouillé shared the opinion of Mirabeau, who also recognized that he had little choice but to cooperate with the commander of "the only public force with the aid of which a degree of order might be restored out of the general confusion."[65]

The aim of the royal court in inducing Bouillé to stay with his army fitted into the program that had already led it to hire Mirabeau as an adviser and promise Lafayette confidence so long as he worked toward the preservation of a strong monarchical executive within a constitutional regime. If the reforms that resulted from the joint effort of Lafayette and Mirabeau proved acceptable to the court, no harm would be done by keeping a loyal, regular army available at Metz, and if the reforms were unacceptable, a royal army under a devoted general might serve as a persuasive argument for a change of program. Reconsidering his own behavior in the spring and summer of 1790, Bouillé in later years decided that he too had made a mistake: he should have regularly accepted the leadership offered to him in the federations around Metz and then gone personally to Paris to work out with Lafayette a plan to fortify the king's position.[66] In actuality, however, he yielded to Latour du Pin's none too subtle advice to stay in Metz, fearing that Lafayette might want to detain him in Paris if he went there

---

[64] *Ibid.*, p. 118.

[65] Bacourt (ed.), I, 152.

[66] F. C. A. de Bouillé, *Mémoires*, p. 121 .

himself, but he sent his son, Comte L.-J.-A. de Bouillé, instead, with a letter which frankly pledged that if Lafayette's program proved helpful as he presumed, he would support it.[67]

Perhaps Lafayette recognized what was afoot, and, if so, he probably did not object. What seemed to be going on was friendly connivance toward the common objective of a strong monarchy within a constitutional regime. The principals in this joint endeavor were the king or, more likely, the queen and their advisers (Mercy-Argenteau, Latour du Pin, La Marck, and Esterhazy), Mirabeau (encouraged by La Marck and Mercy-Argenteau), Bouillé (prompted by the king and Latour du Pin), and Lafayette (both directly and through intermediaries like Esterhazy, La Marck, and perhaps Adelaïde de Simiane). The royal couple were aware of the activity of nearly all participants in this four-cornered operation, and Lafayette could easily have guessed about the activities in which he was not personally participating, but in any event all five principals were tugging in tandem toward the same general goal, the king supposedly in front, but all differing upon who of them should, at least until the goal was reached, chart the intervening course.

In the midst of keeping order in the Paris region and trying to push through a satisfactory bill on the making of war and peace, Lafayette had to deal with the possibility that Bouillé might drift into the counterrevolutionary current. Not content that young Bouillé report to his father in detail when he returned to Metz (which he did not do anyway until July 1), Lafayette asked Ternant, who was being sent to Alsace to try to reconcile German property-holders there with the agrarian reforms of the Revolution, to act also as his intermediary with Bouillé. Ternant delivered to Bouillé a written appeal. After expressing his pleasure upon receiving Bouillé's son, Lafayette expounded his own program: "Believe me, if I care above all for liberty and the principles of our constitution, my second wish, my very ardent wish, is for

[67] Comte de Bouillé to Achille de Chastelet, May 13, AN: former Fabius Collection, Correspondance Bouillé-Lafayette, No. 31; Marquis de Bouillé to Lafayette, May 13, *ibid.*, No. 32; L.-J.-A. de Bouillé, *Souvenirs,* p. 131; and René de Bouillé, *Essai sur la vie du marquis de Bouillé* (Paris, 1853), pp. 227–32.

the return of order, of calm, and the establishment of public vigor."
He then went on to explain that the current disorders arose in
part from the aristocratic party's hope to profit by making trouble
and in part from the persuasion of some of the popular party that
revolutionary methods and factious views were in consonance with
the constitution. Lately, the question who had the authority to declare war and make peace had markedly divided "our party" (by
which he meant all those who were in favor of a new constitution)
"into monarchists and republicans." "We have been the strongest,
but this situation and many others show us that the friends of public welfare will not easily be able to unite." So he made an *ad
hominem* exhortation: "Since you have no repugnance to espous-
ing our constitution, let us serve it, my dear cousin, with all our
power by warding off whatever may interfere with the happiness
and tranquility of our fellow-citizens from no matter what quarter
such efforts may come."

Bouillé thus had his answer. He had asked for Lafayette's program, and Lafayette had replied that it was liberty, the constitution,
and order, and, besides, he had explained that if public order were
lacking, the fault lay with aristocrats no less than Jacobins and that
Bouillé should be guided accordingly. His closing sentence should
have made clear his readiness to cooperate with his "dear cousin":
"It is with very great satisfaction that I see the bonds of our friendship become stronger."[68]

On the same day (May 20) that this letter went off with Ternant,
Mirabeau delivered his anticipated speech in the National Assembly. He pleaded for a high degree of power in the conduct of foreign affairs for the monarch: he should be enabled to appoint all
diplomatic agents and to make all agreements with foreign powers,
though subject to ratification by the legislative body; he should
notify the legislative body of the imminence of war and get its
consent for whatever extra appropriations were needed; and the

---

[68] Lafayette to Bouillé, May 20, F.-C.-A. de Bouillé, *Mémoires,* pp. 123–24, and
Mémoires, II, 461–62. On the émigrés' fears, see Vaudreuil to Artois, Mar. 20, Pingaud
(ed.), I, 143, and Daudet, *Émigration,* I, 37. A letter of introduction, dated May 20, by Lafayette for Ternant on his way to Alsace is contained in the Ball Collection at Indiana
University.

legislature should be empowered both to punish a minister responsible for an offensive war and at any time to require the executive to make peace.[69]

The following morning (May 21) when the National Assembly resumed the debate, Barnave attacked Mirabeau's proposal on the grounds that it gave the king the exclusive right to declare war, leaving to the legislature only the power to stop a war after it had started—a power that would be futile, since if it dared to refuse subsidies, the legislature would cause the war to be lost. Barnave proposed, therefore, that while the king might be empowered to defend the country and conduct international negotiations, the legislature should have the exclusive right to declare war or make peace and to ratify treaties. "Consult public opinion today," Barnave admonished. "You will see on the one hand men who hope to advance in the army [probably meaning to include Lafayette] [or] to get to handle foreign affairs [probably meaning to include Mirabeau], [and] men who are linked to the ministers and their agents [probably meaning to include both]. Such are the advocates of the system which consists of giving to the king—that is to say, to the ministers—this awesome authority. But you will not see the people among them."[70] Barnave pronounced the name of Mirabeau again and again, but never that of Lafayette. Nevertheless, William Short described his speech as "an indirect crimination of the Marquis de la fayette."[71]

Barnave's speech was hailed with enthusiastic approbation in the galleries. He was carried in triumph to his carriage on leaving the Manège, and for the moment he was so glamorous a hero that, according to Short, his triumph "was considered by many as the signal of the decline of the Marquis de la fayette's popularity and gave real alarm to all parties, because all agree, even those who are opposed to the revolution and consequently his enemies, that it

---

[69] According to Alexandre de Lameth (*Histoire*, II, 477–79) the text in the *Moniteur* (May 21, 22, pp. 570–74) is the one delivered in the National Assembly and sent by Mirabeau to that paper for publication. It differs somewhat from that in *AP* (XV, 618–26).

[70] *AP*, XV, 644.

[71] Short to Jay, May 23, Boyd (ed.), XVI, 438.

is his influence alone which preserves the order and security which is enjoyed in the capital."[72]

By the following morning (May 22) public excitement had mounted. News-vendors were peddling a pamphlet entitled *Trahison découverte du comte de Mirabeau,* which described that erstwhile idol as an enemy of the people, suborned by the court. Crowds poured into the Manège and nearby streets and gardens to hear Mirabeau's rebuttal or to get news of it, and they openly jeered him on his way to the Assembly.[73] Lafayette took his place among the deputies, and since he too wished to rebut Barnave's "indirect crimination," he had written out a speech he intended to deliver.[74]

Before Mirabeau spoke, Le Chapelier, trying to effect a compromise, moved that Mirabeau's motion be amended so as to give the king the power to propose and the legislature the power to decide that war be declared. Mirabeau then spoke "with an eloquence of which there has been no [other] example in the assembly."[75] At the outset he dismissed the pamphlet *Trahison découverte du comte de Mirabeau:* "I did not need that lesson to teach me that the distance from the Capitol to the Tarpeian Rock is short." He then "pulverized" (Short's word) Barnave's plan, pointing out that to place the right to declare war exclusively in the legislative body was contrary to the provision of the constitution that gave the king the veto of legislation. He accepted Chapelier's amendment, however, and thus amended, his motion stipulated that the legislature vote whether war should be declared but did not leave the final decision to the legislative body alone.[76]

The Lameth group wanted Barnave to answer Mirabeau, but the majority of the Assembly preferred that the debate be closed. Several nevertheless favored hearing Barnave, and Lafayette, obviously

---

[72] *Ibid.*

[73] *Ibid.*

[74] See below, p. 365, where Lafayette indicates that his speech was read from a prepared manuscript.

[75] Short to Jay, May 23, Boyd (ed.), XVI, 438.

[76] *AP,* XV, 654–59. See also A. de Lameth, II, 321, and Ferrières, II, 33.

playing the role of gallant opponent and also perhaps of would-be conciliator, joined in the protest: "It seems only fair to me that when M. Barnave asks to reply to M. de Mirabeau, he should be allowed to do so. I ask that he have leave to speak, and since I am not in favor of his proposal, I ask to speak after him."[77] Nevertheless, the Assembly decided that Barnave should not be heard.

Twenty-two different proposals had been presented, and the Assembly's parliamentary practice led to the assumption that a vote to give one of them priority on the day's agenda would mean a tactical victory for that one. In the discussion on which of them should have priority, Barnave got his chance to reply to Mirabeau and Le Chapelier—which he did at considerable length. The right to initiate legislation had hitherto belonged to members of the legislature, he argued, and if the king were now granted the right to initiate as well as to sanction legislation concerned with questions of war and peace, the balance of power between the executive and the legislative would swing too far in the executive's favor.[78]

As anticipated, Lafayette's turn came next. He read his prepared speech, which again, without compromising his position, appealed for unity. He preferred Mirabeau's proposal as amended by Le Chapelier, it said, because he thought it appropriate to "the majesty of a great people,[79] the ethics of a free people, and the interests of a numerous people, whose business, possessions, and associations abroad require effective protection." He found in the Mirabeau-Le Chapelier plan "that division of power which seems to me most conformable to the true constitutional principles of liberty and of monarchy, best suited to put off the scourge of war, and most advantageous for the people." This was a time, he contended when debate over "this metaphysical question" seemed to be confusing the nation, "when those who, though regularly joined in support of the popular cause, differed on the current issue while nevertheless subscribing to the same basic principles," and when one side to the controversy was attempting to persuade the people that

[77] *AP*, XV, p. 659, and *Mémoires*, II, 404.

[78] *AP*, XV, 659–60.

[79] *Ibid.*, p. 660, says *majorité d'un grand peuple*, but this is an obvious error. See also below, n. 80.

"those alone are its true friends who approve such and such a decree." Undaunted by the derision to which he probably expected to expose himself by his self-righteous rhetoric, he asserted that "it was appropriate that a different opinion should be clearly enunciated by a man to whom some experience and some labor in the furtherance of liberty have given the right to have an opinion." He obviously meant once more to stress that mere semantic nuances divided the friends of constitutional government—nuances that were not so weighty as was the need for them to work together— but he nevertheless considered his views on the question under discussion as the right ones: "I have thought I could in no better way pay the immense debt that I have contracted toward the people than in refusing to sacrifice for a day's popularity the opinion which I believe to be most beneficial for them. I wanted these few words written out in order not to surrender to insinuations of slander the great responsibility which I have toward the people, to whom my entire life is devoted."[80] Few hearers could have failed to understand that "these few words" were his retort to Barnave's "indirect crimination."

At that point the opposition collapsed. If Short's account to his government was correct (and he probably mirrored Lafayette's interpretation of the event), "the leaders of the more popular party finding that the plan which had obtained the priority would certainly obtain the preference of the assembly, and not chusing to have the appearance of having lost the victory, gave in to the current of Mirabeau's decree with slight verbal alterations which they proposed."[81] Thus, the Assembly finally arrived at an almost unanimous decision. While it declared that the right to make peace and war belonged to "the nation" (the sovereign people, in other words), it stipulated that "war could be declared only by a decree of the legislature voted upon the formal and necessary pro-

---

[80] *AP*, XV, 660, which corresponds with the accounts in contemporary newspapers. *Mémoires* (II, 404–5) omits the final sentence given above. The speech was printed under the title of *Opinion de M. de La Fayette dans la séance d'aujourd'hui* (*22 Mai 1790*) and is in the Jefferson papers in the Library of Congress: see Boyd (ed.), XVI, 440n. See also [Bérenger (ed.)], pp. 197–99.

[81] Short to Jay, May 23, Boyd (ed.), XVI, 439.

posal of the king and subsequently sanctioned by His Majesty" and that hostilities once begun had to cease immediately upon the demand of the legislature. The king, being required to defend the realm in times of peace as well as of war, was vested with the direction of the diplomatic corps, international negotiations, and military movements. The legislature was to have the authority, however, to fix the period of military demobilization after a war, and treaties were to be binding only if ratified by the legislature. The French nation, it was also decreed, renounced the right to wage any war of conquest and undertook never to employ its forces against the liberty of any other people. Hence the king was to notify the legislature whenever any threat of hostilities or need to sustain an ally was imminent, so that the legislature might determine beforehand whether the ministers or other executive agents were guilty of aggression and, if so, whether to prosecute them for the crime of *lèse-nation*.[82]

The session at length adjourned "amid the applause of the Assembly and shouts of joy from the spectators."[83] Lafayette and Mirabeau had worked together, and they had won a resounding success. The debates had been heated, the public had been in ferment, and yet the vote in favor of the articles that finally passed had been almost unanimous. The friends of a strong though constitutionally limited monarchy seemed at last to be in the ascendant. Short informed his government that "many who from their suspicions of Mirabeau feared there was treachery in his plan, adhered to it from their confidence in the Marquis de la Fayette."[84]

Since early morning of May 22 crowds had waited in the Tuileries Gardens and the nearby street for news of what was happening in the Manège. From time to time, men came out of the National Assembly and reported what was going on, and the occasional applause of the galleries revealed that some at least of those on the inside approved of points being made in the discussion

---

[82] *AP*, XV, 661–62, and *Mémoires*, II, 405–6n.

[83] *AP*, XV, 662.

[84] Short to Jay, May 23, Boyd (ed.), XV, 438–39.

of the bill. By six o'clock the session ended, and not long after news-vendors peddled a little sheet, the *Postillon,* carrying the news, which sold for six livres. For the most part the crowd was on the side of the Triumvirate. Thousands rushed to cheer "the generous defenders of the people" as they emerged from the Manège, among them the Lameths, Barnave, and Pétion, while others marched upon the print shop of the *Gazette de Paris,* which had upheld the monarchical side, seized the day's issue, and burned it in the Rue Saint-Honoré before a detachment of National Guards arrived to prevent further violence.[85]

The journals differed in their evaluation of Lafayette's role in the debate. He had been careful to provide the press with a copy of his speech.[86] The *Journal de Paris* published the full text in a most conspicuous place in its issue of May 24, and the *Point du jour* like-wise published it that day. Both printed a footnote (which may have been suggested in the copy Lafayette furnished) calling atten-tion to his appeal for unity within the popular party.[87] In contrast, Loustalot declared that Mirabeau, Le Chapelier, and Lafayette had apparently joined forces against Barnave, Pétion, and the Lameths, and out of this battle had come a bad decree, but, he hoped, the result would be to show the danger of the division in the popular party. Lafayette's few high-sounding phrases, Loustalot main-tained, had been without substance but had made a deep impression and had diverted the deputies' attention from the force of Barnave's arguments. Perhaps, the journalist suggested, the commander of the troops in the city where the National Assembly sat should thereafter abstain from voting in the Assembly, for his expression of opinion deprived others of complete freedom of deliberation.[88] Marat was considerably less temperate in his criticism of Lafayette's preponderance. The commandant general, he said, had 36,000 men at his back; why should he also have a decisive voice in the legisla-

---

[85] *Moniteur,* May 24, p. 586, May 26, p. 594. See also *Courier français,* May 23, p. 184, and *Point du jour,* May 24, p. 182.

[86] *Journal de Paris,* May 23, p. 574.

[87] *Ibid.,* May 24, p. 577, and *Point du jour,* May 24, pp. 170–77.

[88] *Révolutions de Paris,* No. 47, May 29–June 5, pp. 480–83. See below, p. 391.

ture? He should, rather, have had the delicacy to abstain on critical occasions, for anyone who combined so much civil and military power was suspect.[89]

If they had not realized it before, Lafayette's opponents certainly realized now that he held a dominant position not merely because the National Assembly, the Commune, the king, and the people of Paris but, above all, because the National Guard wanted him for commandant general. Let his troops once grow lukewarm or insubordinate, and his influence would diminish. The Triumvirate and its adherents began to consider him the man to beat just as in royal circles he began to appear as the man to join. The Swedish Count Hans Axel Fersen, colonel of the Royal-Suédois Regiment and an intimate friend of Marie Antoinette, wrote to his father from Paris: "Just now, one section of the fanatics, with M. de La Fayette at their head, may be won over for the king. We must not miss the opportunity if it should seem to bring any hope."[90]

BIBLIOGRAPHICAL NOTES

In De Sacy's biography of the Comte d'Angiviller, director-general of the royal buildings, the account of Mirabeau's effort to reach the king through Angiviller is based upon Angiviller's subsequent recollection of it. Despite the relative obscurity of Angiviller, choosing him as intermediary can be explained, if the account is true, as due to Mirabeau's effort to leave no channel untried, particularly since presumably he did not know of La Marck's simultaneous negotiations and had to be doubtful of success with Lafayette. What makes us suspicious of Angiviller's account is this quotation (pp. 209–10) from a letter ascribed to Mirabeau, setting forth the terms he was submitting for Louis XVI's consideration: "We have to be careful of Lafayette. He thinks he is fooling me, but he will fool me so little and I will fool him so much that of the 400,000 livres that I am asking to pay off my debts, he will lend me 200,000, and by paying them to him when the time comes, the king will be square with me." Among the puzzling things about that quotation is that nowhere else (Lafayette's and La Marck's memoirs and Lafayette's and Mirabeau's correspondence included) have we found mention of a loan by Lafayette to Mirabeau of 200,000 livres. On the contrary, in Bacourt (ed.), I, 159, La Marck states that Mirabeau's "full listing of his debts" in May 1790 totaled altogether only 208,000 francs (a sum almost equal to the same number of livres), including 400 louis (12,000 francs) owed to La

[89] *Ami du peuple,* May 26, p. 8. See below, p. 391.

[90] O. G. de Heidenstam (ed.), *Letters of Marie Antoinette, Fersen and Barnave,* tr. Winifred Stephens and Mrs. Wilfred Jackson (New York, n.d.), p. 26.

Marck himself. Nor is there any mention of a debt to Lafayette in the details La Marck gives (*ibid.*, pp. 163–64) of the payments Louis XVI agreed to make to Mirabeau. If the Angiviller story, then, is correct, either Mirabeau was not telling the truth on one or the other accounting of his debts or Lafayette was not as easily fooled as he expected. Nor are both suppositions incompatible.

In Constant Pierre (ed.), *Les hymnes et chansons de la Révolution* (Paris, 1904), a lengthy essay on the song "Ça ira!" examines the numerous legends which have sprung up about it. He doubts that it was sung to an older air that was a favorite of Marie Antoinette or that it was suggested to the composer by Lafayette, though he thinks the expression *Ça ira* might have been popularized by Franklin (pp. 480 and 483). He believes that the reference to "le prudent La Fayette" was in the earliest version (p. 486), but he is unaware that the tune at least (if not the words) was known as early as the fête of May 13 (see above, p. 355 and n. 53). The music and a full set of verses is given in Constant Pierre (ed.), *Musique des fêtes et cérémonies de la Révolution française* (Paris, 1889), p. 478. Pierre Barbier and France Vernillat, *Histoire de France par les chansons* (Paris, 1957), IV, 78–82, gives an account of the song that is primarily based on Pierre's research.

The letter of Lafayette to Latour-Maubourg that is cited above, chapter XIV, n. 66, as of March 18 may conceivably be of May 23. It was obviously written after Lafayette read a speech in the National Assembly and had reason to feel satisfied with its reception. We have, however, preferred to place it in chapter XIV rather than here because the hopefulness it expresses of a reconciliation with the Duport-Lameth faction seems more appropriate for the earlier than for the later date.

Bouillé's letters to Lafayette and Lafayette's comments on Bouillé's *Mémoires* are in the Lafayette Archives in the Cornell University Library, Carton V, in microfilm; the originals are in the Archives Nationales. They are more complete than any published set, but those parts that are published do not vary markedly from the manuscript versions .

Maurois (French ed., p. 215) quotes Lafayette (*Mémoires,* II, 365) directly and correctly as follows: "Lafayette eut des torts avec Mirabeau." The English edition, however, translates this passage: "Lafayette was wrong about Mirabeau." A more accurate translation would be: "Lafayette did Mirabeau some wrongs," and possibly one of the instances that Lafayette had in mind was that narrated above, pp. 347–52.

CHAPTER XVI

A Setback for the Triumvirate

A LEADER in the construction of a new regime may also be a servant of the old and as such, even when his loyalties seem not to be in conflict, may yet feel obliged to decide which of the two regimes merits the greater measure of devotion. To Lafayette the choice had so far been easy, for his objective had been to build a new liberal edifice upon a monarchical foundation, and since the foundation was already available but the edifice was not, the establishment of the new liberty had so far exerted the prior claim. Now, however, liberty appeared firmly ensconced: the constitution was well under way; the elective principle had extensively displaced the principle of heredity or royal preferment, and equality that of privilege; monarchical absolutism had, no matter how reluctantly, yielded in legislation, including the making of war and peace, to cooperation with the representatives of the sovereign people; and the rights of the people had been set forth in a ringing declaration. What was not yet explicit was the extent to which royal prerogative and prestige would be retained. If Lafayette as a deputy in the National Assembly and as a municipal official in Paris and Versailles often acted as a servant of the people, he was not permitted to forget that he was also a general appointed by the king and subject to the orders of the king's ministers.

Consequently General Lafayette was in the anomalous position of preserving the old forms while promoting revolution. When the wife of the commandant at Saint-Denis wished to make her home there,[1] she was not free to move until as commanding general of the king's forces in the area he gave her permission. When the old

[1] AMG: AH Carton LXII, chemise Intérieur, avril 1790, pièce No. 9, Apr. 1. The request was not granted.

police of Versailles raised questions regarding their relations to the new National Guard, they asked Lafayette, who drew a parallel to the police of the City of Paris, which he described as "a department absolutely independent of the National Guard."[2] Nevertheless, in reality the Paris Department of Police did not act independently. For instance, when smugglers appeared at the city barriers with arms, ready to force their way through and the tax collectors asked the commandant general to meet force with force, Lafayette, true to his revolutionary principles, felt that such orders should come not from him but from the civil authorities, and so, he presented the case to the Bureau de Ville, and finally the old Department of Police asked the new National Guard to furnish the old tax authorities with the force necessary to enforce the old laws on smuggling.[3]

The ministers, too, continued to consult him from time to time, as traditional practice required. He had to be asked in formal terms, for example, whether he would permit two companies of the Regiment of Armagnac to return from his jurisdiction at Mélun to their barracks at Condé, and in equally formal terms he granted permission, whereupon the minister of war issued the necessary orders.[4] When he proposed that the Regiment of Rohan-Soubise be withdrawn from Nantes, the minister formally consented provided that Lafayette was confident their removal would create no inconvenience for the city's people or government.[5] When the old Dragoon Regiment of the Duc de Luynes quarreled with the new municipality of Chateaudun, Lafayette had to be consulted before the dragoons could be removed.[6]

Sometimes these matters were handled through the minister of war alone; sometimes the minister of the king's household was in-

---

[2] Lafayette to the muncipal officers composing the Section of Police at Versailles, May 11, Bibliothèque de Versailles (courtesy of M. Bréchin).

[3] Lacroix, V, 644 and 648 (June 1).

[4] Latour du Pin to Lafayette, Apr. 19, AMG: AH Carton LXII, chemise Minutes, avril 1790; Lafayette to Latour du Pin, Apr. 27, *ibid.,* chemise Intérieur, avril 1790, pièce 180; and Latour du Pin to Lafayette, Apr. 29, *ibid.,* chemise Minutes, avril 1790.

[5] Latour du Pin to Lafayette, Apr. 21, *ibid.,* chemise Minutes, avril 1790.

[6] Latour du Pin to Lafayette, May 3, *ibid.,* chemise Minutes, mai 1790. (A reconciliation took place, and they were not removed.)

volved. Saint-Priest called Lafayette's attention to such matters as that women carrying wood passed through the customs barriers every day or that the police needed support in tax controversies.[7] When disturbances occurred in the market place at Lagny, Saint-Priest asked him to send a detachment there from Meaux, but unwilling to weaken the small force at Meaux, he received permission to send a detachment from a stronger regiment at Compiègne instead.[8]

Lafayette's honored position among the leaders of the Revolution did not always ease the burden which the lack of precedent continued to present him as commandant general of an unprecedented citizen army. If a battalion complained that its men were without adequate barracks,[9] if a worried mayor or other city official demanded that a guard be set up somewhere against disorder or that special attention be given to some citizens' grievances,[10] if suspicion that "aristocrats" were disguising themselves in National Guard uniforms led the suspicious to insult the wearers, or if genuine Guards complained of instances when these insults were overzealously directed against them,[11] ultimately it fell to him to find a satisfactory remedy, and the Representatives commended "his usual wisdom and circumspection."[12]

And how was a proud military man to deal with blows to a citizen-soldier by other soldiers? When a Paris National Guardsman on leave was killed by a local officer at Sens on the ground that the

---

[7] Saint-Priest to Lafayette and Cellerier, May 16, Tuetey, III, 265, No. 2748, and June 5, *ibid.*, I, 23, No. 209.

[8] Lafayette to Latour du Pin, May 21, AMG: AH Carton LXII, chemise Intérieur, May 1790, pièce 144; Lafayette to Saint-Priest, May 22, AN:F[7] 36894; and Latour du Pin to Lafayette, May 27, AMG: Carton LXIII, chemise Minutes mai 1790.

[9] Lacroix, V, 500–501 (May 21).

[10] Apr. 10, Tuetey, II, 400, No. 3775; Apr. 20, *ibid.*, p. 387, No. 3636; Apr. 24, *ibid.*, p. 391, No. 3686; Apr. 30, Collection Parent de Rosen, Bibliothèque du XVIᵉ Arrondissement, Vol. XVIII, fol. 18; May 2, Tuetey, II, 432, No. 4093; May 7, *ibid.*, I, 196, No. 1717; May 9, *ibid.*, II, 420, No. 3982; and May 17, *ibid.*, No. 1783. See also Blancheteau catalogue, p. 61, item 207; Robiquet, pp. 54–76; Lacroix, IV, 237 (Mar. 19), 506, 509 (Mar. 26), V, 24 (Apr. 16), 181 (Apr. 28), and VI, 242 (Apr. 30).

[11] *Procès-verbal du Comité militaire*, Part II, p. 62 (Apr. 12), and Lacroix, IV, 708–9 (Apr. 13), 712–13, 715–16 (Apr. 14).

[12] Lacroix, V, 230 (May 4).

Parisian had interfered with the Sens Guards' performance of their duty, Lafayette felt the case was clear: the officer at Sens had merely been doing his duty.[13] The case was not so simply solved when trouble broke out between the National Guard and the Swiss Guards. Some of the Swiss had left their regiments to join the Paris National Guard as chasseurs, and the Swiss in the palace guard considered them deserters. When a Swiss palace guard insulted a chasseur, a duel ensued in which the chasseur was wounded. Thereupon the two corps took up the fight. Lafayette investigated the case, gave strict orders to his chasseurs to cease quarreling with the Swiss, and appealed to the king, who ordered the Swiss confined to their barracks. Besenval, former commander of the Swiss Guards in Paris, also intervened, asking them to treat the National Guard with respect. The pleas of the two generals were effective; a regimental court martial condemned the victorious Swiss Guardsman to death; Lafayette and the National Guard entered a plea for his pardon; and the regimental officers granted the pardon as a step toward "peace, concord, and fraternity."[14]

By the spring of 1790 the usefulness of the Paris National Guard was generally recognized by the royal bureaucrats, but it could do little unless the Paris districts approved. Sometimes they approved unhesitatingly. A proposal to organize a voluntary battalion of old men to be known as the Veterans of the National Guard received the hearty support of the Cordeliers and over forty other districts. They asked Lafayette to endorse the enterprise, and he did. After the first company of the Veterans had elected officers and sent a deputation to the National Assembly to pledge its loyalty, Lafayette sent them to confer with his staff on the details of their organization.[15] Their enterprise thus advanced smoothly.

On the other hand, the Assembly of Representatives was disappointingly slow in reaching decisions that Lafayette thought de-

---

[13] *Ibid.*, IV, 642–43 (Apr. 8), and Charles Porée (ed.), *Sources manuscrites de l'histoire de la Révolution dans l'Yonne* (Auxerre, 1918), I, 361–62.

[14] Among other sources, see *Courrier de Paris*, Apr. 23, pp. 273–75, Apr. 25, pp. 308–9, Apr. 27, p. 347; *Journal général de la cour*, Apr. 22, pp. 171–73, Apr. 24, pp. 187–91, Apr. 25, p. 197; and *Gazette universelle*, Apr. 24, p. 583.

[15] Lacroix, IV, 521, 531–43 (Mar. 29), and *AP*, XII, 665–66 (Apr. 11).

sirable but the districts might oppose as additional financial burdens. He still wanted the National Guard to have a band. After
the French Guard went out of existence, the District of the Filles-
Saint-Thomas took the regiment's musicians under its wing and
provided for all their current expenses, since the National Guard
budget did not do so. On March 26 the commandant general requested the Bureau de Ville to compensate the musicians for at
least their past services. Only weeks later did the Bureau, without
committing itself for the future, authorize the payment of their
back pay. Notwithstanding, Lafayette continued to call upon the
band for ceremonial occasions, and they were commonly referred
to as "the band of the National Guard."[16] Similarly, when Rulhière
requested more commissioned officers for the cavalry, Lafayette
could see no way of securing the necessary funds, and only after
Rulhière found enough qualified men willing to act as lieuten-
ants without additional pay if the municipality would confirm their
commissions did the Assembly of Representatives promise consideration of their offer.[17] With like delays the Representatives
came to a decision about relatively simpler matters such as the
construction of additional guard houses. Not until April did they
begin to discuss a set of regulations for sentinels and patrols, submitted by the Military Committee in December, and they adopted
it in May only after an urgent request by the committee, and even
then merely provisionally. A proposal on clothing for noncommissioned officers and men of the paid companies, likewise presented to the Representatives in December, was pigeonholed until
May, when it was referred to the Department of the National
Guard.[18]

The completing of the National Guard was all the more urgent
because the unemployed crowding into the cities were sometimes
said to be agents of the aristocrats. Stories that under normal circumstances would have appeared ludicrous now roused serious
anxiety. The National Guard, seeing potential treason in every ship-

---

[16] Lacroix, V, 235, 242–45 (May 4).

[17] *Ibid.*, pp. 253–54 (May 6).

[18] *Ibid.*, pp. 124–25 (Apr. 24), 204–7 (May 1), 247–48, 251–52 (May 5), 256 (May 6).

ment of arms, seized some wagons loaded with guns that were leaving the city and stopped others loaded with powder believed to be going to Metz, and only the intervention of the commandant general persuaded them that the shipments were legitimate.[19] Lafayette's unwillingness to regard every unexplained shipment as a counterrevolutionary plot rendered him suspect in certain eyes. They looked upon him with particular suspicion when shipments of money from the Treasury were reported to be destined to aid the Austrian Cabal or other counterrevolutionaries. On one occasion the National Guard on duty at the Treasury refused to let several wagonloads of silver leave until he assured them that the money was going to the frontier posts to pay French soldiers.[20]

That episode gave Lafayette's opponents still another reason to question his motives. The patrol commander, Collard, who had originally stopped the convoy, protested that the division chief, Aumont, had been too brusque in ordering him to let it pass. The next day one of Aumont's staff, Division Major Bazancourt, challenged Collard to a duel, but though the men actually met on the dueling ground, they did not fight. A journalist who described Bazancourt as a bully and Collard as a patriot wrote an open letter to Lafayette, accusing him of ulterior motives: "If you aim to acquire a dangerous preponderance in the state and to surround yourself with faithful satellites in order to be able, when you choose, like the traitor Monk, to re-establish royal despotism or, like the traitor Cromwell, to dissolve the legislature, you will pretend to ignore this deed, but if you are a friend of liberty, you will take account of it and the bully will not go unpunished."[21] Later Collard himself wrote an open letter to Lafayette:"You may quite skillfully appear not to know of the irritating manner that an officer of your staff permits himself toward a citizen officer, but certainly you will permit me to inform the nation and posterity that you do know about it."[22]

[19] *Journal général de la cour*, Apr. 14, p. 111, Apr. 20, p. 159–60.

[20] *Journal de Paris*, Apr. 14, p. 418.

[21] *Révolutions de Paris*, No. 42, Apr. 24–May 1, pp. 217–19.

[22] Collard to Lafayette, May 5, *ibid*., No. 48, June 5–12, p. 546.

The District of the Cordeliers stubbornly persevered as the vanguard of opposition to Lafayette, and he was careful to avoid antagonizing it unnecessarily. On May 21, Bailly passed on to him a matter that involved the Ségurs.[23] The Pensions Committee of the National Assembly had recently allowed publication of some information contained in the *Livre Rouge,* the private account kept by the crown of certain sums paid in pensions. Large amounts, it revealed, had been granted to, and larger ones asked by, the Maréchal de Ségur. The marshal now tried in a letter to the press to justify his grants on the ground that his services had merited them; the Comte de Ségur wrote to the Pensions Committee in support of his father; and the Vicomte de Ségur, a deputy in the National Assembly, endorsed his elder brother's letter. Some members of the Pensions Committee were stung by the count's calling their publication unjust, and an indignant deputy proposed to denounce him. Lafayette, apprehending that the proposed denunciation was intended to be an indirect attack upon himself through his friends, called upon Latour-Maubourg to head it off: "It is intolerable that these snarlers should interfere with finishing the constitution for the sake of their private quarrels. . . . Someone should point out that a son has a good right to complain of a wrong done to his father, that anyhow the Assembly does not have the time to occupy itself with everything, that it must get on with the constitution, and that it is out of order to deliberate on his matter."[24] No mention appears in the minutes of the National Assembly of further attention to Ségur's letter, but under date of April 10 the Pensions Committee published an *Addition au Livre Rouge,* quoting the letters of the Ségurs and giving the details of the pensions they had received.

At this point the municipality of Belleville complained that two cannon from the Château de Romainville then in the possession of the battalions of the Cordeliers and the Bonne-Nouvelle, had

---

[23] Bailly to Lafayette, May 17, BN: Fr. 11697, pièce 59.

[24] Lafayette to Latour-Maubourg, [*post* Apr. 8], AN: F⁷ 4767, and *Le Curieux,* I (1884), 96. See also *AP,* XIII, 177–78, 190, and cf. *Mémoires,* IV, 188–89, where Lafayette correctly doubts that the *Livre rouge* was itself published in 1790; a fair amount of information from it was published, however.

been taken from Belleville, and it wanted them back. Romainville was the country home of the Ségurs. When asked to reclaim these cannon taken from the Ségurs' château and held by the District of the Cordeliers, Lafayette felt somewhat hesitant. He politely invited the battalion commanders of the Cordeliers and the Bonne-Nouvelle to accede to Belleville's request. The records do not show whether this mixture of tact with discipline succeeded, but they do indicate that Lafayette considered it wise to treat the matter gingerly. As he explained to the mayor: "Under the circumstances I did not allow myself to order them to return the cannon. You know, Monsieur, how delicate this matter is, and I fear that a refusal would compromise my authority."[25]

Episodes like the Collard and Ségur affairs joined with the bitterness of the debates on authority over war and peace to intensify the hostility to Lafayette in certain quarters. In large part that hostility was reflected by, if not due to, Marat, who, upon resuming publication of the *Ami du peuple,* began to flay the commandant general unreservedly.[26] A series of pamphlets denouncing the National Guard and its chief also appeared about this time. One of them, entitled *Vie privée imparatiale . . . du marquis de La Fayette,* was anything but "impartial." It was eighty-eight pages of vituperation that not only made Lafayette out to be an unscrupulous libertine and overweening imitator of Cromwell but attributed his treacherous ambition largely to the alleged infidelities of Adrienne. It called Lafayette "General Towhead" (*Blondinet,* literally *near blond*), and the National Guards "Little Boys Blue" (*Bleuets,* literally *cornflowers*).[27]

[25] Lafayette to Bailly, May 21, BN: Fr. 11697, pièce 60.

[26] See, for example, May 18, p. 2, May 19, p. 3, May 26, p. 8. In May L.-S. Fréron began to put out the *Orateur du peuple,* which was soon to imitate the *Ami du peuple,* but at first, Fréron was not unfriendly to Lafayette: see especially his No. 3, p. 19, and No. 5, p. 39.

[27] Lacroix, VI, 7–9 (June 9). The full title was *Vie privée, impartiale, politique, militaire et domestique du marquis de La Fayette, général des Bluets, pour servir de supplément à la nécrologie des hommes célèbres du dix-huitième siècle, & de clef aux Révolutions françaises & américaines. Dediée aux soixante districts de Paris.* We place its publication in May because the last episode it mentions is the dispute of the Swiss and the chasseurs. See also Victor Glachant, "Un pamphlet révolutionnaire anonyme contre le général marquis de La Fayette," *Annales romantiques,* V (1908), 126–31, and below, p. 415, n. 35. The

Nevertheless, the attacks of Lafayette's detractors, though multiplying, rarely dampened the ardor of his admirers. He had an especially effective medium for rousing public approval in the custom he had developed of reviewing the National Guard Sunday mornings. On April 18, the Fifth Division passed in review at Vincennes, where a group of about fifty students in uniform also paraded before him, winning his commendation. The review of the following Sunday was to be a special attraction, for the papers announced in advance that the Corsican hero, General Pasquale Paoli, would be present.[28]

Since 1769, after France had bought Corsica from Genoa, the French army had controlled the island, and Paoli, the leader of Corsican resistance, had lived as a political refugee in England. Deputies from Corsica, however, now sat in the National Assembly, and as the Revolution progressed in France, Corsicans everywhere sought to secure for their country the liberties accorded to the citizens of metropolitan France. In the autumn of 1789 Paoli's secretary had entreated Lafayette to support the Corsican cause, Lafayette promised to do what he could, and Paoli wrote from London thanking him for his interest. Praising his conduct as "a model for souls tormented by the love of liberty and the true happiness of mankind," the exiled leader urged him to lend protection to Corsica's deputies in the National Assembly: "In your eyes, the claim of the Corsicans to liberty ought to have greater merit than that of the Americans; in this century of oppression, Corsica was the first to raise the standard of liberty against tyranny."[29]

At least partly because of Lafayette's influence the Assembly had decreed that Corsicans would enjoy the benefits of the new constitution as French citizens and that Corsican refugees would be allowed to return to their homes.[30] Lafayette sent this good news

---

sobriquet *Blondinet* was bestowed on Lafayette, says Glachant (*ibid.*, p. 152, n. 1), by Desmoulins. On the series of pamphlets attacking Lafayette see Ferrières to Mme de la Messelière, June 14, Ferrières, *Correspondance inédite (1789, 1790, 1791)*, ed. Henri Carré (Paris, 1932), p. 203.

[28] See below, p. 379.

[29] Paoli to Lafayette, Nov. 16, *Mémoires*, II, 426.

[30] Lafayette to unknown, [*ca.* Oct. 25], *ibid.*, p. 432; *ibid.*, IV, 179–80; *AP*, X, 335–37 (Nov. 30), 411–13 (Dec. 7); and Duquesnoy, II, 109–12.

to Paoli with a warm letter greeting him as a hero whom he had admired since childhood and to whom every friend of liberty was indebted and lauding the union of France and Corsica as a social contract sustained by the will of a free people. He invited Paoli to come personally to Paris to receive the plaudits of the French nation.[31] Paoli did not accept this or any similar invitation for several months, and when he finally reached France and was presented to Louis XVI at the Tuileries (April 8), it was not Lafayette but Latour du Pin who presented him. Lafayette was not even present at the beginning of the ceremony, but, as he informed Mme de Simiane: "My good luck allowed me to arrive in time to keep them from speaking nonsense to him."[32]

The review of the National Guard on April 25 gave Lafayette a better opportunity to share the stage with the veteran patriot. The thirty-two-year-old Parisian general rode out on the Champ-de-Mars with the sixty-five-year-old Corsican general, as spectators cheered and applauded. Ten thousand men then passed in review before them and maneuvered for three hours. Paoli seemed pleasantly impressed, and other witnesses too believed that the love of liberty had given the neophyte bourgeois soldiers of Paris the precision of troops with many years' training.[33] Loustalot stressed the emotion of "true patriots" upon comparing "a young warrior who has yet borne arms only for liberty" with "a hero who for a long time has been a martyr for it."[34]

On May 5 Lafayette took Paoli to visit the site of the Bastille. All the men working on the demolition of the fortress, with the contractor Palloy at their head, lined the road, shouldering their tools. They presented each of the generals with cards, adorned with tricolor ribbons and other symbols of French unity, that served as passes to the ruins. On the back of the ribbons were inscribed the

---

[31] Dec. 11, *Mémoires*, II, 433–34.

[32] [Apr. 9], *ibid.*, II, 456, and *La vie et les mémoires du général Dumouriez*, ed. MM. Berville and Barrière (Paris, 1822–23), I, 404.

[33] *Journal général de la cour*, Apr. 25, p. 198, Apr. 26, pp. 199–200, and *Courrier de Paris*, Apr. 26, pp. 329–30.

[34] *Révolutions de Paris*, No. 42, Apr. 24–May 1, pp. 236–39. See also *ibid.*, No. 44, May 8–15, pp. 307–8, and Desmoulins, *Révolutions*, No. 22, pp. 391–93, No. 25, p. 545.

words *Donné par les ouvriers de la Bastille.* The two heroes made boutonnieres of the cards and, upon the workers' request, administered the civic oath to them. Palloy, who had previously presented Lafayette with the first stone wrenched from the Bastille, now presented him with the last one, wrenched from the cells.[35]

In the tangle of reforms that France confronted, one of the most delicate was the reorganization of the municipalities, and because of the capital's size the National Assembly was expected to draw up a special set of regulations for Paris. In the city this expectation intensified the debate over a deep-seated, moot issue: Was the Commune to be vested with greater control over the districts? A majority of the districts wanted the National Assembly to preserve the independence of the district assemblies, while the Assembly of Representatives wanted the National Assembly to place superior authority in the elected officials at the Hôtel de Ville.[36] The National Guard was only incidentally concerned with the outcome. Some of the districts maintained that the National Guard, distributed as it was among the districts, could function only if the integrity of the districts were guaranteed, but a number of battalions disagreed.[37]

The Battalion of Saint-Etienne-du-Mont was foremost among those that promised the Military Committee loyal performance of whatever the National Assembly might require, and the committee submitted a copy of that pledge to its president, Lafayette, with the request that he communicate it to the National Assembly. It also had copies dispatched to the Assembly of Representatives and to the commander of each of the other fifty-nine battalions urging them to secure a similar pledge from their men. The Battalion of the Capucins-du-Marais thereupon delivered to Lafayette, his staff, the Assembly of Representatives, and the other battalions a declaration giving its adherence.[38] The Battalion of the Sorbonne sent a

[35] *Chronique de Paris,* May 7, p. 506, and *Gazette universelle,* May 8, pp. 639–40. According to the *Courrier de Paris,* Apr. 16, p. 173, Lafayette had been greeted with equal enthusiasm on a visit to the Musée de Paris; we have found no other evidence of this visit.

[36] Lacroix, IV, 401, 404–8 (Mar. 13).

[37] *AP,* XII, 377 (Mar. 27). See also Lacroix, IV, 523, 543–44 (Mar. 29).

[38] *Procès-verbal du Comité militaire,* Part II, pp. 61–62 (Apr. 1).

deputation directly to the Assembly of Representatives to reconfirm its devotion to duty whatever form of government might be prescribed for Paris, and the president of the Representatives praised it as "worthy of its chief, [who was] at the same time an enlightened legislator and an intrepid hero."[39] Shortly afterward the Battalion of Saint-Severin, "commanded [it said] by a chief who can justly be given the title of 'hero of liberty,' " renewed its oath to destroy the enemies of the constitution.[40]

In this power struggle between the district assemblies and the Assembly of Representatives Lafayette was careful to avoid committing himself. Not so Bailly, who openly sided with the districts and thus incurred the displeasure of the Paris Assembly of Representatives, who regularly accorded greater deference to the commandant general. For the time being, however, the breach between the mayor and the Representatives was discreetly kept from public view. On April 18, Lafayette joined the former Electors of the Commune to confer a singular honor on Bailly. They presented a bust of him by the illustrious sculptor Houdon to the city of Paris, to serve as a companion piece to the bust of Lafayette presented in 1786 by the State of Virginia.[41] The Electors formally asked the Assembly of Representatives for permission to present Bailly's bust in the Grande Salle, but some Representatives demurred, preferring a similar ceremony in the smaller Salle des Gouverneurs. The Electors insisted, however, upon the Grande Salle, already graced by the busts of Louis XVI, Necker, Lafayette, and other famous men, and the Representatives conceded. Accordingly, an impressive ceremony was arranged for the Grand Salle. Lafayette ordered a detachment of the National Guard to serve as a guard of honor, and he also escorted his wife to the occasion. The bust was placed on the secretary's desk with a flourish of trumpets amid vigorous applause. President Delavigne of the Electors recalled the difficult July days when Bailly had been unanimously elected by all the districts as the first mayor of Paris: "We thought it would

[39] Lacroix, V, 123–24 (Apr. 24).

[40] Ibid., p. 166 (Apr. 27).

[41] Gottschalk, Between, pp. 250–52.

be fitting to place the likeness of the man so wisely chosen to administer the city in this temple of liberty beside the image of the
hero chosen to command its forces." This reference to Lafayette
elicited enthusiastic approval. The Abbé Bertolio, replying as
president of the Representatives, praised the Electors for their
leadership in the July uprising: "But, among all the acts that your
patriotism inspired, I do not hesitate to put in first place the choice
of the two men that your fellow citizens, with your consent, raised
to the two eminent posts on which the success of the revolution
depended, Bailly and Lafayette." Then, although the ceremony
was in Bailly's honor, the president went on to extol Lafayette: "For
some years, we have had the bust of M. de Lafayette. It was given
to us by men who were in a good position to appreciate his merit.
It seems to me that when the free Americans offered it to our capital, they were saying to us, by one of the premonitions that the love
of liberty can inspire: 'Soon he will do for you what he has done for
us.'" Thanking the Electors for Bailly's bust, Bertolio ordered that
it "be placed beneath that of the most beloved of kings, beside that
of M. de Lafayette," and so it was taken from the secretary's desk
and placed upon the spot that Bertolio had designated.[42]

The Representatives then invited the Electors to remain for another ceremony, the award of medals to six women of Paris for
patriotic behavior during the October Days. One of the assemblage,
seeing Adrienne in the audience, proposed that she present the
medals. She was shy, however, and to cover her embarrassment, Lafayette gallantly observed that while he was far too much attached
to her to wish to deprive her of the distinction, he felt that a principle was involved: "It was not consistent with the dignity of a free
people to take, as was possible in the Old Regime, the pleasure of
receiving a medal from a citizeness as the equivalent of the honor
of receiving it from the hand of the president of the Paris Commune."[43] The president thereupon proceeded to award the decorations. Even so, whoever the nominally honored had been that day,
Lafayette's had been the name most often pronounced.

---

[42] Lacroix, IV, 636–41, 643–46; (Apr. 8), and *Patriote français*, Apr. 11, p. 4.
[43] Lacroix, IV, 641–42 (Apr. 8).

Yet honors conferred by the Electors even under the patronage of the Representatives, no matter how welcome, were of dubious substance, for the Assembly of Electors was defunct and the Assembly of Representatives was moribund. In view of the impending municipal reform the Representatives had become increasingly reluctant to incur expense or to take any action that the districts might challenge, while opposition from the districts had not abated. Indeed, in mid-April the Assembly of Representatives submitted its resignation to the National Assembly,[44] persuaded that that was a possible way to unite "powers which are divided among several assemblies and which in fighting each other destroy each other."[45] The National Assembly, however, did not pass the law reorganizing the government of Paris for over five weeks, and so uncertainty about relative authority continued to exasperate the intermittent struggle between the Representatives and the districts.

Meanwhile, sheer economic distress also augmented the popular tension in the capital as a multitude of poor and unemployed refugees from the provinces reinforced the wretched of Paris, and the blame for recurrent disorders was easily attributed to these transients. After Foucault's denunciation of the Paris National Guard[46] it became doubly important to shift that blame from Paris citizens to others, and one of the Representatives stoutly maintained that the Paris National Guard had been called out that day to defend the National Assembly not against the citizens of Paris but against "vagabonds" who had invaded the capital. Thereupon his colleagues passed "with rapture" a vote of thanks to the Paris National Guard "for its indefatigable zeal and its noble courage on every occasion in defending the liberty of the public and of the individual citizen" and sent its resolution to the commandant general, his staff, the Military Committee, the sixty district assemblies, and the sixty battalions of the National Guard.[47] Lafayette in turn personally thanked the Representatives for their confidence in the Na-

---

[44] *Ibid.,* V, pp. 1-2 (Apr. 15).

[45] *Ibid.,* p. 131 (Apr. 26).

[46] See above, pp. 321-22.

[47] Lacroix, V, 23-24, 30-31 (Apr. 16).

tional Guard, he too claiming that they had protected the deputies of the National Assembly not from Paris citizens but from "that vagabond troop of outside mendicants who at this moment are flooding the capital." The presiding officer replied that the Representatives had not expressed their gratitude nearly so often as the soldier-citizens "under your command deserved."[48]

On May 21 the National Assembly finally passed an act reorganizing the government of Paris. It abolished the districts and created forty-eight new subdivisions of Paris to be called "sections," but the National Guard, essentially unaffected, continued to perform what they considered their duty as before. It rescued from angry bystanders a man who had trampled a tricolor cockade under foot, and on May 24, in the aftermath of the debates on war and peace, it saved two persons from lynching in the Place de Grève, though only after two others accused of theft had been hanged and a third stoned to death.[49] Lafayette felt constrained to put additional companies of the National Guard under arms, and none too soon. The following afternoon as he and his aide Louis Romeuf were driving to the Hôtel de Ville, word reached them that a mob had gathered on the Quai de la Ferraille (now part of the Quai de la Mégisserie) and was trying to take away from a National Guard patrol a man accused of stealing a sack of oats. They drove there at once and found the National Guards overpowered by a mob that had already beaten the prisoner unconscious. Despite the warnings of bystanders, Lafayette drove his carriage as far into the crowd as he could. Then he and Romeuf jumped out, Romeuf, though himself threatened by one of the lynchers, took charge of the lifeless body, and Lafayette turned upon the crowd. Since he could not believe them all guilty, he declaimed, they must designate the ones that were. By that time some National Guardsmen had pushed through to their general, and they pointed out one of the guilty men. Lafayette seized him by the collar and, addressing the bystanders,

<hr/>

[48] *Ibid.*, p. 87 and n. 2 (Apr. 20).

[49] *Révolutions de Paris*, No. 46, May 22–29, pp. 228–29, 426–28; *Courier français*, May 26, pp. 204–5; Desmoulins, *Révolutions*, No. 27, 625–26; Lacroix, V, 545–47 (May 26), 582–84, 590–91 (May 25); *Journal général de la cour*, May 26, p. 146, June 1, pp. 233–34; and *AP*, XV, 676 (May 26).

announced: "I am going to show you that any act is honorable in enforcing the law,"[50] and he took him to the Châtelet, which was nearby. Part of the crowd and the National Guard patrol followed him. The battered body still lay on the quay.

Having delivered his man to the Châtelet, Lafayette went out to face the onlookers. The National Guardsmen insisted on escorting him, but he ordered them off, went alone into the throng, climbed on a low parapet, and, an easy target for any ill-intentioned among them, proceeded to berate them: They were the dupes of troublemakers and brigands who wanted to force the National Assembly and the king to leave Paris and to place the city in an uproar, but the property of the city and the preservation of order within it were his responsibility and he would crush any who dared disturb the public peace; he expected to have the necessary backing, but even if alone, he would demand respect for the law to his dying gasp.

If Lafayette's behavior was theatrical, it was perhaps in part because he was indeed a living embodiment of Sir Charles Grandison. But the theatrics were also deliberately calculated.[51] Yet all seemed in vain, for immediately he learned that the people left behind on the quay were lynching another victim. He and Romeuf ran there, with National Guards behind them, and they found the thief whom they had left for dead hanging by a rope to a lamp post. The frustrated rioters had found he was still alive and were trying to finish him off. Lafayette and his men cut him down and sent him to the infirmary of the Châtelet. Lafayette again railed at them indignantly. When he had finished, he ordered them to disperse, and they did, shouting, "Long live Lafayette" as they left.[52]

The commandant general and the mayor decided that the time

[50] Lafayette to [Mme de Simiane], May [26], *Mémoires*, II, 462–64. See also Short to John Rutledge, Jr., May 26, Landin, p. 363; [Bérenger (ed.)], pp. 265–72; and Lacroix, V, 547–49 (May 26). The letter in *Mémoires*, II, 462–64, is dated May 25, but the contents make clear that it was written the day after the attempted lynching, and it is given the correct date in *Mémoires*, III, 242 n. Our account of this episode follows that given by Lafayette in this letter for the most part. The numerous press reports differ from it only in minor details, except for the *Gazette de Paris* (May 26–31, p. 3), which accused Lafayette of lynching the man.

[51] See below, p. 386 and n. 54.

[52] Lafayette to Mme de Simiane, May [26], *Mémoires*, II, 464.

had come when every feasible step must be taken to prevent disorder and, if possible, to remove its causes. In the meantime they agreed to keep all available forces under arms throughout the night. Lafayette sent extra detachments to the Palais Royal, the Châtelet, the Faubourg Saint-Antoine, and other places where assemblages were likely to become unruly. The National Guard had seen no such alert for months, and when morning came on May 26, Paris was quiet.[53]

The rest of the day Lafayette breathed more easily. When a worried Adelaïde de Simiane wrote one of her *bien aimables billets* to find out what had happened, he could even be witty about his adventure: "I am more pleased . . . for your sake than for mine about the inviolability of my person. . . . The efforts of the ill-intentioned will break up once more against the phlegmatic barrier that I put up against them." Since he had already learned that the lynching victim was not going to die, he could afford to be pleased with himself, and he gave her a good-natured, none too modest account of his action, speaking of his indignant oratory as *ma mercuriale* ("my Wednesday speech"):[54] "That's my little adventure of yesterday. It's my friends' property that I risked in a toss-up, but if they are the proprietors of my life, they are jointly responsible for my duties, and I think I achieved a great objective."[55]

The lynchings of recent days underscored, if indeed they were not caused by, the misery that unsettled times had brought to the capital, but Lafayette, despite his philanthropic efforts for the poor, shared a widespread opinion that conspiracy rather than desperate want explained the violence of the rioters, "composed at least in part of vagabonds."[56] Short, still probably relaying Lafayette's opinions, asserted that "the riots . . . were certainly a combined system . . . intended as a battery against the popularity— perhaps against the life of the Marquis de la fayette."[57] Bailly

[53] *Ibid.*, p. 462, and *Courrier de Paris*, May 27, p. 363.

[54] *Mémoires*, II, 464. (A *mercuriale* was a solemn speech given before the Parlement of Paris on Wednesdays on affairs of the week.)

[55] *Ibid.*, p. 464.

[56] *AP*, XV, 676–78 (May 26).

[57] Short to Cutting, June 9, Boyd (ed.), XVI, 508.

appealed to the National Assembly and the people of Paris for a united front against the "vagabonds," who, he insisted, were bought with silver to cause trouble, and the National Assembly heartily applauded his appeal.[58]

That day (May 26), while the Assembly of Representatives was considering a vote of thanks to the National Guard and its commandant general for the measures that they had taken to check disorder, Lafayette walked in. He was received with "the applause which his presence never fails to inspire."[59] He had come not only to report upon the measures he had taken to restore order but also to introduce representatives of three provincial National Guard units asking to affiliate with the Paris National Guard. Although in the past the commandant general had presented similar deputations, this occasion seemed an especially timely recognition of the prestige of the Paris National Guard. Calling attention to "the zeal of the National Guard during the unhappy troubles of the two last days," their commander announced that calm had been restored.[60] A member of the Assembly proposed that now that the commandant general was present, it proceed to adopt the proposed vote of thanks to him and the National Guard. Lafayette's "modesty" did not allow him to stay for that deliberation, and so, amid accompanying applause, he left the building. As he walked into the Place de Grève, the people took up the applause and cheered until he had driven away. After he left, the Representatives declared that they found "no occasion more appropriate" to express their admiration "than that when the citizen-troop, on the days of the twenty-fourth and twenty-fifth, displayed with complete success its courage and its prudence, when its worthy chief, strong in the love of his fellow-citizens, quieted by his presence and his courage alone the outbursts of impatience," and they unanimously passed a vote of thanks to him and his men "for the vigorous and intelligent acts of patriotism which have characterized all their career." The Conseil de Ville also applauded the measures taken

[58] *AP*, XV, 676–78 (May 26).

[59] Lacroix, V, 528 (May 26). See also *ibid.*, pp. 525–26, 552–53.

[60] *Ibid.*, p. 531.

by the commandant general, along with the mayor and the Department of Police, to restore order, and it instructed Lafayette and other municipal officials, if in the future any extraordinary emergency should threaten, to go at once to the Hôtel de la Mairie to concert measures for preserving the peace. The Conseil decided, furthermore, that three of its members should be in continuous attendance at the Hôtel de Ville, ready to act in emergencies.[61]

Among other steps the city authorities took to stem the popular excitement was an appeal to the king to use his influence toward that end. Since the tricolor cockade was the accepted symbol of loyalty to the new regime, it seemed proper that he should urge all other citizens to follow his example and wear it. Lafayette was designated to place that request before His Majesty. The queen, upon hearing of the exploit on the Quai de la Feraille, ironically commented upon Lafayette's being "sensitive to everyone except kings,"[62] but the royal council, he learned, was less ambiguously well disposed. When he submitted to Necker and Champion de Cicé a draft of a formal proclamation in favor of wearing the tricolor cockade, they approved. In submitting the draft, he took the opportunity to make other proposals as well. Recalling Louis XVI's earlier pledge to work earnestly for freedom and the people, he warned that any other policy would alienate the king's servants, "and me first of all"; besides, in order to forestall plots "which make every good citizen shudder," the king should neglect nothing that would enhance his popularity, for "little things often have great effects" and "short delays are sometimes irreparable."

Lafayette therefore suggested a number of "little things." The National Guard would be "infinitely flattered to be reviewed by the king," and a review would create "the best possible effect." He also requested the abolition of the obsolescent requirement that persons wishing to be presented at court furnish a proof of a satisfactory genealogy. It had been rumored that, although the king was willing to provide a horse for a division commander of the Paris National Guard who had been duly presented at court, he would refuse to extend similar favor to division chiefs who had

[61] *Ibid.*, pp. 532–33, 535–36.
[62] *Mémoires*, III, 242.

not been presented, and Lafayette requested that they all receive the same consideration when on duty at the palace. He also urged that Louis the next time he visited the Château at Vincennes give an order to tear down its old dungeon.

Explaining that he had put these ideas in black and white because he thought a written statement convenient for the king, Lafayette apologized for his importunity. Once more he assured Lous XVI that he was ready to give the last drop of his blood to remove the "dangers of faction," just as he would give it to assure the liberty of his country, but he was importunate because he feared he had not been sufficiently insistent in the past. "Our situation is critical," he wrote. "I am sure that we will pull out of it if the king deigns to trust me, but at all times he will see that I do not fear to compromise myself, and I beg him to deign to give me his help in all matters that concern him by doing whatever depends upon him."[63]

On May 27 Lafayette went to the Conseil de Ville and assured it also that tranquility seemed re-established,[64] and the next day the proclamation requested of Louis XVI regarding the cockade was ready.[65] Since His Majesty had learned, it announced, that wearing a cockade differing from the one which he himself wore stirred up discord, he forbade his subjects to wear any other. The proclamation seemed to reflect a royal devotion to the Revolution that could not but have pleased Lafayette. On May 29, it was read in the National Assembly and was greeted with repeated cries of "Long live the king!" After the session the spectators went from the galleries of the Assembly to the Tuileries and, standing under the king's windows, repeatedly shouted "Long live the king!"[66] Lafayette seemed to have advised the monarch well.

Lafayette's heroism in the face of a lynching bee evoked general

---

[63] Lafayette to Louis XVI, May 26, *ibid.,* II, 464–66, and AN: C 184, Dr. 117, pièces 67, 68. Pièce 68 is quoted in part in Charles Braibant (ed.), *La Fayette: exposition organisée par les Archives nationales . . . pour la célébration du bi-centenaire de la naissance de La Fayette* (Paris, 1957) (hereafter cited as Braibant [ed.], *Exposition*), p. 88, item 255. Clermont-Gallerande (I, 443) says that Champion de Cicé drew up the proclamation though Lafayette suggested it to the king.

[64] Lacroix, V, 573 (May 27).

[65] Tuetey, I, 197, No. 1724, and Lacroix, V, 615–16 (May 31).

[66] *AP,* XV, 696–97, and Lacroix, V, 616 (May 31).

admiration. The *Journal général de la cour* reported—erroneously, it proved—that the National Assembly was going to make Lafayette *grand prévôt* of France with full power to keep the peace,[67] and the *Journal du diable* that he would not accept the post and that since for him to do so would cause trouble, the rumor must have been started by the aristocrats.[68] Desmoulins, while wishing he could praise Lafayette more often, lauded his success in arresting disorder.[69] Loustalot even shared the commandant general's opinion that paid brigands were causing the city's troubles.[70]

Lafayette's popularity was perhaps not won by calculation and artifice, but it was certainly not unsought. Nor was it unenvied. According to current reports and Lafayette's own intelligence, his enemies were already grooming Charles de Lameth to succeed him. That purpose, he was convinced, was being carried out by a skillfully contrived agency of the Jacobins. "The Sabbat" he called it, and he described it as a network of cells of ten men in each battalion of the Paris National Guard who took orders from ten dedicated men who in turn every day took orders directly from the Lameths.[71] Whether or not such a fifth column was actually boring from within the National Guard, Lafayette had no doubt it was, and he gave ear to widespread rumors about Charles de Lameth's aspirations.

Latour-Maubourg, devoted to the general but also friendly to the Lameths, undertook to find out whether the rumor had any basis in fact.[72] Charles personally denied that he had ever had such a thought and gave Maubourg a letter for Lafayette which said so positively: "I learn that with regard to the divergence which for some time has been manifest in our opinions in the National Assembly, and particularly in the deliberation relative to authority in

[67] May 27, p. 455. See also *ibid.*, May 26, pp. 446–47, May 28, pp. 460–61.

[68] No. 28, pp. 6–7.

[69] *Révolutions*, No. 27, p. 630, No. 28, p. 664.

[70] *Révolutions de Paris*, No. 46, May 22–29, pp. 424–35.

[71] *Mémoires*, II, 371. This plot, if Lafayette's sources of intelligence were correct, probably began no earlier than the end of May, for Lafayette here refers to the "sections" of Paris, which were created only on May 21.

[72] Theodore de Lameth, p. 115.

peace and war, the report has circulated widely in Paris that I aspire to replace you in the command of the National Guard." He was far from believing, he professed, that men would cast their eyes upon him for that honor; nor, highly though he prized the distinctions his fellow-citizens might bestow, had he ever conceived of becoming commander of the Paris National Guard; and, if the honor were offered him, he would not accept it: "I would blush if anything in my conduct ever could justify the belief that I have been guided by any motive of personal interest." Since he also meant to publish this letter in the newspapers, he added as a postscript: "You will find it easy to understand, Monsieur, that at a time when I see my intentions impugned by obscure schemings and slanderous innuendoes, I try to refute them with whatever publicity is consistent with my character."[73]

Lameth's letter seemed to imply that the post of commandant general was one which an honorable friend of liberty ought not to aspire to if he were already a deputy. It was on the next day (May 26) that Marat's *Ami du peuple* explicitly declared that Lafayette's great military power made it desirable that he abstain from voting on crucial issues in the Assembly; Loustalot followed suit, though more moderately, a few days later; and on May 28 the idea was aired briefly in the Assembly of Representatives.[74] Lafayette felt that he should make clear that whatever influence he had as a deputy was quite distinct from his authority as commander of the Paris National Guard. Furthermore, since both he and Charles had voted for the bill on the declaration of war and peace as finally passed, Charles's letter seemed to him to overstress the differences in their political objectives, making the compromise painfully reached on that bill seem short-lived and ineffective indeed. Nevertheless, he replied to Lameth in a conciliatory tone:

I do not see, Monsieur, what the command of the National Guard or any

[73] Lameth to Lafayette, May 25, *Mémoires*, III, 126. The letter was printed also, among other journals, in *Moniteur*, May 29, p. 604, and *Actes des Apôtres*, pp. 10–16 (in the latter with a mock "projet de réponse de M. de la Fayette"). The postscript does not appear in the version published in Lafayette's *Mémoires*, and perhaps it was added only after Lameth decided to publish his letter, which did not appear in the papers until May 28, two days after the date of Lafayette's reply (see below p. 392 and n. 75).

[74] See pp. 367–68 above, and Lacroix, V, 581, 588–89.

rumor of your nomination to that post could have in common with any difference of opinion on two versions of a decree, especially since you adopted the
one that I preferred. But I hope that the friends of liberty will always agree
on the right principles, and I would like them to come to an understanding
likewise on the best means of establishing the constitution.[75]

By minimizing the genuine differences between their preferences
for the constitutional provisions on declaring war and peace and in
overestimating Lameth's satisfaction with the compromise that
they had accepted, Lafayette was—perhaps all too patently—trying
to make the rift in the Patriot party look more reparable than in
fact it was.

Fortunately for the commandant general, his exchange of implied rebukes with Charles de Lameth came at a time when his defiance of a lynching bee was fresh in everyone's mind. Several
districts of Paris followed the example of the Assembly of Representatives in expressing gratitude to him. The District Sainte-Mar-
guerite announced that it seized "with enthusiasm and satisfaction the occasion when the enemies of the Revolution or perhaps
its extravagant partisans, guided by ambition or interest, seek to
diminish the confidence so legitimately due to the virtuous general"
to send to him "the most sincere expression of the attachment of
the inhabitants of the Faubourg Saint-Antoine and the assurance of
its entire devotion."[76] The more prosperous District of Saint-Germain-l'Auxerrois, "alarmed by the rumors, as false as they are injurious, which float about regarding citizens who are known by
their many acts of patriotism and disinterestedness," declared:
"[We can] not even conceive the idea that another person could
aspire to the place of commandant general. That place seems to
have been made for the Marquis de Lafayette alone; it is Providence that has given him to us. May that Providence preserve
him!" Each of these districts sent its resolution not only to Lafayette but also to the other fifty-nine districts for their adhesion.[77]

Danton and the other Cordelier leaders adopted the resolution of

[75] Lafayette to Lameth, May 26, *Mémoires*, III, 127. See also, among other newspapers, *Moniteur*, May 31, p. 612.

[76] Lacroix, V, 553–54 (May 26).

[77] *Ibid.*, p. 554.

Saint-Germain-l'Auxerrois, but they did so with some reservation. The Cordeliers, they claimed, had even greater faith in the goodness of Providence than Saint-Germain-l'Auxerrois had: Should the capital, by some distressing fatality, lose the commander whom it had placed at the head of its military force, no doubt it would be able to find another citizen worthy of that post, for when the citizens unanimously chose a man, that choice was an expression of the general will and as much a guarantee of excellence as the election of Lafayette had been. Nevertheless, the Cordeliers conceded, they could not "without injustice refuse to M. de Lafayette the eulogies merited by his zeal, his patriotism, and his frankness," and they sent their statement of those sentiments, signed by the officials of the district, including Danton as president, to the other districts.[78]

Some battalions of the Paris National Guard readily joined the districts in pronouncing their appreciation of Lafayette. The Battalion of the Filles-Saint-Thomas proposed that all the battalions join in presenting him with an address promising their support.[79] The Battalion de Saint-Gervais, in response to that proposal, passed a motion vehemently condemning those who were attacking him. Proclaiming its own "sentiments of confidence, love, respect, and obedience for that brave general" whom "a signal blessing of Heaven" had placed at its head, it called for a holy confederation of the National Guard units of the realm to meet with their hero under the flags of liberty as the most effective way to reduce the enemies of the constitution to despair. This resolution was dispatched to Lafayette, the Assembly of Representatives, the division chief, the general staff, and the other fifty-nine battalion commanders. Later that day, when it was read to the Representatives, the president praised the battalion's zeal, remarking that Lafayette's virtue would always shield him against slander.[80]

Apparently also in response to the proposal of the Filles-Saint-Thomas battalion, the battalion commander of Saint-Germain-

[78] *Ibid.*, pp. 554–55.

[79] *Ibid.*, pp. 555–56.

[80] *Ibid.*, p. 598 (May 29). See also below p. 445 and n. 53.

l'Auxerrois asked his fifty-nine colleagues to join in an address to the commandant general to be presented at the next review of the National Guard. Such an address was in fact drafted and circulated. The Paris National Guard, it stated, confident of the disinterestedness of their chief, eager to share the influence he now exercised for the second time in a revolution that gave to the people their imprescriptible rights, admiring the courage with which he hazarded not only his fortune but his life and the readiness with which he risked his popularity rather than lead the people into error, and resenting the doubts cast upon the feelings of the National Guards for their chief, solemnly declared that they regarded the Marquis de Lafayette as the strongest support of the constitution, and so, persuaded that no more worthy commander of the soldiers of liberty could be found, they unanimously renewed their oath of loyalty.[81]

If Charles de Lameth had ever really thought that he might displace Lafayette as commandant general, he could not confidently think so now. At any rate, in his reply to Lafayette's letter of May 26 he made no mention of that matter, and instead, he shifted the ground for dispute in a way that William Short (and so probably Lafayette also) considered a studied maneuver to insinuate that Lafayette had abandoned the people's cause.[82] He expressed wonder how Lafayette could believe that their views on the right to make peace or war were similar. He had not stopped opposing the original motion, he pointed out, until it had been amended to permit "the exercise of the nation's right through the legislative branch." But he too wanted to seem conciliatory: "I hope with you, Monsieur, that the friends of liberty will never cease to cooperate on the true principles already consecrated by the National Assembly."[83]

Lafayette did not answer Lameth in the press; he had a more

---

[81] *Ibid.*, pp. 557–58, and see the Bibliographical Notes below, p. 401. The allusion to Lafayette's sacrifice of his fortune might have been to his recent *contribution patriotique* (Apr. 28) of 25,000 livres (see receipt in Huntington Library, HM 9439), but since this voluntary tax was not publicly announced, the allusion was probably only to Lafayette's well-known financial generosity. See also Girodie catalogue, p. 35, item 49.

[82] Short to Paine, June 8, Landin, p. 367.

[83] [*Ca.* May 27], *Journal de Paris*, May 31, p. 608; *Courrier de Paris*, June 1, pp. 440–41; and *Mercure historique et politique*, June 5, p. 65.

effective channel. His answer was to display his influence with the National Guard and the king. On Sunday morning, May 30, some six or seven thousand of his men reported to the Champ-de-Mars. The king's proclamation on wearing the national cockade had appeared on the bulletin boards of the city the previous afternoon, and the feeling of devotion to Louis XVI ran high. Formerly the king had made a practice of reviewing the French and the Swiss Guard in the month of May, and he now had yielded to Lafayette's request that he review the National Guard. Paris saw in the forthcoming review an implicit recognition of the importance in his eyes of its citizen army.[84]

Lafayette rode onto the reviewing field beside Louis XVI at 10:30. His troops were drawn up in order, and on all sides stood masses of spectators. They welcomed the king with cheers. Louis wore a modest green suit, and as subsequent developments were to make plain,[85] the soldiers were disappointed that he did not appear in a resplendent uniform. But they could take consolation in the king's single ornament—a large, handsome, tricolor cockade on his hat. When Louis, Lafayette, their escorts, and their staffs took their places, the Guards began their maneuvers, and when drill was over, they marched in review. Their precision delighted their commander, and the king too seemed pleased. In the course of the review one of the divisions presented to Lafayette an address, which Short described as "couched in terms of the severest censure against his enemies & the warmest applause of himself" and a journalist (perhaps with hyperbole) described as "the unanimous resolution of all their companions in arms to sacrifice, under his orders and following his example, their fortunes and their lives for the establishment of the French constitution."[86]

After an hour and a half of maneuvers, the last Guardsman swung by, and the spectators took over. They cheered the king, crowded around his escort, and followed him all the way to the

---

[84] *Révolutions de Paris*, No. 47, May 29–June 5, pp. 453–54. Cf. Saint-Priest to Lafayette, May 30, Tuetey, I, 197, No. 1724.

[85] See below, pp. 455–57.

[86] Short to Paine, June 8, Landin, p. 367, and *Gazette de Leide*, June 15. See also *Gazette de Leide*, June 11, and Bibliographical Notes below, p. 401.

Tuileries Palace, crying "Long live the king." Such evidence of affection Louis XVI had rarely seen in recent days. When they reached the palace, it was already 12:15 P.M. Some thought that Louis' eyes were moist as he asked the commandant general to tell the National Guard of his satisfaction.[87]

The next day Lafayette did so:

> The commandant general, having derived a most lively satisfaction from the appearance and the bearing of the troops who appeared Sunday before the king, as well as the manner in which they passed in review, takes still a new pleasure in carrying out the orders of His Majesty, who has charged him to make known to the National Guard how content he was with the review in every regard and how much he counts on your attachment to the constitution, your respect for the law, your affection for his person, and your zeal to maintain the public tranquility.[88]

That day too the Assembly of Representatives, having adopted a resolution lauding His Majesty's proclamation on the tricolor cockade, also sent a deputation to convey to Lafayette and the National Guard their indebtedness for "the active and clear patriotism that marked all their actions." Lafayette in turn thanked the deputation and asked them to assure their colleagues of "his homage and his gratitude."[89]

The king himself, outwardly at least, went a step farther to exhibit his approval of recent innovations. If there were among his retinue any who resented the service that since October the Paris National Guard had rendered as palace sentinels, he wanted it publicly known that he did not share their sentiments. In fact, as if to demonstrate that he no longer regarded himself as a prisoner, he also decided to go to his palace at Saint-Cloud for a few days, and he asked that a detachment of the National Guard accompany him. Through his minister of the household he informed the mayor of his capital of his intentions, and the mayor in turn informed the commandant general. Upon requesting Lafayette to give the necessary orders, Bailly went on:

[87] *Journal de Paris*, June 1, pp. 611–12; *Révolutions de Paris*, No. 47, May 29–June 5, pp. 453–54; Desmoulins, *Révolutions*, No. 28, pp. 665–66, No. 30, p. 260; and Fernan Nuñez to Floridablanca, May 30, Mousset, p. 233.

[88] Lacroix, V, 559 (May 31).

[89] *Ibid.*, pp. 532–33 (May 26), 603–5, 615–17 (May 31), 640 (June 1).

I am also charged, Monsieur, to make known to the National Guard the king's complete satisfaction with the service they perform near his person. I take pleasure, at this time, in carrying out the most pleasant as well as the most honorable of all my duties in asking you to impart this new proof of His Majesty's good will to the National Guard, whose patriotism, prudence, and courage are the surest rampart of our liberty. If this testimonial of the king's goodness can acquire in the estimation of the Parisian army an additional value, it will be, no doubt, when the general who is the object of their love just as he is of their gratitude and of the admiration of every good citizen will be charged to transmit it to them. I shall be obliged to you, Monsieur, if you would please send to each of the battalion and squadron commanders a copy of the letter which I have the honor to write to you and which for my part I shall take care to have published.[90]

In short, the review of May 30 was an unmistakable victory for Lafayette. Whether or not Charles de Lameth had been justly suspected of coveting Lafayette's post or of making him look like a traitor to the popular cause, the pride of Paris in its National Guard and the loyalty of the Guard to Lafayette could scarcely be questioned. In William Short's opinion, "Fortune, who has never yet abandoned the Marquis," had turned the schemes of his opponents "in his favor or at least averted them." Short anticipated that the outcome would be to win him enthusiastic support from the aristocrats, "a class where he hitherto had only enemies," while "the popular faction in the assembly which began to be alarming, seem already to have lost favor even among the lower classes of people," and the National Guard, "who, it was feared, had some kind of attachment . . . to the principles supported by this faction have lately . . . pronounced in the most positive manner contrary sentiments."[91] Lafayette's popularity (and along with it Louis XVI's) seemed to be unassailable.

By the end of May 1790 the split in Patriot ranks was a matter of common knowledge. At court the impression arose that Lafayette and Mirabeau were already united with other leading deputies like Sieyès, Le Chapelier, and Talleyrand against Barnave, Duport, and Lameth.[92] Reflecting that impression, the Austrian ambassador

[90] Bailly to Lafayette, June 1, BN: Fr. 11697, pp. 59 bis–60 bis, and Robiquet, pp. 62–63.

[91] Short to Cutting, June 9, Boyd (ed.), XVI, 508.

[92] Lescure (ed.), II, 449–50 (May 29).

informed his chancellor that the Jacobin Club was "composed of two parties, the Duc d'Orléans' and the Marquis de la Fayette's."[93] Under the same impression though derived from another source, the American chargé d'affaires wrote his superiors that the Triumvirate "had formed a separate party" and now as Lafayette's "most violent enemies" were "not on speaking terms" with him.[94] Émigré circles took heart in the belief that Charles de Lameth's supposed effort to replace Lafayette in the *généralat* would force Lafayette to take the king's side and thus bring about "a happy issue if only the king is firm."[95]

Others were fearful that the king might be too firm. When Bailly's letter announcing the king's intention to go to Saint-Cloud appeared in the newspapers, it provoked mixed editorial comment. The more unfavorable expressed alarm lest the king might not stop at Saint-Cloud but would go on to Rambouillet, still farther from Paris, even if he had asked to be accompanied by a detachment of the National Guard. Others thought that the projected trip, innocent in itself, was really intended to accustom Parisians to seeing the king leave the city so that, after several such trips, he could slip away to a more remote place and renounce the Revolution. Marat sarcastically contended that while the royal ministers' intentions indeed were not good, yet the people should not be alarmed, for Lafayette's love of glory, the advantage to him of retaining his command, and his satisfaction in playing a great role in history would tie him to his duty, even if nothing was to be expected from his *civisme* and *vertu*.[96]

In fact, guarding the person of the king, though a burdensome duty, also was a glorious honor. June 3 would be Corpus Christi Day (*Fête-Dieu*), and on that day His Majesty was expected to attend

---

[93] Mercy-Argenteau to Kaunitz, May 29, Alfred d'Arneth and Jules Flammermont (eds.), *Correspondance secrète du comte de Mercy-Argenteau avec l'empereur Joseph II et le prince de Kaunitz* (Paris, 1891), II, 302.

[94] Short to Jefferson, June 5, Boyd (ed.), XVI, 474.

[95] Vaudreuil to Artois, June 5, Pingaud (ed.), I, 201. Cf. same to same, June 17, *ibid.*, pp. 208–10.

[96] *Ami du peuple*, June 1, pp. 6–7, June 5, pp. 4–5. See also *Révolutions de Paris*, No. 27, May 29–June 14, pp. 456–57; *Moniteur*, June 4, p. 663; *Courrier de Paris*, June 3, p. 469, June 4, p. 7, June 5, p. 19; and *Gazette de Leide*, June 15.

high mass at his parish church, Saint-Germain-l'Auxerrois, and from there, if an ancient custom was followed, the Holy Eucharist would be paraded through the streets to the Tuileries and back. Never before in living memory had a king followed the Holy Sacrament in that procession in the capital. The fete this time might have special significance in view of the charge in certain quarters that the Revolution was hostile to the Christian faith and the Roman Catholic Church. The clergy of Saint-Germain-l'Auxerrois invited the National Assembly to attend in a body, and the mayor and the commandant general desired to make the occasion dignified and appropriate. Accordingly, Lafayette consulted Louis XVI, the clergy of Saint-Germain-l'Auxerrois, and the National Assembly. He had recently presented the Battalion of Veterans to the king, who had been pleased with them, and Louis now asked that they serve as his escort. Lafayette thereupon reminded the battalion to take the civic oath, and it did so on June 2 in the Grande Salle before the Assembly of Representatives.[97]

Lafayette also inquired into the plans of the curé of Saint-Germain-l'Auxerrois. As a result he estimated that 4,200 National Guards would be needed for the Fête-Dieu procession, and he ordered each division to designate 700 in such a way as to distribute the honor among all battalions, ranks, and branches of the command.[98] Since the Assembly of Representatives would have its own services at the Church of Saint-Jean-en-Grève, Lafayette ordered National Guard units to provide a proper escort for them too. Other parish churches made plans for their own services, with National Guard companies participating.[99] He and Bailly also consulted the National Assembly on its wishes regarding its escort, but the Assembly agreed with the Vicomte de Noailles that "being among our fellow citizens, we need no guard."[100]

By 8 o'clock on the morning of June 3 the National Guard began lining the Rue Saint-Honoré and the parvis of the Église

---

[97] Lacroix, V, 642–43, 647–48 (June 1), 653 (June 2). For the presentation of the Veterans to the king see Lacroix, IV, 541 (Apr. 26).

[98] *Courrier de Paris*, June 2, pp. 449–51.

[99] Lacroix, V, 663 (June 2).

[100] *AP*, XVI, 40 (June 1), and *Moniteur*, June 3, p. 624.

Saint-Germain-l'Auxerrois, and at 8:30 the deputies, proceeding from the Manège, took their places in the church nave. Lafayette was among them. When finally the king drove from the Tuileries to the church, a dense crowd gathered along the street acclaimed him.[101] The carriages of the queen and the Comte de Provence followed his, and the church's dignitaries greeted the royal party at the church door as cloisters and square echoed with shouts of "Long live the king!" After Louis and his party took their places near the altar, the priests chanted a solemn high mass, at the close of which each of the deputies as well as of the royal party received a blessed lighted taper to carry.

The ushers then led the deputies out of the church. Headed by some National Guard cavalry and part of the National Guard band, the procession started down the street to the Quai du Louvre. The deputies followed, and behind them the rest of the National Guard band. The clergy, chanting and escorted by National Guard infantry, carried the Holy Sacrament. After them, on foot and singly, came the royal family. On either side of His Majesty marched his escort, the Battalion of Veterans, resplendent in new uniforms. The procession ended with more National Guard cavalry and infantry. As the parade went by, the bands played, church bells pealed, cannon saluted, and the massed crowds cheered. Among the deputies Lafayette and Bailly walked side by side, each bearing his taper. "One could not without admiration," a witness exulted, "see the hero of America honor himself by appearing in a religious ceremony, and one smiled to see a hand accustomed to handling a sword humbly holding a blessed candle that it had received from the hand of a cleric in the house of the Lord."[102]

But the cynosure of the day was the king. Repeatedly shouts broke out along the line: "Long live the king!" Louis XVI returned to the Tuileries only about half-past one. According to the same witness, never before had Paris seen so august a ceremony, never had law or religion enjoyed a more beautiful triumph, never

[101] Details of the events here described are derived from *Courrier de Paris*, June 4, pp. 3–7; *Gazette de Leide, supplément*, June 15; *Révolutions de Paris*, No. 47, May 29–June 5, p. 457; and *AP*, XVI, 92 (June 3).

[102] *Courrier de Paris*, June 4, p. 5.

had the king received a more ardent display of the people's love.[103] A king who had been fervidly hailed by the people of his capital three times within less than a week surely had reason to feel confidence in himself, the Paris National Guard, and its commander. And those whom the alliance of monarch, church, and National Guard appalled had reason to feel uneasy.

BIBLIOGRAPHICAL NOTES

Lacroix (V, 556–58) thinks that the address of the Paris National Guard was not presented to Lafayette at the review on May 30, for although an *Adresse de la Garde nationale parisienne à M. le marquis de La Fayette au Champ de Mars le 30 mai 1790* exists, (1) he found no mention of it in the contemporary press except in the *Gazette universelle ou papier-nouvelles* of June 2 (pp. 739–40), (2) the *Chronique de Paris* of June 4 stated that a "pretended address" of the National Guard had been circulated in Paris, and (3) a copy which he found (BN: Lb 39/8892) was not signed and therefore was presumably only a draft. In its issue of June 15, however, the *Gazette de Leide* published the entire text of the address, and its version conforms with that given in Lacroix, V, 557–58. Furthermore the *Gazette* said that it was delivered to Lafayette at the review. Short also said in a letter to Paine, June 8 (Landin, p. 367) and in another to Cutting, June 9 (Boyd [ed.], XVI, 508) that "the national guards" delivered it to Lafayette, though in the letter to Paine he specified that the delivery took place "in a review of one of the divisions." Lacroix therefore was mistaken in thinking that the *Gazette universelle*'s account was the only contemporary mention of it. The relative silence of contemporaries about its presentation to Lafayette can perhaps be explained by its not being in fact a "unanimous resolution" of the Paris National Guard but only of some battalions, which, however, had had it printed in the hope that it would eventually be unanimous. That explanation would make clear also why the *Chronique de Paris* called the address "pretended," and the circulation of the printed *Adresse* in Paris would corroborate Short's and the *Gazette de Leide*'s testimony that it actually was delivered to Lafayette. We assume that it was delivered but that its delivery escaped widespread notice largely because the review was intended to honor Louis XVI rather than Lafayette.

[103] *Ibid.*, p. 3.

CHAPTER XVII

A Modern Richelieu?

SINCE his letter of May 13 Mirabeau had remained on good terms with Lafayette. They met at intervals at La Rochefoucauld's home along with others of the group that had come to be called the "Comité de La Rochefoucauld," and their secretaries also kept them in touch with each other.[1] One of Mirabeau's secretaries, J.-J. Pellenc, intimated to Lafayette his willingness to cooperate "in the work under consideration related to bringing the constitutional articles together."[2] In a conversation they had on May 28[3] they talked about the disorders at Marseilles, which, according to a dismaying report by Saint-Priest that day to the National Assembly, were still going on.[4]

By that time the Marseilles municipality, as instructed by the National Assembly, had sent a deputation to explain its failure to preserve order. Upon learning from Pellenc that Mirabeau intended to reprimand Saint-Priest for mishandling the crisis, Lafayette informed the secretary about his own views, which, we can readily guess, were less sympathetic to Marseilles and more sympathetic to Saint-Priest than Mirabeau's. Pellenc quickly sought out Mirabeau, informed him of Lafayette's attitude, and then wrote Lafayette that Mirabeau would not consent to any course that would seem to blame the municipality of Marseilles. Mirabeau's reasons for this stand favorably impressed his secretary, who re-

---

[1] Pellenc to Lafayette, [May 28], *Mémoires*, II, 460. See below, n. 3.

[2] *Ibid.*

[3] *Ibid.* We have dated this letter May 28 because the session of the National Assembly that it describes (except for minor differences, which may perhaps be attributable to inaccuracy on Pellenc's part) fits the one for that date reported in *AP*, XV, 704–7.

[4] *AP*, XV, 704–5.

layed the most telling one: the Lameths and Barnave must not be allowed the advantage of proposing a decree that would increase their influence in Marseilles. Mirabeau also sent word by Pellenc that he would be at the "Comité de La Rochefoucauld" that evening and would explain his position to Lafayette there.[5]

What the two men agreed upon at that evening's encounter, if there was one, they did not reveal, but the next day the deputation from Marseilles protested that their fellow-citizens' behavior had been only a justifiable display of patriotic indignation against the symbols of tyranny, and Mirabeau again persuaded the National Assembly to vote his way: the Assembly sent the whole matter to the Comité des Rapports for study and, despite vigorous opposition, approved his request that "the special deputies of the Marseilles municipality receive the honor of being admitted to the session."[6]

If Lafayette was present in the National Assembly on that occasion, he took no part in the debate. But apparently he was not happy with the outcome, for he began again to avoid meeting Mirabeau. He did not even keep an appointment that Mirabeau thought was fixed for May 31, giving as his excuse that he was too busy. Mirabeau assumed, however, the real reason was that Lafayette's circle of advisers had again warned him to beware of an alliance. The next day he sent the commandant general a letter asking indignantly why he could see him only at the "Committee of La Rochefoucauld," and even there rarely alone. Meanwhile matters were getting more critical, he protested, because of the contagious example of "the most active, the most perverse, and most tenacious men this country conceals" (he probably meant the Triumvirate), and Lafayette, he intimated, was not competently coping with the situation. Among many partisans, Mirabeau warned, Lafayette had few dependable servants; of his numerous paid personnel none was a weighty adviser or a distinguished agent; his trusted aides-de-camp might well have the military merit to carry on another successful campaign in America, and his friends did

---

[5] Pellenc to Lafayette, [May 28],*Mémoires*, II, 459–60.

[6] *AP*, XV, 721–24 (May 29).

honor to his reputation as a private citizen, but none of them was capable of understanding men or affairs of state. "Our times, our revolution, our circumstances resemble nothing that has been," Mirabeau admonished. "It is not by wit or by rote or by social graces that a man can guide his conduct these days. It is by combinations of plans, inspiration of genius, and omnipotence of character. Do you recognize any of [those qualities in] your committees? Do you conceive of a possible committee that follows that prescription?"

Having thus implied that Lafayette's "committee" was a clique of mediocrities, Mirabeau, with a frank admission that he was by common standards being immodest, pointed out his own merits: "I am more necessary to you than all your committees put together." Committees might be useful to spread ideas but not to consult as a privy council, for deliberation by many led to indecision or precipitate action, and at the present juncture decisiveness was the sole means of safety. If Lafayette did not trust him, at least he must have no confidence in them. But what good could Mirabeau do if called upon to use his talents only on occasions embarrassing to Lafayette? What good could he do if Lafayette left him in the discard until some crisis arose that hampered the policy he might have advised had he been Lafayette's "regular counselor" and "the dictator in short (allow me the expression) of the dictator?"

Mirabeau then came to the crux of his appeal. There had been a time in French history, early in the previous century, when, in a period of monarchical weakness, Cardinal Richelieu had been a sort of dictator and with the help of his "Grey Eminence," the Capuchin monk Joseph, had made the monarchy strong again. Mirabeau drew a parallel to that time:

Oh, M. de Lafayette! Richelieu was Richelieu against the nation on behalf of the court, and though Richelieu did much harm to public liberty, he did a great deal of good for the monarchy. Be Richelieu toward the court on behalf of the nation, and you will re-make the monarchy while increasing and consolidating public liberty. But Richelieu had his Capuchin Joseph, so have your Grey Eminence, or you will be lost without saving us. Your great qualities need my drive; my drive needs your great qualities; and you trust to petty men who out of petty considerations by petty maneuvers and with petty views seek to render us useless to each other, and you do not see that you need to espouse me and trust me the more your stupid partisans have discredited me, the more they have pushed me aside! Ah, you are jeopardizing your destiny!

And he ended with a request, almost a demand, for an "appointment in the near future at which you will be prompt, alone, and in person . . . and determined to make decisions, since we must make decisions or perish."[7]

If Mirabeau ever deserved the reputation he had in certain quarters as a profound political tactician, it was not in this letter, for all its eloquence and logic. The patronizing, even peremptory, air was hardly calculated to win the self-confident, self-righteous Lafayette. Lafayette did not aspire to long-term power such as Richelieu had wielded; his model was not Richelieu but Washington. Lafayette, who admired Mirabeau's "sublime talents" even if he did not trust him,[8] may well have been made still more distrustful now. For in his opinion those whom Mirabeau called petty and ineffective were honest and upright citizens, and, moreover, they were staunch friends. If Mirabeau meant to call petty such men as Latour-Maubourg, La Rochefoucauld, Bailly, and Gouvion, Lafayette was likely to rally to them more loyally than ever before.

Distrust of Mirabeau was, in fact, more justified than Lafayette could have divined. On the very day that he thus lectured Lafayette for failing to play Richelieu to his Joseph, he tried to undercut Lafayette's influence at court—though, consistently enough, because he considered Lafayette's judgment of men to be deficient. This he did in his first letter as a paid adviser to the royal family. Reiterating his devotion to monarchy as "regulated by the laws," Mirabeau outlined a plan for dealing with "the idol of the day, the pretended general of the Constitution, the rival of the monarch, M. de Lafayette in short."[9]

It was no secret that a change of ministers was still in the offing. Recently, for example, Condorcet had (semi-seriously, it would appear) counseled Lafayette: "It is absolutely necessary that you

---

[7] Mirabeau to Lafayette, June 1, Bacourt (ed.), II, 19–22.

[8] *Mémoires*, II, 365.

[9] "Première note du Comte de Mirabeau pour la cour, June 1," Bacourt (ed.), II, 25–26. That this "note" was intended especially for the queen is clear from Mirabeau to La Marck, June 1, *ibid.*, pp. 32–33.

keep two ministries all ready, one inside, the other outside the Assembly, in order to be prepared against all the accidents of death, treason, water cures, etc. that can upset an assembly of twelve hundred metaphysicians."[10] Mirabeau detected in the impending ministerial crisis a chance to get himself named a minister if the decree prohibiting selection of ministers from within the Assembly could be lifted or ignored.[11] But, he now advised, "after the power which the court's weakness rather than the law has permitted to M. de La Fayette," it would be "a conspicuous error, a delusive idea" to come to an understanding with him about a choice of ministers. Since Lafayette was already master of the Paris National Guard and thereby of a great part of the National Guards elsewhere, would he not, if the ministers were also men of his choice, have complete executive authority and so become in fact "the most absolute, the most redoubtable dictator"? If Lafayette would choose "skilled pilots capable of saving us from shipwreck," Mirabeau would remain silent or even lost in praise, but he feared that Lafayette would select "weak or unskilled or ignorant, I dare not say perverse, ministers."

Lafayette derived his strength, Mirabeau went on, chiefly from the confidence of his army, which he enjoyed only because he seemed to share the preferences of the multitude. To keep his power, he would always be constrained to follow Parisian public opinion, which was molded by a flock of writers and luminaries of Paris, the city least likely to remain under the influence of a single man. Hence, "this man, although no demagogue, will be dangerous for the royal authority as long as public opinion in Paris, of which he can be only the instrument, will impose its sway upon him." Should national sentiments become saner, Paris would be the last city in the realm to change, and so Lafayette was "of all citizens the one on whom the king can least count, the one who, even while entertaining them, will be the last to put into practice the principles of monarchical government." A ministry of Lafayette's choice would put the realm under the domination of Paris,

---

[10] Condorcet to Lafayette, [May 1], Charavay, pp. 568–69. See also *ibid.,* p. 218.

[11] "Première note," June 1, Bacourt (ed.), II, 26.

"though the only way to safety is to bring Paris back into the realm." Such a ministry would make Lafayette chief of the army, commander of all the National Guard units of the kingdom, lieutenant-general of the realm, distributor of all patronage, and prime minister (with the other ministers for his clerks). "Being at the same time slave and despot, subject and master, he would become the most formidable of tyrants."

Mirabeau nevertheless assured Louis XVI that no such tyrant need be feared: "The multitude is entirely unaware of the dictatorship which M. de La Fayette has the clumsiness to exercise." If it knew of his relations with some ministers and "the kind of irresponsible ministry that he has wanted to assume," it would repudiate him, and to avoid his secret's becoming known, he would be forced to keep silent or dissemble if his nominations were turned down. All his efforts as commander of the Paris Guard, all the sums liberally granted him (with which he bought the services of "a thousand spies in Paris, makers of resolutions in the public squares, spectators in the galleries of the Assembly to applaud at his will, aides-de-camp in the provinces to perform I know not what, and writers, pamphleteers of all kinds to serve him and his friends exclusively") would be of no avail if ministers were appointed who would have majority support in the National Assembly. Then, thrown back upon "the inertia of his thought and the nullity of his talent," the "pretended hero" would be able "neither to seduce with his wealth nor to corrupt with his influence." And so he would, if ambition alone prompted him, give up his post, and his now most ardent collaborators would abandon him.

Mirabeau then recommended that Louis XVI build up a rival to Lafayette. He nominated for that honor the Marquis de Bouillé, who was not dependent upon a single city as was Lafayette and was "unblemished by any of the stains that the other has contracted." If the court was bold enough to follow his advice, Mirabeau undertook to make daily commentaries intended to show "how the man who has been built up and is feared might soon be shrunken, nullified, and scarcely dangerous if we put some steady effort . . . into giving him confidence as he harms himself, into resisting him methodically as he seeks to serve himself rather than to serve."[12]

If Mirabeau really was persuaded that Lafayette's popularity was bought, flourished only in Paris, and had no force in the provinces and that his ambition was to control the ministry for his own aggrandizement, why was he trying at the same time to form an alliance with him? And if he really wanted to be the Grey Eminence of a modern Richelieu, why was he attempting to undermine the confidence of the king in his candidate for power-behind-the-throne? The answer obviously was that Mirabeau was engaged in duplicity. He thought of Lafayette as an essentially naïve self-seeker whose voracious appetite for approval he could manipulate and whose popularity he could exploit to his own advantage and, therefore, his country's (for it is easy for a political leader to identify the two). And he was prepared to do so either in an alliance with him or in an alliance against him, as circumstances might dictate.

Furthermore, if Mirabeau was serious when he claimed that the popular regard for Lafayette was derived solely from his control of the Paris National Guard, he suffered from the blindness of those who will not see. The papers were full of evidence of Lafayette's influence upon all elements of the population in many corners of the realm—in the National Assembly and in the Paris Assembly of Representatives, in Paris and in the provinces, inside and outside the National Guard units. It happened that on the very day Mirabeau was trying to convince Louis XVI that Lafayette's popularity was flimsy and ephemeral, the commandant general on the other hand, consulted the king about a great "Federation" planned for July 14—an all-France demonstration of loyalty to country, constitution, and monarch (which, incidentally, when it did take place, was to prove, though that was not its purpose, how mistaken Mirabeau was).[13]

On June 3, the day of the Fête-Dieu, after the procession was over, Lafayette went to the home of the Duc de La Rochefoucauld, where "the Committee" were gathered, Mirabeau among them.[14]

[12] *Ibid.*, pp. 26–32.
[13] See below, chap. XXII.
[14] Mirabeau to La Marck, June 4, *ibid.*, p. 34.

"The Committee" discussed a proposal to introduce a bill abolishing hereditary nobility. Some of the popular journalists had reached a point of unconditional hostility to the old aristocracy, Desmoulins among the most outspoken of them. Why should titled persons, he wanted to know, be chosen so frequently to fill important offices, even when they deserved it, as Lafayette and some others did? And why should even a trustworthy aristocrat like Lafayette be constantly referred to as "M. le Marquis."[15] A letter to the editor of the more dispassionate *Moniteur* warned that the Revolution had not changed the hearts of Frenchmen: not all the privileged were like Lafayette, and in spite of philosophies and revolutionary triumphs a title and a ribbon were still much sought after in Paris.[16]

The discussion at La Rochefoucauld's revealed that "the Committee" were prepared to support the move to abolish titles and other hereditary privileges. Mirabeau alone objected and even scoffed at it. He egged them on a bit, he later confessed, because he thought it a little strange that "these gentlefolk" should "always and in everything" oppose him. At the end of the meeting, still displeased not to have had a private conversation with Lafayette, he was again asked to postpone his wish—this time until the following evening. He felt balked and contemptuous of "the man of indecisions" and "his committee." "In short," he concluded, "there is nothing to do with those curs but to let them yap in a discordant manner. When the king gets tired of being a prisoner, we shall see."[17]

On the same day that Lafayette thus put Mirabeau off, Talon, apparently acting on behalf of the royal court, wrote to La Marck about a potential alliance of the two leaders. Lafayette did not see clearly into the future, he agreed; the bandages that he had over his eyes must be torn off, and by a concerted effort they could hope to do so.[18] So it appeared that the Tuileries entourage was not yet ready to follow Mirabeau's advice to undermine Lafayette and still

---

[15] *Révolutions,* No. 22, pp. 391–93, No. 23, p. 436.

[16] *Moniteur,* Apr. 25, p. 468.

[17] Mirabeau to La Marck, June 4, Bacourt (ed.), II, 34.

[18] Talon to La Marck, June 3, *ibid.,* p. 33. That Talon was probably acting for the court is shown in Talon to Louis XVI, [1791?], *AP,* LV, 442.

hoped to get the two of them to work together. Yet all was uncertainty at the beginning of June, as Louis XVI wavered between alliance with and opposition to the Revolution.[19]

Meanwhile, as Bailly had informed Lafayette, the royal family prepared to go to Saint-Cloud, about seven miles down the Seine River from the Tuileries. Louis XVI took pains to let the National Assembly understand that he would return to Paris on Sundays in order to keep in touch with its work and to disarm any suspicion that he might not return. On the eve of his departure, because of that very suspicion, some hostility was expressed against Louis and Lafayette, but when the royal family actually left, it was amid the cheers of a large crowd gathered at the Tuileries to bid them farewell.[20]

On Friday, June 4, the day set for the departure, Minister of War Latour du Pin appeared before the National Assembly to complain about the deterioration of army discipline, and Lafayette occupied himself with that complaint. So he did not accompany the royal family, and Gouvion took charge of the National Guard detachment that went along. Suspecting that some of the National Assembly's Military Committee had what seemed to him extremist ideas about the reorganization of the army, Lafayette talked with a few of its more friendly members on the morning after Latour du Pin's speech, and they agreed that the minister should meet with the committee before any army bill went up for debate.[21] That day also, in considering a finance bill, the Assembly decided that it must know the sums to be appropriated for the king's civil list.[22]

Lafayette sent a letter immediately to the king at Saint-Cloud about both subjects. On the civil list he observed merely that the matter ought to be settled promptly, and the next day being Sunday, when Louis was expected to visit Paris, he indicated that he

[19] Mirabeau to La Marck, June 4, Bacourt (ed.), II, 34.

[20] *Ami du peuple*, June 5, pp. 4–5; *Orateur du peuple*, No. 13, p. 99; *Courrier de Paris*, June 5, pp. 17–19; *Révolutions de Paris*, No. 47, May 29–June 5, p. 460; and *Gazette de Leide*, June 15.

[21] Lafayette to Louis XVI, June 5, *Mémoires*, II, 468–69.

[22] *AP*, XVI, 95–97 (June 4), 111 (June 5).

would take the liberty to submit some relevant reflections. The rest
of the letter was concerned with the forthcoming army bill. In order "to calm the zeal of the makers of projects," Lafayette made
bold to suggest what the king should do: Latour du Pin should be
authorized to write to the National Assembly's Military Committee
at once asking for an interview on the following Monday; if his
request were received before six o'clock that very (Saturday) evening (June 5), it would keep the Leftist opposition in the committee from taking any steps until after the requested conference;
a minister's request for a mere conversation with a committee
would not bind the king, who would anyhow have the whole of
the intervening Sunday to consult with his advisers. Lafayette desired, he stated, that "the Committee should not exceed its constitutional functions, which would set a bad example for future
legislators."[23] Whether or not Louis XVI and Latour du Pin acceded to Lafayette's suggestion, no discussion of the army bill took
place at the evening session of the National Assembly on June 5,
and for the time being the Left brought about no radical reconstruction of the royal army.

When Louis XVI, as promised, returned from Saint-Cloud to
Paris on Sunday, Lafayette at the head of a detachment of the National Guard rode out to meet him and escorted him to the Tuileries, where he was welcomed by a large crowd. Lafayette presumably took the opportunity to talk with His Majesty about the civil
list, as he had asked permission to do, and since he agreed with
the National Assembly that the king's personal expenses should
be determined by the dignity of his office rather than by considerations of economy, the two men probably saw eye to eye on that
matter.[24] Perhaps on this occasion they also settled another delicate matter, which would hardly have been arranged without
royal consent. The public had recently become exercised because
the Regiment of the Cent Suisses and the Gardes de la Prévôté de
l'Hôtel—the men who, except for the National Guard on duty at

---

[23] Lafayette to Louis XVI, June 5, *Mémoires*, II, 468–69.

[24] *Ibid.*, III, 206, and see *AP*, XVI, 111 (June 5). For details of Lafayette's escorting
of the king see *Courrier de Paris*, June 7, p. 52, and *Journal général de la cour*, June 7,
pp. 542–43.

the palace, were the ones most closely attached to the Tuileries and the Manège—had not yet taken the civic oath. At any rate, on Monday morning (June 7) Lafayette attended a special meeting at the Hôtel de Ville, called, the mayor explained, to administer the civic oath to those two units. The assembly thereupon went down to the Place de Grève, where the Cent Suisses were already drawn up. One of the officers read the oath in German, and then the whole unit, officers and men, vowed to abide by it. Shortly afterward the Gardes de la Prévôté arrived, and they also took the oath.[25]

By that time a rumor had already started that the National Guard had been badly treated at Saint-Cloud. Captain J.-P.-V. Féral of the Battalion of Saint-Louis-en-l'Ile had been with the contingent that had gone to Saint-Cloud to guard the king. Having returned from that tour of duty, Féral made no secret of his discontent: no adequate quarters had been provided for the Paris troops, and unlike the Swiss they had had to sleep in tents; National Guard officers had been denied the privileges extended to other officers; the king's sister, Mme Elisabeth, had been rude to a National Guard officer; and one of the king's valets had shouted along the streets of Saint-Cloud that the National Guard would betray the king. Before the Sunday evening of Louis XVI's return was over, some Parisians were proposing that the king be brought back to Paris— if necessary, by forcing the gates at Saint-Cloud.[26]

By the next day public resentment was high enough to constrain the city officials to take action. The mayor wrote to the commandant general suggesting that a public statement of the facts in the case might be wise.[27] Lafayette began an investigation at once, ordering Charton, Féral's division chief, who also had been at Saint-Cloud, to come to his home that evening. Charton claimed to know of no disrespect to the National Guard at Saint-Cloud, but

---

[25] Lacroix, V, 684–85 (June 7); *Moniteur*, June 10, p. 656; *Journal général de la cour*, June 8, p. 548.

[26] Lacroix, VI, 285; *Courrier de Paris*, June 9, p. 73, June 10, pp. 90–91; *Chronique de Paris*, June 11, pp. 646–47, June 16, p. 666; *Révolutions de Paris*, No. 48, June 5–12, pp. 536–38; *Journal du diable*, No. 32, pp. 2–3; Co. national, June 8, pp. 1, 7; Desmoulins, *Révolutions*, No. 29, pp. 217–18; and *Ami du peuple*, June 9, pp. 2–3, 5–6.

[27] Bailly to Lafayette, June 7, Tuetey, I, 199, ᴺ ᴼ: Lacroix, VI, 286; *Courrier de Paris*, June 10, p. 90; and *Chronique de Paris*, June ᴵᴺ, p. 646–47.

to make doubly sure, he and Lafayette agreed to call the officers of the detachment together and question them.

Actually not only the officers but some enlisted men reported to Charton's house the next day (June 8). Gouvion as the senior officer present presided. He asked the division chief about the way the men and officers had been treated at Saint-Cloud, and Charton's reply was a complete denial of ill treatment. When Gouvion then asked for other opinions, Captain Féral spoke up. He repeated his accusations, but one by one they were denied by Gouvion on the basis of his own knowledge and of Charton's testimony. No one supported Féral's charges; on the contrary, all declared that they would be willing to do duty at Saint-Cloud again. Gouvion wanted Féral to be personally censured, but the others were content to adopt a resolution formally repudiating the current rumors as inventions of ill-intentioned persons. Apparently, everyone at the meeting with the exception of Féral signed the resolution and agreed that copies of it be sent to the National Assembly, the mayor, the commandant general and his staff, and the Assembly of Representatives. Charton wished to keep Féral's name out of the press, but Gouvion insisted that the public ought to know who had caused the trouble. When Gouvion reported the outcome of the meeting to Lafayette and Bailly, they agreed with him.[28]

A series of pamphlets arguing the Féral affair pro and con soon made it a *cause célèbre*,[29] and their impact was intensified by a stream of other pamphlets that betrayed such a degree of either anti-Orleanist or anti-Fayettist bias as to lead to recriminations by each side that the other had bought up the press.[30] Desmoulins, whose

---

[28] Lacroix, VI, 286–88 (June 26).

[29] See, for example, *Précis de ce qui s'est passé dans l'assemblée des officiers et soldats volontaires et du centre formant la garde de Leurs Majestés à Saint-Cloud, convoqués par ordre de M. le Commandant général chez M. Charton, chef de la Première Division, le 8 juin 1790; Lettre d'un officier [Féral] du détachement de Saint-Cloud à M. le Commandant général . . . ce 9 juin 1790;* and *Arreté pris dans la seconde assemblée des officiers et soldats volontaires et des compagnies du centre, de la Garde à Saint-Cloud, lors des premiers voyages de Leurs Majestés (14 juin).*

[30] [Estienne], *Interrogatoire de M. de La Fayette,* pp. 21–22. See also Jean Duetry, "Sebastien Lacroix," *AHRF,* X (1939), 49–60; Passy, pp. 37–38; and McClelland, pp. 160–79.

journal at this time was sometimes favorable[31] and sometimes unfavorable[32] to Lafayette, alleged that Lafayette's friends had tried
to win him over. In an issue that appeared early in June, he declared that some men who claimed to be speaking for Bailly and
Lafayette had offered him a post in the municipality and that he
had learned from Mirabeau that Lafayette was also protecting
him from arrest by the Châtelet. At first he used this story only to
plead for freedom of the press, that journalists should not be beholden to others for protection,[33] but later he asserted that someone
who, he thought, came from Lafayette had offered him 10,000 livres
a year for his support and took him to Lafayette's home, where he
was well received by one of Lafayette's secretaries and accepted the
offer. Neither version of this story seems wholly implausible, but
if a bargain was struck, it was not kept. Desmoulins maintained
that he did not surrender his right to criticize Lafayette (and in
fact he did criticize him frequently thereafter),[34] and his troubles
with the Châtelet continued.

The fear that the Féral affair was part of a plot to undermine the
control by Bailly and Lafayette of Paris was magnified by the libelous nature (already noted) of the particularly incendiary *Vie privée,
impartiale, politique, militaire et domestique du marquis de La
Fayette.* On June 9 the Assembly of Representatives, shocked by
"such an infamous production," denounced it to the king's pro-
curer at the Châtelet, instructing him to seek out its authors, printers, and distributors and to give the greatest publicity to the
Representatives' indignation. On June 30 a printer named Le Normand was arrested. Mme Le Normand begged Lafayette, addressing him as the "rival" of the "virtuous Washington," to have her

---

[31] Desmoulins, *Révolutions,* No. 22, pp. 392–93, No. 23, p. 471, No. 24, p. 512.

[32] *Ibid.,* No. 20, p. 301.

[33] *Ibid.,* No. 29, pp. 245–49. See also *Patriote français,* June 5, p. 3, and Jules Claretie
(ed.), *Oeuvres de Camille Desmoulins* (Paris, 1906), I, 285–86.

[34] Desmoulins to his father, Dec. 31, 1789, Claretie (ed.), II, 350. For the claim of
subsidy, see *ibid.,* I, 285–87 and n., and Ogé Barbaroux (ed.), *Mémoires (inédites) de
Charles Barbaroux* (Paris, 1822), p. 9. The claim is doubtful as it was made by Desmoulins,
on the basis of a guess, to discredit Brissot, and by Barbaroux to discredit Desmoulins, because of their antagonistic stands in the Girondin-Jacobin conflicts of 1792–93. We have
found no reliable evidence of payments to Desmoulins.

husband released. Having just established his shop, he had agreed to print a manuscript without reading it, but by the time he reached the second page, she claimed, he realized that it was "a tissue of lies" and thereupon returned it. Lafayette instructed an aide to take up the matter with the Châtelet, and the aide assured Mme Le Normand that Lafayette was not sensitive about what was printed about him and would ask that M. Le Normand be set free. The Châtelet, in fact, with Lafayette's consent, released him on July 20, and the case died.[35]

Meanwhile, however, the pamphlet had brought on a stormy reaction. On June 12 the District de Saint-Louis-en-l'Ile, Féral's district, passed a resolution endorsing its denunciation by the Representatives. Five days later, the District des Récollets, while professing that the pamphlet was a "new trophy" for Lafayette (for what could be "more glorious for a patriot than the clamors of the aristocracy"?), nevertheless asked not only the Châtelet but also the Investigations Committee of the National Assembly to prosecute its authors.[36] A group at one café, upon reading the "infamous libel" against the general "dear to the nation," threatened to lynch anyone found reading it, and a group at another tore it up and burned it in the street.[37]

Féral likewise resorted to the press. In a letter to Lafayette he claimed that he had been falsely accused of having made inflammatory speeches. He sent copies of his letter to the newspapers, and it appeared in a few.[38] Some of the other battalions that had sent detachments to Saint-Cloud now took a hand in the controversy. The Battalion of Saint-Magloire asked the commandant general himself to investigate the matter, and, on June 10, Féral's own battalion circulated to Lafayette, other city officials, and the other Paris battalions a statement that Féral had been a courageous and

---

[35] See above, p. 377; Lacroix, VI, 7–9 (June 9); Tuetey, I, 155–56, No. Q; Mme Le Normand to Lafayette, and Masson de Neuville to Mme Le Normand, [July 8], AN:BB[30] 160.

[36] Lacroix, VI, pp. 9–10 (June 9).

[37] *Journal général de la cour,* June 12, p. 580, and [Bérenger (ed.)], p. 261. See also *Mercure historique et politique de Bruxelles,* June 26, pp. 321–22, and Charavay, pp. 230–31.

[38] Féral to Lafayette, June 9, Lacroix, VI, 288; *Chronique de Paris,* June 16, p. 666; and *Ami du peuple,* June 26, pp. 4–7, June 24, pp. 1–3.

patriotic defender of the Revolution and should be absolved of all blame.[39] Féral's friends remonstrated that only paid Guardsmen had been present at Charton's home on June 8 and had signed the resolution. To undercut that argument Charton on June 11 assembled a larger group, taking special care to include unpaid soldiers, and submitted the whole case to them. They too added their signatures to the resolution previously adopted, and Charton thereupon sent a letter to the editors of the *Journal de Paris* decrying the current "literary brigandage," reaffirming the good treatment of the National Guard at Saint-Cloud, and calling statements to the contrary untrue and malicious.[40]

Charton obviously thought that his letter would put an end to the Féral affair, but he was disappointed. Soon other National Guard units became exercised. Under Danton's leadership the District of the Cordeliers unanimously endorsed the statement that Féral's battalion of Saint-Louis-en-l'Ile had issued in his favor and sent their endorsement to (among others) Féral, the other sections, Lafayette, and the commandant of Saint-Louis-en-l'Ile to be read to his battalion. On the other hand, on June 17 the Battalion des Mathurins asked for a trial of the case by court-martial; the Battalion de Saint-Nicolas-du-Chardonnet proposed that Féral be suspended pending a decision by court-martial; and the Battalion des Petits-Augustins requested that the matter be put before a committee of surveillance chosen from the entire National Guard.[41]

By that time Lafayette had decided to take personal charge of the investigation. He called together at the Hôtel de Ville two hundred officers from the three divisions of the National Guard that had sent detachments to Saint-Cloud, and after fully discussing the affair, they addressed a letter to Féral denying his account of what had happened, condemning his spreading of false reports in speeches and print, and asking the commandant general to convene a court-martial to try the case.

Feelings ran so high that on June 25 Féral and Charton fought

[39] Lacroix, VI, 289 (June 26).

[40] *Ibid.*, pp. 289–90, and *Journal de Paris*, June 12, p. 656.

[41] Lacroix, VI, 291–93 (June 14), and *Ami du peuple*, June 26, pp. 4–7, June 27, pp. 1–4. See also *Moniteur*, July 1, p. 744.

a duel. No one was hurt, and it ended in a reconciliation of the two men. But the districts and the press were not equally gallant. Some joined in the demand for a court-martial, others claimed that Lafayette had been unfair to Féral and was shielding Saint-Priest and other courtiers at Saint-Cloud. In due course the Féral case went before the Assembly of Representatives, who referred the matter to its Comité des Rapports.[42] Full though the papers had been until then about the Féral affair, it suddenly was almost completely forgotten.

Meanwhile the king had, perhaps unwittingly, helped to assuage the contestants. On June 9, the National Assembly had received his reply to its request on his preference regarding the civil list. He estimated the expense for his family's households at 25,000,000 livres (in addition to the revenues from the crown lands), and his estimates met no opposition in the Assembly. Lafayette voted for the civil list—"with alacrity," he admitted, because it was a token of good will toward "legal royalty"—though, later at least, he called it "exorbitant."[43] Doubtless, too, even if he never indicated it directly, he was pleased by the king's remark, when dealing with the cost of guarding the royal family, that he found in the National Guard all the zeal and devotion he could want and hoped that they would never be removed from his person. A friendly word from the king about the National Guard could hardly have come at a more opportune moment, for in the midst of the Féral controversy it underlined the alliance of king and commandant.

On June 10, Paris celebrated the Octave of the Fête-Dieu. The Assembly of Representatives invited Lafayette to join them at the Church of Saint-Jean-en-Grève, but he sent his regrets: as a deputy he again felt obliged to attend the ceremony at Saint-Germain-l'Auxerrois with the king and the National Assembly.[44] Once more Louis XVI won great applause; even the queen received a little; and the people cheered their favorite deputies as they passed. Lafayette and Bailly again walked side by side, each with his taper, to

[42] Lacroix, VI, 274–75 (June 26).

[43] *Mémoires,* III, 206.

[44] Lacroix, VI, 20 (June 11).

the amusement of at least one journalist: "Take care, general, that they do not make a monk out of you!"[45]

Bailly had feared that an Orleanist plot might spoil the ceremony,[46] but all went off smoothly. The Paris National Guard had never been more popular. As the mayor wrote to the commandant general: "The National Guard, which you have the honor, Monsieur, to command, is always the object of admiration of good citizens," and since he wished to express to it "the gratitude of the citizens of Paris," he asked that on the following Sunday three divisions pass in review before him as mayor; later on he hoped to review the other divisions. Lafayette replied that he would gladly arrange the review, though the Guard's duties were so onerous at the moment that he could assemble only two divisions. Bailly, quite satisfied, agreed to go to Lafayette's home on Sunday morning, June 13, and thence to the Champ-de-Mars.[47]

Before the review took place, France learned that Benjamin Franklin had died in Philadelphia on April 17. Franklin had left France in 1785, but before that time he and Lafayette had worked closely together to promote Franco-American friendship and trade.[48] Lafayette mourned the loss of an old friend, and the Duc de La Rochefoucauld was no less saddened. Both of these Americanophiles wanted the National Assembly to pay an appropriate tribute to Franklin's memory, and in order to make the occasion as impressive as a celebrated orator could, they asked Mirabeau to deliver a brief eulogy.[49] On June 11 Mirabeau did so, asking the French Assembly to unite with the American Congress in homage to a man he described as a friend of Lafayette and La Rochefoucauld, as a *philosophe* who had done the most to spread the rights of men over the world, as one of the greatest thinkers ever to have served both learning and liberty. The Left applauded eagerly, and

---

[45] *Courrier de Paris*, June 11, p. 114. See also *AP*, XVI, 159–60; *Courrier français*, June 11, p. 328; and *Journal général de la cour*, June 11, pp. 571–72.

[46] Lacroix, VI, 287 (June 26).

[47] *Ibid.*, pp. 40–41 (June 12), and Tuetey, II, 420, No. 3985.

[48] Gottschalk, *Between*, pp. 29–219, *passim*.

[49] Paine to Short, June 4, Landin, p. 365, and *Courrier national*, June 12, p. 7. See also below, Bibliographical Notes, p. 433.

as both Lafayette and La Rochefoucauld rose to support the motion, the entire Left rose with them. The Assembly agreed upon three days of mourning and ordered Mirabeau's address sent, with a covering letter by the Assembly's president, the Fayettist Abbé Sieyès, to the American Congress.[50] For several days the papers praised Franklin, noting that the illustrious champion of mankind had been a friend of Lafayette.[51] In a letter which Sieyès wrote to President Washington, enclosing a copy of Mirabeau's address and the Assembly's resolution, he added the hope that nations as they became free would join in peace: "May the Congress of the United States and the National Assembly of France be the first to furnish this fine spectacle to the world! And may the peoples of the two nations join together in a mutual affection worthy of the friendship which unites the two men most illustrious in our time for their exertions on behalf of liberty, Washington and Lafayette."[52]

It so happened that a German electress also had recently died, and the French court had ordered a period of mourning for her, but Lafayette thought that respect for a mere princess ought not to diminish the honor due to a sage. So again he made bold to write to Louis XVI suggesting what should be done: It would gratify the National Assembly if Saint-Priest would inform its president that the court would defer mourning for the electress in order to avoid confusion with the Assembly's tribute to Franklin, adding a word about His Majesty's personal regard for Franklin.[53] Again, however, there is no evidence that the minister sought to win Lafayette's good will by taking his advice.

To share the limelight with the commandant general, nevertheless, was a widely coveted honor, as the pending arrangement for

[50] *AP*, XVI, 170–71, and *Moniteur*, June 12, p. 664. Cf. Short to Cutting, June 9, Boyd (ed.), XVI, 508 n.

[51] *Journal de Paris*, June 12, pp. 654–55; *Courrier français*, June 12, pp. 340–41; *Courrier national*, June 12, pp. 6–7; *Point de jour*, June 12, pp. 470–71; *Gazette de Leide*, June 22; *Révolutions de Paris*, No. 48, June 5–12, p. 540, No. 49, June 12–19, pp. 565–68; and *Gazette de Paris*, June 13, pp. 3–4.

[52] Sieyès to Washington, June 20, Jared Sparks (ed.), *Writings of George Washington* (Boston, 1834–37), X, 497–99.

[53] Lafayette to Louis XVI, June 11, *Mémoires*, II, 469–70.

the mayor to review the National Guard illustrated. It provoked unexpected jealousy on the part of the Conseil de Ville, which, at a meeting on June 12, opposed his doing so without them. The Conseil resolved that since the National Assembly had granted to the municipality as a whole the right to assemble the National Guard, the mayor's action in alone assembling it was illegal. Bailly agreed that the resolution might be right, but since all preparations had already been made, the Conseil decided in a hastily summoned meeting the morning of the review (June 13) to legalize his action by going with him. So off they went to Lafayette's house, where Bailly was expected to stop on his way to the Champ-de-Mars.[54]

Lafayette, they discovered, had already left with his staff. Since it was Sunday, the royal family was coming in from Saint-Cloud, and with a detachment to serve as an escort, he went to meet them at the city gate. As the king, the queen, and their suite drove to the Tuileries, cheers greeted them on every side. Leaving the royal couple at the palace, Lafayette and his men rode back to the Champ-de-Mars to await the mayor, now joined by the Conseil.[55] When Bailly and the municipal officers left their carriages and, escorted by their guard, marched out on the field, Lafayette and his staff joined them. The civil authorities then took their designated places, and Lafayette led his men in review before them. After that, the mayor and the president of the council delivered eulogies of Lafayette and the Guards as "citizens whose efforts and patriotic work so effectively contribute to the safety and the maintenance of public affairs."[56] About five o'clock that afternoon Lafayette ushered the king and his family back to the city gate on their return to Saint-Cloud.[57] Sometime that day he also visited the Faubourg Saint-Marceau, where he received an address promising to cooperate "with all good citizens for the good of the cause" and with his "arrangements for the general welfare."[58]

[54] Lacroix, VI, 38–39 (June 12), 42–45 (June 13).

[55] *Journal général de la cour,* June 14, pp. 598–99.

[56] Lacroix, VI, 44 (June 13).

[57] *Journal général de la cour,* June 15, p. 607.

[58] *Adresse des habitants du Faubourg St.-Marceau à M. de La Fayette . . . 13 juin 1790.* Cf. Charavay, p. 227 and n. 2.

By now some of the La Rochefoucauld Committee were prepared to propose the abolition of hereditary titles.[59] Noble titles and decorations (except those commemorating the Revolution) had long been mere trifles in Lafayette's estimation,[60] but the initiative in abolishing titles did not come from him. In fact, the intention of those who did take the initiative might have been to embarrass him.[61] He attended the evening session of the National Assembly on June 19 only to support a motion on behalf of the Vainqueurs de la Bastille,[62] who sought a place of honor in the forthcoming anniversary celebration of July 14. Bailly had asked Lafayette to intercede for them,[63] and the Assembly voted them by acclamation a place that perhaps more than befitted their exploits.[64] A group of foreigners likewise petitioned to take part in the celebration— which occasioned speeches on the spread of liberty abroad and on the removal of symbols of conquest at home. Inspired by the prevailing mood, a relatively unknown deputy introduced a proposal that apparently neither the Lameths nor Lafayette expected:[65] "This is the day for the burial of vanity. I ask that all persons be forbidden to take the titles of count, baron, marquis."[66] Before he had finished, Lafayette and Charles de Lameth, both noblemen but now recognized rivals, hastened to the tribune to support his motion.

Lafayette yielded precedence to Lameth. Titles, Lameth remarked briefly, were contrary to the equality that formed the basis of the constitution and as feudal survivals should be abolished. Lafayette's speech was briefer still: "I hope there is no need here to quarrel over the constitution. The motion, which has been pre-

[59] See above, n. 16, and A. Lameth, II, 445–46.

[60] See Gottschalk and Maddox, p. 200. Buchez and Roux (XXIX, 8) quote Brissot as stating at his trial in 1793 that Lafayette had frequently spoken of a republic but did not consider France ready for one.

[61] See below, pp. 424 and nn. 71, 72, 430 and n. 88. Cf. *Mémoires*, IV, 153–54.

[62] *Mémoires*, IV, 153 (written in 1821 or later) says "clercs de la bazoche," but the Basoche had already been technically disbanded; see, however, below pp. 450–51.

[63] Bailly to Lafayette, June 8, Tuetey, I, 39, No. 393; Charavay, pp. 225, 569–70; Lacroix, VI, 238–39 (June 25); and Robiquet, p. 63.

[64] *AP*, XVI, 371 (June 19). For the sequel to this action see below, pp. 460–61.

[65] *Mémoires*, IV, 153 (correcting the account in the 1821 edition of Ferrières, II, 70–71).

[66] Speech of Joseph-Marie Lambel, *AP*, XVI, 374.

sented to you and which M. Lameth supports is so necessary a consequence of the constitution that it cannot create the slightest difficulty; I merely wish to join in it with all my heart." Foucault protested that titles of nobility were desirable as rewards for public service: a deserving man could be honored by making him "a noble and a count for saving the state on a given occasion." Lafayette answered that in such a case it would suffice to indicate simply that such a one "had saved the state on such and such an occasion"; it seemed to him "that words like these have something of that American character, precious fruit of the New World which ought to help a great deal in the rejuvenation of the Old."

The debate that ensued was essentially one between the Right and the Left. Goupil de Préfeln moved the abolition of all titles except for the brothers of the king and the princes of the blood. That exception was too much for Lafayette. To honor the king's relatives, such as Provence, Artois, and Orléans, in preference to men who had labored for the state as ministers, magistrates, or soldiers seemed inconsistent with his concept of a citizen-king. For the third time, he spoke up: "No one is more convinced than I of the need to give great éclat and great strength to the great hereditary office held by the king, but in a free country there can be only citizens and public officers. I cannot conceive on what ground distinctions and titles, which henceforth ought to appertain only to functions and to offices, would be accorded to the brothers of the king and the princes of the blood, who are not born public functionaries and officials. If they have otherwise fulfilled the conditions required by law, they will be active citizens, and that is all they can be."[67]

That did not end the debate. At one point a speaker reminded the Assembly that it had agreed not to decide constitutional issues in its night sessions. Lafayette then addressed his colleagues for the fourth time: "After several observations, we shall all be in agree-

---

[67] We follow the accounts in *Mémoires*, II, 408 (which quoted almost verbatim *Journal de Paris*, June 21, pp. 693–95), and IV, 153–54. *Point du jour*, June 21, pp. 135–36, and *Courrier de Provence*, June 18–21, pp. 60–61, give a largely similar account. The text in the *Moniteur*, June 21, pp. 702–3, quoted in *AP*, XVI, 374, is shorter but similar. The *Gazette de Leide's* version (June 29) differs incredibly from the others.

ment. We are not concerned with a new constitutional article but a regulatory decree resulting from the constitution. We do not want to waste the morning sessions, reserved for the constitution, on such subjects, but we are here engaged only in making a necessary deduction from it." His purpose obviously was to bring the proposal to a vote, but his contention that the abolition of titles was a mere corollary of certain constitutional articles already enacted shocked those who set greater store by their social privileges than he, and the debate went on. After additional egalitarian demands from the Left and heated opposition from the Right the Assembly closed debate and voted. The outcome was a decree that hereditary nobility was forever abolished, all titles forbidden (only real family names to be used thenceforth), and all display of liveries and coats of arms prohibited—in Paris by July 14 and in the provinces within three months. Applause drowned out the voices of several who still sought to protest.

The Revolution was now over a year old, and anniversary commemorations were in order. In a tennis court in Versailles on June 20, 1789, the self-styled National Assembly had sworn not to separate until it had drawn up a constitution. Recently a group of citizens, calling themselves the Society of the Tennis Court, had requested Lafayette's permission to go to Versailles "in order to renew their oath of liberty, fraternity, and loyalty to the law in that very tennis court sanctified by the memorable oath taken by the National Assembly." They now had come to the National Assembly to exhibit a bronze plaque which they proposed to place as a marker in that sanctified tennis court. The president thanked them, and the meeting adjourned, amid applause and shouts of joy.[68] When Lafayette walked out of the Manège, no longer a marquis but merely Monsieur du Motier, he was triumphant; other deputies left clutching the hope that Louis XVI would veto the Assembly's bold decree.

The Paris journals responded to the National Assembly's action

---

[68] Facsimile of the request of the Societé du Jeu de Paume to Lafayette [June], in Castaing's catalogue of Nov. 22, 1968, No. 155; *AP*, XVI, 378; *Mémoires*, IV, 154; and Brissot, I, 200–201. See also *Details des circonstances relatives à l'inauguration du monument placé le 20 juin 1790 dans le Jeu de Paume à Versailles*.

in accordance with their political affiliations. In the popular press Lafayette had to share the limelight with Charles de Lameth.[69] The *Révolutions de Paris* divided the credit among several deputies including those two.[70] Marat's approval was moderate; he could understand the Lameths' support of the measure but thought Lafayette's action "very strange." He was joined by others who seemed to imagine that, counting upon Lafayette as a rich, powerful noble to vote against the proposal, the Lameth faction had deliberately sprung it on him with the intention of exposing what they presumed to be his fundamentally aristocratic prejudices.[71] The conservative *Gazette de Paris,* naming the supporters of the measure, added in parentheses after his name "Tu quoque, Brute!" but the *Ami du roi* praised him for understanding that "to be the object of the admiration of the universe as of the love of his fellow citizens, he did not need the splendor of his ancestors."[72]

Mirabeau had been absent from the Assembly that evening. The next morning, before he or La Marck had learned what had happened, La Marck still felt that Lafayette had revealed in a recent conversation a hesitantly friendly attitude toward Mirabeau,[73] and they apparently believed that they might yet win him over entirely. But their good will vanished when Mirabeau thought he saw in the decree of June 19 a good chance to profit at Lafayette's expense. In a note to the queen he condemned the decree with unconcealed vehemence: The "madness" in the National Assembly, in which Lafayette had been "either stupidly or treacherously but wholly an accomplice," would be "the firebrand of civil war." In his opinion the decree was "still more insane because of the way it was passed than because of its provisions." He had enough evidence, he asserted, to show that Lafayette was "equally ambitious and incapa-

---

[69] In addition to the papers cited below, see *Journal de Paris,* June 21, p. 692; *Courier national,* June 21, p. 1; *Courrier de Provence,* June 18–21, pp. 55–57; and *Courier français,* June 21, p. 408.

[70] No. 50, June 26–July 3, p. 715.

[71] *Ami du peuple,* June 23, p. 7. For those who came to share Marat's opinion see Charavay (ed.), *Mémoires de Paroy,* pp. 180–87; Bertrand de Moleville, III, 192; and *Argus patriote,* Oct. 22, 1791, pp. 339–40.

[72] *Gazette de Paris,* June 23, p. 2, and *Ami du roi,* No. 21, p. 83.

[73] La Marck to Mirabeau, June 20, Bacourt (ed.), II, 36–37.

ble" and aspired to be generalissimo and dictator: "His whole purpose, for the present, is that. A plan he has not. His means he takes wherever and whenever he can. His policy is exclusively to raise such a fuss among neighbors that they will leave him free to spread the influence of his little tea-garden throughout the kingdom. He has no qualification for that level of affairs but the imbecility of his character, the timidity of his soul, and the short dimensions of his head."

The king, Mirabeau continued, had "only one man" about him, and that one was the queen, who "would not want to live without her crown but, I am certain, will not stay alive if she does not keep her crown." She must speak to Lafayette in the presence of the king, who must be "prepared and resolute," and Mirabeau wrote out what the king should say: Lafayette's duties absorbed all his faculties, time, and strength; he must look for assistance from others than his henchmen ("and your henchmen are feeble"); "Mirabeau is the only statesman in the country, . . . no one has his make-up, his courage and his character," and "for him to be on our side, we must be on his." Hence the queen must demand that Lafayette work with Mirabeau openly and fully in everything, and the king must bind himself to follow their joint advice. If Lafayette would enter into such a relationship, then Mirabeau undertook "to regulate, modify, and perhaps circumscribe Lafayette's influence during the coming Federation," to lead the National Assembly through the crisis of imminent war, to build up a public opinion favorable to monarchy in the provinces, to increase his own influence in the National Guard, and to participate in the direction of foreign affairs "without compromising anything or anybody." Although the friends of Lafayette would at first find it hard to cooperate with him, Mirabeau conceded, eventually he would get control of the press and, once he was accepted by both sides, he would be able "to consult, to investigate, to advise, to dictate," while keeping closely in touch with the throne.[74]

In effect, Mirabeau was saying: "Make me a crypto-dictator so as to avoid Lafayette's becoming an openly recognized dictator."

[74] Mirabeau to the court, June 20, *ibid.*, pp. 38–44. See also *ibid.*, I, 174.

Perhaps he was consciously only trying to say that if given sufficient power, he could save the monarchy, which he thought Lafayette was perhaps unintentionally but certainly undermining. But was Lafayette as unaware of the realities as Mirabeau thought or pretended to think? Was the monarchy at this point in fact being undermined? Over two years later, to be sure, Mirabeau proved right, since the queen did not hold on to her crown and did lose her life, but that was hardly because what Lafayette was doing now was unstatesmanlike but rather because the royal family, contrary to his advice, attempted to countermand the Revolution. In fact, at this point the king was as popular as he had ever been, and the queen more than she had ever been, and for the time being, they were neither so trustful of Mirabeau nor so distrustful of Lafayette as the former hoped. Nor was it likely, if they had been, that they could have carried off the program he urged. Lafayette was still the man of the hour.

Mirabeau was not alone in expecting violent opposition to the decree abolishing titles of nobility. On the morning after its passage Short witnessed at court "a degree of fermentation produced by this decree among the foreign ministers and courtiers little short of a mob."[75] Some of Lafayette's friends too thought that abolishing armorial bearings and liveries was likely to cause private bitterness and was, in any case, an interference with personal liberty. Induced by this argument, some members of the Constitution Committee contemplated revising the bill and asked Lafayette to request the keeper of the royal seals to delay the king's sanction long enough to allow time for a new proposal. Lafayette promised to do so. He now remembered that he had seen family emblems used freely in America without in any way detracting from the spirit of equality.[76]

Several days went by, however, before the pressure of other affairs permitted him to keep his promise. On top of all his activity as a military and a municipal officer, he was kept busier than was usual as a deputy. On June 22 the Ecclesiastical Committee sub-

[75] Short to Morris, June 20 Davenport (ed.), I, 546 n. Cf. the reaction of Mallet du Pan: letter to Mounier, June 24, Irisson d'Herisson, pp. 114-15.

[76] *Mémoires*, II, 410, 473-74 n., IV, 154, 204.

mitted a schedule of salaries to be paid by the state to the various
ranks of the now nationalized clergy, but Thouret had proposed
a higher schedule. Lafayette was not a religious man, but he was
tolerant and generous, and Adrienne was devout. Hence, when
the subject was debated on June 23, he spoke in favor of the higher
schedule. He went to the tribune only after other deputies had
aroused mutual resentments in a lengthy debate, and only, he said,
to hasten a decision. So far as he could see, a single genuine difficulty remained—to pay churchmen enough to enable them to meet
their needs. For that purpose he favored Thouret's plan. The Left,
however, prolonged the discussion, condemning the higher schedule as more favorable to opulent than to poor clerics, and after
further debate, the Assembly adopted the committee's schedule
rather than Thouret's. Though not a major defeat, this vote was a
setback for Lafayette, since it enabled some of his detractors to picture him as a friend of the rich.[77]

Mirabeau took no part in the debate on the salaries of the clergy,
but the general impression prevailed that he and Lafayette were
still working in harness.[78] They soon definitely parted company
again, however, over the honor of being president of the National
Assembly when the Federation was celebrated. Since a new president was chosen every two weeks, the deputy who would have that
title on July 14 would be the one who was to be chosen on July
5, and electioneering began in June. Mirabeau had decided that he
wanted to be elected, but Talleyrand had the same ambition, and
so did Cazalès and others. Mirabeau anticipated that the Federation would bring on "a great fermentation"[79] and might very well
create a civil crisis that would show up "the ineffectual swaggerer,"[80] Lafayette, whose popularity might then collapse; and if that
were to happen, the president of the National Assembly might well
replace him in public esteem.

[77] Desmoulins, *Révolutions,* pp. 346–47, and Robespierre, *Oeuvres,* VI, 428. For details
of the debate see *AP,* XVI, 407–8, 412–13, 446, and Short to Jefferson, June 25, Boyd (ed.),
XVI, 573.

[78] Lescure (ed.), II, 452 (June 12).

[79] "Troisième note du comte de Mirabeau pour la cour," June 23, Bacourt (ed.), II,
46.

[80] Mirabeau to La Marck, June 25, *ibid.,* p. 52.

On June 24 Mirabeau attended a meeting of the La Rochefoucauld Committee, and the question of the next Assembly president
came up. All present agreed that Mirabeau deserved to be president
someday—not, however, for the Fourteenth, as he wished, but for
a term after that. Mirabeau refused to consider this consolation
prize. Lafayette took aside another member of the committee,
Frochot, and, as Mirabeau learned afterward, expressed his displeasure over the importunity with which Talleyrand was courting
his support, but when Frochot asked why then he opposed Mirabeau, Lafayette replied (in words that Mirabeau must have learned
from Frochot but considered an exact quotation): "I have over-
come the king of England in his power, the king of France in his
authority, the people in its fury; certainly I shall not yield to M.
de Mirabeau." Whether or not, in a bit of bad humor or priggish-
ness, Lafayette actually made that histrionic comment, Mirabeau
believed he had, and when he told La Marck about it, he was furious: "Believe me, my dear Count, sooner or later he will pay for
those words, which reveal . . . his pettiness and . . . his vanity."[81]

A couple of days later, obviously unaware that Lafayette and
Mirabeau had reached a definite rift, some of their mutual friends
tried to push Mirabeau's cause upon Lafayette. Ségur, whom both
Mirabeau and La Marck had been busily cultivating of late because they thought he had influence at court, and Lacoste, whom
Lafayette consistently regarded as a friend, urged him to form an
alliance with Mirabeau and let it be known publicly. But in La
Marck's account of the episode to Mirabeau (probably at third
hand), Lafayette "behaved very badly toward you." La Marck was
thus led to wonder whether a deliberate effort should not be made
to turn the Fourteenth into a fiasco or a disaster: "Combustible ma-
terial is piling up day by day," he confided to his fellow-conspirator,
"and how believe that it will not encounter some spark or other?
What is more, by stating that the affair of the Fourteenth is dangerous, one increases the chances and occasions of danger. Is it or is it
not necessary to preserve the glory of the ineffectual swaggerer?

---

[81] June 26, *ibid.*, p. 54. See also *ibid.*, I, 154. Charavay (*Lafayette*, p. 228, n. 4) con-
siders at least the wording of the remark attributed to Lafayette doubtful; it was not in
Lafayette's usual style. Cf. *Mémoires*, II, 365.

In that you know my preference."[82] To which Mirabeau replied:
"What is said about the dangers of the Fourteenth can never re-
dound to Lafayette's glory, for if he is maladroit enough to gamble
on their probability (and this is possible; he is up to hoping for a
popular commotion in order to show his almightiness), he will
not put out the fire without burning his imprudent hand."[83]

Later that day, Mirabeau tried to make a deal at his brother's
house with Cazalès, who favored a scheme for fusing their follow-
ings alternately behind them, but Mirabeau found that scheme
impractical since he considered himself the only logical candidate.
On his way home he met Lafayette and Talleyrand talking together, but apparently that encounter did not discourage him, for
he still hoped that Cazalès might withdraw in his favor.[84]

Only on June 25 did Lafayette find the time to keep his promise
to the Constitution Committee to try to get a delay in the king's
sanction of the decree regarding the nobility. On that day he went
to see Necker and Montmorin first and then Champion de Cicé. He
apparently advised them to use the bill as a good opportunity to
exercise the royal veto power,[85] but he found out from them, if he
did not already know, that the king's council had decided that
Louis XVI should promptly approve the bill. Lafayette was led
to believe that the reason for this haste was counterrevolutionary:
the bill was considered so extreme that, it was hoped, it would
crystallize the nobles' opposition to the Assembly. Champion de
Cicé, without hiding his own adverse views, recommended that
Lafayette appeal directly to Louis XVI, and Lafayette did so by
letter. He himself, he informed His Majesty, had given the three
ministers some fresh information about the resolution of June 19
and they thought it desirable that the king reconsider his decision;
therefore he begged Louis to delay announcing his sanction to
the Assembly until after His Majesty had talked about it with
Montmorin.[86]

[82] La Marck to Mirabeau, June 26, Bacourt (ed.), II, 53.

[83] Mirabeau to La Marck, *ibid.*, pp. 54–55.

[84] Mirabeau to La Marck, June 26 (a later letter), *ibid.*, pp. 59–60.

[85] See below, n. 88, and Bertrand de Moleville, IV, 192.

[86] Lafayette to Louis XVI, June 25, *Mémoires*, II, 471–72. See also *ibid.*, pp. 410,

The king soon made clear to Lafayette that he had no intention of vetoing the disputed measure, but he took the trouble to write to inquire confidentially why Lafayette wanted it delayed.[87] In reply Lafayette admitted that the members of the Assembly, beginning with himself, had been at fault, for they should have asked for a more reasonable bill; he was now endeavoring to repair the damage by pleading that the king grasp this opportunity to use his veto power to advantage: a bill considered very popular might be amended as a result of the king's criticism—to the still greater satisfaction of the public. If enough time thus were granted, Lafayette now promised to try to secure the passage of an explanatory decree that would stave off rigorous application of the law. For that reason, he requested that the keeper of the seals hold up communication of the royal sanction to the Assembly until late in the session. In language that hardly befitted a "republican," still less a "would-be dictator," Lafayette closed his letter with an expression of his "keen appreciation of the confidence His Majesty had deigned" to show him and of the justice the king had rendered to his sentiments: "I am devoted to him to my last breath by gratitude and the most profound attachment."

The king was not persuaded, and in later years Lafayette came to believe that he had been tricked, that Louis XVI had disguised his real purpose in honoring him with a quasi-confidential correspondence. Hindsight led him to conclude that his own letter of explanation actually had hastened the sending of the royal sanction to the Assembly. Moreover (though perhaps he was too cynical here) he suspected that the king kept his letter of explanation only in order to compromise him if the occasion should arise.[88] At any rate, the bill on titles, emblems, and liveries re-

---

472–73 n. The original of Lafayette's letter is in AN: C184, Dr. 117, f. 66. The editor of the *Mémoires* says (II, 471) that the letter was dated by the king, but it is also dated in Lafayette's hand "Paris Ce 25."

[87] The king's letter is not available; its content is inferred from Lafayette's reply: see below, n. 88.

[88] Lafayette to Louis XVI, June 27, *Mémoires*, II, 473–74, and *AP*, LIV, 491–92, LV, 687. According to a note by Lafayette written long afterward, this letter, which was found in the *armoire de fer* (AN: C184, Dr. 117, f. 54), might have been subjected to some alteration, since its form, he then thought, was not that which his other letters followed

mained the law, no royal veto or legislative revision modifying it
essentially until the Napoleonic Empire. Few, however, dropped
the famous name Lafayette for the practically unknown family
name of Motier.

All this time Lafayette's young cousin, Comte de Bouillé, had
remained in Paris, trying to act as intermediary between the royal
entourage and the commandant general,[89] and he saw the commandant general frequently. Perhaps the young man was one of
the several aristocrats who glamorized their role as confidants of
the king, but he believed that he really enjoyed the court's confidence and was charged to make Lafayette most brilliant offers. He
acknowledged, however, that Lafayette was not impressed, having
already refused several offers such as a marshal's baton and even
the office of constable. Whether or not young Bouillé had been
commissioned by the court to make these flattering offers, Lafayette, while always courteous to his cousin, repeated that his purpose
was to see the Assembly finish the constitution and then to retire.[90]

When after almost two months the Comte de Bouillé decided
to return to his father's headquarters, Lafayette sent along with him
a brief note explaining why he could not sent a lengthier one. Only
that morning (June 26), he complained, he had had to deal with
five or six disturbances that had been deliberately fomented in order to break the peace and make the forthcoming Federation of
July 14 "an occasion for a fuss." The unrest in the realm, he con-
jectured, had been created either by the enemies of the Revolution
(meaning the aristocrats) or by the Orleanist party, but there was
reason to believe that they would be of no consequence, for the
celebration of July 14, although it might prove a little risky, would
turn out well: "*Constitution and public order* ought to be the rallying cry of all good citizens," and the Federation would present "a
beautiful opportunity to put that slogan across." He expected his

(but he did not deny its substance): *Mémoires,* II, 473–74 n. There is no indication on
the original that the text has been tampered with though subsequent investigators have
put additional (and easily distinguishable) marks on it. Vaudreuil (Pingaud [ed.], I, 239)
also suspected ulterior motives for the king's rapid sanction.

[89] Maleissye, pp. 205–6.

[90] Louis de Bouillé, pp. 124–25. Cf. Maleissye, pp. 205–6.

own followers in the end to prove stronger than "those who torment us."[91]

By this time Lafayette thoroughly distrusted Mirabeau, and if he did not yet know that Mirabeau was conspiring with the queen against him, he was one day to find out.[92] Of Bouillé's part in that conspiracy he still suspected nothing, and he closed his letter with a pledge of "a confidence and a friendship that will last all my life."[93] Eventually, when he learned that Bouillé too was an enemy, he nevertheless regarded him as "an enemy more loyal" than some of the others.[94] But at this stage he had small reason to fear any enemies, loyal or disloyal, though he himself was feared by them. "Everything goes from bad to worse," the queen lamented. "The ministry and M. de la F[ayette] take wrong measures every day. We anticipate them in everything, and far from pleasing these monsters, they become more insolent every minute, and in the eyes of decent people we degrade ourselves proportionately. I am in despair."[95] So she lent her ear to Mirabeau rather than to Lafayette.

BIBLIOGRAPHICAL NOTES

The manuscript of Theodore de Lameth on which Eugène Welvert's edition of Theodore de Lameth's *Mémoires* (Paris, 1913) is based is now in the Bibliothèque Nationale (NAF 1388). It states (fols. 198–99) that Baron d'André (later know as Dandré) was the chief agent through whom the Lafayette partisans worked to oppose the Lameth partisans. For this period at least we have found no evidence of such an agency.

Loménie (V, 153 n.) says that about June 1 the relations of Lafayette and Mirabeau were complicated by *une rivalité d'amour . . . auprès de Mme de Condorcet*. Loménie gives no evidence for this statement, and we have found none other than an assertion that Lafayette was the *amant de Madame de Condorcet* (p. 11, n. 3) in a rhymed pamphlet entitled *Entrevue de Messieurs le duc d'Orléans avec le marquis de La Fayette* [Paris, 1790], but that assertion seems very insubstantial.

Among a large number of anecdotes of the kind that seems *ben trovato*

[91] Lafayette to Bouillé, June 26, *Mémoires,* II, 472–73. Bouillé wrote Lafayette letters on Mar. 14, June 3, and June 24 (all mentioning the uneasy situation in Metz), to which Lafayette seems not to have replied: CU: Lafayette Archives, Carton V.

[92] Lafayette to [Mme de Simiane?], [early in 1816], *Mémoires,* VI, 9–10.

[93] *Ibid.,* II, 473.

[94] *Ibid.,* p. 421 n. See also *ibid.,* IV, 98–117.

[95] Marie Antoinette to Mercy, June 12, Maxime de La Rocheterie and Marquis de Beaucourt (eds.), *Lettres de Marie-Antoinette* (Paris, 1896), II, 178.

to show either the brutal but shrewd frankness of Mirabeau or the naïve but gentlemanly delicacy of Lafayette several are narrated in Francis Bickley (ed.), *The Diaries of Sylvester Douglas (Lord Glenbervie)* (London, 1928), I, 288. They are not implausible, but as tales told a decade or more after the events by a French contemporary who possibly was not a direct witness and recorded subsequently from memory by an English diarist they are suspect.

One of the fullest studies, though unfortunately not complete, of the hostility to Lafayette of Marat and his supporters is contained in Albert Mathiez, *Le Club des Cordeliers pendant la crise de Varennes et le massacre du Champ de Mars* (Paris, 1910): see especially pp. 2, 8, and 24–30.

Lacroix gives a detailed account of the Féral affair (VI, 282–98).

The spurious *Mémoires de Condorcet* contains (II, 76–77) a story to the effect that Marie Antoinette expressed a preference for the choice of Le Peletier de Saint-Fargeau as a candidate for president of the National Assembly during the Federation and Lafayette differed with her. The story probably is fiction, but it reflects Lafayette's satisfaction with the eventual choice.

Gilbert Chinard, *L'Apothéose de Benjamin Franklin* (Paris, 1955) gives a detailed account of the ceremonies in France in honor of the deceased sage.

CHAPTER XVIII

Commandant General of the Realm?

THE PRIDE of his native province, Auvergne, in Lafayette could easily be anticipated; after all he was a local boy who had made good. It was typified in a petition to the National Assembly from the municipality of Saint-Julien-de-Fix, when the old provinces of France were reorganized into the new subdivisions called departments; the municipality begged to be allowed to remain in the canton of Paulhaguet, where Lafayette's Château de Chavaniac was located, because they wished "never to separate themselves from him."[1] Likewise a report had it that Lafayette had asked to be admitted as a simple fusilier in the National Guard at Riom, whence he had gone to Versailles as a deputy of the Nobility to the Estates General in the dim days of 1789, but at almost the same time that Passy (near Paris) was doing much the same,[2] the Riom Guard proclaimed him general instead, crowned his bust, and carried it in triumph in a military parade.

Less easily anticipated was the zeal that towns in other provinces all over the country exhibited to associate with Lafayette. The practice of "federations"—meetings of deputations from two or more National Guard units to promote solidarity among friends of the Revolution—which had begun in the latter months of 1789, had consistently gained ground. Frequently these meetings led to patriotic addresses, communicated sometimes to the National Assembly, sometimes to the king, but nearly always to Lafayette as well. A "federation" in February of the National Guard of Romans in Dauphiny sent such an address to the king and the Na-

[1] March 21, quoted in Louis de Romeuf, *Au pays de Lafayette* (Paris, 1921).

[2] *Annales patriotiques et littéraires*, Apr. 11, p. 3, and *Révolutions de Paris*, No. 49, June 12–19, p. 600.

tional Assembly which described Lafayette "as the best as well as the most illustrious citizen."[3] A delegation from two towns in the Department of Yonne appeared early in April before the Assembly of Representatives and declared that the success of the Assembly's work for liberty could not be doubted under the leadership of Bailly and the "generous warrior who in two hemispheres has defended the rights of the people and assured their liberty and now commands an army of patriots, ever ready to repel the enemies of the public welfare."[4]

By that time federations of contiguous communities were so common throughout the realm that the idea of a nationwide federation suggested itself. On March 20 a deputation from the National Guards of Brittany and of Anjou read to the National Assembly a "pacte fédératif" drawn up by young citizens of the two "ci-devant provinces" who had met at Pontivy. They bound themselves, the "pacte" announced, in a "holy fraternity" to defend the constitution, the laws of the National Assembly, and the "legitimate authority" of the king. They solemnly declared: "Being no longer Bretons or Angevins but French and citizens of the same empire, we renounce all our local and private privileges as unconstitutional," and they appealed to all Frenchmen to adhere to this federative pact. Deeply touched, the deputies ordered enough copies of the pact for each of them to send four to his constituents.[5] The response of the Paris press was enthusiastic,[6] and the Assembly of Representatives agreed not merely to adhere to the pact but also to invite all the districts of Paris to do likewise.[7]

Some of the Paris districts needed no such prompting. As far back as November, the District des Récollets had sent to Lafayette and the fifty-nine other districts a resolution proposing that all the National Guards of the realm be invited to enter a fraternal pact in

---

[3] Baron de Gillier to Lafayette, Mar. 30, *Journal des Impartiaux*, No. 15, [*ca.* Apr. 10], p. 24.

[4] Lacroix, IV, 587 (Apr. 1).

[5] *AP*, XII, 264–65 (Mar. 20).

[6] *Journal de Paris*, Mar. 22, p. 321; *Moniteur*, Mar. 22, p. 331; *Courier national*, Mar. 22, pp. 1–2; *Point du jour*, Mar. 22, p. 106; and *Courier français*, Mar. 22, pp. 169–70.

[7] Lacroix, IV, 484–88 (Mar. 22).

support of the Revolution. At that time the proposal had elicited no response, but now, the example set by Anjou and Brittany proved contagious. Enthusiasm for federation spread with amazing speed through the sometimes lumbering district assemblies,[8] and requests for affiliation with the Paris National Guard continued to come in from outlying communities.[9] The district assembly of the Jacobins-Saint-Honoré, while adhering to the Angevin-Breton pact, passed a resolution which was considerably more far-reaching. It petitioned the Commune and the Paris National Guard to invite the municipalities and the National Guard units within a day's journey of the capital to join in a pact that should be part of an ultimately nationwide confederation. Copies of this resolution went to the mayor, the Assembly of Representatives, the other districts of Paris, and Lafayette.[10]

On April 16 the Military Committee of the Commune caught the enthusiasm. It unanimously resolved to ask the districts to co-operate in inviting the eighty-three departments to join in a national federation which "in the name of all the National Guards of the realm" and "under the eyes of the august National Assembly" would "take the most solemn oath to support to the last drop of their blood" the decrees sanctioned by the king. Before dispatching the address to the districts, the Military Committee sent a deputation to its president, Lafayette (for he was generally too busy elsewhere to attend their meetings), to get his approval.

Lafayette was not so enthusiastic as the committee might have expected. Although he was pleased with the new evidence of the committee's zeal in support of the constitution and the National Guards throughout the realm, he feared, for one thing, that the expense of sending deputies might be embarrassing to some of the more remote provinces. He was primarily concerned, however, lest the celebration be premature; it might be better to postpone a national pledge of support until there should be a finished constitution for the National Guard to support. Recognizing, however,

---

[8] *Ibid.*, pp. 268–78 (Nov. 17), 589 (Apr. 1), 599 (Apr. 3), 647 (Apr. 9), 673, 674 (Apr. 12), 715 (Apr. 14), and V, 2 (Apr. 15), 82 (Apr. 20), 113 (Apr. 22).

[9] *Ibid.*, IV, 622–23 (Apr. 7).

[10] *Ibid.*, V, 113–14 (Apr. 22).

that the committee's proposal would unite the National Guards in an impressive display of solidarity, he thought such a pledge might be useful at some future time, and so he advised the deputation to hold it in abeyance while he looked for an appropriate occasion.[11]

Nevertheless, throughout April and May news of additional fraternal gestures in the provinces continued to whet the enthusiasm of Paris. The National Guards of over eighty communities joined in a federative pact at Poitiers, and soon over one hundred others concurred.[12] The National Guard of Marseilles published a patriotic missive and sent it to Lafayette. A deputation from the National Guard of Troyes, declaring that their city would feel honored to join its flags with those of Paris "under the orders of a general whose destiny it is . . . to make liberty triumphant in two worlds," asked for an "alliance of fraternity," and the Paris Assembly of Representatives unanimously accepted the proffered affiliation.[13] Sent to participate in a federation held at Orléans on May 9, forty Paris Guardsmen joined comrades from four provinces in taking an oath before a huge outdoor altar, and they brought a burst of applause when they promised a gift of a marble bust of Lafayette;[14] a deputation from this Orléans assembly assured the Paris Assembly of Representatives of its confidence in Lafayette as one who for fifteen years had worked nobly to defend liberty and to counteract its enemies.[15] The town of Sézanne-en-Brie won particular approval from the Paris Representatives by denouncing the "pernicious advice, writings, plots, or protestations" of "enemies of the nation" and pleading for the good order that the municipality and the commander of Paris approved.[16] The National Guard officers of Hennebon in Brittany, having heard of "the Maillebois conspiracy," promised to bring help to "brave General Lafayette," although Hennebon was more than one hundred

---

[11] *Procès-verbal du Comité militaire*, Part II, pp. 63–67 (Apr. 16–19).

[12] *AP*, XV, 457–59 (May 10).

[13] Lacroix, V, 194–96 (Apr. 30).

[14] *Ibid.*, pp. 193–94 (Apr. 30), 364, 374–75 (May 14).

[15] *Ibid.*, p. 512 (May 22).

[16] *Ibid.*, pp. 216–18, 225–36 (May 3).

leagues distant.[17] At Limoges an ardent citizen proposed that "the Limousin patriotic army" elect Lafayette "commander in chief."[18] The National Guard of Cherbourg swore at the first call to unite with their "dear comrades" in the capital "under the orders of a hero" in guarding the king and the National Assembly; this pledge was signed also by the noncommissioned officers of the royal garrison at Cherbourg.[19] The Commune of Saint-Malo avowed to the National Assembly its devotion to it, the king, the Paris Commune, and Lafayette.[20] The commander of the National Guard of Narbonne sought affiliation for his unit with "those generous soldiers, intrepid and worthy of the brave chief who commands them, of that warrior without fear and without reproach, the hero of America, the shield and the honor of the French empire."[21] The community of Château-Renard (Provence), repudiating the intolerance of some Catholics at Nîmes, announced its devotion to the National Assembly, the king, the Commune of Paris, and Lafayette.[22] When an aristocratic faction in Briançon (Hautes Alpes) attempted to choose for command of its National Guard an enemy of the Revolution, the inhabitants indignantly demanded that the command be given to Lafayette instead.[23] The province of Poitou, "federating" at Fougère, addressed Lafayette as a "hero-legislator."[24] At Lyons tens of thousands of *fédérés,* claiming to represent half a million, sent a letter to "the noble soldier who gave his early years to the defense of a foreign people in order to prepare himself someday to promote that of his own country."[25] A federation for

[17] Desmoulins, *Révolutions*, No. 22, pp. 412–13.

[18] *Courrier de Paris*, May 3, p. 436.

[19] *Supplément au Journal de Paris*, No. 130, p. 2. Numbers of the *Supplément au Journal de Paris* by 1790 had ceased to correspond with those of the *Journal de Paris:* see Louis Gottschalk, "Problems of Textual Criticism," in R. E. Stevens (ed.), *Research Methods in Librarianship* . . . (Urbana, 1971), pp. 91–92.

[20] *Point du jour*, May 24, p. 183.

[21] Lacroix, V, 431 (May 19).

[22] *AP*, XV, 627 (May 20).

[23] *Annales patriotique et littéraires*, May 21, p. 4.

[24] Émile Gabory, *La Révolution et la Vendée* (Paris, 1925), I, 45, and C.-L. Chassin, *La préparation de la guerre de Vendée, 1789–1793* (Paris, 1892), I, 129.

[25] *Adresse et serment fédératif prêté dans la ville de Lyon à l'Assemblée nationale, et lettre de la fédération à M. de la Fayette* (May 30: Chez Brebion, imprimeur du Roi et de la Ville). See also Albert Metzger, *Lyon en 1789–1795* (Lyons, 1882–87), pp. 115–28.

Burgundy at Dijon did much the same.[26] And Lafayette, nothing loath to indulge his now studiously controlled "canine appetite for popularity and fame,"[27] answered some of these addresses with appropriate words of appreciation.[28]

The zeal of the National Guards of the provinces for local federations and for affiliation with Paris made the Paris districts increasingly eager for a national federation. On May 1 the District of the Mathurins resolved (and three others quickly agreed) that the sixty districts of Paris should invite every department of the realm to send a deputy to join in "a general federative pact."[29] Some private individuals as well as district assemblies envisaged a grand fete at which representatives of the National Guards and the regiments of the royal army would take the civic oath. All agreed upon some date in July commemorating the fall of the Bastille as the proper time for the fete. A Committee of Representatives for the Federative Pact—two representatives from each of the sixty districts—was quickly created, and it invited Lafayette and Bailly to meet with it—which they did on May 8.

Lafayette again advised postponement of the proposed ceremony. The anniversary of the fall of the Bastille still seemed to him a less fitting occasion for a national oath-taking than some future date when the completed Revolution would have inaugurated a constitutional system whose provisions all Frenchmen would know and could conscientiously pledge to support. Bailly agreed with him. The districts were nevertheless intent upon commemorating the July 1789 uprising and paying tribute to the defenders of liberty, including the commandant general himself. Lafayette was grateful for their desire to do him honor, but, he protested, he had no wish for the glory which, he reminded them, should go not to a man but to liberty and to the constitution. The deputies of the districts, recognizing that Lafayette could not be

---

[26] *Procès-verbal de la Confédération des Gardes nationales des quatres départements formant ci-devant la Province de Bourgogne et pays adjacens, faite sous les murs de Dijon, le 18 mai 1790* in Blancheteau catalogue, p. 62, item 211.

[27] Jefferson to Madison, Jan. 30, 1787, quoted in Gottschalk, *Between*, p. 285.

[28] Cf. Lafayette to M. de Courpon, commandant at Moissac, *ca.* May 26, cited in *Gazette nationale,* June 4, p. 745, and see below, p. 449 and n. 65.

[29] *Annales patriotiques et littéraires,* May 4, p. 2.

persuaded to promote a celebration that could be misrepresented as a device to flaunt his own accomplishments, asserted their understanding of his sensitiveness. So, with apparent agreement on all sides, the meeting adjourned.

A week later, however, the committee insisted upon a July 14 ceremony, and on May 17, undeterred by Lafayette's sensibilities, they proposed that Paris as the residence of the king and the seat of the National Assembly be the center of a general federative pact; the mayor and the commandant general would sign an invitation to all the civil and military bodies of the realm to send representatives to the capital, and every department and municipality, besides, would assemble all its citizens and troops of the line as well as its National Guard in a local ceremony intended to permit them to pledge allegiance to the federative pact at the very moment that in Paris their representatives were pledging theirs.[30]

Lafayette did not formally consent to that arrangement until May 26. On that day he presented to the Assembly of Representatives deputations from the National Guard units of Sens (Yonne), Brive (Corrèze), and Barbonne (Marne), each of which delivered an address urging the federation of all National Guard units. That of Brive begged the Representatives to tell Lafayette "of the ardent desire we have of acknowledging him as our general and of being affiliated with the National Guard of which he is the chief and the idol," and the president replied that the Representatives were always grateful to receive requests for affiliation from the National Guards of other cities. Then the Assembly passed a resolution somewhat different from the one that by this time had become customary in granting affiliation—different because Lafayette was present and voted for it: "The General Assembly of the Representatives of the Commune, . . . considering the enormous value of this federation and taking in this union the great interest it inspires, resolves unanimously, in the presence of M. le Commandant General, whom it has the satisfaction to see concur in its decision by his vote, that the proposed affiliation . . . be adopted."[31]

---

[30] Notes in Lacroix, V, 273–78, 721.

[31] *Ibid.*, pp. 528–31 (May 26).

The next day the Committee of Representatives for the Federative Pact held another meeting, at which the proposed invitation, entitled *Address of the Citizens of Paris to All Frenchmen,* was adopted. In it "the assembled citizens of all the districts of Paris" invited their "dear brothers and friends" to come together to promote the firm establishment of the constitution. For, it declared, they were no longer Bretons, Angevins, or Parisians, but Frenchmen, brothers, and regenerators of the empire: "On July 14 we conquered liberty, on July 14 we shall swear to conserve it. On the same day, at the same hour, a general cry, a unanimous cry will echo in all parts of France: 'Long live the nation, the law, and the king.'" The mayor and the commandant general were to sign at the bottom of the *Address* "Bailly, mayor of Paris," and "Lafayette, commandant general of the Paris National Guard."[32] In forty-eight days, it was thus assumed, a formal "national Federation" would take place, Lafayette's compliance apparently being taken for granted.

Obviously the commandant general's duty was now to take such measures as lay within his jurisdiction to make the forthcoming Federation a brilliant success. He had to provide specific arrangements for the attendance of not only the National Guard units but also the troops of the line under his command. But any order regarding the attendance of royal troops had to have the approval of the king and the minister of war. On June 1 the commandant general undertook to consult with Louis XVI about the desirability of such a nationwide demonstration of loyalty. He and the king apparently considered the matter at great length, and when their conversation was over, Lafayette felt authorized to inform the National Assembly of their conclusions. Accordingly, he submitted for the king's approval a draft of the sort of letter that he thought should be sent to the National Assembly. His Majesty was gratified, this draft asserted, with the *fédérés'* devotion to the constitution, respect for law, and attachment to his person; he saw in the forthcoming ceremony not a mere association of the district federations but a veritable rally of all Frenchmen for liberty and general

---

[32] *Ibid.,* pp. 722–23 (June 8), and see below, Bibliographical Notes, p. 461.

prosperity; having already authorized a large number of regiments to take part in local federations, he now intended to authorize all royal forces, wherever they might be stationed, to participate in the proposed national Federation. Such a civic fete, Lafayette's wording ran, was but an anticipation of the day when "your great tasks having ended, the deputies of all France will be able in concert with the king to renew the pledge that the nation and its chief have already taken to the constitution." The draft thus reflected Lafayette's abiding concern that no premature celebration of the success of the Revolution should preclude a pledge by the king as well as the people and their representatives to abide by the constitution when it would at length be completed. But Louis (or his advisers) seemed less concerned about that eventual pledge. They crossed out the words that bound him to it—"with the king" and "and its chief"—and what was left ("the deputies of all France will be able to renew in concert the pledge that the nation has already taken to the constitution") seemed intended to bind the deputies but not the king.[33]

In the end the letter Lafayette proposed was not sent to the National Assembly.[34] Instead, on June 4 Latour du Pin, appeared before the National Assembly and after a detailed description of the deterioration of discipline in the army, stated, in words largely similar to those Lafayette had suggested, that the king had instructed him to send a circular to all the armed forces authorizing every regiment to take part in the forthcoming Federation. The National Assembly thanked His Majesty for permitting his forces to federate with the National Guard and sent the matter of military insubordination to its committees.[35] Lafayette's purpose to bind the king no less than the rest of France to the new constitution when once it reached a final form thus made only small progress.

The public, however, knew nothing of this temporary check, for artists, musicians, and writers continued to glamorize the com-

[33] Draft of letter to the president of the National Assembly, June 1, AN: C184, Dr. 117, pièce 69 (*armoire de fer*).

[34] At least we have found no record of it elsewhere than in the *armoire de fer*.

[35] *AP*, XVI, 96–97 (June 4).

mandant general. New medals engraved with his image were available in bronze for forty sous, in silver for ten livres, and in gold for two hundred livres;[36] Adrienne received as a gift a bust of him engraved on agate;[37] and the grenadiers of the District of the Filles-Saint-Thomas asked his permission to place his likeness on the metal buttons of their uniforms.[38] Portraits of him were widely advertised for sale, and the papers published verses to place below them.[39] Masers de Latude, now basking in the dubious glory of having been a prisoner for thirty-five years in the Bastille, dedicated his *Mémoires* to Lafayette, whose fame in America, he said, had even penetrated the walls of his prison.[40] As musician to the king, Anton Stamitz dedicated six duets for the violin to Lafayette.[41]

Not all the notice the generally adored idol received, to be sure, was favorable. A few journalists' editorials continued to complain —some because a deserving man (in their eyes) had not received a post in the Paris National Guard,[42] others because the personality cult of Lafayette went too far.[43] Some caricatures, pamphlets, poems, epigrams, and editorials attacked him.[44] A caricature that gained particular notoriety showed a candle shaped into a bust of him, below which was the legend "Bon mot of an ambassadress

[36] *Supplément au Journal de Paris*, No. 128, p. 1.

[37] *Moniteur*, Apr. 26, p. 476, Apr. 29, p. 480.

[38] *Ibid.*, June 15, p. 680. See also Lacroix, V, 559 (May 26); addendum, *ibid.*, VI, 778; and Paul Olivier, *Iconographie metallique du général Lafayette . . .* (Paris, 1933), p. 6.

[39] See, for example, Desmoulins, *Révolutions*, No. 23, p. 471, No. 24, p. 512. For other poems composed about this time see [Béranger (ed.)], pp. 281–83; *Couplets faits et chantés le 18 mai 1790 par M. Fardeau; Journal général de la cour*, Jan. 12, p. 96; *Moniteur*, Jan. 29, p. 115; and *Mercure de France*, Feb. 6, p. 37, Mar. 20, pp. 52–53. See also Pierre, *Hymnes et chansons*, pp. 33, 463, 498–99, 503, 551, and Barbier and Vernillat, pp. 66, 76, 78, 81.

[40] *Supplément au Journal de Paris*, No. 148, p. 3; *Mercure de France*, June 26, pp. 129–32; and *Mémoires de Henri Masers de Latude*, ed. M. Thiery (Paris, 1790), I, 6.

[41] *Supplément au Journal de Paris*, No. 148, p. 4.

[42] *Courrier de Paris*, May 27, p. 356. See also Desmoulins, *Révolutions*, No. 26, pp. 606–8.

[43] *Annales patriotiques et littéraires*, May 20, pp. 2–3, June 1, pp. 3–4; *Courrier de Paris*, June 3, p. 469; and *Chronique de Paris*, June 4, p. 650.

[44] See, for example, *Actes des apôtres*, No. 98, pp. 11–12, and *Courrier de Paris*, June 3, pp. 472–73.

[Mme de Staël?]: 'The reputation of the great general resembles a candle which sends out light only among the people and smells bad on going out.' "[45] Another caricature entitled "Two hanged in the moonlight" showed him and Bailly swinging on gallows, with quotations from each of them: "Insurrection is the soundest [*sic*] of duties" under Lafayette, and "Publicity is the people's safeguard" under Bailly.[46] Other caricatures showed Lafayette as a young cock courting a young hen (sometimes supposed to represent the queen, sometimes Mme Bailly).[47] A few letters to newspaper editors adopted a sardonic tone: an "alarmed husband" semi-facetiously complained that Lafayette so entranced the ladies that domestic tranquility was endangered;[48] another contended that the head of the national militia should be plebian and not an aristocrat.[49] Moreover, the number of pro-Orléans, anti-Lafayette pamphlets multiplied during the summer of 1790.[50]

On June 5 the National Assembly turned its attention again to the forthcoming Federation. Bailly as spokesman of a deputation from the Paris Commune read the *Address of the Citizens of Paris to All Frenchmen* and asked the Assembly to determine the number of deputies from the National Guard, the civil personnel, and the troops of the line to be sent from the several departments to participate. He then held up the local federations as excellent precedents, inspiring a feeling of fraternity in all departments of the realm: "We can discern it here in the Parisian army. . . . In observing the composition and the bearing of this corps, which has suddenly grown up among us, we perceive a citizen general commanding a citizen army." He then went further than anyone had so far gone: he proposed a federation of civic bodies as well as National Guards, to take place in the presence of the king and the

[45] Reproduced in Charavay, p. 231. André Blum, *La caricature révolutionnaire* (Paris, n.d.), p. 137, cites two variations of this caricature.

[46] Blum, p. 139.

[47] *Ibid.*, p. 138, and Augustin Challamel, *Histoire-musée de la République française depuis l'assemblée des Notables jusqu'à l'Empire* (Paris, 1842), I, 68.

[48] *Journal général de la cour*, Apr. 6, p. 44. See also [Bérenger (ed.)], pp. 288–89.

[49] *Moniteur*, Apr. 25, p. 468.

[50] See below, pp. 491–93, 500 and n. 75.

National Assembly on July 14. The Assembly gave its approval in principle to the Paris plan and left the more detailed points Bailly had raised for further examination by its Constitution Committee.[51]

The next afternoon (Sunday, June 6), after Lafayette had escorted the king and his retinue to the outskirts of Paris on their return to Saint-Cloud, he went to the meeting of the Constitution Committee.[52] He had reason to suspect that the Paris National Guard wanted to proclaim him generalissimo of all the National Guards of France before the altar of the *patrie* at the Federation; only a few days before, the Battalion of Saint-Gervais had called upon the country's National Guard to form "a holy and new confederation . . . with the hero from whom it is inseparable."[53] In the past he had expressed the opinion that no one except the king should hold the power that such a combined command might bestow, and he made clear that he had no intention of changing his mind now. The committee shared his point of view and asked him to submit a resolution to that effect to the National Assembly the next morning.[54]

The National Assembly's principal business that next morning was the Constitution Committee's report. Talleyrand, as the committee's spokesman, made a brief speech urging that the Federation be solemn and glorious but at the same time not ruinously expensive for the localities that would send deputations. Then he introduced the first articles of the committee's report, proposing that every district send one representative for every two hundred Guardsmen and each regiment of the line one officer, one noncom, and one private. Finally he announced that Lafayette had suggested to the committee a principle which it endorsed, and he asked Lafayette to present it.

[51] *Confédération nationale: Adresse des citoyens de Paris à tous les François* (Paris, 1790), pp. 5–7, and *AP*, XVI, 117–19 (June 5). For a description of *Confédération nationale*, see below, p. 461.

[52] This is clear from Talleyrand's report on June 7: *AP*, XVI, 136, and *Moniteur*, June 8, pp. 649–50. The editors of the *Mémoires* (II, 406 n.) have erroneously placed Talleyrand's report on June 8.

[53] See above, p. 393 and n. 80. See also *Mémoires*, II, 406; *Journal de Paris*, June 8, p. 640; and Short to Paine, June 8, Landin, p. 368.

[54] See n. 52 above.

According to the Fayettist *Journal de Paris,* as Lafayette went to the tribune, a sudden stir followed by a conspicuous silence betrayed the hopes of some, the fears of others, in the National Assembly: "A general confederation of all the National Guards had spread widely among the public the notion of a single commandant general for more than a million citizen soldiers, and everyone knew on whom a great number of the National Guard units, in addition to that of the capital, had conferred the right to command them."[55] Lafayette immediately made clear that he did not share that notion. He began by reminding the National Assembly that their main task was to finish the constitution promptly: "However eager I may be to celebrate the gala days of liberty, and notably July 14 and 15, I would have wished that an epoch-making general confederation were determined less by the desire to commemorate than by the desire to advance our labors, and I do not speak here of regulatory or legislative decrees but of that declaration of rights, of that organization of the social order, of that distribution of the exercise of sovereignty which form the essentials of the constitution." The quest for that constitution, he reminded his listeners, was why Frenchmen had taken up arms and would bind themselves together in a confederation: "Let us, Gentlemen, inspired by the idea of that sacred reunion, show that we can make haste and deposit on the altar of the *patrie* a more complete work." The articles regulating the National Guard would be a part of that work—a part that would assure French liberty forever, and in order to forestall the risk that a commander of the National Guard might use his command for private purposes, Lafayette proceeded to lay down the principle Talleyrand had mentioned: "The National Assembly decrees as a constitutional principle that no one may have command of the National Guard in more than one department, and it reserves the right to decide whether this command should not be limited to a single district"[56] (i.e., to a subdivision of a department).

Hardly had Lafayette finished reading his resolution than ap-

[55] *Journal de Paris,* June 8, p. 640.

[56] Lafayette (*Mémoires,* II, 406–8) quotes the text, with its introduction, from the *Journal de Paris,* June 8, p. 640, but a number of other contemporary journals give essentially the same text.

plause burst forth from floor and galleries, and it kept up for a long time after he left the tribune.[57] The debate on the committee's report carried over to the next day, when Talleyrand's proposals were adopted. An amendment to the effect that a command in the National Guard be restricted in fact to a single district was proposed but was quickly quashed out of consideration that such a restriction would abbreviate Lafayette's own command in the Department of the Seine. His motion was then adopted unchanged.[58]

For some time thereafter the refrain ran in the press that Lafayette had brought honor to himself by his motion. The *Courier national,* eulogizing his "neat gesture of disinterestedness," went on: "Everybody ... applauded that act of modesty, which silenced the mob of the envious and those who dared to suspect him of ambitious views," and it compared him to Washington, "who after having assured liberty to his country returned modestly to the ranks of simple citizens."[59] Even some of "the mob of the envious" reacted favorably to Lafayette's speech.[60] William Short, reporting it to their mutual friend Thomas Paine, had every reason to be candid. He was positive that Lafayette now stood "on more firm ground than ever," for, in addition to the popular party, which was attached to him because of his principles, several of the aristocratic party were "now disposed to enlist under his standard because of the rising power of the faction headed by the Lameths, Barnave, and Duport." According to Short, many now were saying openly "that the whole revolution depends on him; that he himself must make it or that it will fail." To be sure, the American chargé d'affaires observed, those who took that position belonged with the kind of person who feared any political institution "that depends on the many" and consequently were ready for the sake of order to submit to one man, whoever he might be. Lafayette him-

---

[57] The *Mémoires* do not mention the applause that greeted Lafayette's speech, but several other contemporary journals do. See also Lindet to the municipal officers of Bernay, June 9, Montier (ed.), p. 178; Short to Paine, June 8, Landin, pp. 366–68; and *Annales patriotiques et littéraires,* June 30, p. 81.

[58] *Moniteur,* June 9, p. 653.

[59] *Courier national,* June 8, pp. 1, 7.

[60] See, for example, *Courrier de Provence,* June 7–9, pp. 382–83, and Barnave cited in *Chronique de Paris,* June 8, p. 635.

self was not one of that kind, however; instead he had taken full advantage of the opportunity "of showing his moderation and of silencing such of his enemies as accused him of ambitious designs."[61]

All the same, some observers found Lafayette's reasoning faulty. Desmoulins pointed out that barring a citizen from the honor of commanding more than one unit of the National Guards conferred that power exclusively on the king: "It is impossible to take more precautions than this pretended republican has done for a long time to keep us from ever having a republic."[62] Marat cast doubt upon Lafayette's modesty: How could a man who still retained command of 40,000 men and dominated the capital be modest? "Our general has become the arbiter of public liberty; his moderation tends to cement his power, to conserve his empire," and should he ever turn against the *patrie,* the people would have no course but insurrection.[63]

Marat's apprehension that too much power was being concentrated in one man's hands was not without foundation. The idea of federation had advanced to the stage not only where Paris was inviting provincial National Guards to send *fédérés* to the capital but also where provincial National Guards were inviting the Paris National Guard (and that meant Lafayette) to participate in their local reunions. In Alsace-Lorraine pronounced aristocratic hostility to the Revolution made support of the Metz and Strasbourg units especially imperative. In May the Paris National Guard had enthusiastically agreed to send a delegation to a federation in Metz,[64] and in June the Strasbourg unit specifically asked Lafayette himself to attend theirs. He felt that he could not leave Paris, but he sent an officer named Chaumont with a letter of friendship and encouragement. It explained that the service which he and his troops had to perform and the continual plots that they had to counteract required them to forgo the pleasure of attending federations in different parts of the kingdom. Yet he would have

---

[61] Short to Paine, June 8, Landin, pp. 366–68.

[62] *Révolutions,* No. 29, pp. 248–49 n.

[63] *Ami du peuple,* June 10, pp. 3–5.

[64] *Moniteur,* May 15, p. 546.

liked to go especially to that of Strasbourg, recognizing the debt the whole realm owed to its National Guard for repressing local attempts to restore inequality, privilege, and servitude. Instead, he issued to Strasbourg his personal invitation, the first of many, to attend "that great and magnificent Federation of all the National Guards of the realm," counting upon welcoming "with all the sentiments of most tender fraternity our companions in arms from Strasbourg, and upon consecrating that alliance, so frightening to the enemies of the constitution, so reassuring to the friends of the *patrie*."[65]

Chaumont also carried 4,500 livres, part of which was for the translation and printing of works favorable to the Revolution, from the fund put at Lafayette's disposal by the National Assembly's Comité des Recherches.[66] Lafayette's letter, printed in both French and German, soon was combined in the same brochure with the official invitation of the Paris municipality[67] to publish the glad tidings of fraternity throughout the German-speaking provinces. And when he returned to Paris, Chaumont brought back from the Strasbourg National Guard an acknowledgment of indebtedness which must have particularly pleased Lafayette: "Happy are the Americans who have seen the establishment of their liberty hastened by you; happy the French! In calling forth the first Declaration of the Rights of Man you laid the foundation of their constitution; in directing the National Guard amid factions and danger you saved us from oppression at the same time that you kept us from the horror of anarchy. You have always loved the people; you have protected them; you have never beguiled them."[68]

With the Federation little more than a month away, the Paris Committee for the Federative Pact now confronted the enormous task of preparing a site for it, providing for the housing and feed-

---

[65] "Copie de la lettre de M. de la Fayette à MM. de la Garde nationale de la ville de Strasbourg," June 9. See also Lafayette to Baron de Dietrich, June 10, Albert Mathiez, "Un complice de Lafayette, Frédéric Dietrich," *Annales révolutionnaires*, XII (1920), 390.

[66] Papers of the Comité des Recherches, AN: Dxxix bis 34, dossier 357, pp. 1, 13, 15.

[67] Adresse des citoyens de Paris à tous les François," [*ca.* June 5], in *Confédération nationale*, pp. 1–4. See also below, p. 450.

[68] Quoted in *La Révolution française*, I (1881), 328.

ing of thousands of delegates, policing a mass of celebrants, and at the same time creating a tone of solemnity worthy of a festival in honor of the rights of man. Eight members of the Conseil de Ville had been assigned to cooperate with the committee, lending it the authority of the Commune. On June 12 Lafayette attended a meeting of the committee and "was received with the applause he so justly deserved." The committee chairman asked him to use his good offices to secure the prompt cooperation of the king's ministers, and "with that grace that won every heart," he invited the committee to meet at his home the following day.[69] Thus prompted, the committee immediately began announcing its plans. The *Address of the Citizens of Paris to All Frenchmen,* signed by Bailly, Lafayette, and the representatives of the districts and supplemented by relevant instructions and speeches, was now printed and dispatched to all the districts and municipalities of the realm.[70] The committee chose the Champ-de-Mars as the site for the Federation and, knowing that to get the field in order would require a great deal of labor, decided to distribute the work among the districts of Paris.[71]

By this time the National Guard had reached a sufficiently high degree of efficiency to make a few remaining paramilitary companies seem dispensable. One of the hitherto most useful of them, the Basoche of the Palais de Justice, had been permitted to survive despite the measures intended to eliminate such units, pending the decision of the National Assembly. Finally, the Assembly passed a measure definitively suppressing unofficial companies, and so the Basochiens were constrained to disband. On June 12 they formally asked the Assembly of Representatives for permission to surrender their arms and flag.

Determined that the unit should end its distinguished career with as much éclat as the National Guard could lend, Lafayette ordered detachments of National Guard cavalry and infantry to participate in the ceremony.[72] On the afternoon of June 17, he

[69] *Journal de la municipalité,* June 15, quoted in Lacroix, VI, 204–5 (June 21).

[70] *Ibid.,* p. 206. See also above, p. 444 and below, p. 461.

[71] Lacroix, VI, pp. 207–8 (June 21), 460–66 (July 10).

[72] *Ibid.,* pp. 91–92, 102–4 (June 16), and *AP,* XVI, 478 (June 26).

went to the Hôtel de Ville to receive the Basoche's arms and flag. When he entered the Grande Salle, he was greeted with "the applause that his presence always inspires." The spokesman of the Basoche then formally announced that they wished to place in the Cathedral of Notre Dame the standard under which they had served since the fourteenth century and to enroll as individuals in the National Guard. He pledged to Lafayette as a general "more admirable for his moral virtues than for those superior [military] qualities which have raised him to the honorable rank where we now see them conspicuously displayed . . . the deference due to wisdom when true merit turns it to account." After the president had responded fittingly, Lafayette spoke: The corps that he had the honor to command always had felt that the Basochiens were its brothers at heart and would feel honored to have them join; their well-demonstrated gallantry would make them welcome to the companies they would enter. The National Guards in the galleries showed their approval by loud applause, and the Representatives readily voted each member of the disbanding army a certificate of service.[73]

Then Lafayette and a deputation from the Assembly of Representatives joined the National Guard and the main corps of the Basoche waiting in the Place de Grève. The Basochiens turned over to him their cannon and small arms, and he led the Guard, the Basoche, and the Commune officials out of the square to the Cathedral of Notre Dame. There the commander of the Basoche asked that its banner be placed in front of the statue of King Philip the Fair, its founder, and the spokesman for the cathedral, promising to comply, accepted the flag as a symbol of the fraternity that bound the nation's defenders together. The National Guards thereupon broke ranks to welcome the men of the Basoche as comrades. Before the month ended, the Basoche informed the National Assembly of the final dissolution of their corps and of their entry into the National Guard, where under the orders of Lafayette they hoped to merit the friendship of the good citizens and brave soldiers with whom they were now united.[74]

[73] Lacroix, VI, 123–25 (June 17).
[74] Ibid., pp. 128–29, 133–36. See also Moniteur, July 27, p. 556.

On June 21 another paramilitary company, the Chevaliers de l'Arc of Montmartre, asked permission to deposit its flags in the Cathedral of Notre Dame and to join the Paris National Guard as individuals. The Chevaliers' spokesman's reference to "the services, the virtues, and the patriotism of the commandant general" evoked the now customary round of applause whenever Lafayette was mentioned.[75] A few days later the Chevaliers de l'Arc came to turn over their standards, and again the entry of Lafayette was greeted by "a new testimonial of the satisfaction that his presence never failed to inspire." The company spokesman affirmed its continuing intention to support the constitution, the president of the Representatives praised the company for its public spirit, and the commandant general expressed his satisfaction over their compliance with the constitution, which owed so much to their patriotic efforts. When he announced that a detachment of the National Guard was ready to escort the Chevaliers to the Cathedral of Notre Dame, where they would deposit their ancient standards, he brought on a new burst of applause; "the Assembly was touched to see that in the midst of the manifold duties that public order placed upon him, he never failed to take care of details that gave the citizens satisfaction."[76]

Before the parade actually started, another private company, formed by men of the parish of Saint-Jean-de-Latran the previous July, came likewise to deposit its flags in the cathedral. The commandant general permitted the Company of Saint-Jean to fall in behind the Chevaliers de l'Arc, and then the National Guard led the procession to the cathedral. After the two companies had presented their flags and the church had received them, Lafayette addressed the Company of Saint-Jean-de-Latran, as he had the Chevaliers, thanking them for their services since the beginning of the Revolution.[77] Thus, for the sake of discipline and of systematic organization within the citizen militia, volunteer companies were obliged to put an end to the proud records they had won in both the old regime and the new.

In the process of reorganizing the National Guard, the National

[75] Lacroix, VI, 182–83.
[76] *Ibid.*, pp. 305–6 (June 28).
[77] *Ibid.*, p. 313.

Assembly forced upon Lafayette himself a probably less painful sacrifice. Because of his own initiative in forbidding anyone to command National Guard units in more than one department he felt obliged to resign as commander of the Versailles National Guard. To the Municipality of Versailles he explained that he hoped that the citizens of Versailles would "maintain the principles to which my resignation renders homage."[78] And to the Versailles National Guard he wrote: "When I proposed the decree to the National Assembly . . . , I was pleased to think that in losing the title of your commander, I would keep that of your brother in arms and your friend." With lifelong devotion to "the holy cause of liberty" and to "a constitution that gives the people their rights and assures their happiness" he waited impatiently, he said, for the day "when all the National Guards united through their deputies in the presence of the National Assembly and the king will together renew the oath to defend and love one another."[79]

Others too were impatient for the great day. The Paris press had published a promise of generous welcome by their Paris comrades to incoming National Guardsmen, whether they were chosen to represent their districts or not,[80] and the flocking of unofficial, self-appointed *fédérés* into Paris created a new challenge. Although no violent outbreaks disturbed the city's tranquility at the moment, officials could not afford to relax their vigilance. The Paris Investigations Committee urged the commandant general to give the strictest orders to his troops to enforce the regulations against deserters and vagabonds, and the minister of war informed him that deserters from the royal army were in the capital,[81] some of them probably among the exuberant *fédérés* prematurely celebrating the anniversary of the capture of the Bastille. Doubtful of the ability of the city authorities to prevent disturbances, the more timorous Parisians began an exodus from the city.[82]

[78] Lafayette to the municipal officers of Versailles, June 17, Bibliothèque de Versailles (courtesy of M. Bréchin).

[79] Lafayette to the Versailles National Guard, June 17, *loc cit.*

[80] Lacroix, VI, 46 (June 14), and *Courier national,* June 17, pp. 7–8.

[81] Investigations Committee to Lafayette, June 16, Tuetey, II, 325, No. 2998, and Latour du Pin to Lafayette, June 17, *ibid.,* p. 437, No. 4138.

[82] *Gazette de Paris,* June 12, p. 2, and *Journal général de la cour,* June 25, p. 684.

On the evening of June 17 Lafayette went to a banquet of the Society of 1789 to mark the first anniversary of the crucial occasion when, with Bailly presiding, Sieyès had proposed that the Third Estate and its adherents constitute themselves the National Assembly. Bailly proposed the first toast: "To the National Assembly." June 17 was the first great anniversary of the Revolution; June 20 was to be another;[83] but the next one, as everyone present realized, was to be the greatest. So Bailly proposed a second toast—to the forthcoming Federation. Other toasts followed—to the memory of Benjamin Franklin, to the National Guards of the realm, to all friends of mankind, and so forth. A collection for the poor was, as customary, taken up and turned over to the mayor. A concert of martial music and songs suitable to the occasion followed, and the crowd outside the dining room called for the celebrities inside to appear on the balcony. As their favorites came out to take their bows, the people applauded, with greatest applause and cheers for Bailly and Lafayette. The Dames of the Halles presented bouquets to some of their heroes, among them, "our good General, to whom the constitution owes a new life, for without him, without his efforts, fine laws might be made but never executed."[84]

June 20 was eagerly awaited not merely because it was the anniversary of the Tennis Court Oath or because it was the first day after the abolition of noble titles but also because it was the Sunday arranged for Louis XVI's second review of the National Guard. Several contretemps, however, jeopardized the success of that review. Days before, it was feared that the devoted Adrienne, who was ill, might have the measles—which, if true, would have obliged Lafayette to absent himself.[85] The Assembly of Representatives, learning of Adrienne's illness, expressed "its desire to give to M. the Commandant General proof of its interest in everything that concerned him" and sent two of its members to inquire about her,[86]

---

[83] See above, p. 423.

[84] *Chronique de Paris,* June 21, pp. 684–87. See also *Journal général de la cour,* June 18, p. 631; *Moniteur,* June 22, p. 708; *Courrier de Paris,* June 19, pp. 242–43; and *Journal de la Société de 1789,* June 26, p. 38.

[85] Lafayette to Louis XVI, June 19, *Mémoires,* II, 470–71.

[86] Lacroix, VI, 185 (June 21), 214 (June 22).

thus making her health a matter of official concern. For a time, indeed, her life was feared to be in danger.[87]

An additional cause for concern centered upon doubts of Louis XVI's good will. The National Guard had felt disappointed that the king had appeared at his last review[88] in ordinary dress instead of the red costume he had been accustomed to wear in the old days when reviewing the French Guard and other troops of the line. The National Guards, many of them former French Guards, felt that the king's plain coat and hat had been deliberately intended as a reminder of their lack of military status. They had spoken so freely about this assumed slur that the commandant general felt he should raise with the king the wearing of something more distinctive than an ordinary walking costume. On the day before the review he sent Louis a note which, after explaining that Adrienne's illness was not measles and so would not interfere with his paying his court at the review, then made a plea regarding the royal *habit de revue:* "My attachment for the king and the keen desire I have to prevent anything that might produce a bad effect forces me to impress upon him a point that will appear minute to him but which circumstances and the turn of certain minds render *very important,*" and he asked the king to "come to the review not as if on an ordinary outing" but in his review costume.[89] In response, Louis XVI promised no more than that he would be at the review at ten in the morning, and accordingly the commandant general ordered three divisions of the National Guard to report to the Champ-de-Mars at nine.[90]

The king, not happy about the unusual interest his fellow-citizens, once his subjects, were taking in what he wore, let his displeasure fall upon Adrienne's cousin and Lafayette's friend the Prince de Poix, a commander of the King's Bodyguard. Having learned of the resentment in the National Guard, Poix was fearful that something unpleasant might happen if the king again ap-

[87] Short to Jefferson, July 7, Boyd (ed.), XVII, 12.

[88] See above, p. 388.

[89] Lafayette to Louis XVI, June 19, *Mémoires,* II, 470–71. See also Bibliographical Notes below, p. 461.

[90] *Gazette de Leide, supplément,* June 29.

peared in mufti at a National Guard review. Expecting to accompany Louis XVI at the review, he took the liberty of trying to
find out what His Majesty intended to wear, giving as his excuse
that he himself wanted to dress conformably. Poix expressed his
anxiety more openly to the queen, and Louis XVI, upon learning
of Poix's solicitude, rebuked him orally for his officiousness. Indignant, Poix wrote His Majesty a letter which, while apologizing
and professing loyalty, nevertheless repeated his desire that the
king wear the same kind of costume at the forthcoming review as
he wore at reviews of troops of the line and stated that, having been
rebuked, he intended to resign his command as soon as the King's
Bodyguard returned to Paris.[91]

In answer to Poix's apology Louis scribbled on the face of
Poix's letter a crushing reprimand, which, however, was an indirect compliment to Lafayette: Regardless of whatever confidence
he might have in Lafayette, the king wanted Poix to know that he
was able to disagree with Lafayette on many points; besides, he
had already discussed the matter with Lafayette, and Poix did not
enjoy the same confidence. Without any pretense of subtlety in his
reprimand Louis professed a preference for those who, even if they
disapproved of acts that circumstances forced upon him, did not
blame him but were content, not being able to change things, to
keep their opinions to themselves.[92]

Although the king declared that he considered the matter closed,
Poix answered, protesting that since his conduct had been irreproachable, he would overlook any personal slights until the day
when the King's Bodyguard returned, and then, he repeated, he
would ask permission to retire from court.[93] Thus a petty detail—
what the king would wear at a National Guard review—became
a point of honor for a courtier torn between loyalty to his monarch
and friendship for Lafayette, mirroring a struggle between the

[91] Poix to Louis XVI, [June 19?], *AP*, LIV, p. 491, No. 107. The original is in AN:
C184, Dr. 117, f. 15.

[92] Louis XVI to Poix, [June 19?], *AP*, LIV, 490. See above, n. 91.

[93] Poix to Louis XVI, [June 20?], *ibid.*, p. 491, No. 108. The original is in AN: C184,
Dr. 117, f. 16.

old and the new that must have been harrowing many other souls of the time.

Early on Sunday morning Lafayette rode out to the Champ-de-Mars. About 15,000 National Guardsmen were trooping in, prepared to be reviewed by the king. Taking a detachment from those already arrived, Lafayette proceeded to the gates of Paris to meet the royal party coming from Saint-Cloud. Louis had characteristically yielded to pressure, but not altogether: he wore a red cloak, not the heavily embroidered one he had been accustomed to wear at military reviews but a *uniforme de Trianon,* trimmed with gold.[94] If any of the former French Guards recognized that it was not the one he had worn at earlier reviews, there might still be trouble.

When the red-cloaked monarch and his blue-coated escort reached the Champ-de-Mars, a huge crowd greeted them. The Guard was drawn up in line on the parade ground—the best uniformed troops of all Europe, the *Gazette universelle* observed, because some of them had goodly incomes.[95] Louis XVI rode down the lines, not skipping a single rank, and "everything ended without disorder or accident."[96] Whether or not he realized it, Lafayette had won another victory, for that was the very day Mirabeau wrote to the court prophesying civil war;[97] if the king had worn a grey coat and had been embarrassed by a display of resentment at the review, Mirabeau's prophecy probably would have sounded inspired and persuasive to those who read it that Sunday.

Amid dramatic events like military reviews, legislative crises, and Adrienne's illness Lafayette remained the harried administrator of a humdrum routine. The flood of communications from and to the mayor—on courts-martial of Guardsmen, on funds for the renovation of uniforms for the paid Guards to wear at the Federation, on permission for the publication of extracts from the minutes

[94] Esterhazy, *Mémoires* (Daudet), pp. 272–73 (or in the Feuillet de Conches edition, IV, 43–44).

[95] *Gazette universelle,* June 21, p. 814.

[96] *Gazette de Leide, supplément,* June 29.

[97] See above, p. 424.

of the Paris Military Committee, on patrolling Paris streets against beggars, on commissions in the National Guard, on certificates of merit for deserving officers, on the date for the election of the Paris *fédérés,* on arms deliveries to Paris, and so forth—remained unabated, and his correspondence with other officials, while less frequent, was often equally time-consuming.[98] The obligation to police the precincts of the National Assembly, of course, required at times much more than regulation service. It rose above the routine again when the unpopular Vicomte de Mirabeau, brother of the orator, once again needed protection. He had gone, so he said, to restore discipline in his regiment, stationed at Perpignan, but the Perpignan municipality had taken him into custody on the ground that only in that way could they protect him from harm. The National Assembly issued an order to the vicomte to return and took the occasion to remind the municipalities of the nation of the inviolability of deputies. Accordingly, the Paris Conseil de Ville ordered the mayor and the commandant general of Paris to take special precautions to safeguard the deputies in the capital.[99]

On June 21 the Conseil de Ville gave a good deal of attention to the impending celebration of July 14. It authorized Lafayette to arrange that for every one hundred National Guardsmen of Paris there should be six delegates (about 2,000 in all) who should meet on July 5 in the Cathedral of Notre Dame to choose their representatives in the Federation.[100] The members of the Conseil appointed to work with the Committee for the Federative Pact were

[98] Lafayette to Bailly, June 1, BN:Fr 11697, p. 59 bis; Champion de Cicé and Lafayette to Latour du Pin, June 8, Catalogue of Michel Castaing, No. 702 (Nov. 1959), p. 23, item 27,372; Saint-Priest to Lafayette, June 4 and 5, Tuetey, I, 23, No. 209; Bailly to Lafayette, June 9, *ibid.,* II, 325, No. 2997; AN:F⁷ 36894, dossier marked "Seine et Marne: Lagny" (correspondence with Saint-Priest of May 22–June 12); Lafayette to Bailly, June 15, Tuetey, II, 444, No. 4200; Bailly to Lafayette, June 19, *ibid.,* p. 442, No. 4174; *ibid.,* p. 387, No. 3636, and AN AF¹¹ 48, liasse 375, p. 20; Bailly to Lafayette, Apr. 20, BN: Fr. 11697, p. 56, and Lafayette to Bailly, [June 19?], *ibid.,* p. 66; C.-L. Chassin and L. Hennet, *Les Volontaires nationaux pendant la Révolution* (Paris, 1899–1906), I, 95, n. 3; Lacroix, VI, 228–29 (June 23); *Procès-verbal du Comité militaire,* Part II, 79–81; Bailly to Lafayette, June 22, AN: AF¹¹ 48, liasse 375, pièce 23; same to same, June 25, *ibid.,* pièce 24; same to same, June 28, *ibid.,* pièce 25; same to same, *ibid.,* July 1, pièce 29; same to same, June 23, BN: FR 11697, pp. 67–68.

[99] *AP,* XVI, 364 (June 19), and Lacroix, VI, 191 (June 21).

[100] Lacroix, VI, 191–92, 202, n. 3 (June 21), and see below, pp. 000, 000.

instructed to take whatever action they deemed wise to speed up preparations, and the Conseil also asked Bailly and Lafayette to request the National Assembly to consider the Federation a national event whose costs would be paid by the public treasury.

Then the Conseil turned to the long-delayed organization of the National Guard cannoneers. The districts so far had refused to authorize the creation of an artillery corps,[101] but Lafayette had assigned twenty cannoneers to each of the six companies (one per division) of paid grenadiers. Lafayette and Gouvion now proposed a regulation that would be provisional pending the organization of the National Guard by the National Assembly. It stipulated that each contingent of twenty cannoneers be commanded by a sous-lieutenant, to be chosen by the Conseil de Ville but responsible to the grenadier captain. The cannoneers were to receive the same treatment as the grenadiers, wear the same uniform except for difference in hats and insignia, and serve along with them; the municipality was to set aside a special field for artillery drill. This emphasis upon artillery was in keeping with the best military theories of the day, but little had yet been done to put theory into practice. The Conseil adopted the plan that Lafayette and Gouvion proposed.[102]

Although official Paris had begun to look forward to July 14 as a day on which many difficulties would at least momentarily dissolve in a glowing burst of patriotism and fraternity, among those who most eagerly awaited the anniversary of the fall of the Bastille keen rivalries arose over seemingly petty issues. The former Electors of Paris, the men who had formed themselves into a quasi-government to meet the crisis of July 1789, had decided early in the spring, before the same idea spread abroad, to celebrate July 14 as the day of their glory by holding a commemorative anniversary service at Notre Dame.[103] But now they found themselves sidetracked, and so on June 25 they decided to hold a *Te Deum* and a banquet on July 13 instead, inviting the National Assembly, the officials of Paris, the staff of the National Guard, the presidents of

[101] See above, pp. 163–64, 263.
[102] Lacroix, VI, 193–95.
[103] See above, p. 244.

the districts, and other dignitaries.[104] And some of Lafayette's opponents thought they might profit from the jealousy created by the special recognition that the Vainqueurs de la Bastille had recently received as favored heroes of July 14, 1789.[105]

In this instance it was the former French Guards and other members of the National Guard who felt aggrieved. Some of the districts of Paris took up the French Guards' cause, declaring that they were the real conquerors of the Bastille. Others citizens who were neither former French Guards nor Vainqueurs claimed to have played an equally deserving part on July 14. Some (and a few observers believed that the Triumvirate were prominent among them) hoped that Lafayette as a patron of the Vainqueurs de la Bastille would be embarrassed. Mirabeau thought that the Lameths "had raised this ridiculous episode only to stir up his [Lafayette's] National Guard,"[106] and La Marck suggested that the animosity against the Vainqueurs could "with money and skill" be used advantageously against Lafayette, "worthy patron of those ridiculous heroes."[107] But he was mistaken. The Vainqueurs volunteered to renounce the special privileges granted them,[108] and although the former French Guards had been most indignant, they passed a resolution decrying the effort of disturbers of the peace to make trouble between them and the Vainqueurs de la Bastille.[109] When the commandant general learned what his men had done, he praised their action as "a new proof of their zeal and their patriotism,"[110] and Mirabeau had to inform La Marck that Lafayette had, in fact, not been the patron of the Vainqueurs but, on the contrary, had had the good sense to induce them to give up their claims, and, by doing so, had foiled the Lameths.[111] Mirabeau and the Triumvirate,

---

[104] Bailly and Duveyrier, III [appendix], 389–94.

[105] See above, p. 421.

[106] Mirabeau to La Marck, June 25, Bacourt (ed.), II, 51–52.

[107] La Marck to Mirabeau, June 25, *ibid.,* p. 51.

[108] Earl Gower to Leeds, June 25, *Despatches of Earl Gower,* ed. Oscar Browning (Cambridge, 1885), p. 7, and *AP,* XVI, 463–66 (June 25).

[109] Lacroix, VI, 241–60 (June 25).

[110] *Ibid.,* pp. 255–57.

[111] Mirabeau to La Marck, June 25, Bacourt (ed.), II, 51–52.

though perhaps equally disappointed, had little in common but their desire to overtake, or at least to slow down, Lafayette, who, whether he wished to be or not, was obviously the front runner in the race for prestige and power.

BIBLIOGRAPHICAL NOTES

The "Imprimerie de Lottin l'ainé & Lottin de S.-Germain, Imprimeurs-Libraires Ordinaires de la Ville," published a twelve-page quarto pamphlet entitled *Confédération nationale* (1790 or 1791; see below, p. 526), which contained the *Adresse des citoyens de Paris à tous les François* and the decisions of the National Assembly and the king on June 5–8 regarding the Federation, with an "Observation" (p. 12) that the documents the pamphlet contained be circulated among all the military and read in all the parishes of the land. While in Lacroix's note (V, 723) Lafayette's signature (printed "La Fayette") is indicated below Bailly's, in *Confédération nationale* (p. 3), it is on the same line and to the left of Bailly's. Desmoulins (*Révolutions,* No. 29, p. 237 n.) complained that Lafayette's name thus preceded Bailly's. Both are followed by over a page of signatures (pp. 3–4) of Paris district officials, National Guard officers, deputies to the Federation, and others. The version of the *Adresse des citoyens de Paris à tous les François* in this pamphlet differs in some insignificant details from that read in the National Assembly on June 5 (see above, p. 444), but it is contained in full in [Bérenger (ed.)], pp. 199–202.

According to Esterhazy (see n. 94 above), Lafayette went to Saint-Cloud on June 19 and asked Louis XVI to wear his red review costume when reviewing the former French Guards, but the king, displeased at that request, dismissed him without giving a definite answer. Since Lafayette that evening attended the meeting of the National Assembly which abolished aristocratic titles, it seems unlikely that he went back and forth to Saint-Cloud the same day, but Esterhazy's story is not otherwise improbable.

The Blancheteau collection is now in the Cornell University Library.

CHAPTER XIX

Friends and Foes Abroad and at Home

I F LAFAYETTE could give some of his friends abroad, like Tom Paine,[1] but little time and attention, they found plenty of time to pay attention to him. Morris not only sent him gratuitous advice from London but talked about him patronizingly with the French ambassador and entered dire thoughts in his diary about his "want of genius" in particular and about French ineptitude in general.[2] Americans at home were far more favorably impressed. In the first letter that Jefferson sent him on his arrival in New York from Europe he wrote: "Behold me, my dear friend, dubbed Secretary of state, instead of returning to the far more agreeable position which placed me in the daily participation of your friendship," but "wherever I am, or ever shall be, I shall be sincere in my friendship to you and to your nation." While "we are not to expect to be translated from despotism to liberty in a feather-bed," Jefferson remained confident of the ultimate success of France's revolution. He worried, however, about Lafayette's personal safety: "Take care of yourself, my dear friend. For tho' I think your nation would in any event work out her salvation, I am persuaded were she to lose you, it would cost her oceans of blood, and years of confusion and anarchy." He urged Lafayette to teach his children "to be as you are a cement between our two nations."[3] He wrote also to Adrienne, saying that he had now given up all hope of revisiting France but wished she would visit America: "You will find here a people warmly attached to your husband,

[1] See above, p. 291.

[2] Feb. 28, May 30, June 24, July 2, Davenport (ed.), I, 529, 532, 554–55. The quotation is from p. 555.

[3] Apr. 2, Boyd (ed.). XVI, 292–93.

yourself, and all your family."[4] That his admiration for his young French friend was due to more than epistolary courtesy was shown by his request soon afterward of Short: "My pictures of American worthies will be absolutely incomplete till I get the M. de la fayette's." He asked Short to find an artist to paint a portrait matching the half-length of Washington that had hung in his Paris dining room.[5] Yet, while apologizing for taking up time "too much and too usefully occupied" for "ordinary ceremonies of civility," Jefferson did not scruple to ask Lafayette for "the favor of your name" on behalf of a young American visitor to Paris[6] or to ask Short (in code) to intimate "under the rose" to Lafayette that it would be a mistake to reappoint Moustier as minister to the United States.[7]

About this time President Washington again received heartening news about Lafayette from mutual friends in Europe. John Paradise, a Greco-American then in London, wrote him: "There is not a more popular man in France than our gallant Marquis, your pupil; nor indeed can popularity be more justly merited. His actions are directed by the purest views, and his glory consists in doing good to mankind."[8] And from Joseph Mandrillon, a French writer of travel literature, came almost the same message: "The Marquis de Lafayette, the worthy emulant and friend of your Excellency, covers himself with glory in France; and if the guardian genius of France preserves him to them, he will enjoy the sweet satisfaction of having done that for his fellow-citizens which your Excellency has done for America."[9]

For his part Lafayette's "patron and master" (to use Paine's description of Washington)[10]—at this stage at least—made no

[4] Apr. 3, *ibid.*, p. 295.

[5] Apr. 6, *ibid.*, p. 318.

[6] Apr. 24, *ibid.*, p. 376. The "young gentleman of South Carolina" was a Mr. Horry, nephew of General Charles C. Pinckney; Washington wrote a similar letter, Apr. 26: Fitzpatrick (ed.), XXI, 38 n.

[7] June 6, 1790, Boyd (ed.), XVI, 476.

[8] Received in June, Sparks, *Correspondence of the American Revolution,* IV, 343. See also A. B. Shepperson, *John Paradise and Lucy Ludwell of London and Williamsburg* (Richmond, Va., 1942), p. 421.

[9] June 1, *ibid.*, pp. 339–40.

[10] See above p. 288.

secret of his feeling that the Revolution in France had his enthusiastic approval: "Nor is it without the most sensible pleasure I learn that our friend the Marquis de la Fayette, has, in acting the arduous part which has fallen to his share, conducted himself with so much wisdom and apparently to such general satisfaction."[11] In reply to one of Lafayette's letters[12] Washington apologized for troubling him with correspondence "merely of a private nature," since he considered the marquis' time much better employed than in answering communications: "I felt no solicitude but that you should progress directly forward and happily effect your great undertakings. How much, how sincerely am I rejoiced, my dear Marquis, to find that things are assuming so favorable an aspect in France! Be assured that you always have my best and most ardent wishes for your success." He described "the happy progress of our affairs" and the cooperation therein of several of Lafayette's American friends, and he took occasion to thank France for recent concessions to American trade with the French West Indies.[13] Lafayette could consider that expression of gratitude a personal compliment, since he had taken a leading part in winning those concessions.

Over ten months after it was written Lafayette finally received this letter, and he was shocked to learn from it that Washington had been ill:

What would have been my feelings, had the news of your illness reached me before I knew my beloved General, my adoptive father was out of danger! I was struck with horror at the idea of the situation you have been in, while I, uninformed, and so distant from you, was anticipating the long waited for pleasure to hear from you, and the still more endearing prospect to visit you, and present you with the tribute of a Revolution, one of your first offsprings. For God's sake, my dear General, take care of your health. . . . Your preservation is the life of your friends, the salvation of your country . . . and you may easley [*sic*] guess what I am exposed to suffer, what would have been my

---

[11] Washington to La Luzerne, Apr. 29, Fitzpatrick (ed.), XXXI, 40.

[12] Gottschalk (ed.), *Letters,* p. 209. Lafayette thought his letters "must have miscarried, or been detained": See n. 14 below.

[13] June 3, Fitzpatrick (ed.), XXXI, 44–46. For Lafayette's part in the West Indies concessions see Gottschalk, *Between,* pp. 39–51, 69–73, 155–60, 223, 240–41, 255–56, 421–22.

situation had I known your illness before the news of your recovery had comforted a heart so affectionately devoted to you.[14]

On the same day that Washington wrote to Lafayette he had also written to Adrienne. She had asked for a captain's commission for Lafayette's secretary Poirey, who had served in the American War of Independence and was now an officer in the Paris National Guard, and Washington promptly had asked the Senate to accede to her request. He now enclosed a brevet commission, assuring her that aside from Poirey's services in America, which alone might have entitled him to this distinction, "his attachment to the Marquis de la Fayette and your protection added claims that were not to be resisted." He was glad to be able to give this mark of attention "to so good a friend to America and so excellent a patriot as Madame la Marquise de la Fayette" in whose welfare, he assured her, no one was "more deeply interested" than himself.[15]

Everywhere among Americans and Americanophiles, Morris being the outstanding exception, "the Marquis" was considered, as Jefferson called him, "a hero."[16] When Franklin died, Dr. Benjamin Rush, of Philadelphia, procuring a lock of the sage's hair, sent some of it to Franklin's European friends, Richard Price in London and Lafayette in Paris.[17] When Washington made his will the following July, he left "to General de Lafayette . . . a pair of pistols taken from the enemy during the Revolutionary War."[18] Princeton University conferred upon America's marquis (as well as on Necker) the degree of Doctor of Laws *in absentia,* and he made a contribution to its endowment fund[19]—though which of these acts was cause and which effect is not clear. In Paris he was regarded as the principal arbiter of matters pertaining to the United

---

[14] Aug. 23, Gottschalk (ed.), *Letters,* p. 348.

[15] Washington to the Senate, May 31, Fitzpatrick (ed.), XXXI, 42, and to the Marquise de Lafayette, June 3, *ibid.,* pp. 46–47.

[16] See above, n. 5.

[17] Benjamin Rush, *Autobiography,* ed. George W. Corner (Princeton, N.J., 1948), p. 183.

[18] July 9, Jared Sparks, *The Life of George Washington* (Boston, 1857), p. 552. See the description of them in the Girodie catalogue, p. 48, item 69.

[19] V. L. Collins, secretary of Princeton University, to S. W. Jackson, Aug. 26, 1929, in Gottschalk collection (microfilm).

States. Thus in May he was assigned the responsibility of passing upon all applications of French officers who felt entitled to admission into the Society of the Cincinnati because of having been commissioned in the American army by the Continental Congress.[20] And when John Paul Jones returned from his service under Tsarina Catherine of Russia, he brought one set of furs for Lafayette and another for Louis XVI, which he asked Lafayette to present.[21]

If, however, Lafayette was an almost impeccable hero to most Americans, less republican foreigners did not always share their enchantment. In June, while the Nootka Sound controversy was threatening to embroil France in war with Britain, Lafayette had a conversation with the British chargé d'affaires in Paris, Lord Robert Fitzgerald. He candidly informed the embarrassed envoy that in his opinion Britain was exploiting the controversy as an opportunity not merely to help the Spanish-American colonies throw off Spain's control but also to thwart the French Revolution. But Britain would never succeed in stopping the Revolution in France, Lafayette contended, because the spirit of liberty burned in every French peasant's heart. Britain's plans to free the Spanish colonies, though premature, appeared to him to be laudable, and France, he expected, might someday aid Britain in such an enterprise, since France sincerely wanted a revolution similar to her own to take place all over the world. According to Fitzgerald, Lafayette regretted the necessity of preserving monarchy even in France and did not despair of someday seeing a more perfect equality among men through "an impartial division of landed property." The shocked British envoy reported these "extravagant" ideas to his government in order, he said, to give "an idea of the principles entertained by a principal character in the present Revolution."[22]

Lord Robert was perhaps needlessly startled, for Lafayette's immediate aim during the Nootka Sound controversy was not the redistribution of property but the preservation of some of the royal prerogative in the conduct of foreign affairs. At the end of June,

[20] Baron de Contenson, "L'Ordre américain de Cincinnatus en France," *Revue d'histoire diplomatique*, XXVII (1913), 527.

[21] S. E. Morison, *John Paul Jones: A Sailor's Biography* (Boston, 1959), pp. 394–96.

[22] Fitzgerald to Leeds, June 4, Browning (ed.), p. 325, and Thompson, pp. 80–81.

Fernan Nuñez, the Spanish ambassador, hoping for the speedy corroboration of the Family Compact that bound the French Bourbons to support the Spanish Bourbons, sounded out the queen, Lafayette, and Montmorin on separate occasions and found them in disheartening agreement. They were loyal to Spain—or at least hostile to Britain—but averse to putting the matter promptly before the National Assembly. A premature move, they feared, could be expected to precipitate comments unfriendly to the Bourbon dynasties and might lead to a hostile demonstration at the forthcoming Federation. In a conversation which lasted well over an hour and in which Lafayette used "all his eloquence and charm" to convince the Spanish ambassador, he proposed that Louis XVI, taking the initiative, request the Spanish king to defer asking for France's decision until after July 14. For he expected the Federation to make the king's party stronger in the National Assembly, which would then be ready to approve a union with Spain that would thereby be binding upon not only the French king but also the French nation. Lafayette assured the ambassador that he had himself always been a partisan of such a union because he was an avowed and irreconcilable enemy of the British nation and king, who would never forgive France for the loss of the American colonies.[23] Shortly afterward Montmorin, in fact, sent a letter to the Spanish government indicating that a satisfactory outcome in the National Assembly could be anticipated if consideration of France's obligation under the Family Compact were postponed until about July 18.[24]

Fernan Nuñez, upon reporting this proposed postponement to his government, described the situation in the National Assembly. Of its three parties (he meant the Right, the Jacobins, and the Fayettists) the group led by Lafayette professed what might now be regarded as moderate opinions, though formerly they would not have been considered moderate. In general, he expounded, it stood for loyalty to old treaties and would certainly favor maintaining the Family Compact so far as the actual situation permitted, but it

[23] Fernan Nuñez to Floridablanca, June 28, Mousset, p. 213.

[24] Montmorin's letter was enclosed in a letter of Louis XVI to the Spanish government, [*post* June 28], *ibid.*, p. 216.

entertained "chimerical theories on peace," drew distinctions between offensive and defensive wars, and would thereby probably weaken the effectiveness of the Family Compact as a source of prompt and certain aid to Spain. The ambassador described the second party as nominally dependent upon the Duc d'Orléans though actually led by the Lameths, Barnave, and others; it was hostile to the king and his family, intent upon establishing a federal republic in France under the leadership of Orléans, and antagonistic to the Family Compact; only by bribery could enough votes be mustered in the Assembly to ensure its support of the Family Compact. The Right was divided, and so, he concluded, Lafayette's party was the only one able to save the king.[25]

The Spanish ambassador's analysis of the French partisan programs, perceptive though it was, was no more than a reflection of what by this time was fairly common knowledge. Barnave, in a detailed account to his constituents in Grenoble of the nascent political clubs, indicated that the Society of 1789 was more friendly to the royal ministry than the Jacobins.[26] The king's sister, Elisabeth, drew a distinction between the parties she called "that of La Fayette and that of M. le duc d'Orléans, otherwise called that of the Lameths"; although she thought that the two were less antagonistic to each other than the general public believed, Lafayette's "is much more numerous, . . . is less sanguinary, and appears to want to serve the king."[27] About the same time a conservative journalist, Jacques Mallet du Pan, maintained that despite efforts to reunite the two revolutionary groups and despite the republican inclinations of both, they were divided by the rivalry for leadership between Lafayette and the Triumvirate.[28]

Although these observers' opinions were based upon mere guesswork rather than accurate information, they make clear that the scission between Fayettists and Jacobins was no longer an insiders' secret. Lafayette's disagreement with the Lameths, Barnave, Du-

---

[25] *Ibid.*, pp. 214–15.

[26] Barnave to the municipality of Grenoble, June 25, *Oeuvres de Barnave,* ed. M. Bérenger de la Drôme (Paris, 1843), IV, 334–42.

[27] Elisabeth to Mme de Bombelles, July 10, Feuillet de Conches (ed.), III, 288.

[28] Mallet du Pan to Montmorin, June 21, 24, Irisson d'Herisson, pp. 116, 134–35.

port, and their friends, born amid disagreements over the repression of domestic disorders, nourished by the dispute over the distribution of the power to make war and peace, had been greatly exacerbated by the controversy over Captain Féral. The mounting, though far from preponderant, dissatisfaction with Lafayette was conspicuously demonstrated on July 1 by three resolutions which the District of the Cordeliers, led by Danton, presented to the Assembly of Representatives. One protested against the treatment of Captain Féral; another condemned the arrest of an author of incendiary articles in Fréron's *Orateur du peuple* impugning the commandant general and others; and a third complained about the new proposal for a corps of cannoneers[29]—all three matters with which Lafayette was directly or indirectly involved. A new organization generally known as the Cordeliers Club (more formally, the Club of the Rights of Man) rapidly assumed leadership among the opponents of Lafayette.

By June of 1790 some popular journals had adopted a consistent policy of finding fault with the commandant general. Loustalot, who in the past had praised him about as often as he had chided him, now not only took Féral's part again but also held other "wrongs" against Lafayette—his opposition to the Belgian Congress, his disapproval of the Marseilles uprising, his pro-monarchical stand on the making of war and peace, his attempts to stifle the complaints of citizen-soldiers in the name of military discipline.[30] The *Orateur du peuple*[31] and the *Journal du diable* joined the chorus of those who defended Féral and the freedom of the press, accused Lafayette of arrogantly surrounding himself with spies and a subservient staff, and went to the defense of Orléans.[32]

Desmoulins often served as the Cordeliers Club's spokesman, al-

---

[29] Lacroix, VI, 338, 350–56 (July 1).

[30] *Révolutions de Paris,* No. 32, Apr. 24–May 1, pp. 217–20; No. 48, June 5–12, p. 546; No. 50, June 19–26, pp. 613–23, 639–40; No. 51, June 26–July 3, pp. 685–93.

[31] See Blancheteau catalogue, p. 62, item 212; p. 64, items 217, 219; p. 68, item 231; p. 69, items 233, 234, 236; and note of Lacroix, VI, 350–57 (July 1).

[32] *Journal du diable,* No. 33, pp. 1–3, No. 36, p. 6, No. 38, pp. 4–8, No. 40, pp. 1–7, No. 41, pp. 5–8, No. 42, pp. 1–2, No. 44, p. 6.

though for a time he continued to vacillate between the friends and the enemies of Lafayette. When he was told—erroneously, it proved—that Lafayette had secured the passage of a bill providing that everyone enrolled in the National Guard would have the rights of an active citizen whether he met the tax qualifications or not, that single act, he declared, made Lafayette as good a citizen as Marat. He soon learned, however, that the National Assembly had given active citizenship only to Paris National Guards who had purchased their own uniforms, and only because uniforms cost more than the amount of the tax required to qualify as an active citizen; thus the right to vote in the forthcoming elections still belonged only to men of some property. Desmoulins, disapproving of such discrimination in favor of the uniform, then referred to Lafayette as his "ex-hero."[33]

Marat had no such compunctions as Desmoulins. He had not forgotten Lafayette's share in the frustrated attempt to arrest him in January, and with all the vehemence that had become his journalistic trademark he condemned Lafayette, Charton, the National Guard staff, and the others who had disavowed Féral. In an "Address to the Patriots of the Army of Paris," he warned them against the "ambition, . . . perfidy, and dark plots" of top National Guard officers, their "mortal enemies," most of whom had been appointed by the commandant general or, if elected, had nevertheless joined the cabal to subject citizen-soldiers to a military code designed to serve the commandant general and an insolent court.[34] In his next issue, Marat continued this attack with a "Denunciation of M. de la Fayette," accusing him of duplicity: he pretended to serve the people but was really devoted to the court; he had favored the *loi martiale* in order to keep the people from resisting their oppressors; he intended that the Châtelet should indict "the good citizens who had saved France on October 6"; he had "vowed implacable hatred" to Barnave, Duport, Robespierre, and the Lameths, who were "the incorruptible supporters of the constitu-

[33] *Révolutions*, No. 32, pp. 367–74, 392–97. See also No. 30, pp. 296–97, No. 31, pp. 32–50, No. 32, pp. 389–92; and below, p. 505 and n. 11.

[34] *Ami du peuple*, June 27, pp. 1–8.

tion"; he had plotted to acquire for the crown the right to make war and peace; he had appointed to his staff a group of unworthy men whom he bound to himself by enormous salaries and had filled the ranks of the National Guard with paid men ready to become "royal soldiers"; he had insisted on forming special corps that would menace public security; he sent citizen-soldiers on oppressive expeditions against their fellow-citizens but reserved all honorable activities for the paid troops; he had persuaded his officers to demand the trial of the admirable Captain Féral for upholding the honor of the National Guard. In short, by following the "tortuous path of a consummate courtier" he had destroyed his image as "the pretended patriot." Marat was running a personal risk, he dared say, in denouncing the commandant general, but he challenged Lafayette to silence him: "I vow an eternal hatred of you as long as you plot against liberty. . . . My last breath will denounce you as one of our most dangerous enemies."[35]

At the meeting of the Conseil de Ville on June 28, the procureur-syndic indicted the *Ami du peuple,* and the Conseil decided to ask the National Assembly to consider passage of a law "remedying such abuses of the press."[36] The procureur-syndic immediately moved against Marat, but the printer of the *Ami du peuple* claimed not to know the journalist's whereabouts, and, unrelenting and untamed, Marat continued to publish his paper subterraneously. The writer who had attacked Lafayette in the *Orateur du peuple,* however, was arrested, and his imprisonment lent color to the complaint of several Paris newspapers that only counterrevolutionary pamphleteers went unpunished.[37] From hiding Marat protested that while a man arrested for distributing a pamphlet directed against the Lameths had been acquitted, another who had sold the *Vie privée, impartiale . . . de La Fayette* had been sentenced to six months in jail; on the other hand, "atrocious libels" against "the faithful representatives of the nation," he alleged, were fabri-

---

[35] *Ibid.,* June 28, pp. 1–4.

[36] Lacroix, VI, 314–15, 320–23 (June 28).

[37] *Journal du diable,* No. 37, pp. 1–3; Desmoulins, *Révolutions,* No. 31, pp. 309–14; and *Patriote français,* July 1, pp. 2–3.

cated in the Society of 1789, where Lafayette and the other followers of the "pretended Impartials" held forth.[38] In addition to the old theme that Lafayette was restricting the liberty of citizen-soldiers by imposing upon them a strict military discipline, he introduced a new one by asking by what right Bailly, Lafayette, and the National Guard staff wore the medal of the French Guards, a decoration exclusively for soldiers who had really participated in the capture of the Bastille.[39]

But Lafayette had his journalistic defenders, too. The *Chronique de Paris* made a point of agreeing with him that "it is important that we live peacefully and that the Revolution be achieved."[40] The *Courrier de Paris,* accusing the disaffected of spreading ideas designed to produce an explosion on the day of the forthcoming national fete, rebuked not only the aristocrats and extremists but also other journalists, and especially Marat, who denounced Lafayette, it asserted, merely because he loved his king.[41]

Lafayette, meanwhile, went on his way, giving no public indication that he knew of the battle of the journalists, although privately it distressed him greatly. About this time he wrote, corrected, and recorrected an order to the National Guard that "any person who hawks anything other than acts emanating from the National Assembly, the king, or a legal authority shall be arrested and brought before the police committee of his district" with a view toward repressing "the efforts of some perverse and misled men," who "in the last few days" have multiplied "the daggers of calumny" and preached insurrection, having been hired by "criminal maneuvers and corrupting money" to create an "artificial unrest." Reconfirming the municipality's regulations concerning the restraint of beggars and urging National Guardsmen to wear their uniforms even when not on duty, the draft continued: "The commandant general leaves it to their vigilance and their patriotism to thwart the attempts of the ill-intentioned. By redoubling our

[38] *Ami du peuple,* July 1, pp. 1–3.

[39] *Ibid.,* July 2, p. 4, July 3, pp. 1–8, July 4, pp. 2–3, July 6, p. 6 n.

[40] July 1, p. 726.

[41] July 1, pp. 451–52, July 3, pp. 6–11, July 4, pp. 26–27.

zeal, by manifesting more than ever our determination to repress all disorder, we shall place public liberty, prosperity, and general tranquility on unshakable foundations." The order seems never to have been formally issued, however.[42]

Mirabeau did not publicly join in the attacks upon Lafayette, for his attitude regarding domestic order and foreign affairs was much more like Lafayette's than like that of Lafayette's opponents. He privately disapproved, however, of the commandant general's influence at court. While he too thought that new conditions required the Family Compact to be made more palatable to the National Assembly, he wanted the court to conduct the negotiations with Spain quietly—without the participation of Montmorin, who was too close to Lafayette. A new ambassador, he counseled, should be sent to Madrid with the draft of a new treaty, which he volunteered to help prepare; knowledge of the selection of the ambassador should be withheld from Lafayette, and Montmorin should be bound by secrecy at least long enough to permit a little time before counter intrigue might thwart the new envoy and to allow the king alone to reap credit for the outcome.[43] Mirabeau suggested Ségur, former ambassador at St. Petersburg, for the Madrid post; although the Spanish court might at first distrust him as a friend of Lafayette, a personal letter from the queen would suffice to set it right.[44] If Lafayette was aware of Mirabeau's maneuver, he did nothing to balk it; his primary concern was to postpone debate on the Family Compact until after the Federation.

In the tug-of-war between factions straining in opposing directions to realign constitutional authority in France the Franco-Austrian alliance was no less in jeopardy than the Franco-Spanish Family Compact. At this juncture the alliance hinged upon the

[42] Huntington Library: HM 9443. This document (4 pp., unsigned but in Lafayette's hand) is obviously a rough draft, for words, phrases, and whole sentences have been crossed out and some reworded more than once. Although the Huntington Library has dated it tentatively 1789, it must be of late June or early July 1790 because it mentions in a crossed-out passage "l'Honneur [of the commandant general] de se retrouver le lendemain de la fédération simple soldat dans la garde nationale." Because it is otherwise unknown, we assume that it was never published.

[43] Mirabeau to the court, June 26, Bacourt (ed.), II, 55–59.

[44] *Ibid.*, and La Marck to Mirabeau, June 26, *ibid.*, p. 53.

Belgian crisis, and upon the outcome of that crisis hinged the balance of power in Europe. Lafayette's course with regard to the Belgian provinces continued to center on Count Cornet des Grez, who was still a refugee at Douai. It was important to know whether the count would support the popular Vonckist party, which was now leaning toward acceptance of Emperor Leopold's concessions, or the aristocratic Congress party, which proposed to fight for independence. Late in May a letter from Cornet des Grez informed Lafayette that the military affairs of Belgium were in a sorry state, and shortly afterward Lafayette's agent La Sonde indicated that Cornet des Grez was about ready to cooperate with the advocates of independence in Brussels if they would agree to certain conditions. Among them were the release of the Vonckist General van der Mersch and, if Lafayette could persuade him, the acceptance of Ternant as a leading military figure in Belgium.[45]

The Brussels Congress also kept suing for Lafayette's support. The Comte de Thiennes came again to see him, this time bearing a letter from "the Sovereign Congress of the United Belgian Estates" which, while admitting recent reverses, revealed its determination to fight to a finish for Belgium's independence. The Congress too hoped that Lafayette would send an officer of distinction to investigate the situation and would be pleased if he were to fix upon the Chevalier de Ternant. In this way, the letter contended, France could assure itself that Belgium was worthy of support and the two countries could join in forming a bulwark against the enemies of liberty.[46]

Cornet des Grez himself came to Paris shortly afterward, and Lafayette made clear to him that he would not support the Congress party, would undertake no formal conversations with repre-

[45] Cornet des Grez to Lafayette, May 29, CU: Lafayette Archives, Carton IV, env. 2489–2531, and "Mémoire concernant l'état actuel des provinces belgiques," June 2[?], *ibid.*, env. 2556–2576. Both documents are dated at Douai. Tassier (p. 377) states that Lafayette went to Douai and spoke to a meeting of Belgian leaders on May 31. One of the citations given to support that statement (p. 378, n. 1) is Secretary Pistrich to Archduke Albert and Archduchess Marie Christine, June 17, Hans Schlitter (ed.), *Briefe der Erzherzogin Marie Christine . . . an Leopold II* (Vienna, 1896), pp. 291–92, but this letter describes Lafayette's participation in a meeting held in Paris in June and not in Douai on May 31.

[46] Congrès souverain des États belgiques unis to Lafayette, June 3, *Mémoires*, III, 42–44.

sentatives of the Belgian Congress, and would persist in demanding the release of General van der Mersch. Eager to do what he could to strengthen the popular party in the Belgian provinces, he consented, if Cornet des Grez would get the Flemish refugees in Paris together, to attend their meeting and explain his position.[47]

Acting upon Lafayette's suggestion, Cornet des Grez invited him to such a meeting at his lodgings on June 15. The host opened the meeting with a long speech sketching the course of the Belgian revolt and insisting that his party was not yet ready to compromise with Leopold II. Then, called upon by Cornet des Grez for his opinion, Lafayette declared his sentiments in favor of liberty, condemned some of the measures of the Belgian estates, but urged the two parties to coalesce upon liberal principles. Others present pointed out that despite its overtures to the liberal leaders at Douai, the Brussels party continued to keep Van der Mersch and other popular leaders in prison. Lafayette then again took the position that the release of Van der Mersch and other patriots must precede any reconciliation. After a great deal of further discussion the meeting resolved to send La Sonde to Brussels with a statement that cooperation would be contemplated only after political prisoners were released. An Austrian agent in Paris, having learned of this conference, reported that Lafayette had apparently attended it only to give it weight and to add to his renown.[48]

Dumouriez had recently importuned Lafayette again to be sent to Belgium as his *homme de confiance,* promising to enhance his influence there, "an influence essential to the success of the French constitution to which your destiny is thoroughly linked."[49] When he learned, apparently through Cornet des Grez, that Lafayette meant not to designate a French general to serve the cause of Belgian independence but was demanding the release of Van der Mersch as a precondition to any kind of cooperation whatsoever, he was displeased. Dumouriez was no friend of the Bourbon-

---

[47] See below, n. 48.

[48] Pistrich to Marie Christine, June 14, 17, Schlitter (ed.), pp. 291–92. See also Tassier, pp. 377–78.

[49] Dumouriez to Lafayette, May 31, is (in a somewhat garbled version) in *Mémoires,* III, 41–42. The original is now in CU: Lafayette Archives, Carton IV, env. 2531–2543.

Habsburg alliance. In a letter consisting of twelve numbered paragraphs he protested against Lafayette's having reduced the Belgian
negotiations to "sterile compliments," and with unconcealed disappointment he berated him for following a "policy lagging two
years behind the Revolution." According to Dumouriez, although
Lafayette had by several actions involved leading figures in the
Belgian upheaval, yet he, who was "chief of the patriotic party in
France," was "refusing to send them even a single man to guide
them." If, however, they would be overwhelmed, "you will be in
their eyes an Austrian" and "they will consider themselves betrayed by France [and] beguiled by you." Brabant would become
a center for French émigrés, and the Low Countries would become
the point of departure for "the most disastrous plots against the
Revolution," plots which would spread into Switzerland and
Germany. "Thus from the Savoy boundary to Dunkirk we will
be encircled in an unbroken line by enemies of the Constitution. . . .
Consider what strength you will give not only to the enemies of
the Constitution but to your personal enemies."[50]

By this time, however, Lafayette had set his course against the
Belgian Congress. In his mind the Belgian insurrection had become "an intrigue of aristocrats and clergy, in which the interests
of the people had been forgotten and where he discerned no principle of liberty or of the rights of nations."[51] Nor could he have
overlooked the advantage for the alliance of Bourbons and Habs-
burgs that lay in a reconciliation of the Belgians with Emperor
Leopold.

When Lafayette finally got around to answering the letter of the
Belgian Congress which Thiennes had delivered, he at first thought
of sending a lengthy reply pleading for Van der Mersch and sub-
stituting Dumouriez for Ternant. Whether or not he ever received
Dumouriez's protest letter, it was now evident that they were in
opposing camps regarding the future of Belgium. In the end he
decided not to commit himself to the Congress. While thanking

[50] Dumouriez to Lafayette, June 30, AN: F⁷ 4691. This letter is in the papers of neither
Dumouriez nor Lafayette. Perhaps it was never sent or, if sent, never received. It nevertheless reveals Dumouriez's reaction to Lafayette's Belgian policy.

[51] *Mémoires*, III, 46 n. See also below, n. 53.

it for the confidence shown him and for the opportunity to express his views, he made clear that its policy was not his. Although he spoke, he claimed, as a private individual whose only title to a public role lay in his being a friend of liberty, his interest in the prosperity of the Belgians and in the speedy termination of their internal divisions obliged him to insist upon the release of General van der Mersch as "the first and the indispensable way of satisfying those views which ought to animate all patriotic hearts." As for the request that he nominate Ternant for a high post at Brussels, he contented himself, while vicariously expressing "the gratitude that your confidence will not fail to inspire in him," with the terse observation that Ternant was at the moment in Germany.[52] When Thiennes carried Lafayette's stiff note back to the Congress, it made clear that Lafayette had committed himself to Belgian reconciliation with Austria.

Montmorin's views on the Belgian situation were in principle much like Lafayette's. He looked upon Belgium's destiny with the eyes of a minister of the Old Regime, anxious for the success of France's ally Austria. Dumouriez continued to disagree. He inferred that Montmorin, exaggerating the mistakes of the Belgian Congress, yielded too readily to the suasion of the Austrian ambassador. Lafayette's personal position, however, Dumouriez believed (or pretended to believe), was entirely different. As "a man of the Nation" Lafayette had to keep an eye out for the dangers threatening France from outside, "and no step you take in that regard can compromise you." Having tried in vain to see Lafayette and get his approval to go to Brussels as his agent, Dumouriez finally left without seeing him (July 9). He apologized for doing so, on the grounds that he had to keep an appointment for the evening of July 10 in Brussels even if preoccupation with the Federation left Lafayette no time for a conference. Since he would need more money than he himself could provide, he presumed that Lafayette would place six thousand livres to his credit in Brussels: "I am too well acquainted with the delicacy of your feelings

[52] See "Projet de réponse de M. le Mis de la F. au Congrès," in CU: Lafayette Archives, Carton IV, env. 2642–2763 (not in Lafayette's hand). The letter actually sent to the Congress is in *Mémoires*, III, 44–45.

to have the slightest concern in that regard."[53] Giving Lafayette gratuitous advice on the alliance with Spain and on the choice of ministers, and warning him against the "intrigues . . . of false friends who make ... dangerous proposals,"[54] Dumouriez promised to stay in Belgium only a very short time if he found himself unable to accomplish something useful to both the French and the Belgian nation.[55] And, in fact, he soon returned to Paris, disillusioned.

Mirabeau, inadequately informed, watched these developments with unconcealed disapproval. Did the king and the queen know, he asked in some dudgeon, that Lafayette had sent Dumouriez directly to the Belgian Congress? Dumouriez had left, he stated positively but incorrectly, in company with La Sonde, who for many months had been Lafayette's "political jockey—and surely, it would have been difficult to select one more base and more perverse." Mirabeau saw in this alleged high-handedness another example of Lafayette's arrogance. Sending a *maréchal de camp* such as Dumouriez with the avowed purpose of dealing with the Congress was "the most glaring act of a mayor of the palace who unquestionably wished to pass, in the eyes of strangers, as master of everything and of everybody." If the king and the queen had known of Lafayette's decision but had concealed it from him, Mirabeau felt constrained to remonstrate: if he were but "half informed," he could give only bad advice, and if he were misled, even worse; and if they had merely forgotten to tell him, he must point out that he could be really useful only if carefully kept *au courant.*[56]

Thus, it appears, not only did Mirabeau suspect that Louis XVI

---

[53] Dumouriez to Lafayette, July 4, CU: Lafayette Archives, Carton IV, env. 2531–2543, and July 9, *Mémoires*, III, 45–46. Lafayette (at least subsequently) thought Dumouriez's behavior in Belgium hypocritical: see *ibid.*, p. 46 n., and cf. Dumouriez, II, 84–85, 90–91.

[54] Dumouriez to Lafayette, July 9, CU: Lafayette Archives, Carton IV, env. 2531–2543. This passage is one of the several omitted from the version of this letter in *Mémoires*, III, 45–46.

[55] *Mémoires*, III, 46.

[56] Mirabeau to the court, July 9, Bacourt (ed.), II, 94–95. Cf. *Orateur du peuple*, No. 58, quoted in Blancheteau catalogue, p. 69, item 233, which erroneously stated that Lafayette had sent Dumouriez to Brussels and was reported to be preparing to lead 10,000 National Guards to the frontier.

failed to consult him about some of his decisions but he also was less well informed than he wanted to be or wanted others to think that he was. As a matter of fact, as Dumouriez recognized, Louis XVI in the conduct of foreign affairs relied on neither Lafayette nor Mirabeau, even if Marie Antoinette seemed willing to rely upon the latter rather than the former.[57] The king took his cue from Montmorin, whose views in these matters largely determined Lafayette's. For the nonce, however, Mirabeau's scoldings of the court and his denunciations of Lafayette produced but small effect, for foreign affairs were temporarily of secondary importance. The great national Federation was in the offing, and all of Paris seethed with an expectation that made the controversies over Nootka Sound and the Belgian provinces seem subordinate and remote—even to Mirabeau.

BIBLIOGRAPHICAL NOTES

The collection of Dumouriez' letters to Lafayette in the Cornell University Library and the Archives Nationales contains at least two letters and several passages from others that were omitted from the versions published in Lafayette's *Mémoires*. The omissions do not seem to be of major significance, and it would appear that wherever the editors of the *Mémoires* intentionally left anything out, they did so largely to soft-pedal Dumouriez's mixture of mendicant with patronizing tones toward Lafayette, who was about eighteen years his junior, and his severe criticisms of the Montmorin-Lafayette policy regarding Belgium. Dumouriez' *Vie et Mémoires* (II, 84–91) gives an account of his relations with Lafayette at this time and of his intercession in the Belgian crisis which, as is to be anticipated, is more favorable to himself and less favorable to Lafayette than we think justifiable.

[57] According to P. Vogt d'Hunolstein (ed.), *Correspondance de Marie Antoinette* (Paris, 1864), pp. 185–87, the queen wrote out a memoir in her own hand from passages copied verbatim from Mirabeau's letter of July 9.

CHAPTER XX

The Return of Orléans

WHEN, at the end of June, Lafayette tried to assure the Marquis de Bouillé that the disorders which had recently rent France would probably have no serious consequences,[1] he nevertheless admitted that he did not want Orléans to return to Paris before the great Federation. Orléans, however, had become restless in London. The Belgian affair had brought him no laurels, and with the possibility that Leopold's peace overtures might succeed, it became less explosive as an international crisis and correspondingly less likely to produce fame and glory. On the other hand, the Châtelet's investigation of the insurrection of October 5–6 had produced no convincing evidence that incriminated the prince. So he now considered it both useless to stay in London and safe to return to Paris. Lafayette nevertheless intended that he should not return. "I still count upon his cowardice to retain him in London," he confided to Bouillé.[2]

Lafayette's aide Boinville had been in London for six months shadowing Orléans, but he now asked permission to come home, and Lafayette, though reluctant to leave Orléans in England unwatched, allowed him to do so.[3] Shortly after Boinville arrived in Paris, it was noised about that Orléans proposed to return to France for the Federation.[4] The question of Orléans' future had already

---

[1] Lafayette to Bouillé, June 26, 1790, *Mémoires,* II, 477.

[2] *Ibid.*

[3] See above, pp. 296–97, and Morris diary, May 11, 13, 28, June 9, 20, 21, 22, Davenport (ed.), I, 512–14, 529, 538, 546–48.

[4] Lafayette to Bouillé, June 26, *Mémoires,* II, 472; La Marck to Mirabeau, June 26, Bacourt (ed.), II, 52. See also Lafayette's speech in the National Assembly, July 6, *AP,* XVI, 720.

come to Montmorin's attention as minister of foreign affairs, for the prince had asked, if he were not allowed home, to be made the formal and actual head of the French mission in Britain, the Belgian crisis being no longer critical enough by itself to serve as a convincing pretext for keeping him from the National Assembly. On June 25, he forced the issue by writing to the king that he definitely planned to return to France soon.[5]

Although many—Lafayette probably among them—still suspected that Orléans had been responsible for the uprising of October 5–6, continual ferment in Paris after his departure made it less plausible that his presence alone had been or would be sufficient to cause unrest in the capital. Furthermore, the restored popularity of the king made Orléans now seem less formidable than previously as a figure around whom anti-Bourbon sentiment might rally. All the same, though the Triumvirate and their Jacobin following might have little use for Orléans personally, his return might induce them to join him in making political capital out of professing that his record as a friend of the Revolution entitled him to more respectful consideration than he had so far received. Hence, to oblige Orléans to remain in London seemed less hazardous to Lafayette (and apparently also to Montmorin and the king) than to permit him to become active once more in Paris.[6] Lafayette therefore had to weigh carefully how far he dared to go in intimidating Orléans.

At this juncture the attacks upon Lafayette in both *ad hoc* pamphlets and regular journals began to reach unprecedented bitterness, partly doubtless in expectation of Orléans' return. Probably because the court agreed with Mirabeau that Lafayette was inept and would play into the hands of the Orleanists unless all the royal supporters combined their forces, the king seriously considered enjoining Lafayette to work with Mirabeau.[7] In words

---

[5] Orléans to Liancourt and Biron, Mar. 6, Apr. 3, *Correspondance de Louis-Philippe-Joseph d'Orléans avec Louis XVI . . .* (Paris, 1800), pp. 115–17, 120–26; Orléans to Montmorin, Mar. 6, May 28, *ibid.,* pp. 113, 141–44; Montmorin to Orléans, May 31, *ibid.,* pp. 144–48; Orléans to Montmorin, June 7, *ibid.,* pp. 149–52; Montmorin to Orléans, June 17, *ibid.,* pp. 152–54; and Orléans to Louis XVI, June 25, *ibid.,* pp. 155–57.

[6] Lafayette to Bouillé, June 26, *Mémoires,* II, 472.

[7] See above, pp. 424–25.

that seemed to echo those which Mirabeau had urged upon the queen,[8] Louis XVI wrote out in his own hand a draft of a statement (somewhat akin to an order) which, while claiming to have "complete confidence" in Lafayette, would, if obeyed, have obliged him to share some of his burden with Mirabeau:

You are so occupied by the duties of your post . . . that it is impossible for you to provide for everything. We must therefore make use of a man who has talent, energy, and who can fill in for whatever, for lack of time, you are not able to do. We are strongly persuaded that Mirabeau is the one who would be most suitable, because of his vigor, his talents, and the way he has of handling affairs in the Assembly. We therefore wish, and require of the zeal and attachment of M. de Lafayette, that he prepare to work with Mirabeau on matters concerning the welfare of the state, that of my service and of my person.[9]

Before her husband's instructions could be delivered, Marie Antoinette arranged to see Lafayette in person. On the evening of June 29 she asked him face to face to join forces with Mirabeau.[10] Perhaps, too, they talked about what should be done regarding Orléans.[11] At any rate, on the following day Montmorin in a dispatch to London supported Lafayette's position that Orléans should not return at that time;[12] and Louis XVI personally wrote the prince that things had not changed and he was to continue to cooperate with La Luzerne.[13] Shortly afterward the queen let La

[8] See above, p. 425. Lafayette thought the words were dictated by Mirabeau: *Mémoires*, II, 367, n. 1; see also below, n. 10.

[9] Louis XVI to Lafayette, June 29, *AP*, LV, 444, and *Mémoires*, II, 496. This draft was found in the king's *armoire de fer* after his suspension. The several versions of it differ only in minutiae. Lafayette said that he never received it (*Mémoires*, II, 367), and at the king's trial and elsewhere it was referred to as only a "project": *AP*, LV, 687, LVII, 244.

[10] Marie Antoinette to Mercy, June 29, La Rocheterie and Beaucourt (eds.), II, 182; La Marck to Mirabeau, June 30, Bacourt (ed.), II, 67; and *Mémoires*, II, 367. It is possible that the king's draft of June 29 was not intended as a letter but rather as a script for Louis' part in the interview with Lafayette; it does not have the usual epistolary salutation and close.

[11] Marie Antoinette to Mercy, June 29, La Rocheterie and Beaucourt (eds.), II, 181–82.

[12] Montmorin to Orléans, June 30, BVP: (old call number) 29417, folio, Part II (enclosing a letter of the king), and Orléans to Louis XVI, July 5, Orléans, *Correspondance*, p. 169. See also Marie Antoinette's memoir, July 9, Vogt d'Hunolstein (ed.), pp. 186–87, and Staël-Holstein to Gustavus III, July 4, Staël-Holstein, p. 165.

[13] Louis XVI to Orléans, June 30, BVP: (new call number) Ms. 934, Observation No. 23.

Marck see a lengthy report of the interview she had had with Lafayette, and she permitted La Marck to show it to Mirabeau likewise. "You will be pleased with it," La Marck wrote him,[14] and
Mirabeau was. "Gilles-César is caught in his own trap," he exulted,
and the main question for him now became: "To what point do we
need to help him there?"[15] On his side, however, Lafayette perceived the trap, and his repugnance to Mirabeau now combined
with his suspicion of the court to frustrate them. In the end he
refused to comply with the court's request that he collaborate with
Mirabeau, and it was never renewed. The draft of Louis XVI's
behest to that effect remained undelivered and was put in the
king's iron chest, perhaps with the intention of using it on some
opportune occasion.[16]

Mirabeau's apprehension of Jacobin intrigue grew as he became
more certain of having worsted Lafayette. He had heard and
heeded (or pretended to heed) a batch of rumors of dubious origin: bread had been distributed for much less than the regular
price fixed by Necker's "juggling"; money was being clandestinely
distributed among the troops of the line; subversive agents were
being sent from Paris to the provinces; incendiary pamphleteers
were being subsidized in the capital; the Lameths had had a long
conference with officers of the paid National Guard; Orléans had
borrowed millions in Holland, part of which had already reached
Paris; and so on. Stressing the imminence of catastrophe, he advised Louis XVI to adopt a policy that showed not only his contempt for both Lafayette and Orléans but also his intention to play
the one against the other. If Orléans had made up his mind to return, Mirabeau expostulated, the court could not well prevent it.
Besides, he declared, Orléans had ceased to be dangerous, since
he no longer had a following; the Jacobins had never been his
partisans even though they were the only ones he might still look
to for support. For that very reason the prince ought to be treated
well, for if his relations with the court were good, the Jacobins

---

[14] June 29, Bacourt (ed.), II, 67.

[15] Mirabeau to La Marck, June 29, *ibid.*, p. 66.

[16] See above, n. 10.

would distrust him, and even if they did not, they would lose the confidence of the "democrats." Besides, Orléans' presence at court would be a source of embarrassment to Lafayette, for the two would impede each other. Let Lafayette therefore seem to be Orléans' persecutor, thus making the friends of the one the enemies of the other. If, on the contrary, the court placed obstacles in Orléans' way and so seemed to be persecuting him, Orléans would join the "democrats" as an ill-used prince, thus providing a now leader-less party with a martyred leader and pushing the royal party more than ever under Lafayette's control. Mirabeau advised the king, therefore, to say to Orléans that he was welcome to return, "but I do not want your name to be any longer in the mouth of the factious."[17]

As Mirabeau foresaw, Lafayette played into his hand by accept-ing the role of Orléans' persecutor (though only at first). The com-mandant general recognized that Orléans and the Orleanists were his political opponents, that the Jacobin leaders were more sympa-thetic to the Orléans party than to himself, and hence that to keep the prince out of France was a way of keeping reinforcements from his own political enemies. He sent his aide Boinville back to Lon-don with instructions to urge, cajole, or threaten Orléans into a degree of anxiety that would induce him to postpone his return until after the national Federation. To that end he provided Boin-ville with instructions designed to show the prince that his return would be dangerous not merely to public order but, in view of the animosity in certain quarters, perhaps to his person as well.[18]

Upon his arrival in London Boinville, accompanied by the French ambassador, promptly called upon the Duc d'Orléans. He told his host, among other things, that Lafayette was afraid that ill-intentioned persons might foment trouble in Paris if Orléans returned, and as Lafayette's envoy he urged the prince, for the sake of public tranquility, to delay his return. La Luzerne spoke in the

---

[17] Mirabeau to the court, July 1 (2 letters), Bacourt (ed.), II, 67–72. See also *ibid.*, I, 183–88. The queen made a résumé of this letter of Mirabeau in her own hand: Vogt d'Hunolstein (ed.), pp. 180–81.

[18] Inferred from La Luzerne to Lafayette and same to Orléans, July 4, *Mémoires*, II, 475–79. See also Orléans to Levassor de La Touche, July 3, Orléans, *Correspondance*, p. 160; *Mémoires*, II, 480–82; and below, n. 32.

same vein. Not yet having received Louis' instructions to continue to cooperate with La Luzerne,[19] Orléans agreed to wait in London, at least until he had time to learn the wishes of the king and the National Assembly regarding the course he should follow. La Luzerne thought "everything went off as well as could be."[20]

Boinville then left London to report to Lafayette. Two hours after he had gone, La Luzerne received a visit from Orléans, who had come to say that he had changed his mind—having been persuaded, La Luzerne surmised, by his friends to do so.[21] This time, Orléans professed that he felt honor-bound to return to Paris for the Federation by his now publicized statement that he would do so; if he remained in London, people might infer that he did not leave because he did not dare rather than because his attachment to king and country made him anxious to avoid causing trouble at home. He intended, therefore, to go to France at once, unless La Luzerne would help him justify his remaining in England. To get such a justification he had brought with him a prepared statement, to which he asked La Luzerne to attest. The ambassador recognized that statement as a partly true recital of their conversation with Boinville, but he feared that it might give a reader an erroneous impression. It implied that although Boinville had vainly tried to frighten the prince with imaginary dangers, what had really persuaded Orléans to remain in England was none of Boinville's threats but the French ambassador's opinion that his return to France might create public disturbances—in other words, that the prince had canceled his proposed return to Paris not out of cowardice but out of a patriotic desire to forestall trouble. La Luzerne at first refused to sign this prepared state-

[19] See above, p. 482.

[20] La Luzerne to Lafayette, July 4, *Mémoires*, II, 475. La Luzerne seems to place the interview with Orléans on July 1 (*ibid.*, p. 476), but see "Copie de l'écrit remis à M. le duc d'Orléans par M. le chevalier de La Luzerne, July 4," *ibid.*, pp. 479–80; Orléans to Levassor de La Touche, July 3, Orléans, *Correspondance*, pp. 160–62 (given also in *Mémoires*, II, 480–82, and *AP*, XVI, 749–50); and Dard, pp. 250–52. See also the Bibliographical Notes below, p. 502.

[21] La Luzerne to Lafayette, July 4, *Mémoires*, II, 476. See also Dard, pp. 216–18. The ablest of Orléans advisers at this time was Choderlos de Laclos; Grace Dalrymple Elliot (*Journal of My Life during the French Revolution* [London, 1859], p. 284) thought that Biron also was among them.

ment, but after much persuasion he reluctantly did so. Orléans gave him his word that he would make no use of the statement thus confirmed other than to send a copy of it to Lafayette and to show it on future occasions as testimony that he had remained in England for commendable reasons.[22] In the end, however, Orléans did not keep his word.[23]

The day after his conversation with Orléans, La Luzerne, worried that perhaps he had made a mistake by yielding to the prince, wrote Lafayette a circumstantiated explanation of his conduct. Even if he had been mistaken, he apologized, he felt relieved that the prince had been kept from going to Paris, "which was our only aim," and Lafayette, by making public what La Luzerne now wrote, could forestall "meddlers" who might try to exploit the ambassador's certification. Thus, La Luzerne felt, he had probably served Lafayette better by giving it than he would have done by refusing to give it. With the explanatory letter he sent Lafayette a copy of Orléans' statement by special courier.[24]

Orléans also sent the certified statement with a covering letter to his friend and chancellor, the deputy Levassor de La Touche, and true to his promise to keep Lafayette informed, sent copies of both documents to Lafayette as well as to Montmorin.[25] By July 6 La Touche had received these documents, and presumably Lafayette had likewise. By that time Lafayette probably had La Luzerne's communication as well, and in addition had already received or soon was to receive a personal report from Boinville. Meanwhile, despite the honors pouring in upon him in advance of the great Federation, Lafayette had some reason to detect a few ominous straws in the wind. Many persons were leaving Paris out of fear that riots would occur on July 14,[26] and the grapevine telegraphed that the center companies of the National Guard were going to ask for the Duc de Biron, an avowed Orleanist, to sup-

[22] Cf. below, pp. 486, 487–88.

[23] See below, pp. 488–89.

[24] La Luzerne to Lafayette, July 4, *Mémoires*, II, 475–78; "Copie de l'écrit remis à M. le duc d'Orléans," *ibid.*, p. 479; and "Note remise . . . ," *ibid.*, pp. 480–82. See also n. 32 below.

[25] See n. 24 above.

[26] *Journal général de la cour*, July 4, p. 27.

plant Lafayette as commandant general.[27] On July 5 the National Assembly inflicted an indirect defeat upon Lafayette by naming the *ci-devant* Marquis de Bonnay as president for the period that would include the day of the Federation, with La Rochefoucauld, who, everyone knew, was Lafayette's close friend, running third, and Menou, whom Lafayette had once called "un président orléanais"[28] second. Bonnay was regarded as the king's choice and hence presumably was more acceptable to Lafayette than Menou, though certainly less so than La Rochefoucauld, but La Marck, overlooking the complete absence of Mirabeau's name from the balloting,[29] got some consolation from the election returns: "Menou won more votes for the presidency than the Duc de La Rochefoucauld. New proof of what the party of La Fayette is in the Assembly."[30] Perhaps even more disturbing to Lafayette were the reports of secret meetings of the court with Mirabeau, which, despite inaccuracies, were essentially true: Mirabeau had in fact had a secret meeting with the queen at Saint-Cloud on July 2.[31] In brief, temporarily Lafayette could no longer count upon either the court's support or a majority in the Assembly, while he could feel certain of opposition in some of the press and in the Cordeliers.

At the same time, from his copy of Orléans' letter of July 4 to La Touche,[32] if not from other sources, Lafayette could easily infer that Orléans was going to appeal his case to the highest authorities.[33] Orléans' note, the one certified by La Luzerne, was, as La Luzerne had warned, a "mighty adroit" one,[34] and Orléans' letter to La Touche, frankly intended to be read in the National Assem-

---

[27] *Courrier de Paris*, July 4, pp. 26–27.

[28] Lafayette to [Mme de Simiane], [Apr. 5?], *Mémoires*, II, 458, and see above, p. 313.

[29] See above, pp. 427–29.

[30] La Marck to Mirabeau, July 4, Bacourt (ed.), II, 79. See also *ibid.*, p. 60 n., and *AP*, XVI, 691.

[31] *Journal général de la cour*, July 5, p. 45; *Ami du peuple*, July 6, p. 8; Mirabeau to the court, July 7, Bacourt (ed.), II, 83; and Marie Antoinette to Leopold II, July 7, Vogt d'Hunolstein (ed.), pp. 154–55.

[32] This letter is described in *Mémoires*, II, 480, as addressed "to the National Assembly, the king, and General Lafayette," but a correction, *ibid.*, III, 516, indicates (as do the contents) that it was "addressed to . . . La Touche," copies going to the others.

[33] See above, n. 32.

[34] La Luzerne to Lafayette, July 4, *Mémoires*, II, 476.

bly as well as by the king, was no less so. It asserted that after the prince had decided to leave England and had made a formal farewell call upon the British king, Boinville, accompanied by the French ambassador, had urged him not to return to France, giving "among several [other] reasons which could not have engaged my attention . . . that of the disorders which ill-intentioned persons who could be certain to make use of my name would rouse," and he enclosed a copy of La Luzerne's certification that such was indeed what Boinville had said.[35]

La Luzerne, it will be recalled, had thought that his having certified Orléans' account of their meeting with Boinville had engaged Orléans to stay in England, but Orléans' letter to La Touche gave a different impression. Stating that he did not wish to run the risk of creating public disorder, it requested the National Assembly "to regulate the course I am to take." Anyone who remembered that Mirabeau had intended to make a similar request on behalf of Orléans the previous October and was prevented only by Orléans' unwillingness to defy Lafayette[36] would have recognized the strategy Orléans was now employing—that of a member of the National Assembly who, having taken formal leave for a specific purpose, now wanted formal permission to return. Orléans' letter argued that he could not have been the cause of disorders in Paris, for despite his lengthy absence abroad, Paris was still not peaceful. "It is high time," he demanded, "to find out who are the ill-intentioned whose schemes are always known—without, however, anyone's ever being able to find any clue to their identity. It is time to learn why my name would serve better than any other as a pretext for popular movements. It is time finally that I should no longer be faced with this phantom without being given any clues of its reality." If, therefore, the Assembly did not object, he intended to abide by his announced intention of returning for the great event of July 14, and even if, as he did not expect, the Assembly took no action on his request, "I would ... conclude from that that whatever has been said to me by Sieur de Boinville is to be considered

---

[35] *Ibid.*, p. 480.

[36] See above, pp. 22–24.

null and void and that nothing stands in the way of my going to rejoin the assembly of which I have the honor of being a member." Not only did he ask La Touche to submit this letter and its enclosure to the Assembly but he indicated that he also intended to publish immediately an exposé of his conduct, including his conversation the previous October with Lafayette, depositing the original with the secretariat of the National Assembly.[37]

The Assembly gave La Touche a place on its agenda for the afternoon of July 6, and Lafayette attended that session. There La Touche read aloud the prince's letter, which, as obviously intended, put Lafayette in a position where he would either have to produce evidence against Orléans or admit that he had none. Thereupon Lafayette went to the tribune to respond, and he seemed embarrassed.[38] An observer remarked that his speech ("a discourse which he had learned by heart") lacked spontaneity.[39] After what had passed between him and the Duc d'Orléans in October, he declared ("and I would not permit myself to bring it up if he himself were not entertaining the Assembly with it"), he had thought that he owed it to Orléans to inform him that the very considerations which had led to his mission to London might still prevail. He himself did not share the current fear of potential disorder, he asserted, but every good citizen desired to avoid risks at the time of the Federation, "dedicated to confidence and common rejoicing," and that was why Boinville had undertaken "to say to M. le duc d'Orléans what I have just repeated to the Assembly."

With that statement (the truth but not the whole truth) the speaker cut his explanation short; instead, he tried an appeal to his colleagues' patriotism. Although the appeal might have seemed irrelevant to the issue then before the Assembly, it was a lucky stroke if unplanned, and clever if planned. It conveyed the sentiment that what happened to Orléans at this point was a minor con-

---

[37] *Mémoires*, II, 480–82. See n. 47 below. A copy of Orléans' letter to La Touche is now in AN: C184, Dr. 116, pièce 27 (armoire de fer).

[38] Ferrières, *Mémoires*, II, 84. [Montjoie], V, 67, says Lafayette went to the tribune "smiling," but he does not indicate whether the smile was one of embarrassment or of pleasure.

[39] *Courier français*, July 7, p. 56.

sideration. "As the one charged by the Assembly to keep public order during this great event," Lafayette now went on to explain why he felt that he no longer needed to share the fear that disorder might result from Orléans' return: "The nearer I see July 14 approach, the more convinced I become that it ought to inspire a sense of security as well as of satisfaction. That feeling is based particularly upon the attitude of all citizens [and] upon the zeal of the Paris National Guard and of our brothers in arms, who are coming in from all parts of the realm, and since the friends of the constitution and of public order have never been united in such great numbers, never shall we be stronger." With that patriotic appeal, Lafayette returned to his seat. The numerous accounts of that session of the National Assembly do not indicate that this time his hearers received his speech with the applause to which he had become accustomed.[40]

On the contrary, the comments that followed were unmistakably unfriendly. The Duc de Biron expressed the opinion that while under a despotic and arbitrary government mere suspicion might drive a good citizen into exile, under a rule of liberty such an excessive use of authority was not permissible, and since in the eight months since Orléans' departure his accusers had not come forward with a single fact to justify their accusations, Orléans ought to be asked to come home to give an account of his conduct and to participate in the Federation. Duquesnoy, usually an admirer of Lafayette, remarked that if all the deputies against whom charges were levied had absented themselves, the Assembly would have broken up months ago. He recalled that when Orléans had left for London, the National Assembly had taken no action and when, a little later, Menou had asked that Orléans be recalled to explain his conduct, it had likewise decided not to deliberate on the matter, and he now thought that it should continue that policy. He therefore moved to pass to the order of the day—i.e., to take no

---

[40] See, among others, *AP*, XVI, 720–21; *Journal de Paris*, July 7, pp. 760–61; *Moniteur*, July 7, pp. 771–72; *Point de jour*, July 7, pp. 408–9; and *Mémoires*, II, 483–84. Desmoulins (*Révolutions*, No. 33, pp. 434–35 n.) says that when a rising vote was taken on Orléans' readmission, Lafayette kept sitting almost alone, but no other paper reports such conspicuous behavior.

action.[41] The Assembly adopted that motion, thereby playing into Orléans hand, since he had declared that he would consider a decision to take no action as meaning that he could regard himself as free to come home. Contrary to what Mirabeau had expected, however, Lafayette chose not to play the role of Orléans' nemesis and refrained from asking for any other decision.

Lafayette's speech on this occasion, unlike others, received but little favorable comment in the press as well. Asserting that Orléans' letter explained some "extraordinary" events, the *Courrier de Provence,* founded by Mirabeau and still regarded as his organ, printed it entire and followed it with the text of Lafayette's speech without comment.[42] The *Courier français* claimed to be mystified: "We, like many others, did not understand."[43] The *Courrier de Paris,* criticizing Lafayette's having sent an agent to warn Orléans to stay away from Paris and maintaining that if the prince heeded "those perfidious councils" and stayed away, he would lend credence to the slanders circulating in Paris, reasoned that if Orléans were guilty, he should be punished but if innocent, vindicated.[44] Marat, describing Lafayette's opposition to Orléans' return as one of "those secret underhanded dealings" which the commandant general and other enemies of the Revolution continually carried on, went a step further and argued that if Orléans proved to have been oppressed by the powerful faction of which Lafayette was the chief, he should be protected and his persecutors punished.[45] Desmoulins stigmatized Boinville's warning to Orléans as a "kind of lettre-de-cachet, delivered by the commandant general of the Parisian militia to M. Philippe Capet."[46]

True to his word, Orléans published his *Exposé* immediately and some newspapers republished it. It reviewed his conduct during the course of the Revolution, adding nothing to the account

[41] *AP*, XVI, 720–21.

[42] *Courrier de Provence*, July 6–9, p. 174.

[43] *Courier français*, July 8, p. 56.

[44] *Courrier de Paris*, July 6, pp. 49–53, July 7, p. 80, July 8, pp. 81–82.

[45] *Ami du peuple*, July 10, p. 8.

[46] *Révolutions*, No. 33, pp. 435 n.

which had already become public property. A considerable part of it was devoted to denying charges made by several pamphlets circulating in Paris, especially that of having incited the uprising of October 5–6.[47] Quoting extracts from it, Loustalot censured both Orléans for not having replied to his slanderers sooner if he were innocent and Lafayette for not having defended him if he had indeed gone to England to facilitate the restoration of order in Paris or for not having revealed his guilt if he was indeed a conspirator. He even implied that Lafayette's purpose might have been to keep the prince in London in order to deprive the French of a fellow-citizen who might have won some of the homage which Lafayette wanted to keep for himself alone.[48]

Lafayette had been scolded by the Leftist press before but never so consistently or for so long as in late June and early July 1790. Having already exploited the Féral case and now exploiting the Orléans affair to the full, the Leftist press apparently meant to strike Lafayette down at this strategic moment before the Federation. Each side accused the other of having bought pamphleteers and bribed agitators to present its side of the story. An anonymous pamphlet entitled *Adresse d'un aide-de-camp de la Garde nationale à ses concitoyens* was so unfriendly as to arouse protest from all of Lafayette's aides. They decided that Jauge, the senior member of their group, should send a letter to the press explaining that none of the commandant general's aides could have had anything to do with such an insulting publication. Jauge's letter to that effect soon appeared in the papers.[49]

The pamphlet warfare, intensified by the far-flung comings and goings of travelers to the Federation, helped to aggravate the uneasy forebodings of violence. One of the pamphlets predicted that the Battalions of Saint-Marcel and Saint-Antoine were going to resort to "most cruel excesses," and the officers of the Saint-Marcel

[47] "Exposé de la conduite de M. le duc d'Orléans dans La Révolution de France," in *AP*, XVI, 729–34. The "Exposé," sent on June 11 from London to be published in Paris, appeared about July 6 as a pamphlet.

[48] *Révolutions de Paris*, No. 52, July 3–10, pp. 743–50.

[49] Jauge to the editor, *Moniteur*, July 6, p. 768, and *Journal de Paris*, July 5, p. 754. Cf. [Estienne], *Interrogatoire de Lafayette*, pp. 25–26 n.

battalion came to consult Lafayette on what to do to counteract this accusation. He advised them to publicize their determination to live up to their oath to combat the enemies of the constitution, and accordingly the battalion commander wrote a letter to the press proclaiming the devotion of his men to the revolutionary cause.[50] The editor of the *Annales patriotiques et littéraires* sent a personal letter to Lafayette asking him to make a thorough search for sabotage in the École Militaire, the Tuileries, and the Luxembourg and to post a heavy guard throughout the École Militaire until after the Federation.[51] About the same time a newspaper reported that Lafayette was about to arrest a man in whose home three thousand daggers had been discovered. The report gave rise to further consternation that a conspiracy was afoot to foment an uprising on July 14, and alarm did not cease until, two days later, the newspaper corrected the story: the arrested man was merely manufacturing daggers.[52]

Less publicly than the press of the Left, Mirabeau continued to snipe at Lafayette. When, for example, Talon resigned from his office at the Châtelet, Mirabeau, expecting him to be named keeper of the king's privy seal, wrote to the queen to oppose Talon's appointment to so high a post, giving among his several reasons that Lafayette was Talon's patron.[53] Another occasion for opposing Lafayette originated with the expectation that the king and the National Assembly would attend the Federation, which raised for Mirabeau (as for others) the delicate problem of precedence. The heart of the ceremony would be the taking of the oath—by the National Guards, the soldiers, the sailors, the deputies of the National Assembly, and the king, thus binding the whole nation directly or vicariously to the future constitution and to each other. Mirabeau, constantly seeking to circumscribe the Jacobins' influence in the Assembly and Lafayette's on the king and queen and to

---

[50] *Journal de Paris*, July 8, p. 766.

[51] J.-L. Carra to Lafayette, July 8, *Annales patriotiques et littéraires*, July 8, pp. 113–14.

[52] *Courrier de Paris*, July 5, p. 43, July 7, pp. 66–67. See also *Annales patriotiques et littéraires*, July 7, p. 108.

[53] June 28, Bacourt (ed.), II, 64.

increase his own, wrote to the court on this subject as well. Painting the Lameths, Barnave, Duport, and Menou as spying enemies
who must in turn be spied upon, he proposed that the king call
together a committee from the National Assembly to prepare,
among other things, the oath that the Constitution Committee
should prescribe for the Federation. The committee should include Bonnay (as president of the Assembly), Sieyès, Bureau de
Pusy, Talleyrand, Le Chapelier, and Mirabeau himself (all members of the Society of 1789), as well as Lafayette. It should also
consider what place the dauphin and the queen were to occupy
at the Federation and whether to extend an invitation to the diplomatic corps. Such a committee, Mirabeau wrote, would be very
popular and accord perfectly with the authority vested in Lafayette,
but at the same time it would limit him to doing publicly no more
than the committee would require of him. Moreover, Mirabeau
cautioned: "It is supremely important that he know nothing of
this proposal [to leave these matters to a committee] unless it be
irrevocably accepted, and only one hour before this [suggested]
meeting."[54]

The same day Mirabeau urged upon La Marck the importance
of Louis' extending to the ambassadors in Paris an invitation to accompany him at the Federation. The attendance of the diplomatic
corps would lend éclat to the ceremony in the eyes of the spectators,
who would ascribe it to the king's great popularity, while the absence of foreign ambassadors would lead to charges that it was
due to an "Austrian Cabal." The king, Mirabeau warned, should
personally get the credit for inviting the ambassadors and not allow
himself to be anticipated in this matter by Lafayette.[55]

The approach of the Federation apparently led some mutual
acquaintances to hope that Lafayette and Mirabeau, despite their
reciprocal animosity, might still be persuaded to work together.
Whether upon the initiative of Condorcet or some other would-be
peacemaker, a group of leading citizens was invited to meet at his

[54] Ninth note to the court, July 7, *ibid.*, pp. 83–85.
[55] *Ibid.*, pp. 86–87.

home on the evening of July 7. Among them were Lafayette, Talleyrand, Sieyès, and Mirabeau (but apparently none of the Jacobin leaders). Mirabeau attended, he later claimed, because he had been led to believe that the meeting would discuss only the future purpose and program of those present. From the outset, however, Lafayette called their attention to details pertaining to the Federation. The major question quickly became how to proceed in drafting the pledge that the king was to take at the Federation, and Talleyrand had a proposal ready. He took special pains, Mirabeau thought, to explain the route that he had taken to come to the meeting (so as to indicate that he had not come with Lafayette), and then he made the motion ("cunning," Mirabeau thought it) that the king himself in a letter to be agreed upon in advance (and of which Talleyrand had prepared a draft which in Mirabeau's opinion was "pitiable") should propose to the National Assembly the text of the oath that he "would like to take." According to Mirabeau, the text proposed by Talleyrand began: "I, first citizen, king of the French, swear to maintain, with all the power the nation has delegated to me, the constitution. . . ."

The debate on the king's oath, thus begun, went on for hours. As Mirabeau reported the meeting to La Marck, Lafayette then rambled on, giving the impression that his purpose was only to provide himself with grounds for pretending to the king and the queen that he had made overtures to Mirabeau; in reality, however, he had made no change in either his views or his clique of revolutionary ineffectives, whom he expected to follow his lead but who would in fact be good for nothing. Although Mirabeau admitted that he did not object to the wording of the royal oath that Talleyrand proposed, he and Sieyès were of the opinion that it would be inappropriate for the king to seem to ask legislative approval for it. In the end they were able to win the others over, and the group finally agreed unanimously that it would drop Talleyrand's proposal. After the meeting Mirabeau, afraid that Lafayette or the Constitution Committee of the National Assembly might "juggle" the decision reached, took care that La Marck (and through him, presumably the court also) should know of that decision, in the firm persuasion that the king should remain inflexibly opposed to seeking legislative approval.[56]

The differences between Mirabeau's and Talleyrand's plan for the royal oath reflected the rivalry of Lafayette and Mirabeau for the approbation of the throne. If Talleyrand's proposal had prevailed, Lafayette, as the one who had dominated the discussion at Condorcet's, would probably have received the major credit for requiring that the king in formulating the text of his special oath should seek the consent of the National Assembly. According to Mirabeau's plan, however, the king would seem to act of his own accord, Mirabeau would be one of the deputies called to the palace for consultation, and he rather than Lafayette would get credit for the arrangement. In the end Louis XVI was neither to take Mirabeau's advice nor to follow any procedure resembling Talleyrand's proposal. But if the purpose of the meeting at Condorcet's house had been to bring the two leading advocates of strong constitutional monarchy together, it failed.

In his next (the tenth) letter of advice to the royal court (July 9) Mirabeau continued his effort to undermine Lafayette. He bitterly decried what he termed Lafayette's assignment of Dumouriez to the Congress at Brussels (although in fact Dumouriez had departed without Lafayette's approval, lamely pretending that Lafayette's silence gave consent).[57] In Mirabeau's judgment Dumouriez was a totally unhappy choice, and if it had been made with the knowledge of the court, he must once more protest that his usefulness was being undercut by his being left in ignorance of the court's intention. Similarly, Mirabeau stressed, he would have disapproved of the instructions, if he had known about them, that the king had sent Orléans to remain in London—but if Orléans now failed to return to Paris, Mirabeau advised that those instructions should be attributed, if they became public, to "the mayor

---

[56] Mirabeau to La Marck, July 7, *ibid.*, pp. 88–89. This letter perhaps was written before the ninth letter to the court (see n. 54 above), in which case that letter to the court was a reaction to the meetings at Condorcet's house, but otherwise the order in which they were written makes little difference.

[57] See above, pp. 477–78.

of the palace," thus seeming to establish the "preponderance of the vizier and the impotence of the master."[58]

In this letter to the court Mirabeau again urged the queen to persuade the king to follow his advice. All would be lost if she merely confirmed her husband's indecision without imparting to him some of her own drive. By way of illustration of the king's baffling failure to act decisively the letter cited his not yet having followed Mirabeau's suggestion to invite a group of deputies to consider the part His Majesty should take in the Federation, and now it was too late. Moreover, Mirabeau added, so long as the queen did not install close to the king an able secret agent of her own choice and so long as the royal couple did not have in the ministry a dependable councillor (patently meaning himself) with whom they could consult every day and who had no other purpose than to restore the monarch's legitimate authority, they would continually run the risk of error, and the king and queen would be only timid prisoners, always obliged to bargain with their jailor (meaning Lafayette) and always at the mercy of insurrection, ambition, and demagoguery.[59] Mirabeau entrusted this letter to La Marck to deliver to the court, enclosing it in a brief one addressed to La Marck himself, in which again he voiced the opinion that Louis XVI should make a speech at the Federation and, moreover, frankly indicated that he himself be asked to write it.[60]

So, it appeared, Mirabeau sought to profit from the commandant general's temporary setback in the Orléans affair—the most palpable blow to Lafayette's popularity since the Revolution had begun. But in the end Lafayette's strategy proved correct—not to form an alliance with Mirabeau but to submerge all other considerations to the heart-stirring solidarity of Frenchmen to be symbolized by the great Federation of July 14, eagerly anticipated in some quarters, anxiously dreaded in others. Thousands of *fédérés* poured into Paris, apparently not fatigued by their long marches

[58] "Dixième note du comte de Mirabeau pour la cour," July 9, Bacourt (ed.), II, 94–95.

[59] *Ibid.*, pp. 95–96.

[60] *Ibid.*, pp. 96–97.

from the four corners of France, and explored the marvels of the capital most of them had never seen. They usually went promptly to pay their respects to their celebrated leaders, and the mayor and the commandant general felt called upon to announce that they would be at the Hôtel de Ville every morning to receive them except on Sunday, July 11.[61]

The reason for that exception was that Louis XVI intended to review three divisions of the Paris National Guard that day. Since the Champ-de-Mars was now reserved for the Federation, the review was scheduled for the Plaine des Sablons,[62] outside the Porte des Ternes. It was to be a very special occasion, for half of Lafayette's men, over 15,000 of the oldest National Guard unit of the realm, would pass in review before not only the king but also thousands of comrades in arms from the provinces. Each Paris Guardsman issued a personal invitation to two *fédérés* to attend the review as his guests.[63]

That Sunday an enormous number of Parisians and *fédérés* assembled on the Plaine des Sablons, and the three even-numbered divisions of the Paris National Guard already occupied the field when the commandant general rode up. Louis XVI arrived shortly afterward, escorted by several gentlemen of the court, and was greeted with joyous cheers. Even though she understood that she was to receive no military honors, Marie Antoinette came too, accompanied in her carriage by her two children. Never before had Lafayette's troops paraded before so large or so eminent a gathering. When the king with his retinue and the general with his staff had taken their places, the drums began to roll, and the Second Division filed past in review, followed by the Fourth and the Sixth. As the troops paraded before the king, they gave him the proper military salutes. When the last battalion had marched by, the crowd clapped and cheered, and some of the spectators surged toward the king and even toward the queen's carriage shouting "Vive le roi!" "Vive la reine!" Louis XVI, deeply touched, bowed

[61] *Journal de Paris*, July 8, p. 764.

[62] *Ibid.*

[63] *Journal général de la cour*, June 11, p. 84.

and smiled.[64] These spectators were *fédérés,* a witness observed, "not the vile slaves of a voluptuous and bloody tyrant" but free men expressing their gratitude to "the best of princes."[65] Marie Antoinette presented the dauphin, and as the pretty five-year-old boy smiled from his carriage upon the sea of faces before him, Parisians and *fédérés* responded with "Vive M. le dauphin!"[66] That morning Louis XVI seemed to have reconfirmed his place as head of the nation.

When the review was over, Lafayette escorted Louis XVI back to the Tuileries, and there the king found the Duc d'Orléans. His visit was not unexpected. He had arrived at the Palais Royal at four o'clock that morning, and shortly after his arrival he had written to the king to announce his advent and to ask permission to pay his respects as soon as possible.[67] He was accompanied by Montmorin. While Lafayette waited in the antechamber,[68] the prince spent a few moments with the king and then went to call upon the queen. Mirabeau had not preached his lesson in vain: both Louis XVI and Marie Antoinette received Orléans in a fashion "rather friendly than unfriendly," La Marck reported to Mirabeau, "as you advised."[69]

But the king's courtiers had not had the benefit of Mirabeau's instruction. Only the day before, Mme Elisabeth, the king's sister, had expressed what probably was still the prevalent feeling within the court, if not that of the king and the queen, when she wrote that

[64] *Moniteur,* July 14, p. 799. See also *Courier français,* July 13, pp. 103–4; *Révolutions de Paris,* No. 53, July 10–17, pp. 2–3; *Chronique de Paris,* July 12, p. 775; and *Journal général de la cour,* July 11, pp. 83–84, July 13, p. 102.

[65] *Courier français,* July 13, p. 104.

[66] *Révolutions de Paris,* No. 53, July 10–17, p. 3. The *Courrier de Paris dans les 83 départemens,* July 11, 1792, p. 183, reported (two years later) that on this occasion by-standers kissed the queen's gown and Lafayette's horse, but contemporary accounts mention no such exuberance.

[67] Orléans to Louis XVI, July 11, BVP: (new call number) Ms. 934, Observation No. 47.

[68] See below, n. 73.

[69] La Marck to Mirabeau, July 10 [*sic*], *ibid.,* p. 99. This letter is apparently misdated; every other account places the interview on July 11, and the letter of Orléans to the king announcing his arrival is dated July 11: see above, n. 67. See also *Gazette de Leide, supplément,* July 20; Staël-Holstein to Gustavus III, July 11, Staël-Holstein, p. 165–66; Ferrières, *Mémoires,* II, 88; *Chronique de Paris,* July 11, pp. 770–71; and *Journal général de la cour,* July 14, p. 110.

letter (already quoted)[70] in which she rejoiced that Lafayette's party was larger than that of Orléans because it was the less sanguinary and seemed to wish to serve the king.[71] The ladies in the queen's chamber therefore greeted Orléans only with silence, and at the entry to the king's apartments a gentleman of the court deliberately insulted him. The report soon went around that Lafayette, who was still in the antechamber, hearing of the prince's discomfiture, sent two of his aides to protect him,[72] and another report had it that after seeing the queen, Orléans passed into the anteroom where Lafayette was waiting, and the meeting of the two men was "most friendly."[73]

From the Tuileries Orléans went to the National Assembly. He took his seat on the left amid some applause. Shortly after his arrival he asked permission to take the civic oath and, permission granted, he first made a brief speech avowing his devotion to liberty, his loyalty to the king, and his approval of the decrees of the Assembly. He then took the oath, and the majority of the deputies applauded.[74]

In the end the impact of Orléans' return upon political events, as Lafayette preferred and as Mirabeau apparently had not anticipated, was feeble. Some suspected that a pamphlet answering his *Exposé* was written by Lafayette or at least published with his consent.[75] Other pamphlets attacked or defended the prince;[76] and

[70] See above, p. 468.

[71] To Mme de Bombelles, July 10, Feullet de Conches (ed.), III, 288–89.

[72] Ferrières to Mme Ferrières, July 13, Ferrières, *Correspondance*, pp. 237–38, and Simolin to Osterman, July 23, Feuillet de Conches (ed.), I, 332. See also Ferrières, *Mémoires*, II, 88; Bacourt (ed.), I, 186; Clermont-Gallerande, II, 22; Montjoie, II, 156–57 and n. 1; and Short to Jefferson, July 11, Boyd (ed.), XVII, 27.

[73] *Journal général de la cour*, July 14, p. 110. See also *Gazette universelle*, July 13, p. 904.

[74] *AP*, XVII, 46; *Gazette de Leide*, July 20; *Point du jour*, July 13, p. 33; and Ferrières to Mme Ferrières, July 13, Ferrières, *Correspondance*, p 237.

[75] Ferrières to Mme Ferrières, July 13, Ferrières, *Correspondance*, pp. 237–38, and *Journal général de la cour*, July 11, pp. 84–86. Among the pamphlets to which this suspicion might apply are *M. de la Fayette et Phillippe d'Orléans jugés par la nation*, *Réponse à l'Exposé de la conduite de M. le duc d'Orléans*, and *Examen impartial de l'Exposé de la conduite de M. le duc d'Orléans dans la Révolution actuelle*.

[76] Cf. *Gazette universelle*, July 10, p. 890; *Courrier de Paris*, July 14, p. 179; and *Journal général de la cour*, July 11, pp. 84–86.

for a time there was fear of an open breach that would do damage
to the public welfare.[77] The Swedish ambassador, Necker's son-in-
law, reported to his king that if Orléans were able to secure popular support, he might yet ruin Lafayette but only by stirring up
violent agitation.[78] The Marquis de Bouillé perhaps had already
begun to believe that, although the worst was yet to come, Lafayette
was losing popularity as a result of the attacks of the Orleanists,[79]
whom he like others among the aristocrats apparently thought
of as Jacobins. In Italy the émigré Vaudreuil, similarly mistaken,
piously hoped that rivalry between the Necker-Lafayette party,
which was that of revolution, and the Orléans party, which was
that of conspiracy, might convert the intended signal for joy and
intoxication at the forthcoming Federation into a signal for massacre instead. Like Mirabeau, though for different reasons, he con-
jectured that if the king were actually counting upon Lafayette,
then everything was ruined, but, if the king were only creating
an impression that he counted upon Lafayette, that would be a wise
and promising course,[80] obviously tending to exploit the commandant general's strength without strengthening him further.

Yet, despite the rumors, guesses, charges, innuendos, fears, and
hopes that filled the air and despite the numerous pamphlets for
or against Orléans and for or against Lafayette (some of which
doubtless were made to order) Lafayette did not rise to the bait,
and the periodical press soon became relatively inattentive to the
issue. Those who had intrigued to bring Orléans back for the Federation with the intention of raising a rival to Lafayette had chosen
the wrong time. Largely to the exclusion of other matters, news
about the Federation filled the journals,[81] and Lafayette remained
the uncontested cynosure of the *fédérés* and their well-wishers. Orléans, having been received with due courtesy by the commandant
general as well as by the royal court and the National Assembly,

---

[77] *Mercure historique et politique de Bruxelles,* July 17, p. 213.

[78] Staël-Holstein to Gustavus III, July 11, Staël-Holstein, pp. 165–66.

[79] F.-C-A. de Bouillé, *Mémoires* [1890 ed.], p. 178.

[80] Vaudreuil to Artois, July 10 ,14, Pingaud (ed.), I, 228, 238.

[81] See below, p. 555.

and thus no longer a candidate for martyrdom, ceased for a long time to be a subject of major public interest.

BIBLIOGRAPHICAL NOTES

McClelland (pp. 116–18, 186–87) analyzes the numerous pamphlets in the Lafayette-Orléans controversy of June–July 1790 that he was able to find in American libraries.

A copy of some of the correspondence of the Duc d'Orléans relative to his mission in London in 1789–90 and his return to Paris is in the Bibliothèque de la Ville de Paris; its old call number 29411, folio, has been changed to Ms. 934. Some of this correspondence has been published: see above, n. 5.

Dard, pp. 251–52, quotes an alleged conversation between Boinville and Orléans on July 3 in which Lafayette's aide threatened the duke with attempts upon his life by members of the National Guard and the King's Bodyguard if he returned to Paris, let him have a glimpse of an extract from the depositions impugning him in the Châtelet investigation of the October insurrection, and revealed that Lafayette had suspended the investigation three months earlier. It is highly unlikely that Boinville could have made such comments without their being reported by either Orléans or La Luzerne, the other participants, both of whom gave accounts of their interview (see above, pp. 484–86). Furthermore, the Châtelet had not suspended its investigation. Dard gives as his source a "Procès-verbal en anglais," indicated as located in AN: W 294, dossier 222. We have had that dossier and other dossiers in that carton searched without uncovering any such procès-verbal.

Nevertheless, the report did get around that Boinville had made some such threats and promises. Simolin (letter to Osterman, July 23, Feuillet de Conches [ed.], I, 332–33) says that Boinville carried with him an extract from depositions given in the Châtelet, with which he was to threaten Orléans; Simolin claims to have seen the original of this extract. Earl Gower, the British ambassador, also reported that certain papers derived from the Châtelet investigation were sent to Orléans (letter to Leeds, July 2, Browning [ed.], p. 9). According to gossip that Morris heard shortly afterward (July 5, Davenport [ed.], I, 556) Orléans was told that if he returned to Paris, Lafayette would challenge him to a duel. After Orléans returned to Paris, rumor had it in England that Orléans had been or soon would be challenged to a duel by one or more National Guardsmen (Walpole to Mary Berry, July 23, *Horace Walpole's Correspondence with Mary and Agnes Berry and Barbara Cecilia Seton,* ed. W. S. Lewis and A. D. Wallace [New Haven, 1944], I, 99). Mazzei believed (*The Memoirs of the Life and Peregrinations of the Florentine Philip Mazzei, 1730–1816,* tr. H. R. Marraro [New York, 1942], p. 336) that Lafayette himself challenged Orléans. We do not consider these reports credible.

CHAPTER XXI

Preparations for the Federation

AS THE anniversary of the fall of the Bastille drew closer, the Paris National Guard made heroic efforts to get everything ready. Some battalions could expect to perform the prosaic task of patrol duty, while others would have the distinction of marching in the parade and participating in the ceremonies on the Champ-de-Mars. The commandant general decided that each division should draw lots to determine its battalions' initial assignments, but since at least three days of festivities were planned and a rotation of duties prescribed, every battalion might look forward to occupying a post of honor at some time.[1] Every battalion was to be represented also by its chaplain at the ceremony around the altar on July 14.

The choice of the Champ-de-Mars for the ceremony was logical, but its uninterrupted vastness presented its own complications. The Paris Committee for the Federative Pact decided to enlarge the flat field in front of the École Militaire and convert it into an amphitheater with a parade ground in the center, sloping mounds of earth covered with tiers of seats on three of its sides, the fourth side to be occupied by a covered pavillion for the invited dignitaries. Opposite the covered pavillion a triumphal arch would provide entrance into the field. Architects, engineers, and laborers began work at the end of June, and by July 1 thousands of men were busy digging, hauling dirt, and building.[2]

While busy with plans for the Federation, Lafayette kept up with the endless red tape of police and military affairs. For exam-

[1] *Courrier de Paris*, July 2, p. 451.

[2] *Ibid.*, July 1, p. 435; *Journal général de la cour*, July 2, p. 11; and *Moniteur*, July 8, 9, pp. 776, 777.

ple, when Bailly, jealous of his prerogatives, wrote that he wished to be consulted if a commander of the Gardes des Portes were named, Lafayette tactfully replied that if such a nomination were contemplated, the mayor would be among the first to be informed. The mayor also prodded him to take additional police measures inside Paris, and the minister of war continued to ask for orders for royal troops outside Paris.[3] In keeping with Bailly's opinion and his own, Lafayette instructed the courts-martial to see that soldiers dismissed from the Paris National Guard should answer to the proper civil tribunal for their offenses.[4] When the Battalion of Saint-Séverin discovered that it had no chaplain, it chose one, and Lafayette and Bailly signed his brevet. They awarded other commissions as well, sometimes in response to some kind of public pressure,[5] and they were continually called upon to greet visitors to the capital.[6]

On July 1 the mayor reminded Lafayette that the assemblies of the forty-eight sections of the city (newly created to take the place of the old sixty districts) would meet for the first time that day, and he asked him to take whatever measures would be necessary to preserve order pending the election of the new municipal officers.[7] Not only a mayor and a representative assembly but also possibly a commandant general were to be elected. The manner of election of the commandant of a National Guard unit, however, was not clear: Was he to be chosen by National Guardsmen whether or not they met the property qualification for the suffrage, or by those who met that qualification (active citizens, as they were called) whether or not they were Guardsmen? At Versailles, since Lafayette had

[3] Bailly to Lafayette, July 3, BN: Fr. 11697, p. 71; Lafayette to Bailly, July 5, *ibid.;* Bailly to Lafayette, June 30, Tuetey, I, 307, No. 2726; July 4, *ibid.,* II, 420, No. 3987; July 5, *ibid.,* p. 454, No. 4292; July 9, *ibid.,* I, 205, No. 1791; and [Latour du Pin] to Lafayette, July 3, AMG: AH Carton LXV, chemise Minutes, July 1790.

[4] Bailly to Lafayette, July 1, 8, Tuetey, II, 437, No. 4148, and Lafayette to Bailly, July 8, BN: Fr. 11697, p. 72.

[5] Brevet as *aumonier* for Lambert in the Bibliothèque Publique de Calais, courtesy of Monsieur G. Tison. For other appointments see Lacroix, VI, 430; Desmoulins, *Révolutions,* No. 33, pp. 438–40; and *Annales patriotiques et littéraires,* July 9, III, 127.

[6] See below, n. 12.

[7] Bailly to Lafayette, June 30, Tuetey, I, 307, No. 2726.

resigned as commander of the National Guard and a successor was to be elected,[8] that issue at first seemed pressing, for the old animosity between the supporters of Berthier and of Lecointre had rekindled, and Lecointre's supporters were proposing Charles de Lameth for the command.[9] But the National Assembly recommended that since the Versailles National Guard actually had a commander (Berthier), it should postpone the election until the issue could be settled by the contemplated decree on the organization of the National Guard of the realm.[10] The advocates of Charles de Lameth were thus once more frustrated.

The precedent established for Versailles implied that the incumbent commandant of a National Guard unit would have to stand for re-election only after the National Assembly had completed its regulation of the whole of France's National Guard. In the capital's pending elections of other municipal officers, however, that outcome left the issue of a National Guardsman's right to vote unresolved. The feeling ran strong that volunteer Guards, having already made financial sacrifices for the good of the service, ought to be permitted to exercise the privileges of active citizens, and the Constitution Committee of the National Assembly decided that any man who had served in the National Guard and had purchased his own uniform should, until the National Assembly enacted a new law on the subject, be considered an active citizen, having contributed to the public welfare a greater sum than that required to qualify as such. Bailly notified Lafayette of the committee's decision, and on July 1, the commandant general sent a circular to the forty-eight sections relaying this advice.[11]

The commandant general's preoccupation with the Federation nevertheless left him little time for less urgent affairs, and on more than one occasion he apologized for his neglect of other matters. On one such occasion he explained: "The guardianship of

[8] See above, pp. 95–96.

[9] Ferrières to Mme de Ferrières, July [10?], Ferrières, *Correspondance*, p. 232; Desmoulins, *Révolutions*, No. 32, pp. 359–62; and *Courrier de Provence*, June 27–30, p. 117.

[10] AP, XVI, 576–77 (June 30); *Assemblée nationale*, June 30, p. 8; *Courier français*, June 30, p. 487; *Moniteur*, July 1, pp. 744–45; and *Révolutions de l'Europe*, July 8, p. 56.

[11] Desmoulins, *Révolutions*, No. 32, pp. 392–94; *Moniteur*, July 7, p. 770.

the Sacred trusts for which we are responsible to France, the vigilance we must exercise to Safeguard the Capital City, these duties have but too often forced me to give them my entire mind. . . . I . . . can find no comfort except in the honor that the National Guard of Paris will enjoy in celebrating . . . the anniversary of that great day which has been of such meaning to France and to the whole world. . . . May the Oath of the Federation, the New Pledge of our fidelity to the Nation, to the Law, to the King be also a lasting guarantee of our liberty and of public order, the end of all faction, and the sign of a general tranquility."[12]

Toward the end of June the Paris Guardsmen chose the delegates who in turn were to select the official representatives of the Paris National Guard in the Federation. The law dividing Paris into sections had scheduled the election of the new municipal officers for July 5, and the Assembly of Representatives had instructed the commandant general to assemble the delegates of the Paris National Guard also on that day to choose their representatives in the forthcoming Federation. In order to avoid having both elections take place on the same day, however, the mayor later requested him to hold the National Guard elections on July 3.[13] Accordingly, on the morning of July 3 Lafayette went to the Cathedral of Notre Dame, where about two thousand delegates of the Paris National Guard had assembled, and the mayor and the Conseil de Ville had come to supervise the election. Lafayette presented several acceptable methods of voting, but the delegates unanimously agreed that a choice by lot, giving each battalion an equal chance, would be best. The question arose whether only those present as delegates were eligible, and the Conseil so ruled. Then, and again unanimously, it was decided that each battalion would choose its quota of representatives separately.

The prevailing good will induced Lafayette to remark that no one could say there was division in the National Guard. This ob-

[12] Lafayette to "Gentlemen," July 1, in the A. J. Marino collection, announced in the American Art Association–Anderson Galleries, sale no. 4389, Apr. 18–19, 1938, and quoted in full in *Hobbies*, Apr. 1941. See also his apology for not sending a model of the Federation flag to the deputies of the Vendée, July 9, Charavay catalogue 39, item 481.

[13] Bailly to Lafayette, June 28, AN:AF[11] 48, liasse 375, p. 25. See also above, p. 504.

servation elicited a volley of applause, and the Guardsmen asked that their commander's words be mentioned in the minutes. Lafayette thought the differences in size of the battalions ought to be taken into account, but when the Conseil was consulted on this point, it expressed the opinion that "the National Guard be represented in proportion to its courage, patriotism, and service." Those generous words led to the unanimous vote that each battalion choose as many representatives as the largest battalion was entitled to have—that is, one for every two hundred of its Guardsmen. The Battalion of the Abbaye de Saint-Germain-des-Pres, which proved to be largest, reported that it contained eleven hundred unpaid troops besides its center company, thus making it eligible to a representation of six men. Accordingly, the sixty battalions and the four corps (guards of the port, chasseurs, grenadiers, and cavalry) proceeded to draw lots for six representatives each, thus providing 384 representatives for all the Paris National Guard. This was a greater number than strict adherence to the ratio of 1:200 would have warranted, and as might have been expected, it comprised more privates than officers.[14]

The next evening, at a meeting of the Conseil and the delegates especially called for that purpose, the minutes of the election meeting were approved and then were signed by the mayor, the commandant general, and the secretary of the Conseil.[15] But the air was too full of noble sentiments and cheerful expectation for the meeting to end there. One of the already chosen representatives asked permission to resign in favor of another member of his unit. Lafayette consulted the delegates, who after much palaver concluded that no representative could transfer his election, and the Conseil approved that decision. Lafayette also reported to his assembled colleagues that their comrades in arms from various departments were already on the march to the capital. Thereupon, the Conseil de Ville resolved, amid fervent acclamation, that detachments of the Paris National Guard be sent to the city gates to welcome the provincial deputations and escort them to the quar-

---

[14] Lacroix, VI, 202–3 (June 21), 379–82 (July 3).

[15] *Ibid.*, pp. 396–99 (July 4).

ters assigned to them. The Assembly asked the commandant general to find out when each detachment from the departments could be expected and to give the necessary orders for their friendly reception.[16]

Then Bailly addressed the gathering. When, he announced, all voices joined in celebrating the perfect accord that reigned among Frenchmen, when the military of the capital testified their devotion to their general and received in turn their general's cordial appreciation of the feelings that united them, then he, their mayor, took pride in having become one of their fellowship, and he displayed the certificate of his own fresh enrollment in the Battalion of the Jacobins-Saint-Honoré, the district in which his own official residence was located. That a fifty-four-year-old celebrity, member of three learned societies, former president of the National Assembly, and mayor of the capital of France, should find glory in becoming a simple fusilier in the Paris National Guard touched his hearers, who replied to his speech with round after round of applause.[17]

Then Colonel A.-E. Haÿ and a deputation of his Garde de la Ville came to petition the Commune, as they had already petitioned the National Assembly, to recognize the Garde's claim to having served the Revolution well and to accord them a place in the ceremonies of the Federation. The National Guards begged to participate in supporting Haÿ's petition to the National Assembly, and the Conseil instructed the commandant general and the mayor to obtain for the Garde de la Ville the favor which its services had earned. A member of the Conseil then moved that, in token of the friendliness that united the military and the municipal corps, the minutes of the meeting be signed by all the officials, printed, sent to all the sections of Paris, and distributed to all the deputies to the Federation.[18]

The National Assembly meanwhile was considering the matter of defraying the cost of the Federation. As requested by the Conseil de Ville, Bailly and Lafayette had presented to the Finance Com-

[16] *Ibid.*, pp. 397–98.

[17] *Ibid.*, p. 398.

[18] *Ibid.*, pp. 398–99.

mittee of the National Assembly a request that since the Federation would be a national fete, its expense should be borne by the national treasury and not by the city of Paris. The Finance Committee agreed that the fete was a national responsibility and favored asking the king to place a sum not to exceed 100,000 écus (300,000 livres) at the disposal of the mayor and other officials of the Paris Commune for that purpose. The matter was then referred to the Constitution Committee, which approved the Finance Committee's proposal. When it was submitted to the National Assembly, however, that proposal ran into some Jacobin opposition, Duport contending that since Paris had sent out the invitations, Paris ought to pay the resulting costs. The Assembly, therefore, adjourned discussion of this subject to the following day, but it accepted the wording of the oath which the representatives of the National Guard, the army, and the navy should take at the ceremony. This new wording both reaffirmed the oath of civic loyalty commonly taken by the military since February 4 and added a pledge to act also as civic-minded policemen.[19] The next day the National Assembly authorized the municipality of Paris to incur the necessary expenses for the Federation and formally enjoined the mayor and the commandant general to maintain good order on that occasion.[20]

Although thousands of hired laborers were hard at work preparing the Champ-de-Mars for the great event, uneasiness nevertheless grew that the field could not be made ready in time. A week before the awaited celebration heavy rains slowed up progress, while Lafayette and his men spent ill-spared hours looking after the National Guard deputations that poured in from the provinces ahead of schedule. To meet the emergency, volunteers from all walks of life presented themselves. The Battalion of the Petits-Augustins resolved that it would relieve the laborers early every evening and, if necessary, work by torchlight, and they sent copies of their resolu-

---

[19] Minutes of the Finance Committee, July 2, Camille Bloch (ed.), *Procès-verbaux du Comité des finances de l'Assemblée constituante* (Rennes, 1922–23), Part 1, pp. 282, 287, and *AP*, XVI, 675 (July 3), 696 (July 4). See also above, p. 227. For the wording of the oath see below, p. 542.

[20] *AP*, XVI, 696 (July 4).

tion to Lafayette and the commanders of all the other battalions. National Guard units as well as district assemblies followed the precedent this provided. Each of the sixty battalions of the Paris National Guard detailed willing men to help. They served in relays, sometimes working until midnight and reporting again during the day. The National Guard of Montreuil-sur-Vincennes also offered to send a detachment to help out every day until the job was done.[21] Nuns came from their convents, monks from their cloisters, actors and actresses from their theaters, veterans from the Invalides, fashionable ladies from their salons, fishwives and porters from the Halles. The butchers of Paris brought with them a huge sign warning aristocrats to beware their wrath. The publisher Prudhomme sent his employees with a banner inscribed on one side "Printers of the *Révolutions de Paris*" and on the other "For liberty." Whole families came with their parish priests at their head, and gilds of workmen with drummers leading the way, each with a banner displaying patriotic slogans such as "Live free or die," "For the *patrie*," "For liberty."[22]

The paid workmen resented the competition of the volunteers, and with rival thousands assembled on the Champ-de-Mars, disorder could be anticipated at any moment. A dispute among the paid workers over the number of hours they should donate without pay almost led to a riot, prevented only by Lafayette's intervention.[23] Consequently he ordered a National Guard patrol to keep order on the field at night,[24] and no further disorders broke out. On the

---

[21] Lacroix, VI, 411–15 (July 5), 432 (July 8).

[22] *Chronique de Paris*, July 6, p. 747; *Patriote français*, July 7, p. 3; *Courrier de Paris*, July 8, pp. 59–60; *Journal général de la cour*, July 7, p. 53; *Courier national*, July 9, pp. 1–3; *Journal de Paris*, July 8, pp. 765–66; *Moniteur*, July 8, p. 776, July 12, p. 794; Ferrières to Mme de Ferrières, July 9, Ferrières, *Correspondance*, p. 228, and July 12, *ibid.*, p. 234; *Révolutions de Paris*, No. 52, July 3–10, pp. 752–55; and R. L., "Discours des forts de la Halle à M. de la Fayette, en terminant leurs travaux au Champ-de-Mars," *Annales révolutionnaires*, IV (1911), 541.

[23] *Journal général de la cour*, July 4, p. 30; *Courrier de Paris*, July 6, p. 59; Gaston Maugras (ed.), *Journal d'un étudiant pendant la Révolution de France* (Paris, 1910), p. 68; Deux amis de la Liberté, *Histoire de la Révolution de France* (Paris, 1792–97), V, 385; and Henri Leclercq, *La Fédération (janvier–juillet 1790)* (Paris, 1929), p. 316.

[24] *Courrier de Paris*, July 8, p. 59, and *Moniteur*, July 10, pp. 781–82.

contrary, work progressed rapidly. Through the glare of long summer days and under flares at night, devoted men and women shoveled huge piles of earth into wheelbarrows and unloaded them on gradually mounting slopes at the sides of the parade ground. Carpenters built the designated altar, pavillion, and tiers of seats. Some sang as they worked, their favorite song being *Ça ira*.[25] Half of Paris seemed to be on holiday, digging, shoveling, hauling, pounding away in a festive mood. At midnight work would stop, and men and women of the same district or of the same trade would march off together, with torches flaring, voices raised in song, and feet keeping time to their singing. National Guard companies stayed behind until the field was cleared, then posted guards, and marched home.

One day Lafayette rode out on his now famous white horse to the Champ-de-Mars. National Guards stopped work to salute him as he rode by, and civilians crowded to welcome him. "Well, general, *ça ira-t-il?*" someone shouted. "Oui, mes enfants," the general replied. And then the crowd burst into song: "Ça ira, ça ira!" And as the handsome horse carried its triumphant young rider from group to group, the sound of *Ça ira, ça ira* followed him. He had not come, however, merely to parade before gratified spectators but also to encourage them on the job. Slipping off his horse, he took up a pickax and began to dig beside the workmen. Then, grabbing a shovel, he filled a wheelbarrow and pushed it along to the mound at the side of the field.[26]

Lafayette's gesture was not lost on other eminent men. Dom Gerle went there to work with a group of fellow Cistercians. Le Chapelier, along with the peasant deputy Michel Gérard, led a troop from the Breton National Guard there, with pickaxes and wheelbarrows.[27] Shortly after his own visit, Lafayette brought Louis XVI to see the Champ-de-Mars, accompanied by a number

[25] Pierre, *Hymnes et chansons*, pp. 480–81, 486.

[26] *Courrier de Paris*, July 9, p. 107; *Journal général de la cour*, July 10, pp. 77–78; *Courrier national*, July 9, p. 2; *Orateur du peuple*, Nos. 41, 42, pp. 326, 335; and Maugras (ed.), p. 68.

[27] *Révolutions de Paris*, No. 52, July 3–10, pp. 754–55.

of gentlemen of the court. When the people spied the royal party, they stopped work and shouted "Vive le roi!" and amid repeated cheers Louis rode around, inspecting the field. He did not conceal his pleasure at these spontaneous demonstrations of his people's affection.[28]

Despite widespread good will, however, things did not go altogether smoothly, for a dispute arose regarding admission to the Federation. The Paris Committee for the Federative Pact had decided that entry for all except officials and deputations should be only by ticket. The best estimates had it that although places would be available to thousands, other thousands would be unable to get in, and the committee believed that fairness and order would best be served if tickets were divided equally among the sixty former districts of Paris.

As soon as the committee's decision was known, however, protests began to roll in. Some clamored for tickets; others opposed tickets of any kind. Marat thought he divined in the distribution of tickets a plot to limit admission to the supporters of Lafayette and the city administration.[29] Bailly's staff reported that unless measures were taken to quiet public resentment, the police could not be responsible for the security of the capital, and one of Lafayette's aides confirmed the danger. Some districts ordered drummers into the streets to tell the people to disregard tickets.[30]

Thus challenged, the Paris Committee for the Federative Pact put the matter before the Constitution Committee of the National Assembly, which referred it to the mayor and the commandant general. Lafayette felt that admission by tickets would be more likely to create disorder than to prevent it, and Bailly agreed with him that every citizen should have an equal right to a place as long as there was room. So they decided that there would be no tickets. When the decision to permit entry without ticket became known, the poor expressed gratitude to Lafayette with a new verse to *Ça ira:*

[28] *Courrier de Paris,* July 10, p. 122, July 11, p. 139, and *Journal général de la cour,* July 10, p. 76.

[29] *Ami du peuple,* July 22, p. 3.

[30] Lacroix, VI, 489–99 (July 13).

For all the people will share the joy
Of witnessing that celebration.
Because of the sagacious Lafayette
All difficulties will subside.[31]

By that time thousands of *fédérés* had arrived in Paris. Between July 9 and 12 bands of uniformed, armed, and enthusiastic men came swinging through the city gates almost every hour. As instructed by the Commune, Lafayette placed detachments of Paris National Guards at the barriers to welcome the visitors and escort them to their designated lodgings. Louis XVI opened the royal library, botanical gardens, and museums to the visitors; the National Assembly invited them to its galleries; the Opéra offered special programs; the theaters touched up their plays to give performances a more patriotic tone; artisans and shopkeepers stood ready to supply choice wares and souvenirs of the impatiently awaited commemoration, now sometimes called "the Federation of the Year II of Liberty."

That men of the royal army might take advantage of the enthusiasm generated by the Federation to desert was easy to foresee, and Lafayette felt that he "must take all possible measures against the introduction of persons who would be suspect and dangerous" and against "the soldiers who in the present circumstances abandon their colors." Accordingly he asked Berthier, for example, as the commander at Versailles to arrest deserters and send them back to their regiments and to instruct troops of the line, if they were to come through Versailles, to set out at dawn the very day after the Federation to return to their barracks. Berthier, however, was not to discourage Versailles National Guardsmen who were alternate delegates to the Federation from attending: "There will be places reserved for all National Guardsmen of the realm who come out of curiosity without being named deputies."[32] Likewise Lafayette

---

[31] *Ibid.*, pp. 495–99. The new verse of *Ça ira* was printed early in July 1790: see Pierre, *Hymnes et chansons*, pp. 480–81, 486–87. The original runs:

> Car tout le peuple jouira
> En voyant cette fête-la.
> Par le prudent La Fayette . . .
> Tout trouble s'apaisera.

[32] Lafayette to Berthier, July 8, Bibliothèque de Versailles (courtesy of Monsieur Bréchin).

excused the Military Committee of Paris from duty on July 14, and the mayor reserved a special block of seats for them in the Champ-de-Mars.[33] Some of the provincial delegates to the Federation offered, during their sojourn in the capital, to share with the Paris National Guard in guarding the National Assembly, and Lafayette wrote to the president of the National Assembly presenting their request. Bonnay replied that such an offer could be nothing but pleasing to the National Assembly, and his colleagues, upon learning of the offer, unanimously approved of it.[34]

On the morning of July 9 the Constitution Committee submitted to the National Assembly its plans for the Federation. One of the steps it recommended was that the king take command of the National Guards and the regular troops at the Federation and designate the officers who would exercise the command in his name and under his orders, and with only little debate, this recommendation was adopted. The seating of the queen, the dauphin, and other members of the royal family, however, roused heated discussion; it was finally arranged that the Assembly's president should sit on the king's right, the deputies grouping themselves to the right of the president and to the left of the king, and that Louis XVI should be asked to determine a "convenient place" for the royal family. The National Assembly also adopted the recommendation that after the National Guards and the troops of the line had taken the prescribed oath, the president of the National Assembly should repeat the oath of February 4, whereupon all the deputies, standing with hands upraised, would announce: "I so swear!" The wording of the oath that the king should take was also adopted.[35]

These resolutions of the National Assembly seemed to complete the major plans for the Federation. The king, now declared chief of the Federation, authorized Lafayette to act in his name at the

---

[33] *Procès-verbal du Comité militaire*, Part II, pp. 82–83 (July 8).

[34] *AP*, XVI, 746 (July 8). See also *Procès-verbal de l'assemblée nationale*, July 9, p. 11; *Point du jour*, July 10, p. 478; *Révolutions de l'Europe*, July 14, p. 128; *Moniteur*, July 11, p. 786; *Le Postillon*, No. 131, p. 7; and *Annales patriotiques et littéraires*, July 10, p. 123.

[35] *AP*, XVII, 12–17. See also below, pp. 539–40. For the wording of these oaths, see below, pp. 542–44.

forthcoming ceremony.[36] So it still remained uncertain whether Lafayette or Louis XVI was to be the Federation's headliner. In any case, it was not to be Mirabeau or Charles de Lameth. If ever Lafayette had been apprehensive that calling the *fédérés* together might profit his opponents, that apprehension was a thing of the past. Most of France now looked forward to

> That day when all hearts with joy unconfined . . .
> Will solemnly swear at one time to an oath . . .
> Of peace and of union, of lasting accord. . . .[37]

Not all Frenchmen, however, were equally rhapsodical. The thronging of *fédérés* to Paris led some Jacobins, Cordeliers, and others to become increasingly suspicious of the commandant general's purposes. Chief among the critics was Marat. The *Ami du peuple* continued to pile accusation upon accusation, some old, some new, against Lafayette: he had sheltered a food speculator from the righteous indignation of the citizens of Vernon; he was a tool of Necker, who was now trying to force the people again under the despot's yoke; he had suppressed the truth about the insult to the National Guard at Saint-Cloud and had unjustly punished Féral;[38] he was trying to make the king a dictator, giving him the veto power and the right to make war and peace.[39]

The entire number of the *Ami du peuple* for July 11 was a condemnation of the Paris National Guard commander. The people of Paris, it declaimed, being inexperienced in governing themselves, had been misled by Lafayette's false reputation as a defender of liberty in America; the Friend of the People had been assured it was Lafayette's debts that had driven him to seek refuge in America. "This magnanimous hero, this burning patriot, this

---

[36] "Proclamation du roi," *Procès-verbal de l'Assemblée nationale,* July 11, and *Courrier de Paris,* July 12, p. 151.

[37] M. Cambon, *Poëme sur la Révolution française* (Beziers, 1790), p. 35. The lines translated above read:
> Ce jour où tous les coeurs, au sein de l'allegresse . . .
> Prêteront à la fois ce serment solennel . . .
> De paix et d'union, une amitié durable.

[38] *Ami du peuple,* July 8, pp. 3–4, 7–8, July 9, pp. 1–2.

[39] *Ibid.,* July 9, pp. 1–6.

incorruptible defender of liberty" now was planning to enchain
the nation. The "foes of public happiness" had required the National Guards to wear uniforms which only the opulent could
afford, and thus the Guard consisted of "solicitors, notaries, attor-
neys, magistrates, nobles, raised by the cabal to the rank of captain,
major, and commander of the citizen legions, dolts interested in
perpetuation of the abuses of despotism." To that army, "almost
all of them mortal enemies of liberty," six thousand paid troops
had been added, along with a general staff whose enormous salaries made them Lafayette's satellites. In order to subjugate the citizen-soldiers more thoroughly the commandant general had divided them into different corps distinguished by special uniforms,
had made captious rules of discipline, and had sworn his men to
obedience to their chiefs. The citizen guard, in short, had become
a praetorian cohort: "Soon the Parisian army will succeed in destroying liberty, which the National Assembly is secretly undermining, which the ministers are boldly attacking, which the general
so often places in peril, and which the creatures of the court, the
tools of the Old Regime, mortally oppose."[40]

On July 13, the very eve of the Federation, in an article entitled
"New Denunciation of M. de la Fayette," Marat declared that Lafayette's aides-de-camp were thugs hired to get rid of good patriots
who displeased him. He accused the aide Desmottes of having
challenged Alexandre de Lameth to a duel for having cast reflections on the general and then of having like a coward failed to
show up at the dueling field. Anyone who thus threatened the defenders of the Revolution roused Marat's particular animostiy: "To
hang him on the first lamppost is a way to get to heaven, a reward
which the patriots of the Faubourg Saint-Antoine ought to seek."
For such an enemy Marat considered proper punishment to be
"that the people tear him to pieces as a wild beast."[41]

How much influence the diatribes of the *Ami du peuple* had at
this time or who regarded them as the sincere warnings of a zealous
patriot and who as the rantings of a frustrated demagogue can

[40] *Ibid.,* July 11, pp. 1–8.
[41] *Ibid.,* July 13, pp. 1–7.

only be guessed. Marat claimed that because of his denunciations of the general "the creatures of that sincere friend of liberty" had paid newsboys to destroy issues of the *Ami du peuple* but that the outcome of their efforts had been only to raise the price of the journal: the issues of the previous five days had sold for as high as an écu (60 sous) at the Palais Royal, though the regular price was only two sous.[42] The claim is not altogether incredible; that Lafayette's friends would try to buy up a sensational attack upon him and that the result of their attempt at repression would be an increased demand for the journal they intended to repress might have been presumed. There was just enough truth in Marat's accusations to make them sound plausible to those who were already prepared to believe them.

Other popular journalists likewise tried to stem the brimming paean to Lafayette. The *Journal du diable* accused him of trying to sow dissension among all classes of citizens so that he might "divide and rule," but his "dark schemes" were now becoming well known.[43] Loustalot was second only to Marat in the vehemence of his denunciations. The *fédérés,* he grumbled, were not received with becoming hospitality; their baggage on their backs, their faces covered with dust and sweat, their eyes sparkling with expectation, they encountered only neglect upon arrival. And the constitution they were being marshaled to swear allegiance to was far from perfect: it established a property qualification for suffrage; it gave the king excessive power; because of Lafayette's influence in the National Assembly it failed to provide trial by jury for soldiers; it did not leave the press free. Moreover, according to the *Révolutions de Paris,* Lafayette had failed to clear up his relations with Orléans, and the adulation bestowed on him was far from deserved. Loustalot therefore proposed to let the people "see that hero naked": the Bastille had been taken without him; although hailed as the "defender of liberty in two worlds," he had actually served America only with the connivance of the rulers of France; in France the only military expedition he had headed had been that

---

[42] *Ibid.,* July 12, p. 8.
[43] *Journal du diable,* No. 44, pp. 3–4, 7.

against Marat the previous February; during the October Days he had hesitated to lead Paris to Versailles to avenge the insults to the national cockade and then had failed to protect the Château; he had permitted his staff to plot against Féral and had sought to ruin Collard; he had tried to please the "Austrian Committee" by opposing the Belgian revolutionaries; he had favored summoning the patriots of Marseilles to answer charges at the bar of the National Assembly; he had supported Mirabeau on giving the king the power to make peace and war. In short, Loustalot contended, although Lafayette continually talked about the welfare of the people, whatever he did was for his own interest or for that of the royal ministry.[44]

Some contemporary observers perhaps failed to appreciate that Loustalot, Marat, Desmoulins, the *Diable,* Mirabeau, Orléans, the Cordeliers, the Jacobins, the Triumvirate, and the queen, though for different reasons and in different ways, were fighting for the same cause—to make the soaring Lafayette fly an ordinary pitch. What no one could easily overlook, however, was that the opposition to Lafayette was not succeeding. His lofty flight was only in part the product of his own volition, for, despite the skeptics, most of the people of revolutionary France seemed eager to bask in the solace of hero-worship. From the stones of the Bastille the house-wrecker Palloy had made a series of models of the demolished prison, which he intended to present to the departments, the National Assembly, and the commanding general, and he deferentially asked Lafayette's permission to display one of them on the altar of the *patrie* at the Federation.[45] The journals continued to advertise the sale of pictures of Lafayette and Bailly. The royalist *Journal général de la cour,* decrying the rumor that aristocrats were plotting to rise on July 14, expressed (or perhaps sarcastically feigned) confidence that all would be well: "Lafayette will be there, so we can sleep in peace in the soothing certainty that our beloved general for his part will not sleep at so critical a moment."[46]

[44] *Révolutions de Paris,* No. 52, July 3–10, pp. 725–28, 730–50, 752.

[45] Palloy to Lafayette, July 4, and Lafayette to Palloy, July 8, BVP: Liésville Collection, carton marked "Rev. Registres relatifs à Palloy et à la Bastille," No. 5, pièces 1391–92.

[46] July 11, p. 83.

Deputies in Paris and municipal officers in Bordeaux expressed their certainty that Lafayette was taking the most appropriate measures to maintain order.[47] Chénier wrote a "Hymne pour la fête de la Révolution," a stanza of which read:

> In the midst of [liberty's] dangers, Lafayette is her guide;
> Since in America he became her defender
> She has everywhere followed his fearless advice;
> Wherever he is, she is there too.[48]

Parisians and guests from the provinces attending a performance at the Comédie Française found a new verse added to the text of a contemporary drama:

> The fête of a great people is that of a good king.
> Of all who would oppress, this day marks the defeat;
> All our wishes have been fulfilled: Paris like Boston
>   Has in Bailly, in Lafayette
> Its Franklin and its Washington.[49]

The curé of a remote provincial parish proposed and the local municipality approved that a new church bell should bear the inscription "To the new French Joshua, la Fayette."[50] About this time an "Ode en marche nationale" was dedicated to Lafayette, and a long poem which appeared in Béziers, recounting the story of the Revolution and extolling the forthcoming Federation, described Lafayette as "a magnanimous hero," "the conqueror of Albion, that generous warrior" who had destroyed the "infamous cabal" of October 5–6.[51]

---

[47] Ferrières to Mme de Ferrières, July 12, Ferrières, *Correspondance*, p. 235, and municipality of Bordeaux to Lafayette, July 12, Gaston Ducaunnès-Duval (ed.), *Inventaire-sommaire des archives municipales, period révolutionnaire (1789–An VIII)* (Bordeaux, 1910). p. 234.

[48] *Journal de la Société de 1789*, July 10:
> Au milieu des perils La Fayette est son guide:
> Depuis qu'en Amérique il devint son appui,
> Elle a suivi partout sa prudence intrépide;
> Elle est toujours auprès de lui.

[49] *Révolutions de Paris*, No. 53, July 10–17, p. 40.

[50] *Courier français*, July 13, p. 104.

[51] Cited in Pierre, *Hymnes et chansons*, p. 197. The poem was Cambon's *Poëme sur la Révolution française:* see above, n. 37.

Upon reaching Paris, each of the deputations of *fédérés* sought out the national celebrities from its part of the country, but all hoped to catch a glimpse of the commandant general, and he did not make it difficult to see him. He rode on his white horse from his home on the Rue de Bourbon to many points of the city—to the Place de Grève, the Tuileries, the Champ-de-Mars, the Plaine des Sablons—dressed in royal blue uniform coat, lined and trimmed in red, with white underdress, bright epaulets, and a hat with tricolor cockade. As he passed, Parisians and visitors would clap their hands and shout friendly greetings, to which the general, hat in hand, would reply with a bow and a smile.[52] Officers from the provinces went to see him at the Hôtel de Ville, and they often left with invitations to dine with the Lafayettes. The deputation from Lyon brought a gift of a Roman ensign inscribed *Cives lugdu-nenses optimo civi* ("The citizens of Lyon to the best citizen"). The deputation from Avignon received a personal invitation to dine with him the day after their arrival.[53] The deputations from Riom and Clermont, eager to call upon their illustrious fellow Auvergnat, asked the Paris detachment which welcomed them at the city gate to take them first to his home. With the flourish of drums they marched to the house on the Rue de Bourbon, and their officers went in to call upon the commandant general. He welcomed them and invited the whole contingent, over a hundred strong, to dine with him, fifty the next day and the remainder the day thereafter, so that every man from Auvergne would have broken bread at his table.[54] Short feared that he was "running through his fortune" and would be financially ruined: "He has a large tent spread in his garden which holds a table of an hundred plates. He intends that it shall be filled every day as long as the deputies of the gardes nationales continue here."[55] Unless Short was mistaken, Lafayette

[52] *Révolutions de Paris*, No. 52, July 3–10, p. 750.

[53] *Mémoires*, IV, 324–25 n.; Metzger, p. 146; and N.-J.-B. Lescuier and Jean Duprat to the municipality of Avignon, July 13, P. Vaillandet (ed.), *Correspondance des deputés d'Avignon près l'Assemblée nationale* (Avignon, 1933–34), I, 45.

[54] Mège, II, 327, and see below, p. 525.

[55] Short to Jefferson, July 7, Boyd (ed.), XVII, 12.

had "tables in every room in his house below stairs; so there are daily two and three hundred persons who dine there."[56]

On July 7 the National Guardsmen of each of the 544 districts of France had been invited to choose one of their number to represent them at meetings to be held in the Hôtel de Ville, where they would confer with the general staff of the Paris National Guard on matters pertaining to the "federative pact."[57] On the morning of July 10 these representatives met for the first time in the Grande Salle. Acting as presiding officer, Lafayette expressed the pleasure that the Paris National Guards derived from being joined by their brethren from all over the nation—a sentiment that called forth hearty applause. The representatives of the National Guards then proceeded to organize more formally. First of all, it was proposed that the commandant general of the Paris National Guard be chosen president. Lafayette held back, but the Guards insisted again and again. Finally he accepted and was proclaimed president by unanimous consent. Then, after electing eight secretaries, the assembly decided to send committees to present the respects of the National Guards to the National Assembly and to the king, and it commissioned its president to find out when such committees would be received. Lafayette was also vested with authority to arrange the *fédérés'* share in policing Paris, every *fédéré* standing ready to act, without distinction of rank, as a simple fusilier in performing that service. Various members of the assembly then, with enthusiastic support, moved further honors for their presiding officer, but he, refusing to put those motions to a vote, adjourned the meeting.[58] False modesty? Genuine modesty? Or good politics? Probably a mixture of all three, but it did not matter; he needed no new titles to be assured of his hold upon the country's National Guards.

That afternoon a long column of Bretons, in full battle dress,

---

[56] Same to same, July 16, *ibid.,* p. 213.

[57] Lacroix, VI, 561.

[58] *Procès-verbal de la Confédération des François à Paris, le quatorze juillet mil sept-cent-quatre-vingt-dix* (Paris, 1791), pp. 3–4, and Lacroix, VI, 561 (July 23). See the Bibliographical Notes below, p. 526.

came marching down the road from Versailles. A Paris National Guard detachment awaited them at the Barrière de la Conférence and led them through the streets of the capital straight to the Tuileries. Outside the palace window they cheered the king, who then appeared at the window and was greeted with renewed vivas.[59] They next paraded to the square of the Hôtel de Ville. On his mother's side Lafayette was a Breton. He had sat for a brief moment in the Provincial Assembly at Rennes on his return from America in 1785[60] and still owned extensive estates in Brittany. He therefore had a rather special interest in the Breton *fédérés*. When word came that they had arrived, he went down to meet them. He extended them a welcome that was "most tender and most fraternal," and they responded with obvious pleasure.[61]

That day work on the Champ-de-Mars ended.[62] At the entrance towered the triumphal arch, fittingly decorated with patriotic inscriptions. Opposite it stood the amphitheater, ready to receive king, National Assembly, and Paris officials. In the center twenty-four steps reached upward to the great altar. Around the field loomed stands huge enough to accommodate 30,000 spectators. When the last carpenter had driven the last nail, the workers left, and Lafayette stationed detachments at the entrance with orders to admit no one until dawn on July 14.[63]

By July 10 the parade orders also were ready, drawn up by Lafayette and his staff with the approval of Bailly. The first section of the procession was so planned as to emphasize the role of Paris in the capture of the Bastille. It would comprise a detachment of the Paris National Guard cavalry, half of the Paris National Guard band (whose pay and status Lafayette had not yet been able to get formally approved by the municipality),[64] a detachment of Paris

---

[59] *Révolutions de Paris*, No. 53, July 10–17, p. 2.

[60] Gottschalk, *Between*, pp. 151–52.

[61] *Courier national*, July 12, p. 7. See also *Révolutions de Paris*, No. 53, July 10–17, p. 2; *Journal général de la cour*, July 13, p. 103; *Chronique de Paris*, July 13, p. 778; and Ferrières to Mme de Ferrières, July 13, Ferrières, *Correspondance*, p. 238.

[62] Forts de la Halle to Lafayette, July 10, *Annales révolutionnaires*, IV, (1911), 541.

[63] *Révolutions de Paris*, No. 53, July 10–17, pp. 5–7.

[64] He had last asked on June 28: Lacroix, VI, 315.

National Guard grenadiers (former French Guards), and representatives of other heroes of July 14, 1789, and of the Paris military and officialdom. The second section would be composed of *fédérés* and representatives of the royal service. The oldest member of each departmental deputation of *fédérés* would carry a banner provided by the Commune of Paris and inscribed with the department's name. Midway between the eighty-three departmental deputations would come the king's color guard, the marshals of France, other high military officers, deputations from the various branches of the royal army, and the general officers and the deputations of the royal navy. A company of Paris chasseurs and a company of Paris cavalry would close the procession.[65] The head of the parade would move from the Boulevard Saint-Martin, proceed via the Place de Louis XV to the Cours de la Reine, and then across the Seine by a pontoon bridge to the Champ-de-Mars. Louis XVI and the royal family would then enter through the École Militaire (but Bailly and Lafayette refrained from indicating when or how he would take part). After the king's arrival, the color bearers would bring their standards to the altar to be consecrated, and the ceremony would end with a *Te Deum*. Special instructions would be given for artillery salutes at appropriate times.[66]

The king accepted this procedure and agreed to its being published as by his command. He gave Lafayette the title of "major-general of the Federation," with Gouvion as "major *en second*." He also designated Talleyrand to celebrate the mass, assisted by the chaplains of the Paris National Guard. He commissioned the major-general of the Federation to pronounce the civic oath, according to the formula decreed by the National Assembly, not only in the name of the deputies of the National Guards but also in the name of those of the royal army and navy. Then the president and the deputies of the National Assembly would likewise pronounce the oath, and, finally, His Majesty would take a special oath. A proclamation specifying these royal wishes was printed, posted,

---

[65] *Courrier de Paris*, July 14, pp. 182–89, and *Confédération nationale. Ordre de marche*, pp. 1–4.

[66] *Confédération nationale. Ordre de marche*, pp. 4–7.

and distributed throughout Paris, with the "Order of March" signed by Bailly and Lafayette appended to it.[67]

Obviously Lafayette so far was victorious over Mirabeau in the competition for the ear of the king. The queen was less amenable, however. Offended that the assembly had not placed her on a throne beside her husband, she broached the question with Lafayette, but he made plain that he believed such prerogatives as sitting with the National Assembly at a public ceremony belonged only to the king as the first magistrate of the nation. Louis XVI, though he must have known her preferences, arranged that a prominent but less exalted place be set aside in the amphitheater for Marie Antoinette, the dauphin, and other members of his family, and she, placing the blame where she thought it belonged, made no secret of her displeasure with Lafayette and his "royal democracy."[68]

On July 11, at the second meeting of the delegates of the *fédérés,* Lafayette announced that both the National Assembly and the king had consented to receive a delegation of all the National Guards. Since the spokesman of the Guards would be expected to deliver an address on both occasions, Lafayette as president was designated to act with the secretaries in preparing drafts of the addresses for the *fédérés'* approval.[69] The address he helped prepare for delivery to the National Assembly urged the early completion of the constitution and pointed to the contribution of the National Guards toward a constitutional regime by maintaining order while the Assembly destroyed the old and slowly built the new.[70] The draft of the address to Louis XVI was much shorter.[71] It said nothing about the events of July 1789, since they comprised episodes that might be embarrassing to the king, but it was calculated to remind him as the citizen-king of a free people that there could be no turning back, that the National Guard gave him obedience only because obedience was dictated by their respect for his virtues and their devo-

[67] Saint-Priest to Bailly, July 12, 13, Tuetey, I, 206, 207, Nos. 1803, 1805, 1810.

[68] *Mémoires,* III, 208–9, 213–15, and see Bibliographical Notes below, p. 526.

[69] Lacroix, VI, 562–63 (July 23), and *Procès-verbal de la Confédération,* pp. 5–6.

[70] *AP,* XVII, 77 (July 13).

[71] *Ibid.,* p. 83.

tion to the law. The intent in both speeches was to appeal for free-dom under a constitution and a system of law still to be perfected.

At the next meeting of the delegates of the *fédérés* (July 12), the "Order of March" for July 14 was read so that each of them might inform his comrades of their assignment for the day, and then La-fayette submitted the texts of the two proposed addresses. The dele-gates accepted them unanimously, asking only for greater emphasis upon the need to determine the organization and equipment of the National Guard. Since the addresses were to be delivered in the name of all the *fédérés,* the assembly agreed that a larger representa-tive body should be given the chance to consider the approved texts. For that purpose Lafayette had already reserved the Church of Saint-Roch, big enough to accommodate at least three *fédérés* from each district of the realm, and he invited the assembled dele-gates to come the next morning to the church and bring their com-rades along. Invitations to the meeting were posted throughout the city.[72]

In the hope of further cementing the ties of ruler and nation Lafayette requested the king to hold a review of the National Guard delegations, and Louis readily consented.[73] Some of the Guards preferred a private review of only selected units, but con-siderable uneasiness regarding such exclusiveness had developed, and Lafayette shared it. He had had occasion at the numerous din-ners which he gave to the *fédérés* to display "a great deal of impa-tience" with royal partisans among them. Some of the guests first drank to the health of Louis XVI and only then to that of the Na-tional Assembly or applauded the king more loudly than the na-tion's deputies.[74] On the afternoon of July 12, when he entertained half of the *fédérés* in the Auvergnat deputations at a table set for fifty-one diners, the conversation turned to the issue of a limited or a general review, and he voiced his preference for a general review. The commander of the Clermont contingent agreed, and Lafay-

---

[72] *Procès-verbal de la Confédération,* pp. 7–11, and Lacroix, VI, 562 (July 23). The invitation is quoted in full in Charavay, p. 570.

[73] Saint-Priest, II, 37.

[74] *Mémoires,* III, 213. Cf. Short to Morris, July 27, Davenport (ed.), I, 565.

ette asked him to impart his opinion to any *fédérés* he might encounter.[75]

The subject of concern was not merely the even distribution of royal approval, it was also the possibility that the king's favor might be used in such a way as to court selected *fédérés'* support for his cause. Partisans of royal power thought they had good reason to hope, just as Marat and the Leftist opposition thought they had good reason to fear, that as chief of the Federation Louis XVI, with Lafayette's connivance, might yet be the one to profit the most from the celebration. But on the eve of the Federation Lafayette himself intended that the chief beneficiary should be no man but the limited monarchical constitution.

BIBLIOGRAPHICAL NOTES

Leclercq's *La Fédération* as well as his *Vers la Fédération* is subject to the same criticism as his *Les Journées d'Octobre* (see Gottschalk and Maddox, pp. 293 n., 306, 327 n., 348 n., 386–87); they are the most detailed secondary studies of the events leading to and including the Federation but are subject to correction in a number of details.

Some of Lafayette's account of the events related to the Federation of 1790 was contained in an essay in *Mémoires,* III, 191–215, entitled "Sur la démocratie royale de 1789 et le républicanisme des vrais constitutionnels." Although the footnote *ibid.,* p. 191, says it was written about 1799, it would appear from *ibid.,* IV, 395, n. 2, that it was enclosed with a letter of Lafayette to Bureau de Pusy dated December 25, 1797.

In the *Ami du peuple* of July 9, pp. 1–2, Marat pretends to quote from an address of Lafayette to the battalions of the Paris National Guard, which he described as the commandant general's "confession of faith." We have been unable to find any other mention of this address. No such title is listed in André Monglond, *La France révolutionnaire et imperiale: Annales de bibliographie methodique et description des livres illustrés* (Grenoble, 1930–63) or in Martin and Walter or in Jackson.

The date of publication of the *Procès-verbal de la Confédération* (see n. 58 above) is given on the title-page as 1790 and on the last page (p. 96) as 1791. We consider the later date the more likely since it must have taken a considerable length of time to compile the "Liste de Messieurs les Gardes-nationales élus députés à la Fédération," which comprises (pp. 33–96) thousands of names arranged by departments and by districts within the departments.

[75] Mège, II, 37.

CHAPTER XXII

"Zenith of His Influence"

ON July 13 Lafayette set out early for the Church of Saint-Roch. Rain had fallen steadily, but hundreds of National Guards had already assembled there. As president of the Assembly of the Fédérés he opened the session with an account of the work so far accomplished. Bailly and Joseph Charon, chairman of the Paris Committee on the Federative Pact, entered while he was speaking, and he introduced the mayor, who, upon welcoming the deputies, announced that the Commune would present to each of them a medal commemorating the great event they had come to celebrate, and Charon seconded the mayor's words. Lafayette then made known the king's decision to review the National Guard deputations later that day on the Champs-Elysées, which he proposed to do without distinction among them, in the order of their arrival. The assembled *fédérés* then considered the final drafts of the addresses Lafayette had prepared for delivery to the National Assembly and to Louis XVI and unanimously approved them. After determining that its other officers and one deputy from each district (about six hundred National Guardsmen in all) would accompany the president on both occasions, the meeting adjourned, and the deputation started off for the Manège.[1]

Thus it happened that Lafayette missed the midday thanksgiving service of the former Electors of Paris at the Cathedral of Notre Dame. They had invited the commandant general, along with the other officials of the city, and in honor of these leaders the vast cathedral was packed. The sermon recalled the events of the preceding July, when, the preacher said, the Electors of Paris in

---

[1] *Procès-verbal de la Confédération*, pp. 12–13, and Lacroix, VI, 562 (July 23).

choosing Bailly mayor had given France its Franklin and in choosing Lafayette commandant general had given France its Washington. Then the wives of three leaders of the Revolution—Adrienne de Lafayette among them—took up an offering for the poor. After a short performance entitled "La prise de la Bastille," the choir chanted the *Te Deum,* the audience joined in, and the service ended.[2] To wind up their celebration the former Electors gave a banquet for five hundred persons at the Cirque of the Palais Royal, where toasts were drunk to the nation, the king, the mayor, the commandant general, the presidents, the Electors of Paris, all the citizens of Paris, and the deputies to the federative pact.[3]

Meanwhile Lafayette and his little army of National Guard deputies were carrying out their assignment. "The most profound silence fell upon the Assembly" when they appeared in the Salle du Manège.[4] Going to the tribune, Lafayette first offered the National Guards' "homage of respect and gratitude" and then described the part that they had played in protecting the country from anarchy: "The nation, seeking to be free at last, charged you to give it a constitution. But it would have waited for one in vain, if its enlightened will, of which you are the medium of expression, had not created that loyal force which rests in our hands and if the happy cooperation [of the one force with the other], suddenly replacing the old order that the initial stirrings of liberty were rendering obsolete, had not become the first of the laws to take the place of those which were vanishing." The coming fete was a reward, he dared say, of the National Guards' zeal; it would unite many widely scattered brethren, who, guided by the National Assembly's influence and by the imperious need to preserve the unity of the state, had unceasingly directed their common efforts toward a common goal: "Certainly also the unanimous accord with which the National Guards today bring to France's constituent assembly, their adhesion to the principles which tomorrow they will swear to

[2] Lacroix, VI, 457–59 (July 10); *Courier national,* July 16, pp. 9–10; *Moniteur,* July 20, p. 828, Aug. 18, pp. 951–52; *Journal de Paris,* July 17, pp. 801–2; *Journal général de l'Europe,* July 25, pp. 138–39; and *Journal de la municipalité,* July 17, pp. 985–90.

[3] *Moniteur,* July 20, p. 828.

[4] *Point du jour,* July 14, p. 59.

maintain and defend, is a reward that you have earned by your work. You recognized, Gentlemen, both the needs of France and the wishes of Frenchmen when you destroyed the Gothic edifice of our government and our laws and respected only the monarchical principle, while an attentive Europe learned that a good king can be the prop of a free people just as he had been the solace of an oppressed people."

Lafayette next raised the point which for him was the heart of his address: "Finish your work, Gentlemen, and selecting from among your decrees those which should form the essentials of the French constitution, make haste to present to us, who are justly impatient, that code of laws which the first Legislature should soon receive as a sacred trust and which your foresight will render the more stable the more exactly the constitutional ways of revising it will be indicated." He then made clear the provisions which he thought should be kept in the constitution: "The rights of man have been declared, the sovereignty of the people has been recognized, the [governmental] powers have been distributed, the bases of public order have been established. Now carry on and put strength into authority of the state. The people owe to you the glory of a free constitution, but they ask of you, they expect, that stability at last which cannot exist without a strong and thorough organization of government." Since the Assembly had so far recognized the National Guards only by indirection, Lafayette, describing them as "united in the name of liberty, guardians of individual property as well as of common property, of the safety of all and the safety of each," voiced their plea "to find our place in your constitutional decrees, to read and study our duties there, and to learn how citizens will be armed to carry them out." Meanwhile, he promised, the Guards would fulfill their trust: "Called from all parts of France by the most pressing of all [duties], proportioning our confidence to your wisdom and our hopes to your accomplishments, we unhesitatingly bring to our country's altar the oath you prescribe for her soldiers." At the very moment, he continued, that the National Guards in Paris would raise their hands in solemn oath, their brethren in every part of the realm would also be taking an oath that would unite them. "May the solemnity of that great day be the signal for the conciliation of parties, for the oblivion of resentments, for peace, and for public happiness!" And his peroration aimed at reassuring those who still feared disturbances: "Have no fear that our blessed enthusiasm will carry us beyond the limits prescribed by public order. Under the influence of the law the standard of liberty will never become that of license. We pledge to you, Gentlemen, respect for the law, whose defenders we are. We pledge it to you on our honor, and free men, Frenchmen, do not promise in vain."[5]

The address had been interrupted several times by applause. When it was over, the Assembly and the spectators expressed their warm appreciation again, and when the applause slackened, it burst forth anew with greater enthusiasm. Lafayette's friends among his fellow deputies were jubilant.[6] In reply to his address Bonnay, as president of the National Assembly, embellished the same themes and seconded their desire for the prompt re-establishment of public order and the completion of the constitution: "The finest day of the National Assembly will be the one on which it will be able to turn over to its successors the obligation to stabilize the majestic edifice which it now is hastening to complete." He then invited the delegation to come to the floor of the Assembly as honored guests and to remain for the rest of the session.[7]

Bonnay's speech too won hearty approval, and the Assembly passed a vote of thanks to the National Guards of France in "recognition of the support which they have given to our labors." It also ordered Lafayette's and Bonnay's speeches printed. Lafayette then led the Guards onto the Assembly floor amid the vigorous clapping of deputies and spectators. Soon thereafter, the session adjourned, and he headed the deputation out of the hall and to the Tuileries.[8]

[5] We have followed the text given in *Adresse des Gardes nationales de France, lue par M. de La Fayette à la séances du 13 juillet 1790*. . . . (Paris, 1790), pp. 1–4, but see also, among others, *Procès-verbal de la Confédération*, pp. 14–15; *Mémoires*, II, 4–6, 205; and *Moniteur*, July 16, pp. 808–9.

[6] *Point du jour*, July 14, pp. 59–63.

[7] *Adresse des Gardes nationales lue par M. de La Fayette*, pp. 4–6.

[8] *AP*, XVII, 77–78; *Point du jour*, July 14, p. 63; *Courier national*, July 14, p. 6; and *Gazette de Leide*, No. 59, July 23.

Louis XVI received the deputation courteously, and Lafayette delivered a second address. Mentioning "imprescriptible rights," "the energy of the people," and "the virtue of their king," he declared that Louis XVI's finest titles were "Chief of the French" and "King of a Free People": "May that pure homage which despotism cannot command be the glory and recompense of a citizen-king. You have wanted us to have a constitution based on liberty and public order. All your wishes, Sire, will be realized. Liberty is assured to us; our zeal assures you of public order. The National Guards of France pledge to Your Majesty an allegiance recognizing no limits but the law and a love having no end but that of our lives."[9]

Although Mirabeau had hoped that he would write and the king would deliver a fitting speech at the Federation itself,[10] Louis had chosen to reply to Lafayette's address on this occasion and the next day at the Federation to make no further remarks beyond taking the oath. Having learned in advance approximately what Lafayette would say, he had shaped his reply accordingly, preparing his own speech, modified only slightly upon the queen's recommendation.[11] He now read the reply he had carefully composed:

I greatly appreciate the assurances of love and attachment that you give me in the name of the National Guards assembled from all parts of France. May the solemn day on which as a body you renew your oath to the constitution witness the disappearance of all dissensions, restore calm, and make law and liberty prevail throughout the realm. Defenders of public order, friends of law and liberty, remember that your first duty is the maintenance of order and submission to law; that the benefits of a free constitution should be equal for all; that the freer one is, the more serious are the offenses he commits against freedom [and] the more criminal the acts of violence and force that are not required by law.

He would have liked, he assured them, to tell all of France "that their king is their father, their brother, their friend; that he can be

---

[9] *Procès-verbal de la Confédération*, p. 16; *Mémoires*, III, 6–8; *AP*, XVII, 83; *Moniteur*, July 19, p. 821; *Gazette de Leide*, July 13; *Journal de Paris*, July 18, p. 806; *Courier national*, July 16, p. 7–9; *Courrier de Paris*, July 16, pp. 194–96; *Journal de la municipalité*, July 20, pp. 993–95; *Courier français*, July 14, p. 111; and *Ami du roi*, July 17, p. 192.

[10] See above, p. 497.

[11] Archbishop of Toulouse to La Marck, July 13 (2 letters), Bacourt (ed.), II, 100–102.

made happy only by their welfare, great only by their prosperity, sick only by their ills." He asked the *fédérés* to relay his sentiments especially to the cottages and hovels of the unfortunate, where he wanted to be "in order to look after them, to live for them, to die, if need be, for them," and he promised, as soon as circumstances permitted, to visit the provinces with his family.[12]

The king's friendly reception of the *fédérés* bade fair to make of the National Guards even stauncher monarchist sympathizers. When the audience was over, on the king's request they filed past him, and finding themselves in the queen's corridor, they urged Lafayette to take them to pay their respects to her. Such a courtesy would have been in keeping neither with the function they had been charged with by the Assembly of the Fédérés nor with their president's view of the queen's place in a "royal democracy." He replied, nevertheless, that he would gladly go with them but would not deliver a formal address, for such an address was due only to the National Assembly and to the king. Accordingly, he arranged for the Guards to be received by Marie Antoinette, who had brought the dauphin with her. After presenting them, he gave up his place at their head and mingled with the rest of the queen's callers. Some of the Guards kissed the little prince's hand, whereupon his mother began to lead him around so that others might do likewise. But when she looked up and saw Lafayette, she immediately stopped and confined herself to the ordinary amenities.[13] The incident could hardly have diminished Marie Antoinette's aversion to Lafayette, but the Guardsmen were pleased with her "most gracious reception."[14]

The reaction of most journals to that morning's events must have pleased Lafayette. They praised his eloquence in expounding the "sentiment of true liberty,"[15] described him as a "worthy de-

---

[12] See n. 9 above. Here we have followed the text given in *Procès-verbal de la Confédération* (pp. 16–17).

[13] *Mémoires*, III, 214–15 n.

[14] *Procès-verbal de la Confédération*, p. 17, and *Mémoires*, III, 6. See the Bibliographical Notes below, p. 554.

[15] *Courier national*, July 14, p. 5.

fender of liberty and legitimate authority,"[16] and considered no one more worthy to express the aspirations of the armed citizens of the empire.[17] Even the *Courrier de Provence,* which was unlikely to express an opinion not shared by Mirabeau, approved of both Lafayette's liberal monarchical principles and his plea for a completion of the constitution.[18] Louis XVI had his response to Lafayette's address printed and scattered all over Paris that evening, and it was well received. Members of the king's household,[19] the minutes of the National Guards' assembly,[20] and some of the press[21] gave almost equally favorable accounts of it.

Not all journalists were wholly friendly, however—least of all, Marat. He described Lafayette's speech to the National Assembly as "a captious discourse," transforming the National Guards "into satellites of a corrupt legislature, into satellites of an inept prince." The address to the king he considered an audacious sacrilege on the part of a shallow courtier, and he accused the speaker of having played "the role of a vile flatterer, of a dastardly seducer, of a traitor to the *patrie.*"[22]

Despite the persistent rain the National Guards gathered that afternoon on the Champs-Elysées, prepared to pass in review before Louis XVI. The bad weather, however, obliged officers to call off the outdoors review and, instead, to lead various units through the Tuileries Gardens and into the palace lobby, where Louis waited to receive them. Again His Majesty's friendliness captivated the *fédérés.* Noticing three men in line dressed as peasants, Louis asked one of them where he came from. "Sire," the young man answered, "I am from Auvergne." Whereupon Louis XVI clapped his hands

[16] *Journal général de l'Europe,* July 25, p. 138.

[17] *Point du jour,* July 14, p. 58. For another favorable report see *Mercure historique et politique de Bruxelles,* July 24, p. 259.

[18] July 13–16, pp. 215–17.

[19] Archbishop of Toulouse to La Marck, July 13, Bacourt (ed.), II, 101–2, and Bertrand de Moleville, III, 232.

[20] *Procès-verbal de la Confédération,* p. 17, and *Mémoires,* III, 6. See the Bibliographical Notes below, p. 554.

[21] See n. 9 above.

[22] *Ami du peuple,* July 19, pp. 3–6.

and shouted: "Vivent les Auvergnats!"[23] He could hardly have failed to remember that Lafayette was an Auvergnat.

That evening at the Hôtel de Ville Lafayette presided over a meeting of the National Guard representatives that crowded into the Salle de la Reine. The Paris Assembly of Representatives deliberately adjourned early so as to let them have its larger meeting place, to which they went, but no business of importance was transacted.[24] All expectantly awaited the morrow.

Apparently a last-minute attempt was made to disrupt the Federation. According to a letter purporting to have come from a National Guardsman,[25] copies of one of Marat's pamphlets were distributed that night among his comrades on guard on the Champ-de-Mars. Entitled "Infernal Project of the Enemies of the Revolution," it accused Lafayette and the inner circle of the Society of 1789 of plotting to make the king an absolute dictator and called upon the *fédérés* to resist.[26] As the pamphlet passed from tent to tent, the Guardsman's letter said, his comrades "drank to the health of the Friend of the People." Three hours later, the letter went on, many spies came into the camp in disguise and, mingling with the Guards, denounced Marat as an unscrupulous hireling paid to instigate the assassination of Necker, Bailly, and Lafayette, but the soldiers defended Marat as a "fanatic for liberty" and drove the spies away.[27] Doubtless the story had some elements of truth. Some of the Paris National Guards presumably read Marat and defended him, but it seems highly unlikely that more than a few of them would at this point have felt that Lafayette was the self-seeking royalist henchman that the wary Friend of the People portrayed. And if the Guardsman's letter was genuine, perhaps agents-provacateurs were busy, though fruitlessly, plotting dissension among the guardians of the peace.

[23] *Révolutions de Paris*, No. 53, July 10–17, pp. 3, 32, No. 54, July 17–24, pp. 81–82. See also *Courier national*, July 16, p. 9; *Courrier de Paris*, July 14, p. 189, July 16, p. 194; and "Proclamation du roi," July 13, *Procès-verbal de la Confédération*, pp. 12–13.

[24] Lacroix, VI, 489 (July 13).

[25] *Ami du peuple*, July 22, p. 3.

[26] Charles Vellay (ed.), *Les pamphlets de Marat* (Paris, 1911), pp. 197–210.

[27] See above, n. 25.

Another plot that night had somewhat greater success. An officer named Bonne-Savardin, accused of being an agent of the Maillebois conspirators, had been arrested on his way to Savoy in May and had recently been returned to Paris and imprisoned in the Abbaye de Saint-Germain. During the evening of July 13, two men, both wearing the uniform of the Paris National Guard and one representing himself as an aide of Lafayette, delivered an order authorizing the keeper of the Abbaye to turn his prisoner over to them to be taken at once to the Hôtel de Ville and returned later to prison. The keeper complied, and the professed officers escorted the prisoner to the waiting carriage and drove off. Only the next night, when his prisoner failed to return, did the keeper make inquiries. Although it created another scandal, Bonne-Savardin's freedom was short-lived, however; he was recaptured and returned within a fortnight.[28]

Neither Marat's accusation of an "infernal plot" nor the escape of the alleged royalist plotter came to Lafayette's notice until after the Federation. On the eve of that gala event he had every reason to feel that things were in good train for the next day. All looked propitious, except the weather; it was still raining.

By 2:30 the next morning, a few people had already assembled at the entrance to the Champ-de-Mars asking to be admitted. The National Guard officers in charge let them in, and they took their choice of the unreserved seats to wait in the rain for the spectacle scheduled to begin only at midday. Long before dawn a steadily increasing stream of civilians moved along the streets and quays of Paris to the parade ground, and National Guardsmen left their barracks and homes to take up patrol duty. By six o'clock troops of the line and sailors were heading toward the boulevards to find their places in the huge parade that was to initiate the first anniversary of the capture of the Bastille, and *fédérés* from the eighty-three departments of France fell in behind their departmental banners, each emblazoned with the slogan "Constitution." Days before, special convoys of meat and flour had poured into the Halles of

---

[28] Lacroix, VI, 604, 609–14 (July 29). See also *Orateur du peuple*, No. 46, p. 367, and *Journal général de la cour*, July 12, p. 132. In the next volume in this series we shall deal with the consequences of Bonne-Savardin's escape at greater length.

Paris bringing provisions for the thousands of Parisians and visitors so that no commercial traffic should impede the marching of the thousands of men commemorating the dawn of the Second Year of Liberty. Carriages, carts, and wagons were prohibited, as were also the carrying of arms and (except for domestics and foreigners) the wearing of livery, and shops were required to remain closed.[29]

About eight o'clock Lafayette arrived at the Porte Saint-Martin with his staff. As soon as all was ready, he took his place at the head of the cavalry and gave the order to march.[30] The procession moved down a lane formed by two lines of blue-coated Paris National Guardsmen, as spectators cheered from windows, doorways, and rooftops. Whenever the marchers stopped for a few moments, grateful people brought them cakes, bread, and wine. For over three hours the parade advanced briskly, despite bursts of rain, Lafayette from time to time bowing with hat in hand to applauding spectators. Even Marat admitted that the commandant general won all hearts, although he himself considered it "childish" for a man of Lafayette's age so to "imitate" the manners of a courtier.[31]

It was ten o'clock when the head of the column entered the Rue Saint-Honoré. There Lafayette sent an aide ahead to inform the president of the National Assembly that the parade would soon reach the Place de Louis XV. On its way there it passed the Manège, where Lafayette dismounted and entered to inform his fellow deputies that it was time for them to take their places.[32] Dressed in plain black coats, escorted by the mayor and the municipal Committee on the Federative Pact, the deputies immediately set out across the Tuileries Gardens. The wind was strong, and the rain coming down hard, but the deputies, trying to keep dry under their umbrellas, pushed on.

In the meantime, Lafayette had again caught up with the procession, which had halted at the Place de Louis XV. There the students of the École Militaire—the Bataillon des Enfants—moved

---

[29] Municipal ordinances, July 8, Lacroix, VI, 468–69.

[30] *Ami du peuple*, July 22, p. 3.

[31] *Ibid.*, pp. 3–4.

[32] *AP*, XVII, 84–85 (July 14); Ferrières to Mme de Ferrières, July 18, Ferrières, *Correspondance*, pp. 240–41; and *Journal de Paris*, July 15, pp. 791–94.

out of line and took a post at the bridge across the Seine, and the Bataillon des Vétérans stationed themselves nearby. The color guards of the sixty Paris battalions, the senior National Guard units of the realm, drew up in the center of the spacious square in a double line to form a lane of escorts for the National Assembly. Thus, with the Élèves Militaires symbolizing France's future hopes, the Vétérans symbolizing her past glory, and the color guards of the Paris National Guard symbolizing her present resolve, the commandant general, mounted on his white horse, awaited the deputies of the nation. When all were drawn up in order, he took a post close to the Élèves Militaires and faced the Tuileries Gardens.

As the National Assembly entered from the Gardens into the square, Lafayette and all the troops saluted. The representatives of the French nation, one of them recorded, were filled with profound pride upon beholding "that general who so well fulfilled the prom- ise that he had given in his earliest youth" mounted close to "a bat- talion of heroes who were not much taller than their sabres and their grenadiers' bonnets, ... twelve or thirteen-year-old soldiers."[33] When the deputies had made their way into the lane of color guards, the advance to the Champ-de-Mars resumed.

Windows, doorways, and roofs still were filled with onlookers, waving and shouting "Vive l'Assemblée nationale!" "Vive la Na- tion!" Handsomely gowned ladies tossed flowers at deputies and soldiers as they passed. Other spectators, soaking wet, stood two and three rows deep behind the Guards lining the Cours de la Reine, cheering or singing "Ça ira! ça ira!" "It would not have been easy to say whether there were more [spectators] under the trees or in the trees."[34]

Somewhere along the line of march to the Champ-de-Mars, as Lafayette, with beads of perspiration on his face, was giving out his orders, a man, pushed through the crowd and ran up to him with

[33] Letter of an unidentified deputy in *Journal de Paris*, July 15, p. 792. The letter is quoted in full in J.-B. Regnault-Warin, *Mémoires pour servir à la vie du Général La Fayette et à l'histoire de l'Assemblée constituante* (Paris, 1824), II, pièces justificatives, pp. 91–96, and in [Bérenger (ed.)], pp. 210–20. Maurice Tourneux, "La Fédération parisienne du 14 juillet 1790 (Essai bibliographique)" *Révolution française*, XIII (1887), 86, says the writer was J.-D. Garat.

[34] *Journal de Paris*, July 15, p. 792.

a bottle of wine and a glass. The intruder filled the glass with wine and held it out to Lafayette: "General, you are warm. Have a drink." Lafayette, hesitating only an instant, drained the glass and thanked the stranger as he handed it back. The unknown man had noted and understood the general's hesitation; he refilled the glass and drank from it himself. The spectators applauded. They probably shared the reaction of the several witnesses who recorded their feeling that Lafayette intended by his gesture to demonstrate that he had confidence in all his fellow-citizens.[35]

After the general and his staff crossed the bridge over the Seine, he ordered the artillery to signal that the National Assembly was coming. So when the deputies reached the bridge, cannon salutes announced their approach to the long-expectant people in the Champ-de-Mars, and the soldiers on duty there went to their posts. Volley after volley boomed forth as Lafayette led the parade through the triumphal archway. It was a classical monument of three arches side by side in a tall masonry structure. It commemorated no military triumph, however; its bas-reliefs and inscription were designed, rather, to celebrate the cult of the Revolution, the victory of liberty, the constitution, and the rights of man. Beyond it, in the center of the huge field, loomed the Altar of the Patrie, bearing on all four sides appropriate sentiments, symbols, and allegorical pictures.[36]

At 10:30, the spectators, some of whom had already been waiting for hours, had seen the first sign that they had not waited in vain. A company of grenadiers escorted onto the Champ-de-Mars from the École Militaire a large body of clergy, including the chaplains of the Paris National Guard and priests from the provinces, wearing white cassocks and tricolor sashes. At the end of the line came Talleyrand, bishop of Autun, wearing his episcopal robes. As the

[35] Among others, Ferrières, *Mémoires*, II, 93; *Gazette de Paris*, July 17, p. 4; *Gazette universelle*, July 18, p. 922; and Maugras (ed.), p. 72 n. *Mémoires*, IV, 154–55, says that Ferrières' account was correct.

[36] The description of the Champ-de-Mars is based upon *Journal général de l'Europe*, July 25, pp. 141–42; *Ami du peuple*, July 19, pp. 1–2; *Moniteur*, July 16, pp. 807–8; *Courrier national*, July 16, pp. 11–14; *Patriote français*, July 15, p. 1, July 17, pp. 3–4, July 18, pp. 3–4; *Courrier de Paris*, July 16, pp. 196–200; and Helen Marie Williams, *Letters on the French Revolution* . . . (Boston, 1791), pp. 3–14. See also note 42 below.

spectators applauded, the priests and their escort proceeded in the rain across the field and took their posts, four ranks deep, on the platform at the foot of the altar facing the triumphal arch.[37] For the next three hours the crowd loyally watched the huge parade march to its assigned places as hundreds of musicians and drummers played a long repertoire of martial airs.

At last Lafayette with the Bataillon des Enfants, followed by President Bonnay and the National Assembly, came through the center arch.[38] As if by prearrangement, this day was understood to be the one for cheering the representatives of the nation, and the stands shouted "Vive l'Assemblée nationale!" This was, however, the first time that day that the spectators in the stands had seen Lafayette, and though they did not yell his name, they increased their applause in his honor. A Breton spectator asked why the applause had grown so great, and the man next to him explained that it was principally for Lafayette, also a deputy. But, the Breton asked, weren't there 100,000 men in the realm who were as good citizens as Lafayette? Indignant bystanders cried out that the Breton was a "bad citizen" and hustled him off to the police.[39]

When the last detachment of grenadiers had crossed the field and the last troop of cavalry had taken its post at the entrance, the crowd waited for their king. In the center of the pavilion, covered with a brilliant canopy ornamented with fleur-de-lys and tricolor bands,[40] a single white banner designated the king's place. It was a chair resembling a throne, elevated on a dais, behind which and to the right was the chair for the National Assembly's president. Resisting what he thought to be Lafayette's "ridiculous idea" to locate the president above the king, Saint-Priest had made this change in interpreting the National Assembly's order.[41] The king's "throne" was draped in purple velvet embroidered with gold fleur-de-lys, while Bonnay's seat was an undecorated armchair. The deputies were expected to sit in the tiers below. A solid block in the cen-

---

[40] Bertrand de Moleville, III, 236.

[37] *Moniteur,* July 23, p. 842.

[39] *Patrote français,* July 25, pp. 2–3. See also Jackson, p. 87.

[38] *Chronique de Paris,* July 16, p. 786. See also *Patriote français,* July 18, p. 3.

[41] Saint-Priest, II, 36–37. Cf. above, p. 514.

ter of the amphitheater was thus occupied by the king and the National Assembly. The officials of Paris and the wives of notables, including Adrienne, occupied the remaining seats. A special box was reserved for the queen and her family and the ambassadors. Thousands of spectators filled every spot in the stands on the other sides of the field, and though their umbrellas offered little protection against the wind and the rain, they were gay and elated. Umbrellas, dresses, tricolor sashes and ribbons added brightness and variety of hue. A deep, solid line of Paris National Guards was posted all around the field just in front of the stands.[42]

While the crowd waited for the king to make his entry, the band played and the people sang "Ça ira, ça ira." The National Guards on the field joined in the singing, some of the soldiers began to dance, and soon clusters of *fédérés* all over the field were performing the steps of their provinces to the tune of "Ça ira" or of their provincial folksongs. The stands chanted back, clapping in time to the music, laughing to see the soldiers prancing on the wet and muddy field. Cheers floated back and forth. When the crowds in the stands shouted "Vivent nos amis!" "Vivent nos frères!" the *fédérés* answered: "Vivent les Parisiens!" "Vivent les Vainqueurs de la Liberté!" and they all joined in "Vive la Nation!"[43]

Finally a salvo of artillery announced that the king was coming. As he walked to his seat from the École Militaire, resplendent in his robe of state and jewels, the crowd shouted "Vive le roi! Vive le roi!" For a moment Louis stood by his "throne," his bright regalia contrasting with the black coats of the National Assembly, acknowledging the cheers of soldiers and spectators. Then, though the cheers did not let up, he sat down. Several gentlemen of the court sought to group themselves around him, but the members of the National Assembly objected. Saint-Priest and one or two others were allowed to stand behind him.[44] The queen and the rest of the

[42] The description of the pavilion and the crowd (where not otherwise indicated) is based upon *Révolutions de Paris*, No. 53, July 10–17, p. 9; *Ami du peuple*, July 18, pp. 2–3; *Courrier de Provence*, July 13–16, p. 299; and *Patriote français*, July 17, p. 3. See also n. 36 above.

[43] *Chronique de Paris*, July 16, pp. 785–86; Desmoulins, *Révolutions*, No. 35, p. 514; and *Journal de Paris*, July 15, p. 793.

[44] *Courrier de Provence*, July 13–16, p. 229, and Saint-Priest, II, 36–37.

royal family went to their box. They too were splendidly—some thought too splendidly—attired.[45]

With the king in his place, the artillery gave the signal to the *fédérés* to dress their lines and prepare for the mass. The rain was beating down hard, as if "Heaven were washing away the sins of the nation," and patriots were to accuse the skies of being aristocratic.[46] Finally, attendants lighted the incense in the urns at the four corners of the altar. The priests followed by the bishop of Autun passed Lafayette on their way from the platform to the altar. The priests' white cassocks were soggy with rain, the bishop's robes clung to him in limp, wet folds. The assisting priests took the covers off the sacred vessels, and as the bishop of Autun began to celebrate mass, the thousands of communicants quieted down. The officiating bishop was said—at least, long afterward—to have been cynically amused,[47] but whether he was or no, the ceremony seemed majestic and reverent, reminding some of Old Testament solemnities.[48]

While the spirit of veneration still moved the spectators, Lafayette gave the signal for blessing the standards. The bearers of the eighty-three departments' colors and of the royal oriflamme formed a line before the altar, and Talleyrand pronounced the blessing of the church upon their standards. The bands then began to play, artillery boomed outside the field, and the spectators clapped their hands, as the color-bearers marched from the altar, passed before the king, and took their banners back to their comrades.[49]

It was almost five o'clock when Lafayette gave the signal for the

---

[45] *Patriote français*, July 18, pp. 3–4.

[46] Desmoulins, *Révolutions*, No. 34, p. 466, No. 35, p. 515; F. L. d'Escherny, *Correspondance d'un habitant de Paris avec ses amis . . .* (Paris, 1791), p. 318; and *Patriote français*, July 15, p. 1.

[47] A persistent tradition has it that in passing Lafayette on the steps toward the altar, Talleyrand muttered, "Don't make me laugh." We have found no contemporary source, however, that reports this alleged remark. It is first found in the *Mémoires du Chancelier Pasquier* (Paris, 1893–95), I, 247; Pasquier claimed to have learned it from Lafayette himself. It does not sound plausible for 1790, though it might have appeared characteristic of the later Talleyrand. See G. Lacour-Gayet, *Talleyrand, 1754–1836* (Paris, 1928–31), I, 108–9.

[48] *Journal de Paris*, July 15, p. 792.

[49] *Révolutions de Paris*, No. 53, July 10–17, p. 7, and *Journal de Paris*, July 15, p. 792.

next event. Paris National Guards, two abreast, formed a lane that stretched symbolically from the steps of the altar to the steps of the "throne." Lafayette rode down the lane, dismounted within a few yards of the king, and ascended the stairs to the "throne." Saluting the king as chief of the Federation, he asked for orders. One of the National Assembly was reminded of the sentiment in Tacitus' *Agricola* that nothing so much enhances the splendor of a throne as the sight of a proud and noble man, still young but able to look back upon a series of triumphs, bowing before it.[50] Louis XVI gave Lafayette the text of the oath to be taken by the *fédérés* and ordered him to administer it. Saluting once more, the general moved away from the throne, turned, drew his sword, and holding it high before him, walked slowly between the lines of Guardsmen to the foot of the altar. He mounted the steps and laid his sword upon the altar, while trumpets sounded on the platform below. As the last note died away, silence descended upon the great arena. In a firm, confident voice Lafayette recited the oath prescribed for the *fédérés*:

We swear to be forever faithful to the Nation, to the Law, and to the King; to maintain with all our power the Constitution decreed by the National Assembly and accepted by the King; to protect, in keeping with the Laws, the safety of persons and of property, the circulation of grain and of other supplies within the realm, the collection of public taxes in whatever form they may have; [and] to remain united with all Frenchmen by the indissoluble bonds of brotherhood.[51]

As he finished, thousands of swords flashed, and thousands of voices pronounced: "I so swear."

Thereupon, an aide on the altar platform signaled the artillery, "and France was told that in the Hero of Liberty as well as in his numerous brothers in arms she would find not only defenders of the constitution but also friends and brothers whom the same zeal had united for the glory of the nation, for the maintenance of the law, and for the splendor of the French throne."[52] Artillery thun-

---

[50] *Journal de Paris*, July 15, p. 794. See above, n. 33.

[51] *Procès-verbal de la Confédération*, p. 18. See also above, p. 509.

[52] *Moniteur*, July 23, p. 842. See also Fernan Nuñez to Floridablanca, July 15, Mousset, p. 109; *Chronique de Paris*, July 16, p. 786; and *Gazette de Paris*, July 16, p. 2.

dered along the Seine, and people cheered. Frenchmen in other cities, celebrating their local federations about the same moment took a similar oath. And the spirit of federation spread even beyond France. Among the marchers and spectators at the Champ-de-Mars were more or less formally recognized delegates of foreign countries; in London about that hour over six hundred men raised their glasses to Lafayette and other leaders of the Revolution; in Hamburg, in the Low Countries, and elsewhere friends of the French Revolution rejoiced over the rebirth of liberty.[53]

Lafayette now descended the steps and returned to the chief of the Federation for new orders, while the music played on, the *fédérés* swung their hats on the points of their swords, and the spectators shouted and sang. The royal wish was that the National Assembly should next take the civic oath. At Lafayette's signal the band stopped playing, a short volley of shots rang out, and the arena grew quiet once more. President Bonnay and the deputies of the National Assembly rose in their places, and Bonnay pronounced the oath of the deputies of the nation:

I swear to be faithful to the Nation, to the Law, and to the King, and to maintain with all my might the Constitution decreed by the National Assembly and accepted by the King.

The deputies responded: "I so swear." Again salvos of artillery rang out, and again spectators and *fédérés* shouted "Vive l'Assemblée national!" "Vive la Nation!"[54]

The next event was to be the oath of Louis XVI. Lafayette had all along preferred that the king take the oath standing in the midst of the nation's deputies, but he believed that the Jacobins, failing fully to realize the potential danger of a solitary and separate act, wanted Louis to take the oath standing alone at the altar, and he suspected that some aristocrats also had advocated that

---

[53] Letter from Hamburg, July 19, in *Courrier de Paris*, Aug. 1, p. 455, and *Chronique de Paris*, Aug. 2, p. 854; Pierre Jolly, *Du Pont de Nemours* (Paris, 1956), p. 105 (describing the "American section of humanity," which was led by Thomas Paine and John Paul Jones, bearing the United States flag); Auguste Dide, "Les fédérations rurales en 1790 et la fête du 14 juillet," *Révolution française*, I (1881), 9–30; Feuillet de Conches, I, 329–30; and Earl Stanhope to La Rochefoucauld, n.d., *Moniteur*, July 30, p. 867.

[54] *Procès-verbal de la Confédération*, pp. 18–19.

procedure.[55] It now was clear that the king had chosen to act as Lafayette hoped. Seated on his horse once more, Lafayette gave the signal for a third oath-taking. By that time the rain had stopped, and the sun had come out. The cannoneers upon signal fired a short volley to announce another part of the program. Louis XVI rose and waited for silence. Then with arm raised toward the altar, he pronounced in a firm, loud voice:

I, King of the French, swear to employ all the power delegated to me by the constitutional law of the state, to maintain the constitution decreed by the National Assembly and accepted by me, and to attend to the execution of the laws.

When the king had finished, a roar sounded from one end of the field to the other, so loud that the artillery was almost drowned out. The National Assembly, the *fédérés,* the municipal officials, and the Paris National Guards joined with the people in the stands in cries of "Vive le Roi!" Then came cries once more of "Vive l'Assemblée nationale!" "Vive la Nation!" The nation's deputies hugged each other in glee. It was "a touching spectacle of a family of brothers who had just sworn to an indissoluble union, an eternal friendship."[56] So great was Louis XVI's popularity at that moment, one of his aristocratic partisans believed, that had he dared to mount a horse and ride out on the field, he could have won the *fédérés* to his cause.[57] Some revolutionary journalists afterward fretted that the popularity of Louis XVI had overshadowed that of the National Assembly, that Lafayette and others had perhaps even designed the ceremony to plant royalism in the hearts of the *fédérés.*[58]

[55] *Mémoires,* III, 214. See also [Estienne], *Interrogatoire de La Fayette,* p. 38. Virieu thought that Lafayette feared the king might have been trampled by a rush of admirers toward him at the altar while his courtiers feared an attempt by Orleanists on his life: Grouchy and Gillois (eds.), p. 207. Lescure (ed.), *Correspondance secrète,* II, 459 (July 16), is the only source we have found that says Lafayette wanted the king to take the oath at the altar.

[56] *AP,* XVII, 85 (July 14), and *Procès-verbal de la Confédération,* p. 19.

[57] Daudet (ed.), pp. 281–82, and Saint-Priest, II, 37.

[58] *Courrier de Provence,* July 13–16, p. 227; *Révolutions de Paris,* No. 53, July 10–17, p. 12, No. 54, July 17–24, pp. 1–2; *Journal général de la cour,* July 16, p. 123; and *Ami du peuple,* July 19, pp. 5–6. See also Maximilien Robespierre, *Lettres . . . à ses commetans,* No. 7, [1792], p. 316.

At that juncture Marie Antoinette took her chance to share in the people's affection for their king. Rising in her box and holding her little boy in her arms, she presented him to the cheering people. The spectators responded ardently: "Vive la reine!" "Vive le dauphin!" The picture of a magnificently gowned queen with a little prince in a soldier's uniform charmed the *fédérés*. Some of them broke ranks and thronged toward the queen's box.[59] Lafayette galloped to the spot and ordered them back to their posts around the altar. He afterward maintained (though whether on intelligence he then had or learned only later is not clear) that the queen had planned to stir up a popular demand that she take her place beside the king.[60]

The Federation was almost over now, and the priests returned to the altar to chant the *Te Deum*. When they had finished, Louis XVI arose to depart, and cries of "Vive le roi!" followed him all the way back to the École Militaire. Lafayette watched the parade lines reassemble. Officers of the royal troops came up to ask him what to do with the royal oriflamme. Lafayette told them to put it overnight in the Château de la Muette, where the next gala event was to take place, and carry it the next morning to the Manège.[61]

So far the stars of the gala occasion had been the National Assembly and the king, Lafayette basking in the reflection of their glory. But now that the king was gone, exuberant *fédérés* gathered around their president, the conspicuous embodiment of their part in the unique pageant in which they had just so gloriously participated. Desmoulins looked askance at this idolatry of mere men— for Lafayette, he feared, had received even more worship than the king—rather than of principles, and he imagined that the general, catching sight of him as he was leaving the Champ-de-Mars, read

---

[59] *Patriote français*, July 18, p. 4.

[60] *Mémoires*, III, 213–14. Marat says (*Ami du peuple*, July 18, p. 8) that Lafayette had to order the troops back into line on two separate occasions, the other one being when the king started for the altar. He alleged that on that other occasion many of them were so annoyed that they turned their backs on the general, whereupon some paid officers cried, "Vive Lafayette!"—to which the general responded, "Gentlemen, there is no longer a Lafayette." Of the numerous other accounts none tells of this episode, which could hardly have escaped notice if it had indeed occurred.

[61] *AP*, XVII, 86 (July 15).

in his face his "bitter reproaches" and perhaps felt remorse.[62] But Desmoulins probably egocentrically exaggerated the significance of a lone face in an overflowing crowd to a preoccupied, triumphant general, who, it would seem, at that moment had no reason to feel any pangs of guilt.

When the Paris color-bearers and the National Assembly were ready, Lafayette took his place in the parade once more, and the marchers passed through the triumphal arch, across the bridge, and along the Cours de la Reine back to the Place de Louis XV and the Tuileries. Meanwhile Louis XVI and his party drove from the École Militaire along other streets to the Tuileries, receiving a continual ovation on the way. The aristocratic party was encouraged. The *fédérés,* they gathered, had shown far more attachment to the king and the royal family than to the National Assembly and they seemed to have reason to hope that "Lafayette had been brought down."[63] They discovered room also to speculate whether, this time by placing himself at the head of the *fédérés,* Louis might be able to dissolve the National Assembly, punish the leaders of subversion, and recover his authority.[64]

Which side, indeed, had won the tug-of-war that the pageantry of the Federation betokened—the aristocratic monarchists or the cause of "royal democracy"? Each apparently considered itself the victor, and the Cordeliers' journalists clearly implied that both sides in fact had been pulling in the same direction. The *Orateur du peuple* called the major-general of the Federation *le dictateur la Fayette.*[65] Desmoulins charged that Lafayette was guilty of "complicity in debasing the majesty of the French people."[66] Marat held that the president of the National Assembly and not the commandant general should have administered the oath to the *fédérés* and that it was time for "informed and courageous men" to re-

---

[62] *Révolutions,* No. 34, pp. 464–65. See also *ibid.,* pp. 521–22.

[63] Daudet (ed.), p. 281. Cf. Tourzel, I, 162–68.

[64] Saint-Priest, II, 37, and Marie Antoinette to Mercy, July 20, La Rocheterie and Beaucourt (eds.), II, 184.

[65] No. 47, pp. 382–83.

[66] *Révolutions,* No. 34, p. 465.

mind monarch, commandant general, and president of their proper places and functions.[67] The commandant general himself had little evidence of the aristocrats' speculations, but he suspected that they resented his conspicuous refusal to exalt the king above the National Assembly.[68]

As president of the *fédérés,* however, he had little time to be concerned with that matter, for he had other duties to perform. He was expected at the Château de la Muette, where the Commune of Paris was tendering a banquet to the *fédérés,* and he accompanied Bailly there. Many of the National Guards were already gathered in the château garden and came out to greet them. To Bailly they paid a becoming respect, but for Lafayette they evinced a warm affection. They crowded about him, jostling and cheering, patting his horse, trying to touch his hands, or to throw their arms about him. For a moment it was feared that he and his horse would be suffocated, but his friends extricated him.[69] With Bailly he made his way to the château, mingling with the thousands of Guardsmen scattered among numerous tables set out in the garden, greeting some of them personally, and praising at least one of them for vigilance in putting down counterrevolution.[70]

Lafayette left the Muette before the dinner was over, possibly called away to attend to the escape of Bonne-Savardin, by this time discovered. When later that evening he went home, he rode through a Paris gaily decorated and brightly illuminated in celebra-

---

[67] *Ami du peuple,* July 18, p. 3.

[68] *Mémoires,* III, 214.

[69] *Révolutions de Paris,* No. 53, July 10–17, pp. 10–13; Duc de Doudeauville, *Mémoires* (Paris, 1862), III, 174; Desmoulins, *Révolutions,* No. 34, pp. 464–65, 521–22; *Ami du peuple,* July 22, pp. 4–5; Bertrand de Moleville, III, 241–42; *Journal de la municipalité,* July 15, p. 978; *Journal général de l'Europe,* July 25, p. 147; *Journal général de la cour,* July 16, p. 123; *Patriote français,* July 18, p. 4; *Courrier de Paris,* July 16, p. 207; *Mercure historique et politique de Bruxelles,* July 24, p. 297; the *fédérés* of Lyon to the municipality of Lyon [*ca.* July 14], Metzger, pp. 147–48; and Felix Hézecques, *Recollections of a Page at the Court of Louis XVI,* trans. C. M. Yonge (London, 1878), p. 317. For a rumor that some aristocrats tried to stifle Lafayette, see Williams, pp. 13–14. [Montjoie], V, 76, says that Lafayette tried to get himself named chief of the National Guard of the realm at this dinner, but no other source corroborates him.

[70] J. Walletz (commander of the deputation from the Gironde) to Baron Soubervie, Aug. 10, 1830, Indiana University, Ball Collection.

tion of the Federation, with transparencies of himself and Bailly in the most conspicuous places.[71] He had every reason to feel proud of his first year as commandant general and confident of the road he still had to travel. The minutes of the Assembly of the Fédérés (which he signed as president) stated: "On this memorable day, which should forever honor and unite the French Nation, not the slightest blow at public order has been attempted."[72] For Lafayette the year since the preceding July had been a glorious one indeed! A mutual friend of Lafayette and Jefferson wrote to the latter from The Hague:

The day of the Fourteenth went off happily, thank God, to the satisfaction of the kindly people and of its good king, to the honor of Lafayette, to whom security, public order, the safe outcome of the whole thing had been confided. . . . Everyone is united here in saying, but each according to his inclination and system, some blessing, some cursing, that the French are copying the Americans and Lafayette their Washington.[73]

The Federation did not mark the close of the celebrations of the *fédérés* in Paris. It was followed by a series of festivities that lasted until July 24,[74] ten days after Bastille Day. Then, the fetes having ended and most of the *fédérés* having left, the Assembly of the Fédérés, acting through the deputation that had accompanied their president on ceremonial visits, deposited all their formal papers with him. The papers included the official minutes of their meetings, the speeches made by Lafayette as their spokesman, and the responses of king, president, and other notables. By order of the Assembly of the Fédérés Lafayette had these documents published as the *Procès-verbal de la Confédération des François, 14 juillet 1790*. The authors of the *Procès-verbal* did not always strive to attain the sober, unenthusiastic, detached tone which official minutes generally convey; the events they recounted apparently left them too deeply affected for dispassionate reportage.

The public did not have to wait, however, for this at times ef-

---

[71] Thompson (ed.), p. 85.

[72] *Procès-verbal de la Confédération*, p. 19.

[73] C.-W.-F. Dumas to Jefferson, July 20, Boyd (ed.), XVII, 209.

[74] The narrative of these festivities is reserved for presentation in a forthcoming volume.

fusive, at times formal, account to read of the thrilling events of July 14. Several other brochures carried all over France, and well beyond its boundaries, the joyful tidings of the first anniversary of the memorable date destined to become the recurrent national holiday of France. The newspapers gave detailed narratives of much that had actually happened and of some things that were merely rumored or feared or invented. And numerous participants and spectators wrote home about the stirring ceremonies.

Despite the hours of rain and fatigue that had dampened the celebration, nearly always the tone of the newspaper accounts was rhapsodic. One journalist announced: "Never had Paris enjoyed a truer peace and never had there been so much fraternity."[75] Others declared that the fete had been "magnificent,"[76] "sublime,"[77] not only the "most beautiful day in the history of France" but also "unique in history and a model to other peoples who would break their chains."[78]

Private letters were no less enthusiastic. A Parisian wrote to friends abroad:

That day may be regarded as the fete of liberty, the triumph of law, as an august and solemn pact, a great confederation, a religious ceremony, a new contract between the people and the king, a renovation, a renaissance of the political body, a renewal of the social order, a national congress, the inauguration of democracy. What then have I seen in the Champ-de-Mars? . . . The most moral picture that may ever be presented for the reflection and meditation of the philosopher.[79]

A *fédéré* informed his father:

This event may perhaps justly be regarded as the establishment of the constitution. . . . The court is greatly changed; the former arrogance has given way to the greatest popularity. The king has declared himself more than ever the chief of the Revolution.[80]

[75] *Courrier de Paris*, July 14, p. 178. See also *Journal de la municipalité*, July 15, p. 978.

[76] *Journal de Paris*, July 16, p. 795.

[77] *Orateur du peuple*, No. 46, p. 368.

[78] *Journal général de l'Europe*, July 25, pp. 144, 147.

[79] Baron d'E*** to L***, Aug. 10, Escherny, pp. 316–17.

[80] Delamare de Crux to his father, Vassière (ed.), p. 200.

A participating deputy of the National Assembly declared: "I believe there has never been a more beautiful spectacle on earth, nor have more souls ever been filled at the same moment with the same joy."[81]

Witnesses nostalgically remembered "that day without precedent" the rest of their lives. A Paris Guardsman who had been on duty all that night and day and had been "soaking wet twenty times" nevertheless recalled it in after years as "incontestably the most beautiful day of the Revolution."[82] A page of the king who had come to scoff afterward admitted that he had remained to praise.[83] The Comte de Ségur, long past the event, when tragedy had cooled his revolutionary ardor, still thought: "Never in antiquity had a fete demonstrated more solemnly the enthusiasm of a people for its laws, for its legislators, for its chief, and for its liberty."[84] Lafayette himself always believed: "The Federation of 1790 was one of the greatest events of the Revolution. Fourteen thousand deputies formally chosen by more than three million National Guardsmen, deputations from all land and sea forces, came in the name of armed France to abjure the Old Regime and to pledge allegiance to constitutional liberty and equality."[85] He estimated that 300,000 spectators had attended the Federation and their acclamations "were reechoed from one end of the empire to the other."[86]

Nor was it Frenchmen alone who basked in the fraternal spirit that had warmed the rain-soaked spectators at the Federation. An enthusiastic English spectator pronounced the judgment that the Federation had been "the most sublime spectacle which, perhaps, was ever represented on the theater of this earth."[87] Foreign diplo-

---

[81] [Garat to a friend, undated], *Journal de Paris*, July 15, p. 794.

[82] Baron Thiébault, *Mémoires*, ed. Fernand Calmettes (Paris, 1893), I, 261–64.

[83] Hézecques, p. 317.

[84] *Décade historique*, ed. P. Tardieu (Paris, 1824–30), I, 242.

[85] *Mémoires*, III, 3. Cf. Lafayette to M. Ternaux, Sept. 13, 1816, in Charavay catalogue, sale of Mar. 26, 1971, item 168.

[86] Lafayette to M. d'Hennings, Jan. 15, 1799, *Mémoires*, III, 251, where the number of National Guardsmen is put at four million. The original of this letter, now in the Huntington Library (HM 21654), says "plus de quatre million."

[87] Williams, p. 3.

matic emissaries, having more reason to weigh their words, were nonetheless electrified. The Spanish ambassador assured his government: "The spectacle was the most magnificent and the most novel that could possibly be witnessed. . . . I know of no spectacle given by the Romans that surpassed, that even equaled, this one."[88] Nor, indeed, had any modern people (the Americans perhaps excepted) "surpassed" or "even equaled" the spectacle of their massed representatives pledging national fraternity and "allegiance to constitutional liberty and equality." The American chargé d'affaires, although keenly disappointed that "those who wished to see a patriot, & sober legislator in every *fédéré*" sometimes saw instead only "the votaries of Mars, Bacchus, & Venus," was no less astonished that where disorder had been widely expected, "the most perfect order and harmony reigned" and that "the spectacle . . . was really sublime and magnificent."[89] Even the chary British ambassador praised the harmony and the "astonishing regularity" that had characterized the day.[90]

As one might have expected, the American envoy attributed to Lafayette the principal credit for the lift to Louis XVI's popularity that resulted. He was glad to report to Gouverneur Morris, who doubtless was glad to learn, that the *fédérés'* "principles of *Royalism*" were "very observable" and that they were "far from shewing those democratic principles which prevail in a part of the National Assembly." Those principles he attributed to "the demagogues of the assembly" (he meant the Jacobins), who had "never remained more silent or more quiet" than at this time when "everything was feared from their manoeuvres." The victory over these "demagogues" belonged to "the Marquis de la fayette," who "seemed to have taken full possession of the fédérés" and was "adored by them." The Federation, Short decided, "may be regarded as the zenith of his influence."[91]

Other witnesses of the day's events confirmed Short's opinion

[88] Fernan Nuñez to Floridablanca, July 15, Mousset, pp. 109–11.
[89] Short to Morris, July 27, Davenport (ed.), I, 565.
[90] Gower to Leeds, July 16, Browning (ed.), p. 14.
[91] Short to Morris, July 28, Davenport (ed.), I, 565.

that Lafayette's influence was at its zenith.[92] His very critics, by their disapproval of his "deification"[93] and "adulation"[94] and of his overshadowing the king and all other rivals for popular acclaim,[95] confirmed the general esteem in which he was held. Pictures, poems, songs, and pamphlets glorifying him were sold out more rapidly than ever.[96] Every *fédéré* carried home with him a medal commemorating the Federation, awarded by the Commune of Paris, along with a certificate of participation in the great occasion, signed by Lafayette and other municipal officials.[97] At that moment in the history of the Revolution, only the king, if even he, could have commanded a greater loyalty from the French people. As Lafayette on his spirited white charger pranced from point to point on the Champ-de-Mars that day of triumph, one of the Paris National Guard, the future general and baron Paul Thiébault, found all eyes fixed upon horse and rider, and, as he afterward recollected, a wit standing near him, pointing at the equestrian cynosure, exclaimed: "Look at M. de Lafayette galloping down the centuries to come!"[98]

The centuries to come, perhaps, but not the years immediately to follow. Despite all Lafayette's pre-eminence the moment was not yet ripe for the "royal democracy" he wanted, for royalists dreaded democracy and democrats distrusted royalty. William Short, if not

[92] *Gazette de Paris*, July 16, p. 2; Delamare de Crux to his father, July 15, Vaissière (ed.), p. 200; Mme de Corny to Jefferson, July 23, and Mme d'Enville to Jefferson, July 27, Boyd (ed.), XVII, 261, 287.

[93] *Révolutions de Paris*, No. 53, July 12–17, p. 13.

[94] Robespierre, *Défenseur de la constitution*, ed. G. Laurent, No. 10, [c. July 25, 1792], p. 294. See also No. 6 [*ca.* June 22, 1792], *ibid.*, pp. 172–83.

[95] Mirabeau to the court, July 29, Bacourt (ed.), II, 120–21, and Desmoulins, *Révolutions*, No. 35, pp. 501–9.

[96] Ferrières, *Mémoires*, III, 134 n.; Charavay, illustration between pp. 234 and 235; *Révolutions de Paris*, No. 53, July 10–17, pp. 13, 40; *Courrier de Paris*, July 17, p. 230, July 18, p. 8; [Béranger (ed.)], p. 287; *Courier national*, July 20, p. 8; and *Journal général de l'Europe*, July 25, p. 147.

[97] Lacroix, VI, 473–74 (July 10).

[98] Thiébault, I, 261. The white horse eventually became the property of Thiébault's livery stable (*ibid.*, note). Thiébault thought it a mean animal by that time.

the others who bore testimony to Lafayette's triumph,[99] perhaps recognized the ambiguity in the metaphor which spoke of his "zenith." Short complained that Lafayette made no use of his influence:

The time will come perhaps when he will repent having not seized that opportunity of giving such a complexion to the revolution as every good citizen ought to desire. It would have been easy for him to have engaged the [National] Assembly to have fixed the epoch of the elections for the next legislature. I fear now that nothing but some crisis which I do not foresee will engage them to do it.[100]

Several months later Short, convinced that the National Assembly would prolong its existence as long as it could, saw no Cromwell to dominate "this new Long Parliament":

The only man who could have placed bounds to the duration of this Assembly let slip the moment at which he could have done it, at the time of the late Federation. He erred from too much virtue and from too little of what the French call *caractère*. If he had followed the advice of one of his friends at least [Short himself] he would have saved his country much misfortune, much blood perhaps, and would have added to the kind of immortality he had already acquired. But there are moments which never return and now things must take their own long and apparently perilous course.[101]

What Short perhaps did not recognize was that Lafayette had deliberately chosen not to be a Cromwell. Instead, he sought to be a Cincinnatus, a Washington, a leader who would use his hold on the people only to fulfill their will and then, having tided them over a crisis, would return to his own domestic affairs. He never took the position that he should give orders to the civil authorities, but rather that he should take orders from them. He as yet had little reason, Short's hindsight to the contrary notwithstanding, to believe that his policy would not soon bring a happy ending.

Indeed, at the time of the Federation the Revolution with which

---

[99] Cf. Tourzel, I, 162.

[100] Short to Morris, July 27, Davenport (ed.), I, 565–66. See below, n. 101.

[101] Short to William Nelson, Jr., Feb. 21, 1791, Princeton University Library (courtesy of Joseph H. Harrison, Jr.). For clarity we have occasionally modified spelling and capitalization in quoting Short's letters.

he had merged his life, fortune, and sacred honor and in which he had risen to an unrivaled prestige both among his fellow-citizens and abroad seemed to promise a bright future for France. In a period of less than fifteen months since the Estates General had convened, it had wiped out many abuses. The good will of the king and the support of the people seemed to be rapidly bringing about a devoutly wished consummation. The Constituent Assembly had passed decrees that made nobles, clergy, and people into a single estate, a "nation": all were alike mere citizens; titles and privileges had disappeared; the law was the same for everyone. France looked as if it would soon be the constitutional monarchy that Lafayette desired, with a representative legislature and a strong king. For all their defects, the newly enacted constitutional provisions so far seemed sound. And France was free and united. If some men, in high places and low, still were malcontent, they appeared unlikely to achieve their ends, too frustrated to break that freedom and unity.

So in mid-July 1790 the Revolution seemed to be well on its course, headed in the right direction. At the zenith of his influence Lafayette might well have looked to even an informed observer to be prancing confidently on his white horse down the centuries to come. But, unfortunately for him and for those who counted upon him, the zenith of a celestial body marks not only the culminating point in its ascent but also the beginning of its descent. The Federation marked the acme of Lafayette's influence, but his primary aim—a completed constitution—dragged far behind.

BIBLIOGRAPHICAL NOTES

In addition to appearing in full in many contemporary newspapers (see nn. 5–9 above) Lafayette's addresses to the National Assembly and to the king of July 13 were both printed as separate pamphlets, not only in Paris but in other cities such as Lille, Evreux, and Brussels, in more than one edition, sometimes with the king's response appended. The king's response was also printed separately, not only in Paris but also in other cities. Some of these items are catalogued in such bibliographies as Jackson (pp. 87, 111, 126, 166), Martin and Walter (II, 612), and Monglond (I, 927). The versions of these addresses given in *Mémoires,* III, 4–6, depart occasionally from those in their source, which Lafayette (somewhat inaccurately) called *Le Procès-verbal de la fédération* [*sic*] *des Français* and dates 1790; see above, p. 548.

Bibliographies of the accounts of the Federation are numerous: see, *inter alia,* Maurice Tourneaux, "La Fédération parisienne," pp. 75–93, and Le-clercq, *Fédération,* pp. 356–58 nn. Various items of iconographical as well as bibliographical interest are described in Blancheteau catalogue, pp. 70–77, items 237–64; Braibant (ed.), *Exposition,* pp. 90–92, items 264–75; Bruel (ed.), II, 617–45, *passim;* and Girodie catalogue, pp. 106–15, items 160–83.

The National Assembly's official account is the "Procès-verbal de la cérémonie de la Fédération du mercredi 14 juillet 1790" (*AP,* VII, 84–85). We have depended more upon the *Procès-verbal de la Confédération,* signed by Lafayette and the eight secretaries of the Assembly of the Fédérés. De-tailed accounts may be found also in *Journal de Paris,* July 15, pp. 791–94 (see above, n. 33); *Courier national,* July 16, pp. 5, 10–15; *Courier français,* July 16, pp. 117–20; *Moniteur,* July 16, pp. 807–8, July 23, p. 842; *Courrier de Paris,* July 16, pp. 196–207; *Journal général de l'Europe,* July 25, pp. 139–47; *Chronique de Paris,* July 15, 16, pp. 783, 785–87; *Gentleman's Magazine,* LX, Part II (1790), pp. 754–58; *Journal de la municipalité,* July 20, pp. 995–97; *Gazette de Paris,* July 15, pp. 1–2, July 16, pp. 1–4; *Gazette de Leide,* July 23; and *Mercure historique et politique de Bruxelles,* July 24, pp. 296–97.

Among the letters describing the Federation soon after July 14 are Dela-mare de Crux to his father, July 15, Vaissière (ed.), pp. 199–200; Mlle de Givey to her brother, July 16, *ibid.,* pp. 201–4; Edmond Géraud to his father, July 17, Maugras (ed.), pp. 70, 71 n.; Ferrières to Mme Ferrières, *Corre-spondance,* pp. 240–41; Staël-Holstein to Gustavus III, July 15, Staël-Holstein, pp. 166–67; Short to Morris, July 27, Davenport (ed.), I, 565–66; Gower to Leeds, July 16, Browning (ed.), p. 14; Fernan Nuñez to Floridablanca, July 15, Mousset, pp. 106–10; Escherny, pp. 305–25; and Williams, pp. 10–13.

The list of accounts by witnesses written after a lapse of time includes A. Lameth, II, 462–66; *Mémoires,* III, 251, IV, 154–55; Saint-Priest, II, 36–38; Ferrières, *Mémoires,* II, 91–95; Bertrand de Moleville, III, 233–40; and Ester-hazy, pp. 275–82.

Marat claimed in his account of the Federation (*Ami du peuple,* July 22, pp. 1–6) that after the banquet at La Muette Lafayette led the *fédérés* to the Tuileries to cheer for the king under the palace windows. Doudeauville (III, 174) also reports such a royalist demonstration but does not seem to in-clude Lafayette in it. We doubt that Lafayette would have led a royalist demonstration at this point.

APPENDIX I

The Fund of the Comité des Recherches

The Archives Nationales (D xxix bis 34, dossier 357) contain a set of papers entitled on the cover "Pièces contenant des états des dépenses secrètes du Commandant général et du Maire de Paris" and on the next page "Emploi des cent soixante treize mille six cent livres touchées au Trésor royal sur les mandats de M. De la Fayette." It is divided into several numbered items. Item 1 is a narrative in seven unnumbered pages of the uses made of the fund; item 2 gives accounting details—sums paid, to whom, and date; items 3–21 are receipts signed by the recipients of each sum. The first entry is of October 23, 1789, and the last of July 23, 1790.

A large part of the money seems to have been paid for (1) agents to keep watch on counterrevolutionaries, counterfeiters of Caisse d'Escompte notes, foreign bribers, deserters, vagrants, several foreign ambassadors (including Mercy), suspected Frenchmen abroad (e.g., Laclos, Calonne, and other émigrés in England), and foreigners believed to be transporting money from France, (2) officers sent to various points to make arrests, (3) escorts for prisoners or witnesses transported to Paris, (4) investigators of the army in the area close to Paris, and (5) searchers for grain in the same area.

A list of *complots de contre révolution ou d'exciter des troubles* is given on the first two (unnumbered) pages. The list contains several familiar names of persons, but since for nearly all of them we have no knowledge of their having been involved in conspiracy, we conclude that they were only temporarily suspected of being accessory to "plots" that subsequently either proved negligible or were frustrated by Lafayette's agents without producing significant consequences. They may even have been unknown to Lafayette until the actual accounting since some of the principal agents (e.g., Delaborde, item 3) indicate that they sub-employed others and received their money not directly from Lafayette but from his aide Desmottes (e.g., Sommellier, item 1; Delaborde, item 6; and Vaugien, items 11–12).

The persons who signed for sums received from this fund are, for the most part, unknown to us, but some names of known officers of the Paris National Guard or of the royal army appear among them—for instance, Cottin, Ermigny, D. M. Jullien, Boinville (see above, pp. 101 and 102), Ternant (see above, p. 275), and Chaumont (see above, p. 449). A sum of 12,000 livres was furnished in December to the Paris Comité des Recherches, and another sum (of 30,000 livres) in April. The various items are regularly endorsed by Bailly and Lafayette, and sometimes by M.-L.-F. Du Port (i.e., Duport-Dutertre), apparently in his capacity of *lieutenant de maire du Département de la Police,* or (in an instance when the expenditures appear to be for diplomatic purposes) by Montmorin, or (in another instance involving the Paris Comité des Recherches) by Perron (of the Paris committee).

If any of the money was used directly to suborn the press, we have not been able to detect it, unless the payment to some printers at Strasbourg by Chaumont (Part 1, pp. [6–7], and Parts 14–15) of 3,600 livres for "the printing of several works for the Revolution" was beyond the reasonable charge for such printing. Unless Mathieu d'Agoult, Rutledge, Poupart-Beaubourg, and Laclos are to be considered journalists (and they are listed not as paid agents but as suspects under surveillance among those possibly engaged in *complots de contre révolution*), none of the names mentioned is known to us to have been that of a journalist.[1] If Lafayette hired Paris journalists (see above, pp. 299 n. and 414), he apparently did not use these funds for that purpose. If they were used at all to influence the press, it was more likely to have been to suppress opposition than to buy support.

The total sum of the expenditures accounted for is 173,154 livres and 5 sous. The care taken to account for each livre is impressive.

[1] The name Hérault appears among the paid agents (item II, p. 27) as having received 3000 livres on July 28. If this is the Hérault *imprimeur* mentioned in Lacroix, IV, 101, then he is the sole exception to this general statement. We think, however, because all the other recognizable persons named in this item were National Guard officers, that Hérault was too.

APPENDIX II

Myths after Favras

When Favras and his wife were sent to the Abbaye, Augeard was already imprisoned there. In his *Mémoires* Augeard claims to have talked with each of them separately, and if he is to be believed, they both told the same story: that the Comte de Luxembourg had been in the Favras plot from the beginning but when he was refused Lafayette's place as commandant general if the conspiracy succeeded, he betrayed the whole affair to Lafayette; that Lafayette had then called in his spies, who, without any basis of fact, accused Favras of engaging to kill him and Bailly, although the conspiracy's objective had been only to save the king; and that to the latter end the Comte de Provence's treasurer had begged Favras to make a loan for Provence.[1] Except that Morel and not Luxembourg had first called the plot to Lafayette's attention, the story ascribed by Augeard to the Favras couple is not implausible. If Augeard's account of his conversations with the Favras couple is true, Favras believed that Luxembourg betrayed him.

Nevertheless, Augeard told of another conversation which, if truthfully recollected, would exculpate Luxembourg. Long after it took place, Augeard recorded the details of a meeting that he said took place in 1798 with Gouverneur Morris. According to this record, Morris told him that the evening after the banker Chomel had consulted Lafayette about lending money to Favras, Lafayette spoke to Morris about it. Thereupon Morris asked the general to send Chomel to see him, and when the banker arrived, he advised him to be on his guard against Favras but to promise a loan provided it was guaranteed by competent and important people. In Morris' story as relayed by Augeard, Favras later told Chomel (and Chomel told Morris) that he had employed three former sergeants of the French Guards, now National Guardsmen, Morel, Turcati, and Jean-Pierre Marquié, to recruit three or four hundred men to secure the person of the king and get rid of Lafayette and Bailly, and Morris then advised Chomel to require notes signed by the Comte de Provence before handing over any money. Morris also, in the same alleged conversation with Augeard, said that after he and Lafayette found out what was going on, they counseled the Comte de Luxembourg to have nothing to do with the affair, for the conspirators wanted the head of a prince of the blood to finish off the Revolution and if they could not get Provence's, they would settle for a lesser one such as his. At first Luxembourg denied knowing any-

[1] Augeard, pp. 212–30.

thing about the conspiracy, Morris allegedly continued, but when Lafayette and Morris named the conspirators, he agreed to see no more of them, and he kept his word;[2] his subsequent absence from their circle led the conspirators to believe that it was he who had betrayed them.[3] But in Augeard's version of Morris' account it was not Luxembourg but Chomel who informed Lafayette and Morris of what was going on.

This account is highly implausible, however. Although Morris' diary contains many personal details, it does not mention the name of Chomel, and it gives no indication of his dealings, of which Augeard says Morris knew so much in 1789. On the contrary, it indicates that Luxembourg frequently offered information which Morris preferred not to know and regularly discounted.[4] Morris' diary, as published only long after his death, gives the impression that in 1789 he was unaware of the details of the Favras plot before he learned of them from Lafayette. "I don't believe a Word of the Plot," he recorded for his own consumption on the day it broke.[5] Morris might, of course, have discreetly avoided mentioning the alleged information as too incriminating to allude to even in a private diary, but it is more probable that Augeard was confused, since much that he claims Morris told him in 1798 could easily have been imagined on the basis of information made public as early as 1790, and if in fact Morris gave Augeard the account he recorded, that account provided little more than by 1798 was commonly known, except to put Morris into the picture as a principal confidant of Lafayette. In doing so, however, it makes Lafayette have more confidence in Morris, and Morris in the Revolution, than the otherwise available evidence would warrant. Augeard, we think, was led to color the story in the desire to exculpate Luxembourg from the suspicion of the counterrevolutionaries that he had betrayed them.

Feuillet de Conches (III, 471–77), Cleray (pp. 169–77), and Braesch[6] discuss a document purporting to be a letter of Monsieur to Favras, dated November 1, 1790 (which, whether the letter is genuine or not, must be a slip for 1789), and they conclude that it is a hoax.[7] Louis Blanc was the first to tell about such a letter,[8] and his story was apparently substantiated later by Alexandre Dumas' account of a conversation with Lafayette in 1830.[9] If true, it would mean that Lafayette either kept the letter which, according to

---

[2] *Ibid.*, pp. 217–20. Augeard's conversation (1798) was with someone he designated as "Morin," but obviously Gouverneur Morris is meant.

[3] See Maleissye, pp. 121–33. Cf. *Journal général de la cour*, Dec. 29, p. 812.

[4] See above, pp. 105–6.

[5] Morris diary, Dec. 25, Davenport (ed.), I, 343. See also *ibid.*, p. 346 (Dec. 27).

[6] F. Braesch, "Un faux historique, prétendue lettre du comte de Provence à Favras," *Révolution française*, LXXII (1919), 201–2.

[7] Cleray gives a facsimile of it, facing p. 128.

[8] *Histoire de la Révolution française* (Lahure edition; Paris, n.d.), I, 307. The first edition began to appear in 1847.

[9] *Mes mémoires,* ed. Pierre Josserand (Paris, 1967), IV, 56–58. The first edition began to appear in 1852. See also Cleray, pp. 173–74.

Morris' diary (I, 346), he claimed to have returned to Provence or found and kept another letter of a similarly incriminating nature which he nowhere else mentioned, with a view to exploiting it as a gage of immunity from future prosecution by Provence in return for keeping silent about it. Aside from the violence which the existence of such a letter does to the character of both the shrewd Provence for having written it and the high-minded Lafayette for using it as blackmail, one wonders[10] why Lafayette should have wanted to keep such a letter secret all his life. He otherwise never hid his suspicion that Provence was accessory to the Favras plot, and after the death (1824) of King Louis XVIII (the former Comte de Provence) the threat to reveal the alleged letter no longer would have been an effective means of blackmail against him, while its publication might have done some damage to the Bourbon reputation under his brother and successor, Charles X, whom Lafayette opposed.

[10] As does, e.g., Feuillet de Conches (ed.), III, 474–75.

APPENDIX III

Lafayette and the Bankers

Edmund Soreau claimed in 1928 that Lafayette was among the persons associated with the banker J.-G. Schweizer of Zurich.[1] Mathiez added to this statement that Schweizer often entertained Lafayette at his residence in the Paris Swiss colony.[2] Jean Bouchary[3] and Philippe Sagnac[4] indicated that Schweizer received Lafayette at his "table ouverte." The source of all of these statements seems to be one by Frédéric Barbey that Schweizer went to Paris in 1786 and established a well-attended salon there, and among the prominent persons he freely entertained was Lafayette.[5]

We have looked for associations of Lafayette with Schweizer and other bankers and can document remarkably few. As we have indicated in a previous volume[6] Jauge was one of his aides-de-camp, and above we have indicated that Cottin *fils* was too; hence Lafayette had through them associations with the house of Cottin and Girardot, and perhaps they were his own bankers.[7] He also learned from Chomel about Favras' attempted loan,[8] he seems to have considered engaging Jacob van Staphorst, of Amsterdam, to spy upon Favras,[9] and it is apparent, besides, that he was associated with bankers in promoting Morris' financial plans[10] and as a member of some of the clubs to which he belonged. He perhaps associated with Kornmann as a fellow Mesmerist,[11] and there undoubtedly were bankers in the Society of

[1] "Veymerange ou chronique de la bourgeoisie," *AHRF*, V (1928), 222.

[2] *La Révolution et les étrangers* (Paris, 1918), p. 9.

[3] *Les manieurs d'argent à Paris à la fin du XVIIIe siècle* (Paris, 1939), p. 104.

[4] *La fin de l'Ancien régime et la Révolution américaine (1763–1789)* (Paris, 1947), p. 458.

[5] Frédéric Barbey, *Suisses hors de Suisse, au servce des rois et de la Révolution . . .* (Paris, 1914), pp. 234–35.

[6] *October Days*, p. 289.

[7] Pp. 119–20. On April 15, 1790, the mayor and commandant general reimbursed Cottin *fils* 600 livres for expenses on a trip to Sens: AN: D xxix ^bis 34, dossier 357, item 20.

[8] See above, p. 120.

[9] Morris diary, Nov. 27, Davenport (ed.), I, 315.

[10] See above, p. 138 nn. See above also p. 307, n. 32, for a letter from M. de Seneffe as spokesman for a society of foreign capitalists.

[11] See Brissot, II, 54. We have contended (*Between,* p. 82) (and still contend) that

1789.[12] Necker, who had been associated with the house of Thélusson, doubt-less as minister of finances continued to be interested in banks and bankers, and Lafayette was closely associated with Necker during all of the period of this volume. In addition, Gouverneur Morris tried on one occasion and offered on another to interest Lafayette in candidates for the position of treasurer of the newly created Caisse Extraordinaire, though without success.[13] Some of these instances rest upon very tenuous evidence indeed, but all of them to-gether do not add up to a guilty alliance, during this period at least, with the monied interests. We have no evidence other than that given above for any special link of Lafayette with Schweizer during the period under considera-tion in this volume.

Brissot is "highly doubtful" as a source on this matter, but Robert Darnton, *Mesmerism and the End of the Enlightenment in France* (Cambridge, 1968), pp. 78–79, credits him.

[12] Cf. Herbert Lüthy, *La banque protestante en France de la révocation de l'Édit de Nantes à la Révolution française* (Paris, 1961), II, 618, and Georges Lefebvre, *La Révolution française* (Paris, 1951), p. 147.

[13] Morris diary (Feb. 4, 7), Davenport (ed.), I, 404–5, 407.

APPENDIX IV

Some Additional Lafayetteana

Usually, when its contents have enabled us to assign at least an approximate date to a pamphlet, a verse, or a picture and have appeared worthy of substantive consideration, we have mentioned it somewhere above. A considerable number of pamphlets, verses, or pictures, however, were not easily dated or, if datable, could be made to fit only awkwardly into our context. Merely to list them would add nothing to biographical or bibliographical knowledge, for the interested reader will find many, if not all of them, already listed in the catalogues or bibliographies of Blancheteau, Braibant, Bruel, Girodie, Jackson, Martin and Gérard, Olivier, Pierre, and Tuetey. For the period between the October Days and the Federation a few items not already mentioned in the text above nevertheless seem to us worthy of special consideration.

Several pamphlets not expressly mentioned above directly or indirectly accused Lafayette of trying to make the Paris National Guard a personally dependent and politically repressive praetorian guard. One of these was *L'Ecouteur aux portes No. 2*, dated October 10, which, although lauding Lafayette personally, accused the National Guard of being spies for questionable purposes.

This attack was apparently from the Left, but the Right was no less active. *Grandes questions à resoudre par les amis de MM. Necker, Bailly, Lafayette, et par tous ceux qui se piquent un peu d'Aristocratie, ou de démagogie, d'égalité républicaine ou de royalisme* asked questions which were obviously intended to embarrass the advocates of reform. The *Lettre intéressante de M. de la Fayette suivie de la VIIe et VIIIe d'un commerçant à un cultivateur sur les municipalités* [March (?) 1790] quoted a perhaps genuine letter of Lafayette to the Swedish ambassador for the purpose of embarrassing the commandant general. Lafayette's letter explained that the property of a royal regiment captured in the July uprising of 1789 was a legitimate prize of war and probably would not be returned. "This letter," the pamphleteer then declared, "needs no comment; it ought to allow the French soldiers to appreciate how they will be judged and treated by the king's jailer." The *Lettre impartiale de M. [F.-L.] S[uleau] à M. Necker, augmentée de deux post scriptum et une lettre à M. d'Orléans* [1790] is an attack upon the law abolishing titles of nobility. Poupart-Beaubourg published *Mes onze ducats d'Amsterdam, mes quatre cent quatre-vingt livres à Versailles, et mes quinze cents livres de Paris à déposer sur l'autel de la Patrie dans la quinzaine de*

Pâques, par M. le comte de Mirabeau (1790), which attacked Lafayette (among others), belittling his part in the American Revolution.

It would take considerably more space than would perhaps be justifiable to cite all the verses of this period (in addition to those cited in the text above) that glorified him. Two, however, are worth special attention. The first (by M. Durand *fils*) is found in the *Mercure de France*,[1] some lines of which read:

> Dans des temps orageux, sous un autre hémisphère,
> Tu braves les hasards, vengeas la Liberté;
> Nous la demandons tous, cette Liberté chère.
> Elle est entre tes mains; ta brillante carrière
>   Doit te conduire a l'immortalité. . . .
>   Et le Héros du Nouveau Monde
> Sera toujours le Héros des François.

The second, under date of October 21, is found in *Lettres à Monsieur le comte de B*****. It reads:

> Mars et Minèrve ensemble ont inspiré ce choix.
> Oui, d'un jeune Héros nous devons tout attendre;
> Il sut, bon citoyen, voter de sages loix.
> Et, guerrier valeureux, il saura les défendre.

Lafayette's more dramatic actions were often commemorated in the various visual art media. Perhaps the event most frequently represented graphically was the disarming of the mutineers on January 12 (see, among others, Blancheteau catalogue, pp. 56–57, items 191–95). Charavay (between pp. 246 and 247) gives a facsimile in color of an engraving showing Lafayette "receiving from the hands of Prudence the Crown of Immortality due to his genius and to his foresight." The catalogue of the Fogg Museum of Art (February–May 1944) lists (item 105) a Sèvres porcelain signed "Houdon 1790" and modeled upon his marble bust of Lafayette. A medal struck in 1790 commemorates the review of the National Guard on June 20.[2] Desmoulins' *Révolutions de France*[3] describes a picture, said to have been commissioned by the widow of Favras, which portrays her in mourning showing her ten-year-old son her husband's body as the boy, hand on sword, looks menacingly at Lafayette.

For two caricatures that may be of this period see Blum, p. 138, item 366, and p. 140, item 377. The first is entitled "Le général à la mode" and shows a monkey playing a violin in front of a bookstore; the legend states that monkey tricks and crimes "are the worthy results of Blondinet's courage." It apparently refers to Lafayette's surveillance of the press. The second

---

[1] Oct. 10, p. 25.

[2] Olivier, p. 4, item 4, thinks that the review in question was that of either March 21 or June 20, but March 21 was a cavalry review and thus seems ruled out.

[3] No. 26, p. 574 n.

shows soldiers listening to an orator who resembles Lafayette; it bears the legend: "I stand between the people and the law. I have principles, character, and colleagues. Will that do, Jacobins? [*Ça ira-t-il, Jacobins?*]" It probably belongs to this period of conflict with the Jacobins, but it may be of a later period as well.

INDEX

(Italics are used for bibliographical data.)

LOUIS GOTTSCHALK is Gustavus F. and Ann M. Swift Distinguished Service Professor Emeritus of History at the University of Chicago. He is a past president of the American Historical Association, recipient of many awards in the United States and abroad, and the author or the editor of numerous books.

MARGARET MADDOX, a research associate with the rank of assistant professor at the University of Chicago, worked with Professor Gottschalk for many years. She died in January 1973 while this volume was in production.